Human Rights and 21st Century Challenges

Human Rights and 21st Century Challenges

Poverty, Conflict, and the Environment

Edited by

DAPO AKANDE
JAAKKO KUOSMANEN
HELEN McDERMOTT
DOMINIC ROSER

OXFORD
UNIVERSITY PRESS

OXFORD
UNIVERSITY PRESS

Great Clarendon Street, Oxford, OX2 6DP,
United Kingdom

Oxford University Press is a department of the University of Oxford.
It furthers the University's objective of excellence in research, scholarship,
and education by publishing worldwide. Oxford is a registered trade mark of
Oxford University Press in the UK and in certain other countries

First Edition published in 2020

Impression: 1

Published in the United States of America by Oxford University Press
198 Madison Avenue, New York, NY 10016, United States of America

British Library Cataloguing in Publication Data
Data available

Library of Congress Control Number: 2019947219

ISBN 978–0–19–882477–0

Printed and bound by
CPI Group (UK) Ltd, Croydon, CR0 4YY

Preface

This collection of essays came out of the Oxford Martin Programme on Human Rights for Future Generations research programme, at the University of Oxford. The programme focused on the appropriateness of a human rights framework for addressing three major challenges to human security in this century and beyond: poverty, armed conflict, and climate change. Drawing on the disciplines of law, philosophy, and international relations, the programme contributed to academic thinking and the development of policy with respect to these three challenges. The overarching question addressed in this programme was whether and how a human rights framework can deal with these interrelated global challenges facing current and future generations. In particular, the programme investigated the normative, legal, and institutional human rights and justice frameworks to face these challenges.

As with the Human Rights for Future Generations Programme, the approach adopted in this book is multi-disciplinary, in the belief that there is much to gain from approaching human rights research from different perspectives. Contributors to the book include members of the programme as well as friends of, and collaborators with, the programme.

At the time we began work on the programme, the three challenges we address in this book were clearly going to be major challenges for this century. It also seemed clear to us that the role of human rights in this century would need serious and sustained thinking from a number of disciplinary perspectives. What was less clear was that sustaining support for the value of promoting and protecting human rights would itself come to be a major challenge. In our view, this further challenge makes the book all the more important. The value and relevance of human rights frameworks and ideals cannot be assumed. Those frameworks and the intellectual foundations on which they rest must be analysed, critiqued, and debated with rigour. We hope this book provides all of this.

We are grateful to the Oxford Martin School who generously funded the programme for the four years of its existence, and to all those who contributed to the programme's activities. In particular, we wish to thank Professor Sandra Fredman and Professor Simon Caney, who (together with Dapo Akande) co-directed the programme and provided invaluable academic leadership. We are also indebted to Zoe Davis-Heaney, our programme administrator who was essential in so many ways, including in the organization of the workshop where the papers in this book were first presented. Our thanks go to Susan Power who provided great assistance with copy-editing of this book, including ensuring consistency of referencing. Finally, we wish to express our gratitude to all those at Oxford University Press involved with the publishing of this work, including John Louth, Merel Alstein, and Jack McNichol

Contents

List of Contributors

Dapo Akande is Professor of Public International Law and co-Director of the Oxford Institute for Ethics, Law and Armed Conflict at the University of Oxford. He was a co-Director of the Oxford Martin School Human Rights for Future Generations Project.

Simon Caney is Professor of Political Theory at the University of Warwick. He was a co-Director of the Oxford Martin School Human Rights for Future Generations Project. His main focus is the application of political philosophy to global politics with a particular emphasis on climate change.

Thompson Chengeta is a European Council Research Fellow at the University of Southampton where he researches on ethics and legal implications of autonomous weapon systems. He is also an Adjunct Senior Lecturer on international law at Midlands State University. Thompson also serves as a member of the International Panel on the Regulation of Autonomous Weapon Systems and the International Committee for Robot Arms Control."

Fiona de Londras is Professor of Global Legal Studies at Birmingham Law School, the University of Birmingham. She publishes widely on human rights, including in the context of counter-terrorism. In 2017 she was awarded the Philip Leverhulme Prize in Law.

Kate Donald is the Director of the Economic and Social Policy program at the Center for Economic and Social Rights (CESR). Previously, she worked as Adviser to the UN Special Rapporteur on Extreme Poverty and Human Rights.

Sandra Fredman FBA QC Hon is the Rhodes Professor of the Laws of the Commonwealth and the USA, Oxford University and Director Oxford Human Rights Hub. She was a co-Director of the Oxford Martin School Human Rights for Future Generations Project.

Hilary Greaves is Professor of Philosophy at the University of Oxford. Her current research focuses on issues in ethics and economics that are relevant to global prioritization, as well as on more foundational topics in ethics.

Hurst Hannum is Professor of International Law, Fletcher School of Law and Diplomacy, Tufts University.

Christof Heyns is Professor of human rights law at the University of Pretoria and a member of the United Nations Human Rights Committee. Heyns was UN Special Rapporteur on extrajudicial, summary, or arbitrary executions 2010–16.

Lawrence Hill-Cawthorne is Associate Professor in Public International Law at the University of Reading. Lawrence's current research focuses on the intersection between international humanitarian law and general international law, and more specifically the nature of rights and obligations under international humanitarian law.

John H Knox is Henry C. Lauerman Professor of International Law at Wake Forest School of Law. In 2012, he was appointed a three-year mandate as the United Nation's first Independent Expert on the issue of human rights obligations relating to the enjoyment of a safe, clean, healthy, and sustainable environment. In 2015, his role was extended for another three years as special rapporteur.

Harold Hongju Koh is Sterling Professor of International Law, Yale Law School; Legal Adviser, US Dept of State (2009–13); Assistant Secretary of State for Democracy, Human Rights and Labor (1998–2001).

Jaakko Kuosmanen is an Academy Secretary at the Finnish Academy of Science and Letters. He is also an Adjunct Professor at the University of Helsinki.

Liora Lazarus, BA (UCT), LLB (LSE), DPhil (Oxon) is an Associate Professor in Law, a Fellow of St Anne's College, and Head of Research at the Bonavero Institute for Human Rights. Her primary research interests are in comparative human rights, security and human rights, comparative theory, and comparative criminal justice.

Helen McDermott is an Assistant Legal Adviser at the UK Foreign & Commonwealth Office. She was previously a Visiting Scholar at the Blavatnik School of Government, University of Oxford, and Research Associate with the Oxford Institute for Ethics, Law & Armed Conflict, University of Oxford. *She writes in her personal capacity, the views expressed in her chapter are her own, and not those of the Foreign & Commonwealth Office or any other Government Department.*

David Rodin is Co-Founder of the Oxford Institute for Ethics Law and Armed Conflict and was Part-Time Professor at the European University Institute in Florence.

Dominic Roser is a Senior Lecturer and Researcher at the Interdisciplinary Institute for Ethics and Human Rights of the University of Fribourg.

Margot E Salomon is Associate Professor in the Department of Law at the London School of Economics and Political Science and director of the interdisciplinary Laboratory for Advanced Research on the Global Economy at LSE Human Rights. Her latest book is *The Misery of International Law: Confrontations with Injustice in the Global Economy* (with J Linarelli and M Sornarajah), (OUP 2018).

Magdalena Sepúlveda Carmona is the Executive Director of The Global Initiative for Economic, Social and Cultural Rights (GI-ESCR) and a member of the Independent Commission for the Reform of International Corporate Taxation (ICRICT). From 2008 to 2014 she was the United Nations Special Rapporteur on Extreme Poverty and Human Rights.

Kerri Woods is Lecturer in Political Theory at the University of Leeds. Her publications include *Human Rights* (Palgrave Macmillan 2014) and *Human Rights and Environmental Sustainability* (Elgar 2010).

Introduction

Dapo Akande, Jaakko Kuosmanen, Helen McDermott, and Dominic Roser

The interlocking threats of armed conflict, environmental degradation, and poverty constitute a central part of the political and moral challenges facing the world in the twenty-first century. However, anyone who considers that these challenges should be confronted with approaches that incorporate and are built upon human rights faces a difficult task. High regard for human rights seems to have developed in a particular and bygone political context. The rise of populism and nationalism in recent years may be seen as having created myriad novel and complex realities. These developments suggest that work now needs to be done to apply human rights to new realities but may also indicate that we need to adapt our understanding of human rights in light of them.

Conflict-related deaths have reportedly trebled since 2008, with more countries experiencing violent conflict in 2016 than at any time in the nearly thirty years before that. According to the World Bank, 1.25 billion people live in countries facing fragile and conflict-affected situations. The nature of armed conflict has also changed significantly as the majority of conflicts are not fought by clearly defined actors or in confined geographical locations, and recent technical progress has given rise to unprecedented means of warfare. The scale of environmental problems continues to escalate. Global greenhouse gas emissions increased by around 2.2 per cent per year in the first decade of the twenty-first century, despite years of warning about the associated risks. These increases yield a significant probability of missing the 2°C warming target beyond which climate impacts such as extreme weather, disease, and migration are particularly likely to materialize. Political solutions have been slow in the making: humanity is inexperienced at dealing with the unfamiliar features of this challenge, particularly those risks which come with a small probability but a high impact and which are caused by aggregating innumerable individual actions across the globe and over decades. Poverty too remains intensely challenging. An estimated 795 million people are undernourished with over 1 billion of the world's population living on less than US$1.25 a day. The shape of the poverty challenge has changed over the past decades, too. For example, the relative share of the poor in the world population has decreased significantly and the relative share of the poor who live in countries with significant domestic capacity has increased strongly.

Dapo Akande, Jaakko Kuosmanen, Helen McDermott, and Dominic Roser, *Introduction* In: Human Rights and 21st Century Challenges. Edited by: Dapo Akande, Jaakko Kuosmanen, Helen McDermott, and Dominic Roser, Published by Oxford University Press 2020.
DOI: 10.1093/oso/9780198824770.003.0001

The interwoven nature of these three core twenty-first-century challenges complicates efforts to address them. For example, it has been estimated that on average, countries experiencing major violence have a poverty rate that is over 20 per cent higher than countries with no major violence and, conversely, poverty is a driver of conflict in the first place. Moreover, the World Bank estimates that conflict drives 80 per cent of all humanitarian needs and it projects that the share of the extreme-poor living in conflict-affected situations will exceed 50 per cent by 2030. Add to this the fact that environmental degradation often hits the poor disproportionally, thus not only leading to backlashes in the fight against poverty but also providing further fertile grounds for conflict. At the same time, policies to mitigate global environmental problems face heavy scrutiny by leaders of poor nations who fear that their poverty-eradication efforts will be stifled by being pushed into accepting an unfair share of the task. Global challenges like climate change will not be solved without a massive increase in cooperation across borders and state-building within borders, both of which are threatened by current and future conflicts.

The contributions to this volume consider what human rights might have to say about how states, and the international community more broadly, should tackle these three big challenges. While some contributors are skeptical about the role of human rights in these fields, others consider whether we should recognize new human rights, and many examine how these challenges shape our understanding of human rights. As various chapters emphasize, individual rights cannot be analysed in isolation since efforts to protect some rights often encroach upon other rights. This also underscores the importance of looking at these intertwined challenges in conjunction. Ideally, the development of both the content and the spirit of human rights should evolve in step across these various domains. Of course, whether real-world developments should affect our view of human rights at all depends on these views in the first place, for example on whether respect for human rights should primarily be seen as an instrument for furthering other goals. This is a topic taken up in Part I of the book.

The challenge of ensuring coherence in the progression of human rights applies not only to the various domains such as poverty, environment, and conflict but also to the unwieldy patchwork of participants in the discourse on human rights. This book seeks to contribute to greater engagement, across disciplines, of perspectives on human rights by including lawyers, philosophers, and political theorists. Each of the book's parts includes contributions by those who have served as Special Rapporteurs within the United Nations human rights system on the challenges under consideration. By including scholars who have also served in policy-making roles, the book makes a determined effort to integrate academic and policy conversations on these issues.

In the following, we provide an overview of the various contributions to the book. The book is divided into four parts. Part I covers foundational questions which are relevant to all the following parts. It features an evaluation of the 'big picture' legal developments of recent times as well as two philosophical pieces offering competing visions of the point of human rights.

It should not be taken as a given that reliance on human rights is the correct, or even a useful, approach to addressing these challenges. While the question of whether human rights in general, or human rights law in particular is an appropriate framework for these issues is addressed in part in some of the contributions, it is the central focus of Chapter 1 by Hurst Hannum. Unlike some of the other contributors, Hannum argues against 'expansive calls' for new rights and against attempts to address many societal problems from a human rights perspective. In his view, such 'expansive calls' are not only likely to lead to a backlash against human rights but are also unlikely to be unsuccessful in providing answers to these pressing problems. He takes the view that the contemporary content of human rights is defined most clearly and powerfully by law, and adopts a narrow vision of what that body of law should seek to do, should be invoked for, and who it should be invoked against. In his view, arguments that poverty is a human rights violation or a human rights approach ought to be taken to environmental protection are likely to lead to little more than slogans and platitudes that fail to solve real-world problems. Such calls would detract attention from more concrete social and economic obligations (such as forced evictions or the right to health) and may leave important environmental issues (such as the conservation of species) untouched.

Chapter 2 by Hilary Greaves focuses on one of the big philosophical questions about human rights: are rights bedrock features of our moral experience such that it is not possible to provide further normative explanation for or justification of them (rights-primitivism) or do they ultimately rely on a consequentialist rationale; that is, are rights a mere means for improving the world? She sides with the latter option, though with a version that is just as far from simple act consequentialism as it is from rights primitivism. This version is global consequentialism. It does justice to our intuitions about rights and avoids the various problems of act consequentialism. It is global in the sense that any performance, attempt to display, declaration of being in conformity with a right, etc, of any act, rule, motivation, etc, is to be evaluated according to its consequences. Greaves illustrates the distinctiveness of global consequentialism by examining the legal principles in the case of war. Michael Walzer holds the questionable view that these legal principles straightforwardly mirror the content of the underlying morality of war. Jeff McMahan and Henry Shue offer alternatives to this and Greaves illuminates their differences from the perspective of global consequentialism.

In Chapter 3, David Rodin, too, looks at the big picture in order to compare two fundamentally different philosophical visions of rights: the dominant beneficiary approach and his own relational approach. Neither is a consequentialist account in Greaves' sense. Both agree with rights primitivism that there are brute facts about rights. However, they disagree with Greaves' account of primitivist views by considering an explanation or justification of rights feasible. Indeed, that is where

Rodin's two approaches diverge. The beneficiary approach sees rights as ultimately grounded in the rights-bearer's status, such as her dignity or autonomy, or the rights-bearer's needs or interests. The relational approach, in contrast, sees rights as emerging from and grounded in relationships of mutual respect and consideration. A major weakness of the beneficiary approach is that our supposedly universal and equal rights—deriving from our equal status or equal needs—actually seem to have a dynamic nature. They change due to forfeiture and liability arising from the responsible decisions of the rights-holder. The relational approach can capture this better.

After Part I dealing with foundational issues, the next three parts turn to more applied issues: conflict and security; poverty; and protection of the environment. Each of those parts features an introduction to the general themes discussed within that part.

The five chapters in Part II on conflict and security focus on the legal and human rights challenges that arise out of armed drone warfare, cyber conflict, securitizing human rights, and sustainable security. All these chapters are to be read against a background of modern challenges arising out of the fight against terrorism and the use of new technologies for conducting conflict. This part begins with an overview of all the chapters by Harold Hongju Koh in Chapter 4, which draws not only from academic expertise but from substantial experience of working in the United States Government.

The chapters by Heyns, Akande, Hill-Crawthorne, and Chengeta (Chapter 7) and McDermott (Chapter 8) draw out tensions between security and human rights in situations of armed conflict, setting forth legal frameworks and specific rules within them capable of reconciling these tensions. It should be noted that in Koh's view, both of these chapters do not pay sufficient attention to state practice in setting out the international law rules they consider. Broadly speaking, these chapters examine how legal frameworks related to human rights might come into play in limiting the actions of participants in situations of conflict and insecurity. By contrast, the chapters by Lazarus (Chapter 6) and de Londras (Chapter 5) examine the relationship between security and human rights from the opposite perspective, examining how human rights and the goals of sustainable development (itself seen as being underpinned by consideration of human rights) are being used or could be used to enhance (rather than limit) state power. Examining the concepts of 'sustainable security' and 'securitizing human rights', these chapters examine, as Koh notes, conceptual tensions between human rights and security more broadly, with the aim of achieving a synthesis.

Fiona de Londras' Chapter 5 addresses the challenge that is the realization of Sustainable Development Goal (SDG) 16. This Goal commits the international community to promoting 'just, peaceful and inclusive societies' with a clear focus on security. She explores what is sought to be achieved in security terms through these stronger institutions; whether this goal enables the imagination and pursuit of something that might be called 'sustainable security'. de Londras finds that the very notion of 'sustainable security' may be antithetical to basic human rights. She argues that in the absence of a shift towards sustainability in our pursuit of security, the transformative potential of SDG 16 will be difficult to realize; indeed, the Goal may instead be used to legitimate oppressive, repressive, and often fundamentally undemocratic measures and institutions said to be needed to prevent violence and combat terrorism and crime. The chapter calls for appropriate governance strategies. She suggests reorienting SDG 16 and the underpinning concept of security to license, encourage, and support a movement towards sustainable security and towards designing, implementing, and maintaining institutions that have sustainable security at their heart. In this way, Goal 16 might just be able to effect an important, but difficult, shift in how we assess states' approaches to tackling insecurity and, consequently, their operational approaches thereto.

Liora Lazarus' Chapter 6 addresses the twenty-first-century trend of 'securitization of rights'. She argues that human rights are being transformed from concepts originally embodying the idea of state limitation to those underpinning state coercion, the latter trend being spurred most recently by the 'war on terror'. Lazarus concludes that we must resist the temptation to leverage security for the protection of rights. The right to security should be distinct from the other rights it is supposed to protect. It should not securitize other rights: if security constitutes such an essential element of all other rights, then let us secure those rights in the first instance, instead of deploying the language of security to arrive at their protection. The right to security, and other protective duties, needs to be specific: these rights should correlate to reasonable and well-balanced expectations of what citizens can expect from state actors. Finally, she recommends that a non-instrumental and value-based language of rights, of equality, dignity, and liberty needs to be placed front and centre in human rights discourse.

In response to de Londras and Lazarus, Koh in Chapter 4 argues that the tension between the competing imperatives of security and rights is best reconciled by 'humanizing security'. This concept suggests that security *decisions* should be made by decision-makers sensitive to concerns of non-combatants; that they should adopt *means* that carefully discriminate between civilians and combatants; and that they should be driven by the *end* of preserving not just freedom from fear but also the fundamental freedom of civilians to achieve personal fulfilment in society through the full exercise of their civil, political, economic, social, and cultural rights.

Chapter 7 provides a holistic examination of the international legal frameworks which regulate targeted killings by drones. It argues that for a particular drone strike to be lawful, it must satisfy the legal requirements under all applicable international legal regimes, namely: the law regulating the use of force (*ius ad bellum*), international humanitarian law, and international human rights law. It is argued that the legality of a drone strike under the *ius ad bellum* does not preclude the wrongfulness of that strike under international humanitarian law or international human rights law, and that since those latter obligations are owed to individuals, one state cannot consent to their violation by another state. The chapter then considers the important legal challenges that the use of armed drones poses under each of the three legal frameworks mentioned earlier. It considers the law relating to the use of force by states against non-state groups abroad and examines the principles of self-defence and consent, in so far as they may be relied upon to justify targeted killings abroad. It next turns to some of the key controversies in the application of international humanitarian law to drone strikes such as the threshold for non-international armed conflicts, the possibility of a global non-international armed conflict, the question of who may be targeted in a non-international armed conflict, and whether there is a duty to investigate killings by drones. The final substantive section of the chapter considers the nature and application of the right to life in armed conflict as well as the extraterritorial application of that right particularly in territory not controlled by the state conducting the strike.

Helen McDermott addresses the challenge posed by cyber technologies to individual human rights, and the difficulty associated with regulating these cyber operations. The question at the heart of the Chapter 8 is: can international law effectively respond to advancements in technology so as to prevent and redress human rights violations in cyber space? McDermott draws out this tension between individual human rights and potential security threats posed by cyber operations, and identifies certain characteristics of the cyber context that are likely to pose barriers to the operationalization of human rights. She concludes that although many of the challenges posed to the realization of rights are not unique to cyber operations, this context serves to highlight its potential to bring about a vacuum in protection and in turn, the need for a reconsideration of how the law is currently applied in this area. McDermott suggests that in order to ensure redress for violations associated with hostile cyber activities, reconsideration of the state-centric approach to international law is needed. The plausibility of conferring enforceable human rights law obligations on non-state actors requires serious consideration as the current landscape may breed proxy cyber armies with states operating behind a curtain of plausible deniability.

Part III turns to poverty, which has not traditionally been regarded as a human rights issue. Rather, it has been considered as a question relating to charity. In recent decades, however, there has been a shift towards a human rights approach to poverty alleviation. This has been facilitated by the increasing recognition of socio-economic human rights around the world after the end of the Cold War. In 1993, the Vienna Declaration from the World Conference on Human Rights reaffirmed that 'all human rights are universal, indivisible and interdependent and interrelated'. There have also been systematic efforts to render the content of the rights enshrined in the International Covenant on Economic, Social, and Cultural Rights (ICESCR) more determinate (eg through General Comments and national adjudication), and to link them to other development initiatives such as the SDGs.

Yet, it is safe to say that still in the second decade of the twenty-first century, the link between human rights and poverty remains incomplete and problematic in many ways. All chapters in this part highlight the difficulties and the potential for a human rights approach to poverty. Plenty has been done, but there is much work still ahead. In the twenty-first century, agile non-state actors are becoming increasingly powerful, markets are becoming more interconnected, the nature of work is changing due to automation and robotics, and climate change is transforming many regions in radical ways. In such a rapidly changing global environment, the human rights approach to poverty becomes particularly important. Those affected by the changes deserve more than an assurance of charity, they deserve the protection they are entitled to on the basis of their human rights.

The challenges in formulating a human rights approach to poverty are related to both the conceptual dimensions of human rights as well as their implementation. Margot Salomon's Chapter 9 opens the part on poverty by highlighting three key impediments present in the following chapters. She emphasizes the fact that a forceful human rights approach to poverty requires also addressing a multi-level democratic deficit, a harmful commitment to growth, and a categorical absence of accountability for the state of poverty and inequality.

In Chapter 10, Sandra Fredman argues that the limitations of a human rights approach to poverty can be attributed to a set of background assumptions relating to the idea of human rights. She suggests that a notion of human rights according to which their primary aim is to protect each person's freedom against state intervention leads to an individualistic and formal understanding of rights abstracted from the social context of power and inequality. Fredman suggests that these background premises need to be reconfigured in terms of their understanding of freedom and equality. On this reconfigured approach, freedom requires the state to facilitate genuine fulfilment of individual capabilities. In turn, equality is considered as substantive rather than formal. Fredman concludes that from these starting points, poverty can be seen as a violation of human rights. She further emphasizes the importance of recognizing the mutually supportive link between SDGs and human rights. SDGs become more than aspirations when viewed through the lens of human rights. Simultaneously, the content of SDGs can be used to render the content of binding human rights more determinate. In many ways, the ideas in Fredman's chapter are in tension with those presented in Chapter 1. Similarly, the articulation of a mutually supporting link between the SDGs in general and human rights can be contrasted with the tension that de Londras notes in Chapter 5 between one of the SDGs and human rights.

In Chapter 11, Jaakko Kuosmanen explores how deliberation can facilitate interdisciplinarity and can provide an avenue for rendering a human rights approach to poverty more determined in terms of its content. He suggests that deliberation can clarify the nature of rights and their correlative obligations in a particular context, and it can be utilized in the drafting of budgets that are in compliance with human rights obligations. Yet, deliberation is not a magic wand that necessarily solves all contestation relating to human rights and budgets. Various challenges remain, including the challenge of participatory deliberation, rigid governance structures that complicate deliberation in practice, lack of transparency, and compliance.

In Chapter 12, Magdalena Sepúlveda and Kate Donald expand the enquiry on the link between human rights and SDGs. They explore how looking at some of the goals and targets in the SDGs from a human rights approach can help fulfil their transformative potential. While recognizing that a rights approach does not provide answers to all the challenges in the realization of SDGs, Sepúlveda and Donald suggest that it does provide an opportunity to rethink some of the policy responses implemented so far. They conclude that human rights have the potential to provide a common language and framework for action, and highlight the importance of emerging from silos and embracing interdisciplinarity—something that is a central theme throughout this book. Fully embracing a rights-based approach to poverty reduction requires policy-makers and researchers to deepen the analysis of poverty and its causes, and to forge better collaboration.

Part IV of the book, finally, brings a human rights perspective to the environmental domain. In the introduction to this part, Chapter 13, Kerri Woods notes that this might be met with scepticism since the liberal ideology at the roots of human rights is also at the roots of environmental degradation. If, however, one takes this liberal ideology as given then it should be acknowledged that most of the reasons for bringing a human rights perspective to the contexts to which it has traditionally been applied also apply to the environmental context. This is especially important given how there are few developments that currently affect humans' core concerns as much as the rapid and deep changes to our environment. Alas, taking a human rights approach to environmental questions is not as straightforward as it might seem. The chapters in this part underscore this point. The factors that bedevil squaring human rights and the environment are many. For example, there is the fact that the cause and effect of many environmental changes are spatially and temporally far removed from each other; that both cause and effect are often dispersed across innumerable persons; that there is often much uncertainty about the cause-effect relationship; that environmental harm is often an unintended side effect (and sometimes even an—inculpably—*unknown* side effect) of otherwise benign actions; or that many environmental issues force us first to work out a stance on the relation of the rights of humans to the rights of non-humans.

Kerri Woods observes that contemporary debates invoking intergenerational environmental human rights are primarily about the duties justified by rights, rather than the rights themselves. Chapter 14 by Dominic Roser on the topic of uncertainty is an instance of this. In many cases of environmental change there is large uncertainty about the impact of this change on humans and their rights. Intuitively, this uncertainty calls for cautiousness, which many translate into a call for the application of a precautionary principle. However, many versions of the precautionary principle are beset by grave problems. Roser argues that a human rights approach provides a good rationale for the intuition behind the precautionary principle. If high uncertainty means that there is a high probability both of violating rights and of providing benefits that go beyond the fulfilment of rights, then a rights-based approach will generally be averse to a high degree of uncertainty. This is so because the former probability is not simply offset by the latter.

Chapter 15 by John Knox, the first UN Special Rapporteur on Human Rights and the Environment, provides an overview of the development of human rights and the environment, in particular climate change. This development culminated in the Paris Agreement which is the first international environmental agreement to recognize human rights as an integral element. Knox notes that this attention to human rights sets a precedent for further international regimes besides the climate change regime. He argues that while the obligations of each state to protect against the effects of climate change within its own jurisdiction receives the necessary attention in the Paris Agreement, the same cannot be said of the collective obligation of states to cooperate to mitigate climate change. The chapter closes by discussing two fields where the intersection of human rights and climate change will remain prominent in the years to come: climate finance mechanisms and domestic litigation.

Chapter 16 by Simon Caney tackles the question of population growth from a human rights perspective. He emphasizes that we need to do both: protect human rights from the threat of climate change but also choose methods to do so which honour human rights themselves, including procreation-related rights. He avoids two extremes. He neither dismisses population growth as an irrelevant issue that will be solved automatically as a by-product of fulfilling human rights nor does he consider population growth to be the famous elephant in the room, an elephant which might call for drastic measures such as strict limits to the number of children each person can have. Rather, a balanced solution depends on the precise shape of one's theory of intergenerational justice as well as on empirical facts about ecological constraints. In Chapter 13, Kerri Woods observes that notions of the good life have taken up much attention in the history of environmental ethics. While questions about the good life are usually absent in a human rights approach, contributions such as those by Simon Caney can be interpreted to open up reflection about it, in particular by delineating which visions of the good life are compatible with realizing human rights.

Taken together, the chapters in this volume reveal that strengthening the place of human rights in our world not only faces obstacles by individual humans who disregard them or intellectually oppose them. Equally important are the shifting contexts to which human rights must apply. If we are truly committed to human rights, we cannot avoid the hard work of refining and reshaping our understanding of this commitment in the light of evolving challenges ever anew.

I

FOUNDATIONS

1

Reinvigorating Human Rights for the Twenty-First Century*

Hurst Hannum

I. Introduction

The imagining, proclamation, and eventual codification of international human rights law (IHRL) rank among the most significant accomplishments in international relations of the post-1945 era. While the concept of rights on the domestic level had been evolving for centuries, the notion that all people in the world possessed certain rights—that their own government is obliged to protect—was nothing short of revolutionary.

The intrusion of human rights into the heretofore sacrosanct realm of national sovereignty upended 350 years during which sovereignty was understood primarily as a shield against outside influence. While sovereignty was never absolute, its limits were few. One of the only limits related to rights was the customary international law norm that required states to protect aliens within their jurisdiction, although this protection stemmed from respect for the sovereignty of the aliens' state rather than from any broader concern for the rights of all individuals within a state's territory. Other limits reflected the 'sovereign equality' of states (eg state responsibility for acts within its territory that might harm another state) or the perceived necessities of conducting international relations (eg immunity of diplomats, freedom of the high seas).

Human rights, on the other hand, are not in their essence 'international'. Their violation affects other states only indirectly, and the idea that how a state treats its own citizens within its own jurisdiction is a legitimate matter for international concern was truly novel. Illustrative of this approach is the long struggle to outlaw slavery, which initially focused on the transnational slave trade. Abolitionist campaigns within countries began to bear fruit in the late eighteenth and early

* This chapter is a slightly revised and updated version of Hannum (2016), 'Reinvigorating Human Rights for the Twenty-First Century' 16 Human Rights Law Review 409. For a fuller exploration of many of the issues discussed, see Hurst Hannum, *Rescuing Human Rights: A Radically Moderate Approach* (Cambridge University Press 2019).

Hurst Hannum, *Reinvigorating Human Rights for the Twenty-First Century* In: Human Rights and 21st Century Challenges. Edited by: Dapo Akande, Jaakko Kuosmanen, Helen McDermott, and Dominic Roser, Published by Oxford University Press 2020.
DOI: 10.1093/oso/9780198824770.003.0002

nineteenth centuries, but the first international treaty that banned slavery itself was adopted only in 1926.[1]

The origins and growth of international human rights norms and what became the international human rights movement have been analysed by a number of scholars, and it is not particularly relevant to a contemporary understanding of the content of human rights to decide whether the meaningful internationalization of rights began in the 1930s, 1940s, or 1970s.[2] Formally, however, identifying as one of the purposes of the United Nations 'promoting and encouraging respect for human rights and fundamental freedoms for all without distinction as to race, sex, language, or religion' was surely a landmark.[3] The language of the Charter left implementation of this goal primarily in the hands of states themselves, but it made clear the fact that human rights were no longer solely within the domestic jurisdiction of states.

While some contemporary states continue to complain that international human rights norms violate traditional norms of state sovereignty,[4] sovereignty today no longer permits states to act in any way they wish with respect to the treatment of individuals within their jurisdiction. This fact is reflected not only in hortatory declarations and diplomatic speeches but also in practice. The United Nations and many other multilateral international organizations include the promotion of human rights within their mandates, and regional human rights courts exist in Europe, Africa, and the Western Hemisphere. Every country in the world has ratified at least one of the nine global treaties adopted under the auspices of the United Nations; as of mid-2015, more than 160 states had ratified the two core conventions on civil and political rights and economic, social, and cultural rights, respectively; 177 states had ratified the Convention on the Elimination of All Forms of Racial Discrimination; 189 had ratified the Convention on the Elimination of All Forms of Discrimination Against Women; and 196 states[5] had ratified the Convention on the Rights of the Child.

[1] Slavery Convention (adopted 25 September 1926, entered into force 9 March 1927) 60 LNTS 253.

[2] Cf eg Elizabeth Borgwardt, *A New Deal for the World: America's Vision for Human Rights* (Harvard University Press 2005); Mary Ann Glendon, *A World Made New: Eleanor Roosevelt and the Universal Declaration of Human Rights* (Random House 2001); Lynn Hunt, *Inventing Human Rights: A History* (WW Norton and Co Ltd 2007); Micheline Ishay, *The History of Human Rights: From Ancient Times to the Globalization Era* (University of California Press 2008); Johannes Morsink, *The Universal Declaration of Human Rights: Origins, Drafting, and Intent* (University of Pennsylvania Press 1999); Samuel Moyn, *The Last Utopia: Human Rights in History* (Harvard University Press 2010) including the useful Bibliographical Essay, 311–21; Aryeh Neier, *The International Human Rights Movement: A History* (Princeton University Press 2012).

[3] Charter of the United Nations (adopted 24 October 1945) 1 UNTS XVI art 1.3.

[4] See eg the comments of the government of Sri Lanka regarding a Commission of Inquiry created by the UN HRC to examine alleged human rights violations and international crimes committed during the Sri Lankan civil war: the resolution of the Council 'challenges the sovereignty and independence of a member state of the UN [and] violates principles of international law.' Statement by HE Mr Ravinatha AT Aryasinha, Permanent Representative of Sri Lanka, to the UN HRC, Geneva, 10 June 2014, para 22.

[5] The United States is the only country in the world that has not ratified the Convention.

In 2006, the UN Human Rights Council (HRC) adopted a new procedure, the Universal Periodic Review (UPR), under which the human rights situation in every member state of the United Nations is reviewed on a regular basis, irrespective of which—if any—treaties the state has ratified. The UPR was adopted by consensus, and all 192 UN members submitted reports on their domestic human rights practices and participated in the initial four-year review process.

Whatever quibbles or questions remain about the legal impact of human rights treaties, the relevance of 'soft law' principles and declarations, or the lack of sufficiently robust implementation or compliance mechanisms, the argument that human rights are purely a domestic matter is no longer sustainable.

A. Human Rights as Law

'Human rights' as a phrase is extraordinarily broad and can encompass many understandings of what 'rights' are. As implied by the first sentence of this chapter, however, the contemporary content of human rights is defined most clearly and most powerfully as law. The relationship of law to other regulatory or aspirational frameworks—politics, ideology, religion, social justice, equality, or fairness, to name only a few—is a recurring theme of the present work. The underlying assumption is that the status of human rights as law needs to be protected and that the distinction between legal obligations and other obligations of a moral or political nature needs to be maintained. 'Human rights' may mean all things to all people, but 'international human rights law' cannot.

This understanding of human rights as denoting IHRL is necessarily narrow; it does not encompass every right that someone or some group seeks to assert. As discussed below in section V on the flexibility inherent in human rights norms, this narrowness should not be confused with uniformity in interpretation and application. Law does, however, provide a structural context in which human rights can be best understood in today's world. Law also provides (i) the best evidence of the content of human rights and (ii) the best evidence of the essential universality of human rights commitments that states have actually undertaken. As aptly put by Allen Buchanan, '[h]uman rights law, not any philosophical or "folk" theory of moral human rights, is the authoritative lingua franca of modern human rights practice' (emphasis deleted).[6]

This approach does not seek to minimize the role of human rights understood more broadly as an aspirational moral framework that has inspired activists and ordinary people around the world. It also recognizes the political value that many governments have found in human rights, whether it is to promote them or to hold

[6] Allen Buchanan, *The Heart of Human Rights* (OUP 2013) vii (hereafter Buchanan, *The Heart of Human Rights*).

them up as foils for nationalist rhetoric that rejects any influence by foreigners on the sacred homeland. However, understanding the role of human rights as law is essential if one hopes to clarify the other roles that human rights may play, as ideology, utopia, or political weapon.

Law can change, and IHRL is no exception. Neither the Universal Declaration of Human Rights (UDHR) nor any other human rights instrument was handed down on golden tablets or otherwise revealed through divine intervention. The continuing evolution of IHRL is demonstrated by the adoption of numerous treaties at the global and regional levels that expand, nuance, or occasionally limit the broad norms articulated in the UN Charter or by the 1948 UDHR. New norms await further elaboration and agreement, and interpretations of existing norms may shift—just as many domestic statutes and constitutions acquire new meaning in order to respond to new situations and new problems. We should welcome this process, although proclaiming too many new norms without ensuring that meaningful consensus exists within all regions of the world can be problematic, as discussed further in section IV on new rights.

The arguments that follow are pragmatic rather than philosophical, realist rather than visionary. They assume that the constraints of the current international system of states will continue to exist for the foreseeable future and that neither a world government nor a new 'super' or 'hyper' state will have either the capacity or the legitimacy to mould the world into any particularly orderly shape.

The arguments also are premised on the proposition that IHRL has had a positive influence on the situation of individuals across the globe and that maintenance and better implementation of that law should be encouraged.[7] It does not presume that either human rights or law is the primary agent of change within or across societies, but it does argue that human rights norms can facilitate the development and influence of other socio-economic, political, moral change agents in ways that are more likely to respond to the needs of most people in the world.

B. Today's Problem

Human rights are on the verge of becoming a victim of their own success. Unless there is a conscious attempt to return to the principles of consensus and universality, the increasingly strident calls from European and other 'Western' human rights activists for adherence to the contemporary liberal European construct of society is likely to create a backlash in the rest of the world. This tendency is concurrently exacerbated by activists who see an expansive concept of 'rights' as the

[7] See eg Beth Simmons, *Mobilizing for Human Rights: International Law in Domestic Politics* (CUP 2009); Thomas Risse, Stephen Ropp, and Kathryn Sikkink (eds), *The Persistent Power of Human Rights: From Commitment to Compliance* (CUP 2013).

primary means to effect domestic social and political change, as well as by governments that wish to burden human rights with broader geopolitical initiatives. The result will be, ironically, to strengthen anti-human rights governments and others who have challenged the universal application of human rights by privileging cultural relativism over globally shared values.

A few recent examples may be useful. Mainstream academics have called for the extension of human rights obligations not only to international organizations but to corporations, other non-state actors, and even individuals.[8] An analysis of potential conflicts between human rights and other international norms, such as those set forth in trade or bilateral investment treaties, holds that the 'constitutionalisation of the international human rights regime' in South America has led to state obligations to, *inter alia*, 'adopt affirmative actions, preventative measures and adequate and transformational compensation measures to address widespread situations of systematic patterns that produce or reproduce inequality among citizens[,] … produce public information … [and] prevent undue media concentration'.[9] A court in Mexico declared that the killing of dozens of protesters by soldiers at a Mexico City student demonstration in 1968 was 'genocide', a stunning expansion of the ultimate international crime far beyond what was originally envisioned.[10] Amnesty International, one of the oldest and most well-respected international human rights non-governmental organizations (NGO), has promoted drafting a treaty to control the arms trade[11] and called for the 'full decriminalization of all aspects of consensual sex work'.[12] After losing its bid to host the 2000 Games, a Chinese government official claimed that it was a 'human right of the Chinese people' to host the Olympics in the future.[13] The UN HRC has appointed individual experts to consider the relationship between human rights and, eg transnational corporations, dumping of toxic waste, the use of mercenaries, extreme poverty, the effects of economic reform policies and foreign debt, and 'international solidarity'.[14]

[8] See generally Andrew Clapham, *Human Rights Obligations of Non-State Actors* (OUP 2006) (hereafter Clapham, *Human Rights Obligations*).

[9] Victor Abramovich (2015) 'State Regulatory Powers and Global Legal Pluralism' 12(21) Sur J <http://sur.conectas.org/en/state-regulatory-powers-global-legal-pluralism/> accessed 25 February 2017.

[10] See Kevin Sullivan, 'Mexico to Seek Genocide Charges Against Officials in 1968 Massacre' *Washington Post* (14 January 2005).

[11] See Amnesty International, 'Global Arms Trade Treaty—A Beginners' Guide: 50th Ratification Update' (25 September 2014) <http://www.amnesty.org/en/latest/news/2014/09/global-arms-trade-treaty-beginners-guide-th-ratification-update/> accessed 25 February 2017.

[12] See Amnesty International, 'Global Movement Votes to Adopt Policy to Protect Human Rights of Sex Workers' (11 August 2015) <http://www.amnestyusa.org/news/press-releases/global-movement-votes-to-adopt-policy-to-protect-human-rights-of-sex-workers> accessed 7 August 2019.

[13] 'Olympics: In 2008, it will be China's turn' *Associated Press* (28 February 2006) <http://english.sina.com/sports/1/2006/0228/67435.html> accessed 7 August 2019.

[14] A list of all the Council's Thematic 'Special Procedures' may be found at <http://spinternet.ohchr.org/_Layouts/SpecialProceduresInternet/ViewAllCountryMandates.aspx?Type=TM> accessed 7 August 2019 (hereafter thematic 'special procedures'). Also see the section on new rights.

Some of these initiatives or claims are morally defensible, indeed admirable, and calling for greater social equity or punishing soldiers who kill protesters is laudable and necessary. However, it stretches the imagination to believe that these issues were foremost (or even present) when the UDHR was adopted by the UN General Assembly in 1948. That instrument, although not in and of itself legally binding, remains the most widely accepted articulation of human rights, but the popularity of the term 'human rights' as a mantra for change has led to a significant expansion of the rights proclaimed in 1948. The consequences or 'blowback' of such an expansion may be to set back an entire movement that is based on the proposition that all human beings enjoy certain rights simply because of their status as humans.

Of course, interpretations of international norms change over time, and we should welcome the fact that we have a much fuller understanding of human rights than we did in 1948. Just as 'equal protection' in the United States was understood to permit racial segregation until the Supreme Court issued its famous 1954 judgment in *Brown v Board of Education*,[15] international human rights bodies today are unlikely to tolerate inequities and ill-treatment that were common a half-century ago. Calls for restraint in formulating new rights should not serve as cover to justify attempts to turn the clock back to an earlier time, when women, children, minorities, and other disempowered groups 'knew their place'.

II. Criminal Punishment, Coercion, and Force

A. Confusing Human Rights Violations with International Crimes

The prevalent confusion between the responsibility of a state to protect human rights and the culpability of an individual who commits a crime is paradigmatic of attempts to infuse human rights into unrelated concepts, usually to the detriment of both. For example, it is common to find references to 'human rights crimes' in the context of violent conflicts, without any explanation of what the adjectival characterization of a crime as a 'human rights' crime adds to our understanding of either criminal justice or international law. A similar approach may be found in discussions of transitional justice or post-regime-change situations, when the issue of punishing past 'human rights violations' arises.[16]

International law has imposed obligations on individuals for centuries, and such criminal liability pre-dates concern with international human rights and the

[15] 347 US 483 (1954).

[16] For a recent article that assumes that 'human rights accountability' means criminal prosecution, see Leigh Payne, Francesca Lessa, and Gabriel Pereira (2015) 'Overcoming Barriers to Justice in the Age of Human Rights Accountability' 37 Human Rights Quarterly 728.

obligations of governments to those within their jurisdiction. It is difficult to see, for example, what punishing the pirate, hijacker, drug trafficker, terrorist, money launderer, or polluter has to do with human rights. Of course, all involve harm to people or property, combined with widespread international agreement that punishing such acts need not be restricted by the normal limitations of state sovereignty. (Most states exercise jurisdiction over crimes only if the crime occurs within that state's territory or if either the victim or perpetrator is a citizen of the state.) On the other hand, most harms are neither international crimes nor human rights violations, even if they may give rise to personal civil or criminal liability at the domestic level.

The rejoinder of many human rights activists is that only certain kinds of crimes are human rights crimes, that is those that involve either widespread killing or particularly heinous acts. The most common examples given are genocide, war crimes, crimes against humanity, and torture. However, the body of law concerning the first three of these crimes arose independently of and prior to the articulation of the human rights obligations of governments. We may bemoan the lack of enforcement, but the international community has attempted to define and punish war crimes at least since the nineteenth century, including what might now be termed 'human rights' crimes such as rape and torture, in addition to crimes of mistreating prisoners of war or attacking civilian targets.

The primary concern of human rights advocates, particularly in Latin America, has been to overcome the impunity of government officials who escape punishment for the crimes they committed during their reign. This view crystallized around the case of General Pinochet and his henchman in Chile, who granted themselves amnesties before leaving office after a murderous seventeen years in power; a similar situation obtained in Argentina and elsewhere in Latin America in the 1970s and 1980s.[17] Local human rights activists and the relatives of victims were in the forefront of campaigns to reverse these amnesties, and combatting impunity became a new 'human rights' mantra. The human rights 'hook' was that human rights norms require the prevention of future abuses and that victims have the right to an appropriate remedy for violations that occurred in the past.[18]

The conflation of criminal punishment with human rights violations deepened when UN negotiators began in 1999 to refuse to approve amnesty clauses in peace agreements that immunized perpetrators of internationally recognized war

[17] See generally Naomi Roht-Arriaza, *Impunity and Human Rights in International Law and Practice* (OUP 1995).

[18] See eg*Case of Aguirre et al. v Peru* Inter-American Court of Human Rights Series C No 75 (2001). For a contrasting view, which rejected a challenge to the conditional amnesty provisions of South Africa's Truth and Reconciliation Commission, see *Azanian Peoples Organisation (AZAPO) and others v President of the Republic of South Africa*, Constitutional Court of South Africa (1996), 4 South Africa Reports 671. Cf Serpa Soares, 'An Age of Accountability' (Special Editorial) (2015) 13 Journal of International Criminal Justice 669, 673 (asserting 'that it is clearly established that there is a direct connection between accountability and achieving sustainable peace').

crimes and crimes against humanity.[19] This stance led UN Secretary-General Ban Ki Moon in July 2007 to threaten to boycott cooperation with the Indonesia-East Timor Commission of Truth and Friendship, unless the commission ruled out recommending amnesties for 'human rights' crimes.[20] Also controversial has been dealing with the situation in Northern Uganda, where leaders of the rebel Lord's Resistance Army have been indicted by the International Criminal Court (ICC), despite objections from many of the victims of their crimes, who would prefer to seek peace through reconciliation rather than retribution.[21]

This categorical rejection of impunity for international crimes—as well as human rights violations—is heralded by many as a universally applicable norm, although such a position is unsupported by state practice and certainly does not constitute a norm of customary international law.[22] For example, the Belfast Guidelines on Amnesties and Accountability, adopted by a group of experts in 2013, note that '[w]ithin international human rights law, there are differences in the approach of the regional human rights courts on whether there is an obligation to prosecute gross violations of human rights or whether it is sufficient that states investigate such violations and provide remedies for those affected. Amnesties enacted in different regions of the world may be subject to different standards.' The Principles do refer to human rights, but they clarify that '"[g]ross violations of human rights" is used here to denote acts that constitute serious crimes under national or international law and, if committed by a government, would violate the state's human rights obligations.'[23]

Rather than being based on illusory norms of international law, decisions regarding amnesties are better left to domestic authorities (assuming that the alleged criminals do not adopt 'auto-amnesties' simply to protect themselves), who are better positioned to determine whether punishment, forgiveness, or something in

[19] Guidelines for UN Representatives on Certain Aspects of Negotiations for Conflict Resolution (1999) UN Department of Political Affairs. The Guidelines have never been published in full, but they are referenced in the UN Juridical Yearbook 2006, Annex E, item 8: 'These Guidelines include a discussion of amnesty provisions and note that the UN "cannot condone amnesties regarding war crimes, crimes against humanity and genocide or foster those that violate relevant treaty obligations of the parties in this field."' This standard was reiterated and made more explicit in the Report of the Secretary-General, 'The Rule of Law and Transitional Justice in Conflict and Post-Conflict Societies' (2004) UN Doc S/2004/616 para 10: 'UN-endorsed peace agreements can never promise amnesties for genocide, war crimes, crimes against humanity or gross violations of human rights, and, where we are mandated to undertake executive or judicial functions, UN-operated facilities must scrupulously comply with international standards for human rights in the administration of justice.' Gross violations of human rights are not defined.

[20] See Earthtimes.org, 'Indonesia Criticizes UN Chief' (*Global Policy Forum*, 31 July 2007) <http://www.globalpolicy.org/component/content/article/163/29222.html> accessed 7 August 2019.

[21] See eg Barney Afako, 'Negotiating in the Shadow of Justice' in Elizabeth Drew and Alexander Ramsbotham (eds), *Conciliation Resources, An international Review of Peace Initiatives 2002–09 and the Juba Peace Process* (Conciliation Resources 2010) 21.

[22] Principle 6(e), Belfast Guidelines on Amnesty and Accountability (2013) <http://www.ulster.ac.uk/__data/assets/pdf_file/0005/57839/TheBelfastGuidelinesFINAL_000.pdf> accessed 7 August 2019.

[23] Ibid, Principle 1(a), Fn 3.

between is more likely to lead to a more stable, rights-respecting polity in the future. What is ultimately required is the much more difficult and time-consuming task of helping to change the behaviour of governments, and demands to put all human rights violators in prison may or may not contribute to this goal.[24]

Since the 1990s, international crime and punishment have spawned hundreds of international jobs and cost billions of dollars, including the aborted trial of Slobodan Milosevic and the successful prosecution of many individuals who committed crimes in former Yugoslavia and Rwanda. A permanent international criminal court, based in The Hague, was created in 2000, and 122 countries have submitted to its jurisdiction as of mid-2019 (two countries, Burundi and Philippines, which were previously parties to the Court's Statute have withdrawn from it). Its jurisdiction extends not to 'human rights' violations but to the three traditional categories of international crimes already mentioned, namely genocide, war crimes, and crimes against humanity (a fourth crime, that of aggression, was added in 2010, although it had been accepted by only thirty-eight states as of mid-2019). In the Rome Statute itself, human rights are mentioned only in the context of ensuring that the court interprets applicable law in a non-discriminatory manner and consistently with 'internationally recognized human rights' (article 21(3)); prohibiting, in most instances, evidence obtained by means that violate human rights norms (article 69(7)); and, oddly, as being an area of competence relevant to the selection of judges (article 36(3)(b)(ii)).

Another goal of this 'new direction in human rights advocacy' was described by the International Center for Transitional Justice when it was founded in 2001 as 'helping societies to heal by accounting for and addressing past crimes after a period of repressive rule or armed conflict'.[25] Without entering fully into the 'peace versus justice' debate, the point is simply to reiterate that 'human rights violations' or even 'serious' or 'gross' violations are often not crimes and are attributable to governments, not to individuals. No-one believes that international law mandates

[24] It is perhaps worth recalling that apartheid is a crime against humanity, defined in a treaty ratified by 109 states. International Convention on the Suppression and Punishment of the Crime of Apartheid (adopted 30 November 1973, entered into force 18 July 1976) 1015 UNTS 243 (Apartheid Convention). However, when South Africans decided that a 'truth and reconciliation' commission was more appropriate in most instances than individual criminal prosecution, foreign states, NGOs, and international organizations unanimously accepted this determination—despite the fact that article IV(b) of the convention specifically demands that states 'adopt legislative, judicial and administrative measures to prosecute, bring to trial and punish in accordance with their jurisdiction persons responsible for, or accused of' apartheid as defined in the treaty.

[25] This was the original articulation of ICTJ's mission, as quoted in the History portion of Wikipedia's entry on the organization. See <en.wikipedia.org/wiki/International_Center_for_Transitional_Justice> accessed 7 August 2019. The mission is now couched somewhat differently, emphasizing human rights rather than crimes: 'ICTJ assists societies confronting massive human rights abuses to promote accountability, pursue truth, provide reparations, and build trustworthy institutions… We strive for societies to regain humanity in the wake of mass atrocity. For societies in which impunity is rejected, dignity of victims is upheld, and trust is restored; where truth is the basis of history. We believe that this is an ethical, legal, and political imperative and the cornerstone of lasting peace.' See ICTJ, 'Vision and Mission' (2017) <http://www.ictj.org/about/vision-and-mission> accessed 7 August 2019.

criminal punishment for every government official who authorizes or tolerates religious or gender discrimination, denies free expression, or suppresses trade union activity, for example, although such acts certainly constitute serious violations of human rights and may also constitute crimes under domestic law.

The United Nations has not been immune to this conflation of human rights norms with criminal justice. For example, it may not be coincidence that the three most recent UN High Commissioners for Human Rights (before the current holder of that post) had significant experience with international criminal tribunals prior to their appointment; none had served on an international human rights body.[26] High Commissioner Navi Pillay offered to help Haiti prosecute former dictator Jean-Claude Duvalier[27] and warned Nepal against granting amnesties to those who committed 'serious human rights violations' during the conflict in that country.[28] The UN HRC has created commissions of inquiry into the armed conflict in Syria[29] and the June 2014 conflict in Gaza,[30] and it ordered an investigation of crimes and human rights violations in Sri Lanka that occurred during and after the end of that country's civil war in 2009.[31] The mandates of all three refer more often to crimes against humanity and criminal prosecution than they do to human rights violations.[32] The Council also created a US$1.2 million fact-finding

[26] Louise Arbour (2004–2008) served as Chief Prosecutor for the International Criminal Tribunals for Rwanda and the former Yugoslavia; Navi Pillay (2008–2014) was a judge on both the International Criminal Tribunal for Rwanda and the ICC; and Zeid Ra'ad Al Hussein (2014–present) played a central role in the establishment of the ICC and served as the first President of the Assembly of States Parties of the ICC.

[27] 'UN Offers to Help Haiti Prosecute Duvalier Crimes' *Reuters* (1 February 2011) <af.reuters.com/article/worldNews/idAFTRE7103RZ20110201> accessed 7 August 2019.

[28] 'UN Warns Nepal Against Amnesty for Civil War Crimes' *Reuters* (15 April 2014) <http://www.reuters.com/article/us-nepal-un-amnesty-idUSBREA3E0ED20140415> accessed 7 August 2019.

[29] UNHRC Res S-17/1 (2011).

[30] UNHRC Res S-21/1 (2014).

[31] UNHRC 'Promoting Reconciliation, Accountability and Human Rights in Sri Lanka' (9 April 2014) A/HRC/RES/25/1 (2014).

[32] There have been three separate mandates for the Syrian Commission of Inquiry. The initial mandate was 'to dispatch urgently an independent international commission of inquiry . . . to investigate all alleged violations of international human rights law since March 2011 in the Syrian Arab Republic, to establish the facts and circumstances that may amount to such violations and of the crimes perpetrated and, where possible, to identify those responsible with a view to ensuring that perpetrators of violations, including those that may constitute crimes against humanity, are held accountable'. UNHRC Res S-17/1 (2011) para 13. The second resolution requests the commission to 'conduct a . . . special inquiry . . . into the events [of an alleged massacre] in *El-Houleh* and, if possible, to publicly identify those who appear responsible for these atrocities, and to preserve the evidence of crimes for possible future criminal prosecutions'. UNHRC Res S-19-1 (4 June 2012) A/HRC/RES/S-19/1, para 8. The third resolution, asks the commission to follow up on its report, 'with a view to hold to account those responsible for violations and abuses, including those that may amount to crimes against humanity and war crimes'. UNHRC Res 21/26 (17 October 2012) A/HRC/RES/21/26, para 10. While each of the resolutions also refers to human rights violations, the emphasis on criminal liability is clear. The Gaza resolution similarly requests the commission 'to investigate all violations of international humanitarian law and international human rights law in the Occupied Palestinian Territory . . . to establish the facts and circumstances of such violations and of the crimes perpetrated and to identify those responsible . . . all with a view to avoiding and ending impunity and ensuring that those responsible are held accountable . . .'. UNHRC Res S-21/1 (24 July 2014) A/HRC/RES/S-21/1, para 13. The Sri Lanka resolution mandated 'a comprehensive investigation into alleged serious violations and abuses of human rights and related crimes by

commission to investigate alleged crimes committed by the Islamic State in Iraq[33] and recently requested the High Commissioner to document gross human rights abuses and violations of international humanitarian law (IHL) by Boko Haram.[34] On the government side, the US Department of Homeland Security created a 'Human Rights Violators and War Crimes Unit' as part of its US immigration and customs authorities, in order to prevent the entry into the United States of 'foreign war crimes suspects, persecutors and human rights abusers'; one of its missions is to 'identify and prosecute individuals who have been involved and/or responsible for the commission of human rights abuses across the globe'.[35]

Of particular concern is the increasing focus on international crimes and accountability on the part of the HRC and the Office of the UN Commissioner on Human Rights (OHCHR), which are ill-suited and often unqualified to determine whether or not criminal violations of IHL have occurred.[36] In addition, there is very little that these bodies can do to influence situations of widespread violence and armed conflict, which are certainly not being ignored by other UN actors, states, or the media. Appeals to 'human rights' in such conflicts are unlikely to yield much fruit, which risks diminishing the value or effectiveness of human rights in the minds of many.

both parties in Sri Lanka ... and to establish the facts and circumstances of such alleged violations and of the crimes perpetrated with a view to avoiding impunity and ensuring accountability ...' UNHRC Res 25/1 (9 April 2014) A/HRC/25/1, para 10(b).

---

[33] John Heilprin 'UN Backs Inquiry of Alleged Islamic State Atrocities' *New York Times* (2 September 2014) A4. Also see UNHRC Res RES/S-22/1 (3 September 2014) HRC/RES/S-22/1. The press release announcing release of the 2015 report does not even mention the phrase 'human rights'. OHCHR 'ISIL May Have Committed War Crimes, Crimes Against Humanity and Genocide: UN Report' (OHCHR, 19 March 2015) <http://www.ohchr.org/EN/NewsEvents/Pages/DisplayNews.aspx?NewsID=15720&LangID=E#sthash.ySLpAFFm.dpuf> accessed 7 August 2019.

[34] OHCHR 'Human Rights Council Concludes Special Session on Atrocities Committed by the Terrorist Group Boko Haram' (OHCR, 1 April 2015) <http://www.ohchr.org/EN/NewsEvents/Pages/DisplayNews.aspx?NewsID=15790&LangID=E> accessed 7 August 2019.

[35] US Immigration and Customs Enforcement 'Overview, The Human Rights Violators & War Crimes Unit' <http://www.ice.gov/human-rights-violators/> accessed 7 August 2019.

[36] A recent example of this trend is a proposal by two former ambassadors to the United Nations to 'strengthen the conflict prevention and peacebuilding roles of the International Court of Justice and UN Human Rights Council'. This idea is even more surprising in light of their proposal in the same article also to create a UN 'Peacebuilding Council' out of the current Peacebuilding Commission; Madeline Albright and Ibrahim Gambari, 'To Confront the Crisis in Global Governance, the UN Needs Key Reforms' *USA Today* (16 June 2015) <http://www.usatoday.com/story/opinion/2015/06/16/united-nations-climate-change-peacekeeping-security-council-column/71258730/> accessed 7 August 2019. In the report from which this op-ed is drawn, 'human rights' appears three times in the three-page table of contents, once in 'human rights and transitional justice' and twice as 'international courts and human rights bodies'. See Commission on Global Security, Justice & Governance, 'Confronting the Crisis of Global Governance' (*The Hague Institute for Global Justice and the Stimson Centre*, 16 June 2015) <http://www.thehagueinstituteforglobaljustice.org/thinking-doing/publication/commission-on-global-security-justice-governance/> accessed 7 August 2019. To '[s]treamline the global human rights architecture,' the report encourages 'a human rights dialogue between the Security Council, HRC, and International Criminal Court ... [in order to respond to] large-scale human rights abuses,' ie international crimes. Ibid, 90, s 7.3.4.3.

B. Human Rights Hawks

Human rights can affect the use of force in two primary ways. First, severe or mass human rights violations may be utilized to justify the use of force by one state or coalition of states against another. Such a justification would either modify or serve as an exception to the prohibition of the threat or use of force 'against the territorial integrity or political independence of any state' contained in article 2(4) of the UN Charter.[37] Second, the simultaneous application of IHRL and IHL (also known as the law of war) in armed conflicts may modify one or the other body of law. The first issue involves *jus ad bellum*, or the legality of the use of force. The second implicates *jus in bello*, or the modalities of using force once hostilities have begun.

1. *Jus ad bellum*

In his book *Freedom on Fire: Human Rights Wars and America's Response*, John Shattuck proudly proclaims, 'I am a human rights hawk.'[38] A well-respected human rights lawyer and activist for decades, Shattuck served as Assistant Secretary for Democracy, Human Rights, and Labor under US President Bill Clinton in the challenging years 1993 to 1998. Citing the rise in chaos and repression that followed the end of the Cold War, along with the mass killings epitomized by the conflicts in Bosnia and Herzegovina, Haiti, Rwanda, and Kosovo, he argues that international security must be redefined 'to include the global protection of human rights, as we face an ever increasing threat of instability and terror emanating from failed states'.[39] In fact, the 'human rights wars' of which Shattuck speaks are more often cases of genocide or massive crimes against humanity, and his use of the much more expansive notion of 'human rights' wars is unfortunate; the confusion is increased by his definition of humanitarian intervention as 'a combined military and civilian effort by a coalition of countries to protect a civilian population *from severe human rights abuse* at the hands of their own government' (emphasis added).[40] While Shattuck supports multilateral action, Ruti Teitel observes that the 'drumbeat for humanitarian intervention' after Bosnia and Rwanda also was supported by 'human rights activists [who] were unabashed unilateralists, arguing for humanitarian intervention with or without procedural authorization or multilateral political backing'.[41] Michael Glennon notes the 'veritable cottage industry [that]

[37] The only clear exceptions to the use of force are individual or collective self-defence, as set forth in article 51 of the UN Charter, or when force is authorized by a binding decision taken by the UN Security Council pursuant to article 25 and Chapter VII of the UN Charter.

[38] John Shattuck, *Freedom on Fire, Human Rights Wars and America's Response* (Harvard University Press 2005) 7.

[39] Ibid, 289.

[40] Ibid, 297.

[41] Ruti Teitel, *Humanity's Law* (Oxford University Press 2011) 114–15.

has sprung up [after the 1999 NATO bombing in Kosovo] among manufacturers of new sets of rules concerning humanitarian intervention'.[42]

Another well-known hawk is Anne-Marie Slaughter, a supporter of the use of force in Kosovo in 1999, Iraq in 2003, Libya in 2011, and former Director of Policy Planning in the US Department of State 2009–2011. Complaining that international law has been too slow to legalize humanitarian intervention, she, too, goes well beyond genocide and crimes against humanity when she defines an intervention as 'legitimate' (not 'legal') 'when it responds to a gross and systematic violation of human rights that offends our common humanity'.[43] Noting the danger of 'aggression masquerading as humanitarian intervention', she argues that 'it is necessary to keep the requirement of collective authorization' for the use of force, on the assumption that, once we 'spell out the global conditions for legitimacy over legality ... the law will catch up with the reality of state practice'.[44] Like so many other theoretical justifications for force, however, the devil is in the details: despite Slaughter's recognition that '[i]t is impossible to strike Syria legally', she advocates US attacks on Syria and urged US President Obama 'to demonstrate that he can order the offensive use of force in circumstances other than secret drone attacks or covert operations ... [t]o lead effectively, in both the national and the global interest, the US must demonstrate its readiness to shoulder the full responsibilities of power'.[45]

2. The responsibility to protect

For over a decade, the debate over humanitarian or human rights intervention has largely evolved in the context of the doctrine of the 'responsibility to protect' ('R2P'). Unfortunately, the vagueness, hyperbole, and neo-colonial undertones of R2P may have the consequence of making it more, not less, difficult to reach consensus on criteria for humanitarian intervention in the future. As R2P continues to evolve within the labyrinthine corridors of the United Nations, what little potential the concept might have had as a catalyst for action is diminishing rather than increasing.[46] Finally, it may make it even more difficult to promote and protect human rights, properly understood, if a clear distinction is not maintained between the moral and political aspirations of R2P and the legally binding norms of IHRL.

[42] Michael Glennon, *The Fog of Law: Pragmatism, Security, and International Law* (Stanford University Press 2010) 98.

[43] Anne-Marie Slaughter, 'A Regional Responsibility to Protect,' in David Held and Kyle McNally (eds), *Lessons from Intervention in the 21st Century: Legality, Legitimacy, and Feasibility, Global Policy* (*e-book* Wiley Blackwell 2014) <http://www.princeton.edu/~slaughtr/Articles/RegionalResponsibilitytoProtect.pdf> accessed 7 August 2019.

[44] Ibid.

[45] Anne-Marie Slaughter, 'Stopping Russia starts in Syria' *CNBC* (23 April 2014) <http://www.cnbc.com/id/101605835> accessed 7 August 2019.

[46] Cf Margaret DeGuzman, 'When Are International Crimes Just Cause for War?' (2014) 55 Va J Int'l L 73 (hereafter DeGuzman, 'International Crimes').

The genesis of R2P lies in the 2001 report of the International Commission on Intervention and State Sovereignty (ICISS), which was created a year earlier by the Canadian government to consider how the international community 'should respond in the face of massive violations of human rights and humanitarian law'.[47] The Commission argued that substituting the concept of the 'responsibility to protect' for that of 'humanitarian intervention' better reflected the desired focus on victims, rather than the intervener, and was more likely to be acceptable to states.

While the primary public arguments for the invasion of Iraq in 2003 by the United States and its 'coalition of the willing' (which included such European human rights stalwarts as the United Kingdom, the Netherlands, Spain, Portugal, Italy, and Denmark) initially rested on illusory claims of weapons of mass destruction and support for terrorism, the case for invasion also included Saddam Hussein's admittedly heinous violations of human rights and the need to establish democracy by overthrowing the regime.[48] Whatever the true motives for invading Iraq, the mantra that emanated from Washington during the George W Bush administration, at least, was that the United States should assist in replacing dictatorships with democracy—implicitly, anywhere it can. With democracy would come tolerance and open societies, although the path to achieve these goals is strewn in Iraq with thousands of dead Americans and hundreds of thousands of dead Iraqis.[49] The overuse of 'democracy' and 'freedom' by President Bush sounded suspiciously like 'human rights' to many beyond Washington, DC, although the Bush administration's understanding of the latter term was myopic, at best.

The Obama administration has not been immune to resolving human rights dilemmas by force, although it does seem more reluctant to do so. A 2014 op-ed article went so far as to conclude that 'some of the most outspoken warmongers in Washington are self-proclaimed human rights advocates', citing arguments for the use of US military power 'to capture a warlord in Uganda, impose order in the Ivory Coast, crush rebels in South Sudan, and locate kidnap victims in Nigeria'.[50]

[47] International Commission on Intervention and State Sovereignty, 'The Responsibility to Protect' (*ICISS*, 2001) A at B, at 81. The full text of the report and related documents are available at: <https://www.idrc.ca/en/book/responsibility-protect-report-international-commission-intervention-and-state-sovereignty> accessed 23 August 2019.

[48] See eg President George W Bush's statement to the UN General Assembly, 12 December 2002, in which he cites the UN Commission on Human Rights' finding that 'Iraq continues to commit extremely grave violations of human rights, and ... the regime's repression is all pervasive ... Events can turn in one of two ways: If we fail to act in the face of danger, the people of Iraq will continue to live in brutal submission ... The regime will remain unstable ... the region will remain unstable, with little hope of freedom, and isolated from the progress of our times ... If we meet our responsibilities, if we overcome this danger, we can arrive at a very different future. The people of Iraq can shake off their captivity. They can one day join a democratic Afghanistan and a democratic Palestine, inspiring reforms throughout the Muslim world.' <https://georgewbush-whitehouse.archives.gov/news/releases/2002/09/20020912-1.html> accessed 7 August 2019.

[49] For a stinging condemnation of the 'apocalyptic legacy' of the Iraq war, see Frank Rich, 'Iraq Everlasting' *New York Magazine* (4 June 2014).

[50] Stephen Kinzer, 'Are Human Rights Activists Today's Warmongers?' *Boston Globe* (25 May 2014).

In 2005, the 'responsibility to protect' was limited by the UN General Assembly to the responsibility of individual states to protect their populations from the four international crimes of genocide, war crimes, ethnic cleansing, and crimes against humanity.[51] The international community's responsibility was limited to 'appropriate diplomatic, humanitarian and other peaceful means', unless coercive measures were authorized by the Security Council.[52]

Despite the circumspect manner in which the General Assembly delineated R2P, a 2009 report by the UN Secretary-General on R2P curiously added the phrase 'and violations' to most mentions of the four crimes, apparently as a means of tying the 2005 Summit Outcome's version of the responsibility to protect against certain international crimes to the broader responsibility of states to respect, ensure, and recognize international human rights.[53]

The only authorization by the UN Security Council of the use of force by non-UN forces occurred to protect civilians in Libya in 2011 was initially hailed as the high point of R2P. The Council authorized 'all necessary measures … to protect civilians and civilian populated areas under threat of attack', based on Muammar Qaddafi's threats against rebels in the city of Benghazi and with the support of the Arab League.[54] However, the subsequent de facto expansion of that mandate by US and European countries to legitimize the overthrow of Qaddafi and their support for the insurgents robbed R2P of much of its precedential value.[55] The subsequent civil war, deterioration of security, and resulting anarchy in Libya tarnished the concept of R2P further, and Libya should be remembered as a warning about unintended—perhaps even inevitable—consequences of using force, even to save lives.[56]

By linking the new concept of R2P to the widely accepted principle of state responsibility for human rights, the Secretary-General and others risk undermining the latter for no apparent reason. Fortunately, the platitudes that infused the Secretary-General's 2009 report have not been expanded or given more specific content in subsequent iterations of R2P, although the linkage of R2P with 'gross' or 'severe' or 'systematic' human rights violations continues. Implementing human

[51] See UNGA 2005 World Summit Outcome, GA Res 60/1 (24 October 2005) A/RES/60/1, para 138. For a cogent criticism of this limitation, see DeGuzman, 'International Crimes' (n 47).

[52] Ibid, para 139.

[53] UNGA 'Implementing the Responsibility to Protect, Report of the Secretary-General' (12 January 2009) A/63/677. The phrase 'crimes and violations' is repeated on numerous occasions in the report; See Ibid, paras 10(b), 10(d), 17, 18, 19, 23, 29, 32, 35, 38, 43, 49, 50, 54, 56, 57, 58, 59, 60, 66, and Annex, paras 1, 4, 5, and 7.

[54] UNSC Res 1973 (17 March 2011) UN Doc S/RES/1973, para 4.

[55] See eg Alan Kuperman (2003) 'A Model Humanitarian Intervention?: Reassessing NATO's Libya Campaign' 38 International Security 105.

[56] On the impact of R2P with respect to Libya, see Aidan Hehir (2013) 'The Permanence of Inconsistency: Libya, the Security Council, and the Responsibility to Protect' 38 International Security 137. ('Action taken on the basis of altruistic individual impulses cannot reasonably be cited as constituting a precedent or new norm. Rather, it is more accurately described as aberrant behaviour impelled by a unique constellation of necessarily temporal factors.' Ibid, 155–56.)

rights is difficult enough without the baggage of the responsibility to protect, and linking the concept of R2P with the law of human rights is unlikely to help either gain adherents.[57]

3. *Jus in bello*

It is clear that IHRL applies in time of armed conflict, alongside IHL, a position upheld by the International Court of Justice in several recent judgments.[58]

> The Court considers that the protection offered by human rights conventions does not cease in case of armed conflict, save through the effect of provisions for derogation of the kind to be found in Article 4 of the [International Covenant on Civil and Political Rights]. As regards the relationship between international humanitarian law and human rights law, there are thus three possible situations: some rights may be exclusively matters of international humanitarian law; others may be exclusively matters of human rights law; yet others may be matters of both these branches of international law … [T]he Court will have to take into consideration both these branches of international law, namely human rights law and, as *lex specialis*, international humanitarian law.[59]

These interpretations have been reinforced by the European Court of Human Rights (ECtHR), which has slowly expanded its extraterritorial jurisdiction over state actions outside its own territory.[60] The recent case of *Hassan v UK* alleged violations of the applicant's right to life, the prohibition against torture, and the legality of his detention by British forces in Iraq in 2003.[61] The court first followed its precedents in finding that, during his detention, Hassan was within the jurisdiction of the United Kingdom for the purposes of the European Convention on Human Rights. It then rejected the British argument that only IHL and not the human rights norms of the European Convention applied 'in the active hostilities phase of an international armed conflict, where the agents of the Contracting State are operating in territory of which they are not the occupying power'.[62] Consistent with the opinions of the International Court of Justice referenced earlier, the Court concluded that, given 'the co-existence of the safeguards provided by international

[57] For a fuller critique of R2P, from which parts of this section are drawn, see Hurst Hannum (2009) 'The Responsibility to Protect: Paradigm or Pastiche?' 60(2) Northern Ireland Legal Quarterly 135.

[58] See *Legality of the Threat or Use of Nuclear Weapons*, Advisory Opinion [1996] ICJ Rep 226 para 25; *The Legal Consequences of the Construction of a Wall in the Occupied Palestinian Territory* (Advisory Opinion) [2004] ICJ Rep 148, para 106 (hereafter *Legal Consequences of the Construction of a Wall*); *Case Concerning Armed Activities on the Territory of the Congo (Democratic Republic of Congo (DRC) v Uganda)* (Merits) Judgment [2005] ICJ Rep 168, paras 215–16.

[59] *Legal Consequences of the Construction of a Wall* (n 59) para 106.

[60] For brief descriptions of these cases, see European Court of Human Rights, 'Extra-territorial Jurisdiction of States Parties to the European Convention on Human Rights' (*Fact Sheet* 2014) 4–9.

[61] *Hassan v the United Kingdom* App no 29750/09 (ECtHR, 16 September 2014).

[62] Ibid, paras 76, 77.

humanitarian law and by the Convention in time of armed conflict, the grounds of permitted deprivation of liberty set out in subparagraphs (a) to (f) of [article 5 of the Convention] ... should be accommodated, as far as possible, with the taking of prisoners of war and the detention of civilians who pose a risk to security under the Third and Fourth Geneva Conventions'.[63] Finding that the detention was not arbitrary and was consistent with IHL, the Court found no violation of the European Convention.[64]

A final related issue is how the much the broader goals of 'humanitarian' or 'human rights' intervention (as opposed to a 'normal' armed conflict where military victory is the primary goal) may complicate existing norms of both IHRL and IHL. In a recent article, Gabriella Blum identifies the crux of the problem:

> Somewhat paradoxically, by making human rights violations within any single country a matter of international interest—and by deeming gross human rights violations a grave offence that implicate a duty to intervene on the part of the international community— human rights came to operate as both a limitation on war and a cause for war. They limited the targets and scope of deliberate harm in war, but also revived an earlier interest in the plight of individuals as a just cause for waging wars of 'humanitarian interventions'.[65]

In 'human rights wars', to use John Shattuck's phrase, structural changes, both political and economic, have become 'necessary components of victory, not merely post-war missions'.[66]

Structural changes mean not only stopping mass killing or creating more honest and functional government institutions; they also implicate 'regular' human rights. For example:

> Confiscation [of property] is allowed [under IHL] only for 'military necessity'. And yet, once gender equality, aid, and reconstruction are made part of the goals of the war [in Afghanistan], no less so than chasing after Al Qaida operatives, it is unclear why confiscation of property for... [military necessity] should be allowed, while for ... [the construction of a school for girls] it should not. Nor, for that

63 Ibid, para 104.

64 Ibid, paras 110, 111. A dissenting opinion by four judges argued that the norms of the European Convention could not be displaced by IHL without a formal derogation from Convention norms, as permitted by Article 15. The court must 'give priority to the [European] Convention ... By attempting to *reconcile the irreconcilable*, the majority's finding today does not, with respect, reflect an accurate understanding of the scope and substance of the fundamental right to liberty under the Convention, as reflected in its purpose and its historical origins in the atrocities of the international armed conflicts of the Second World War.' Ibid, dissenting opinion of Judges Spano, Nicolaou, Bianku, and Kalaydjieva, para 19; emphasis in original.

65 Gabriella Blum (2013) 'The Fog of Victory' 24 European Journal of International Law 391, 404 (hereafter Blum, 'Fog of Victory').

66 Ibid, 408.

> matter, is it clear why that same goal of gender equality would not justify the use of armed force against those who are fighting against it …
>
> With the extension of the war into the political and civilian realm, the principle of proportionality—if weighed against those interests—risks becoming meaningless. After all, how can one weigh how many lives the rights of women in Afghanistan are worth?[67]

As Blum demonstrates, conflating human rights and IHL may not be such a good idea. Beyond the obvious concern of each body of laws to protect the rights of individuals, their purposes are quite different. While derogation or temporary suspension of rights may be justified in states of emergency, human rights law generally assumes that states exist in conditions of relative peace and that governments are capable of acting to effectively (if not perfectly) ensure rights. IHL, on the other hand, is predicated on the existence of an armed conflict, and its major concern is regulating how that conflict should be conducted. Blum's not-so-rhetorical question is incapable of being answered by human rights law, and IHL is better at quantitative comparisons than qualitative moral judgments. We are left either with no law or the need to develop new law; the former situation would be disastrous, while the human rights hawks too often tend to ignore the latter in favour of rhetoric, 140-character tweets, and YouTube video appeals.

4. Concluding remarks

As the final quotation suggests, it is difficult, perhaps impossible, to balance the worth of one life against another. It is just as difficult to predict whether a particular use of force will be 'successful' or not, and at what cost.[68] Not only political but technological considerations determine which countries will be targeted for armed intervention; millions died in the Democratic Republic of Congo and Sudan, while intervenors tried to save thousands in Kosovo and Libya. Even if an international consensus could be reached over the criteria for intervention —just the four crimes identified by the UN General Assembly or a lower threshold?—any decision to

[67] Blum, 'Fog of Victory' (n 66) 416, 420. If this sounds overly theoretical or dramatic, consider the opinion of US Air Force General Michael Short during the 1999 NATO bombing of Serbia, who told journalists that 'hitting civilian morale was crucial to success. His tactic was going to be "no power to your refrigerator, no gas to your stove, you can't get to work because the bridge is down—the bridge on which you held your rock concerts and all stood with targets on your heads. That needs to disappear …"' *The Observer* (16 May 1999) 15, quoted in Costas Douzinas, *Human Rights and Empire: The Political Philosophy of Cosmopolitanism* (Routledge Cavendish 2007) 206 (hereafter Douzinas, *Human Rights and Empire*).

[68] For example, one of the criticisms of the 1999 NATO bombing in Kosovo/Serbia concerned the fact that NATO war planes flew at high altitudes in order to protect the pilots. This tactic was successful, in that NATO suffered not a single casualty during the three-month bombing campaign. However, approximately 500 innocent civilians were killed by NATO jets, and an additional 5,000–10,000 people, mostly Albanians, died as a result of the Serb campaign of ethnic cleansing that was unleashed immediately after the bombing began.

intervene will reflect national priorities, politics and capabilities, not only the extent of suffering of the victims.

Advocates of the responsibility to protect pretend that its adoption is an innovative limitation on national sovereignty, the sovereignty that 'allows' genocide and mass murder to be committed without consequence. However, this simplistic equation ignores another basic principle of international law that is held dear not only by criminals but also by former colonies and less powerful states whose history has been one of too much intervention rather than too little; that is, the prohibition against the use of force that is one of the cornerstones of the United Nations. The history of the past several decades provides little support for the claim that loosening or legalizing the norms against armed force will mitigate disaster, but it is almost certain that government intervention based on 'humanitarian' or 'R2P' justifications will be used to hide much less laudable goals on the part of the interveners.

Sovereignty has been limited by IHRL for decades. The obligations accepted by states under human rights treaties are legally binding, not just political statements mouthed by the UN General Assembly. That they do not include provisions that would authorize invasion or bombings is not a weakness but a recognition of the fact that implementation of human rights norms is a complex, often long-term process that cannot be accomplished by outsiders. Even if violations within a state are serious—such as widespread discrimination, regular use of torture, unfair trials and elections, a preference for elite enrichment rather than fulfilment of socio-economic rights—the answer cannot be found in the neo-colonial imposition at the point of a gun of others' ideals of rule of law or development.

Using the protection of human rights as an excuse for bombs and forced regime change is almost never a good idea. Neither the international community nor 'coalitions of the willing' have been particularly successful in (re)constructing states in accord with human rights principles.

A properly defined international responsibility to protect—directed towards preventing widespread loss of life, whatever the cause—could be a meaningful advance in the humanization of international law. However, calls for the use of force in order to 'do something' in the face of widespread human rights abuses raise unrealistic expectations and may deter adoption of less drastic actions that will be slow and frustrating but that may, in the end, be more fruitful and sustainable.

III. Marginalizing Government

Just as it may be easier to punish individuals than to change governments, human rights activists often find it easier to go after softer, more readily identifiable targets rather than governments. Transnational or multinational corporations (TNCs) have long been accused of either conspiring with governments to violate human rights for economic gain or simply ignoring governments and infringing 'rights' directly. Oddly, they are rarely given credit for contributing to the fulfilment of economic rights when development goes well, but that lack of balance need not detain us here.

A TNC may collaborate with a repressive government in many ways, and there is no doubt that many TNCs are willing to do so.[69] When the collaboration amounts to complicity or aiding and abetting an international crime, then the individuals involved (not the company) may be subject to international criminal law.

The UN attempted on a number of occasions to address corporate responsibility for human rights, culminating in adoption of the Guiding Principles on Business and Human Rights by the HRC in 2011. Prior to that initiative, the General Assembly spent many years in the 1970s and 1980s discussing a Code of Conduct for Transnational Corporations, an initiative that eventually foundered on north–south divisions, continuing disagreements over the New International Economic Order that was proclaimed by the UN General Assembly in 1974,[70] and a growing desire on the part of developing countries to encourage rather than discourage foreign investment.[71]

The most rights-oriented attempt to articulate the relationship between business and human rights were the Norms on the Responsibilities of Transnational Corporations and Other Business Enterprises with Regard to Human Rights, adopted by the UN then-Sub-Commission on the Promotion and Protection of Human Rights in 2003.[72] According to their primary author, US law professor and member of the Sub-Commission David Weissbrodt, the norms 'applied human rights law under ratified conventions to the activities of … [businesses]. Moreover, the language of the document emphasized binding responsibilities through the use of the term "shall" rather than "should," and the draft norms included measures for implementation.'[73]

While many NGOs welcomed the norms, they received a chilly reception from the business community and the Sub-Commission's parent body, the Commission

[69] See eg UNHRC 'Report of the Special Representative of the Secretary-General on the Issue of Human Rights and Transnational Corporations and Other Business Enterprises, Corporations and Human Rights: A Survey of the Scope and Patterns of Alleged Corporate-Related Human Rights Abuse' (23 May 2008) A/HRC/8/5/Add.2. The website of the Business and Human Rights Resource Centre is an excellent source for, *inter alia*, contemporary allegations regarding corporate behaviour <https://business-humanrights.org/en> accessed 7 August 2019.

[70] Declaration on the Establishment of a New International Economic Order, UNGA Res 3201 (S-VI) (1 May 1974) A/RES/S-6/3201.

[71] For a brief summary, see generally Sean Murphy (2005) 'Taking Multinational Corporate Codes of Conduct to the Next Level' 43 Columbia Journal of Transnational Law 389.

[72] UNCHR 'Norms on the Responsibilities of Transnational Corporations and Other Business Enterprises with Regard to Human Rights' (26 August 2003) Doc E/CN.4/Sub.2/2003/12/Rev.2.

[73] UNCHR 'Responsibilities of Transnational Corporations and Other Business Enterprises with Regard to Human Rights' (2002) Doc E/CN.4/Sub.2/2002/13 (2003), 6. Also see David Weissbrodt and Muria Kruger (2003) 'Norms on the Responsibilities of Transnational Corporations and Other Business Enterprises with Regard to Human Rights' 97 American Journal of International Law 901.

on Human Rights. Nonetheless, it was not politically feasible for the Commission simply to drop the issue, and it subsequently requested the Secretary-General to appoint a special representative on human rights and business, whose work over the next several years resulted in adoption by the UN HRC (which succeeded the Commission in 2006) of the Guiding Principles on Business and Human Rights.[74]

The principles were drafted by the special representative, US professor John Ruggie, after extensive research and a series of consultations with governments, businesses, NGOs, and other stakeholders. The principles are organized to implement the 'protect, respect and remedy' framework approved by the Council in 2010.[75] The special representative's introduction to the principles states that their 'normative contribution lies not in the creation of new international law obligations but in elaborating the implications of existing standards and practices ... [and] integrating them within a single, logically coherent and comprehensive template'.[76]

The three pillars of the principles are 'the *State* duty to protect against human rights abuses by third parties, including business ... the *corporate* responsibility to respect human rights, which means to act with due diligence to avoid infringing on the rights of others; and greater access by victims to effective remedy, judicial and non-judicial' (emphasis added). [77] 'The term "responsibility" to respect [re businesses], rather than "duty", is meant to indicate that respecting rights is *not* an obligation that current IHRL generally imposes directly on companies ... [although it reflects] a standard of expected conduct acknowledged in virtually every voluntary and soft-law instrument related to corporate responsibility' (emphasis added).[78] A Working Group of the Council created in 2011 now monitors compliance with the principles.

The Guiding Principles look much like what one would expect from a decent set of guidelines articulating corporate social responsibility. As noted earlier, they do not purport to extend the legal obligation to ensure human rights to business; for this reason, many NGOs were disappointed. At the same time, however, they have reinforced social and political pressures on business to pay attention—'due diligence'—to human rights norms, and the principles themselves have been widely supported by the business community.

In 2014, the HRC decided to create an open-ended intergovernmental working group 'to elaborate an international legally binding instrument to regulate, in IHRL, the activities of transnational corporations and other business entities'.[79]

[74] UNHRC Res 17/4 (2011) A/HRC/RES/17/4.

[75] UNHRC 'Report of the Special Representative of the Secretary-General on the Issue of Human Rights' and 'Transnational Corporations and other Business Enterprises, John Ruggie' (9 April 2010) UN Doc A/HRC/14/27 (2010), (hereafter John Ruggie, 'Report 2010').

[76] UNHRC 'Report of the Special Representative of the Secretary-General on the Issue of Human Rights and Transnational Corporations and other Business Enterprises, John Ruggie' (21 March 2011) UN Doc A/HRC/17/31 (2011), para 14.

[77] John Ruggie, 'Report 2010' (n 76) para 1.

[78] Ibid, para 55.

[79] UNHRC Res 26/9 (2014) A/HRC/RES/26/9, para 1.

The first meeting of this group, which was 'to collect inputs ... on possible principles, scope and elements of such an international legally binding instrument',[80] was in July 2015, and it remains to be seen whether this initiative will bear fruit in any meaningful way.

In the United States, a more direct means of attempting to hold corporations accountable for harm that they cause was 'discovered' when, in 1979, a US Court of Appeals was called upon to interpret the 1789 Alien Tort Claims Act (ATCA). ATCA grants original jurisdiction to federal district courts over 'any civil action by an alien for a tort only, committed in violation of the law of nations or a treaty of the United States'.[81] The court in *Filartiga* held that this jurisdiction could be exercised over a Paraguayan national and a Paraguayan victim (both resident in the United States at the time) for torture that had occurred in Paraguay.[82]

This set the stage for dozens of cases filed under ATCA against both individuals and corporations for torts committed outside the United States (any tort committed within the United States would be actionable under domestic tort law), so long as they allegedly violated international law. The US Supreme Court subsequently affirmed that an ATCA suit is permissible so long as the alleged violation of the law of nations (today known as customary international law) is widely accepted 'and defined with a specificity comparable to the features of the eighteenth-century paradigms we have recognized' (piracy, violations of safe conducts, and infringement of the rights of ambassadors).[83] However, a subsequent Supreme Court decision in 2013 narrowed the scope of ATCA further, by holding that the statute does not have extra-territorial application. [84] It noted, in passing, that there was 'no indication that the ATS [ATCA] was passed to make the United States a uniquely hospitable forum for the enforcement of international norms'.[85]

While the responsibility of the foreign government is implicit in ATCA suits, even a successful case does not directly require the offending government to do anything. In addition, shifting the focus to corporations may make it easier for the government itself to shift blame for the harm. Further, the prospect of using corporations to control governments rather than the reverse raises serious concerns, and attempts to impose human rights obligations directly on companies (whether foreign or domestic) may empower just those entities—corporations—that are the least accountable and transparent of all.[86]

80 Ibid, para 5.

81 28 USC sec 1350.

82 *Filartiga v Peña-Irala*, 630 F2d 876 (2d Cir 1980). Filartiga also was ground-breaking in that it held that the prohibition of torture was a norm of customary international law.

83 *Sosa v Alvarez-Machain*, 124 SCt 2739 (2004).

84 *Kiobel et al. v Royal Dutch Petroleum*, 133 SCt 1659 (2013).

85 Ibid, 12.

86 Cf the comments of Professor Ruggie in his first report, where he states that making corporations 'in effect, co-equal duty bearers for the broad spectrum of human rights ... may undermine efforts to build indigenous social capacity and to make Governments more responsible to their own citizenry'. UNCHR 'Interim Report of the Special Representative of the Secretary-General on Human Rights and

Many other non-state actors—criminals, terrorists, armed opposition groups beyond the control of governments, intergovernmental organizations, religious groups, and others—harm individuals. The issue is not whether ways should be found to hold such entities responsible for the harm that they cause, whether through criminal sanctions, civil sanctions, or both, but whether it is useful to characterize such acts as 'human rights violations'. One of the strongest arguments for extending 'human rights' obligations to non-state actors has been made by Andrew Clapham, who would extend human rights to the UN and other international organizations, corporations, non-state actors in times of armed conflict,[87] and even individuals.[88] While Clapham makes a strong case for why such entities should care about 'human rights' broadly construed, the 'obligations' he proposes most often fall within the scope of moral and political obligations, rather than legal ones.[89]

Given the limits on international enforcement mechanisms and the ultimate responsibility of states to control activities within their jurisdiction, it would seem better in the long run to insist that governments live up to their obligations to prohibit and punish certain conduct, rather than expecting international law to mandate corporate or other non-state conduct in human rights matters. Improving corporate social responsibility has already had an impact on the activities of many businesses, and there is no need either to limit corporate social responsibility (CSR) to international 'human rights' norms nor to impose legal obligations to protect and ensure human rights on entities that have neither the capability nor the authority to do so.

Bringing pressure to bear on all political and economic actors who may be able to contribute to making the world a better place is a worthy endeavour. Ensuring that individuals, organizations, and businesses that harm others are held responsible for that harm is laudable. Much of such work is related to the economic, social, cultural, civil, and political rights guaranteed by IHRL, but it also reaches—and should reach—much further, addressing issues of morality, social justice, equity, and use of national resources, in order to enable individuals and groups to achieve a better life.

Transnational Corporations and Other Business Enterprises' (22 February 2006) UN Doc A/EN.4/2006/97 (2006), para 68.

---

[87] With respect to individual government, police, or military officials, a comprehensive study published by the International Committee of the Red Cross in 2005 observed that 'it is the majority view that international human rights law only binds governments and not armed opposition groups'. This does not detract from the idea that individuals may commit and be held responsible for international crimes, as discussed above, but it is far from clear what expanding human rights obligations to individuals is designed to achieve. Jean-Marie Henckaerts and Louise Doswald-Beck, *Customary International Humanitarian Law, Vol. 1: Rules* (ICRC 2005) 299.

[88] Clapham, *Human Rights Obligations* (n 9).

[89] See eg Hurst Hannum (2007) 'Book Review: Human Rights Obligations of Non-State Actors' 101 American Journal of International Law 514.

Government's job is to oversee a legal and political system that is fair, non-discriminatory, accountable, and tolerant of minority views, so that these more far-reaching demands can be responsibly brought to bear on all organs of society and individuals within society. Both advocacy and the targets of advocacy enjoy rights that enable free choice on both sides; the *outcome* of advocacy is not guaranteed, except insofar as the human rights of all are ensured. However, it remains true that '[h]uman rights can meaningfully survive only within the context of the nation-state'.[90]

Struggles between government and civil society are inevitable—this is called democracy, which assumes that disagreement among different segments of society is better than enforcing an artificial consensus that only consolidates the power of those who already exercise it. Providing support, assistance, expertise, and resources to government are an essential part of ensuring human rights, and we should not expect the private sector—whether business, religious, or civil society actors—to accomplish or be held accountable for what is properly within the domain of government.

IV. Undermining Old Rights with New Ones

Both critics and some supporters of the human rights movement have expressed concern over what Eric Posner terms the 'hypertrophy' of rights: 'The more human rights there are, and thus the greater variety of human interests that are protected, the more that the human rights system collapses from an undifferentiated welfarism in which all interests must be taken seriously for the sake of the public good.'[91] Michael Ignatieff argues that 'rights inflation—the tendency to define anything desirable as a right—ends up eroding the legitimacy of a defensible core of rights'.[92] Allen Buchanan similarly observes that 'unbridled proliferation damages the very idea of international human rights by abandoning the notion of extraordinarily high priority norms in favour of an ever-expanding list of protected interests'.[93]

Perfection was not achieved with the adoption of the Universal Declaration in 1948, nor with the adoption of the two covenants in 1966. There is a great deal of room for new rights, and there have been welcome advances in articulating new international norms for minorities and indigenous peoples, to name only two recent initiatives. In addition, the rights of certain vulnerable or historically

[90] Douzinas, *Human Rights and Empire* (n 68) 231. Steven Ratner's articulation of a moral standard for international justice based on peace and basic human rights, although couched in a somewhat different context, also recognizes that 'the interests and standards of states ... deserve serious consideration alongside the interests and claims of individuals'. Steven Ratner, *The Thin Justice of International Law: A Moral Reckoning of the Law of Nations* (OUP 2015) 85 (hereafter Ratner, *The Thin Justice*).

[91] Eric Posner, *The Twilight of International Human Rights Law* (OUP 2014) 94.

[92] Michael Ignatieff, 'Human Rights as Idolatry' in Gutmann (ed), *Human Rights as Politics and Idolatry* (Princeton University Press 2003) 90.

[93] Buchanan, *The Heart of Human Rights* (n 7) 286.

marginalized groups—women, children, persons with disabilities—have been articulated in greater detail through the adoption of treaties that expanded on the covenants' focus on 'everyone'.

These treaties adopted under the auspices of the UN[94] retain the 'human' in human rights; they do not address broad economic or political issues that are incapable of being rationally debated in the context of rights. However, the list of topics today addressed by the most important UN human rights body, the HRC, goes well beyond further explication or examination of adopted treaties and puts in sharper perspective the rights-inflation criticism. Beginning in 1990, the Council (then Commission) has created working groups and individual experts (collectively known as 'special procedures') on an ad-hoc basis to address a number of thematic issues. The early special procedures were concerned with physical security (eg, disappearances, torture, arbitrary execution, and detention) and civil rights (eg, independence of judges and lawyers, freedom of religion and belief, racism). A number of socio-economic rights followed, including the rights to health, food, water, education, and housing.

By 2017, the list of special procedures had grown to forty-four,[95] and the issues addressed include even narrower categories (eg, African descendants, persons with albinism, human rights defenders), as well as a number of what might be termed 'rights and' issues. The latter include special procedures on the implications for human rights of the environmentally sound management and disposal of hazardous substances and wastes (created in 1995); extreme poverty and human rights (1998); effects of foreign debt and other related international financial obligations of States on the full enjoyment of all human rights, particularly economic, social, and cultural rights (2000); human rights and international solidarity (2005); the use of mercenaries as a means of violating human rights and impeding the exercise of the right of peoples to self-determination (2005); human rights and transnational corporations and other business enterprises (2011); human rights obligations relating to the enjoyment of a safe, clean, healthy, and sustainable environment (2012); the promotion of a democratic and equitable international order (2011); the promotion of truth, justice, reparation, and guarantees of non-recurrence (2011); and the negative impact of unilateral coercive measures on the enjoyment of human rights (2014).

One of the most questionable—yet universally accepted—of the new human rights is set forth in the 1986 UN General Assembly Declaration on the Right to Development,[96] the first article of which proclaims:

1. The right to development is an inalienable human right by virtue of which every human person and all peoples are entitled to participate in, contribute

[94] Other UN-developed treaties address torture, migrant workers, and the protection of persons from 'enforced disappearance'.
[95] A complete list may be found at OHCHR website, Thematic 'Special Procedures' (n 15).
[96] UNGA Res 41/128 (4 December 1986) A/RES/41/128.

to, and enjoy economic, social, cultural, and political development, in which all human rights and fundamental freedoms can be fully realized.

2. The human right to development also implies the full realization of the right of peoples to self-determination, which includes, subject to the relevant provisions of both International Covenants on Human Rights, the exercise of their inalienable right to full sovereignty over all their natural wealth and resources.

The conflation of development with 'inalienable' human rights is evidence of the increasing political character of human rights even in the 1980s, and it reflects the concern of developing countries (and the United Nations in general) to create a more equitable international economic order. While there is no doubt that a country's level of development is relevant to its capacity to fulfil its human rights obligations, as explicitly recognized in the Covenant on Economic, Social and Cultural Rights (CESCR), it is difficult to reconcile the myriad aspects of international development with the primary focus of human rights on the relationship between individuals and their own government. Nonetheless, the rhetoric of the right to development enjoys broad support, and the resolution creating the position of UN High Commissioner for Human Rights specifically mandates that the High Commissioner shall 'promote and protect the realization of the right to development'.[97] However, the right to development remains in the realm of 'soft law'; it has not yet been proclaimed in any UN human rights treaty and certainly does not form part of customary international law.

As is evident from the partial list of special procedures above, many of the 'human rights and' issues are related to economic policy, trade, and interstate relations.[98] Given the dire conditions in which billions of people in the world survive, it is not surprising that reducing or eradicating poverty has increasingly become linked to the concepts of human rights and human dignity.[99] In 2001, the Committee on Economic, Social and Cultural Rights bluntly declared that 'poverty constitutes a denial of human rights'.[100] The following year, High Commissioner Mary Robinson stated, '[e]xtreme poverty to me is the greatest denial of the exercise of human

[97] UNGA Res 48/141 (10 December 1993) A/RES/48/141, para 4(c).

[98] This connection purportedly reflects article 28 of the Universal Declaration of Human Rights: 'Everyone is entitled to a social and international order in which the rights and freedoms set forth in this Declaration can be fully realized.'

[99] The Universal Declaration of Human Rights refers to dignity five times. Article 1 proclaims 'All human beings are born free and equal in dignity and rights. They are endowed with reason and conscience and should act towards one another in a spirit of brotherhood.' Article 22 refers to the right of everyone to realization 'of the economic, social and cultural rights indispensable for his dignity and the free development of his personality'.

[100] UNCESCR 'Substantive Issues arising in the Implementation of the International Covenant on Economic, Social, and Cultural Rights: Poverty and the International Covenant on Economic, Social, and Cultural Rights' (10 May 2001) E/C.12/2001/10, para 1.

rights'.[101] Louse Arbour, Robinson's successor as High Commissioner, similarly called poverty 'the gravest human rights challenge in the world' and stated that '[t]he realization of human rights—including the fight against poverty—is a duty, not a mere aspiration'.[102] Arbour's successor, Navi Pillay, stated that 'poverty itself represents a complex of human rights violations'.[103] A panel of eminent human rights experts declared in 2011, '[t]he goal of eradicating poverty must be transformed from a merely voluntary development target into a legally binding human rights obligation of rich and poor countries and of other actors in the international community alike'.[104] Many NGOs have joined in, with Amnesty International using 'poverty is a human rights violation' as a campaign slogan.[105]

A useful publication by the New York-based Center for Economic and Social Rights suggests that poverty can be a cause of human rights violations, that it can be a consequence of human rights violations, or that it can be seen as, 'in itself a negation of human dignity and therefore a denial of human rights'.[106] Among the challenges in identifying the existence of poverty per se as a violation of human rights are the range of rights involved, the range of responsible actors (both national and international), and the 'overlapping and multiple determinants [of poverty] that cannot all be ascribed to state or non-state actors'.[107] The report persuasively concludes that 'poverty is not in and of itself a violation. Rather the violation occurs when certain (usually government) actions or inaction breaches human rights obligations in a way that creates, exacerbates or perpetuates poverty'.[108]

[101] 'Mary Robinson, UN Human Rights Chief' *BBC News* (United Kingdom, 21 November 2002) <http://www.news.bbc.co.uk/2/hi/talking_point/forum/1673034.stm> accessed 7 August 2019.

[102] 'Statements on the occasion of the UN's celebration of Human Rights Day 2005'.

[103] Letter of Navanethem Pillay, High Commissioner for Human Rights to all UN Permanent Missions in New York and Geneva, concerning Human Rights in the Post-2015 [Sustainable Development] Agenda (6 June 2013) 4 (on file with author).

[104] The Panel on Human Dignity 'Protecting Dignity: An Agenda for Human Rights' (Geneva 2011) para 86 (hereafter Panel on Human Dignity, 'Protecting Dignity') <https://www.geneva-academy.ch/joomlatools-files/docman-files/GB-ADH%20Brochure%20Agenda%20Human%20Rights-17x17.pdf> accessed 7 August 2019.

[105] Remarks of Marianne Mollmann, Senior Advisor, Amnesty International, at ILSA/ILA International Weekend, Panel 'Fair and Balanced: The Ethics of International Human Rights Fact Finding' (21 October 2011) (author's notes). Mollmann noted that human rights have 'different expression in different contexts', distinguishing fact-finding from adoption of a campaign slogan. AI's website describes its current Secretary General, Salil Shetty, as a 'long-term activist on poverty and justice', citing his work with the UN Millennium Campaign and ActionAid, 'one of the world's foremost international development NGOs'. See <http://www.amnesty.org/en/who-we-are/our-people/secretary-general> accessed 7 August 2019.

[106] Centre for Economic and Social Rights, 'Human Rights and Poverty: Is poverty a Violation of Human Rights?' (*Human Rights Insights No 1*, 2009) 3 <http://www.palermo.edu/Archivos_content/2015/derecho/pobreza_multidimensional/bibliografia/Sesion4_doc3.pdf> accessed 7 August 2019.

[107] Ibid, 4.

[108] Ibid, 7. This is similar to the situation of private domestic violence against women or the kidnapping (or enforced disappearance) of persons by, eg criminals or vigilantes. In and of itself, such acts are merely crimes, not human rights violations. However, if the government is unable or (more commonly) unwilling to punish and prevent such crimes, its refusal to 'ensure' a woman's right to physical security

The issue is not whether poverty should be combatted but whether it is useful to identify it as a human rights violation, along the lines of the simplistic AI slogan. For the reasons just mentioned, the answer is no, from both a pragmatic and legal perspective. Pragmatically, poverty-reduction policies involve much more than stopping 'violations', and focusing on human rights misleadingly implies that there are simple solutions to the complex problem of structural poverty. The 'poverty-is-a-human-rights-violation' slogan detracts from the attention that should be paid to a state's concrete obligations with respect to economic and social rights (such as forced evictions, violations of labour rights, or the right to health) that may exacerbate or create poverty. Finally, calling on states to 'end poverty' without any consideration of competing rights or the complexities of macroeconomic policy (such as balancing a temporary increase in poverty against a good faith attempt to address longer-term structural issues) misrepresents the totality of a state's human rights obligations, implying that poverty always trumps everything else. While reminding states of their obligations to protect the human rights of all those within their jurisdiction is appropriate and welcome, when human rights experts offer gratuitous advice on economic policy, it simply supports the nefarious notion that 'human rights' offer the answer to all the world's problems.[109]

Another issue frequently linked to human rights is protection of the environment, ranging from holding companies responsible for oil spills and other environmental degradation to asserting an obligation on—someone? everyone?—to address climate change. Since most UN human rights treaties were drafted before environmental protection became a matter of international concern, there are few specific references to environmental matters, and environmental concerns are most often addressed as part of the rights to life or health.

or its tolerance of disappearances (in which security forces often collude) becomes an internationally cognizable violation of human rights.

[109] For example, in responding to the release of a European study on the structure of the EU banking sector, three UN special procedures offered advice that seems to go well beyond their competence and the mandates of international human rights law. The Special Rapporteur on extreme poverty and human rights called on states categorically not to use 'budgetary resources' to bail out financial firms; the independent expert on foreign debt and human rights called for regulatory reforms to be extended to 'other financial sector actors' in addition to banks; and the independent expert on a democratic and equitable international order simplistically suggested 'perfectly viable alternative solutions to the financial crisis, such as reducing the so-called "defense" budget and significantly reducing all military expenditures'. 'UN Experts call for EU Banking Sector Reforms in Line with States' Human Rights Obligations' *UN News Centre* (5 October 2012) <http://www.un.org/apps/news/story.asp?NewsID=43220#.WLIdbBicZfg> accessed 7 August 2019. A somewhat similar approach was offered by the Deputy High Commissioner for Human Rights during HRC consideration of a devastating drought in the Horn of Africa in 2011. She opined that 'the crisis has provided an opportunity to examine grievances such as the debt burden, trade, representation in international financial institutions, toxic waste dumping and illegal fishing'. OHCHR, 'The Crisis in the Horn of Africa: A Human Rights Perspective' *News and Events* (26 October 2011) <http://www.ohchr.org/EN/NewsEvents/Pages/CrisisHornAfrica.aspx> accessed 7 August 2019.

More recently, regional instruments have referred explicitly to environmental issues. The African Charter on Human and Peoples' Rights recognizes the right of '[a]ll peoples' (not persons) to a 'general satisfactory environment favourable to their development'.[110] The African Women's Convention recognizes in greater detail the right of women 'to live in a healthy and sustainable environment'.[111] The additional protocol to the American Convention on Human Rights on socio-economic and cultural rights provides:

1. Everyone shall have the right to live in a healthy environment and to have access to basic public services.
2. The States Parties shall promote the protection, preservation, and improvement of the environment.[112]

As a component of the right to an adequate standard of living, the 2012 Association of Southeast Asian Nations (ASEAN) Human Rights Declaration guarantees the right to a 'safe, clean and sustainable environment'; it also mentions the environment in the context of the right to development.[113]

As discussed with respect to poverty, human rights violations may either cause or result from environmental degradation, but the right to a clean/healthy/sustainable environment per se is difficult to define. As one leading expert on both environmental issues and human rights has stated:

> The substance of environmental rights involves evaluating ecological systems, determining the impacts that can be tolerated and what is needed to maintain and protect the natural base on which life depends. Environmental quality standards, precaution and principles of sustainability can establish the limits of environmental decision-making and continue to give specific content to environmental rights in law.[114]

It is certainly possible to develop 'environmental rights in law', as evidenced by the number of environmental protection laws at both domestic and international levels. However, the obligations owed to humans—the subjects of human rights—are perhaps better articulated by continuing reference to existing rights, such as to

110 African Charter on Human and Peoples' Rights (adopted 27 June 1981, entered into force 21 October 1986) (1982) 21 ILM 58 (African Charter) art 24.

111 African Union, Protocol to the African Charter on Human and People's Rights on the Rights of Women in Africa (adopted 28 March 2003, entered into force 11 July 2003).

112 Additional Protocol to the American Convention on Human Rights in the Area of Economic, Social and Cultural Rights (Protocol of San Salvador) (entered into force 16 November 1999) OAS Treaty Series No 69 (1988), 28 ILM 156.

113 Association of Southeast Asian States, ASEAN Human Rights Declaration (18 November 2002) art 28(f); The right to development is found in articles 35–37.

114 Dinah Shelton (2010) 'Developing Substantive Environmental Rights' 1 Journal of Human Rights & Environment 89, 120.

health and life.[115] A human rights approach to the environment is likely to leave many legitimate environmental issues untouched (eg conservation of species, preservation of 'natural' beauty), while inserting the environment into human rights without relatively specific norms may lead to little more than platitudes. Calling for Royal Dutch Shell to 'clean up its human rights mess in the Niger Delta'[116] may be useful to an NGO looking for support and new sources of income, but confusing civil wrongs and damages with government obligations and peoples' rights is unlikely to help.

Scores of countries suffer from varying degrees of official corruption, and the resulting damage to the economy, government accountability, and rule of law can be enormous. High Commissioner Navi Pillay called corruption 'an enormous obstacle to the realization of all human rights ... [t]he impact of corruption on development and human rights is multifaceted; so too must be our response'.[117] At the same time, merely including a concept as broad as 'corruption' within IHRL simply adds to the list of rights whose definition and implementation are extremely problematic.[118] Ensuring good governance is not the same as ensuring human rights, and the latter will never be sufficient to protect us from corrupt or ignorant government officials.

One human rights academic has stated that 'it is legitimate to draw on philosophical arguments or activist agendas to claim any global social issue as a human right',[119] but one should be careful what one wishes for. Nearing the end of her time as UN High Commissioner for Human Rights, Navi Pillay observed that 'all [states] argued that she should avoid creating new rights. "That came up again and again," she said'.[120] Examples of either new or extended rights that have been

[115] According to the first UN Independent Expert on the issue of human rights obligations relating to the enjoyment of a safe, clean, healthy and sustainable environment, John H Knox, this has been the approach consistently adopted by UN human rights bodies, which 'have concentrated not on proclaiming a new right to a healthy environment, but rather on what might be called "greening" human rights—that is, examining and highlighting the relationship of existing human rights to the environment.'

UNHRC 'Report of the Independent Expert on the Issue of Human Rights Obligations Relating to the Enjoyment of a Safe, Clean, Healthy and Sustainable Environment, John H. Knox Preliminary Report' (24 December 2012) UN Doc A/HRC/22/43, para 16 (hereafter Knox, 'Preliminary Report').

[116] Amnesty International USA, 'Shell Oil: Own up, Pay Up and Clean Up', email from <alerts@takeaction.amnestyusa.org> 10 November 2011 (on file with author).

[117] OHCHR, 'The Human Rights Case Against Corruption' (*Summary of Panel Discussion,* 27 March 2013) <http://www.ohchr.org/EN/NewsEvents/Pages/HRCaseAgainstCorruption.aspx> accessed 7 August 2019.

[118] For brief arguments on both sides of the issue, cf Mathew Murray and Andrew Spalding, 'Freedom from Official Corruption as a Human Right' (*Governance Studies at Brookings,* January 2015) <http://www.brookings.edu/~/media/research/files/papers/2015/01/27-freedom-corruption-human-right-murray-spalding/murray-and-spalding_v06.pdf> accessed 7 August 2019, with Anusha Pamula, 'The Problem With Framing Freedom From Corruption as a Human Right' (*GAB/The Global Anticorruption Blog,* 29 May 2015) <globalanticorruptionblog.com/2015/05/29/the-problem-with-framing-freedom-from-corruption-as-a-human-right/> accessed 26 February 2017.

[119] Stephen Marks, 'Human Rights' in Christopher Bates and James Ciment (eds), *Global Social Issues: An Encyclopedia* (Routledge 2012).

[120] Nick Cumming-Bruce, 'For UN Leader on Human Rights, Finish Line Looks Blurry' *New York Times* (13 August 2014) <https://www.nytimes.com/2014/08/14/world/europe/for-un-leader-on-human-rights-finish-line-looks-blurry.html> accessed 7 August 2019.

identified within the UN system include the Special Rapporteur in the field of cultural rights, who has raised concerns about the impact of commercial advertising 'on cultural diversity and the right of people to choose their own ways of life';[121] a special rapporteur on the right to health stated that the criminalization of sex work violates human rights by, *inter alia*, 'creating barriers to access by sex workers to health services and legal remedies';[122] and the Special Rapporteur on freedom of opinion and expression has called on governments 'to develop effective policies to attain universal access to the Internet' for their populations.[123] An Organization of American States (OAS) draft declaration on the rights of the elderly calls upon states to 'take steps to ensure that public and private institutions offer older persons access without discrimination to comprehensive care, including ... appropriately manag[ing] problems related to the fear of death of the terminally ill'.[124] Advocates and UN agencies continue to strain to link human rights and the environment.[125]

Perhaps the crux of the problem is that many human rights advocates, both 'northern' and 'southern', confuse their own social agendas with the promotion of internationally recognized human rights. For example, requiring women by law to cover themselves and remain in every respect subservient to men violates the international human rights prohibition against discrimination based on sex. On the other hand, even very strong social and/or religious pressures on women to conform to certain social norms do not violate human rights standards—which

[121] UNGA 'Report of the Special Rapporteur in the Field of Cultural Rights' (2014) UN Doc A/69/286, para 96.

[122] UNGA 'Report of the Special Rapporteur on the Right of Everyone to the Enjoyment of the Highest Attainable Standard of Physical and Mental Health, Anand Grover' (2010) UN Doc A/HRC/14/20, para 43. In August 2015, Amnesty International decided to call for decriminalisation of the sex trade, although it will apparently be left to each national section of AI to determine whether or not it will support or lobby for this position. See Doreen Carvajal, 'Amnesty International Votes for Policy Calling for Decriminalization of Prostitution' *New York Times* (11 August 2015) <https://www.nytimes.com/2015/08/12/world/europe/amnesty-international-votes-for-policy-calling-for-decriminalization-of-prostitution.html> accessed 7 August 2019.

[123] UNGA 'Report of the Special Rapporteur on the Promotion and Protection of the Right to Freedom of Opinion and Expression, Frank La Rue' (2011) UN Doc A/HRC/17/27, para 60. Journalists widely, breathlessly—and inaccurately—reported that 'the UN' had declared broadband access to be 'a basic human right, right up there with the right to healthcare, shelter and food'. See Randall Lane, 'The UN Says Broadband Is Basic Human Right' *Forbes* (15 November 2011) <http://www.forbes.com/sites/randalllane/2011/11/15/the-united-nations-says-broadband-is-basic-human-right/#510dc49d4514> accessed 7 August 2019.

[124] Draft Inter-American Convention on Protection of the Human Rights of Older People, OAS Doc OEA/Ser G, CAJP/GT/DHPM/145/14 rev 18 corr 4 (2015) art 6.

[125] See eg Concept Note for a High Level Expert Meeting on the New Future of Human Rights and Environment, co-organized by OHCHR and the UN Environment Program: 'More than 2 million annual deaths and billions of cases of diseases are attributed to pollution. All over the world, people experience the negative effects of environmental degradation ... These facts clearly show the close linkages between the environment and the enjoyment of human rights, and justify an integrated approach to environment and human rights.' The initial report of the Independent Expert on the issue of human rights obligations relating to the enjoyment of a safe, clean, healthy, and sustainable environment appropriately observed that 'the first priority of his mandate is to provide greater conceptual clarity to the application of human rights obligations related to the environment'. Knox, 'Preliminary Report' (n 116) Summary.

constrain governments, not one's family or church or social peers. No-one suggests that international law should force the Catholic church to ordain women priests, for example, and voluntarily accepted Islamic, Jewish, or fundamentalist Protestant tenets regarding the 'place' of women are no different. It is racist behaviour if one's family cuts off all contact with a family member who marries someone of a different ethnicity or caste, but human rights law does not mandate the family's acceptance of such a situation, and the family's racist attitude does not per se constitute a human rights violation under international norms.

Such social constraints and attitudes are indefensible in a modern society populated by diverse cultures and traditions, and I believe that greater equality and tolerance of difference are likely to develop almost inevitably as societies modernize. However, not everything that I (or any other human rights advocate) believe is mandated by international law. There are, of course, limits—enforcing a particular sect's views of morality by using violence against women goes beyond freedom of religion and cannot be condoned. Tradition cannot justify the genital cutting of young girls, and continuing discrimination in work or housing based on caste or social status must be combatted. If a government persistently ignores widespread domestic violence or child abuse, it is violating human rights, since the state is obliged to guarantee rights not only by abstaining from interfering with individual freedoms but also by ensuring an individual's right to physical security in the private sphere.[126]

As societies evolve politically and economically, social mores and cultural norms also change. However, it is a mistake to try to squeeze all socially desirable progress into the human rights framework. Universal human rights norms do not mandate the degree of economic equality that a society should seek; they do not impose a particular view of relationships within the family; they do not tell societies how much to spend on guns versus butter; they say almost nothing about foreign policy and trade. Each of these issues is important (and perhaps even more important to most people than rights), but human rights provide only the context in which these difficult issues should be decided—a democratic society in which free debate is possible and non-discrimination guaranteed.

Similarly, not everything bad (from a 'Western' or modern perspective) is a human rights violation. There is certainly a need to address the root causes of poverty, promote social justice and mutual respect among communities, end

[126] See eg *Velasquez-Rodriguez v Honduras* Inter-American Court of Human Rights Series C 4 (29 July 1988), para 172 ('An illegal act which violates human rights and which is initially not directly imputable to a State (for example, because it is the act of a private person or because the person responsible has not been identified) can lead to international responsibility of the State, not because of the act itself, but because of the lack of due diligence to prevent the violation or to respond to it as required by the Convention'); UNHRC 'General Comment No 31' (29 March 2004) CCPR/C/21/Rev.1/Add. 1326, para 8 ('the positive obligations on States Parties to ensure Covenant rights will only be fully discharged if individuals are protected by the State . . . against acts committed by private persons or entities that would impair the enjoyment of Covenant rights . . . ').

corruption, and lessen global disparities, but this does not necessarily mean viewing everything through the prism of 'rights'—human rights are not designed to provide an answer to every social, political, or ethical question that arises in our increasingly complex world. Insisting that they do so undermines their ability to achieve their more limited (but no less valuable) aims and interferes with the need for societies to continue to reflect their different histories and cultural heritage, within the bounds of what is actually mandated by international law.

In addition, substituting the adversarial absolutism of rights language for the often more fruitful path of dialogue and open political debate may make it less likely that society will be able to arrive at viable solutions. Moreover, problems such as identifying the best way to promote economic development, how to deal with climate change and sustainability, the most appropriate trade and immigration policies for a given country, or how to apportion available resources among competing demands require a much broader, fact-based discussion than is likely to emerge if the only argument is whether my 'rights' are superior to yours. There is a legitimate role for human rights advocacy to ensure that society does not limit recognized rights unduly or in a discriminatory manner, but treating rights as a comprehensive quasi-religious doctrine within which all answers may be found is nonsense.

V. The Inherent Flexibility of Human Rights Norms

Understandably, most human rights advocates (and governments) talk about human rights in summary fashion, referring simply to 'freedom of expression' or the 'right to housing'. Few human rights are absolute, however, and the drafters of the Universal Declaration and subsequent instruments understood that rights may be legitimately limited by other competing rights or interests. Among the reasons identified in treaties that may justify such limitations are protection of the rights and freedoms of others, public order (*ordre public*), public health, public morality, national security, and the general welfare.

Of course, these terms are frequently advanced by states to justify violating rights, not simply limiting them, but their mere invocation does not free a state from upholding its human rights obligations. Rights may be limited only if the limitations are necessary (not merely convenient or desirable), imposed by law (not just at the whim or total discretion of government officials), and for purposes that are essentially democratic (an authoritarian government cannot limit rights merely to keep itself in power). In addition, human rights treaties subject states to at least a degree of international oversight, and it is up to these international bodies, not states themselves, to offer an opinion as to whether a limitation is justified and proportionate.

Restrictions on rights imposed in good faith, for legitimate purposes, enable states to adapt universal human rights norms to specific local conditions. Fair trials must be possible under both common law and civil law jurisdictions. Humane prison conditions may vary from country to country, although a universal floor of minimum treatment may exist. Priorities may need to be set when fulfilling many economic, social, and cultural rights.

Jack Donnelly, a political philosopher who has written frequently and persuasively about the 'relative universality' of human rights, adopts a useful three-tiered description to explain what I refer to as the inherent flexibility of human rights. In Donnelly's analysis, the broadest level is that of the 'concept' of human rights, where there is near universal consensus on broad principles such as the liberty and security of person and the right to social security.[127] At the second level, these concepts have multiple and defensible 'conceptions' of the rights they articulate, in which factors such as history, *ordre public*, and culture may play a role.[128] The lowest level is that of 'implementation', when specific norms are translated into national law and practice.[129] Donnelly offers as a particularly good example of the implementation phase the myriad forms of electoral systems that could be adopted in order to implement the right 'to take part in the government of his country, directly or through freely chosen representatives'.[130]

Donnelly's tiered analysis is not precise, and the distinction between 'concept' and 'conception' may beget a certain degree of confusion, if only linguistic. However, the schema accurately portrays in a general sense the way in which IHRL is translated into practice by states. Thus, universality does not, cannot, and should not be equated with uniformity, at least in a world of diverse societies and sovereign states.

The Covenant on Economic, Social and Cultural Rights (CESCR) makes explicit the distinction between acceptance of legally binding international norms and their implementation. Article 2.1 of the covenant provides as follows:

> Each State Party to the present Covenant undertakes *to take steps*, individually and through international assistance and co-operation, especially economic and technical, to the maximum of its available resources, *with a view to achieving progressively* the full realization of the rights recognized in the present Covenant by

[127] Jack Donnelly (2007) 'The Relative Universality of Human Rights' 29 Human Rights Quarterly 281, 299. Donnelly has pursued and parsed the issue of universality versus relativism in a number of writings spanning more than two decades; see ibid, 282, fn 1, for references to many of his earlier works.

[128] Ibid.

[129] Ibid.

[130] Universal Declaration of Human Rights (adopted 10 December 1948) UNGA Res 217 A(III) art 21.

all appropriate means, including particularly the adoption of legislative measures (emphasis added).

The Optional Protocol to the ESC Covenant, which was adopted only in 2008 and entered into force in 2013, specifically provides that, in its examination of individual communications, the Committee on Economic, Social and Cultural Rights (ESC Committee) 'shall consider the reasonableness of the steps taken by the State Party.... [and] shall bear in mind that the State Party may adopt a range of possible policy measures for the implementation of the rights set forth in the Covenant'.[131]

Because of the broad language employed in the Covenant and the progressive nature of implementation, some commentators (particularly in the United States, which has signed but not ratified the ESC Covenant) question whether these are rights at all, but this is clearly a minority position.[132] Early in its existence, the ESC Committee noted that, 'while the Covenant provides for progressive realization and acknowledges the constraints due to the limits of available resources, it also imposes various obligations which are of immediate effect', among which is the obligation 'to take steps'.[133] These steps 'must be taken within a reasonably short time ... [and] should be deliberate, concrete and targeted as clearly as possible towards meeting the obligations recognized in the Covenant'.[134] In addition, States have 'a minimum core obligation to ensure the satisfaction of, at the very least, minimum essential levels of each of the rights' in the Covenant.[135]

There is no comparable reference to progressive realization in the Covenant on Civil and Political Rights (CCPR), and states are 'to respect and to ensure' the covenant's rights and 'ensure that any person whose rights ... are violated shall have an effective remedy'.[136] In practice, however, it is difficult not to conclude that civil

[131] Article 8.4.

[132] See eg Philip Alston (1990) 'US Ratification of the Covenant on Economic, Social and Cultural Rights: The Need for an Entirely New Strategy' 84 American Journal of International Law 365 ('[T]he US Government, for almost a decade, has categorically denied that there is any such thing as an economic, a social or a cultural human right.'); Susan Kang (2009) 'The Unsettled Relationship of Economic and Social Rights and the West: A Response to Whelan and Donnelly' 31 Human Rights Quarterly 1006 ('recent [US] administrations' rejections of international economic and social rights remain particularly striking'). In 2009, then Secretary of State Hillary Clinton gave a major speech on human rights policy in which she mentioned economic rights only once: when referring to women whom she had met in China, she commented that they were 'working not just for *legal* rights, but for environmental, health, and economic rights as well' (emphasis added). The implication that economic rights are not legal rights is clear, an interpretation reinforced by other references in the speech to 'economic development ... economic empowerment ... [and] economic opportunity' but not to economic rights. Hilary Clinton, 'Remarks on the Human Rights Agenda for the 21st Century' (*US Department of State,* 14 December 2009) <https://2009-2017.state.gov/secretary/20092013clinton/rm/2009a/12/133544.htm> accessed 23 August 2019.

[133] UNCESCR 'General Comment No 3: The Nature of States Parties' Obligations (Art. 2, Para. 1, of the Covenant)' (14 December 1990) E/1991/23, para 1.

[134] Ibid, para 2.

[135] Ibid, para 10.

[136] International Covenant on Civil and Political Rights (adopted 16 December 1966, entered into force 23 March 1976) 999 UNTS 171, arts 2.1 and 2.3.

and political rights also are implemented flexibly, if not explicitly progressively. For example, article 10's requirement that detainees 'shall be treated with humanity and with respect for the inherent dignity of the human person' is likely to be interpreted differently if one is examining prison conditions in Denmark, Brazil, or Chad; the norm is the same, but implementation in such different countries will vary according to both capacity and differing notions of 'dignity'. Even given the fairly specific 'minimum guarantees' set forth in article 14.2 that apply to anyone charged with a criminal offence, the basic obligation to ensure 'a fair and public hearing by a competent, independent and impartial tribunal' in any civil or criminal proceeding (article 14.1) is a relatively broad concept whose precise interpretation and implementation may vary from state to state and as judicial systems within states develop. The prohibition against 'arbitrary or unlawful' interference with one's privacy or reputation in article 17 surely must be balanced by article 19's protection of freedom of expression, and that balance is likely to vary with cultural and social norms.

Variation in interpretation and implementation is evident for many rights, perhaps none more so than freedom of expression. As articulated in article 19.2 of the CCPR, the right includes 'freedom to seek, receive and impart information and ideas of all kinds'. However, the subsequent paragraph notes that the exercise of the right 'carries with it special duties and responsibilities' and that it may be restricted, where necessary, in order to respect the rights or reputations of others, national security, public order (*ordre public*), public health, or public morals.[137]

International human rights bodies recognize flexibility in many ways. For example, the ECtHR will not act as a 'fourth instance' by serving as an appellate court from decisions of national courts applying national law.[138] As discussed shortly, limitations based on public order ('*ordre public*') may recognize the relevance of a state's historical circumstances and cultural or religious foundations.

In the jurisprudence of the ECtHR, the flexible interpretation of rights is achieved through use of the doctrine of the 'margin of appreciation'.[139] 'By reason of their direct and continuous contact with the vital forces of their countries, state authorities are in principle in a better position than the international judge to give an opinion on the exact content' of human rights, when they determine what limitations are necessary.[140] This state discretion is not unlimited, and it goes hand in

[137] Ibid, art 19.3.

[138] See David Harris, Michael O'Boyle, Edward Bates, and Carla Buckley, *Law of the European Convention on Human Rights* (2nd edn, OUP 2009) 14–15 (hereafter Harris *et al*, *Law of the European Convention on Human Rights*).

[139] A brief summary may be found in Harris *et al*, *Law of the European Convention on Human Rights* (n 139) 11–14. Proposed Protocol No 15 to the European Convention on Human Rights, adopted in 2013, adds a specific reference to the 'primary responsibility' of states to secure human rights and affirms that 'in doing so they [the states] enjoy a margin of appreciation, subject to the supervisory jurisdiction of the European Court of Human Rights'. As of December 2015, it had been ratified by only twenty-five states and had not yet entered into force.

[140] *Handyside v United Kingdom* App no 5493/72 (ECtHR, 7 December 1976) Merits.

hand with international supervision, but it reflects the subsidiary role of human rights bodies and the fact that 'the initial and primary responsibility for the protection of human rights lies with the contracting parties' to human rights treaties.[141]

Of course, such deference to the state can be dangerous, and it is often difficult to discern the criteria upon which states are determined to have exceeded or acted within their margin of appreciation.[142] Differences of opinion over whether an act falls with the margin of appreciation frequently depend on one's view of the outcome of the case—confirming or rejecting a state's arguments for limiting the exercise of a right—rather than on the application of well-articulated criteria. Nevertheless, some discretion in interpretation and implementation of human rights norms is essential, unless one believes that every right must mean exactly the same thing in every country at all times.

Country-specific deference has been shown by the ECtHR in permitting Turkey to limit the wearing of headscarves[143] and to retain an electoral system that may result in effectively marginalizing regional parties;[144] permitting France to ban the public wearing of the niqab or burka (through a law outlawing face coverings in most circumstances);[145] and allowing Italy to require that crucifixes be hung on the walls of public school classrooms.[146] Concern for the rights of others was expressed by the court in each of these cases, but the specific circumstances of each state—and the open, democratic manner in which the challenged restrictions had been adopted—led the court to allow the concerned states their 'margin of appreciation' and to recognize the historical realities of each.[147]

[141] Harris *et al*, *Law of the European Convention on Human Rights* (n 139) 13.

[142] For references to varying opinions on the margin of appreciation doctrine, see Alastair Mowbray, *Cases and Materials on the European Convention on Human Rights* (Oxford University Press 2007) 629–33.

[143] *Sahin v Turkey* App no 44774/ 98 (ECtHR, 29 June 2004).

[144] *Refah Partisi v Turkey* App no 41340/98 (ECtHR, 13 February 2003).

[145] *SAS v France* App no 43835/11 (ECtHR, 1 July 2014). The court accepted France's argument that the restriction served the legitimate goal of ensuring respect for the values of an open and democratic society and 'seeking to protect a principle of interaction between individuals . . . essential for the expression of . . . pluralism . . . tolerance . . . [and] broadmindedness . . . ', ibid, para 153. The court declared that it 'has a duty to exercise a degree of restraint' in assessing 'a democratic process within the society in question' and found no violation. Ibid, para 154.

[146] *Lautsi v Italy* App no 30814/06 (ECtHR, 18 March 2011). The court found that crucifixes in school were religious but also a tradition, which the court should protect. Since the educational atmosphere was open and tolerant, the impact of the crucifixes was not deemed to be significant, even though crucifixes gave 'the country's majority religion preponderant visibility in the school environment'. Ibid, para 71. Cf *Folgero and others v Norway* App no 15472/02 (ECtHR, 29 June 2007), in which the court accepted that it was permissible to give Christianity a special place in the curriculum, given Norway's 'national history and tradition'. However, it found a violation of the convention by a nine to eight vote due to the 'not only quantitative but even qualitative differences applied to the teaching of Christianity as compared to that of other religions and philosophies'. Ibid, paras 89, 95.

[147] For an approach that may well have applicability outside Europe, see *Donaldson v United Kingdom* App no 56975/09, Decision as to the Admissibility (ECtHR, 25 January 2011) para 28, in a case concerning the right of a prisoner to wear a political symbol: 'The Court recognises that in the present case the significance of the Easter lily will be relevant to any assessment of the necessity of the interference. It notes that in Northern Ireland many emblems are not simply an expression of cultural or political identity but are also inextricably linked to the conflict and can be viewed as threatening and/

A former president of the ECtHR has observed that 'essentially the Convention guarantees are applied in a context defined by the democratic society in which they function. This is just common sense. Human rights cannot be and should not be divorced from the practical day-to-day functioning of society.'[148] Domestic laws are frequently founded, if only implicitly, on a society's moral and/or religious beliefs, and IHRL permits a great deal of discretion to states in legislating such beliefs. Even in a relatively homogeneous region such as Europe, for example, the ECtHR has consistently been unable to identify a common European conception of morality.[149]

The issue is not that it is wrong to argue that societies and cultures should change, and evolving conditions make resisting any change whatsoever both impossible and undesirable. In particular, outsiders should be able to support domestic efforts to foster social change that is consistent with modern values of tolerance and non-discrimination. However, focusing on what are seen by many cultures as particularly 'Western' rights, such as the rejection of gender role stereotypes, advocacy of same-sex marriage, or prohibiting corporal punishment for children,[150] may undermine efforts to guarantee or restore equally important rights on which one may be able to find a wider degree of agreement. IHRL does not lend itself well to the concept of 'best practices' that often finds its way into UN documents; even if it did, it is foolish to assume that what is 'best' is to be found solely in liberalism or capitalism, as those terms are understood in the United States and much of Europe.[151]

or discriminatory by those of a different cultural, political or religious background. Consequently, the public display of emblems can be inherently divisive and has frequently exacerbated existing tensions in Northern Ireland. Therefore, *as cultural and political emblems may have many levels of meaning which can only fully be understood by persons with a full understanding of their historical background, the Court accepts that Contracting States must enjoy a wide margin of appreciation in assessing which emblems could potentially inflame existing tensions if displayed publicly*' (emphasis added).

---

148 Luzius Wildhaber (2007) 'The European Court of Human Rights: The Past, the Present, the Future' 22 American University International Law Review 521, 535.

149 *Müller v Switzerland* App No 10737/84 (ECtHR, 24 May 1988) para 35. This phrase has been repeated verbatim in many subsequent cases.

150 See eg *A v United Kingdom* App no 25599/94 (ECtHR, 23 September 1998) (finding that UK law allowing the defence of 'reasonable chastisement' insufficiently protected children from physical abuse); Damien Gayle, 'Italian Politician Convicted of Child Cruelty for Pulling his Son's Hair While Eating at Swedish Restaurant in "Culture Clash"' *Daily Mail* (14 September 2011) <http://www.dailymail.co.uk/news/article-2037008/Italian-politician-convicted-child-cruelty-pulling-son-s-hair-eating-Swedish-restaurant-culture-clash.html> accessed 7 August 2019.

151 The debate over cultural relativism versus universality is an old one, and little of substance has changed in the past two decades. Cf Josiah Cobbah (1987) 'African Values and the Human Rights Debate: An African Perspective' 9 Human Rights Quarterly 309; Bilahari Kausikan (1993) 'Asia's Different Standard' 92 Foreign Policy 24; and Makau Mutua (2001) 'Savages, Victims, and Saviors: The Metaphor of Human Rights' 42 Harvard International Law Journal 201; with, eg Aryeh Neier (1993) 'Asia's Unacceptable Standard' 92 Foreign Policy 42 (1993); Rhoda Howard (1993) 'Cultural Absolutism and the Nostalgia for Community' 15 Human Rights Quarterly 315–38; and Amartya Sen (1997) 'Human Rights and Asian Values' New Republic 14–21. For a recent, not entirely satisfactory, UN attempt to balance traditional values and human rights, see UNHRC 'Study of the Human Rights Council Advisory Committee on Promoting Human Rights and Fundamental Freedoms Through a

Assailing the Taliban for violating women's rights was accurate and appropriate, but it missed the point—the Taliban regime violated *everyone's* rights, and change was less likely to result from campaigns directed at violations that also were consistent with entrenched social customs, no matter how distasteful those customs are to modern societies. Similarly, while the sometimes violent rejection by crowds in Cairo in March 2011 of attempts to raise women's rights issues was reprehensible,[152] there was perhaps some justification for a feeling that the broader goals of regime change and democracy were more important than highlighting the concerns of any particular sub-group of the population, no matter how large or how well-founded its complaints.

Even legitimate complaints about rights violations may be lost if the context is muddied. For example, while members of the punk protest group Pussy Riot who were sentenced to years of imprisonment for interrupting a religious service to protest Russian government policies were certainly victims, they were hardly human rights heroes or defenders. Performance art, even if deliberately aimed at political or cultural sensitivities, is protected under the guarantee of freedom of expression, but interfering with the rights of others (the Russian Orthodox clergy and parishioners, in this case) under the guise of free expression can be legitimately restricted. If the band members' imprisonment, as claimed by the *New York Times*, 'elevated their stature into global symbols of human rights and freedom in Russia',[153] one wonders how this resonates with ordinary Russians suffering from daily rights violations far removed from restrictions on punk artists. The impact of IHRL risks being weakened if human rights are highlighted primarily in the context of popular causes and celebrity.[154]

Better Understanding of Traditional Values of Humankind' (6 December 2012) UN Doc A/HRC/22/71 ('States should respect the cultural diversity and pluralism that exist within communities and societies as a source of enrichment and value added . . . this should not, however, justify any breach of universal human rights and fundamental freedoms.' Ibid, para 78).

---

152 See eg Jenna Krajeski, 'Women and Men in Tahrir Square' *The New Yorker* (8 March 2011) <http://www.newyorker.com/news/news-desk/women-and-men-in-tahrir-square> accessed 7 August 2019.

153 Rick Gladstone, 'Pussy Riot Members Take Tour to New York' *New York Times* (5 February 2014) <www.nytimes.com/2014/02/06/world/europe/pussy-riot-memberssay-prison-emboldened-them.html?_r=0> accessed 26 February 2017. A few months later, the Boston Globe enthused that Pussy Riot had become 'synonymous with a new style of activism, one that knew no boundaries and travelled at the speed of social media.' Mark Shanahan and Meredith Goldstein, 'Pussy Riot Bring Message to Harvard' *Boston Globe* (16 September 2014) <http://www.bostonglobe.com/lifestyle/names/2014/09/15/namesriot/r2hHUjV4UctHWB3BveQtAO/story.html#> accessed 7 August 2019.

154 Cf the observation by an unidentified Amnesty International staff member who disagreed with the organization's plans to decentralise, which began in 2010. 'But it's more than that. They [AI's senior management] seem to be moving Amnesty into campaigning mode with big stunts and branding exercises designed to boost membership—at the expense of the detailed research on which our credibility depends. We will launch a campaign on Pussy Riot because it's fashionable, chasing the energy, lurching from one issue to the next.' Quoted in Palash Ghosh, 'Amnesty International: The High Cost of Human Rights Activism and Charity' *International Business Times* (12 June 2013) <http://www.ibtimes.com/amnesty-international-high-cost-human-rights-activism-charity-1301765> accessed 7 August 2019. While celebrities and the causes that they support are often sincere and well-meaning, what happens if a cause cannot attract one? Cf the nearly fifty 'celebrity upstanders' who support the work of Enough, an

Finally, shorthand references to rights also may ignore the content of the obligations that states have actually assumed. While it may be surprising that Saudi Arabia, for example, has ratified the Convention on the Elimination of All Forms of Discrimination Against Women, it has done so with a telling reservation that limits its acceptance of the convention's provisions to those that do not contradict 'the norms of Islamic law'.[155] Other states have objected to this reservation on the grounds that it is incompatible with the object and purpose of the convention,[156] but it is no doubt an accurate reflection of just how far Saudi Arabia is willing to go to comply with international norms. No state has refused to treat Saudi Arabia as a party to the treaty, despite the arguably illegal Saudi reservation. This and similar reservations have not prevented Muslim countries from improving women's status and equality, albeit unevenly and sometimes almost imperceptibly, but neither do they represent a legal commitment to conceptions of gender equality as they are generally perceived in 'Western' societies.

Cultural overreaching also misunderstands—perhaps deliberately—the difference between legal norms and moral, political, or social norms. It is precisely because 'human rights' have been legitimized by their inclusion in legally binding international treaties ratified by states that they are able to command respect—in theory, if not always in practice. The United States cannot claim the right to torture suspected terrorists, and China cannot refuse to provide full educational opportunities for girls—not simply because outsiders think that torture is bad and equal education is good, but because the United States and China formally bound themselves to respect and implement these rights. Law is not the only or even the most important source of societal norms, but it should not be conflated or confused with other norms that may stem primarily from the views of a particular society, religion, or interest group.

Finally, a primarily legalistic, adversarial approach to rights whose content is either ill-defined or deliberately stated in broad terms to accommodate regional and national priorities is unlikely to be received favourably even by states willing to make a commitment to international norms. Rights that are capable of being legally enforced by an international body are a worthy goal, but to many countries they have come to represent yet another example of imposing 'Western' values on systems that are simply incapable of absorbing them. Indeed, concepts

NGO devoted to ending genocide and crimes against humanity <http://www.enoughproject.org/about/celebrity-upstanders> accessed 7 August 2019.

[155] The text of the Saudi reservation is found at <https://treaties.un.org/Pages/ViewDetails.aspx?src=IND&mtdsg_no=IV-8&chapter=4&lang=en#EndDec > accessed 23 August 2017.

[156] Objections to reservations by Saudi Arabia and/or similar reservations by other states have been made by Austria, Belgium, Canada, Czech Republic, Denmark, Estonia, Finland, France, Germany, Greece, Hungary, Ireland, Italy, Latvia, Mexico, the Netherlands, Norway, Poland, Portugal, Romania, Slovakia, Sain, Sweden, and the United Kingdom. See <https://treaties.un.org/Pages/ViewDetails.aspx?src=IND&mtdsg_no=IV-8&chapter=4&lang=en#EndDec> accessed 26 February 2017.

such as democracy and rule of law may have quite different meanings in different contexts.[157]

VI. The Way Forward

Calls for restraint and moderation rarely inspire the emotional commitment that often flows from appeals to absolute truth and fundamentalist conviction. There is a fine line between admirable dedication to a cause and inflexible zealotry, however, whether the cause is human rights or the promotion of moral or religious purity. This chapter is an appeal for radical moderation, which celebrates and promotes human rights norms without distorting or deifying them. It rejects starry-eyed human rights lawyers who aspire to be social reformers, as well as narrow libertarians and positivists who believe that both states and law are nuisances, to be tolerated only so long as they do not interfere with individual greed and intolerance. This moderately radical approach also rejects claims by many domestic social activists that IHRL provides a dispositive answer to addressing internal disparities in political and economic power that would, in many cases, be better resolved through political debate and activism within the society.

This limited view of human rights is consistent with a belief that, first, international law does matter and, second, it is not a bludgeon to be used primarily by the powerful against the weak. This is an avowedly legalistic approach, and its corollary is that maintaining the distinction between law and morality or law and politics is important. Recognizing that these concepts are created and enforced differently does not diminish any of them; if anything, it should reinforce the fact that social progress can only be achieved by appealing to law, politics, *and* morality.

Human rights advocates rhetorically insist that '[a]ll human rights are universal, indivisible and interdependent and interrelated',[158] but this is not realistic in either theory or practice. People demand rights that are most immediately necessary or that are in some manner prerequisites to enjoying additional rights. For example, while a good education is not a formal prerequisite for participating in political decision-making or ensuring an adequate standard of living for one's family, it will probably increase the likelihood that the two latter goals will be achievable.

[157] Rule of law 'is not an attractive concept', said U Pe Myint, a [Burmese] commentator and columnist. 'We do not usually equate the rule of law with justice. It has connotations of pacifying, subjugating people. I think most people don't really understand what it means.' Quoted in Thomas Fuller, 'Those Who Would Remake Myanmar Find That Words Fail Them' *New York Times* (19 July 2015) <https://www.nytimes.com/2015/07/20/world/asia/those-who-would-remake-myanmar-find-that-words-fail-them.html?mtrref=www.google.ie&gwh=3E1BE5CE6578493E1C22110C98C14103&gwt=pay> accessed 7 August 2019.

[158] UNGA 'World Conference on Human Rights, Final Declaration and Programme of Action' (12 July 1993) UN Doc A/CONF.157/23 (1993), sec. I, para 5.

Protecting women from endemic violence and minorities from discrimination are de facto requirements if they are to enjoy other rights.

A more realistic focus for the foreseeable future on the most fundamental and achievable human rights is more likely to lead to progress than is a diffuse approach that plays on momentary outrage or reflects a social agenda that dovetails with the preferences of Western funders and politicians. The notion of fundamental or core rights is both old and controversial, and I acknowledge the weakness of the reference. However, this is a more realistic approach for advocates and practitioners than is simply intoning the mantra that all rights are equal, indivisible, etc.[159] Just as in medical triage, such a focus does not imply a rejection or diminution of the entire gamut of internationally recognized rights, any more than treating the most urgent and curable cases first undermines the physician's Hippocratic Oath. Human rights triage may even have an advantage over medical triage, since effective protection of such rights such as free expression, the prohibition against torture, freedom of trade unions, non-discrimination, and the obligation of government to foster an improving standard of living is likely to have a snowball effect that will make it easier in the future to guarantee all rights.

This approach is not sexy, and it risks losing some of the emotional support for human rights that stems from highlighting war casualties or publicity-friendly global issues such as the plight of children. It may unfortunately be interpreted to support an overly conservative approach that discourages the formulation of new rights that are required to respond to social, political, and technological change. It does not directly address many of the major issues with which the global community and individual societies are faced on a daily basis.

Whether unfortunate or not, the fact is that IHRL per se has had very little impact on the conduct of war, the conclusion of peace agreements, the reconstruction of post-conflict societies, the redistribution of wealth, economic theory, or

[159] I will here mention only two recent and one older work that deal with this issue, although it is a recurrent theme among human rights scholars. Stephen R Ratner grounds his thoughtful proposal for law based on global justice on two pillars, peace and 'basic' human rights. He modestly advocates only a 'thin' morality for international legal norms that is 'a 'moral minimum' —universal in scope, reflecting values shared across cultures that are a baseline from which thicker, community-based morality may be developed'. Ratner, *The Thin Justice* (n 91) 90. These rights, characterized as encompassing 'the *fundamental freedom of the individual* vis-à-vis the states and other powerful actors that threaten him or her, coupled with the *basic material goods and conditions* necessary to a minimally flourishing life,' include non-discrimination based on certain traits, freedom to form a family, freedom of religion and culture, 'some' freedom of political expression, freedom from alien rule, 'some type of' representative government, primary education, and a safe workplace. Ibid, 76–77. Even the grandiose proposal for a World Court of Human Rights observes, 'While all human rights find their moral and philosophical rationale in human dignity, not every violation or denial of human rights also constitutes an attack on human dignity. The present Agenda aims primarily at addressing those core human rights issues directly linked to human dignity, which is characterised by powerlessness, humiliation and dehumanisation. This core is composed of fundamental civil, political, social, economic and cultural rights.' Unfortunately, like most others, the agenda does not identify with greater specificity which rights are 'core'. Panel on Human Dignity, 'Protecting Dignity' (n 105) 82. Finally, see the influential early work by Henry Shue, *Basic Rights* (2nd edn, Princeton University Press 1996).

restructuring power relationships within families. The solutions to most conflicts or malfunctioning societies are too complex to be aided in a significant way by simplistic appeals to human rights law. At the margins, human rights can help design a more responsive and equitable system of government; they may promote transparency and accountability and undermine an atmosphere of privilege and impunity; they may mandate wider participation for more people and diminish at least *de jure* discrimination. But human rights norms are targeted at regulating the relationship between individuals and their governments, not offering grand plans for the (re)construction of society itself.

Despite the obvious difficulties in dealing with the frontiers of human rights law or setting priorities, one should not ignore the consensus that does exist in all regions of the world over the core content and legitimacy of most human rights. Fair trials, respect for privacy, prohibitions against arbitrary killings and systematic racial discrimination, obligations on the state to promote basic socio-economic rights—all of these norms are widely accepted in principle, even if practice leaves much to be desired. They are accepted by governments, at least formally, and by most activist members of civil society, although both government and civil society have goals that transcend the narrow bounds of human rights. However, the debate over the precise scope of human rights law in some areas should not obscure our agreement on its content in many other areas.

At the same time, we cannot assume that the battle for even a reasonably conservative definition of human rights has been won, any more than history ended in the late twentieth century. For example, many Asian and African countries are seeking to reduce the responsiveness of the new UN HRC, not expand its effectiveness. What has been termed a new form of 'authoritarian capitalism' is emerging in Singapore, China, and elsewhere, but both civil-political and economic, social, and cultural rights will be at risk in any country that values free enterprise yet opposes freedom in any other context.

Among many other blatant rejections of human rights norms, suppression of human rights defenders and government critics has increased in Russia and China in recent years. A military coup in Thailand in 2014 overthrew a democratically elected government, in favour of the traditional political and economic elite that had consistently lost elections for the preceding decade. A military coup in Egypt overthrew the government democratically elected after the ouster of Hosni Mubarak in the 2011 'Arab spring'. Trinidad and Tobago withdrew from the American Convention on Human Rights in 1998; Venezuela followed suit in 2012. In 2011, the Council of Ministers of the South African Development Community (SADC) unanimously decided to dissolve its Tribunal and replace it with a tribunal that was expressly prohibited from receiving or hearing human rights complaints from individuals.[160]

[160] This action was motivated by the tribunal's 2010 decision that Zimbabwe's eviction of white-owned farmers from their land violated human rights and constituted illegal racial discrimination;

Regression has also occurred in countries usually deemed to be supporters of IHRL. US President George W Bush formally approved the use of 'enhanced interrogation techniques'—ie torture—to extract information from suspected terrorists in the aftermath of the attacks on New York and Washington on 11 September 2011.[161] His brother and candidate for the Republican presidential nomination in 2016, Jeb Bush, has refused to rule out a return to those practices.[162] While waterboarding and other forms of 'enhanced interrogation' were formally ended by Barack Obama when he took office in January 2009, the Obama administration declined even to investigate, let alone prosecute, those responsible for the torture, in direct violation of US obligations under the Torture Convention.[163] President Obama has been thwarted in his proclaimed goal of closing the detention camp at Guantanamo, Cuba, due to Congressional action making the closure impossible.[164]

The United Kingdom has refused to comply with a number of judgments by the ECtHR that British laws restricting the right to vote of convicted felons violate the European Convention.[165] While claiming that no-one should 'doubt the British commitment to defending human rights,' British Prime Minister David Cameron argued that the European Court's failure to take account of 'democratic decisions by national parliaments' may mean that 'the very concept of rights is in danger of slipping from something noble to something discredited'.[166] The government recently passed a rule that universities that invite speakers 'with extremist views linked to terrorist groups' must ensure that they are challenged by others.[167]

Zimbabwe refused to comply with the judgment and campaigned vigorously to quash the tribunal. *Campbell and Others v Republic of Zimbabwe* (2/2007), 28 November 2008, SADCT 2. The dissolution was subsequently upheld by the African Commission on Human and Peoples' Rights, on the grounds that only access to national courts is guaranteed by the African Charter. 409/12, *Tembani and Freeth v Angola and Thirteen Others*, Decision taken at the 54th Ordinary Session of the Commission (5 November 2013).

161 See generally, Philippe Sands, *Torture Team: Rumsfeld's Memo and the Betrayal of American Values* (Palgrave MacMillan 2008); Karen Greenberg and Joshua Dratel, *The Torture Papers: The Road to Abu Ghraib* (CUP 2005).

162 Associated Press and Spencer Ackerman, 'Jeb Bush Refuses to Rule Out Use of Torture if He Becomes US president' *The Guardian* (14 August 2015) <www.theguardian.com/us-news/2015/aug/14/jeb-bush-refuses-to-rule-out-use-of-torture-if-he-becomes-us-president> accessed 7 August 2019.

163 Glenn Greenwald, 'Obama's Justice Department Grants Final Immunity to Bush's CIA Torturers' *The Guardian* (11 August 2012) <https://www.theguardian.com/commentisfree/2012/aug/31/obama-justice-department-immunity-bush-cia-torturer> accessed 7 August 2019.

164 Max Fisher, 'Why Hasn't Obama Closed Guantanamo Bay?' *Washington Post* (30 April 2013) <http://www.washingtonpost.com/news/worldviews/wp/2013/04/30/obama-just-gave-a-powerful-speech-about-the-need-to-close-gitmo-so-why-hasnt-he/> accessed 7 August 2019.

165 *Hirst v UK (No 2)* App no 74025/01 (ECtHR, 6 October 2005). A summary of cases involving the UK may be found in European Court of Human Rights, 'Prisoners' Right to Vote' (*Factsheet*, February 2015), <www.echr.coe.int/Documents/FS_Prisoners_vote_ENG.pdf> accessed 7 August 2019.

166 'Concept of Human Rights Being Distorted, Warns Cameron' *BBC News* (25 January 2012) <www.bbc.co.uk/news/uk-politics-16708845> accessed 7 August 2019.

167 'Free Speech at University: Intolerance of Intolerance' (*The Economist*, 31 October 2015) <http://www.economist.com/news/britain/21677038-intolerance-intolerance-students-are-ever-quicker-label-offensive-material-hate-speech> accessed 7 August 2019.

The 'war on terror' continues in many countries and all regions of the world, providing a continuing excuse for indefinite detention without trial, torture, killings, and other human rights violations that commonly occur in the name of protecting so-called national security. While it is legitimate (and even required) that governments respond to and attempt to prevent terrorist attacks, the constant drumbeat about terrorism from government officials and in the media has created a climate in which human rights are often lost.[168] '[D]anger and fear are fast replacing dignity and hope as the terms that come first to mind when we describe the shape of the world in which we live … [i]n order to ensure its survival, the human rights idea needs to stand firmly against this kind of distortion of its essence, this move to turn it into a basis for selective aggression abroad and an alibi for brutality at home.'[169]

It would be inexcusable hubris to expect that 'human rights' will look exactly the same in fifty years as they do today—and it would be overly optimistic to assume that future changes will necessarily broaden the list of what we today consider to be rights worth protecting.[170] 'Perhaps instead of focusing exclusively on the flaws of the modern human rights enterprise, including the deficiencies of its legal core, those who are committed to human rights should question their confidence that the system is stable and that the only change to be anticipated in the future is further progress.'[171] In addition, attempting to expand the scope of human rights too quickly plays into the hands of those who exalt stability above all else, and consolidating rights within societies remains a formidable task.

> 'When I use a word,' Humpty Dumpty said, in rather a scornful tone, 'it means just what I choose it to mean—neither more nor less.'

[168] It has been frequently observed that most people are much more likely to be killed by lightning than by terrorism. Useful contributions to the war on terror debate may be found in the reports of the UN's special rapporteurs on the promotion and protection of human rights while countering terrorism, which are available at <http://www.ohchr.org/EN/Issues/Terrorism/Pages/SRTerrorismIndex.aspx> accessed 7 August 2019. Cf Statement by the High Commissioner for Human Rights at the Opening of the March 2015 Session of the HRC: 'The fight against terror is a struggle to *uphold* the values of democracy and human rights—not undermine them. My Office strongly supports efforts by States around the world to prevent and combat terrorism, and to ensure that the perpetrators of terrorism, as well as their financiers and suppliers of arms, are brought to justice. But counter-terrorist operations that are non-specific, disproportionate, brutal and inadequately supervised violate the very norms that we seek to defend. They also risk handing the terrorists a propaganda tool—thus making our societies neither free nor safe' (emphasis in original). OHCHR 'Opening Statement, Item 2, High Commissioner's Annual Report' <http://www.ohchr.org/en/NewsEvents/Pages/DisplayNews.aspx?NewsID=15642&LangID=E#sthash.cWQg7eSN.dpuf> accessed 7 August 2019.

[169] Conor Gearty, *Can Human Rights Survive?* (CUP 2006) 102, 136.

[170] For example, since 1999, the Organisation of Islamic Cooperation (formerly the Organisation of the Islamic Conference) has lobbied for UN recognition that 'defamation of religion' violates human rights. This argument has been contentious, on the grounds that such a prohibition would violate the right to free expression, and resolutions in the UN HRC/Commission and General Assembly have been bitterly fought. In recent years, however, the HRC has adopted resolutions on the issue without a vote, a degree of consensus that was achieved after the focus shifted from religion per se to 'derogatory stereotyping, negative profiling and stigmatization of *individuals* based on their religion or belief.' UNHRC Res 28/18 (7 April 2015) A/HRC/RES/28/18, para 3(c).

[171] Buchanan, *The Heart of Human Rights* (n 7) 303.

> 'The question is,' said Alice, 'whether you can make words mean so many different things.'
>
> 'The question is,' said Humpty Dumpty, 'which is to be master—that's all.'[172]

Words are power, and those who would be masters of the words must be aware of the consequences of their misuse. Good intentions do not excuse bad policies; dedication to an ideal does not excuse acts that render that ideal less realizable. Responsible and effective human rights advocacy, whether by governments or NGOs, requires reinforcing consensus, recognizing limits, and remembering that the goal is to enable individuals and societies to determine their own future in dignity and independence.[173] Without sacrificing the goal of universal compliance with universal standards, a moderate—but persistent—approach to human rights may prevent the erosion of one of the twentieth-century's greatest legacies: the recognition of rights that we all should enjoy, simply because we are human.

Acknowledgements

The opinions expressed herein have been shaped by a great number of conversations—some of them with individuals who would probably disagree with many of this chapter's conclusions. Among the constructive critics have been students and colleagues in a number of academic institutions at which I presented most of the ideas found in these pages, and I wish to thank the Fletcher School of Law and Diplomacy; University of Hong Kong; Central European University; Harvard Law School; King's College, London; Princeton University's Woodrow Wilson School of Public and International Affairs; the University of Minnesota; and the University of Glasgow for allowing me to present my thoughts to a variety of audiences.

A number of colleagues and friends have also contributed in various ways to my thinking (sometimes encouraging, sometimes discouraging), including Malin Oud, Bert Lockwood, Samuel Moyn, Cecile Aptel, Joel Trachtman, David Harris, John Shattuck, the late Nigel Rodley, the late Kevin Boyle, and the anonymous reviewer from Human Rights Law Review. None, of course, is responsible for any of the views expressed here. I also thank my research assistants at Fletcher, Kathrin Strobel, Casey Hogle, Aruni Jayakody, and Aliya Razzawi, without whom I never would have surfaced from beneath the stacks of materials in my office.

[172] Lewis Carroll, *Though the Looking-Glass, and What Alice Found There* (Macmillan 1871) 6.

[173] Although set in the context of US foreign policy, Diane Marie Amann's similar recommendation rings true: '[I]f the global goal is to nurture human rights in ways meaningful within humanity's myriad cultures—as it should be—an approach that proceeds with humility and with attention to tradition seems likely to establish a truer course . . .'. Dianne Amann, 'The Course of True Human Rights Progress Never Did Run Smooth' (2008) 21 Harv Hum Rts J 171, 174.

2

Global Consequentialism and the Morality and Laws of War

Hilary Greaves

I. Introduction

Rights-based approaches and consequentialist approaches to ethics are often seen as being diametrically opposed to one another. This is entirely understandable: simple act consequentialism, at least, just is the thesis that an action is right if it leads to the best consequences (or the highest expected value) overall, while to say that X has a moral right to Y is in part to assert that there are moral reasons for suitably situated agents to provide X with Y *even if doing so foreseeably will not* lead to the best consequences overall. At this level, intuitions in various cases are strongly on the side of the rights theorist: intuitively, for example, one ought not to execute an innocent scapegoat, even if doing so will foreseeably lead to better consequences overall thanks to the act's role in pacifying the mob.

On the other hand, we may well, like Narveson, 'see nothing but darkness and confusion' in a view that takes rights as literally primitive—a view, that is, according to which there are simply *facts* both about which persons have rights to which things and what this implies about what one ought to do, which facts are, on this view, not themselves grounded *in any sense* in any kind of reasons, either for ascribing these rather than those rights or for responding to rights in the prescribed way.[1]

Global consequentialism aims, among other things, to find the appropriate middle ground between these two extremes: simple act consequentialism at one extreme, with no place at all for talk of rights, and primitive rights theory on the other, with no place at all for rationales for rights ascriptions or rights respect. Global consequentialism is also an independently motivated view. In particular, it grows naturally out of familiar concerns that simple act consequentialism, if construed as the whole of morality, might be self-defeating. It is, in any case, *one* natural account of the foundational morality that might underlie rights talk, and hence that might have distinctive implications for how disagreements at the level of practical moral and legal rights theorizing are to be resolved.

[1] Jan Narveson (1973) 'Moral Problems of Population' 57(1) The Monist 69.

Hilary Greaves, *Global Consequentialism and the Morality and Laws of War* In: Human Rights and 21st Century Challenges. Edited by: Dapo Akande, Jaakko Kuosmanen, Helen McDermott, and Dominic Roser, Published by Oxford University Press 2020.
DOI: 10.1093/oso/9780198824770.003.0003

The purpose of the present chapter is to illustrate how this might work. I will apply global consequentialism, by way of a case study, to a recent discussion of the ethics of war. Section II reviews the background theory of global consequentialism. Section III reviews a recent exchange between Jeff McMahan and Henry Shue over the morality and laws of war. Section IV examines what a global consequentialist should say about this particular exchange. I will argue that by global consequentialist lights, each of McMahan and Shue is in some important respects clearly right, in others clearly wrong.

II. Global Consequentialism

A. The Rights Violation Objection

The basic objection to consequentialism based on considerations of *rights*—or, more generally, side constraints—is familiar. Suppose, for example, that a town is gripped by anger at a spate of recent unsavoury crimes. The town sheriff faces the choice between executing an innocent scapegoat (which would pacify the mob) on the one hand, or allowing the riots to continue (in which case many more people will be killed) on the other. At least in hypothetical cases in which, we stipulate, the sheriff's decision will have no knock-on effects on (for example) general respect for the machinery of justice, simple consequentialism will say that the sheriff ought to execute the innocent scapegoat. But most people find this implausible. The scapegoat, intuition screams, has a *right* to be treated fairly; it is *unjust* to punish the innocent. Perhaps with the exception of cases in which the consequences at stake are really extreme, these considerations of rights and justice, intuition says, override considerations of overall good in determining what the sheriff ought to do.

B. The Self-Defeatingness Objection

Aside from the brute intuition against executing scapegoats for the sake of the greater good, however, simple act consequentialism is also subject to a quite different kind of objection: that it is *self-defeating*. The latter worry is that trying to *use* act consequentialism to guide one's decisions on an everyday basis, and/or to formulate laws that are themselves directly consequentialist in content, would itself lead to undesirable consequences. If so, then the consequentialist *even by her own lights* should want to avoid such 'consequentialist' decision procedures, laws, and so on.

There are at least three ways in which this can happen. First, relating to calculation time. Trying to work out, in full gory detail or even to a reasonable approximation, the possible or likely consequences of one's proposed action from here to eternity, together with probabilities for all the relevant possibilities, is clearly an unwieldy task, and not one to which the computational power of human brains is always well adapted. For this reason alone, it would lead to bad consequences if we actually tried to perform full consequentialist calculations before, for example, deciding whether or not to save a drowning child. We will get better consequences if we have adequately reliable 'rules of thumb' worked out in advance and if, in the heat of the moment, we simply apply those rules without (much) further reflection.

Second, relating to personal bias. Because full consequentialist calculations are complex and hence (in practice) require a fair amount of estimation, there is a lot of scope for personal bias to skew the results, if we make case-by-case decisions on the basis of attempts at consequentialist calculations. Suppose, for example, that I have promised an elderly and somewhat tiresome aunt that I will call her at 8 p.m. this evening, but then I receive a last-minute invitation to a party. On self-interested grounds, I would vastly prefer to go to the party. A consequentialist decision procedure, it seems, would have me try to estimate the amount of harm it might do to my aunt if I break my promise, and the likelihood of that harm materializing, so that I can compare these possible consequences with my estimates of the enjoyment and other benefits the party will bring me. But clearly, I have an incentive to underestimate the former and overestimate the latter, so as to get the calculation to deliver the verdict that I ought to go to the party. Therefore, there is a danger here of motivated cognition. I might in general do a better job of choosing actions with the best consequences if my decision procedure is something other than *thinking* about which actions have the best consequences.

Third, relating to alienation: most or all of us are not psychologically well-suited to conducting consequentialist reasoning in our daily lives. Arguably, for instance, we naturally go to visit a close friend or family member in hospital driven by values that are far from impartial: driven, by, for instance, a direct concern for the welfare of the hospitalized party in particular, an enjoyment of his/her company, and/or a high value placed on our own special relationship to this person. There might, in the end, be reasons that even the consequentialist should accept for visiting such a person rather than (say) using the time in question to volunteer for charity: perhaps one's ability to cheer up close friends means that the hospital visit would do more good *even considered impartially* than one could do by serving in a soup kitchen, and/or perhaps one needs to maintain such relationships in order to stay psychologically healthy enough to be productive in one's charitable works in the long run. But the very process of running all our decisions through such an explicit consequentialist algorithm might lead to a sort of 'alienation' between one's affections and one's deliberative self; one that in turn leads to a sense of loneliness and emptiness, is destructive to valuable relationships, and leaves the world overall in a worse state than it would have been in had some not explicitly consequentialist decision procedure been followed.[2]

This discussion has been carried out in terms of the everyday decisions of private individuals, but it is if anything even clearer that similar considerations apply to questions of public morality, and in particular to questions of what the content of our laws ought to be. There are all sorts of reasons for thinking that the consequences of having laws that simply read 'do whatever would have the best overall consequences' would itself be disastrous (relating, for instance, to epistemic and motivational limitations, both on the part of the courts and on the part of those who would be subject to the law in question). Even the consequentialist, then, should not desire laws that are themselves consequentialist *in content*. In *that* sense, 'consequentialism about the law' would be self-defeating.

C. Global Consequentialism: A First Pass

This much seems clearly correct: making all one's everyday decisions on the basis of explicit and case-by-case consequentialist calculations, and/or having laws that themselves simply restate consequentialism, would generally have seriously suboptimal consequences, and so even by the consequentialist's own lights would be undesirable.

It would be too quick to conclude from this, however, that consequentialism itself must simply be rejected wholesale, as internally inconsistent, and therefore a false and misguided ethical theory. The warranted conclusion is more limited: it is simply that the consequentialist, by her own lights, should prefer decision procedures, laws, and so forth that are not themselves simplemindedly consequentialist in content. But of course, this does not render considerations of consequences altogether irrelevant (ie, consequentialism does not, *pace* Bernard Williams, hereby 'usher itself from the scene').[3] The consequentialist should prefer the enactment of whatever set of laws has the property that enacting *that* set of laws would lead to better consequences than enacting any alternative set of laws; she should prefer the adoption of whatever everyday decision procedure has the property that adopting that decision procedure has better consequences than adopting any alternative decision procedure; and so on.

Further, we now see how a framework of rights, in particular, might in one clear sense be reconciled with consequentialism. Once we have granted that the laws, everyday decision procedures, and so forth, whose adoption leads to the best

[2] Peter Railton (1984) 'Alienation, Consequentialism, and the Demands of Morality' 13(2) Philosophy & Public Affairs 134–71.

[3] Bernard Williams, 'A Critique of Utilitarianism' in John Jamieson Carswell Smart and Bernard Williams (eds), *Utilitarianism: For and Against* (CUP 1973).

consequences are unlikely, for the above reasons, to be consequentialist in content, there is no reason to think that their content could not involve a rights framework. Hence, there is no reason of principle to doubt that global consequentialism might amount to the middle ground between simple act consequentialism and primitive rights theory whose desirability I suggested at the start of this chapter. In this approach, rights might find a place at several levels of morality, so that the initial intuitions against simpleminded consequentialism are perhaps accommodated, but the *foundations* for all levels are ultimately consequentialist ones, so that 'darkness and confusion' are avoided.

D. The Structure of Normative Theories

To formulate global consequentialism more generally and (slightly) more precisely,[4] it is useful (roughly following Kagan) to distinguish between *evaluative focal points, roles*, and *normative factors* in the formulation of a normative theory.[5]

- A theory's *evaluative focal point* is the thing whose normative status the theory seeks to assess. We have already considered acts, laws, and everyday decision procedures; one might similarly evaluate character traits, motivations, and so forth. Simple act consequentialism, for example, is a normative theory that seeks to assess only one type of focal point (acts), but other normative theories may be concerned with more or different evaluands.
- The *normative factors* are the factors that the theory considers relevant to the normative status of the evaluative focal point. What is distinctive of *consequentialist* theories is that they, and they alone, take considerations of consequences to exhaust the relevant normative factors. In contrast, a Kantian

[4] Unlike act and, to a lesser extent, rule consequentialism, there is no canonical, widely accepted formulation of global consequentialism. Related ideas have been discussed in: Robert Adams (1976) 'Motive Utilitarianism' 73(14) The Journal of Philosophy 467–48 (hereafter Adams, 'Motive Utilitarianism'); Derek Parfit, *Reasons and Persons* (OUP 1984) 25 (hereafter Parfit, *Reasons and Persons*); Fred Feldman, *Doing the Best We Can* (Reidel 1986); Peter Railton (1988) 'How Thinking About Character and Utilitarianism Might Lead to Rethinking the Character of Utilitarianism' 13 Midwest Studies in Philosophy 398–416 (hereafter Railton, 'Thinking About Character and Utilitarianism'); Roger Crisp (1992) 'Utilitarianism and the Life of Virtue' 42 Philosophical Quarterly 139–60; Fred Feldman (1993) 'On the Consistency of Act- and Motive-Utilitarianism: A Reply to Robert Adams' 70 Philosophical Studies 201–12 (hereafter Feldman, 'Act- and Motive-Utilitarianism'); Shelly Kagan, 'Evaluative Focal Points' in Brad Hooker, Elinor Mason, and Dale Miller (eds), *Morality, Rules, and Consequences: A Critical Reader* (Rowman & Littlefield 2000) 134–55; Philip Pettit and Michael Smith, 'Global Consequentialism' in Brad Hooker, Elinor Mason, and Dale Miller (eds), *Morality, Rules, and Consequences: A Critical Reader* (Rowman & Littlefield 2000) 21–133; Toby Ord, *Beyond Action: Applying Consequentialism to Decision Making and Motivation* (DPhil thesis, University of Oxford 2008) (hereafter Orb, *Beyond Action*); Hilary Greaves, 'Global consequentialism' in Douglas Portmore (ed), The Oxford Handbook of Consequentialism, (Oxford University Press, forthcoming).

[5] Shelly Kagan (1992) 'The Structure of Normative Ethics' 6 Ethics 223–42.

theory might admit, for instance, universalizability (in some more or less precisely specified sense), in addition to or instead of considerations of consequences.

- The need for specification of a *role* arises because there is, in general, more than one thing one might 'do with' the item being evaluated, and in general the evaluation will depend not only on the item but also on what is done with it. For example, the best act to *try to perform* may not be the same as the best act to *perform*, since *trying* to perform an act can have other consequences besides performance. Similarly, the best set of laws to advocate for may not be the same as the best set of laws to enact; and the best set of moral rules to guide one's own actions by may not be the same as the best set of moral rules to use as a basis for ascriptions of praise and blame.

Using this scheme, we can classify (in particular) act, rule, and global consequentialism, and see how they differ. Since these three theories are all forms of consequentialism, they agree about the normative factors; but they disagree along the other two dimensions. Act and rule consequentialism each choose some *particular* evaluative focal point (respectively, acts and rules), and evaluate their chosen focal point relative to a particular role. The relevant role for act consequentialism is of course the act's being performed; rule consequentialists disagree among themselves about the choice of role, but any particular rule consequentialist theory takes on some particular commitment on this matter. For instance, the form of rule consequentialism advocated by Hooker takes the relevant role to be: being 'accepted' by a majority of members of the moral community.[6] In contrast, global consequentialism declines to single out either any particular evaluand(s) or any particular role(s) as primitive: as the name suggests, it amounts to conseqentialist evaluation of *any* evaluative focal point, relative to *any* role.

E. Global Consequentialism: Official Formulation

Global consequentialism can then be formulated, slightly more precisely, as follows:

> **(GC) Global consequentialism**: *For all evaluative focal points F and roles R, the right F in role R is the F such that having that F in role R has better consequences than having any alternative F (or no F at all) in role R.*

[6] Brad Hooker, *Ideal Code, Real World: A Rule-Consequentialist Theory of Morality* (OUP 2000) chapter 3, 72–92. Rule consequentialism then adds a further, *non-consequentialist* criterion for the evaluation of acts, viz that an act is right if it is in conformity with the selected rules.

GC entails, for instance, that the right *act* to *perform* is the act whose performance has better consequences than the performance of any other available act (or no act); and that the right *act* to *try to perform* is the act such that trying to perform that act has better consequences than trying to perform any available act (or no act); and so forth.

So far so good, perhaps; it is a slightly delicate matter, though, exactly what this has to do with such questions as that of whether or not there is a moral right to life. For sure, it follows from the above that according to global consequentialism, the 'right' set of items to *say* that there are moral rights to is that set of items such that saying there are moral rights to those items has better consequences than saying there are moral rights to any alternative set of items, or to no items. That is, we can see that global consequentialism will take a consequentialist line about what it is 'right' to say. But for all that has been said so far, this could simply be the familiar line taken by act consequentialism, viz that it is morally right to say whatever will have the best consequences, regardless of truth or falsity. And, returning to the dilemma with which we started, it will be no comfort to the would-be anti-consequentialist if global consequentialism simply reiterates the simple act consequentialist's claim that ascriptions of moral rights are false, but that (applying act consequentialism to acts of speech) it is often morally right to speak such falsehoods.

To put the worry another way: the global consequentialist has told us what it is 'right' to say, but this notion of 'right' is potentially ambiguous. Clearly there is a distinction, in general, between some utterance's being *expedient* or *morally right* to *say* on the one hand, and its being *true* on the other. The question, then, is whether the notion of 'right to say' that is involved in global consequentialism is merely a matter of expediency, or one of truth; only in the latter case will global consequentialism have proceeded beyond simple act consequentialism on the question of whether there are moral rights.

To have a distinctive view to consider, therefore, let us consider a version of global consequentialism that does indeed take on these more novel commitments. We then have a theory according to which the formula (GC) exhausts or otherwise determines all that can be said on moral matters. It must hold, then, either that there *is* no coherent question of which rights ascriptions are true as opposed to merely expedient, or that the global-consequentialist formula *determines truth conditions as well as expediency conditions*. According to this latter version of global consequentialism, the sentence 'there is a moral right to life' is *true* if and only if the best moral system, for example, to regulate one's behaviour with includes affirmation of a moral right to life. Insofar as there is indeterminacy in the choice of evaluative focal point and role—insofar, that is, as context fails to determine the relevant evaluative focal point ('moral system', or something else?) and role ('regulating behaviour' in precisely what sense?)—whether or not there is a right to life *simpliciter* is itself correspondingly indeterminate (because it is relative to unspecified parameters). On this view, then, while questions of truth and expediency of course in general come apart---whether your haircut is nice is quite a different question from that of whether my saying your haircut is nice would lead to good consequences---in certain normative domains they coincide.

This last claim is fairly radical, and will not be popular with primitive rights theorists. The latter will want to insist that it would, or could, remain fundamentally *true* that there is a moral right to life even if empirical conditions were such that it was in no way expedient to integrate ascription of that right into any system, for any purpose. But disagreement with *primitive* rights theory, of course, is to be expected: a significant part of the point of the exercise, recall, was to move away from that perspective on rights. By the lights of those who were convinced by the case for seeking a middle ground between primitive rights theory and simple act consequentialism in the first place, global consequentialism seems promising.

F. Two Other Issues

Before proceeding to apply global consequentialism to the case of war, I pause to flag two tangential issues.

First, any consequentialist theory presupposes some 'theory of the good'; that is, a ranking of states of affairs (and hence of sets of consequences) in terms of better and worse overall. It is only relative to such a theory of the good that we know what we mean by one thing's having 'better consequences' than another. There are of course numerous controversial issues involved in the question of what is the correct theory of the good. In particular, it is controversial both which aspects of a state of affairs make it better or worse *ceteris paribus* (eg just the well-being of sentient creatures, or other things too?) and how those aspects that each make states of affairs better *when other things are equal* are to be traded off against one another (eg to settle comparisons between a state of affairs that involves more human well-being but also more damaged natural ecosystems, or comparisons that involve trade-offs of the well-being of some persons against that of others). There is a rich literature investigating issues of both of these types in detail, and it is not my purpose here to enter into the details. The present discussion is instead about how, in structural terms, the notion of overall good fits into moral theory. This is a matter about which act, rule, global, and non-consequentialist theories disagree, even when they agree on the theory of the good itself. Readers are free to interpret the discussion in terms of their own preferred theory of the good.[7]

[7] Global consequentialism does, however, require, a 'non-moral' theory of the good—at least in spirit, if not in letter. That is, the theory of the good against which (say) candidate moral rules are to be evaluated should not already take account of issues of (say) desert, since questions of what a given individual *deserves* themselves depend on matters of which moral rules (if any) the individual in question has violated: it should depend in a more straightforward manner on (say) the well-being levels of individuals. In all likelihood, at the end of the day the global consequentialist will agree with the commonsense verdict that there is *some* sense in which it is 'worse' if an innocent is mistakenly imprisoned than

Second, there is a potential worry about internal conflicts within global consequentialism. Any given action, for instance, falls with equal accuracy under a number of different descriptions, and in general, global consequentialism might deem one and the same action to be right relative to one accurate description, but wrong relative to another. Suppose, for instance, one finds oneself in a situation such that the right *act*, according to the global consequentialist perspective, is not the one that would be picked by following the right *decision procedure*, by global consequentialist lights, nor the one that is mandated by the right laws, by the global consequentialist point of view. What then ought one to do? Perform the right act, follow the right decision procedure, or conform to the right laws?

I flag this worry only to set it aside (although the general issue will rear its head again in section IV). The problem of conflicts may or may not, in the end, be sufficient ground for rejecting global consequentialism, and it is beyond the scope of this chapter to try to settle that question.[8] For the purposes of this chapter, I will simply assume that global consequentialism is promising enough for its implications to be worth working out.

Let us see, then, what global consequentialism has to offer by way of commentary on one recent first-order normative discussion. Section III takes a step back from the foundational issues that have been the focus of the present section, and reviews a recent discussion of the ethics and laws of war. Section IV will turn to the task of exploring the connections between this recent discussion on the one hand, and global consequentialism on the other.

III. McMahan and Shue on the Morality and Laws of War

A. The Laws of Armed Conflict

The existing international laws of war recognize the following three key principles:

- *Combatant equality*: While *political leaders* on one side of a war but not the other may be held to account for waging a war that is deemed unjust (that fails to satisfy the agreed principles of *jus ad bellum*), no legal distinction is drawn between 'just combatants' and 'unjust combatants'; combatants on both sides

if a genuine criminal is imprisoned; but that sense of 'worse' is not the one involved in the theory of the good that lies at the foundations of a global consequentialist approach.

[8] For further discussion, see Adams, 'Motive Utilitarianism' (n 4) 467–48; Parfit, *Reasons and Persons* (n 4) 31–4; Railton, 'Thinking About Character and Utilitarianism' (n 4) 398–416; Feldman, 'Act- and Motive-Utilitarianism' (n 4) 201–12; Ord, *Beyond Action* (n 4); Greaves, 'Global consequentialism' (n 4).

of a war are subject to the same rules concerning the conduct of their military operations.

- *Non-combatant immunity*: Combatants may only intentionally attack enemy *combatants*; non-combatants (eg most civilians living in enemy territory) are not legitimate targets.
- *The privileged status of prisoners*: Prisoners of war may not be attacked or killed; they may only be detained for the duration of the war, to prevent them from serving again as combatants on the enemy side.

B. The Orthodox View of the Morality of War

The question then arises of what the relationship is between these *legal* principles on the one hand, and the *morality* of war on the other. According to the now-orthodox view (associated in particular with Michael Walzer) the laws of war straightforwardly mirror the content of the underlying morality of war.[9]

Walzer's view proceeds from putative basic principles of morality concerning the notion of someone's being (morally) 'liable to be killed'. The idea is that (i) by default, one has a (moral) right not to be attacked or killed, but (ii) one loses this right (becomes 'liable to be attacked/killed') if one poses a sufficiently serious, perhaps lethal, threat to others. This is how Walzer seeks to defend the view that in a context of war it is often morally permissible to use lethal force, while in a peacetime context killing is normally one of the most serious of wrongs: killings in war, but not in ordinary life, are generally carried out in settings in which the victim was posing a threat.[10]

Given these principles, the further principles of combatant equality, non-combatant immunity, and the privileged status of prisoners follow immediately. Just combatants, no less than unjust combatants, pose a lethal threat to their adversaries. And neither non-combatants nor prisoners of war *pose* any such threat (although non-combatants may sometimes *contribute* to threats, for example by supporting the army in various ways).

[9] Michael Walzer, *Just and Unjust Wars: A Moral Argument With Historical Illustrations* (4th edn, Basic Books 2006).

[10] Importantly, the condition that someone is 'liable to be killed' is neither necessary nor sufficient for it being *permissible* to kill him—liability to be killed implies only that the person in question has lost his *right* not to be killed, so that *he is not wronged* if he is killed. It would remain impermissible to kill him if, for example, no sufficiently good purpose would be served by such killing. But the idea is that often in a context of war, some sufficiently good purpose would be so served, so that considerations of liability on the one hand and those of the permissibility of acts of killing on the other very often line up with one another in practice.

C. Criticisms of the Orthodox View

Recently, however, there has emerged something of a consensus among moral theorists that Walzer's putative underlying principles of morality are simply not true, *qua* moral principles. 'Posing a threat', these revisionists argue, is neither necessary nor sufficient for becoming liable to be killed.

It is not sufficient, because: (i) if the threat you pose is *justified*, then you are not liable as a result of posing that threat. For example, if you are defending yourself against a violent mugger, and the only mode of resistance available to you is the use of potentially lethal force, you do not lose your right not to be killed by the mugger. That is because your threat is a justified one: it is only the mugger who has lost his right not to be attacked and potentially killed, by posing an *unjustified* threat against you in the first place. (ii) If you are not *responsible* for the threat you pose, then you aren't as a result liable. For example, if you are stuck at the bottom of a well and an innocent third party is thrown down the well, and will crush you to death on landing unless you detonate a bomb that will blow him up *en route*, he poses a lethal threat but (intuitively) is not *liable* to be killed as a result, although your killing him may be *excusable*. In the context of war, the first point suggests (to a first approximation) that only combatants on the unjust side of the war, not those on the just side, are liable. The second point suggests that not all unjust combatants are liable, and perhaps not even most.

Actually *posing* the threat is also intuitively not *necessary* for becoming liable to be killed. If, for instance, you have hired a hitman to kill some third party, then intuitively, you (no less than the hitman himself) have thereby lost your right not to be attacked; you have become liable thanks to your *contribution to* and *responsibility for* the threat, even though you yourself are (arguably) not *posing* the threat. In the context of war, the point would apply, for example, to the politicians who authorized an unjust war, and arguably to some ordinary civilians in virtue of their support of the war and of the armed forces.

D. Revisionist Liability Theory and the Laws of War

Suppose that one tried to take an approach that was structurally like Walzer's—that is, to advocate laws of war that simply follow from a straightforward application of the underlying morality of war—but starting not from Walzer's own (crude) moral theory but from the revisionists' more sophisticated liability theory.

It is clear, in the first instance, that the resulting laws could not look anything like the existing laws of armed combat. For the reasons given above, both the principle of combatant equality and the principle of non-combatant immunity would have to go. Cecile Fabre offers a detailed discussion of precisely which non-combatants would be liable on this view.[11]

Second, however, given the radical uncertainties that soldiers and others will face concerning the questions of who is and is not liable—which side in the war is the just side, and which particular enemy combatants and non-combatants meet the conditions for liability—it seems that on any plausible approach to moral permissibility under conditions of uncertainty, the results of applying the revisionist liability theory will be that just about *any* real-world lethal attack will be morally impermissible ('contingent pacifism'). If so, then the corresponding laws would have to deem all actual wars illegal.

Theorists of the ethics of war thus face the following trilemma. First, they could simply bite the bullet and advocate pacifism at the level of the laws of war, no less than at the level of its morality: that is, they could advocate simply outlawing all war. Second, they could hold that there is a sharp distinction between the morality of war and its laws, even its morally optimal laws. On this view, while the *morality* of war is as given by the revisionists' liability theory, there are good reasons why the morally optimal *laws* will look a lot more like the existing laws of armed conflict. Or, third, they could reject the revisionists' liability theory as an account of the morality of war.

The first horn of this trilemma seems implausible, and I am not aware of anyone who has advocated it. The second horn is grasped by Jeff McMahan; the third by Henry Shue. I turn now to a brief exposition of McMahan's and Shue's views, in turn.

E. McMahan's View

According to McMahan, then, the *morality* of war does indeed track the revisionists' liability theory. However, we are to distinguish sharply between the morality of war on the one hand, and the laws of war on the other. According to McMahan, there is no reason why these two codes should be particularly close in content, and indeed the existing laws of war may, for all McMahan says, be very close to the morally optimal ones.

Since laws are made by conventional agreement, McMahan agrees that the question of which are the morally optimal *laws* is highly sensitive to considerations of what the practical consequences would be of enacting this or that law. And there are many reasons for thinking that any attempt to enact the revisionists' liability principles directly into law, in the way envisaged as the 'first horn' of the trilemma, would have disastrous consequences. In the first instance, epistemic limitations are

[11] See Cecile Fabre (2010) 'Guns, Food, and Liability to Attack in War' 120 Ethics 36–63.

important: since the laws of war must be action guiding, they cannot draw distinctions that soldiers in the heat of battle would not be able to draw. Thus, while they can distinguish between enemy combatants and enemy non-combatants as broad categories, and between friendly and enemy combatants as broad categories, they cannot distinguish between liable versus non-liable individual combatants or non-combatants, nor between the just versus the unjust side of the war. Second, there are also issues of bad faith: laws according to which any killing of 'just' by 'unjust' combatants is illegal would be open to abuse by victorious parties seeking revenge, who will tend to simply declare their own side of the war to have been the just one, regardless of where the moral truth lies. Third, if, as I tentatively suggested earlier, the consequence of insisting that the laws must closely reflect revisionist liability theory would be a legal contingent pacifism, according to which all actual wars are illegal, the laws would in practice simply be disregarded. Better, surely, to have laws that acknowledge the reality of war, and do something to try to limit the corresponding damage.

According to McMahan, however, since the *morality* of war, unlike its laws, is *not* a matter of convention, it just 'is what it is' and pragmatic concerns are here irrelevant.[12] It is, on this view, simply a moral *fact* that just combatants typically have a right not to be killed, notwithstanding the inadvisability of trying to take any account of this fact when devising laws.

The central worry for this view is how to handle the conflicts that, on this view, can arise between morality on the one hand, and law on the other. Each source of normativity (moral and legal) might say, of a given action, that that action is either required, permitted but not required, or forbidden; there is no general guarantee that the two sources will issue the same verdict in any given case.

McMahan is relatively unconcerned by cases in which morality permits some action that the law either forbids or requires, or vice versa: in these cases, he says, one ought to obey the prohibition or requirement, setting aside the mere permission.[13] But conflicts between a requirement from one source and a prohibition from the other are more serious. What *ought one to do*, that is, if and when morality requires some action that the law forbids, or vice versa?

While McMahan thinks that such conflicts are likely to be relatively rare in practice, he concedes that they can arise in principle. For example, he thinks that one might sometimes be morally *required*, not just permitted, intentionally to target liable civilians, when this is required for the success of one's just mission.[14] His verdict is simply that in any and all such cases, one ought to follow the dictates

[12] Jeff McMahan, 'The Morality of War and the Law of War' in David Rodin and Henry Shue (eds) *Just and Unjust Warriors: The Moral and Legal Status of Soldiers* (OUP 2008) 19–43, 35.

[13] For dissent on this count, see Henry Shue, 'Do We Need a "Morality of War"?' in David Rodin and Henry Shue (eds), *Just and Unjust Warriors: The Moral and Legal Status of Soldiers* (OUP 2008) 87–111, 107.

[14] Ibid, 38.

of morality over those of law, while openly acknowledging the legal violation one thereby commits, but pleading leniency on the grounds of one's 'moral justification' for breaking the law.[15]

F. Shue's View

Shue, meanwhile, claims to find McMahan's position unintelligible. According to Shue, while there is always an open question of whether or not one ought to obey *actual* laws—those laws might themselves be immoral—it is always the case that 'one morally ought to obey the morally best laws' in any context in which laws are needed at all.[16] If so, then there is no question of having a separate morality that can sometimes conflict with (the morally best) laws, as proposed by McMahan; the task is simply to work out what the morally best laws are, and morality will then be exhausted by the injunction to obey those laws.

The key distinction for Shue is not between the morality of war on one hand and the laws of war on the other; rather, it is between what morality requires *in the context of ordinary life* on the one hand, and what morality requires *in the context of war* on the other. Shue advocates a picture according to which all of morality—for ordinary life, for war, or for any other context—is grounded in an unchanging set of 'fundamental moral considerations': for instance, principles that are in favour of well-being, and against cruelty.[17] The matter of which 'specific standards' follow from those fundamental considerations, however, can depend on the context: in particular, it could well be that *in a context of ordinary life* a fundamental concern for welfare leads to a specific standard that simply bans (just about) all killing, while *in the context of war* those same fundamental concerns instead lead to specific standards that merely issue guidance on whom one is versus is not permitted to kill. According to Shue, McMahan makes a basic mistake in applying the specific standards that are appropriate to ordinary life to the very different context of war.

IV. Global Consequentialism Meets the Morality of War

What should a global consequentialist make of the exchange between McMahan and Shue? I will argue here that by global consequentialist lights, there are some particular and important respects in which McMahan is correct and Shue incorrect, others in which their status is reversed. The possibility of global consequentialism

[15] Ibid, 39.
[16] Ibid, 110.
[17] Ibid, 88, 90, 95.

as at least *one*, arguably somewhat appealing, account of the foundations of morality therefore has some illumination to offer on the apparent stalemate between these two theorists. Six points are worthy of note.

First, by global consequentialist lights, McMahan overstates the difference between the morality versus the laws of war. Recall that McMahan thinks that it follows, simply from the fact that morality is not the product of any *convention* or *agreement*, that considerations of 'reasons for adopting' one or another moral standard, such as the pragmatic considerations that he allows centre stage in the discussion of the *laws* of war, cannot have any role to play in determining the content of the *morality* of war. But if global consequentialism is correct, this is not right: instead, in the domain of morality no less than in that of law, considerations of (at least) the *consequences of one or another moral standard being advocated/adopted/used as a decision procedure/used as the basis for ascriptions of responsibility and blame/etc.* are highly relevant to the question of which moral statements are true (ie to the content of morality). The admitted fact that morality is not a matter of *convention* does not, on this view, prevent considerations of consequences from playing a role in determining its content.

Second, as we have seen, one of Shue's key objections to McMahan is that Shue regards the very idea of a morality of war that diverges from the prescriptions of the (morally best) laws of war as incoherent. But if global consequentialism is correct, then there is a clear route by which this divergence could easily happen. This is because according to global consequentialism, the question of which are the right standards is intelligible only relative to a particular *role* those standards might play, and morality corresponds to a different role (really, a set of roles) than does law. It could easily be the case, for instance, that the principles whose *enaction as laws* has the best consequences (hence, the content of the 'morally best laws') are quite different from the principles whose *use as a decision procedure by conscientious moral agents* has the best consequences, since considerations of transparency and enforceability are relevant to the former but not the latter. On this point, according to the global consequentialist perspective, Shue is incorrect and McMahan in the end correct, although not for the reason McMahan himself gives.

Third, granted that the content of the morality of war could differ even from that of the morally best laws for war, however, the question remains of *how* different its content will be. McMahan thinks that the content of the relevant morality is *very* different from that of the relevant laws. For most of the 'roles' relative to which we might, as global consequentialists, assess a system of morality, however, such radical difference is unlikely to be the result of applying the global consequentialist formula (GC). The basic reason for this lies in observations already made by McMahan himself: for example, that '[c]ombatants should be reluctant to give their individual judgment [about the permissibility of killing based on judgments of individual liability] priority over the law, for the law has been designed in part precisely to obviate the need for resort to individual moral judgment in conditions that are highly unconducive to rational reflection'.[18] For most *moral* purposes ('roles'), be they ones of individuals' decision-making procedure or ascriptions of moral responsibility, the result of such observations, according to global consequentialism, is not that combatants should defer to the law rather than to morality, but rather that the content of morality of war itself is much closer to that of law than it would be if the context of war involved more ideal epistemic conditions. Thus, while McMahan is correct in his qualitative claim that the content of the morality of war might well diverge from that of the (morally best) laws of war, he significantly overstates the extent of the divergence.

Fourth, while McMahan thinks that morality is fairly unitary (that the morality of war is just the morality of ordinary life, applied to the context of war, but with the same principles of eg conditions for liability applicable in both contexts), Shue sketches the outline of a more complex picture, according to which context-invariant 'fundamental moral concerns' give rise to differing 'specific standards' in different contexts. However, Shue says nothing further about *how* the fundamental concerns he gestures at might 'give rise' to diverging specific standards. Global consequentialism offers one principled way of filling in the picture, and one that seems much within the spirit of what Shue does say. Shue's 'fundamental moral concerns' become a comprehensive theory of the good (so that we know what counts as the best overall consequences), and the notion of this theory of the good 'giving rise' to a particular specific standard is explicated, relative to a role for the standard in question, by the global consequentialist formula (GC). On this point, then, in the global consequentialist view McMahan is incorrect and Shue correct, but global consequentialism is also able to fill in the crucial details where Shue's own discussion leaves matters vague.

Fifth, a minor observation on the structure of the landscape. Commenting on McMahan, Rodin writes that McMahan takes the morality of war to be 'predominantly deontological in character', while the 'morality of public rule formation' is 'predominantly consequentialist in character'.[19] This characterization of McMahan's views, however, is potentially seriously misleading. For McMahan does not think that either the morality of war *or* the 'morality of public rule formation' (the morally best laws for war) is consequentialist *in content*. Indeed, no-one has ever advocated, nor would they ever advocate, laws that are genuinely consequentialist *in content*: a law according to which one is simply legally required to do whatever would promote the best overall consequences would be a laughing stock, and rightly so. The point is rather that, as noted earlier, like the global consequentialist, McMahan takes consequentialist considerations to be *relevant to determining* the content of the laws of war, but in contrast to the global consequentialist, he takes

[18] Ibid, 41.

[19] David Rodin, 'Morality and Law in War' in Hew Strachan and Sibylle Scheipers (eds), *The Changing Character of War* (OUP 2011) 446–63, 453 (hereafter Rodin, 'Morality and Law in War').

such considerations to be irrelevant to determining the content of the morality of war. This distinction is crucial: failure to recognize it seems likely to block all possibility of finding any middle ground between the extremes of an overly simplistic act consequentialism and an overly primitive rights theory.

Finally, we saw that, as a result of admitting that the content of the morality of law might diverge from that of even the morally best laws for war, McMahan was compelled to acknowledge the possibility of conflicts between requirements and prohibitions issuing from the two different sources. This problem is arguably simply the reappearance, in the particular context of war, of the problem of conflicts that plagues global consequentialism quite generally, outlined in section III. To note that the problem is a general one is of course not immediately to say anything about how it is best to be solved, but it may nevertheless prove illuminating.

I note in closing that nothing about the context of war exorcises the purely general worries that we noted in section II for global consequentialism. In particular, those who are dissatisfied with global consequentialism's partial collapsing of truth conditions and expediency conditions in general will be no more happy with this approach in the application to war (for some complaints that are easily interpreted along these lines, see eg Rodin).[20] Global consequentialism is far from uncontroversial. However it is also far from implausible.

[20] Rodin, 'Morality and Law in War' (n 19) 459–61.

3

Two Visions of Human Rights

Relational and Beneficiary-Focused Theories

David Rodin

I. Introduction

There are visions of rights that play a powerful role in shaping how we think about and practice human rights. Broader than a theory, a vision of rights reflects a basic orientation and related set of assumptions that may be shared by a whole family of competing normative approaches that are in other respects very different. Sometimes a theoretical vision can be so pervasive that we are barely aware of the way in which it enables or constrains certain forms of thinking and acting. In this chapter, I will discuss a widespread vision of rights that informs many of the most prominent current theories of rights. I will contrast it with an alternative vision of rights that I will argue to be superior in important respects.

I will call the vision of human rights that I wish to critique the 'beneficiary-focused' view. This is the view that human rights have their normative source in some feature of the beneficiary of the right (the person, agent, or object that the right is intended to benefit). This basic thought is developed in different ways within different theories. Rights may be thought to derive from certain interests or needs of the beneficiary (eg their interest in possessing what is required to lead a decent life) or in exercising distinctive human capabilities. Alternatively, human rights may be thought to stem directly from the dignity, autonomy, or normative status of the rights beneficiary. In both cases, it is features of the beneficiary that forms the basic ground of the right. The beneficiary is thought to hold a normatively privileged position in the derivation of the right: he or she possesses the relevant features (interests or status) and other persons are morally required to orient their behaviour around them.

The alternative vision that I wish to explore is quite different. Rather than viewing human rights as stemming from features of the beneficiary of the right, it holds that they derive from a normative relationship between the beneficiary and the counterparty of the right (the person who holds the correlative duty, no-claim, or liability). Rather than privileging the status and interests of the beneficiary, it focuses on the capacity of normative relations or transactions between persons to generate mutually effective claims, duties, and liberties. I call this vision the 'relational' view. It is

David Rodin, *Two Visions of Human Rights* In: Human Rights and 21st Century Challenges. Edited by: Dapo Akande, Jaakko Kuosmanen, Helen McDermott, and Dominic Roser, Published by Oxford University Press 2020.
DOI: 10.1093/oso/9780198824770.003.0004

reflected in contractarian accounts that see human rights as a product of agreements (either real or hypothetical) between moral agents. It is also reflected in the reciprocity theory of rights that I have defended, and that explains rights as emerging from relations of moral reciprocity between moral agents. Relational approaches reveal a vision of human rights, not as possessed simply by virtue of our being human but rather as normative artefacts that we jointly create through our interactions and intentions. Beneficiary-focused approaches tend to be individualistic because they focus on the needs and status of the individual who is the bearer of the right, and static because they conceive of human rights as inalienable, equal, and universal. Relational approaches tend to emphasize collaboration, in that they view rights as products of mutual creation through processes of normative interaction and exchange, and they are also dynamic in a way that I will explain shortly.

In this chapter, my interest is to explore how these two competing visions inform our ability to provide a substantive normative account of human rights. I will first say a few words about how I understand this task. I will then raise a challenge concerning the ability of beneficiary-focused approaches to provide such an account. A substantive account of human rights, as I conceive it, is distinct from an analysis of rights, whose task is to tell us what rights are (the nature of rights). It is also distinct from a formal account, whose task is to tell us what rights there are (which rights exist). A viable substantive account will have a bearing on both questions, but its role is different. As I understand it, the role of a substantive account is to provide an explanation and a moral ground of rights. This encompasses a number of interconnected tasks. First, the account should stand in a stable reflective equilibrium with our pre-theoretical intuitions about how rights 'present' in moral experience. By the presentation of rights, I mean our apprehension of such things as the particular content of rights possessed by different persons, the extent to which rights are resistant to trade-off against the achievement of the interests and rights of others, the burdens that rights can properly impose on counterparty duty-holders, and the way that conflicts of rights are properly resolved. A key feature of my argument will be that familiar beneficiary-focused accounts of human rights are in tension with the dynamic presentation of many rights, including core human rights. Human rights are dynamic in the sense that they have the capacity to alter their content and configuration over time in characteristic ways, in particular through the phenomenon of forfeiture. Second, a substantive account should provide a normative justification for the constellation of rights so identified by showing how it draws normative support from underlying and adjacent moral principles. Third, a substantive account should contribute practical tools for resolving characteristic forms of moral problems and conflicts. In other words, we should expect a substantive account of rights to possess not only explanatory power (the ability to explain the status and presentation of rights) but also deliberative power (the capacity to help us better deliberate on and resolve practical moral problems).

Hilary Greaves begins Chapter 2 by articulating an ambition to avoid what she calls rights primitivism. Primitivism, in her view, has two features. First, it articulates the belief that there are brute facts about rights. Second, it holds that rights are bedrock features of our moral experience such that it is not possible to provide a further normative explanation or justification of rights. The substantive accounts of rights I canvas here are intended to assert the first of these contentions, but to reject the second: they seek to explain how there can be a matter of fact as to whether rights exist and what is there content, while grounding this in further (underlying or adjacent) normative concepts and principles.

I will consider a substantive account of only a class or subset of human rights, not of human rights in their totality. The reason is that there are commonly recognized human rights that are resistant to relational approaches and are not plausibly explained by the reciprocity account that I will defend. I therefore assume that a complete account of human rights will be pluralistic in form, combining a number of substantive accounts or grounds. The class of human rights that I will address may be loosely characterized as 'central (or core) interpersonal rights'. Examples of central interpersonal rights include negative rights such as the right to life, the right to liberty, the right to bodily integrity, the right to the continued possession of justly acquired property, and also central positive rights, such as the right to receive assistance in the form of sustenance, shelter, and medical care in case of need. By referring to these rights as central, I mean that they are among the most important and stringent of our human rights and they protect some of our most urgent needs and interests. They are paradigmatic human rights that must stand at the very heart of any rights architecture. By describing them as interpersonal, I mean first, that these rights can and ought to be asserted against individual persons and not simply against states, transnational institutions, or other organizations. Second, we can make sense of the possession and exercise of such rights by individual persons in a state of nature unmediated by institutions.

As will be apparent, this project is orthogonal to 'political' accounts of rights that have been advanced by John Rawls, Joseph Raz, Charles Beitz, and others. These approaches eschew the project of providing a substantive or moral account or human rights and instead view human rights as defined by the particular roles that they play within international or domestic politics. On this view, rights function to set limits to a society's internal autonomy and specify the legitimacy of sovereignty that makes a state immune to external intervention (Rawls, Raz) or define those rights that the international community has a responsibility to protect in modern societies (Beitz).[1] In contrast, I take seriously the claim that human rights may exist as aspects of morality independently of the role they play within politics and

[1] Joseph Rawls, *The Law of Peoples* (Harvard University Press 1999) 79–81. See also Joseph Raz, 'Human Rights without Foundations' in John Tasioulas and Samantha Besson (eds), *The Philosophy of International Law* (OUP 2010); Charles Beitz, *The Idea of Human Rights* (OUP 2009).

of their existence within the law, and seek to explain the nature of this existence. While I will make various appeals and reference to the legal status of human rights, it should be remembered that my focus here is on the nature of human rights as pre-legal moral entities.

II. The Beneficiary-Focused Vision: Problems of Forfeiture and Stringency

Theories that reflect the beneficiary-focused vision of rights (beneficiary theories for short) view human rights as arising from, and being justified by, some feature of the beneficiary of the right. Beneficiary theories come in two basic variants. The first views human rights as morally mandated responses to some distinctive status possessed by human beings. A classical example is the theory that human rights arise from the distinctive dignity of humans and the requirement to properly respect this in our actions.[2] A second variant views rights as arising from the requirement to protect certain morally important needs or interests that are universally or characteristically possessed by human persons. These may be variously characterized as interests,[3] the conditions for a minimally decent life,[4] or the fundamental conditions of a good life.[5] Some important beneficiary approaches to human rights may be viewed as combining an appeal to both the concepts of status and needs. Thus, Martha Nussbaum and Amartya Sen, who focus on the importance of essential human capabilities, can be viewed as appealing both to a form of human need and as spelling out the conditions for human dignity.[6] Similarly the important tradition of thought that takes human rights to be rooted in autonomy can be viewed as an appeal to both an essential human status and a fundamental need.[7] Certain contemporary accounts have been explicitly pluralistic combining elements of a dignity and interests.[8]

[2] For a useful contemporary discussion of the dignity approach see Jeremy Waldron, 'Is Dignity the Foundation of Human Rights?' in Rowan Cruft, S Matthew Liao, and Massimo Renzo (eds), *Philosophical Foundations of Human Rights* (OUP 2015).

[3] Joseph Raz, *The Morality of Freedom* (OUP 1986) chapter 7 (hereafter Raz, *Morality of Freedom*).

[4] Cécile Fabre, *Cosmopolitan War* (OUP 2012) section 1.2 ff.

[5] S Matthew Liao, 'Human Rights as Fundamental Conditions for a Good Life' in Rowan Cruft, S Matthew Liao, and Massimo Renzo (eds), *Philosophical Foundations of Human Rights* (OUP 2015).

[6] Martha Nussbaum, *Creating Capabilities: The Human Development Approach* (Belknap Press 2011).

[7] James Griffin, *On Human Rights* (OUP 2008); James Griffin (2000) 'Welfare Rights' 4 Journal of Ethics 27–43; James Griffin (2001) 'Discrepancies Between the Best Philosophical Account of Human Rights and the International Law of Human Rights' 101(1) Proceedings of the Aristotelian Society 1–28; James Griffin (2001) 'First Steps in an Account of Human Rights' 9(3) European Journal of Philosophy 306–27.

[8] John Tasioulas, 'On the Foundations of Human Rights' in Rowan Cruft, S Matthew Liao, and Massimo Renzo (eds), *Philosophical Foundations of Human Rights* (OUP 2015) (hereafter Tasioulas, 'Foundations of Human Rights')

There are significant differences between these approaches but they all share a common commitment to the view that rights are fundamentally grounded in a normatively relevant feature of the right beneficiary. Structurally, all beneficiary theories pursue a substantive account of rights by identifying some significant good associated with the beneficiary, whether that be a human status, need, or interest, that is the object of the right. They then argue that this object is sufficiently morally important to justify the imposition of duties on others. These correlative duties are the content of the right.

Beneficiary theories are attractive for a number of reasons. First, they possess an appealing directness in the derivation of rights. This derivation may draw from consequentialist reasoning, in the case of need and interest variants of the approach, or from the deontological reasoning in the status variant. But in both cases rights emerge directly from the moral status of the object of the right. Second, it puts the focus of the account where it would appear to be most needed–on the needs, status, and interests that are of greatest moral importance. This has the effect of giving prominence to the needs and interests of the most vulnerable, which may be one of the reasons that human rights discourse has had such a transformational political effect.

However, as a class, beneficiary theories also possess severe problems. One problem is their difficulty in explaining the forfeiture of human rights. It is uncontroversial that persons sometimes possess the liberty right to kill others in conditions of self- or other defence. Broadly, these conditions obtain when (i) one person is responsible for posing an unjust threat to another; (ii) there is no morally less costly way of averting the threat; and (iii) the moral costs imposed on the person are not disproportionate to the harm inflicted by the threat. On standard Hohfeldian assumptions, this liberty right to kill in defence *just is* the absence, loss, or suspension of the liable person's right to life. This loss or suspension is most commonly explained as a forfeiture of that right. To be sure, this forfeiture is not necessarily permanent or complete (eg an aggressor who is liable to be killed in self-defence, may regain the right not to be killed if he ceases to be a threat), but it is effective while the conditions for permissible defensive action are met.

Other rights are subject to forfeiture also. If one may kill a responsible person in order to avert a significant unjust threat, then one may also maim, hurt, or insult a person in order to avert lesser unjust threats. Moreover, rights can be forfeit in contexts other than defensive action. The criminal justice system is premised on the principle that we may forfeit liberty rights and become liable to punishment as a result of criminal wrongdoing. Property rights and liberty rights may become forfeit when one is liable to compensate or provide redress for a previous wrongful harm, as in a tort action or a moral duty of restitution after wrongdoing.

The process of rights forfeiture that we observe in these phenomena is both familiar and remarkable. It shows that it is possible for rights bearers to lose the protection afforded by some of our most central rights, including human rights such as the rights to life, bodily integrity, liberty, and possession of property. If this is true, then many canonical beliefs about the nature of human rights must be false, at least with respect to an important class of rights. Foundational human rights documents famously assert that human rights possess certain essential features. First, they are taken to be universal, in the sense that they are possessed by all human beings (or perhaps by all currently living human beings). Second, they are equal, in that human rights are identical in content and status. Third, they are inalienable in the sense that human rights cannot be lost, or abrogated by another party such as the state. The universality, equality, and inalienability of human rights are often taken to adhere in, and in some measure to derive from, the central claim that human rights are rights possessed by persons simply by virtue of their humanity.[9]

If central human rights are forfeitable, then each of these canonical claims, taken at face value, is false. Most obviously, a forfeitable right cannot be inalienable because to forfeit a right *just is* to alienate or cease to possess it. If human rights are forfeitable, then it cannot be the case that human rights are equal (assuming that equality implies identical in content and status). Rather, the content and status of human rights varies between different persons at a given point in time, and varies for a given right holder over time. For instance, the liberty right of a convicted and sentenced tax fraud does not have the same content and status as my liberty right at the present moment, or of his own liberty right prior to his conviction. Similarly, if human rights can be forfeit, then it cannot be the case that each human right is universally possessed by every human person since persons can cease to possess those rights without ceasing to be human. Finally, and for the same reason, it cannot be true that human rights are possessed simply by virtue of our humanity.

The phenomenon of forfeiture raises a significant problem for the beneficiary-focused vision of rights. In its general form the problem is this: beneficiary-focused accounts locate the conditions for the possession of human rights in the moral status, needs, or interests of the bearer of the right in question. But forfeiture shows that a bearer of a human right can lose that right without losing the moral status, or ceasing to possess the underlying needs or interests identified in the account. For example, a person who is liable to be killed for defensive reasons does not cease to be human being. He has no less interest in continuing to live, and has no less dignity or need of characteristic human capabilities, freedoms, and autonomy than he did prior to the attack. Moreover, his interest in possessing these goods is no less than that the defending party. Yet he does not, in the circumstances, possess the right not to be killed. Therefore, it cannot be the case that his moral status, needs, and interests alone provide the conditions for his possession of the right. Other,

[9] In its preamble, the Universal Declaration of Human Rights famously refers to 'the equal and inalienable rights of all members of the human family' echoing Jefferson's Declaration of Independence (1776): 'We hold these truths to be self-evident, that all men are created equal, that they are endowed by their Creator with certain unalienable rights, that among these are Life, Liberty, and the Pursuit of Happiness'.

potentially conflicting, normative features are clearly playing a material role in determining the possession and content of the human right.

Now it is hardly news that human rights such as life, liberty, and property possession are capable of forfeit. Yet this has not typically been perceived as a substantial problem for beneficiary-centred accounts of human rights. Why? My guess is that proponents of these accounts make two assumptions: first, that forfeiture is a relatively peripheral and localized feature of human rights; and second, that beneficiary-centred accounts possess theoretical resources sufficient to account for forfeiture. Both assumptions are false.

Forfeiture is not a peripheral feature of rights. It is central to their normative functioning, and fundamental to the way in which human rights protect their bearers. Rights protect us, not merely through the assertion of claims and liberties but also through the enforceability of correlative duties. There are broadly three normative mechanisms by which duties may enforced and correlative rights and liberties protected. First, persons are morally permitted to take potentially harmful *defensive action* against a responsible person to prevent or avert an imminent threat to some person's rights. Second, those responsible for a breach of rights may be required bear costs in order to provide *restitution* or compensation to restore the rights bearer to the *status quo ante*. Third, *punitive* harm may be inflicted on those responsible for a breach of rights in order to deter that party or others from inflicting future breaches of rights. Each of these three mechanisms consists, at base, in a mechanism of rights forfeiture. We can see this by noting the central role of liability to harm in each case. Although there are exceptional cases in which we are permitted to harm a person who has a right against that harm because it is the lesser evil, in most cases we are morally permitted to inflict defensive, compensatory, and punitive harm only on those who are liable to such harm. To say that a rights-bearing person is liable to suffer a harm is to say that he has forfeit, lost, or alienated his rights against harm in this context and for these purposes.

It is worth pausing to note the extraordinary integrity, elegance, and power of the system of rights revealed in these phenomena. Rights not only specify protected objects consisting in the interests, status, and needs of individuals. Rights simultaneously establish the logically correlative duties required to achieve this protection, and moreover articulate the means and boundaries of the permissible enforcement of those duties through the liberties of defence, forcible compensation, and punishment. All these resources exist within the system of rights as a unified normative whole. Looked at this way, the forfeiture of rights is not a bug but a feature. The *alienability* of human rights is an indispensable component of the necessary means for enforcing duties and securing the goods that are the objects of rights and a central feature of their normative architecture. As we have seen, the problem with the beneficiary theories is that they have difficulty in accounting for forfeiture because one may lose a human right without ceasing to possess the objects which these theories identify as the normative source of the right.

Let us now consider the resources that a beneficiary-centred theorist may deploy to deal with the problem. One potential response is simply to deny the phenomenon of forfeiture. In situations of defence, punishment, and compensation it appears that the person responsible for unjust action has forfeit certain rights, but this may not be true. It may be that the responsible person's rights are extant but are being overridden by other normative considerations in the form of a lesser evil justification. In a lesser evil justification, a person is morally permitted to infringe the rights of another person when this is necessary to achieve a substantially greater good or to avoid a substantially greater evil.

This response enables the beneficiary theorist to avoid the problem of forfeiture, but only at very high cost. First, the phenomena of defence, punishment, and restitution do not look like cases of lesser evil justification. When a right is justifiably overridden as a lesser evil, there is a characteristic moral 'residue' in the form of an obligation to apologize to, or compensate, the party whose right has been infringed. But there is no obligation to apologize to, or compensate, a responsible person who is harmed in the course of justified defence or punishment. It is hard to even make sense of what it would mean to compensate a tortfeasor for harms suffered in fulfilling a valid tort claim.

Second, allowing that central human rights can be justifiably infringed as the lesser evil in such cases would rob them of the characteristic resistance to trade-off that human rights are thought to possess. If an aggressor retains his right not to be killed even as he is permissibly killed as a means to defend the life of his victim, then it would seem that we would have to accept comparable infringements of human rights in other circumstances where this is necessary to avoid lesser evils. For example, why should it not be justified to kill one innocent man as a means to prevent the murder of two others, or to torture one in order to prevent the torture of two others?

Third, it is often not the case that permissible acts of defence, punishment, or compensation are the lesser evil. For example, an innocent victim may kill an aggressor if this is necessary to preserve no more than his own life, and he may even kill to prevent a lesser harm, such as the loss of limb. In neither case does it appear that killing the aggressor is the lesser evil from an impersonal perspective. One might respond that the comparison of harms for a lesser evil calculation must take into account the fact that the aggressor is potentially liable to be harmed, whereas the victim is not. But obviously this response is only available if one already accepts that the aggressor potentially forfeits his rights in the course of defensive action, which is precisely what this approach is intended to deny.

Another potential response to the problem of forfeiture is to accept that those who are harmed in the course of defence, punishment, and restitution do not have the right not be harmed, but to deny that they have forfeit any rights. Instead one may insist that when we properly specify the content of human rights, it will transpire that these permissible harms are consistent with the content of a right that we all possess equally and inalienably. For example, when we talk of the right to life, we should not say that the content of this right is simply the right not to be killed by others. Rather, it is the far more complex right not to be killed provided we are not ourselves posing an unjust threat to the rights of others such that the only way to prevent our unjust action is killing us. Harmful acts of defence, punishment, and the like which appear to require justification because they contravene the rights of those harmed, are, on this approach, entirely consistent with the complex and properly specified content of those rights.

The problem with this specification approach is that it robs human rights of a great deal of their explanatory power. We can no longer explain why defensive action is permissible in one case and impermissible in another by appealing to the operation of a general normative mechanism of rights such as forfeiture. Instead, the content of human rights seems to simply reflect independent judgements about what is permissible and impermissible. Rather than explaining and informing our moral judgements in particular cases, this account would seem to presuppose it. The account therefore lacks the deliberative power that a substantive account of human rights should aspire to, as I said at the outset.

Worse still, the content of rights on this account would appear to be open-ended and indeterminate. The properly specified content of the right to life would have to accommodate and articulate every conceivable circumstance of justified killing (at least all those that are not justified by reason of lesser evil), including some circumstances that have yet to be realized. Such complex rights are probably essentially unknowable in advance, and certainly could not be accurately captured in the documents of law and politics that are their necessary practical medium.

A more promising line of response is to argue that forfeiture is only a problem for beneficiary theories if one identifies the content of a right with the underlying object that the right protects. But beneficiary theorists need not, and do not, make any such a claim. Instead, they view the underlying interests, status, or needs as providing a *pro tanto* reason for the imposition of duties on others to secure those objects. The interests, status, or needs are the ground of the right, but the content of the right consists in the duties that they create in others. A right only exists when the underlying object is sufficiently important to generate duties in others. This is made clear by Raz in his classic formulation of the interest theory of rights.

> 'X has a right' if and only if X can have rights, and, other things being equal, an aspect of X's well-being (his interest) is a sufficient reason for holding some other person(s) to be under a duty.[10]

[10] Raz, *Morality of Freedom* (n 3) 166.

On this view, the reasons provided by underlying objects are feasible. There is an independent question about whether a person's status, interests, or needs do, in any particular case, generate a sufficient reason for holding other persons to be under a duty; in other words, whether they create the conditions for the existence of a right. By spelling out the conditions under which these *pro tanto*, reasons are feasible, one may hope to provide an explanation of the phenomenon of forfeiture of rights.

John Tasioulas has produced a sophisticated account of the feasibility conditions for the imposition of duties on others.[11] He notes that feasibility conditions come in two forms: internal conditions that do not take into account any interests beyond those of the putative right holder, and external conditions that do take into account such broader interests. An example of an internal feasibility condition is a situation in which it is impossible to secure the object of the supposed right. For example, there can be no right to be both alive and dead at the same time, or to engage in intergalactic travel, or (given limited resources) for all persons to enjoy a luxurious standard of living. He further argues that rights must be sensitive to situations in which the attainment of a good or interest is an 'evaluative impossibility', in the sense that having a duty to deliver the object of the putative right is inappropriate to the right-holder's interests, or would destroy the moral value of the object. Thus, there can be no right to be romantically loved, since the value of romantic love is intimately linked to its bestowal as a free gift, which would be destroyed by imposing a duty to love.[12]

If a putative right does not fall at the level of internal feasibility conditions, we must next ask whether it is defeated because it is excessively burdensome on others. The key question is whether the imposition of duties to secure the object of the putative right 'imposes excessive burdens on potential duty-bearers, in terms of other values, including excessive sacrifices in our ability to fulfil other human rights?'[13] For example, Tasioulas argues that a putative right to the highest attainable standard of health is defeated because achieving this objective would impose excessive burdens on others.[14]

Before considering whether some variant of this feasibility account can help to resolve the forfeiture problem, I first want to introduce a second and related problem for beneficiary theories of rights: how beneficiary theorists can explain why rights not to be harmed (negative rights) are in certain respects more stringent than rights to be assisted (positive rights) even when they protect identical needs, status, or interests. Since these two problems are structurally similar, we may hope that a solution to one problem will suffice also to resolve the other.

[11] Tasioulas, 'Foundations of Human Rights' (n 8).
[12] Tasioulas, 'Foundations of Human Rights' (n 8) 59.
[13] Ibid, 60.
[14] Ibid.

There are a number of ways in which negative rights present as more stringent than positive rights. One area of difference concerns their enforceability. For example, compliance with the duty not to harm others is universally enforced through the criminal justice system, but duties to assist others in case of extreme need rarely is ('good Samaritan' laws are rare and are generally restricted to creating legal protections for those who choose to intervene to assist others, rather than generating a positive legal duty for them to do so). The stringency differential that I want to examine, however, concerns the way in which positive and negative rights can generate different requirements to bear costs as a consequence of compliance with a right, even when the moral value of the underlying object of the right is identical. Consider the following hypothetical cases.

> *Bridge*: I am being pursued by a murderer who intends to kill me. My only route of escape is to cross a narrow and rickety bridge on which you are standing. Crossing the bridge to escape the murderer will cause you to fall to your death in the ravine below.

It seems clear that I am not permitted to cross the bridge in order to save myself in *Bridge*. Your right not to be cast into the ravine is sufficiently stringent to require me to accept exceptionally severe harm (including death) as the cost of preserving the goods that are the object of your right (your continued survival).

> *Medicine*: A murderer has attempted to poison you with a drug that causes fatal kidney failure. I possess the only medicine that will reverse the damage to your kidneys, but I need this medicine to manage the treatment of my own, otherwise fatal, kidney condition.

It seems clear that I am not required to give the medicine to you in *Medicine*. Your right to be assisted by me is not sufficiently stringent to require me to accept exceptionally severe harm (such as death) as the cost of preserving the goods that are the object of your right (your continued survival).

For a beneficiary theorist, the right not to be killed and the right to receive life-saving assistance have the same normative source; the needs, status, and interests of the right bearer. Why, then, is your right not to be harmed in *Bridge* so much more stringent than your right to be assisted in *Medicine*? We may look to the feasibility account to explain the disparity. The internal feasibility conditions will be of little help here (it is not the case that achieving the object of your rights in either case is logically, physically, or normatively impossible). But external feasibility conditions look more promising. There is a long tradition of explaining the greater stringency of negative rights by appeal to their supposed lower costs of compliance, since all that is required to comply with a negative right is to abstain from interfering with others, in comparison with positive rights which require costly and burdensome forms of intervention.

But the burdensomeness test will not help us to explain the difference between the rights (positive and negative) that have the object of preserving your life in *Bridge* and *Medicine*. There are three problems. First, any explanation invoking burdensomeness would be viciously circular. When we ask why your right not to be killed in *Bridge* is more stringent than your right to receive assistance in *Medicine*, we are in part asking why the negative right in *Bridge* is capable of imposing greater burdens on the putative duty bearer as a cost of compliance, compared with the positive right to assistance in *Medicine*. We cannot invoke the different burdens that the right would impose on duty bearers in order to explain the difference in stringency because that is precisely what requires explanation.

Second, even if it were possible to deploy the burdensomeness test in a non-objectionably circular way this would take us no further, since the test generates the wrong answer in these cases. The burden that I would be required to bear in order to preserve your status, needs, and interests is the same in both cases: death. We should therefore expect that your interest in continued survival is sufficiently important to generate a duty either in both cases equally, or in neither. It is true that compliance with negative rights is, in most cases, less burdensome than compliance with positive rights. But this fact about what is generally the case cannot explain why in a small but important set of cases the burdens justifiably imposed by negative rights can be equal to, or greater than, those imposed by positive rights.

Indeed, in one respect the burden imposed by your putative rights is greater in *Bridge* than in *Medicine*. If I do not cross in *Bridge*, I will not only die but be murdered (my right to life will be violated and I will be wronged). In *Medicine*, if I give you the medicine then I will die but I will not be wronged, because my right to life will not be violated. We generally believe that it is a greater moral burden to be wrongfully harmed than to be harmed without being wronged. Therefore, we should expect that your interests should generate a stronger duty for me to give you the medicine than to abstain from crossing the bridge. This conclusion is clearly wrong.

Return now to the forfeiture problem. The burdensomeness test is equally unsuccessful at explaining why a person responsible for wrongful harm may be liable to defensive, compensatory, or punitive harm. Take the case of defensive harm. Prior to engaging in a wrongful attack, an aggressor has the right, with respect to the victim, not to be killed. Would it be unduly burdensome (relative to the interest protected) to impose a duty on the victim not to kill the aggressor in self-defence? On the face of it, it would seem not. The cost that such a duty would impose on the victim (death) is no greater than the cost that he will impose on the aggressor by killing him in self-defence. Moreover, as we have seen, self-defensive killing is often deemed just when an aggressor threatens lesser interests such as the destruction of a limb. But a duty to bear such lesser costs does not seem excessively burdensome relative to the aggressor's interest in continued survival. One might argue that the burden imposed on the victim is excessive because the victim has the right not be harmed, whereas the aggressor is potentially liable. But this response obviously assumes the very feature that requires explanation: that the aggressor has forfeit his right.

The burdensomeness test will not resolve the forfeiture or differential stringency problems for beneficiary theorists. But perhaps another feasibility condition can. One potential route out of the forfeiture problem is simply to assert that a person's interests, needs, or status will not generate duties if that person is currently breaching (or has breached) the rights of others. Thus acting wrongfully towards others becomes an independent feasibility condition for the possession of rights.[15] This would explain why being responsible for a breach of other's rights can make one liable to defensive, compensatory, or punitive harm.

The difficulty with this approach is how we can make sense of the normative status of this feasibility condition in the context of the broader beneficiary theory of rights. Recall that beneficiary theories are committed to the claim that the normative ground of a right consists exclusively in the status, need, or interest of the beneficiary of the putative right. As Raz says (in the interests variant) 'an aspect of X's well-being (his interest) is a sufficient reason for holding some other person(s) to be under a duty'. But on the view being considered here, it turns out that this claim is not true. It is not ever the case, for any person X, that his interest in remaining alive is a *sufficient* reason for holding any other person to be under the duty not to kill him. This is because a necessary condition for holding other persons to be under that duty is that X is not currently responsible for a breach of rights. This necessary condition for the possession of the right is independent of the putative right-bearers interests; therefore those interests cannot be sufficient for the imposition of the duty.

Worse still, the beneficiary theorist is unable to explain *why* not currently threatening the rights of others should function as a necessary condition for holding others to be under a duty. On a beneficiary theory, the interest, status, or need of the right bearer is the exclusive source of right's correlative duties imposed on others. Yet whether or not X unjustly threatens the rights of others is independent of these features. The feasibility condition is therefore entirely disconnected from the broader normative theory to which it is appended. Its sole purpose is to provide a solution to the forfeiture problem, but the reason why it functions to defeat the

[15] Cécile Fabre takes this approach: Cécile Fabre (2009) 'Permissible Rescue Killing' 109 1(2) Proceedings of the Aristotelian Society 149, 153.

imposition of duties on others is unexplained and unexplainable in the context of a benefit theory. It is, in this sense, objectionably *ad hoc*.

What is more, we can see that the burdensomeness condition proposed by Tasioulas and others is *ad hoc* in the same way. Why should the fact that a putative duty would be excessively burdensome serve to defeat its imposition? Contrast the burdensomeness test with Tasioulas' 'internal' feasibility conditions for the existence of a right. Each of the internal conditions can be explained in terms of the underlying interests or status that is the source of the putative right. Thus, a good that is impossible to obtain or which would be destroyed by the imposition of a duty cannot generate a reason to impose a duty on others, since such a duty could not possibly achieve the good. But whether a putative right would impose burdens (excessive or otherwise) on duty bearers is a fact entirely independent of the interests, needs, or status of the right-holder. It is therefore unclear why this fact should be viewed as sufficient to defeat the imposition of a duty on a beneficiary theory.

III. Relational Theories of Rights

In section II I argued that beneficiary theories of rights have great difficulty in accounting for ordinary features of human rights such as their forfeitability. I now want to contrast what I the beneficiary vision with an alternative vision of rights that I will call 'relational'. Examples of relational theories of rights include certain contractualist theories, for example David Gauthier's view of morality as arising from agreements between self-interested persons.[16] It also includes the reciprocity theory of rights that I have previously defended, which seeks to explains core interpersonal rights as emerging from reciprocity relations between moral agents.[17]

As we have seen, the defining characteristic of beneficiary theories is their shared commitment to the view that the normative source of rights lies exclusively in a morally relevant feature of the beneficiary of the right (their needs, status, or interests). The defining feature of relational theories of rights is their commitment to the view that the normative source of rights lies in morally relevant relations between moral agents. Because moral relationships are in part constituted by the actions and choices of persons, they have the potential to capture the dynamic nature of rights reflected in phenomena like the forfeiture and the differential stringency of positive and negative rights. I will first briefly summarize the reciprocity theory, showing how it can account for forfeiture and differential stringency rights, before

[16] David Gauthier, *Morals by Agreement* (OUP 1987).

[17] David Rodin (2014) 'The Reciprocity Theory of Human Rights' 33 (3) Law and Philosophy 281–308. The following paragraphs draw from and summarize argumentation developed more fully in this chapter.

reflecting on some of the general strengths and weaknesses of the relational approach that this theory highlights.

According to the reciprocity theory, rights arise from mutually supporting reciprocity relationships between moral agents. In particular, a person possesses rights with respect to X when that person complies with reciprocal rights that X possesses with respect to them. Negative and positive rights are grounded in two different forms of reciprocity relationship. Negative rights have their source in a relationship of actual (contemporaneous or prior) compliance with reciprocal duties. Thus, I have the right that you not kill me *because* and *to the extent* that I comply with the duty that I not kill you. Similarly, you have the right that I not kill you *because* and *to the extent* that you comply with the duty that you not kill me. Positive rights to assistance are grounded in a counterfactual reciprocity relationship. The grounding relationship is counterfactual in the sense that the right holder *would* assist the duty bearer *if* their situations were reversed. Thus, if it is counterfactually true of a person in need, X, that he would assist Y were their circumstances reversed, then this can generate an obligation for Y to provide comparable assistance to X in those circumstances.

The reciprocity theory begins from a basic hypothesis about the genesis of normative obligations: persons can come to possess rights when they comply with the obligations generated by the rights of others. Unlike Gauthier's contract theory, the reciprocity account does not seek to ground morality in self-interested reasons that could be accepted by a pure rational egoist. Instead, it begins with a foundational conception of reciprocity that is already normative, albeit one that is extremely basic and deeply rooted in our moral psychology--the requirement to give respect and consideration to those who manifest appropriate respect and consideration towards us.

A reciprocity approach to rights has a number of advantages. First, it can easily account for forfeiture of rights. If my right to life has its normative source in my observance and compliance with your right to life, then this explains why I may forfeit my right by threatening to inflict on you wrongful harm. By failing to comply with your reciprocal rights, I undermine or negate the existence conditions for my own right, making me morally vulnerable to be used as a means to secure the object of your right. The reciprocity theory also reveals a little noted feature of positive rights, which is that rights to assistance may also be forfeit in certain circumstances. If someone refuses to recognize an obligation to assist me in a situation of need, then he may have no claim that I assist him in an identical situation of need, even if his need were great and the costs to me would be negligible (there may be compelling moral reasons of other kinds to assist--for example, consequentialist or virtue based reasons--but I would not *wrong* him by failing to assist).

Reciprocity also provides an account of the differential stringency of different kinds of rights. Why are negative rights against harm so stringent in comparison with positive rights to assistance (eg they are publicly enforceable through criminal law and are capable of imposing very significant costs on duty bearers as a cost of compliance)? According to the reciprocity theory, this difference stems from their respective source in different forms of reciprocity relationship. Rights against harm are grounded in reciprocity of actual compliance. You can possess rights because you have satisfied the conditions of compliance for the rights of others in the past or, as in the paradigm case of the right to life, because you are satisfying the conditions of compliance for the rights of others at this very moment.

The reciprocity underlying rights to assistance instead stems from a counterfactual reciprocity of compliance, and this explains their lesser stringency in terms of enforceability and the costs that can reasonably be imposed on others as the cost of compliance. Most people we are called on to assist are not currently assisting us and nor have they assisted us in the past. Instead, the obligation to assist them arises from the counterfactual claim that they would assist us in comparable circumstances. This counterfactual reciprocity grounds a genuine duty, but it lacks the stringency deriving from actual reciprocal compliance. The difference between the two forms of reciprocity is both ontological and epistemic. I can know with near certainty that you are currently complying with my right to life because you are currently making no attack on my person. But the counterfactual claim that you would assist me, were I in an identical situation of need, depends on free actions undertaken under alternative circumstances and can only be known with a much weaker degree of certainty. There is a lexical normative priority between the reciprocity of actual compliance and the reciprocity of counterfactual compliance. Counterfactual compliance (or lack of compliance) only plays a role in establishing the existence of a right if there is no relevant right already established through a person's actual compliance with obligations. Thus, a maliciously motivated person who *would* kill me given the opportunity, retains his right not to be killed by me so long as he actually complies with the duty not to harm me.

Like other accounts of rights, the reciprocity theory also has characteristic weaknesses. I will enumerate some of these shortly. Before doing so, I want to emphasize some salient features of the broad 'vision' of human rights implicit in the reciprocity account (and relational approaches more generally), which differ substantially from other accounts, particularly from beneficiary theories. Classical conceptions have long viewed human rights as universal and stringent moral claims possessed equally by all humans simply by virtue of their humanity. Beneficiary theories have, in different ways, each attempted to capture and articulate the moral underpinnings of this view. I have argued, that this classical conception is substantially mistaken. It is a static and undiscriminating view of human rights, which fails to account for the remedial mechanisms of rights forfeiture that are intrinsic to the system of human rights and are a source of their normative strength. Nevertheless, no plausible account of human rights can be entirely disconnected from the legal and philosophical tradition within which they have historically been explicated, and it is incumbent on the defender of revisionist accounts to explain the meaning and status of such concepts as equality, autonomy, and dignity within their theory.

What then can a reciprocity theorist make of the idea of the equal moral status of all persons? Clearly he or she cannot understand this to imply the assertion that every person possesses human rights that are identical in content and status--the phenomenon of forfeiture shows this to be untrue. However, he or she can assert that persons all have an equal *capacity* to bear rights, and moreover that the content and status of their own rights lies within the control of their own agency. Any person capable of acting for reasons and of observing reciprocal moral obligations has the capacity to generate rights-correlative duties in others. And the content of those correlative duties lies preponderantly within that person's own control.[18] I may forfeit a right by acting wrongly and breaching the rights of others, but no other person--be it individual or state--may annul, abrogate, or impede my rights for any other reasons than those relating to my own decisions, actions and agency (at least not without infringing my rights). This is how the reciprocity theorist would characterize the distinctive status of autonomy and dignity that is so tied to the traditional discourse on human rights.[19]

Another clear differentiator of the reciprocity theory of rights, compared with other theories, is the explanatory connection that is made between the possession of rights and the observance of duties towards others. Hohfeldian theory makes explicit that all claim rights are logically connected to correlative duties,[20] but the reciprocity theory makes this connection normative as well as conceptual by invoking the moral principle of reciprocity. It claims that we possess the protection of rights *because* we conform with the duties owed to others. In this sense it

[18] I say 'preponderantly' rather than 'exclusively' because possession of rights, particularly positive rights, can also depend on the agency of counterparties to the putative right. For example, I cannot generate a right to receive from you a benefit by granting that benefit to you if you do not in fact wish to receive it. This explains, among other things, why there is no right for an unrequited lover to have their affections returned. Benefits must be willingly received in order to generate reciprocal positive rights.

[19] A similar point can be made about the notion of the 'equal moral worth' of persons. We might understand moral worth to be linked to the possession of moral rights, or we might conceive of it as impersonal moral value such as weighed in a proportionality calculation or lesser evil justification. In neither case does it seem true that humans have equal moral worth. Thus it is worse from an impersonal perspective for a non-liable person to be harmed than for a liable person to be harmed even if the consequences are otherwise identical. This seems to me to be another way of saying that the liable person does not have the same moral worth (significance, salience, moral weight, etc) in impersonal terms. This observation has important consequences for rule consequentialist accounts of human rights, of which I take Hilary Greaves 'global consequentialist' theory to be an example. On these views, human rights are morally grounded in rules which, if they were to be implemented and institutionalized in certain ways, would generate the morally best overall consequences. However, the proceeding observation casts doubt on this project, since the impersonal value of outcomes is itself partly determined the configuration of rights possessed by affected agents. Thus, in order to know what rules will produce the morally best consequences, we need already to know what rights people have and to understand how they change (eg through processes of forfeiture) and how they guide action.

[20] Wesley Newcomb Hohfeld (1917) 'Fundamental Legal Conceptions as Applied in Judicial Reasoning' 26 (8) Yale Law Journal 710–70.

connects with the conservative tradition of thought that asserts that there can be 'no rights without responsibilities'.

I suspect that some readers will find this rich normative connection between the possession of rights and the compliance with responsibilities towards others an attractive feature of the account, while others will find it substantially less so.[21] What is undeniable is that it creates difficulties for the account in explaining how impaired or undeveloped persons such infants, the mentally ill, or the profoundly disabled can possess rights. This is a weakness that it shares with all theories of rights that give a prominent role to agency and autonomy in the explanation of rights including will theories of rights.

A further problem with the reciprocity theory is that it might appear viciously circular and hence conceptually vacuous. According to the theory, the normative source of a person's right is his compliance (either actual or counterfactual) with the duties correlative to the rights of others. But if the theory already requires the substantive concept of a duty to others, then we have explained nothing: our substantive theory of rights presupposes a substantive theory of rights.

The right way to think about this, I believe, is that the reciprocity theory provides a substantive explanation of rights only in concert with a naturalistic account of how the practice of recognizing rights claims can emerge within communities of moral agents. To see this, imagine of a group of persons who do not possess rights or duties with respect to each other. The absence of rights may be localized (eg we may think of a group of neighbours who possess no rights or duties with respect to each other concerning their ability to make noise at night) or it may be general (eg a 'super state of nature' in which every person possesses universal liberties with respect to every other person). Imagine now that iterated patterns of behaviour emerge within these groups of persons, for example the neighbours generally start to avoid making noise after a certain hour; the persons in the state of nature start to avoid inflicting certain kinds of grievous harm on each other. This may be either because members sense a potential for mutual advantage in the emergence of these iterated patterns of behaviour, or because the patterns develop fortuitously through random variation.

Rights emerge when these patterns of behaviour become reciprocated, that is, when persons start to view these patterns of behaviour as structured by, and generative of, normative reasons. They move from viewing the situation as one of simple concurrence—'I'm not harming him *and* he's not harming me'—to one of reason-based entailment—'I'm not harming him *because* he's not harming me'. We

[21] In Chapter 10 in this book, Sandra Fredman discusses the objectionable Victorian notion of conditionality assumed by notion of 'deserving' and 'undeserving' poor. But it is important to understand that the reciprocity theory does not imply such objectionable notions. The possession of rights, on this view, is not conditional on thrift and industry of those in need of assistance but rather with the commitment of the potential beneficiary to view others as a morally deserving recipient of aid in identical circumstances.

may understand the '*because*' to contain initially an inchoate admixture of normative and prudential reasons--because he's not harming me, I have no *need* to harm him; because he's not harming me I have no *interest* in harming him; because he's not harming me I *ought* to not harm him. Once a person conceives himself as bound in this way by normative reasons distinct from, and potentially opposed to, prudential reason, then rights properly understood are in a position to emerge. The moral principle of reciprocity allows us to draw a strong normative entailment between my acknowledging duties to assist you and duties to not harm you and your obligation to acknowledge those same duties with respect to me.

The naturalistic story is required for the reciprocity theory to avoid vicious circulatory, but it has a number of further consequences, some welcome, some more problematic. One welcome feature is that it can explain the wide range of different configurations of both positive and negative rights that we find operative within different communities across time and space. For example, I have no duty to sacrifice my life to save the life of my neighbour (as we saw in the fictional case of *Medicine*), but a platoon member may be under the obligation to sacrifice his life to save one of his comrades, if the comrade would do the same in those circumstances. A reciprocity account combined with the naturalistic story can explain these right and duties as emerging from the organic recognition of different reasons for action within different communities. Similarly, the reciprocity theory avoids giving an implausibly timeless view of rights that would allocate identical positive and negative rights to prehistoric cave dwellers, simple agrarian societies, and contemporary city dwellers. Because the content of rights reflects patterns of reciprocated assistance, concern, and non-interference, the account is compatible both with the phenomenon of moral progress—the way in which moral rights can develop, strengthen, and become more comprehensive over time—and also with moral regress—the phenomenon by which rights diminish decay and lose normative potency.

However, a less welcome consequence is that the reciprocity theory seems to undermine the historically important role of rights as a driver or motivator of moral progress. We can certainly provide a naturalistic account of how rights may have emerged within a state of nature through organically evolving patterns of reciprocity, and for how particular allocations of rights and duties develop in different social contexts. But we cannot utilize the language of rights to express moral reasons for this evolution, since the rights only come after the stable patterns of reciprocal interaction have already emerged.

Similarly, the account seems to create the possibility for what we might call rights 'ghettos' and rights 'gated communities'. Within a rights 'gated community', a high degree of security and effective institutions for mutual aid create strong relations of reciprocity, which ground a strong and mutually reinforcing network of positive and negative rights. There is thus a virtuous circle, creating highly stable and normatively advantaged communities. In rights 'ghettos' the opposite happens. Poor, insecure, or unstable communities are inhospitable to the possession conditions of positive and negative rights, and therefore persons within those communities actually possess fewer and less efficacious rights. This may be seen as a problematic consequence of the reciprocity theory, since it seems to rob the notion of human rights of its progressive power. We may want human rights to provide the moral reasons for escaping rights ghettos and developing and broadening the resources that are found within stronger communities. It is not clear on the reciprocity view that rights are capable of doing this.

IV. Conclusion

Much contemporary theorizing about human rights has been strongly influenced by a beneficiary vision of rights. On this view, rights not only serve, but derive from, the status, interests, or agency of their beneficiaries. This vision has an obvious attraction for anyone concerned with the welfare and dignity of the most vulnerable. But beneficiary accounts cannot explain some of the most basic features of human rights, such as their ability to change configuration through processes of forfeiture. Moreover, these processes are central to the ability of human rights to protect their bearers and to serve as deliberative tools.

But beneficiary approaches are not the only ways to understand human rights. An alternative approach is provided by relational theories that offer an entirely different vision of what human rights are and what they may do. This is a vision of rights as collaborative, dynamic, and built on self-reinforcing relationships of mutual respect and consideration. The relational approach of rights has weaknesses and difficulties of its own, but it deserves further consideration as we seek to build a truly robust account of human rights appropriate to twenty-first century challenges.

II

CONFLICT AND SECURITY

4

State of Play and the Road Ahead

Humanizing Security

Harold Hongju Koh

In the globalized twenty-first century, just about everything affects human rights, and just about everything affects security. Conflicts large and small, detectable and covert, range across physical and virtual space, spurred by the proliferation of private security contractors and special operations and by dramatic technological developments such as armed drones, lethal autonomous robots, and tools of cyber conflict.[1] Ironically, these emerging counterterrorism tools, which are designed to counter security threats, may end up themselves posing significant threats to human rights. So, how can we best reconcile the imperatives of rights with the demands of security in the future?

The four chapters that follow map the emerging legal and human rights dilemmas that flow from such diverse topics as armed drone warfare, cyber conflict, securitizing human rights, and sustainable security. Each chapter takes a different approach to the challenge of reconciliation. Chapters 5 and 6 address the tension between security and human rights in situations of armed conflict, setting forth legal frameworks with specific rules capable of reconciling the tensions. Chapters 7 and 8 seek to reconcile the conceptual tensions thematically—less with detailed frameworks than with hybrid concepts of 'sustainable security' and 'securitizing human rights' that are intended to synthesize human rights and security principles. After briefly reviewing the approaches offered by these chapters, this chapter suggests a counterpoint to the valid and serious concerns expressed within them: the idea of '*humanizing security*'.

Chapters 5 and 6 outline two emerging armed conflict frameworks posed by new technologies: drones and cyber conflict. Both chapters attempt to regulate the relationship between security and human rights by offering overlapping legal frameworks that translate from established bodies of international law to emerging technological innovations. Chapter 7, by Christof Heyns, Dapo Akande, Lawrence Hill-Cawthorne, and Thompson Chengeta, builds on Heyns' Report to the UN General Assembly as Special Rapporteur on Extrajudicial, Summary or

[1] For a recent effort to map the emerging law in this area, see Harold Hongju Koh, 'Keynote Address: The Emerging Law of 21st Century War' (2017) 66 Emory Law Journal 489.

Harold Hongju Koh, *State of Play and the Road Ahead* In: Human Rights and 21st Century Challenges. Edited by: Dapo Akande, Jaakko Kuosmanen, Helen McDermott, and Dominic Roser, Published by Oxford University Press 2020.
DOI: 10.1093/oso/9780198824770.003.0005

Arbitrary Executions on Armed Drones and the Right to Life.[2] The authors offer an international law framework regulating the use of armed drones in a manner designed to ensure respect for the human right to life. Their chapter is particularly helpful in distinguishing among the distinct legal regimes that should apply to drone strikes: *jus ad bellum*, *jus in bello*, and human rights law. The authors reaffirm that to be lawful, a legal regime governing the use of armed drones must independently meet the standards required by *each* of these human-centred legal regimes. Generally speaking, states and commentators have assumed that if a particular drone strike satisfies the requirements of one legal regime—for example, if it was launched consistent with the rules of *jus ad bellum*—then the entire strike is *per se* legal. But too often they do not carefully assess whether the specifics of that strike also satisfied the additional and independent requirements of human rights law and international humanitarian rules governing *jus in bello*. By analogy, it is just as mistaken for the law of war to assume that a strike becomes *per se* legal if *jus ad bellum* standards are satisfied, as it is for domestic criminal law to assume that when an individual lawfully responds in self-defence to an assailant, then the law imposes no further limits to the degree of force that the defender may lawfully employ.

Helen McDermott's Chapter 8 likewise correctly argues that obligations under international human rights law do not evaporate during cyber conflict. She sets forth a useful typology of cyber operations and then seeks to translate existing European human rights precedents to various forms of cyber operations.

Yet despite their virtues, to my ears (as a former US government lawyer who participated in many interagency debates over drones and cyber conflict), both these chapters lack a certain tactile feel for the actual issues currently being contested among policy-makers who operate daily within and among these frameworks. For example, Chapter 7 says little about whether and to what extent armed groups may join together as associated forces or belligerents in a single non-international armed conflict.[3] Nor do the authors say much about whether and to what extent there are geographical limits on the scope of a particular non-international armed conflict.

For all of its virtues, Chapter 7 makes too little reference to actual state practice and stated *opinio juris* in this field, as opposed to various International Committee of the Red Cross (ICRC) and non-governmental organization (NGO) commentaries. To name just two sources about which Chapter 7 could say much more, take President Barack Obama's 2013 counterterrorism speech at the National Defense University[4] and UK Attorney General Jeremy Wright's January 2017 speech laying

2 UNGA 'Report of the Special Rapporteur on Extrajudicial, Summary or Arbitrary Executions' (2001) A/68/382.

3 The issue is briefly touched upon in Heyns, Akande, Hill-Cawthorne, and Chengeta, Chapter 7 of this book, text accompanying notes 75–80.

4 President Barack Obama, 'Remarks by the President at the National Defense University' (The White House, Office of the Press Secretary, 23 May 2013) <https://obamawhitehouse.archives.gov/

out the views of Her Majesty's Government on the applicability of international law to the use of force against non-state actors.[5] In both far-ranging speeches, first President Obama and then Attorney General Wright made clear their governments' preference for capture over kill and for respect for state sovereignty in the use of drones. Both expressed their nation's commitment to the notion that self-defence may be invoked to use force against a 'continuing imminent threat' against senior operational leaders who are clearly determined to strike against their nation, so long as there is a 'near-certainty that no civilians will be killed or injured'.[6] For the United States, these legal and policy rules were originally embedded in a classified Presidential Policy Guidance, but shortly before the Obama Administration left office in December 2016 it embodied these principles into a comprehensive 'legal and policy frameworks' document, which sought to set forth a detailed explanation of how the various US practices developed during that Administration are consistent with the laws of war.[7]

Shortly thereafter, UK Attorney General Wright affirmed that the United Kingdom remained committed to respond first to threats posed by non-state actors with the tools of criminal justice. Like President Obama, Attorney General Wright affirmed that a government may use self-defence only when it is proportionate and necessary, with 'necessity' connoting first, that law enforcement measures must be plainly inadequate to address the threat and second, that the threat must be imminent. But in assessing 'imminence', the UK government made it clear that it would consider the following questions, originally laid out by Sir Daniel Bethlehem, former Legal Adviser to the Foreign and Commonwealth Office in 2012: 'How certain is it that an attack will come? How soon do we believe that attack could be? What scale of attack is it likely to be? Could this be our *last clear opportunity* to take action? And crucially—is there anything else we could credibly do to prevent that attack?'[8] Similar standards were echoed by my successor as State Department's

the-press-office/2013/05/23/remarks-president-national-defense-university> accessed 11 August 2019 (hereafter Obama, 'Remarks by the President at the National Defense University').

[5] Jeremy Wright, 'Attorney General's Speech at the International Institute for Strategic Studies: The Modern Law of Self-Defence' (Attorney General's Office, 11 January 2017) <https://www.justsecurity.org/36171/read-speech-uk-attorney-general-force-imminence-international-law/> accessed 25 November 2019 (hereafter Wright, 'The Modern Law of Self-Defence').

[6] Obama, 'Remarks by the President at the National Defense University' (n 4).

[7] 'Report on the Legal and Policy Frameworks Guiding the United States' Use of Military Force and Related National Security Operations' (The White House, December 2016) <https://obamawhitehouse.archives.gov/sites/whitehouse.gov/files/documents/Legal_Policy_Report.pdf > accessed 11 August 2019 (hereafter The White House, 'Frameworks Report'). See also President Barack Obama, 'Remarks by the President on the Administration's Approach to Counterterrorism' (The White House, Office the Press Secretary, 6 December 2016) <https://obamawhitehouse.archives.gov/the-press-office/2016/12/06/remarks-president-administrations-approach-counterterrorism> accessed 11 August 2019.

[8] Wright, 'The Modern Law of Self-Defence' (n 5) (emphasis added). See generally Daniel Bethlehem (2012) 'Self-Defense Against an Imminent or Actual Armed Attack by Nonstate Actors' 106 American Journal of International Law 770–72, 774, 776.

Legal Adviser, Brian Egan, in his 1 April 2016, speech to the American Society of International Law.[9]

Like the US President, the UK Attorney General argued that a state may invoke the concept of 'elongated imminence' to act in self-defence when it has a 'last clear chance' against a transnational terrorist network. While preemptive self-defence in response to threats that have not yet materialized is decidedly not permitted, states 'need to be able to take necessary and proportionate action where there is *clear evidence* that armed attacks are being planned and directed against them, and where it is the only feasible means to effectively disrupt those attacks'.[10] Under such a 'last clear chance' test, a state need not wait to be attacked in the same way as it was in a prior attack. After all, it is unlikely that Al Qaeda will attack Western targets again using civilian aircraft, shoe bombs, underwear bombs, cartridge bombs, or any other instrumentalities that it has used before. Instead, if a non-state actor has a proven track record of having repeatedly attacked a state over time, it can be argued to pose a *bona fide* imminent threat to that state, even if the precise details about the next attack are unclear. But the use of force in "self-defence" would be illegal against a group that had never before attacked the affected state or demonstrated its capacity to attack, absent clear evidence about a specific, planned, and imminent attack. And to be acceptable, the state's use of force in such situations would be limited to using only those means that could most feasibly be predicted to effectively disrupt those attacks. In the policy world, the debate over the temporal scope (ie the precise degree of "elongation") that may attach to the *jus ad bellum* definition of imminence is a source of intense discussion, but the authors of Chapter 7 barely address the extent to which the issue is being actively contested.[11]

A similar critique could be lodged against McDermott's cyber conflict chapter (Chapter 8), a topic about which I also opined as a US government official in a 2012 speech stating the position of the United States and its allies regarding currently agreed-upon international rules of cyber conflict.[12] That speech made clear the view of international-law-respecting nations that international law applies in cyberspace, that cyberspace is neither a law-free zone nor a black hole, and that forms of cyber activity can, under certain circumstances, represent a use of force to which the laws of *jus ad bellum* and *jus in bello* apply, with states being responsible for their own actions as well as for the acts of proxy actors.

[9] Brian Egan (2016) 'International Law, Legal Diplomacy, and the Counter-ISIL Campaign: Some Observations' 92 International Law Studies 235. See also Marty Lederman, 'The Egan Speech and the Bush Doctrine: Imminence, Necessity, and "First Use" in the Jus Ad Bellum' (Just Security, 11 April 2016) <https://www.justsecurity.org/30522/egan-speech-bush-doctrine-imminence-necessity-first-use-jus-ad-bellum> accessed 11 August 2019.

[10] Wright, 'The Modern Law of Self-Defence' (n 5) (emphasis added).

[11] The issue is alluded to in Heyns *et al*, Chapter 7 of this book, text accompanying notes 39–44.

[12] See generally Harold Hongju Koh (2012) 'International Law in Cyberspace' 54 Harvard International Law Journal Online 1, 2–7.

McDermott adds to this international humanitarian law analysis a thorough exploration of the contemporary human rights debates regarding cyber operations, particularly the debates regarding jurisdiction versus attribution and about extraterritorial jurisdiction based on effective, as opposed to overall, control.[13] But as with Chapter 7, McDermott's analysis turns more on European human rights jurisprudence than on contemporary state practice. Her typology of cyber intrusions does not clearly distinguish within the spectrum of recognized activity that runs from (i) *cyber monitoring*, defence, espionage, and hacking, which can be done by private parties; to (ii) *computer network exploitation*, which is a form of intelligence; to (iii) pernicious forms of *consumer network attack*, which can have broader, physical consequences, such as using a computer to open a dam or to shut down a hospital. Given that the latter physical effects are no different from those that would result from simply bombing the dam or hospital, the destructive cyber acts that cause them should plainly be governed by the laws of war. Nor, surprisingly, does McDermott explore the extended exercise in cyber-rule-making called the Tallinn Manual (currently in version 2.0), which has sought to elaborate these emerging rules in considerable detail.[14] Nor does she mention regular official standard-setting exercises through diplomatic negotiation before such global fora as the Group of Governmental Experts (GGE)[15] which have been working to keep translating international human rights and humanitarian law in order to constrain rapidly evolving technological capacities.

Perhaps the most visible, and consequential, recent global cyber operation was Russia's hacking of the 2016 US presidential election with an eye toward undermining public faith in the US democratic process, denigrating Hillary Clinton, and helping to elect Donald Trump as President.[16] While multiple ongoing US domestic investigations will doubtless reveal more about possible Russian collusion with US persons around election manipulation, based on what is already known, there seems to be little doubt that the Russian hack violated international

[13] Compare Harold Hongju Koh, Legal Adviser, 'Memorandum Opinion on the Geographic Scope of the Convention Against Torture and Its Application in Situations of Armed Conflict' (United States Department of State, 21 January 2013) 5–6 with Marko Milanovic, 'Harold Koh's Legal Opinions on the US Position on the Extraterritorial Application of Human Rights Treaties' (EJIL: Talk!, 7 March 2014) <https://www.ejiltalk.org/harold-kohs-legal-opinions-on-the-us-position-on-the-extraterritorial-application-of-human-rights-treaties/>.

[14] International Group of Experts, *Tallinn Manual 2.0 on the International Law Applicable to Cyber Operations* (2nd edn, CUP 2017) (hereafter International Group of Experts, *Tallinn Manual 2.0*). See also Michael Schmitt (2012) 'International Law in Cyberspace: The Koh Speech and Tallinn Manual Juxtaposed' 54 Harv Int'l LJ Online 13 (providing a concordance between positions stated in my official speech and the unofficial Tallinn Manual).

[15] See Elaine Korzak, 'The 2015 GGE Report: What Next for Norms in Cyberspace?' (Lawfare, 23 September 2015) <https://www.lawfareblog.com/2015-gge-report-what-next-norms-cyberspace> accessed 11 August 2019.

[16] 'Background to "Assessing Russian Activities and Intentions in Recent US Elections": The Analytic Process and Cyber Incident Attribution' (Office of the Director of National Intelligence, 6 January 2017) <https://www.dni.gov/files/documents/ICA_2017_01.pdf> accessed 11 August 2019.

human rights law. Even if the Russians did not actually manipulate polling results, illegal coercive interference in another country's electoral politics—including the spreading of false news—constitutes a blatant intervention in violation of international law. As the Tallinn Manual authors noted: '[i]llegal coercive interference could include manipulation of elections or of public opinion on the eve of elections, as when online news services are altered in favor of a particular party, false news is spread, or the online services of one party are shut off'.[17] An external attempt to distort the information that voters possess when they go to the polls also plainly violates the human rights of the electors under the International Covenant on Civil and Political Rights.[18] Without mentioning Russia by name, my successor as State Department Legal Adviser publicly cautioned that 'a cyber operation by a State that interferes with another country's ability to hold an election or that manipulates another country's election results would be a clear violation of the rule of non-intervention'.[19] While we do not yet know the full story of this sorry episode, plainly, this should be a non-partisan issue, because it could well recur soon, in the United States or abroad.[20] So it may well be that the cyber operations that most impinge on international human rights in the future will be those that trample upon the right to free and fair elections.

These two initial chapters regarding drones and cyber conflict steer us to the broader conceptual questions that underlie this topic. In Chapter 6, Liora Lazarus argues that growing insecurity has led to the rise of a claimed right of security and a trend toward 'securitizing human rights' that may be inconsistent with the rule of law. Lazarus focuses on the negative concept of tolerable insecurity. Explaining why human rights are prompts for state action, she introduces and explores the idea of a 'right to security' as an explanation for the growing fusion of rights and security.

In Chapter 5, Fiona de Londras goes one step further, suggesting that the very notion of 'sustainable security' may be antithetical to basic human rights. The production of security as a public good, she suggests, may end up infringing on the rights to protest, detention, and due process. More generally, a securitized

[17] International Group of Experts, *Tallinn Manual 2.0* (n 14) 45.

[18] International Covenant on Civil and Political Rights, art 25 ('Every citizen shall have the right and the opportunity, without . . . unreasonable restrictions: (b) To vote and to be elected at genuine periodic elections which shall be by universal and equal suffrage and shall be held by secret ballot, guaranteeing the free expression of the will of the electors.').

[19] See Brian Egan, 'Remarks on International Law and Stability in Cyberspace' (US Department of State, 10 November 2016) <https://2009-2017.state.gov/s/l/releases/remarks/264303.htm> accessed 11 August 2019.

[20] French President Emmanuel Macron claimed that he was hacked during the French presidential campaign. Aurelien Breeden, Sewell Chan, and Nicole Perlwroth, 'Macron Campaign Says It Was Target of "Massive" Hacking Attack' *New York Times* (5 May 2017). According to Republican Senator and former presidential candidate Marco Rubio, the Russians tried to hack him earlier this year. Emmarie Huetteman, 'Marco Rubio Says His Campaign Was a Target of Russian Cyberattacks' *New York Times* (30 March 2017).

concept of the rule of law may be inconsistent with the development and furtherance of a truly just, peaceful, and inclusive society. She rightly calls for appropriate governance strategies. de Londras examines one such strategy in particular, the commitment of United Nations Member States to Sustainable Development Goal 16 (SDG16): a principle of 'sustainable security' through promotion of just, peaceful, and inclusive societies with effective, accountable, and inclusive institutions at all levels.[21] Central to the thinking that underlies SDG16 is the notion that human rights will be dramatically eroded unless stable frameworks of law and institutions are developed to promote security through counterterrorism.

While all these are worthy efforts, let me suggest that the valid and serious concerns expressed within these chapters may best be reconciled by expressing the tension between the competing imperatives of security and rights as 'humanizing security'. Many states have public documents defining their 'national security strategy' as including 'protection of infrastructure', 'protection of the cyber-grid', 'homeland security', and the like. But all too often, these catalogues of interests notably exclude the minimization of harm to human civilians who may be adversely affected by the state's responsive actions. These documents also rarely prioritize the avoidance of discrimination against marginal groups who may be stigmatized by the state's counterterrorism measures. By 'humanizing security', I mean refining the notion that a state has exogenously originating national security interests so as to capture the core concerns of innocent civilians, both those who are affected by counterterrorism measures at home and abroad as well as those domestic constituencies whom security claims are supposed to protect.

While this is not the place to elaborate on this notion at length, at a minimum, the notion of humanizing security should have important implications for national security decision-making, with respect to both means and ends. The concept suggests that security *decisions* should made by decision makers sensitive to concerns of non-combatants; that they should adopt *means* that carefully discriminate between civilians and combatants; and that they should be driven by the *end* of preserving not just freedom from fear but also the fundamental freedom of civilians to achieve personal fulfilment in society through the full exercise of their civil, political, economic, social, and cultural rights.

In concrete terms, a commitment to 'humanizing security' would require first ensuring that humans, not robots, make the key decisions that direct and determine lethal action in counterterrorism activities. By implication, weapons

[21] UN Sustainable Development Goal 16 directs collective action to: 'Promote peaceful and inclusive societies for sustainable development, provide access to justice for all and build effective, accountable and inclusive institutions at all levels'. See United Nations, Sustainable Development Goal 16 <https://sustainabledevelopment.un.org/sdg16> accessed 11 August 2019.

systems that take human beings 'out of the loop' and allow autonomous robots to make lethal targeting decisions must be *per se* unlawful. Second, the concept of humanized security requires that the human beings affected by these actions have channels through which to participate in and oversee the governmental decisions that adversely affect them by enforcing both transparent and fair procedures and substantively fair rules. In some societies, these channels may be provided in the form of judicial review; in others as administrative process. But the total absence of such channels of participation would violate procedural and substantive due process. Third, humanized security requires that international law concern itself as much with minimizing human rights violations that may ensue from particular military actions as with minimizing invasions of state sovereignty and other perceived state interests. So, for example, when Donald Trump, a governmental leader ostensibly committed to state sovereignty, threatens before the UN General Assembly to 'totally destroy' North Korea—a country with whom the United States is not at war and that is populated by more than 25 million people—we should ask not just whether such threats violate North Korea's sovereignty, but also whether they needlessly threaten the security and human rights of millions of innocent civilians.[22]

I could go on, but my point should be clear. When we ask, 'what kind of security do we have a right to enjoy?', the answer should be 'humanized security', not just freedom from internal and external attack. Humanized security resembles sustainable security in that the only kind of security policy that can be sustained over the long term is one that is made by and for human beings. This means strengthening institutions of national security to ensure that they fully take human considerations into account.

Today, we see humanized security in much of everyday state practice, but we need to see more of it. We see it in the internalization of the Geneva Conventions into military training. We see it in the incorporation of international humanitarian and human rights law into international criminal law. We see it when we acknowledge that human rights law has a vital role to play in regulating armed conflict, both *jus ad bellum* and *jus in bello*.

Simply put, humanized security is necessary to a just society. A societal fixation on security threatens rights. Conflict kills human rights. As the last living Nuremberg prosecutor, Ben Ferencz, memorably put it: 'War makes murderers out of otherwise decent people. All wars, and all decent people'.[23] From here on in, if conflict is necessary, as it sometimes is, to protect security, we will need a robust,

[22] 'At UN, Trump Singles Out "Rogue" Nations North Korea and Iran' *New York Times* (19 September 2017).

[23] Lesley Stahl, 'What the Last Nuremberg Prosecutor Alive Wants the World to Know' (*60 Minutes*, 8 May 2017) <http://www.cbsnews.com/news/what-the-last-nuremberg-prosecutor-alive-wants-the-world-to-know/> accessed 11 August 2019.

humanized concept of security to ensure that in times of threat and conflict, security exigencies do not trample human rights.

Acknowledgement

I am grateful to Dylan Kolhoff and Catherine McCarthy of Yale Law School for their fine research assistance, and to Dapo Akande and Sarah Cleveland for their abiding friendship and colleagueship.

5

'Sustainable Security'

A Proposal

Fiona de Londras

I. Introduction

Our planet is in crisis. Climate change, armed conflict, terrorism, poverty, hunger, ill-health, democratic decay; the causes of this crisis are complex and multiple, while sustainability in all aspects of development is key to our collective attempts to address them. The interconnectedness of food, climate, security, equality, healthcare, and so on in the sustainability agenda is clearly reflected in the broad and ambitious programme for action outlined in the United Nations' Sustainable Development Goals (SDGs). Within those, I want to concentrate particularly on Sustainable Development Goal 16 (SDG16). This commits the international community to promoting 'just, peaceful and inclusive societies' including by promoting the rule of law at national and international levels and ensuring access to justice for all, by developing effective, accountable, and transparent institutions at all levels, and by '[s]trengthen[ing] relevant national institutions, including through international cooperation, for building capacity at all levels, in particular in developing countries, to prevent violence and combat terrorism and crime'.[1] An ambitious goal, SDG16 is, then, concerned with security and how we achieve it.[2] It is this element of SDG16 with which I am concerned here.

My focus in this chapter is on the vision of security that might be achieved through successful pursuit of SDG16. What is it that we are trying to achieve in security terms through these stronger institutions? Does this goal enable us to imagine and pursue something I term here 'sustainable security' and, if so, what might the implications of so doing be for rights? And how might we inculcate that into the indicators by which states' realization of the SDGs will be measured?

What motivates this enquiry is my reading of SDG16 in the context of two long-standing debates in the literature, and the opportunity afforded by the lack of clarity within Goal 16 itself. The two debates that must inevitably frame any attempt to

[1] Goal 16 Targets.

[2] This is not to say that SDG16 is *only* concerned with security, but that is the focus of my enquiry and analysis here.

Fiona de Londras, *'Sustainable Security'* In: Human Rights and 21st Century Challenges. Edited by: Dapo Akande, Jaakko Kuosmanen, Helen McDermott, and Dominic Roser, Published by Oxford University Press 2020.
DOI: 10.1093/oso/9780198824770.003.0006

conceptualize 'sustainable security' are, first, the debate as to what security is, and, second, the debate as to what the optimal relationship between rights and security is. These debates are not new, of course, but neither are they resolved. As will become clear throughout this chapter, they are both contested and contestable, and in principle at least SDG16 offers the opportunity to contest still further orthodoxies around them and, perhaps, radically to reimagine and instantiate an approach to both in the form of 'sustainable security'.

At the outset, it must be said that it is not at all clear that SDG16 is designed in a manner that envisages or invites such radicalism. In truth, while some have said that SDG16 offers immense transformative potential,[3] it might as easily be read as a somewhat 'catch-all' provision, the content and aims of which are somewhat less tangible than is the case in relation to other goals such as, for example, Goal 7 which aspires to 'ensure access to affordable, reliable, sustainable and modern energy for all'. What is clear when one places Goal 16 in the context of the two debates mentioned above, however, is that if it is to have and to realize a transformative potential in the context of security, it requires a shift in what have become the dominant international discourses of security and its implications for the rule of law. In Chapter 6 of this collection, Liora Lazarus convincingly shows that security is increasingly becoming seen as something to which 'we' have a right and, as a result, that the state is obliged to pursue (as rights holders have a claim to state action in pursuit of that right), thus legitimizing oppressive and repressive security measures and 'securitizing' or 'hardening' the rule of law so that it is becoming a licence for coercion rather than a limit on state power.[4] Unless we take advantage of the opportunity presented by SDG16 and intervene to rethink security, an approach of that kind might also underpin how security is understood and pursued in the context of the overall attempt to achieve the SDGs. Were this to happen, it would further embed this rights-restricting and limited approach to understanding security to potentially repressive ends. First, however, it is apposite to outline in brief the content, targets, and indicators for SDG16.

II. Sustainable Development Goal 16

As with the other SDGs, Goal 16 is expressed in fairly simple terms on the face of it. The goal is to 'promote just, peaceful and inclusive societies for sustainable development, provide access to justice for all and build effective, accountable and

[3] See eg Cat Tully, 'The Critical Role of Effective, Accountable and Inclusive Institutions in Implementing the Sustainable Development Goals' (*FDSD Provocation*, October 2015) <http://www.fdsd.org/site/wp-content/uploads/2015/10/The-critical-role-of-effective-accountable-and-inclusive-institutions.pdf> accessed 11 August 2019 (hereafter Tully, 'The Critical Role of Effective, Accountable and Inclusive Institutions')

[4] See Lazarus, Chapter 6, this book.

inclusive institutions at all levels'. The goal itself quite clearly has a broad scope; although they create conditions of security that are essential to societal function, just, peaceful, and inclusive societies are about more that security. In its development, it has to be acknowledged, SDG16 was not primarily seen as a goal relating to security *per se*. Rather, it was generally considered that the Millennium Development Goals had erroneously neglected matters of good governance, inclusion, participation, and security and SDG16 is clearly part of the response to this omission. This is reflected in the targets for Goal 16, only some of which are clearly directed towards security *per se*. These are:

16.1 Significantly reduce all forms of violence and related death rates everywhere
16.2 End abuse, exploitation, trafficking and all forms of violence against and torture of children
16.3 Promote the rule of law at the national and international levels and ensure equal access to justice for all
16.4 By 2030, significantly reduce illicit financial and arms flows, strengthen the recovery and return of stolen assets and combat all forms of organized crime
16.5 Substantially reduce corruption and bribery in all their forms
16.6 Develop effective, accountable and transparent institutions at all levels
16.7 Ensure responsive, inclusive, participatory and representative decision-making at all levels
16.8 Broaden and strengthen the participation of developing countries in the institutions of global governance
16.9 By 2030, provide legal identity for all, including birth registration
16.10 Ensure public access to information and protect fundamental freedoms, in accordance with national legislation and international agreements
16a Strengthen relevant national institutions, including through international cooperation, for building capacity at all levels, in particular in developing countries, to prevent violence and combat terrorism and crime
16b Promote and enforce non-discriminatory laws and policies for sustainable development

For some, it is the concentration in SDG16 on governance and inclusion that is really the key to realizing the transformative potential of the SDGs *per se*. In this vein, for example, Cat Tulle writes:

> this Goal is truly transformative, not least because of the failures of top-down, command-and-control approaches to complex global challenges including cybercrime, climate change and unsustainable consumption patterns. Ours is a world of complexity, interdependence and uncertainty that evades centralised

> responses, scorns predictions, and needs solutions fundamentally different to the tried and tested ways that do not work.[5]

While there is plenty of literature, which we do not need to canvass here, that substantiates the claim that multi-level governance, transparency, accountability, and participation are key to good governance in the contemporary world,[6] committing to developing institutions that are, at once, effective, accountable, transparent, representative, and *strong* in the same goal raises some questions and creates some opportunities from the perspective of security.

On the one hand, the commitment to stronger institutions sits apart from the commitment to effective, accountable, transparent, and representative institutions; indeed, strength is mentioned here *only* in relation to security ('Strengthen relevant national institutions, including through international cooperation, for building capacity at all levels, in particular in developing countries, to prevent violence and combat terrorism and crime'). This may be read as suggesting that national institutions to prevent violence and combat terrorism and crime should be *strong* but need not necessarily be *effective, accountable, transparent*, and *representative*. Such a reading would, of course, be deeply problematic, not only because 'strength' of institutions divided from these characteristics of good governance may be taken to suggest that an institution that is strong is robust, well resourced, responsive, but not necessarily well governed or, indeed, part of a good governance framework. Such a reading would do relatively little to assuage the anxieties of anyone familiar with the repressive actions of institutions that are 'strong' and ostensibly have the maintenance and achievement of security as their goal.

Another, rather more palatable and harmonious reading of the targets suggests that national institutions to prevent violence and combat terrorism and crime are strong *when they are* effective, accountable, transparent, and representative. In other words, that the general requirements of good governance outlined in the targets are applied also to these institutions so that they are expected to adhere to principles of good governance but are particularly singled out in SDG16 because of prevailing concerns with high levels of interpersonal violence, armed conflict, and terrorism, and reflecting a concern to ensure that 'developing countries' engage with processes of international 'capacity building' to combat these phenomena more effectively. This reading would suggest that we can infer these institutions should also adhere to the rule of law and ensure access to justice for all, and should be responsive, inclusive, participatory, and representative. In other words, it is possible to read the singling out of national institutions to prevent violence and combat terrorism and crime as nothing more than a matter of emphasis, and not as

[5] Tully, 'The Critical Role of Effective, Accountable and Inclusive Institutions' (n 1).

[6] For a taster see eg Ian Bache and Mathew Flinders, *Multi-Level Governance: Essential Readings* (Edward Elgar 2015).

making these institutions exceptional when compared to other national and international institutions addressed by SDG16.

Whether the concept of a 'strong' institution from a security perspective will, however, be defined by reference to the other governance related goals in the targets for SDG16, remains to be seen. Interestingly, in the development of indicators for Goal 16, this target often attracted little if any attention. For example, the Sustainable Development Solutions Network—a part of the United Nations specifically oriented towards mobilizing expertise to aid in achievement of the SDGs—included *no* proposed indicators whatsoever for Target 16a.[7] In the Virtual Network Sourcebook on Measuring Peace, Justice and Effective Institutions report, 'Goal 16: The Indicators we Want', produced with the support of the United Nations Development Programme (UNDP) and the Federal Republic of Germany, the only proposed indicator for Target 16a was '[p]ercentage of requests for international cooperation (law enforcement cooperation, mutual legal assistance and extraditions) made through existing conventions that were met during the reporting year',[8] thus suggesting a purely operational approach to SDG16. However, the indicators that were actually agreed as starting points for Goal 16 suggest a broader conception of its scope and purpose. These indicators were developed by the Inter-Agency and Expert Group on Sustainable Development Goal Indicators[9] and then agreed as a practical starting point, at the forty-seventh session of the Statistical Commission in the spring of 2016.[10] There are actually twenty-three proposed indicators for Goal 16, but in respect of Goal 16a there is only one: 'Existence of independent national human rights institutions in compliance with the Paris Principles'.[11] On the face of it, the substantive connection between this and Goal 16a itself is not immediately clear; certainly, national human rights institutions (and human rights oversight *per se*) are important to understanding and responding to conditions of insecurity and rights violation, but they are not the only institutions of note in this context. Indeed, when one thinks of institutions to prevent violence and combat terrorism and crime, national human rights institutions are hardly what springs to mind: police, security, and intelligence institutions, oversight bodies, courts, prisons, risk analysis institutions, and so on seem

[7] See 'Indicators and a Monitoring Framework Launching a data revolution for the Sustainable Development Goals' (*SDSN*) <http://www.oneworld.net/sites/default/files/resources/2016-06/150612-FINAL-SDSN-Indicator-Report1.pdf 11 October 2019> accessed 25 November 2019.

[8] Federal Ministry for Economic Cooperation and Development and UNDP, 'Goal 16: The Indicators We Want' 10 <http://www.undp.org/content/dam/undp/library/Democratic%20Governance/Virtual%20Network%20on%20Goal%2016%20indicators%20-%20Indicators%20we%20want%20Report.pdf> accessed 11 August 2019.

[9] UNESC, 'Report of the Inter-Agency and Expert Group on Sustainable Development Goal Indicators' (19 February 2016) E/CN.3/2016/2/Rev.1 (hereafter UNESC, 'Report of the Inter-Agency and Expert Group').

[10] UNESC 'Statistical Commission, Report on the Forty-Seventh Session' (8–11 March 2016) E/2016/24, chap I, sect B, decision 47/101.

[11] UNESC, 'Report of the Inter-Agency and Expert Group' (n 10) 59.

clearly to be included within those that should be 'strong' according to Goal 16 if we are to tackle common instantiations of violence and insecurity. Of course, other targets within Goal 16 are also relevant to reducing insecurity, but the indicators for other governance-related goals do not provide much succour to anyone who might have thought that Goal 16a would mark a sea change in the development approach to security and good governance. We are to indicate whether institutions are effective, accountable, and transparent (Goal 16.6) by reference to primary government expenditure as a proportion of original approved budget by sector, and by the proportion of the population that is satisfied with their last experience of public services. Whether decision-making is responsive, inclusive, participatory, and representative will be assessed by representativeness (in re sex, age, persons with disabilities, and population groups) in public institutions, and the proportion of the population that believes decision-making is inclusive and responsive.[12] Certainly, indicators for Goal 16.1 include the number of conflict-related deaths per 100,000 population by sex, age, and cause, the proportion of the population that experience physical, psychological, or sexual violence in a twelve-month period, and the proportion of people who feel safe walking around the area in which they live.[13] However, nothing in the indicators suggest how, if at all, it is proposed that institutional governance would be related to these goals of reducing insecurity.

Do these indicators, then, mean that SDG16, and particularly SDG16a, need not trouble those concerned with security, insecurity, and rights? I suggest not. In fact, what seems to be a mismatch between the goal, targets, and indicators when it comes to 'strong institutions' relating to crime, violence, and terrorism should, rather, be a matter of some concern. Indicators are effectively mechanisms of measurement; they are, in some ways, the bureaucratic method by which we assess whether or not a certain goal, as interpreted by those developing and applying the indictors, has been fulfilled.[14] But these means of measurement are not determinative of what a state can or will do or attempt to legitimate by reference to the overall policy objective, in this case the goal. So, while a state may claim that it need only devote its energies to that which is specified in the indicators in order to fulfil its commitment to the SDGs, states could just as plausibly argue that the indicators are part *but not all* of what the SDGs provide a *prima facie* justification (if not an obligation) for them to do. When it comes to terrorism, in particular, but also to other forms of pernicious violence such as organized crime, there is a well-worn pattern of states taking an expansive approach to their duty to try to achieve or maintain security (local, national, or international). Thus, there is a real danger

[12] Ibid, 58.
[13] Ibid, 57.
[14] For a critical engagement with indicators as a mode of governance see eg Kevin Davis, Angelina Fisher, Benedict Kingsbury, and Sally Engle Merry, *Governance by Indicators: Global Power through Quantification and Rankings* (OUP 2012); Simon Bell and Stephen Morse, *Sustainability Indicators: Measuring the Immeasurable?* (2nd edn, Earth Scan 2008).

that SDG16a might at the one time legitimate state action in putative pursuit of security, but not make that same state accountable for that action through the indicators. There seems, then, to be a clear case for the revision of the indicators for SDG16a in order to harness fully the potential that this goal offers for the enhancement of security *and* the design of appropriate governance structures relating to security. This is best achieved by considering what it is that we might mean when we think about security from a sustainability perspective ('sustainable security'), how best to protect rights and the rule of law while pursuing it, and then how to assess whether institutional design is such as to serve these complementary goals. Doing this, first, requires us to think closely about what we mean when we talk about security, and how that interacts with rights.

III. Security

The term 'security' is so commonly used that we may no longer wonder what it is that it really means. What does it mean to be 'secure' and, indeed, to be 'insecure'? What is it that we pursue when we pursue security? What is the good that we aim to achieve through measures such as SDG16?

There is certainly a connection of some kind between 'security' and what we might call 'the Peace'.[15] This connection is hardly new and has been reflected in all manner of ways; recall, for example, the performance of Descartes' ballet *The Birth of Peace* in Stockholm to mark the signing of the Treaties of Westphalia,[16] or the licence of the UN Security Council to intervene in situations where international *peace and security* are disrupted.[17] This connection seems relatively straightforward in many ways; 'the Peace' we think (or, perhaps, intuit) is an easily recognizable state of affairs. It is the absence of major systemic insecurities such as (formally declared) war, the use of force, major campaigns of terrorist attacks, and so on. It is also the aversion of such states of affairs, so that even when we stand on the brink of major insecurities of this kind—where, for example, there is a border-based standoff between forces (eg on the border of North Korea), or increased levels of military exercises near a border (eg Russian 'war games' near the Ukrainian border), or a situation of nuclear standoff (eg between India and Pakistan)—we

[15] Recall, eg, Kant's *Perpetual Peace: A Philosophical Sketch* (1795) and its (lesser known) forerunner, Charles-Irénée Castel de Saint-Pierre, *Project for Perpetual Peace* (1729) (originally published anonymously). See also Adrian Bogdan (2013) 'The Right to Peace in the Context of Contemporary International Reality' 40 Revista de Stiinte Politice 46.

[16] See the account of the relationship between the Ballet and the Peace of Westphalia in Lawrence Nolan, *The Cambridge Descartes Lexicon* (CUP 2016). Note, however, that at least some doubt has been cast on whether Descartes' did write the ballet: Richard Watson, *Descartes's Ballet: His Doctrine of the Will and His Political Philosophy* (St Augustine's Press 2004).

[17] United Nations, Charter of the United Nations, 24 October 1945, 1 UNTS XVI, Chapter VII.

consider ourselves to be 'at peace' and secure as long as the situation does not 'boil over' into actual use of force.

Thus, we consider ourselves to be 'at peace' and, hence, 'secure' in these situations, because we are relatively more secure than we would be had the situation not been contained. In this sense, then, security might be understood as a relational concept—as a condition that is relatively more secure than the alternative possibility which we have managed to avert, even if it is still relatively less secure than the other alternative which we have failed to attain (ie the lack of such tensions in the first place). Understood thus, the concept of security may appear at once straightforward and relatively unproblematic. But of course nothing is as simple as it seems, for the connections between internal (or domestic) security and international security are important considerations so that even if we successfully 'manage' international tensions, domestic developments might overtake those attempts and result in force being used in any case.[18] So too are the possibilities that international insecurity will lead to domestic disruption and upheaval, often with a forceful and/or violent response by the state, that is experienced (at least by some) as insecurity.[19]

Thus, even when we think about security in fairly straightforward and, on the face of it, unproblematic terms such as 'the Peace', complex dynamics of national, social, international, and geopolitical risk, politics, resistance, and insecurity demand our attention.

Up to now I have acted as if security is largely about states *per se*, but of course it is also about people; about the everyday micro and macro aggressions experienced by people all over the world. If we were to rescale the concept of 'the Peace' to the individual level, we might say that security can be understood as being about protection from (or the absence of) and resistance to (or resilience in the face of) harm. Taken in this way, we can immediately see that insecurity is widespread; indeed, it is arguably the common experience of humankind, albeit with important variations of experience across context (eg conditions of general political stability where one is located) and characteristics (eg gender, race, socio-economic position, sexual orientation). This kind of quotidian insecurity is both measurable and measured, so that we know (or at least have some sense of) its awesome scale. We know, for example, that inter-personal violence causes 1.6 million deaths a year,[20] not to mention the millions more injuries, indignities, and other forms of harm that result from this.[21] All of this goes to the realization in public health literature and police that violence is a leading public health problem in the world today.[22] Violence here

[18] Perhaps the most notorious example is the impact of the killing of Archduke Franz Ferdinand on European security and, ultimately, the outbreak of the First World War.

[19] Take, eg, 'pre-emptive' action taken in some states to prevent 'contagion' from the 'Arab Spring'.

[20] WHO, *World Report on Violence and Health* (World Health Organization 2002).

[21] Ibid.

[22] See eg WHA 'Preventing Violence: A Public Health Priority' (1996) Resolution WHA49.25.

is self-directed, interpersonal, and collective, and it is both a cause and a result of deep insecurity. Violence and insecurity are a continuum where mass outbreaks of violence emanate from, exacerbate, and are clearly related to everyday experience of insecurity. This is not to say the two are the same—as Catharine MacKinnon famously wrote, '[w]ithout everyday anti-Semitism a Holocaust is impossible, but anyone who has lived through a pogrom knows the difference'[23]—but they are also not entirely different. Any approach to security that aims to be meaningful must, it seems to me, address both of these forms of insecurity and put in place mechanisms of building up resilience in respect of it.

The relationship between insecurity and violence at the geopolitical and personal levels is also important here. We know, as noted earlier, that violence and insecurity exist on a continuum, with developments at any point (or any scale) having potential knock-on effects elsewhere. In this respect, time is also an important scale: a pressing and immediate security problem, and how we respond to it will have implications for (in)security in the future as well, so that what seems an appropriate response to the immediate problem might actually be ineffective by reference to our broader and more long-term conception of security.[24] This does not mean it would always be inappropriate—sometimes immediate action is necessary and, often, it is suboptimal—but it does mean that our assessment of its success *as a mechanism for increasing security* must take time into account as a relevant analytical scale.[25] Security, then, is about both 'the Peace' and about personal protection from and resilience in the face of violent harm, as well as about recognizing and accounting for the causal and correlative relationships that may exist between (in)securities across time and space.

Thus, what I term 'sustainable security' requires us to think broadly and deeply about what security looks like by reference to what insecurity is, and to develop governance structures through which our security solutions (including legal and operational measures to address particular security problems, as well as policy approaches to addressing insecurity *per se*) will be designed with this vision in mind and, indeed, tested against a complex, multi-scalar understanding of security. In this, my proposed conception of sustainable security under SDG16 has a broader focus than sustainable security models that see insecurity in primarily statist terms. Such an articulation of sustainable security—one that focuses on climate change, competition over resources, marginalization of the majority world, and global militarization[26]—is an important part of attempts to address meta-structures and

[23] Catherine MacKinnon, *Are Women Human? And Other International Dialogues* (Harvard University Press 2007) 183.

[24] On the importance of time in all social policy activities (which are taken here to include enhancing security) see eg Tony Fitzpatrick (2004) 'Social Policy and Time' 13(2–3) Time & Society 197–219.

[25] This applies the argument that long-termism is essential for assessing the effectiveness in strategic accounting decisions from Kym Irving (2009) 'Overcoming Short-Termism: Mental Time Travel, Delayed Gratification and How Not to Discount the Future' 19(4) Australian Accounting Review 278.

[26] Chris Abbott, Paul Rogers and John Siobada, *Global Responses to Global Threats: Sustainable Security for the 21st Century* (Oxford Research Group 2006).

manifestations of insecurity but pays inadequate attention to the daily iterations of quotidian insecurity and to their uneven distribution across place, race, gender, age, and social status. My argument for sustainable security made out here addresses such shortcomings.

IV. Security and Rights

The second major debate that necessarily contextualizes any consideration of the security-related aims of SDG16 is that as to the appropriate relationship between rights and security. We might usefully start by stating that which we can tell to be true about this relationship through experience alone: a lack of security has negative implications for rights, and measures and actions taken ostensibly in pursuit of security can have negative impacts on rights.[27] Put baldly in this way, it is tempting to resign ourselves to a conclusion that 'rights lose' either way. To some extent this may well be correct: insecurity and our responses thereto *do* jeopardize rights enjoyment so that the optimal environment for rights enjoyment is 'the Peace' in both statist and personal terms. This is perhaps nothing more than a conventionally Lockean observation, and a naïve one at that. International peace and security, national peace and security, and personal security and freedom from violence (structural, economic, political, and interpersonal) cannot now be achieved without taking measures directed thereto; insecurity is simply too embedded, too common, too widespread, and too pervasive a part of the contemporary human experience for it to disappear organically, but the means we use to try to counter it also have implications for rights. Thus, we are in a quandary.

Esteem for rights, if nothing else, compels us to act to try to counter insecurity. We do not need to decide whether the putative 'right to peace' exists in order to underpin such actions, or even justify them by reference to a right to security (if such a thing exists as a legally enforceable right).[28] A simple acknowledgement of the implications of insecurity for rights is enough. Major outbreaks of insecurity such as war, insurrection, terrorism, or military brutality within a domestic regime all have pernicious effects on rights. The right to life is clearly endangered,[29] not only for combatants but also for civilians, not to mention people whose category status is not easily discernible.[30] In 2016 alone, for example, it is estimated that at least 560,000 people lost their lives in violent circumstances, of which around

[27] See McDermott, Chapter 8 (this book).

[28] On the right to security *per se* see Liora Lazarus, 'The Right to Security: Securing Rights or Securitising Rights' in Rob Dickinson, Elena Katselli, Colin Murray, and Ole Pedersen (eds), *Examining Critical Perspectives on Human Rights* (CUP 2012).

[29] See eg Heyns, Akande, Hill-Cawthorne, and Chengeta, Chapter 7, this book.

[30] Claire McEvoy and Gergely Hideg, *Global Violent Deaths 2017: Time to Decide* (2017; Small Arms Survey).

99,000 were direct conflict deaths.[31] Terrorist organizations' callous disregard for the principle of distinction (and, indeed, most rules governing the use of force in many cases), as well as the apparently insatiable appetite in some terrorist organizations for extra-judicial killings and execution following what are effectively kangaroo court proceedings also clearly endanger and routinely result in violations of the right to life.[32] Of course, armed conflict has rights implications far beyond the right to life. Conflict brings with it a wide range of civil, political, and socio-economic rights violations; typically gender-based and sexual violence spike, there is torture and other forms of ill-treatment, slavery, and bonded labour are not uncommon, there are cases of arbitrary detention, schools and hospitals are often destroyed and/or rendered unsafe, cultural heritage is destroyed, food shortages are common, and there is widespread persecution. In such circumstances the acts of violence that form the armed conflict *per se* of course constitute direct violations of rights, but indirect violations also flow from, for example, the destabilization of the region and economy with consequences for poverty and economic stability, or the breakdown of social bonds of trust and community that are the necessary conditions for human flourishing, curiosity, entrepreneurialism, creativity, and resistance. Thus, the systemic insecurities that arise from armed conflict (whether involving states or non-state actors or both) radically undermine the conditions required to pursue life to the full, exacerbate quotidian violence and insecurity, and are thus deeply troubling from a rights perspective.

It must be said, however, that 'the Peace' at a statist level is hardly a time of rights and security Utopia either. We have already seen how widespread personal insecurity is, and that any meaningful concept of security requires a workable standard of everyday freedom from and resilience in the face of insecurity. For far too many of us living on this planet that is simply not the case. The everyday violence experienced by so many people has clear implications for rights including, but going well beyond, the right to life. The violence in question often (although not always) emanates from sources other than the state, ie is often 'private' within the conventional (and deeply problematic) public/private dichotomy on which so much law and policy is constructed.[33] Fathers, husbands, uncles, brothers, sons, partners, and lovers are some of the greatest perpetrators of the violence that women experience,

[31] 'Armed Conflict Survey 2014, Conflict Numbers and Fatalities' (IISS, 2014) available at <https://www.iiss.org/-/media//images/publications/armed%20conflict%20survey/2015/conflicts%20vs%20no%20of%20fatalities%20copyright.jpg?la=en> accessed 25 November 2019.

[32] The Penal Code of the so-called Islamic State of Iraq and Syria prescribes the death penalty for a wide range of offences, often without due process or any kind of regularized criminal trial. This is reported widely, eg in Anon (2016) 'Justice in the Time of the ISIS' 55 Invisible Dog <http://www.invisible-dog.com/justice_ISIS_eng.html> accessed 12 August 2019. As the penal code is published on websites run by and connected with so-called Islamic State of Iraq and Syria no direct link to this Code can be included here.

[33] For a comprehensive critique of the public/private division in international law see eg Christine Chinkin (1999) 'A Critique of the Public/Private Dimension' 10(2) European Journal of International Law 387.

for example. The scale of violence against women is beyond dispute: one in three women experience physical or sexual violence, mostly imposed by an intimate partner.[34] This is a truly worldwide phenomenon: 43 per cent of women in the European Union report having experienced some form of intimate partner violence over their lifetimes,[35] while a staggering 92 per cent of women in New Delhi report having experienced some form of sexual violence in public spaces.[36] Going beyond the private spaces we call family and home, interpersonal violence is an everyday experience, either in fact or in its apprehension, for many. Police brutality is a clear example, as are gun and knife crime, and violence emanating from organized crime organizations including gangs. The implications for rights that emanate from these forms of insecurity include, but also in some cases go beyond, those related to armed conflict. All too often the state's positive obligation to protect people from a loss of life[37] (and, indeed, the state's other positive obligations[38]) is inadequately (or not at all) performed, either because of corruption, institutional weakness, or plain indifference.

Insecurity, then, is unequivocally bad for rights. A simple logic would suggest, on the basis of this, that rights enjoyment can be improved by increasing security, but of course the instinctive attractiveness of this proposition must be tempered by the common-sense observation that this depends both on how you *define* security and on how you go about *achieving* that which you have defined thus. A singular focus on 'the Peace' as preventing armed conflict, for example, does little for the woman whose husband beats and rapes her, whose local police force fails to act in response, and who has no economic or other resources to take legal action herself to protect herself from such violence. Neither does it aid the Black teenager who is reluctant to drive his car lest a 'routine' traffic stop results in his being shot dead by a police officer whom he perceives as acting with impunity. What is required in order to address rights violations by increasing security is a comprehensive (albeit complex), multi-part, and ultimately long-term approach to addressing insecurity by creating 'just, peaceful, and inclusive societies'. Even if we get that element of the recipe right (ie we accept the complicated and multi-scalar concept of security that

[34] World Health Organization, Department of Reproductive Health and Research, London School of Hygiene and Tropical Medicine, South African Medical Research Council (2013) *Global and Regional Estimates of Violence against Women: Prevalence and Health Effects of Intimate Partner Violence and Non-Partner Sexual Violence* (WHO) 2.

[35] European Union Agency for Fundamental Rights (2014) *Violence Against Women: An EU-Wide Survey* (FRA) 71.

[36] UN Women (2013) 'Safe Cities Global Initiative' (*UN Women Brief*) <http://www.unwomen.org/~/media/headquarters/attachments/sections/library/publications/2013/12/un%20women-evaw-safecities-brief_us-web%20pdf.ashx> accessed 12 August 2019.

[37] On positive duties to protect life in international human rights law see eg *Neira Alegría v Peru*, Inter-American Court of Human Rights Series C No 13 (11 December 1991); *Suarez de Guerrero v Colombia*, Merits, Communication No 45/1979, UN Doc CCPR/C/15/D/45/1979, IHRL 2570 (UNHRC 1982); *McCann v United Kingdom*, App no *18984/91*, 27 September 1995.

[38] On positive duties to protect rights generally see Sandra Fredman, *Human Rights Transformed: Positive Rights and Positive Duties* (OUP 2008).

we ideally aim to achieve), we must also be attentive to the means used to achieve it. All too often, repressive state powers are introduced in the pursuit of security:[39] powers that do nothing to address many of the causes of violence, can exacerbate the crises of social cohesion that often underpin insecurity, and are counterproductive both by violating rights directly and by creating or sustaining conditions of suspicion and perceived injustice that often underpin insecurity with attendant risks for rights into the future.[40]

It is because they both oversimplify 'security' and fail to take complex direct and indirect rights impacts into account, that many of the seemingly attractive models that are posited as helping governments and policy-makers to calibrate the relationship between rights and security properly are ultimately unconvincing. Whether it is the proposition that Pareto-style modelling can be used to identify a point of rights and liberty optimization,[41] or the myth of balance that is founded on an unsustainable and often unarticulated assertion of hydraulicism between rights and security,[42] or even the pseudo-scientific proportionality analysis often favoured by courts,[43] these models falter on their overly narrow and short-termist conception of security. Rather than truly interrogate whether a measure enhances security, these approaches ask whether the measure in question can be justified as a response to a specific security problem that has been identified by government, and fails to put that problem in its broader (in)security context. Such an approach is understandable, but if our aim is really to enhance *security* understood in the multifaceted and sustainable way proposed above, it cannot succeed. Only a commitment to measuring our actions against our aim, and to rethinking our aim (security) in a sustainable way, seems to be likely to succeed to reduce insecurity at both macro- and personal levels in the longer term.[44] The question then is whether SDG16 offers an opportunity to develop such an approach.

[39] For an analysis of how and why this is the case see eg Fiona de Londras, *Detention in the 'War on Terror': Can Human Rights Fight Back?* (CUP 2011) chapter 1 (hereafter de Londras, *Detention in the 'War on Terror*).

[40] On broader societal implications and their contribution to insecurity see eg Méderic Martins-Mazé and JP Burgess, 'The Societal Impact of EU Counter-Terrorism' in Fiona de Londras and Josephine Doody (eds), *The Impact, Legitimacy and Effectiveness of EU Counter-Terrorism* (Routledge 2015) (hereafter, Méderic Martins-Mazé and JP Burgess, 'The Societal Impact of EU Counter-Terrorism').

[41] See Eric Posner and Adrian Vermeule, *Terror in the Balance: Security, Liberty and the Courts* (OUP 2007). For a compelling critique see Alice Ristroph (2008) 'Professors Strangelove' 11 Green Bag 2D 245.

[42] On which see Andrew Ashworth, 'Security, Terrorism and the Value of Human Rights' in Ben Goold and Liora Lazarus (eds), *Security and Human Rights* (Hart Publishing 2007) and Andrew Ashworth and Mike Redmayne, *The Criminal Process* (4th edn, OUP 2010) 45.

[43] On proportionality in this context see eg Mathias Vermeulen, 'Assessing Counter-Terrorism as a Matter of Human Rights: Perspectives from the European Court of Human Rights' in Fiona de Londras and Josephine Doody (eds), *The Impact, Legitimacy and Effectiveness of EU Counter-Terrorism* (Routledge 2015).

[44] See further Fiona de Londras, 'Evaluation and Effectiveness of Counter-Terrorism' in J Peter Burgess, Genserik Reniers, Koen Ponnet, WOm Hardyns, and Wim Smit (eds), *Socially Responsible Innovation in Security: Critical Reflections* (Routledge 2018).

V. 'Strong' Institutions in a Security Context

Regardless of how security is conceptualized it inevitably rubs up uncomfortably against rights and at times the rule of law. In an international project that remains largely underpinned by liberalism (where liberalism is understood almost in Wilsonian terms as a project that is committed to promoting capitalism and democracy as key mechanisms of advancing 'peace'[45]), security easily becomes a 'key category' or a common good to be pursued and against which actions that might otherwise be considered repressive can be justified. In Neocleous' estimation, security's totemic position within liberalism means that balance becomes an assumption, a rhetorical device, and 'a mechanism for working any argument into a fundamentally liberal mode of thought'[46] so that the pursuit of security in its contemporary mode is an activity that 'straddles law and economy, police power and political economy, and becomes the dominant mode of what Foucault calls "governmental rationality" '.[47] Thus, within our current mode of thinking about security and about how we achieve it, including through promoting 'just, peaceful, and inclusive societies', we have a tendency to design institutions in a manner that treats rights as important but ultimately contingent categories—the extent of their effective operation in any given set of circumstances can be determined, at least in part, by reference to perceived (in)security and actions taken in response to that. In this mode of thinking, security-oriented institutions are ones through which state power is exercised, but not necessarily mechanisms for the refinement and application of state power in an appropriately limited and accountable way.

Secrecy is an excellent illustration of this. Secrecy is ultimately anathema to fundamental commitments to participation, transparency, and accountability that underpin a liberal polity, but is still (at least rhetorically) accommodated within liberal constitutional polities on the basis that it is 'necessary' for security.[48] With

[45] On Wilsonian liberalism *per se* see eg Lloyd Ambriosis, *Wilsonian Statecraft: Theory and Practice of Liberal Internationalism during World War I* (Scholarly Resources Ltd 1991). I acknowledge the problématique of referring to Wilson in these foundational, liberal terms given his segregationist, racist, and non-liberationary political philosophy as President of the United States of America, and the indivisibility of this philosophy from his international relations thought. See Lloyd E. Amrosius (2007), 'Woodrow Wilson and *The Birth of a Nation*: American Democracy and International Relations' 14(4) Diplomacy & Statecraft 687–718. Furthermore, Wilsonian liberalism is robustly criticized in international law primarily, although not exclusively, by Third World Approaches to International Law (TWAIL) scholars, critical feminist scholars, and critical race scholars of international law. For a small selection see eg Elizabeth Iglesias (1996/97) 'International Law, Human Rights, and LatCrit Theory' 28(2) University of Miami Inter-American Law Review 177; Adrien Katherine Wing, *Global Critical Race Feminism: An International Reader* (NYU Press 2000); Hilary Charlesworth and Christine Chinkin, *The Boundaries of International Law: A Feminist Analysis* (Manchester University Press 2000); Frederick Snyder and Surakiart Sathirathai, *Third World Attitudes towards International Law: An Introduction* (Martinus Nijhoff 1987).

[46] Mark Neocleous, *Critique of Security* (Edinburgh University Press 2008) 12.

[47] Ibid, 13.

[48] On the role and accommodation of secrecy within liberal states see Lydia Morgan (2018) '(Re)conceptualising state secrecy' 69(1) Northern Ireland Legal Quarterly 59–84.

secrecy, then, comes the construction and empowerment of massive institutions of state power (eg domestic and international intelligence agencies) which are subject to some, but not all, of the 'usual' requirements of governance, review, and oversight, which can act in a manner that is deeply troubling to the protection and enjoyment of individual and collective rights, which have the capacity to undermine democracy fundamentally (eg by making resistance or opposition effectively impossible and certainly dangerous), but which might be presented as being 'strong' on the (often unsubstantiated) basis that they are effective in keeping us safe. It seems unlikely that this is the kind of institutional strength envisaged and called for by SDG16a, but this does not mean that it could not be. In the absence of careful thinking about 'strength', there is a real danger, indeed, that this might be precisely what states perceive strong institutions to be in this context.

A much more productive, and more effective, way of thinking about and conceptualizing strength here would be to start from the premise that a strong institution in the context of violence, crime, and terrorism (ie in the context of security) would be an institution that is designed to instantiate a form of careful reasoning about rights; a form of reasoning that recognizes the relationship between rights and security *as is*, and the relationship between rights and security *as might be* if we committed to a sustainable approach to security. That institutions would play a role in reorienting politics and politicians towards sustainable security is entirely appropriate; they are, after all, 'the kinds of structures that matter most in the social realm; they make up the stuff of social life'.[49] Sustainable security, then, requires attention to all relevant institutions: to police, to intelligence and security services, to courts, to probation services, but also to other institutions that provide resilience in the face of and can help to reduce insecurities such as families, religious communities, sports clubs, the arts, and a robust set of media (formal/traditional and informal/social).[50]

When it comes to the former—the kinds of institutions that we are accustomed to seeing as part of the state and elements of the state's security apparatus—sustainable security requires us to be attentive to the sets of rules or conventions that we expect them to apply (eg the law) and the structures that impose, devise, and instantiate these rules and conventions (eg police forces and the judiciary). Seen in this light, a concern with 'strong' institutions is a concern with strengthening the rules and conventions, and the structures through which they are formed, applied, and given social meaning. A sustainable security approach, then, makes it clear that something like SDG16a cannot be seen in isolation, but should rather be seen in the broader context of Goal 16's commitment to effective governance based

[49] Geoffrey Hodgson (2006) 'What are Institutions?' XL(1) Journal of Economic Issues 1, 2.

[50] On social institutions as sources of resilience see Martha Albertson Fineman (2008) 'The Vulnerable Subject: Anchoring Equality in the Human Condition' 20(1) Yale Journal of Law & Feminism 1, 12–15.

on the rule of law. Thus, a commitment to sustainable security *necessarily* means that strong institutions *are* institutions that are effective, accountable, transparent, and participatory. They *are* institutions that are committed to adherence to the rule of law. And they *are* institutions that instantiate a way of thinking about security across scales of time, space, and place to ensure (i) that all forms of insecurity are recognized as being of concern to the state and as obstacles to development, and (ii) that all security-oriented actions, policies, measures, and operations are undertaken in a manner that properly accounts for and recognizes their impacts on both rights and security in the short, medium, and long term.

This, of course, is not as easy to do as it is to write. On the one hand, political exigencies can operate to distort reasoning greatly in the context of insecurity, particularly for example in the wake of a traumatic events such a major terrorist attack.[51] However, difficult is not impossible. If we break our conception of 'strength' in institutional terms down further into just three categories of effectiveness, adherence to the rule of law, and long-termism, for example, means of strengthening institutions in this mold begin to appear.

A. Effectiveness

In the context of security, effectiveness is hardly a simple notion,[52] but building on previous work[53] we might say that for a measure, action, or institution with a security orientation to be effective it must *work* to achieve its objectives. These objectives fall into two further categories: meta objectives and specific objectives. Meta objectives will ideally be, at a minimum, (i) increasing security, (ii) maintaining legality, and (iii) adhering to the political (rather than the 'cultural') 'values' of the polity in question. Of course, these meta objectives are informed here by a concept of sustainable security, rather than a purely responsive impulse to address instances of insecurity as they arise. Specific objectives will relate more closely to the particular functions and aims of the institution in question, but would range from, for example, enhancing international intelligence cooperation to ensuring effective training of police forces in response to domestic violence allegations. In an effective institution the meta objectives will necessarily inform how the specific objectives are pursued; in other words, they will become the organizing norms for the institution in question.

[51] See generally de Londras, *Detention in the 'War on Terror* (n 40) chapter 1, pp. 8–35.

[52] For a range of analyses from legal, operational, democratic, and societal perspectives see generally Fiona de Londras and Josephine Doody, *The Impact, Legitimacy and Effectiveness of EU Counter-Terrorism* (Routledge 2015).

[53] Fiona de Londras (2016) 'Accounting for Rights in EU Counter-Terrorism: Towards Effective Review' 22(2) Columbia Journal of European Law 237.

Thus, for example, a national institution established for the purposes of reducing domestic violence will have an overall meta objective of increasing security (for victims of domestic violence, with attendant knock-on effects for reductions of gender-based violence and gendered cultural and other harms) in a manner that maintains legality (so that, for example, an appropriate process would be required in order to remove a suspected perpetrator permanently from the family home, or the suspected perpetrator would have a right to due process) and adheres to the values of the polity in question (such as fiscal transparency and the accountability of the director to, for example, parliament or a relevant government minister). Its specific objectives might include objectives such as enhancing police training, inculcating greater trust in the police on the part of victims, deterring domestic violence by potential perpetrators, reducing cases of reoffending, reducing the number of serious injuries and fatalities resulting from domestic violence, and identifying and tackling root and trigger causes of domestic violence such as misogyny or drug and alcohol abuse. The effectiveness of this institution could then be assessed against these meta- and specific objectives, with changes being made as appropriate where shortfalls or missteps are identified either in institutional design or oversight, or in the exercise or design of the powers in question.

Effectiveness, then, builds in concepts of transparency, accountability, and legality as appropriate to the context in question; it requires a constant process of reflection and reflexivity; and it takes various different forms of insecurity and their interconnectedness seriously. It stands to reason, then, that for security-oriented institutions to be 'strong' as foreseen by SDG16a they should be effective, and that a sustainable security approach makes it clear that effectiveness must be seen as a complex, multifaceted, and measurable value.

B. Adherence to the Rule of Law

Strong institutions oriented towards security simply must adhere to the rule of law for the simple reason that undermining the rule of law (by, for example, acting without lawful authority, empowering the state and disempowering the polity, allowing discretion to trump process and the principle that the state may only exercise such powers as it is given, and undermining rights) is ultimately *bad for security*. This kind of approach to security does little to address either systemic, armed conflict-type insecurity or, indeed, everyday insecurity.

In relation to the former, abandonment of the Rule of Law is likely to build resentment and a sense of disenfranchisement, as well as the weakening of the state in terms of the extent to which its members feel allegiance to it rather than to another non-state actor, all of which contributes simply to the exacerbation of insecurity in the longer term.[54] Of course, acting contrary to the rule of law in armed conflict also results in more immediate insecurities and rights violations; manipulation of well-defined rules of law (such as the principle of distinction) through, for example, determining that medical and religious personnel need not be 'counted' in proportionality analyses[55] jeopardizes the entire framework of the law of armed conflict and thus exacerbates civilian insecurity in future conflicts. In a non-armed-conflict situation, acting contrary to the rule of law (by, for example, failing to tackle police corruption, or introducing powers of such discretion that they can be applied in a way that is experienced as discriminatory by a 'suspect community'[56] but nevertheless be legitimated by the law) does nothing to address chronic crises in social cohesion being experienced across states which in turn contribute to the perpetuation of insecurity in the longer term.[57]

Adherence to the rule of law is, then, logical in many ways. However, this must be read subject to the caveat that the rule of law is increasingly becoming a concept that empowers states rather than one that limits their capacity to exercise power. Should, for example, 'strong institutions' in the context of Goal 16a be understood simply as 'institutions that prevent crime, or terrorist attacks', this could easily legitimate an approach to the design and exercise of state power that is anathema to the traditional, liberal conception of the rule of law and that does not necessarily instantiate a way of thinking about rights that makes them part of, rather than in contest with, security. Thus, in assessing adherence to the rule of law we might want to engage with something more sophisticated than, for example, the World Justice Project Rule of Law Index, which takes quite a formalistic approach to the rule of law.[58] Under this Index, rule of law adherence can be measured by reference to the existence of constraints on government powers, the absence of corruption, open government, fundamental rights protection, the right to life and security of the person, regulatory enforcement, civil justice, and criminal justice.[59] These

[54] On the root causes of terrorism and their connections to 'weak' states see, classically, Martha Crenshaw (1981) 'The Causes of Terrorism' 13(4) Comparative Politics 379.

[55] See s 7.8.2.1 of the United States Department of Defense, *Law of War Manual* (Office of General Council Department of Defense, June 2015) which provides '[t]he incidental killing or wounding of [medical and religious] personnel, due to their presence among or in proximity to combatant elements actually engaged by fire directed at the latter, gives no just cause for complaint. Because medical and religious personnel are deemed to have accepted the risk of death or further injury due to proximity to military operations, they need not be considered as incidental harm in assessing proportionality in conducting attacks' (internal references omitted). As Oona Hathaway has commented, 'taken to its logical conclusion, it threatens to eradicate proportionality as a condition of lawful military targeting altogether': Oona Hathaway, 'The Law of War Manual's Threat to the Principle of Proportionality' (Just Security, 23 June 2016) <https://www.justsecurity.org/31631/lowm-threat-principle-proportionality/> accessed 12 August 2019.

[56] Paddy Hillyard, *Suspect Community: People's Experience of the Prevention of Terrorism Acts in Britain* (Pluto Press 1993).

[57] Méderic Martins-Mazé and JP Burgess, 'The Societal Impact of EU Counter-Terrorism' (n 41).

[58] 'Rule of Law Index 2015' (*World Justice Project* 2015) <http://worldjusticeproject.org/sites/default/files/roli_2015_0.pdf> accessed 12 August 2019.

[59] Ibid, 14.

indicators are, however, largely assessed by reference to positive law (rather than the lived experience of state power), and to statistical analyses. Refigured to take greater account of institutional design and societal acceptance/legitimacy such indicia might, however, be useful ways of analyzing rates of adherence to the rule of law.

C. Long Termism

We have already seen that any sustainable approach to security must take temporal scales into account. Indeed, this is hardly unique to security. As many contributors to this volume have shown,[60] the long term is a key analytical framework in all parts of sustainable development. However, for various reasons, long-termism is difficult to properly commit to in the context of security. The reasons vary across contexts, but when a security risk materializes that, for example, results in military attacks on the integrity of the state there is a clear imperative (if not responsibility) to respond in order to protect the state and its polity, even if the response may further damage relations with the belligerent or with an ally.

Long-termism, however, can be a useful dimension in assessing the form, force, and extent of the response; we might ask not only whether the response is proportionate to the attack to which we are responding, but also whether its potential repercussions and the attendant risk of further, future insecurity are justified by the immediate imperative to respond. This is not an exact science—and neither could anyone plausibly claim that it is. It is also not necessarily something that decision-makers do not already take into account, either through formal institutional design or through a personal approach to political decision-making that values long-termism, but it *is* nevertheless critically important to sustainable security.

In the context of security, then, strong institutions should be ones where long-termism is built in; where there is an expectation, a culture, and a requirement to take decisions for the future as well as for now; to value the security of future generations and not only of current policies. From a long-termism perspective institutions that are 'strong' will be institutions that are innovative, open, and reinvigorated;[61] that are independent, accountable, and able to act over a long time period, that must be reviewed to ensure that they are effective,[62] that value participation

[60] See eg in this book, Hurst Hannum, Chapter 1; Liora Lazarus, Chapter 6; Margot E Salomon, Chapter 9; Sandra Fredman, Chapter 10; Magdalena Sepulveda and Kate Donald, Chapter 12; Kerri Woods, Chapter 13; Simon Caney, Chapter 16.

[61] *Now for the Long Term: The Report of the Oxford Martin Commission for Future Generations* (Oxford Martin School, University of Oxford, 2013) 7 <https://www.oxfordmartin.ox.ac.uk/downloads/commission/Oxford_Martin_Now_for_the_Long_Term.pdf> accessed 11 August 2019 (hereafter Oxford Martin School, *Now for the Long Term*)

[62] See further Jessie Blackbourn, Fiona de Londras, and Lydia Morgan, *Accountability and Review in the Counter-Terrorist State* (University of Bristol Press, 2019).

and transparency to the extent possible (and, in this, that value and account for lived experience of insecurity emanating from both state and non-state sources), and that measure the long-term impact of their actions.[63] These are all commitments the achievement of which can be measured and assessed, and which are likely to enhance our likelihood of truly reducing insecurity.

VI. Conclusion

It is quite easy to see why insecurity is a concept ripe for the sustainable development agenda. As already outlined, insecurity of all kinds simply makes human flourishing enabled by the enjoyment of rights more difficult to attain, it harms people and polities, and it drains resources from the broader sustainability agenda. But tackling insecurity is complex. The SDGs are, I submit, on the right track when they identify institutions as key to tackling insecurity, and when they locate those institutions within a broader framework of concern for ensuring that our societies are more just, more fair, and more inclusive.

However, an exhortation to '[s]trengthen relevant national institutions, including through international cooperation, for building capacity at all levels, in particular in developing countries, to prevent violence and combat terrorism and crime' without further appropriate elaboration of what 'strength' means in this context both undermines the likelihood that the transformative potential of SDG16 will be realized in the context of tackling insecurity *and* risks legitimating oppressive, repressive, and often fundamentally undemocratic measures and institutions by reference to the need to prevent violence and combat terrorism and crime. By reorienting this provision and the underpinning concept of security to license, encourage, and support a movement towards sustainable security and towards designing, implementing, and maintaining institutions that have sustainable security at their heart, Goal 16 might just be able to effect an important, but difficult, shift in how we assess states' approaches to tackling insecurity and, consequently, their operational approaches thereto.

Given this, it is perhaps no surprise that Goal 16 was relatively under-considered in the early policy literature that followed the finalization of the SDGs.[64] States, fundamentally, may not *want* a recalibration of how we perceive security and assess

[63] These are modelled on the five principles for the long term outlined in Oxford Martin School, *Now for the Long Term* (n 62). They also build on my proposals for good governance in counter-terrorism as outlined in Fiona de Londras (2016) 'Accounting for Rights in EU Counter-Terrorism: Towards Effective Review' 22(2) Columbia Journal of European Law 237–74; Fiona de Londras, 'Governance Gaps in EU Counter-Terrorism: Implications for Democracy and Constitutionalism' in Fiona de Londras and Josephine Doody (eds), *The Impact, Legitimacy and Effectiveness of EU Counter-Terrorism* (Routledge 2015).

[64] But see now the excellent and extensive work of Pathfinders on 'SDG16+', available at <https://www.sdg16.plus> accessed on 11 October 2019.

states' security action. After all, the *status quo* provides rhetorical legitimation (although not legal justification) for the repression of the media, suppression of academics, murder of opponents, siphoning of funds, and detention without trial of rivals the world over, while simultaneously being ineffective at compelling long-termism, responsiveness to forms of violence and harm considered unimportant (eg domestic violence), or meaningful review of so-called security measures (especially those relating to counter-terrorism). With a little imagination and the reform of the indicators for SDG16 there is a real possibility of stymying the slow progress towards security as a development goal only adding to that already worrying trend.

6
Insecurity and Human Rights

Liora Lazarus

Friends, delegates and fellow Americans: I humbly and gratefully accept your nomination for the presidency of the United States. Together, we will lead our party back to the White House, and we will lead our country back to safety, prosperity, and peace. We will be a country of generosity and warmth. But we will also be a country of law and order. Our Convention occurs at a moment of crisis for our nation. The attacks on our police, and the terrorism in our cities, threaten our very way of life. Any politician who does not grasp this danger is not fit to lead our country. Americans watching this address tonight have seen the recent images of violence in our streets and the chaos in our communities. Many have witnessed this violence personally, some have even been its victims. I have a message for all of you: the crime and violence that today afflicts our nation will soon come to an end. Beginning on January 20th 2017, safety will be restored. The most basic duty of government is to defend the lives of its own citizens. Any government that fails to do so is a government unworthy to lead. It is finally time for a straightforward assessment of the state of our nation. I will present the facts plainly and honestly. We cannot afford to be so politically correct anymore.[1]

I. Introduction

Insecurity, and the promise of security, safety, and order, sit at the centre of contemporary political discourse. Seen as dichotomous paradigms, security is most commonly pitted against human rights. Security, a core rationale of the state, requires coercion and intervention from state actors for its realization. Human rights, on the other hand, are commonly associated with state limitation and, in

[1] Donald Trump Republican National Convention Speech (Politico, 21 July 2016) <http://www.politico.com/story/2016/07/full-transcript-donald-trump-nomination-acceptance-speech-at-rnc-225974#ixzz4GpBehqGS> accessed 12 August 2019.

Liora Lazarus, *Insecurity and Human Rights* In: Human Rights and 21st Century Challenges. Edited by: Dapo Akande, Jaakko Kuosmanen, Helen McDermott, and Dominic Roser, Published by Oxford University Press 2020.
DOI: 10.1093/oso/9780198824770.003.0007

particular, a structure in which to hold the state's coercive power to account. For liberals, human rights are the life-blood of contemporary democratic and constitutional arrangements. For conservatives, they are the 'politically correct' tools of a liberal elite designed to erode social order and 'life as we know it'.

In contrast to this conservative caricature, however, human rights are being transformed from concepts originally embodying the idea of state limitation to those underpinning state coercion. This 'securitization of rights' trend is the twenty-first-century challenge that this chapter seeks to expose and critique. Human rights as prompts to state coercion arise from two directions. On the one hand, there is an emerging emphasis of the notion of the right to security as a meta-right through which all other rights might be realized.[2] On the other hand, a range of protective (and often coercive) duties on the state to protect individuals against private violence are being implied, and promoted, from other basic human rights.[3] The prompts behind these shifts are historical, philosophical, legal, and political, and they deserve further scholarly and critical attention. In section II, the chapter examines the development of the right to security in political discourse, philosophical debate, and within international and comparative law. Thereafter, section III outlines the rise of protective duties under international human rights law and domestic constitutional law in a range of jurisdictions. Section IV then evaluates the shift to coercive human rights. The chapter concludes that while the shift may be a strong counter to the conservative caricature of human rights, there are risks that this development will corrode the human rights project more broadly.

II. The Right to Security

Major international human rights declarations, and domestic constitutions, enacted after 1945 commonly refer to the 'right to security' as an expression of the ancient right of *habeas corpus*—a right to security from the state.[4] More recently, however, the ideal of a positive right to security, in the sense of a right to state protection from private violence, has grown in influence.

[2] Liora Lazarus, 'Mapping the Right to Security' in Ben Goold and Liora Lazarus (eds), *Security and Human Rights* (Hart 2007); Liora Lazarus, 'The Right to Security: Securing Rights or Securitizing Rights?' in Rob Dickinson (ed), *Examining Critical Perspectives on Human Rights* (CUP 2012) (hereafter Lazarus, 'Securing Rights or Securitizing Rights?'); Liora Lazarus, 'The Right to Security' in Rowan Cruft, S Mathew Liao, and Massimo Renzo (eds), *Philosophical Foundations of Human Rights* (OUP 2015) (hereafter Lazarus, 'The Right to Security').

[3] Liora Lazarus, 'Positive Obligations and Criminal Justice: Duties to Protect or Coerce' in Julia Roberts and Lucia Zedner (eds), *Principled Approaches to Criminal Law and Criminal Justice: Essays in Honour of Professor Andrew Ashworth* (OUP 2012) (hereafter Lazarus, 'Positive Obligations').

[4] Liora Lazarus, 'The Right to Security' in *Max Planck Encyclopedia of Comparative Constitutional Law* (OUP 2016) (hereafter Lazarus, 'The Right to Security').

'Freedom from fear'[5] was included in Roosevelt's Four Freedoms ultimately contained in the Universal Declaration of Human Rights and expressed as 'the highest aspiration of the common people'.[6] While at the time this implied a prohibition on international aggression, the notion of an individual subjective right to security, has grown significantly over the last three decades. The move has been spurred first by the fragmentation of international security after the end of the Cold War which generated an alliance of the international human security, the socio-economic rights, and the development movements around the ideal of 'human security', and the right to be 'free from violence'. Second, and more recently, the war on terror has seen politicians invoking the right to security as a 'meta-right' to legitimate coercive state action and provoke a rebalancing between human rights and liberty on the one hand, and security on the other.[7] These politicians have found some support in existing philosophy and law on the subject (Figure 6.1).

A. Political Rhetoric on the Right to Security

My own analysis in 2011 showed an increasing popularity in the use of the term 'right to security' in global political rhetoric since 9/11 as a means to legitimate security measures.[8] Most leading politicians will have engaged the term at some stage. Out of the 400 examples examined, on only one occasion did a politician invoke the right to security in its negative sense as a 'right to security against the power of the state'.[9]

Some politicians went even further and claimed (as John Reid, former UK Home Secretary, did in 2007) that the 'right to security' is 'the basic right on which all others are based'.[10] This 'meta-rights' language is also evident in the preamble of French security legislation promulgated in 2003.[11] The meta-rights premise is used to argue that negative rights ought to be 'rebalanced' in favour of the right to security and to legitimate strong coercive measures. An example of such language can be found in in the introductory speech to the EU counter-terrorism strategy, where it was stated 'our political goal remains to strike the right balance between

[5] Franklin Delano Roosevelt, 'The Four Freedoms' (Speech to the members of the 77th Congress, 6 January 1941) <http://www.americanrhetoric.com/speeches/fdrthefourfreedoms.htm> accessed 12 August 2019.

[6] The Universal Declaration of Human Rights (adopted 10 December 1948 UNGA Res 217 A(III) (UDHR).

[7] Lazarus, 'Securing Rights or Securitizing Rights?' (n 3).

[8] This analysis was conducted in 2011 and is discussed in Lazarus, 'Securing Rights or Securitizing Rights?' (n 3).

[9] Sir Menzies Campbell (House of Commons debates into extending the limits of pre-charge detention) HC Deb 25 July 2007, vol 463, col 851.

[10] Full text of speech reported 'Reid Urges Human Rights Shake Up' *BBC News* (12 May 2007) <http://news.bbc.co.uk/2/hi/uk_news/politics/6648849.stm> accessed 12 August 2019.

[11] Article 1 para 2 of law n°2003-239 of 18 March 2003.

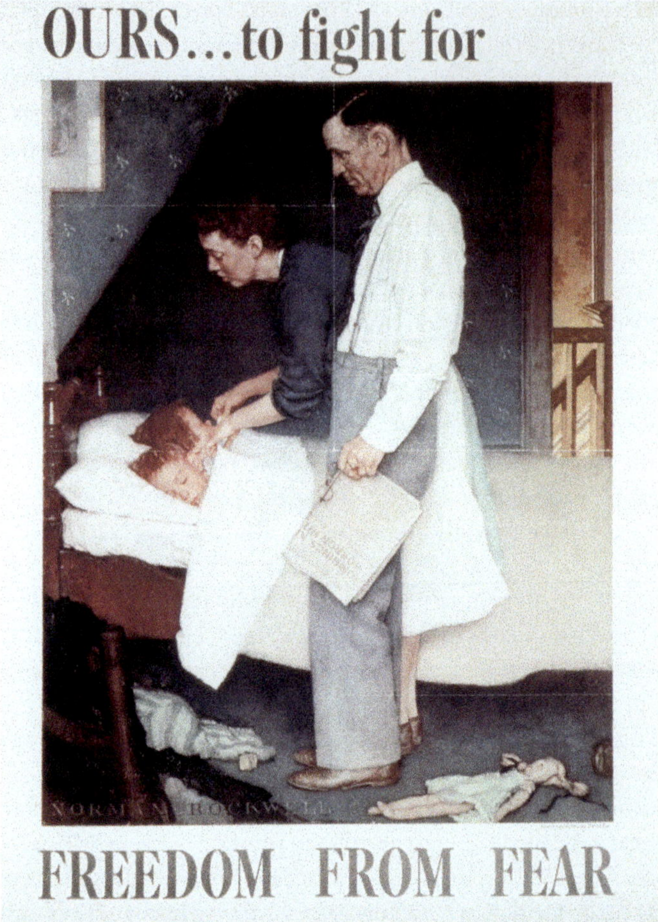

Figure 6.1 Photo by Library of Congress/Corbis/VCG via Getty Images

the fundamental right to security of citizens, which is first, right to life, and the other fundamental rights of individuals, including privacy and procedural rights'.[12] Similarly, John Reid, discussing UK counter-terrorism policy in 2006 stated: 'as we face the threat of mass murder we have to accept that the rights of the individual that we enjoy must and will be balanced with the collective right of security and the protection of life and limb that our citizens demand'.[13]

[12] European Commissioner for Justice, Freedom and Security, 'EU Counterterrorism Strategy' Speech/07/505 (European Parliament, 5 September 2007) < http://europa.eu/rapid/press-release_SPEECH-07-505_en.htm> accessed 12 August 2019.

[13] John Reid, 'Rights, Security Must Be Balanced' *Associated Press Online* (16 August 2006).

The rhetoric of the right to security is not only the preserve of security-minded politicians. Many in the human rights community have been quick to use the right to security as a way to fend off attacks on the human rights project as a whole. Faced with the onslaught on rights that came with early counter-terror strategy, for example, Amnesty International claimed that 'the right to security is a basic human right'.[14] Moreover, as we will see in more detail shortly, the development community has been a key part of the human security movement, as it appears that the concept of security has more political purchase than invoking the language of the right to subsistence, food, or health on their own.[15]

So the rhetorical attraction of the right to security comes from two directions. On the one hand, those seeking to legitimize strong security measures can invoke rights as a legitimizing tool, a process I have previously termed 'righting security'.[16] On the other hand, human rights, humanitarian, and development activists are keen to leverage the politically animating concept of security to preserve the goods they seek to protect, or in simple terms to 'secure' rights.

B. Philosophical Arguments for the Right to Security

While we may be tempted to reject the arguments of hawkish politicians who argue that the right to security is the meta-right upon which all rights rest, and while we may understand the pragmatism of those seeking to secure rights, the arguments of leading philosophers are less easily disposed of. The main contributor in this field is Henry Shue, whose work has been highly influential in the social rights movement.

Shue viewed rights as 'basic' if and when 'enjoyment of them is essential to the enjoyment of all other rights'.[17] He took the instrumental view that 'whether a right is basic is independent of whether its enjoyment is also valuable in itself'.[18] Shue identified security as one of the three basic rights, alongside 'liberty' and 'subsistence'. He makes an instrumental and preconditional argument that security constitutes a basic right because 'being physically secure is a necessary condition for the exercise of any other right, and guaranteeing physical security must be part of guaranteeing anything else as a right'.[19]

The scope of the duties flowing from Shue's positive right to security are potentially wide-ranging. He enumerates three such duties, which includes the key

[14] William Schulz, 'Safer or Scared? Impact of the War on Terror' *CNN* (28 May 2003).

[15] Lazarus, 'Securing Rights or Securitizing Rights?' (n 3) 95–98.

[16] Ibid, 97.

[17] H Shue, *Basic Rights: Subsistence, Affluence, and US Foreign Policy* (2nd edn, Princeton University Press 1996) 19.

[18] Ibid, 20.

[19] Ibid, 21–22.

'duty to protect people against deprivation of security by other people'.[20] Without the state fulfilling these duties, the enjoyment of all other rights (of which security forms a constitutive part) is impossible.

Shue doesn't quite resolve the relationship between basic rights to security and liberty, and the trade-offs that might have to be made between them. For Shue, in order for liberty to attain the same *basic* status as the rights to security and subsistence, it has to be constitutive of the enjoyment of other rights. In this constitutive sense, Shue sees a smaller role for liberty than he does for 'security' and 'subsistence'. Shue identifies those aspects of liberty which constitute essential elements of the enjoyment of other rights: namely rights to participation and rights to freedom of movement.[21] This instrumental account of liberty as a basic right is thus a thinner rendition of the kind of liberty Locke viewed as valuable for its own sake.[22]

As I have argued elsewhere,[23] Shue is particularly vague on the practical forms that the correlative duties might take. He is clearly concerned about coercive overreach and suggests a safeguard in building organizations and society in a way that encourages self-restraint, rather than bolstering the coercive duties of state agents over individuals. It is unclear whether, given the weight Shue places on the attainment of actual security as a precondition to the exercise of other rights, this will entirely resolve the potential for the State's coercive overreach as a duty-based response to such a constitutive right.

C. The Right to Security in Law and Policy

1. International law and institutional approaches

Given the potential to leverage the right to security for the legitimation of strong coercive state powers, both in political rhetoric and in philosophical argument, it is worth looking more closely at how the law treats the idea of the right to security. The following brief survey shows a variation of conceptions, as well as a multiplicity of institutional and judicial approaches.

The right to security is enshrined in most of the major international human rights documents alongside the protection of 'liberty', and they are usually jointly viewed to protect the right against arbitrary detention.[24] In some international

[20] Ibid, 52.

[21] Ibid, 71–82.

[22] Lazarus, 'The Right to Security' (n 3).

[23] Ibid.

[24] See eg Universal Declaration of Human Rights (adopted 10 December 1948 UNGA Res 217 A(III) (UDHR) (1948) art 3; International Covenant on Civil and Political Rights (adopted 16 December 1966, entered into force 23 March 1976) 999 UNTS 171 (ICCPR) art 9; American Convention on Human Rights (adopted 22 December 1969, entered into force 18 July 1978) art 7; African Charter on Human and Peoples' Rights (adopted 27 June 1981, entered into force 21 October 1986) art 6; Convention for the Protection of Human Rights and Fundamental Freedoms (European Convention on Human Right,

documents you can also find references to the idea of social security[25] and the right to security in the context of the right to an adequate standard of living.[26]

After the 1990s, the 'human security' paradigm gained increasing influence over the language of international institutions, and attached the notion of 'security' to a range of previously self-standing goods. Thus, in the United Nations Development Programme (UNDP) Human Development Report 1994 the notion of human security was said to encompass threats in the seven areas of: economic security, food security, health security, environmental security, personal security, community security, and political security. Likewise, the notion of security gained prominence in the Millennium Development Goals (MDGs) which pledged to 'spare no effort to free our people from the scourge of war' and 'eliminate the dangers posed by weapons of mass destruction'.[27] This was reflected also in the conception of 'human security' set out in Article 143 of the United Nations General Assembly 2005 World Summit Outcome Document which states:

> We stress the right of people to live in freedom and dignity, free from poverty and despair. We recognize that all individuals, in particular vulnerable people, are entitled to freedom from fear and freedom from want, with an equal opportunity to enjoy all their rights and fully develop their human potential. To this end, we commit ourselves to discussing and defining the notion of human security in the General Assembly.

Subsequently, the UN System Task Team on the Post-2015 UN Development Agenda (2015) recommended that the post-2015 framework should include a specific target on violence, which is underpinned by the notion that 'freedom from violence is a human right'.[28] The Sustainable Development Goals (SDGs) thus include Goal 16 to 'promote peaceful and inclusive societies for sustainable development' which is measured *inter alia* by target 16.1 to 'significantly reduce all forms of violence and related death rates everywhere'.[29]

as amended) (ECHR) (1951) art 5, and Charter of Fundamental Rights of the European Union (26 October 2012) art 6.

---

[25] UDHR art 22; Charter of Fundamental Rights of the European Union, art 34.

[26] UDHR art 25.

[27] UNGA '55/2 United Nations Millennium Declaration' (8 September 2000) UN Doc A/RES/55/2, para 8.

[28] United Nations 'Transforming Our World: The 2030 Agenda for Sustainable Development' (*Sustainable Development Knowledge Platform*) <https://sustainabledevelopment.un.org/post2015/transformingourworld> accessed 12 August 2019 (hereafter United Nations, 'Transforming Our World').

[29] United Nations, 'Transforming Our World'. In Chapter 5, this book, de Londras discusses the vision of security that might be achieved through successful pursuance of Goal 16.

2. Constitutional provisions

In domestic constitutions the references to security vary.[30] Article 2 of the French Declaration of the Rights of Man 1789 refers to 'sûreté', a term which itself is subject to some dispute within France.[31] The term does not appear explicitly in the French Constitution of 27 October 1946. However, in the Canadian Charter of Rights and Freedoms (1982), section 7 states that everyone has the right to life, liberty and *security* of person'. This reflects the language of the large majority of provisions in domestic constitutional laws.[32] In contrast, however, the South African Constitution protects a positive right to security by enshrining the right 'to be free from all forms of violence from either public or private sources'.[33] Similarly, protection from 'private violence' finds expression in the proposed Draft Bill of Rights of the Northern Ireland Human Rights Commission, a Bill which has never been enacted.[34]

3. Legislative provisions

The preambles of three recent French Statutes make symbolic reference to the 'fundamental right to security'.[35] The 2003 Statute goes as far as asserting that security is a 'meta-right'. It states that 'security is a fundamental right and a condition for the exercise of individual and collective liberties' and underlines 'the duty of the State in this area'.[36]

D. Legal Interpretation of the 'Right to Security'

The language of human security, the MDGs, a number of positive rights provisions and legislative statements surveyed thus far, echo Shue's far-reaching aspirations for the right to security. On their own, they offer little guidance on how such aspirations may be implemented in concrete terms, or how they will be balanced against

30 See more comprehensive coverage in Lazarus, 'The Right to Security' (n 5).

31 See Lazarus, 'The Right to Security' (n 5).

32 Ibid.

33 Constitution of the Republic of South Africa, 1996, s 12(1)(c).

34 Northern Ireland Human Rights Commission, 'A Bill of Rights for Northern Ireland: Advice to the Secretary of State for Northern Ireland' (10 December 2008) 40.

35 Article 1(2) of law n°95-73 of 21 January 1995 d'orientation et de programmation relative à la sécurité < https://www.legifrance.gouv.fr/affichTexte.do?cidTexte=LEGITEXT000005617582> accessed 12 August 2019; Article 1(2) of law n°2003-239 of 18 March 2003 pour la sécurité intérieure (21 octobre 2017) <https://www.legifrance.gouv.fr/affichTexte.do?cidTexte=JORFTEXT000000412199> accessed 12 August 2019; Article 1(2) of law n°2001-1062 of 15 November 2001 relative à la sécurité quotidienne < https://www.legifrance.gouv.fr/affichTexte.do?cidTexte=JORFTEXT000000222052> accessed 12 August 2019.

36 Article 1(2) of law n°2003-239 of 18 March 2003. Nevertheless, the Council of State ('*Conseil d'Etat*') has held that the right to security is not a fundamental freedom ('*liberté fondamentale*') pursuant to Article L 521-2 of the French Code of Administrative Justice; Council of State, ordonnance, 20 July 2011, Commune de Mandelieu-la-Napoule, n°236196. See also Marc-Antoine Granger (2009) 'Existe-t-il un "Droit Fondamental à la Sécurité"?' 2 Revue de Science Criminelle et de Droit Penal Comparé 273.

other competing interests and rights. It is in the granularity of legal interpretation that this guidance has been developed, and in which institutions have had to face up to the inevitable limitations on the right to security. Again, there is much variety in this respect, as despite textual similarity between relevant provisions, norms protecting the right to security are subject to varying judicial interpretations.

1. Human Rights Committee

The International Covenant on Civil and Political Rights (ICCPR) enshrines the right to security in its classic form as a right against arbitrary detention. Nevertheless, ever since its key decision in *Degaldo Páez* in 1990,[37] the United Nations Human Rights Committee (UNHRC) has been active in developing the right to security as a positive individual right to state protection. Its approach to this right has been elaborated now in General Comment No. 35 on Article 9 ICCPR which states that:

> The right to security of person protects individuals against intentional infliction of bodily or mental injury . . . The right to personal security also obliges States parties to take appropriate measures in response to death threats against persons in the public sphere, and more generally to protect individuals from foreseeable threats to life or bodily integrity proceeding from any governmental or private actors. States parties must take both measures to prevent future injury and retrospective measures, such as enforcement of criminal laws, in response to past injury [. . .][38]

2. European Court of Human Rights (ECtHR)

While the wording of the right to security under the ICCPR and the European Convention on Human Rights (ECHR) is almost identical, the ECtHR has not followed the approach of the Human Rights Committee. Consequently, it retains a limited conception of the right to security under Article 5: 'the Court is steadfast in limiting the right to security of person to procedural protections in cases of arbitrary detention'.[39] Early cases demonstrate that the Court did not even wish to read security independently of liberty. In *Adler and Biuvas v Federal Republic of*

[37] *William Eduardo Delgado Páez v Colombia* (12 July 1990), Communication No 195/1985, para 5.5.

[38] UNHRC 'General Comment 35' (14 December 2014) UN Doc CCPR/C/HC/35 para 9. This General Comment synthesizses a range of decisions of the UNHRC related to these issues (*Leehong v Jamaica* (13 July 1999), Communication No 613/1995, para 9.3; *Marcellana and Gumanoy v Philippines* (30 October 2008) Communication No 1560/2007, para 7.7; *Obodzinsky v Canada* (19 March 2007) Communication No 1124/2002 para 8.5) as well as UNHRC observations and reports on particular national jurisdictions see for exampleeg: UNHRC 'Concluding Observations of the Human Rights Committee: El Salvador' UN Doc CCPR/CO/78/SLV (22 August 2003) para 16; UNHRC 'Consideration of reports submitted by States parties under article 40 of the Covenant Concluding observations of the Human Rights Committee' UN Doc CCPR/C/NOR/CO/6 (18 November 2011) para 10; UNHRC 'Concluding observations on the fourth periodic report of the Philippines, adopted by the Committee at its 106th session (15 October– - 2 November 2012)' UN Doc CCPR/C/PHL/CO/4 (13 November 2012) para 14.

[39] Rhonda Powell (2007) 'The Right to Security of Person in European Court of Human Rights Jurisprudence' 6 European Human Rights Law Review 649.

Germany, the Court noted that the terms 'liberty' and 'security' should be read as a whole,[40] while in *Bozano v France*,[41] it stipulated that Article 5 deals with arbitrary deprivation of liberty (see also *X v Ireland*[42]).

More recent cases have accepted arguments articulating security separately from liberty under Article 5 although these cases all relate to examples of arbitrary detention.[43] Tellingly, the ECtHR agreed with the UK House of Lords in rejecting the idea that the broader conception of the right to security as a right to euthanasia could apply under Article 5.[44] While Strasbourg does not have a highly articulated conception of the right to security under Article 5, it has extensive jurisprudence on protective duties under the right to life and right against torture will be discussed shortly.

3. Canada

The jurisprudence on section 7 of the Canadian Charter, which protects the right to security, is extensive. Much of this relates to the negative right to security of person against arbitrary state interference. But the right to security has been broadly interpreted beyond the criminal justice sphere. It includes a right to physical as well as psychological integrity, and can include protection from private actions where a sufficient 'causal connection' is established between state action or inaction and the prejudice suffered by the individual rights holder.[45]

Canadian jurisprudence is clear that the Charter does not impose positive obligations on governments directly.[46] For a breach of the right to security to be established, state action must violate the 'principles of fundamental justice' which apply to all limitations of rights under the Charter. Within these limitations, however, the Canadian Supreme Court has used the right to security as a platform for the creation of a number of rights not expressly included in the Canadian Charter. This has resulted in protective duties on the state in the context, for example, of abortion;[47] child custody proceedings[48] and child care orders;[49] euthanasia;[50] health care;[51] and prostitution.[52]

[40] *Adler and Biuvas v Federal Republic of Germany* App No 5573/72 (ECtHR, 16 July 1976) 102 (146).

[41] *Bozano v France* App No 9990/82 (ECtHR, 18 December 1986).

[42] *X v Ireland* App No 6040/73 (ECtHR, 20 July 1973).

[43] *Kurt (Koçeri) v Turkey* App No 24276/94 (ECtHR, 25 May 1998) paras 122–123; *Tepe v Turkey* App No 27244/95 (ECtHR, 9 May 2003); *Öcalan v Turkey* App No 46221/99 (ECtHR, 12 May 2005) para 88.

[44] *Pretty v United Kingdom* App No 2346/02 (ECtHR, 29 April 2002) para 14; *R (on the Application of Pretty) v DPP* [2001] UKHL 61, para 23.

[45] *Blencoe v British Columbia* [2000] 2 SCR 307 (Can).

[46] *Canada (Attorney General) v Bedford* [2013] 3 SCR 1101 (Can), para 88.

[47] *R v Morgentaler (No 2)* [1988] 1 SCR 30 (Can).

[48] *New Brunswick (Minister of Health and Community Services) v G (J)* [1999] 3 SCR 46 (Can).

[49] *Winnipeg Child and Family Services v K.L.W* [2000] 2 SCR 519 (Can).

[50] *Rodriguez v British Columbia (Attorney General)* [1993] 3 SCR 519 (Can); *Carter v Canada (Attorney General)* [2015] 1 SCR 331 (Can).

[51] *Chaoulli v Quebec (Attorney General)* [2005] 1 SCR 791 (Can); *Canadian Doctors for Refugee Care v Canada* (2014) FC 651 (Can).

[52] *Canada (Attorney General) v Bedford* [2013] 3 SCR 1101 (Can).

4. South Africa

The express positive right to security protected in Section 12(1)(c) of the South African Constitution has been extensively formulated by the South African Constitutional Court. The Court has used this right to develop a broad range of protective duties against violence in various spheres. The archetypal case of *Metrorail*,[53] which dealt with the state's duties in protecting rail commuters from lethal violence, shows the importance of the test of reasonableness and accountability when assessing whether a positive duty under this right has been breached. This acts as a delimiting factor on the potential scope of the positive duties imposed, although not without due justification by the state. The duty was eloquently framed by Justice O'Regan:

> the nature of the duty, the social and economic context in which it arises, the range of factors that are relevant to the performance of the duty, the extent to which the duty is closely related to the core activities of the duty-bearer—the closer they are, the greater the obligation on the duty-bearer, and the extent of any threat to fundamental rights should the duty not be met as well as the intensity of the harm that may result. The more grave is the threat to fundamental rights, the greater is the responsibility on the duty bearer. Thus, an obligation to take measures to discourage pickpocketing may not be as intense as an obligation to take measures to provide protection against serious threats to life and limb... Details of the precise character of the resource constraints, whether human or financial, in the context of the overall resourcing of the organ of State will need to be provided. The standard of reasonableness so understood conforms to the constitutional principles of accountability, on the one hand, in that it requires decision-makers to disclose their reasons for their conduct, and the principle of effectiveness on the other, for it does not unduly hamper the decision-maker's authority to determine what are reasonable and appropriate measures in the overall context of their activities. [54]

The case of *Baloyi* also shows how the South African Constitutional Court has carefully balanced the protective duties of the state in respect of victims of domestic violence, against the perpetrators' negative rights. Justice Albie Sachs was clear that 'the specific inclusion of private sources emphasizes that serious threats to security of the person arise from private sources. Section 12(1) has to be understood as obliging the state directly to protect the right of everyone to

[53] *Rail Commuters Action Group and Others v Transnet Ltd t/a Metrorail and Others* 2005 (4) BCLR 301 (CC) (S Afr).

[54] Ibid, para 88.

be free from private or domestic violence'.[55] However, he was alert to the inevitable balance that had to be struck: 'the Court faces the novel and complex task of establishing the appropriate balance between the state's constitutional duty to provide effective remedies against domestic violence, and its simultaneous obligation to respect the constitutional rights to a fair trial of those who might be affected by the measures taken'.[56]

III. Protective Duties

Alongside the development of the right to security, is a growing recognition internationally of 'protective duties', or as I have argued elsewhere 'coercive duties',[57] arising out of basic rights such as the right to life and freedom from torture. With varying scope, these enjoin states to act to protect individuals at risk of human rights violations by private actors. This jurisprudence shows that courts have developed alternative ways to protect against private violence without recourse to the broadly conceived right to security. While this approach may be more welcome by avoiding the pitfalls of overblown and diffuse claims of a right to security, protective duties nevertheless create duties which engage the state's coercive power, and are often broadly and forcefully drawn. Here again, the question of balance remains key.

A. The German Constitutional Court and Protective Duties

By the 1970s, the German Federal Constitutional Court had fully acknowledged the notion of protective duties (*Schutzpflichten*).[58] Some constitutional theorists and decisions associate these protective duties with the idea, established in the *Lüth* decision in 1958,[59] that German constitutional rights constitute a system of 'objective norms and values' which radiate throughout the legal system as a whole. Others see protective duties as correlative duties derived from subjective individual rights to state protection, and base their argument on the wording of Article 1(1)

[55] *The State v Baloyi* (2000) 1 SACR 81 (CC) (S Afr).<?IBT>

[56] Ibid, para 1.

[57] Lazarus, 'Positive Obligations' (n 4).

[58] See eg: BVerfGE 39,1, 25 February 1975, and BVerfGE 56, 54 NJW 1981. See further Josef Isensee, 'Das Grundrecht als Abwehrrecht und als staatliche Schutzpflicht' in Josef Isensee and Paul Kirchhoff (eds), *Handbuch des Staatsrechts der Bundesrepublik Deutschland, Band IV: Allgemeine Grundrechtslehren* (Müller Heidelberg 1992).

[59] *BVerfGE* 7, 198 (1958).

of the German Basic law which enjoins the State to 'respect and protect' human dignity.[60]

Protective duties have been a consistent aspect of German constitutional jurisprudence since, and their scope was discussed in the German Aviation decision.[61] There, the Federal Constitutional Court rejected the idea that the state was required to shoot down a hijacked plane as a consequence of its protective duty to individuals on the ground at risk of losing their lives. Rather, the Court argued that the broad discretion afforded to states in their fulfilment of protective duties had to include the proportionate protection of the rights to life and human dignity of the passengers trapped on a hijacked plane. The decision was a carefully crafted balance between the state's protective duties, and its duties of restraint.

This balance notwithstanding, German commentators have drawn the conclusion that the range of protective duties recognized by the Federal Constitutional Court when taken as a whole constituted an overarching 'right to security'.[62] This is despite the absence of such an explicit positive right under the German Basic Law.

B. Inter-American Court of Human Rights

The most important international jurisprudence to influence the progression of protective duties lies with the decision of the Inter-American Court of Human Rights in *Velasquez Rodriguez*.[63] Faced with the rise of 'disappearances' across Latin America in the 1980s, and consistent denial of any responsibility by state parties, the Inter-American Court developed the international human rights foundation for protective duties. The Court argued that the inclusion of the phrase 'ensure to all persons subject to their jurisdiction the free and full exercise of those rights and freedoms' in Article 1(1) of the Inter-American Convention resulted in extensive positive obligations upon states which went beyond the mere 'respect' of human rights protected therein'. Rather,

> this obligation implies the duty of the States Parties to organize the governmental apparatus and, in general, all the structures through which public power is exercised, so that they are capable of juridically ensuring the free and full enjoyment of human rights. As a consequence of this obligation, the States must prevent,

[60] Graf von Kielmansegg, 'Grundfälle zu de allgemeinen Grundrechtslehren' [2009] *JuS* 216.

[61] *BVerfGE* (2006) 1 BvR 357/05, 15 February 2006, paras 120–121.

[62] Josef Isensee, *Das Grundrecht auf Sicherheit—Zu den Schutzpflichten des freiheitlichen Verfassungsstaates* (Walter de Gruyter 1983) 33.

[63] *Velasquez Rodriguez Case*, Inter American Court of Human Rights Series C No 4 (29 July 1988) (hereafter *Velasquez Rodriguez*).

> investigate and punish any violation of the rights recognized by the Convention and, moreover, if possible attempt to restore the right violated and provide compensation as warranted for damages resulting from the violation. [64]

The result of this reasoning was a comprehensive list of duties aimed at limiting states' frequent attempts to absolve themselves of responsibility for 'disappearances' done in their name. Thus, the Court argued that 'any violation of rights […] is imputable to the State' including in conditions where there was a 'lack of due diligence to prevent the violation or respond to it as required by the Convention' on the part of the relevant state,[65] or a failure to take 'measures to prevent or punish those responsible'.[66]

In sum, the Court argued that the state has a 'legal duty to take reasonable steps to prevent human rights violations and to use the means at its disposal to carry out a serious investigation of violations committed within its jurisdiction, to identify those responsible, to impose the appropriate punishment, and to ensure the victim adequate compensation'.[67] The duty thus described was broad, including 'all means of a legal, political, administrative and cultural nature',[68] to 'investigate every situation involving a violation of the rights protected under the Convention'.[69] Importantly, and of relevance for future jurisprudence on state liability for the acts of private actors, the court argued that

> if the State apparatus acts in such a way that the violation goes unpunished […] the State has failed to comply with its duty to ensure the free and full exercise of those rights to the persons within its jurisdiction […] the same is true when the State allows private persons or groups to act freely and with impunity to the detriment of rights recognized by the Convention.[70]

There is little question that the approach in *Velasquez Rodriguez* was underpinned by outrage at the impunity with which egregious human rights violations conducted by 'unofficial' state agents were being treated. This accounts for the depth of the obligations created in this decision. Notwithstanding, the Inter-American Court did recognize some limitations in this respect. The Court was prepared to accept that that the 'duty to investigate' is not 'breached merely because the investigation does not produce a satisfactory result'. Nevertheless, it argued, that such a duty must be taken 'seriously', 'have an objective and be assumed by the

[64] *Velasquez Rodriguez*, para 166.
[65] *Velasquez Rodriguez*, para 172.
[66] *Velasquez Rodriguez*, para 173.
[67] *Velasquez Rodriguez*, para 174.
[68] *Velasquez Rodriguez*, para 175.
[69] *Velasquez Rodriguez*, para 176.
[70] *Velasquez Rodriguez*, para 176.

State as its own legal duty' and constitute 'an effective search for the truth by the government'. Moreover, that the duty applies regardless of the status of the actor in question, as 'where the acts of private parties that violate the Convention are not seriously investigated, those parties are aided in a sense by the government, thereby making the State responsible on the international plane'.[71]

The approach in *Velasquez Rodriguez* has continued to apply in the Inter-American Court. For example, the protective duties approach was adopted with particular poignancy in the murdered 'Street Children' case. Here the Court argued that the right to life includes 'the right that [the individual] will not be prevented from having access to the conditions that guarantee a minimum existence'. Thus, 'states have the obligation to guarantee the creation of the conditions required in order that violations of this basic right do not occur and, in particular, the duty to prevent its agents from violating it.[72]

Similarly, the Court found Mexico in breach of various rights under the Inter-American Convention because of its failure to take adequate steps to prevent the disappearance, abuse, and death of three women in the Cotton Field case.[73] Here the Court also relied on the Inter-American Convention on the Prevention, Punishment and Eradication of Violence against women 'Convention of Belem do Para'.[74] This connection to gender violence and the emphasis on the state's duties of due diligence in the investigation of human rights violations was also present in the very recent decision of *Velásquez Paiz et al v Guatemala*.[75] This decision dealt with the failure of the Guatemalan police to investigate cases of suspected violence against women in the first hours of their disappearance adequately.

C. Gender Violence in International Law

As the Inter-American cases suggest, an important source of protective duties is the development of international law protections against violence against women. Since the Convention on the Elimination of All Forms of Discrimination Against Women (CEDAW) was adopted by the UN General Assembly in 1979, gender

[71] *Velasquez Rodriguez*, para 177.

[72] *Villagran-Morales et al v Guatemala*, Inter-American Court of Human Rights (19 November 1999) para 144.

[73] *González et al ('Cotton Field') v Mexico*, Preliminary Objection, Merits, Reparations, and Costs, Judgment, Inter-American Court of Human Rights Series C No 205 (16 November 2009) para 166.

[74] Organization of American States, Inter-American Convention on the Prevention, Punishment and Eradication of Violence against Women ('Convention of Belem do Para') (9 June 1994) <http://www.oas.org/juridico/english/treaties/a-61.html> accessed 12 August 2019.

[75] *Velásquez Paiz et al v Guatemala*, Inter-American Court of Human Rights Series C No 307 (19 November 2015). Decision available in Spanish at <http://www.corteidh.or.cr/docs/casos/articulos/seriec_307_esp.pdf> accessed 12 August 2019. See also Lucia Mazzuca and Keina Yoshida, '*Velásquez Paiz et al v Guatemala*: Gender Stereotypes and Lack of Justice—Part 1' (Oxford Human Rights Hub, 9 August 2016) <http://ohrh.law.ox.ac.uk/velasquez-paiz-et-al-v-guatemala-gender-stereotypes-and-lack-of-justice-part-i/>.

violence has been the subject of extensive international law activity.[76] This includes the 19th General Recommendation of the CEDAW Committee,[77] which notes that states should 'take appropriate and effective measures to overcome all forms of gender-based violence, whether by public or private act' and 'ensure that laws against family violence and abuse, rape, sexual assault and other gender-based violence give adequate protection to all women, and respect their integrity and dignity'.[78] Similarly, the General Assembly Declaration on the Elimination of Violence Against Women (DEVW) enshrines a 'due diligence' standard and enjoins states to 'pursue by all appropriate means and without delay a policy of eliminating violence against women' including: exercising 'due diligence to prevent, investigate and in accordance with national legislation, punish acts of violence against women, whether those acts are perpetrated by the state or by private persons'.[79] The international duty of due diligence with respect to the treatment of violence against women is also supported by the Committee of Ministers of the Council of Europe in their Recommendation (2002) which obliges states to penalize all non-consensual sexual acts, including where the victim does not show resistance.[80]

D. European Court of Human Rights

Protective duties have been extensively developed in the ECtHR since 2000. These stem mostly from the positive aspect of the right to life and the right against torture.[81] These protective duties, relate to the preventative obligations of the state in the policing context as well as strengthening criminal law protections against state-sponsored killing of political dissidents;[82] negligent actions leading to death;[83] parental abuse;[84] rape;[85] and domestic violence.[86] The jurisprudence as a whole, which

[76] Liora Lazarus, 'The Human Rights Framework Relating to the Handling, Investigation and Prosecution of Rape Complaints', Annex A to *The Stern Review* (Home Office, 2010).

[77] UN Committee for the Elimination of All Forms of Discrimination against Women, 'General Recommendation No 19' in 'Note by the Secretariat, Compilation of General Comments and General Recommendations Adopted by Human Rights Treaty Bodies' (29 July 1994) UN Doc HRI/GEN/1/Rev.1.

[78] Ibid, s 24.

[79] UNGA Res 48/104 (20 December 1993) UN Doc A/RES48/104 art 4.

[80] Recommendation no R (2002) 5 adopted by the Committee of Ministers on 30 April 2002 and Explanatory Memorandum, H/Inf (2004).

[81] *Osman v United Kingdom* App No 23452/94 (ECtHR 28 October 1998) (hereafter *Osman*)

[82] *Mahmut Kaya v Turkey* App No 22535/93 (ECtHR 28 March 2000); *Kiliç v Turkey* App No 22492/93 (ECtHR 28 March 2000); *Akkoç v Turkey* App No 22947/93 (ECtHR, 10 October 2000).

[83] *Oneryildiz v Turkey* App No 48939/99 (ECtHR, 30 November 2004).

[84] *A v United Kingdom* App No 25599/94 (ECtHR, 23 September 1998).

[85] *MC v Bulgaria* App No 39278/98 (ECtHR, 04 December 2003).

[86] *Kontrova v Slovakia* App No 7510/04 (ECtHR, 31 May 2007); *Opuz v Turkey* App No 33401/02 (ECtHR, 9 June 2009).

has also been influential in the United Kingdom, has given rise to a range of investigative, preventive duties as well as sharpening criminal law prohibitions against private violence.

The ECtHR, much like the South African and Canadian Courts in respect of the right to security, acknowledges that it cannot place 'an impossible or disproportionate burden on the authorities' as it has to keep 'bearing in mind the difficulties involved in policing modern societies, the unpredictability of human conduct and the operational choices which must be made in terms of priorities and resources'.[87] It also notes that:

> another relevant consideration is the need to ensure that the police exercise their powers to control and prevent crime in a manner which fully respects the due process and other guarantees which legitimately place restraints on the scope of their action to investigate crime and bring offenders to justice, including the guarantees contained in Articles 5 [right to liberty] and 8 [right to private life] of the Convention.[88]

As a consequence, 'not every claimed risk to life can entail for the authorities a Convention requirement to take operational measures to prevent that risk from materialising'.[89] Hence, states are only under a *specific* obligation 'in certain well-defined circumstances' to take proactive 'preventive operational measures to protect an individual whose life is at risk from the criminal acts of another'.[90] This specific obligation only arises where 'the authorities knew or ought to have known of the existence of a real and immediate risk to the life of an identified individual, and that they failed to take measures within their powers which, judged reasonably, might have been expected to avoid that risk'.[91] This delimited specific duty is clearly framed and informed by tortious notions of causation and responsibility.

Notwithstanding, there are times in Strasbourg jurisprudence when the balanced approach to coercive duties is not always evident. In *Opuz v Turkey* the Court, influenced also by the CEDAW committee approach to domestic violence, stated: the Court underlines that in domestic violence cases perpetrators' rights cannot supersede victims' rights to life and to physical and mental integrity.[92]

[87] *Osman* (n 83) 116.
[88] Ibid.
[89] Ibid.
[90] Ibid.
[91] Ibid.
[92] *Opuz v Turkey* App no 33401/02 (ECtHR 9 June 2009) para 147.

E. India

A similarly hard-line approach has been taken in India where a series of cases held the State liable for negligent acts resulting in the violation of the right to life. These are referred to in the jurisprudence as 'constitutional torts', and much the same considerations of proximity and reasonableness apply in their application to state responsibility for deaths of private citizens.[93] The Indian Supreme Court elaborated on the state duty to protect life in the Chakma case. Here the Indian state attempted to side-step its obligations on the basis that the Chakma settlers were foreigners and without constitutional rights. The Court was having none of it:

> We are a country governed by the Rule of Law. Our Constitution confers certain rights on every human being and certain other rights on citizens. Every person is entitled to equality before the law and equal protection of the laws. So also, no person can be deprived of his life or personal liberty except according to procedure established by law. Thus, the State is bound to protect the life and liberty of every human being, be he a citizen or otherwise, and it cannot permit any body or group of persons, e.g., the AAPSU, to threaten the Chakmas to leave the State, failing which they would be forced to do so. No State Government worth the name can tolerate such threats by one group of persons to another group of persons; it is duty-bound to protect the threatened group from such assaults and if it fails to do so, it will fail to perform its constitutional as well as statutory obligations. Those giving such threats would be liable to be dealt with in accordance with law. The State Government must act impartially and carry out its legal obligations to safeguard the life, health and well-being of Chakmas residing in the State without being inhibited by local politics.[94]

IV. Evaluation

What are we to make of this shift in the conception of human rights as mechanisms of state limitation to prompts for state protection and intervention? The implications are mixed and often contradictory. In one sense, this survey acts as a strong and useful counter to the conservative caricature of human rights as 'politically correct' limitations to the essential pursuit of law, order, and security. Human

[93] See *National Human Rights Commission v State of Arunachal Pradesh* AIR 1996 SC 1234; *M Hongray v Union of India* AIR 1984 SC 1026; *Challa Ramkonda Reddy v State of Andhra Pradesh* (1990) ACJ 668; *R Gandhi v Union of India* AIR 1989 Mad 205; *M/s Inderpuri General Stores v Union of India* AIR 1992 J&K 11; *Manjit Singh Sawhney v Union of India* 2005 Indlaw DEL 379; Ken Cooper-Stephenson, 'The Emergence of Constitutional Torts Worldwide' (University of Kwazulu-Natal, Conference on Comparative Constitutionalism, South Africa, 12 December 2005).

[94] *National Human Rights Commission v State of Arunachal Pradesh* AIR 1996 SC 1234, para 20.

rights are no longer exclusively focused on state restraint, and have as much to do with increasing individual security as they have to do with protecting the rights of those who threaten harm. In another sense, this transformation is a welcome and pragmatic evolution in a world where private violence has become just as much of a core threat to individual rights as State power. Vulnerable victims deserve state protection, particularly those (women and children) where inequality threatens their life chances even more. But in another sense, the rhetoric around the right to security and duties of protection also signals the deeper and more corroding influence of security politics within human rights, humanitarian, and development discourse.

Before elaborating on this final point, a clarification: it is not the intention here to criticize all forms of protective duties whether these are derived from the right to security, or whether they are derived from other rights. There are convincing moral and analytical claims that underpin the claim that rights give rise to duties and that these may involve duties of protection towards individuals at risk from private actors or actors who are secretly working on behalf of the state.[95] There is no ambition here to refute or contest these claims. Nor is it the objective here to characterize negatively all state coercion. 'Justified coercion', in Dworkin's language,[96] is essential to the state's social functioning, to the maintenance of equality, fairness, and dignity for individuals. Equally, it is not the aim to characterize all protective duties as inevitably engaging state coercion. There are duties which are derived from rights which do not impinge on the rights of third parties, which are innately protective and can usefully be characterized as such. Duties of due diligence when it comes to the state's treatment of sexual violence, are examples of plainly protective duties. They exist on the softer end of the spectrum we are concerned with here.

But the other end of the spectrum can also give rise to concerns that call for more nuanced consideration. This is when broad undefined protective duties arising from the right to security, or other rights, invoke the sharp coercive end of the state's criminal law enforcement mechanism or military apparatus. It is the coercive sting that exists in a number of the claims to positive rights to security and to protective duties generally, with which we are concerned. The focus here is thus on state coercion directed at potential and actual perpetrators of harm which would engage restriction of their human rights and liberties. These restrictions are commonly imposed as a consequence of a duty of prevention, investigation or adequate punishment which are the consequence of a victim or potential victim's rights. As I have argued more extensively elsewhere,[97] what is not clear without further

[95] See Sandra Fredman, *Human Rights Transformed: Positive Rights and Positive Duties* (OUP 2008) 1; D Bilchitz, *Poverty and Fundamental Rights: The Justification and Enforcement of Socio-Economic Rights* (OUP 2007); A Sen, *Development as Freedom* (OUP 1999).

[96] R Dworkin, *Law's Empire* (Harvard University Press 1986).

[97] Lazarus, 'Positive Obligations' (n 4).

consideration, however, is how these duties ought to be framed, or how they are to be implemented where they conflict with the basic rights of others.

Into this opaque mix comes the politically compelling assertion that the right to security is the fundamental right upon which all others rest. The claim arises not only from hawkish politicians with oppressive motives. It is embedded in a language of human security used pervasively across the human rights and development world, and it comes also with the credentials of philosophical reasoning. Notwithstanding Shue's good intentions, the potential for the state's coercive overreach to be justified in human rights terms, is shaped by the contemporary environment in which the right to security and protective duties are articulated. States seeking to legitimate extensive security measures can and do draw on the right to security and protective duties in their rhetorical justifications of coercive interventions.

As I have argued elsewhere,[98] the claim that the right to security constitutes the meta-right upon which all others rest, and that the realization of rights depends on the state achieving a level of physical security for all, risks securitizing rights as a whole. Instead of grounding rights in non-instrumental values such as dignity, equality, and liberty, rights here are made conditional upon the fact of security's attainment. When politicians argue, as they have, that 'the right to security, to the protection of life and liberty, is and should be the basic right on which all others are based', they are arguing for a subtle reordering of the value of liberty relative to security. They are securitizing all rights by recasting them as derived from the basic security prerequisite. But liberty means something very different to security and the avoidance of risk. If it is seen as the subset of the right to security, then it becomes a lot less adventurous. Liberty may even mean the right to take risks.

Waldron alerts us to the danger that focusing on the precondition of security to the exercise of all rights might steer us away from the meaningful enjoyment of other rights. Because security is a 'voracious ideal',[99] we might skew the balance between security and other important rights in damaging ways. Moreover, without a specific and distinctive conception of the right to security—one which has meaningful content and limits—we do not know what it is we are balancing. What we do know is that the amorphous right to security can be used to legitimate measures in political rhetoric that threaten the other rights that security is meant to be 'securing'. Unless we delimit the scope of the right to security in political discourse, and delimit its status relative to other rights, other human rights which security is meant to be serving will come under threat. The threat is particularly acute because of the right to security's intricate relationship with inscrutable claims of future risks. In order for the state to protect the positive right to security it must pre-empt

[98] Lazarus, 2015.

[99] J Waldron, 'Security as a Basic Right (after 9/11)' in *Torture, Terror and Trade-Offs: Philosophy for the White House* (OUP 2010) 177.

and prevent these risks to individuals. But how much risk must we prevent in order to guarantee the right to security? And how much risk can we live with before we can say that other rights are secure?

V. Human Rights and Tolerable Insecurity

While domestic constitutional conditions may vary, it is clear from this survey of jurisprudence that human rights in international law and a broad range of national jurisdictions are just as concerned with the attainment of security as they are with state limitation. Nevertheless, while human rights are not inevitably about state limitation, their implementation by human rights institutions demonstrate a nuanced awareness of the balance between the state's protective function and its duties of restraint. It is inside these decisions that we might find important guidance on the search for what I want to term *tolerable insecurity*.

The political discourse of security's increasing influence on human rights discourse needs countering. It is essential to establish a political language which can encompass, and even celebrate, a notion of tolerable insecurity or *tolerable risk* into our public conception of human rights. A conception which does not seek to place human rights at the service of security, but one which makes and celebrates the unavoidable link between risk and freedom. Elsewhere, I have argued that we ought to engage with the thought device of a *right to insecurity*.[100] Such a right could be used to emphasize the importance of a life of self-creation, the value of unknowns and surprises, the importance of improvization and innovation, and, most importantly, of freedom. My argument was premised on the idea that if we are to live in a society, where the right to security becomes the meta-right through which we justify our claims to all other social values, we will, inevitably undermine our freedom. The point, is 'with freedom comes risk and insecurity, it is a necessary concomitant of the liberal society'.[101]

The thought device of the right to insecurity was deliberately designed to provoke a discussion about the way in which human rights rhetoric is increasingly becoming securitized. But as a basis for policy, however, we need to move beyond rhetorical flourish, or analytical debate, and establish concrete guidance about the kind of risks and insecurities we can tolerate in a human rights order. In this endeavour, we can learn from the way in which courts are shaping the right to security and protective duties more generally. Locating the shape of tolerable insecurity, objectively understood, is in essence what courts are having to do when they confront the concrete questions of the state's protective obligations arising from

[100] L Lazarus, 'Inspecting the Tail of the Dog' in M McCarthy (ed), *Incarceration and Human Rights* (Manchester University Press 2010).
[101] Lazarus, 'Inspecting the Tail of the Dog', 2010.

human rights. The strongest judicial decisions are those which directly confront, and intelligently balance, the potential conflict between negative rights protections and the protective duties of the state, and which are clear about keeping the duty to protect in a broader perspective, by instituting requirements of causality and reasonableness.

This kind of reasoning is present in the language of *Osman*, *Metrorail*, the German Aviation decision, and in *Velsquez Rodriguez* to name a few. It is also evident in the bounded conception of the right to security issued by the UN Human Rights Committee. It is not open to these institutions to shy away from the inevitable balance that has to be struck between security and rights. They are clear that the state cannot reasonably be expected to secure all of us at all times, and that in this pursuit they cannot simply turn off the rights of those who pose a threat of harm. The challenge now is for this delimited, balanced, and reasonable conception to travel across to political and policy-based arguments, which often displace nuanced arguments of balance.

While many in the human rights world are leveraging security to advance the fight for key basic rights such as the right to food (now recast as food security) or the right to health (now recast as health security), the temptation to exploit the language of security needs resisting. Insecurity, the concomitant of liberty, is a permanent and enduring state of democratic and free societies. The realistic question is how much insecurity liberalism can tolerate before losing its fundamental character. Security and law and order politics, earlier peddled by Donald Trump in his attempt to 'replace randomness with purpose' and 'chaos with peace',[102] is ultimately self-defeating. It exists on a continuous promise of security to an electorate whose perception of insecurity it fuels and exploits. It is a politics premised on the anxiety of its supporters. No matter how skilfully and manipulatively it is deployed, and Trump is following a long line of politicians here, this kind of politics is pursuing a goal of security incompatible with liberal values. Of course it may be possible to build walls, take away all freedoms, and oppress people enough to minimize insecurity to miniscule dimensions, but that is not what liberal democratic societies do. Aharon Barak, former President of the Israel Supreme Court, understood this more than most:

> Terrorism plagues many countries. The United States realized its devastating power on September 11, 2001. Other countries, such as Israel, have suffered from terrorism for a long time. While terrorism poses difficult questions for every country, it poses especially challenging questions for democratic countries, because not every effective means is a legal means. I discussed this in one

[102] Foreign policy speech <http://time.com/4309786/read-donald-trumps-america-first-foreign-policy-speech/>.

case, in which our Court held that violent interrogation of a suspected terrorist is not lawful, even if doing so may save human life by preventing impending terrorist act. We are aware that this decision does not make it easier to deal with that reality. This is the fate of democracy, as not all means are acceptable to it, and not all methods employed by its enemies are open to it. Sometimes, a democracy must fight with one hand tied behind its back. Nonetheless, it has the upper hand. Preserving the rule of law and recognition of individual liberties constitute an important component of its understanding of security. At the end of the day, they strengthen its spirit and strength and allow it to overcome its difficulties.[103]

VI. Conclusion

There is much to be gained from the judicial approaches to protective duties in the formation of policy language around security and rights, certainly as a framework for identifying tolerable risk and insecurity. But we can go further. First, we must dispute the claim that the right to security is the right of rights, a project I have undertaken in greater depth elsewhere.[104] Second, we must contest the politics of security and its alliance with human rights discourse, to challenge overblown claims of the security the State is capable of delivering, and to call for realistic and respectful assessments of risk and insecurity in political discourse. We need also to acknowledge that 'security is not an all-or-nothing matter, but a matter of more or less',[105] and ultimately that it is also possible, if undesirable, to enjoy other human rights in conditions of compromised security. We ought at the very least to argue for restraint in the deployment of rhetoric around the right to security. If there is to be such a right, we must find a way to distinguish it sharply from the right to be secure.

Shue argues that the right to security, as a precondition to all other rights, is in essence the right to secure rights. But it is essential to keep the right in its place, to make it less easily exploited as a basis for the state's coercive overreach. The right to security should be distinct from the other rights it is supposed to protect. It shouldn't securitize other rights: if security constitutes such an essential element of all other rights, then let us secure those rights in the first instance, instead of deploying the language of security to arrive at their protection. The right to security, and other protective duties, needs to be specific: these rights should correlate to reasonable and well balanced expectations of what citizens can expect

[103] (HC 5100/94, Pub. Comm. Against Torture in Isr. v. Gov't of Israel, 53(4) PD 817, 845.) A Barak (2002–03) 'A Judge on Judging—The Role of the Supreme Court in A Democracy', 116 Harvard Law Review 148.

[104] See my own attempts at Lazarus, 2015.

[105] Waldron, 2010, 177.

from state actors. Finally, a non-instrumental and value based language of rights, of equality, dignity, and liberty needs to be placed front and centre in human rights discourse. We must resist the temptation to leverage security for the protection of rights. Instead, we need to celebrate our freedom and the understand the risks that come with it.

7

The Right to Life and the International Law Framework Regulating the Use of Armed Drones

Christof Heyns, Dapo Akande, Lawrence Hill-Cawthorne, and Thompson Chengeta

I. Introduction

States have and will continue to develop new methods of employing lethal force. On the horizon, for example, are developments in autonomous robotic systems[1] and nano- and biotechnology,[2] which raise a plethora of complex issues that the international community must address in coordinated ways. Armed drones (or 'unmanned aerial vehicles', or UAVs, fitted with weapons), called here merely 'drones', have moved from the horizon into the realm of the known. The attraction of drones is clear; in particular, they provide a strategic advantage of the deployment of deadly force against a remote target without exposing one's own forces to risks.

During the past decade or so, many states have become increasingly reliant on unmanned systems and in particular drones to deliver force in the context of military operations.[3] By the end of 2013, the United States, for example, had

[1] UNHRC 'Report of the Special Rapporteur on Extrajudicial, Summary or Arbitrary Executions, Christof Heyns' (9 April 2013) A/HRC/23/47 < https://www.ohchr.org/Documents/HRBodies/HRCouncil/RegularSession/Session23/A-HRC-23-47_en.pdf accessed 26 November 2019> (hereafter Heyns Report).

[2] See Frank Simonis and Steven Schilthuizen, *Nanotechnology: Innovation Opportunities for Tomorrow's Defence* (TNO Science and Industry 2006).

[3] Peter Singer, *Wired for War* (Penguin 2009); Paul Rogers, *Unmanned Air Systems: The Future of Air & Sea Power?* (Institut Français des Relations Internationales 2014); Jeremiah Gertler, *US Unmanned Aerial Systems* (Congressional Research Service 2012) 3; US Department of Defense, 'Unmanned Systems Integrated Roadmap', FY2013-2038 (2013) 19, < https://dod.defense.gov/Portals/1/Documents/pubs/DOD-USRM-2013.pdf accessed 26 November 2019> . See Rob O'Gormann and Chris Abbott, 'Remote Control War: Unmanned Combat Air Vehicles in China, India, Israel, Iran, Russia and Turkey' (Open Briefing, London 2013) < https://www.files.ethz.ch/isn/170021/Remote-Control-War.pdf > accessed 26 November 2019; Shashank Joshi and Aaron Stein, 'Emerging Drone Nations' (2013) 55 Survival 53; Guy Taylor, 'US Intelligence Warily Watches for Threats to US Now That 87 Nations Possess Drones' *Washington Times* (10 November 2013) <http://www.washingtontimes.com/news/2013/nov/10/skys-the-limit-for-wide-wild-world-of-drones/?page=all> accessed 13 August 2019.

Christof Heyns, Dapo Akande, Lawrence Hill-Cawthorne, and Thompson Chengeta, *The Right to Life and the International Law Framework Regulating the Use of Armed Drones* In: Human Rights and 21st Century Challenges. Edited by: Dapo Akande, Jaakko Kuosmanen, Helen McDermott, and Dominic Roser, Published by Oxford University Press 2020.

DOI: 10.1093/oso/9780198824770.003.0008

over 20,000 unmanned systems.[4] Drones have not only been used by the United Kingdom, the United States, Israel, and the North Atlantic Treaty Organization (NATO) in operations outside their territory (in Afghanistan, Pakistan, Yemen, Libya, Iraq, Somalia, Gaza, and Syria), they have also been used by Pakistan, Iraq, and Nigeria within their own territory.[5] In Pakistan, for example, it was reported that between 2004 and 2014, a minimum of 2,300 people were killed by US drone strikes.[6] Of that number, 420 have been identified as civilians, amongst which were approximately 150 children.[7] In Yemen, at least 300 people have been killed to date, amongst them a minimum of 30 civilians.[8]

In spite of concerns that have been raised about them, drones are clearly here to stay. Indeed, it might even be said that unmanned systems, including drones, are the future of warfare. There is broad agreement that drones *per se* are not illegal weapons, in the sense of possessing characteristics that necessarily violate rules of international law.[9] However, despite the fact that drones are now an established technology, there is, in some respects, a lack of consensus on how to apply to drones the various rules of international law that regulate the use of lethal force, notably the *jus ad bellum*, international humanitarian law (IHL), and international human rights law (IHRL). It is the aim of this chapter to contribute toward clarifying the application of these different rules to drone warfare. In particular, this chapter will explore a number of contested issues that arise in these three areas of international law and the implications of these controversies for the regulation of armed drones.

Drones can be expected to become increasingly sophisticated and smaller in form, as well as become cheaper and therefore more accessible. In addition, the technological skills needed to operate these systems are becoming readily available in different parts of the world. Drones are likely to form part of the arsenals of an increasing number of states that may be able to deploy such weapons across international borders in relatively non-intrusive ways, both on traditional 'battlefields' and for the purposes of pursuing targets far removed from what would traditionally be seen as the 'zone of hostilities'. Some states may also wish to use

[4] See Peter Singer, 'The Predator Comes Home: A Primer on Domestic Drones, their Huge Business Opportunities, and their Deep Political, Moral, and Legal Challenges' (Brookings Institution, 8 March 2013) <http://www.brookings.edu/research/papers/2013/03/08-drones-singer> accessed 13 August 2019; US Department of Defense, 'Task Force Report: The Role of Autonomy in DoD Systems' (Defense Science Board, July 2012) 78 <https://fas.org/irp/agency/dod/dsb/autonomy.pdf> accessed 13 August 2019.

[5] See UNGA 'Report of the Special Rapporteur on the Promotion and Protection of Human Rights and Fundamental Freedoms While Countering Terrorism' (18 September 2013) UN Doc A/68/389, paras 25–40 and Clay Dillow, 'All of These Countries Now Have Armed Drones' *Fortune* (12 February 2016) < https://fortune.com/2016/02/12/these-countries-have-armed-drones/ > accessed 13 August 2019.

[6] The Bureau, 'Covert Drone War' (*The Bureau of Investigative Journalism,* 2014) <http://www.thebureauinvestigates.com/category/projects/drones/> accessed 26 November 2019.

[7] Ibid.

[8] Ibid.

[9] This is not the case, for example, with lethal autonomous robots. See Heyns Report (n 1).

armed drones in domestic law enforcement contexts, such as for border patrols, operations against organized crime, and crowd control in demonstrations. Armed drones are also reportedly already within the arsenal of some non-state actors. In sum, the number of states and actors with the capacity to use drones is likely to increase significantly in the near future, underscoring the need for greater consensus on the terms of their use.

One of the most important consequences of the expanding use of drones is that targeted killing across borders appears to be easier than in the past. This creates the potential for undermining the role that state sovereignty, irrespective of the controversies that admittedly surrounds this concept, plays in sustaining the international security system. Indeed, the ready availability of drones may lead to situations where states that perceive their interests to be threatened increasingly engage in low-intensity but drawn-out applications of force that know few geographical or temporal boundaries.

This would run counter to the notion that war—and the transnational use of force in general—is an exceptional situation of limited duration and scope, and that there should be a time for healing and recovery following conflict. An approach in terms of which peacetime is the exception, and armed conflict the norm, could have far-reaching consequences for the protection of the right to life. The laws specifically designed for wartime, IHL, offer less protection of life than does the default regime of IHRL, precisely because war is seen as an exception.[10] To the extent that war becomes the norm, the lower level of protection of life offered by IHL risks becoming seen as the default regime.

II. The Applicable Legal Frameworks and the Relationship Between Them

A number of substantive areas of international law have a direct bearing on the legality of the use of armed drones. The two most directly relevant to the protection of the right to life are IHL and IHRL. Each of these regimes balances, albeit to different degrees, state security concerns on the one hand and the protection of individuals (including the protection of life) on the other. The third area of international law of particular importance to the use of drones is the law governing the use of force by one state on another state's territory (*jus ad bellum*). These *ad bellum* rules form the cornerstone of the international security system and will determine the legality of the inter-state use of armed drones.

The law on the inter-state use of force serves in the first place to protect state sovereignty, but in doing so it also serves to protect individuals. Indeed, one might

[10] Lawrence Hill-Cawthorne (2014) 'The Role of Necessity in International Humanitarian and Human Rights Law' 47 Israel Law Review 225.

think of the *jus ad bellum* as an outer layer of protection of the right to life. The protection of state sovereignty and of territorial integrity—which in other ways often presents a barrier to the protection of human rights—can, in this sense, constitute an important component of the protection of individuals against lethal force, especially with the advent of armed drones, by containing the spread and intensity of armed conflicts. IHL and IHRL, by contrast, speak not to the inter-state use of force, but rather the specific features of a particular drone strike, such as how it is carried out, against whom it is carried out, and the consequences that follow. These differences notwithstanding, all three areas are closely related when discussing the use of lethal force across borders, and both international security and the protection of the right to life depend on the principle that the use of force is a matter of last resort.

In order to examine the legality of a particular drone strike under international law, a holistic approach is therefore needed. For a particular drone strike to be lawful under international law, it must satisfy the legal requirements under *all* applicable international legal regimes.[11] Although a particular drone strike may satisfy the requirements of the *jus ad bellum*, it may still be inconsistent with applicable rules of IHL and IHRL, and thus unlawful under international law. And the opposite may also be true: whereas a drone strike by a state may appear to comply with applicable rules of IHL and IHRL, if it does not satisfy the conditions for lawful force under the *jus ad bellum*, it will constitute an unlawful act under international law, entailing the responsibility of the state.

The importance of taking an holistic approach here is well illustrated by the example of an action by a state taken in self-defence. As discussed in more detail shortly, a valid claim to be acting in self-defence under Article 51 of the UN Charter, in response to an armed attack, may justify a use of armed force in another state's territory. However, a valid claim by a state to act in self-defence for the purposes of Article 51 is *irrelevant* to that state's compliance with those rules of IHL and IHRL that help to protect the right to life of those being targeted. Nor, as a matter of the secondary rules of state responsibility, can a valid claim to act in self-defence preclude the wrongfulness of conduct which otherwise violates applicable rules under IHL or IHRL.[12] This position has been articulated clearly by the International Law Commission (ILC) in its commentary to the Articles on the Responsibility of States for Wrongful Acts. Although Article 21 of those Articles stipulates that lawful measures in self-defence will preclude the wrongfulness of an act, the ILC emphasized that:

[11] Kevin Heller (2013) 'One Hell of a Killing Machine, Signature Strikes and International Law' 11 Journal of International Criminal Justice 89, 91 (hereafter Heller, 'One Hell of a Killing Machine'); Nils Melzer, *Targeted Killing in International Law* (OUP 2009) 51–52 (hereafter Melzer, *Targeted Killing*).

[12] Marko Milanovic, 'Drones and Targeted Killing: Can Self-Defense Preclude their Wrongfulness?' (EJIL: Talk!, 10 January 2010) <http://www.ejiltalk.org/drones-and-targeted-killings-can-self-defense-preclude-their-wrongfulness/> accessed 13 August 2019.

> This is not to say that self-defence precludes the wrongfulness of conduct in all cases or with respect to all obligations. Examples relate to international humanitarian law and human rights obligations... As to obligations under international humanitarian law and in relation to non-derogable human rights provisions, self-defence does not preclude the wrongfulness of conduct.[13]

Similarly, while the consent of a state on whose territory force is used can justify what would otherwise be regarded as an infringement of territorial integrity by the state using force, such consent will not be relevant to the compliance of either state with any applicable rules of IHRL and IHL. The obligations of states under IHRL[14] and IHL[15] are not owed on a bilateral, reciprocal basis, but rather to each and every state party to the relevant treaty, and, for those treaty rules that co-exist under customary international law, to all states. In addition, IHRL and (some) IHL obligations are owed directly to individuals entitled to protection under these legal regimes. This nature of IHRL and IHL obligations means that one state cannot consent to another state violating the rights owed to individuals.[16] Acts which violate these rights violate also the obligations owed to every other state party to the particular treaty (or to every other state in the case of obligations arising under customary international law) and the rights of individuals protected by the rules of IHRL.[17]

[13] On the non-availability of self-defence as a circumstance precluding wrongfulness for breaches of IHL and IHRL, see International Law Commission (ILC), Commentary to art 21, Articles on Responsibility of States for Wrongful Acts (2001) UNYBILC vol II, Pt Two; and James Crawford, *The International Law Commission's Articles on State Responsibility: Introduction, Text and Commentaries* (CUP 2002) 166 (hereafter Crawford, *State Responsibility*).

[14] *Questions Relating to the Obligation to Prosecute or Extradite (Belgium v Senegal)* [2012] ICJ Rep 422, para 68.

[15] The *erga omnes* nature of IHL can be seen in arts 1 of the 1949 Geneva Conventions and of Additional Protocol I of 1977 which impose on states an obligation not only to respect these treaties to but 'ensure respect' of the treaties. The 2016 ICRC Commentaries to art 1 of Geneva Conventions states that: 'The interests protected by the Conventions are of such fundamental importance to the human person that every High Contracting Party has a legal interest in their observance, wherever a conflict may take place and whoever its victims may be... The Conventions thus create obligations *erga omnes partes*, i.e. obligations towards all of the other High Contracting Parties.' Paragraph 119 of the ICRC Commentary to art 1 of Additional Protocol I also states that: 'the [Diplomatic] Conference clearly demonstrated that humanitarian law creates for each State obligations towards the international community as a whole ("*erga omnes*"); in view of the importance of the rights concerned, each State can be considered to have a legal interest in the protection of such rights' (para 45). The ICRC Commentaries are available at: <http://www.icrc.org/applic/ihl/ihl.nsf/Comment.xsp?viewComments=LookUpCOMART&articleUNID=6C86520D7EFAD527C12563CD0051D63C> accessed 13 August 2019.

[16] Similarly, the *erga omnes* nature of these obligations means countermeasures may not preclude wrongfulness for breaches of obligations under IHL and IHRL. See eg Silvia Borelli and Simon Olleson, 'Obligations Relating to Human Rights and Humanitarian Law' in James Crawford, Alain Pellet, and Simon Olleson (eds), *The Law of International Responsibility* (OUP 2010) 1177–96

[17] The ILC has made it clear that: 'In circumstances where the consent of a number of States is required, the consent of one State will not preclude wrongfulness in relation to another': ILC Commentary to art 20, Articles on Responsibility of States for Wrongful Acts (2001) UNYBILC vol II, Pt Two, paras 9 and 10.

Each of the legal regimes explored in this article is therefore relevant to a different aspect of the use of drones, and each must be considered separately. In seeking to contribute towards greater clarity, and at least to take stock of the applicable legal framework as a whole, each of the three international legal regimes identified as relevant to the use of drones will be explored in turn.

III. The Law Relating to the Use of Force on Foreign Territory

We will begin by examining the law governing the inter-state use of force, the *jus ad bellum*, and its relevance for the employment of armed drones. The use by one state of drones to target individuals located in another state must in the first place comply with the rules on the inter-state use of force. While IHL and IHRL speak more directly to protection of the individuals affected by a drone strike, the law on the use of inter-state force focuses on state sovereignty; it serves primarily to protect the legal rights of states. This includes the right and interest of the state to have the lives of its citizens and inhabitants protected from acts of aggression. As was stated earlier, it can thus indirectly serve to protect life by containing the geographical spread of conflict.

Article 2(4) of the UN Charter and customary international law prohibit the threat or use of inter-state force. A state may, however, consent to the use of force on its territory by another state, with the result that Article 2(4) will not be engaged. Where no consent is given, the UN Charter gives two exceptions to the Article 2(4) prohibition: where action is taken lawfully in self-defence under Article 51 and where the Security Council authorizes enforcement action under Chapter VII of the UN Charter. Given that it is in these areas that many controversies especially arise, consent and self-defence will be considered in turn for their relevance to the use of drones by states abroad.

A. Consent

Where a territorial state consents to another state targeting non-state actors on the former's territory with drones, no issue in principle should arise under the *jus ad bellum*, for Article 2(4) of the UN Charter will not have been violated.[18] Indeed,

[18] It has been suggested that a state cannot invite another state to assist it in a civil war, such that where the domestic situation is so severe, the *de jure* government would not be able to consent to force being used on its territory by another state: see Christine Gray, *International Law and the Use of Force* (OUP 2008) 81 (hereafter Gray, *International Law*). However, this rule is supposedly derived not from the prohibition of the use of force but rather from the principle of non-intervention or perhaps the right of self-determination. In any event, it is not clear that there is sufficient state practice and *opinio juris* for such a limitation of the consent principle to be regarded as a part of international law: see Yoram Dinstein, *War, Aggression and Self-Defence* (CUP 2011) 119; Dapo Akande and Zachery Vermeer, 'The Airstrikes

consent has been given by Pakistan, Yemen, and Somalia which has then been relied upon by the United States to justify the use of drones in those territories; regarding Pakistan, this consent was subsequently withdrawn, whereas regarding Yemen and Somalia, though consent has not been withdrawn, the authority of those governments might call the validity of that consent into question.[19]

While consent would seem a simple test that would result in a particular drone strike in foreign territory being consistent with the *jus ad bellum*, in practice there are issues of considerable difficulty surrounding consent, including who may give consent, whether consent must be given publicly and explicitly or could instead be implicit, and when consent could be considered to have been vitiated by coercion.[20]

With regard to who may give consent, the fundamental nature of the prohibition of the use of force for state sovereignty means that only the state's highest authorities may validly give consent—that is, have the *authority* to give consent—to a use of force.[21] One cannot simply rely on the notion of attribution under the secondary rules on state responsibility by analogy. Although the acts of all government officials, acting in that capacity, are attributable to the government, not all parts of the government are entitled to give consent with respect to the use of force. In particular, it is not sufficient to obtain consent from regional authorities or from particular agencies or departments of government. The International Law Commission has made it clear that:

> [w]hether a particular person or entity had the authority to grant consent in a given case is a separate question from whether the conduct of that person or entity was attributable to the State ... For example, the issue has arisen whether consent expressed by a regional authority could legitimize the sending of foreign troops into the territory of a State, or whether such consent could only be given by the central Government, and such questions are not resolved by saying that the acts of the regional authority are attributable to the State[22]

against Islamic State in Iraq and the Alleged Prohibition on Military Assistance to Governments in Civil Wars' (EJIL: Talk!, 2 February 2015); and Raphael Van Steenberghe, 'The Alleged Prohibition on Intervening in Civil Wars is Still Alive after the Airstrikes against the Islamic State in Iraq: A Response to Dapo Akande and Zachary Vermeer' (EJIL: Talk!, 12 February 2015).

[19] Max Byrne (2016) 'Consent and the Use of Force: An Examination of "Intervention by Invitation" as a Basis for US Drone Strikes in Pakistan, Somalia and Yemen' 3 Journal on the Use of Force and International Law 97.

[20] The controversies surrounding the issue of consent more generally are discussed in Crawford, *State Responsibility* (n 13) 163–65.

[21] See Oliver Corten, *The Law Against War: The Prohibition on the Use of Force in Contemporary International Law* (Hart 2010) 259 (hereafter Corten, *The Law Against War*): 'In the case of a military operation, no one contests that only the highest authorities of the State are able to issue such consent validly. It is only on this condition that it can be claimed that a use of force is not directed against the State's independence and so does not violate article 2(4).'

[22] See ILC Commentary to art 20, Articles on Responsibility of States for Wrongful Acts (2001) UNYBILC vol II, Pt Two, para 5.

The answer to the question of which domestic authority is entitled to give consent to what would otherwise constitute a violation of international law depends on the interplay between international and domestic law. In the first place, one needs to consider the nature of the international rule in question and the manner in which that rule is generally applied.[23] As already stated, the importance of the prohibition on the use of force suggests that consent to a departure from this rule will usually need to be established at the highest levels of government. Second, one will need to consider the domestic arrangements made with respect to the matter at hand.[24] Where domestic law or domestic constitutional arrangements are such as to give responsibility on these issues to lower level officials this may be taken into account.

However, it would be natural that where there is a difference of view between the highest authorities in government and lower-level officials, it is the view of the higher-level officials that should be taken as determinative. This arises in part because international law itself assumes that certain organs of government have the capacity to represent the state in international affairs. Thus, the Head of State, Head of Government, and the Foreign Minister are presumed, as a matter of international law, to have plenary competence to conclude treaties on behalf of the state.[25] In addition, these senior government officials are accorded immunity *ratione personae* from the jurisdiction of other states because of their privileged position in conducting international relations on behalf of the state.[26] Thus, it can be assumed that it is the view of these officials, where expressed, that should be determinative of whether the state gives consent or not to the use of force on the state's territory. Importantly, the view that consent to the use of force must be given by the highest authorities in the central government of a state accords with the bulk of international practice.[27]

Regarding the issue of publicity and consent, while there does not appear to be a requirement that consent be made public, it must nevertheless be clear as between the states concerned that consent is being given to the use of force, and the

[23] The ILC has stated that: 'Who has authority to consent to a departure from a particular rule may depend on the rule. It is one thing to consent to a search of embassy premises, another to the establishment of a military base on the territory of a State. Different officials or agencies may have authority in different contexts, in accordance with the arrangements made by each State and general principles of actual and ostensible authority': Ibid, para 6.

[24] It has also been argued that where a state's actions on another's state's territory are consented to by the latter, the former should inquire into whether this consent complies with the latter's domestic law: Ashley Deeks (2013) 'Consent to the Use of Force and International Law Supremacy' 54 Harvard International Law Journal 1.

[25] Vienna Convention on the Law of Treaties (opened for signature 23 May 1969, entered into force 27 January 1980) 1155 UNTS 331 (VCLT) art 7.

[26] *Arrest Warrant of 11 April 2000 (DRC v Belgium)* [2002] ICJ Rep 3, paras 53–55; Dapo Akande and Sangeeta Shah (2010) 'Immunities of State Officials, International Crimes and Foreign Domestic Courts' 21 European Journal of International Law 815, 818ff.

[27] Corten, *The Law Against War* (n 21) 266: 'In respect of all the precedents just examined, it appears clearly that, to be validly given, consent to external intervention must have been given by the highest authorities of the State such as the Prime Minister, the President or the Government as a whole.'

parameters of that consent should also be made clear. Consent must be given in advance.[28] Moreover:

> Certain modalities need to be observed for consent to be considered valid. Consent must be freely given and clearly established. It must be actually expressed by the State rather than merely presumed on the basis that the State would have consented if it had been asked. Consent may be vitiated by error, fraud, corruption or coercion. In this respect, the principles concerning the validity of consent to treaties provide relevant guidance.[29]

Consent on so serious a matter as the use of force is not to be implied. Furthermore, where force exceeds the limits of the consent given, that force will be a violation of Article 2(4).[30] In addition, once consent to the use of force is withdrawn, the state conducting targeting operations is bound by international law to refrain from conducting any further operations from that moment onwards (unless there is a separate justification for using force).[31]

B. Self-Defence

Where no consent is given, Article 2(4) will be engaged by a drone strike on another state's territory, requiring resort to one of two exceptions to the prohibition contained in the UN Charter. The most common exception invoked by states using drones in these situations is self-defence.[32] International law poses stringent conditions on the use of force in self-defence. Under Article 51 of the UN Charter and customary international law, a state may invoke self-defence to justify its use of force to target individuals on another state's territory where an armed attack against it occurs or is imminent (on which see later). The International Court of

[28] 'Consent to the commission of otherwise wrongful conduct may be given by a State in advance or even at the time it is occurring. By contrast, cases of consent given after the conduct has occurred are a form of waiver or acquiescence, leading to loss of the right to invoke responsibility': ILC Commentary to art 20, Articles on Responsibility of States for Wrongful Acts (2001) UNYBILC vol II, Pt Two.

[29] See Ibid, para 6.

[30] Ibid, para 9: 'where consent is relied on ... it will be necessary to show that the conduct fell within the limits of the consent'.

[31] See *Case Concerning Armed Activities on the Territory of the Congo (Democratic Republic of the Congo v Uganda)* [2005] ICJ Rep 168, para 105 (hereafter *DRC v Uganda)*, where the ICJ took the view that Ugandan presence in the DRC was unlawful from the moment when consent was withdrawn (despite an agreement setting out modalities for withdrawal).

[32] The United States and the United Kingdom, for example, rely on self-defence: US Department of Justice White Paper, 'Lawfulness of a Lethal Operation Directed Against a US Citizen Who is a Senior Operational Leader of Al-Qa'ida or an Associated Force' (made public 5 February 2013) (hereafter US Department of Justice White Paper) <https://fas.org/irp/eprint/doj-lethal.pdf > ; Ewen MacAskill, 'Drone Killing of British Citizens in Syria Marks Major Departure for UK' *Guardian* (7 September 2015) (hereafter MacAskill, 'Drone Killing').

Justice (ICJ) has confirmed that, for an attack to constitute an 'armed attack' and thus enable the state's right to use force in self-defence, the scale and effects of the attack must reach a certain threshold of gravity.[33] Thus, not any use of force against a state will necessarily justify a response in self-defence; rather, only grave uses of force can do so.

In addition to the requirement of an armed attack, the state claiming to be acting in self-defence must also satisfy the dual requirements of necessity and proportionality, grounded in customary international law.[34] These requirements, as defined in the context of the *jus ad bellum*, are closely linked to the important issue of the *aim* of an act of self-defence. Thus, 'necessity and proportionality mean that self-defence must not be retaliatory or punitive; the aim should be to halt and repel an attack'.[35] In other words, action taken lawfully in self-defence (eg the use of drones to target individuals in another state's territory) must serve the purpose of halting and repelling an armed attack and must be both necessary and proportionate to this end.[36] Action taken after an armed attack has ended, and which in reality seeks to retaliate against that armed attack, would not constitute a lawful exercise of self-defence, but rather an armed reprisal in violation of Article 2(4) of the UN Charter.[37] In considering the elements relevant to determining whether a particular action is necessary and proportionate to the aim of self-defence, the ICJ in the *Oil Platforms* case placed emphasis on the nature of the objects targeted by the United States and their role in staging any initial armed attacks.[38]

The requirements of necessity and proportionality also help to define the limits of the right to self-defence. The right persists only for so long as it is necessary to halt or repel an armed attack and must be proportionate to that aim. However, that

[33] *Case Concerning Military and Paramilitary Activities In and Against Nicaragua (Nicaragua v United States)* [1986] ICJ Rep 14, para 191 (hereafter *Nicaragua v United States*); *Case Concerning Oil Platforms (Iran v United States)* [2003] ICJ Rep 161, paras 51, 62 (hereafter *Iran v United States*).

[34] The ICJ has on numerous occasions highlighted the need for a response to an armed attack to be necessary and proportionate for that to constitute lawful self-defence: see *Nicaragua v United States* (n 33) para 194; *Legality of the Threat or Use of Nuclear Weapons*, Advisory Opinion [1996] IC Rep 226, para 41 (hereafter *Legality of the Threat or Use of Nuclear Weapons*); *Iran v United States* (n 33) para 74; *DRC v Uganda* (n 31) para 147.

[35] Gray, *International Law* (n 18) 150; see also Albrecht Randelzhofer, 'Article 51' in Bruno Simma, Daniel-Erasmus Khan, Georg Nolte, and Andreas Paulus (eds), *The Charter of the United Nations: A Commentary* (3rd edn, OUP 2012) (hereafter Randelzhofer, 'Article 51'); Dapo Akande and Thomas Liefländer (2013) 'Clarifying Necessity, Imminence, and Proportionality in the Law of Self-Defense' 107 American Journal of International Law 563, 569.

[36] The manner in which the requirements of necessity and proportionality have been invoked by the ICJ confirms this interpretation of the purpose of lawful self-defence: see eg *Nicaragua v United States* (n 33) para 237 (holding that US actions in and against Nicaragua were not necessary as the threat to the Salvadorian government had already been curbed by other means); *Iran v United States* (n 33) para 76 (holding that the US attacks against Iranian oil platforms were not necessary to respond to the attacks against US ships); see also *Legality of the Threat or Use of Nuclear Weapons* (n 34), Dissenting Opinion of Judge Higgins, para 5 ('the concept of proportionality referred to was that which was proportionate to repelling the attack, and not a requirement of symmetry between the mode of the initial attack and the mode of response').

[37] *Iran v United States* (n 33) Dissenting Opinion of Judge Elaraby, para 1.2.

[38] *Iran v United States* (n 33).

is not to say that, in determining what is necessary to bring an attack to an end and what is a legitimate objective for self-defence, states are entitled to continue to act in self-defence until the absolute destruction of the enemy is achieved such that the enemy poses no long-term threats. International law cannot permit states to act until the elimination of long-term threats is secured. The law of self-defence permits responses to emergency situations in which states face immediate or imminent risks. Once the immediate or imminent threats of (continued) attack are resolved, states will need to find other methods of securing long-term peace and stability.

To permit force to be used as a means of achieving long-term security where the threat of immediate or imminent attacks has receded, is to permit perpetual warfare. Therefore, even when drones are used in self-defence, consideration needs to be given to the moment when the group against which drones are being used is sufficiently disrupted such that it no longer poses an immediate or imminent threat.

The question of 'imminence' raises a further controversial point of considerable importance to the use of armed drones abroad. Article 51 recognizes the right to self-defence where 'an armed attack occurs' but also refers to self-defence as an 'inherent' right of states. This has given rise to arguments that the right to self-defence under customary law is not displaced by the Charter. Importantly, the argument that an anticipatory attack against an imminent threat is permissible rests on this basis.[39] There is a significant debate about the legality of action in self-defence prior to an actual armed attack. However, as the Report of the High-Level Panel Established by the UN Secretary-General noted: 'Long-established customary international law makes it clear that States can take military action as long as the threatened attack is imminent, no other means would deflect it, and the action is proportionate'.[40] The United Kingdom, for example, takes the view that action in self-defence can be lawful where an armed attack is imminent.[41]

Importantly, at most, anticipatory self-defence could be lawful only in response to an existing threat. It may not be employed pre-emptively to prevent a threat from arising in the future. The necessity of self-defence, according to the well-known construction, 'must be instant, overwhelming, and leaving no choice of means, no moment of deliberation'.[42] The body of opinion and state practice that rejects the concept of anticipatory self-defence altogether should also be noted, and serves at least as a confirmation of the limited scope of the exception.[43]

[39] UNGA 'Report of the High-Level Panel Established by the UN Secretary-General' (December 2004) UN Doc A/59/565 (2004) at 188–92.

[40] Ibid.

[41] 'Attorney-General's Advice on the Iraq War, Iraq: Resolution 1441' (2005) 54 International Criminal Law Quarterly 767, 768.

[42] Letter from Mr Webster to Lord Ashburton, August 6, 1842 in RY Jennings (1938) 'Caroline and McLeod Cases' 32 American Journal of International Law 82.

[43] Gray, *International Law* (n 18) 160–1.

Finally, it must be emphasized that the imminence requirement in IHRL, which stipulates that intentional lethal force may be used only to *protect* life, is not to be conflated with the requirement of imminence in the law governing the use of force on foreign territory under Article 51. The former is a condition required for all uses of lethal force to be lawful under IHRL. The latter applies under the doctrine of anticipatory self-defence and the legality of a use of force on another state's territory under the *jus ad bellum*.[44] Meeting the requirement of imminence under one regime may not necessarily satisfy the test under the other. This is consistent with one of the key themes of the present chapter, that *separate* assessments of the legality of drone strikes under each applicable branch of international law must be undertaken.

A further controversy that must also be considered here concerns self-defence measures taken in a foreign state against non-state actors who do not act on behalf of that foreign state. This question is of particular importance given that non-state actors are currently being targeted by drones in states that do not necessarily bear responsibility for the acts of those actors.[45] Prior to 9/11, the claim that force could be used in self-defence in response to an armed attack by a non-state group whose acts were not attributable to a state was controversial at best.[46] The International Court of Justice rejected this view of the law in the *Nicaragua* case.[47]

However, state practice since the events of 11 September 2001 suggests that international law now permits such a notion of self-defence. The shift began with the near universal support for the US and UK's response in Afghanistan to the 9/11 attacks, which was based on a claim to be acting in self-defence against a non-state group operating from a state where the actions of that group could not be said to be attributable to the territorial state using ordinary rules of attribution under the law of state responsibility.[48] Indeed, following the events of 9/11, the Security Council adopted Resolutions 1368 and 1373, both of which recognized 'the inherent right of individual or collective self-defence in accordance with the Charter'.[49] This would suggest that a state may use force in self-defence on another state's territory, where that first state has been the victim of an armed attack by non-state groups operating on the latter's territory, even where that attack is not attributable to the 'host' state.

[44] Contrast the US Department of Justice White Paper (n 32).

[45] See references above at nn 3–6 for recent articles detailing drone strikes by the United Kingdom and the United States against non-state actors in a number of different countries.

[46] See discussion of pre-9/11 practice in Gray, *International Law* (n 18) 195–98.

[47] *Nicaragua v United States* (n 33) para 195.

[48] See eg the US letter to the Security Council under art of the UN Charter, in which it referred to its right to self-defence against Al Qaeda and the Taliban regime in Afghanistan that was allowing its territory to be used by Al Qaeda: UN doc S/2001/946. The same claim was made by the United Kingdom: UN Doc S/2001/947.

[49] UNSC Res 1368 (12 September 2001) S/RES/1368/2001, preambular para 3; UNSC Res 1373 (28 September 2001) S/RES/1373 (2001), preambular para 4.

In contrast, the ICJ in its *Israeli Wall* advisory opinion subsequently implied that inter-state force cannot be used in self-defence in response to an armed attack by a non-state actor:

> Article 51 of the Charter thus recognizes the existence of an inherent right of self-defence in the case of armed attack by one State against another State. However, Israel does not claim that the attacks against it are imputable to a foreign State.[50]

Nonetheless, state practice relating to the use of force abroad against non-state actors, since 2001, is now broad and extensive, and indeed it extends beyond the immediate post-9/11 context.[51] Following this practice, and despite academic controversy,[52] the law on this matter, appears to have changed.

However, even if states may, in certain circumstances, lawfully exercise self-defence in response to an armed attack against a non-state actor, this only means that the armed attack requirement can be fulfilled without attribution of the attack to a state. Other customary international law requirements would still need to be fulfilled before a state can respond with force in self-defence on the territory of another state. In particular, it must be necessary and proportionate to respond with force to an armed attack (or imminent armed attack) from a non-state actor. In the context of a use of force against a non-state group, it is suggested that the necessity condition would only be satisfied where the territorial state itself is either unable or unwilling to prevent continued attacks.[53] It is worth emphasizing that this test of whether the territorial state is unable or unwilling to act is not an independent legal standard but merely an aspect of the application of the long-standing criterion of necessity. In determining whether a state is unable or unwilling to take action, the

[50] *Legal Consequences of the Construction of a Wall in the Occupied Palestinian Territory*, Advisory Opinion [2004] ICJ Rep 136, para 139 (hereafter *Legal Consequences of the Construction of a Wall*). It is to be noted that art 51 does not, in fact, condition the notion of armed attack as emanating from a state only.

[51] For example, since 9/11 one may refer to Uganda and Rwanda's use of force in the DRC; Kenya and Ethiopia's use of force in Somalia; Russia's use of force in Georgia; Israel's use of force against Hezbollah in Lebanon; Turkey's repeated use of force in northern Iraq; Saudi Arabia's use of force in Yemen; Colombia's use of force in Ecuador; the use of force by many states in Syria against ISIS. As Christian Tams notes, '[t]he situations in which force has been used (or a corresponding right has been asserted) vary considerably, but have almost exclusively been explained as exercises in self-defence': Christian Tams (2009) 'The Use of Force against Terrorists' 20 European Journal of International Law 359, 378 (hereafter Tams 'The Use of Force against Terrorists').

[52] See generally, Tams 'The Use of Force against Terrorists' (n 51) 359; Ashley Deeks (2012) '"Unwilling or Unable": Toward a Normative Framework for Extraterritorial Self-Defense' 52 Virginia Journal of International Law 483 and Monika Hakimi (2015) 'Defensive Force against Non-State Actors: The State of Play' 91 International Law Studies 1; Noam Lubell, *Extraterritorial Use of Force Against Non-State Actors* (OUP 2010) Pt I (hereafter Lubell, *Extraterritorial Use of Force*).

[53] Kimberley Trapp (2007) 'Back to Basics: Necessity, Proportionality, and the Right of Self-Defence Against Non-State Terrorist Actors' 56 International Criminal Law Quarterly 141; Daniel Bethlehem (2012) 'Self-Defense Against an Imminent or Actual Armed Attack by NonState Actors' 106 American Journal of International Law 770, 776.

state acting in self-defence might be required to request permission for such action prior to the commencement of acts taken in self-defence.[54]

Finally, Article 51 of the UN Charter makes it clear that measures adopted by states in exercise of self-defence must be reported to the UN Security Council.[55] This can be seen as posing an obligation of transparency and justification to the international community, placing the issue formally on the agenda of the Security Council and recognizing its role. All Member States of the United Nations have an obligation under its founding treaty to submit such reports. While failure to report will not render unlawful an otherwise lawful action taken in self-defence, 'the absence of a report may be one of the factors indicating whether the State in question was itself convinced that it was acting in self-defence'.[56] According to Article 51 the right to exercise self-defence shall continue 'until the Security Council has taken measures necessary to maintain international peace and security'. This demonstrates that the end point of an action in self-defence is not only determined by the principles of necessity and proportionality, noted above, but may also be determined by the Security Council.[57]

In addition to its transparency function, it could be argued that the rationale for this reporting requirement is to contribute towards the protection of the legal rights of sovereignty by the international community, since the state using force is required to offer its justification for that use of force. By extension, it must be concluded that a state must report afresh when the material facts have changed—for example, where self-defence is used as a basis for the use of force on the territory of a new state, or where new parties are added to the conflict.

IV. International Humanitarian Law

Having considered a number of the varied issues that arise in applying the rules under the *jus ad bellum* to the use of armed drones by states, this section will now explore the second key body of international law of relevance here, that is, IHL. IHL applies only where there is a situation of either international or non-international armed conflict. As such, whether a particular drone strike is regulated by IHL will depend on whether that strike falls within the context of one of these types of armed conflict. If a drone strike does not take place in the context of an armed conflict, IHL will not apply, and the applicable rules of IHRL will continue exclusively to govern the use of lethal force. The test whether an armed conflict exists is an objective, factual one and is not determined by the subjective views as to the

[54] Ibid, Bethlehem.
[55] *Nicaragua v United States* (n 33) para 235; *DRC v Uganda* (n 31) 222,para 145.
[56] Ibid, para 200.
[57] Randelzhofer, 'Article 51' (n 35) 804.

characterization of the situation by the parties involved. This section will consider some of the key controversies in the application of IHL to drone strikes.

A. The Threshold for Non-International Armed Conflict

Where a state targets non-state actors abroad, that act may, depending on the fulfilment of other conditions, take place in the context of a non-international armed conflict,[58] and thus be governed by the rules of IHL applicable in that type of conflict. Classification of situations as international or non-international armed conflicts depends primarily on the question of who are the parties to the conflict. Conflict between states, are, according to Common Article 2 of the 1949 Geneva Conventions, international armed conflicts. Violence between a state and an organized non-state armed group, or between two or more such groups, may be a non-international armed conflict. It is generally accepted that a non-international armed conflict may take place across state boundaries, with the phrase 'non-international' referring not to the territorial scope of the conflict but to the status of the parties.[59]

Drones have thus far typically not been used in inter-state conflict. The question thus arises whether they are being used in non-international armed conflicts (NIACs). For violence to amount to a non-international armed conflict there must be 'protracted armed violence between governmental authorities and organized armed groups or between such groups within a State'.[60] Two cumulative criteria must thus be satisfied in order for a particular situation to be classified as a non-international armed conflict to which IHL would apply. These two criteria relate to: 'the intensity of the conflict and the organisation of the parties to the conflict'.[61] Thus, an armed group will only be considered to constitute a party to an NIAC if it is sufficiently organized. International jurisprudence has determined the relevant indicative criteria, which include, *inter alia*, the existence of a command structure, headquarters, and a group's ability to plan and carry out military operations.[62]

[58] Unless the non-state group acts on behalf of a foreign state, in which the conflict would be international.

[59] Thus, the wording of Common Article 3 to 1949 Geneva Conventions which speaks of a non-international armed conflict in the territory of *one* of the parties is regarded as requiring only the fighting takes place at least on the territory of one party to the Geneva Conventions. On this, see *Hamdan v Rumsfeld*, 542 US 507 (2004); Noam Lubell, 'The War (?) Against Al-Qaeda' in Elizabeth Wilmshurst (ed), *International Law and the Classification of Conflicts* (OUP 2012) 432–23; Dapo Akande, 'Classification of Armed Conflicts: Relevant Legal Concepts' in Wilmshurst, ibid, 72 (hereafter Akande, 'Classification of Armed Conflicts').

[60] *Prosecutor v Tadić* (Decision on the Defence Motion for Interlocutory Appeal on Jurisdiction) ICTY-94-1 (2 October 1995) para 70.

[61] *Prosecutor v Tadić* (Trial Judgment) IT-94-1-T (7 May 1997) para 562.

[62] *Prosecutor v Limaj and others*, IT-03-66-T (30 November 2005) paras 94–134; *Prosecutor v Lubanga*, (Judgment) [2012] ICC-01/04-01/06, paras 536–538.

Moreover, for a conflict to qualify as an NIAC, armed violence must also reach a certain threshold of intensity which is higher than that of internal disturbances and tensions.[63] The armed violence should not be sporadic or isolated but protracted.[64] The requirement of protracted violence 'refers more to the intensity of the armed violence than its duration'.[65] Like the condition of organization, the intensity of the armed violence is an issue which is determined on a case-by-case basis.[66]

In the context of drones, these requirements mean that IHL will not apply where the threshold levels of violence or organization are not present, leaving IHRL to govern the situation alone. It should be noted that individual drone strikes by themselves are not likely to meet the necessary threshold of violence for a NIAC to come into existence, leaving IHL inapplicable unless a drone strike is used in the context of a pre-existing NIAC.

A number of controversies have, however, arisen with regard to the scope of non-international armed conflicts and the threshold criteria for their existence, as a result of claims made by particular states when employing armed drones abroad. For example, where a state employs armed drones against members of the same non-state group in a number of different territories, the question arises as to whether the violence between the state and non-state group should be treated as a single, global non-international armed conflict.[67] The consequence of following such an approach would be that, when assessing whether the intensity threshold for a non-international armed conflict had been met, one would aggregate the entirety of the violence between the state and non-state group across the globe. It might be argued that where a state targets in different states, members of the same (sufficiently organized) non-state armed group, with which it is already in a non-international armed conflict, a single, global non-international armed conflict exists, with the relevant rules of IHL applying to all such strikes.[68] If this approach

[63] Art 1(2) of Additional Protocol II of 1977; *Prosecutor v Musema* (Appeals Judgment) ICTR-96-13-A (16 November 2001), para 248.

[64] *Musema*, ibid.

[65] *Prosecutor v Haradinaj and others* Judgment (Trial Chamber) IT-04-84-T (3 April 2008) para 49; *Limaj* (n 62) para 90.

[66] *Musema* (n 63) para 249.

[67] See eg the ICRC's criticisms of the view that the international fight against terrorism constitutes a single, transnational non-international armed conflict: ICRC, 'International Humanitarian Law and Terrorism: Questions and Answers' (1 January 2011) < https://www.icrc.org/en/doc/resources/documents/faq/terrorism-faq-050504.htm accessed 26 November 2019> .

[68] See eg Noam Lubell and Nathan Derejko (2013) 'A Global Battlefield? Drones and the Geographical Scope of Armed Conflict' 11 Journal of International Criminal Justice 65 (hereafter Lubell and Derejko 'A Global Battlefield?'). Amongst the many pieces written on this issue from the perspective of drone strikes, see eg Laurie Blank (2010) 'Defining the Battlefield in Contemporary Conflict and Counter-Terrorism: Understanding the Parameters of the Zone of Combat' 39 Georgia Journal of International and Comparative Law 1; Kenneth Anderson (2011) 'Targeted Killing and Drone Warfare: How We Came to Debate Whether There is a "Legal Geography of War"' (Washington College of Law Research Paper No 2011–12); Jennifer Daskal (2013) 'The Geography of the Battlefield: A Framework for Detention and Targeting Outside the "Hot" Conflict Zone' 161 University of Pennsylvania Law Review 1165.

is followed, the intensity requirement could be met by aggregation of violence, rather than by examining the level of violence in each country. The result of such an approach is that, on some views, the less protective rules of IHL will apply in such cases to those targeted and exclude or modify the more protective rules of IHRL. Under this model, unsuspecting communities, far away from any battlefield, may lawfully be significantly affected so long as they are not disproportionately so (on proportionality, see later).

This result does, of course, depends on one's view of the interaction between IHL and IHRL in this area. If the ICJ's approach to the interaction between IHL and the right to life under the International Covenant on Civil and Political Rights (ICCPR) is applied equally in non-international armed conflicts,[69] then the right to life of the person targeted would not be violated so long as IHL is complied with.

The possibility of a non-international armed conflict which spans across more than one country could certainly only exist where the individuals against which the state uses force in those several countries are *actually* members of the same non-state group.[70] This is because the violence can only be part of the same armed conflict if it is between the same parties. Where violence is between entities that are not parties to the same conflict, that violence cannot be part of a single non-international armed conflict. Thus, in a supposed global non-international armed conflict, the fulfilment of the organized armed group criterion would have to be tested on a global basis.[71] Where there is no single organization that groups together all those fighting then the test for an organization would not be met, and one could not aggregate all the violence together for the purposes of the intensity criterion.

There is clearly an incentive for states that are engaged in military clashes to define the group with whom they are engaged so broadly as to capture those not really members thereof, so as to bring them all within the same non-international armed conflict. The way in which the existing organization criterion under IHL has been interpreted to some extent helps to protect against this. An armed group is a party to a non-international armed conflict if, and only if, it is sufficiently organized in accordance with the demands of IHL. An armed group will only be sufficiently organized to be a party to a non-international armed conflict, if there is 'a sufficient body of evidence pointing to the ... [group] being an organized military

[69] See *Legality of the Threat or Use of Nuclear Weapons* (n 34) para 25.

[70] See Lubell and Derejko 'A Global Battlefield?' (n 68) 78 stating that where the individuals targeted by drone strikes are not members of the same non-state armed groups with which the targeting state is already in an armed conflict, 'it will become necessary to show that a separate armed conflict exists between the state and the targeted armed group').

[71] Lubell and Derejko 'A Global Battlefield?' (n 68) ('It is, however, highly questionable as to whether a one-sided drone strike can meet the threshold of intensity for armed conflict ... It is therefore submitted here that drone strikes alone are unlikely to be sufficient for the determination of a NIAC and the ensuing applicability of IHL').

force, with an official joint command structure, [and] headquarters'.[72] Moreover the group should have 'a unified military strategy' and be 'able to speak with one voice'.[73] Importantly, this is a factual, objective test, immune from the political considerations of the attacking state; it is not, therefore, for the state party to an NIAC to define for itself what constitutes the armed group against which it is fighting.

A related controversy arising from the use by certain states of drones against non-state armed groups abroad involves claims by certain states that force may be used not only against an organized armed group in a situation that meets the above requirements but also against its co-belligerents (or 'affiliates' or 'associates').[74] Co-belligerency is a concept that applies in international armed conflicts and entails that a sovereign state becomes a party to a conflict either through formal or informal processes.[75] A treaty of alliance may be concluded as a formal process, while the informal process could involve providing assistance to or establishing a 'common cause' with belligerent forces.[76]

Transposing the concept of co-belligerency into non-international armed conflicts has been met with resistance because it ignores the significant differences between the two types of armed conflict and opens the door for an expansion of targeting without clear limits.[77] Where the individuals targeted are not part of the same command and control structures as the organized armed group or are not part of a single military hierarchical structure, they ought not to be regarded as part of the same group, even if there are close ties between the different groups.[78] As a result, one cannot aggregate the violence between the state and these different armed groups as part of the determination as to whether the threshold for non-international armed conflicts has been met. Violence by different organized armed groups against the same state can amount to non-international armed conflicts only where the intensity of violence between each group and the state individually crosses the intensity threshold.

To illustrate the points made above, one may make reference to the possibility of a single, global non-international armed conflict with Al-Qaeda, for which it was stated that

[72] *Prosecutor v Milosevic* (Decision on Motion for Judgment of Acquittal) IT-02-54-T (16 June 2004), para 23.

[73] *Haradinaj* (n 65) para 60.

[74] 'Remarks by the President in the State of the Union Address' (The White House, 12 February 2013) < https://obamawhitehouse.archives.gov/the-press-office/2013/02/12/remarks-president-state-union-address> accessed 26 November 2019; Curtis Bradley and Jack Goldsmith (2005) 'Congressional Authorization and the War on Terrorism' 118 Harvard Law Review 2112, 2113.

[75] Hersch Lauterpacht (ed), *Oppenheim, International Law: A Treatise* (Longmans, Green & Co 1935) 203, 206.

[76] Ibid.

[77] 'The [US] administration's failure to define what specific organizational features or conduct would lead a group to be classified as an associated force raises concerns that this results in an aggressive and indefinitely expansive scope of targeting authority': Amnesty International, *Statement of shared concerns regarding U.S. drone strikes and targeted killings*, AI Index: AMR 51/017/2013, 6.

[78] For what constitutes an armed group, see *Haradinaj* (n 65) 144–45.

> [t]here is little evidence that the various terrorist groups that call themselves AQ or associate themselves with AQ possess the kind of integrated command structure that would justify considering them a single party involved in a global NIAC with the US ... Indeed, even the US government rejects the idea that AQ is a unified organization, dividing AQ into three separate tiers.[79]

The view of the International Committee of the Red Cross (ICRC) was that, based on the facts, this type of NIAC was not and has not been taking place. Instead, a case-by-case approach to analysing and classifying legally the various situations of violence that have occurred in the fight against terrorism should be applied. Seen in this light, some of these situations may be classified as an international armed conflict, others as NIACs, while the rest may be outside any armed conflict.[80]

A final, important point must be emphasized here, in keeping with the general theme of this chapter that each applicable legal regime must be addressed separately to determine the legality of a particular drone strike under international law. Even if the concept of a global non-international armed conflict is accepted, IHL does not, on its own, determine whether armed force can be used in foreign states. IHL simply governs *how* force may be used and does not regulate *whether* or *when* armed force may be used. It is the *jus ad bellum* which determines *whether* force may be used on foreign territory and which restrains the extraterritorial use of force. Thus, accepting the possibility of a global non-international armed conflict between a state and a non-state group does not in itself give permission to states to use force on foreign territory. Whether a state can carry the fight to a(nother) foreign territory will depend on the law relating to the use of force. The state seeking to carry out a drone attack in a particular foreign state will need to show that there is a sufficient, and indeed, separate justification under the law relating to the use of force for any attacks on each individual foreign state territory. In particular, the necessity of using force in self-defence on the territory of that particular state will need to be assessed separately.

B. Who May Be Targeted Under the Law of Non-International Armed Conflict?

Once it has been established that a non-international armed conflict exists, and thus that the rules of IHL applicable in such situations apply in the specific case, the next question concerns who may be targeted. The law of non-international armed

[79] Heller, 'One Hell of a Killing Machine' (n 11).

[80] ICRC, International Humanitarian Law and the Challenges of Contemporary Armed Conflicts (32IC/15/11, 2011) 10ff.

conflict is less settled in this area than the law of international armed conflict. It is clear that, as a matter of both treaty and customary law, civilians may not be made the object of an attack unless, and for such time as, they take a direct part in hostilities (DPH).[81] This is the principle of distinction and constitutes one of the cardinal principles of targeting under IHL. Where there is doubt as to whether a person is a civilian or is taking a direct part in hostilities, civilian status must be presumed.[82]

The treaty rules applicable in non-international armed conflict, however, do not define 'civilian', and there have been debates about whether members of non-state armed groups may be targeted on the basis of their status alone (eg as combatants can in international armed conflicts). In its Interpretive Guidance on Direct Participation in Hostilities, the ICRC has taken the view that 'civilians' protected from direct attack in a NIAC are all those who are neither members of a state's armed forces nor members of organized armed groups. The latter are then defined as 'individuals whose continuous function it is to take a direct part in hostilities ('continuous combat function' or CCF)'.[83] They may be targeted based on their status alone.

Thus, where a drone strike is carried out against an individual with a continuous combat function in an organized armed group with which the attacking state is engaged in an NIAC, this will be consistent with the principle of distinction in IHL, though of course the other applicable rules of IHL also must be observed. However, 'recruiters, trainers, financiers and propagandists may continuously contribute to the general war effort of a non-State party, but they are not members of an organized armed group belonging to that party unless their function additionally includes activities amounting to direct participation in hostilities'.[84] Such persons, therefore, remain civilians, protected against attack unless they directly participate in hostilities.

In addition to targeting on the basis of status, individuals may be targeted as result of conduct they have undertaken. Civilians lose their protection from direct attack where, and for such time as, they take a direct part in hostilities. According to the ICRC there is a three-stage (cumulative) test for determining when a civilian is directly participating in hostilities and thus may be targeted.[85] In order for activity to qualify as direct participation in hostilities:

[81] Art 13(2) and (3) of Additional Protocol II of 1977. See also Jean-Marie Henckaerts and Louise Doswald-Beck, *Customary International Humanitarian Law Volume I: Rules* (CUP 2005) Rule 6.

[82] Art 13(2) and (3) of Additional Protocol II of 1977; art 50(1) of Additional Protocol I of 1977.

[83] ICRC (Melzer), Interpretive Guidance on the Notion of Direct Participation in Hostilities under International Humanitarian Law (ICRC 2009) 27 (hereafter ICRC, 'Interpretive Guidance'). See also Sandesh Sivakumaran, *The Law of Non-International Armed Conflict* (OUP 2012) 359–62. Others adopt a different approach to defining membership of organized armed groups see eg Yoram Dinstein *et al*, *The Manual on the Law of Non-International Armed Conflict: With Commentary* (International Institute of Humanitarian Law 2006); Keneth Watkin (2010) 'Opportunity Lost: Organized Armed Groups and the ICRC 'Direct Participation in Hostilities' Interpretive Guidance' 42 New York University Journal of International Law and Policy 641 (hereafter Watkin, 'Opportunity Lost').

[84] ICRC, 'Interpretive Guidance' (n 83) 34.

[85] Ibid, 46.

> 1. The act must be likely to adversely affect the military operations or military capacity of a party to an armed conflict or, alternatively, to inflict death, injury, or destruction on persons or objects protected against direct attack (threshold of harm); 2. There must be a direct causal link between the act and the harm likely to result either from that act, or from a coordinated military operation of which that act constitutes an integral part (direct causation); and 3. The act must be specifically designed to directly cause the required threshold of harm in support of a party to the conflict and to the detriment of another (belligerent nexus).[86]

The most important criterion with respect to direct participation in hostilities is the requirement that the civilian either carries out acts that directly cause harm or engages in an operation that directly causes harm.[87] The ICRC has defined this requirement narrowly, stating that 'direct causation should be understood as meaning that the harm in question must be brought about in one causal step'.[88] General production and transport of weapons, or recruiting and training of personnel, are considered too indirect, unless forming an integral part of a specific military operation.[89]

The ICRC also emphasizes the rule that civilians lose their immunity from attack only *for so long as* they directly participate in hostilities, stating that '[c]ivilians lose protection against direct attack for the duration of each specific act amounting to direct participation in hostilities'.[90] However, the ICRC Guidance also states that '[m]easures preparatory to the execution of a specific act of direct participation in hostilities, as well as the deployment to and the return from the location of its execution, constitute an integral part of that act'.[91] As such, a civilian will be participating directly in hostilities both during the commission of the act and for a certain period before and after the act is carried out.

The ICRC's concept of 'continuous combat function' may be criticized because of its lack of an authoritative basis in treaty law. However, it has the advantage of answering the question of who is a legitimate target by referring to activity that directly causes harm to belligerents and/or civilians. This provides some objective basis for determining who may be targeted. It is noteworthy that the ICRC's approach to the concepts of 'members of organised armed groups' and 'direct

[86] Ibid.

[87] Dapo Akande (2010) 'Clearing the Fog of War? The ICRC's Interpretive Guidance on Direct Participation in Hostilities' 59 International and Comparative Law Quarterly 180, 187 (hereafter Akande, 'Clearing the Fog of War?').

[88] ICRC, 'Interpretive Guidance' (n 83) 53.

[89] Ibid.

[90] Ibid, 70. Certain states, including Israel and the United States, have advocated a 'continuous direct participation' standard, arguing that the 'for such time' limit does not reflect what is required under customary international law. Such a view was rejected, however, by the Israeli Supreme Court: *Public Committee Against Torture in Israel v Government of Israel*, Supreme Court of Israel, HCJ 769/02 (13 Dec 2006) paras 12, 30.

[91] ICRC, 'Interpretive Guidance' (n 83) 65.

participation in hostilities' has been followed in recent state practice concerning drone attacks.[92] Indeed, many would accept that members of an organized non-state armed group that is party to a non-international armed conflict are not to be regarded as civilians and are therefore not immune from attack.

However, the ICRC's 'continuous combat function' test has also been criticized for not going far enough[93] in the sense that it provides advantages to non-state groups as compared to state forces and thus promotes inequality between belligerents.[94] There is an imbalance under the combined combat function approach since members of the state's armed forces without a combat role (with limited exceptions) are lawful targets, whereas their counterparts in non-state groups are not. Furthermore, since the continuous combat function is defined by reference to taking a direct part in hostilities, which is then itself narrowly defined, persons who join an organized armed group and perform military functions that do not constitute direct battlefield activity are exempt from targeting on the basis of status. It has therefore been suggested that an analogy should be drawn between members of regular armed forces and members of organized armed groups such that persons who perform the types of functions performed by members of the armed forces would not be considered a civilian. Although superficially attractive as it promotes equality of arms, the problem with this latter approach is that the functions performed by members of the regular armed forces are very broad indeed. Since non-state groups do not necessarily have formal indicia of membership, one would still need some criteria for identifying the membership of an organized armed group.

One of the critical questions with regard to targeted killing in any armed conflict is how to ensure that the persons being targeted are indeed legitimate targets. A loose test of membership of a group that cannot be applied on the basis of objective evidence is likely to lead to greater civilian casualties or at least a lack of public confidence in the operations. In all cases where a state uses lethal force against individuals in a non-international armed conflict there must be objective evidence to support the claim of membership of an armed group, or alternatively that the persons in question are taking a direct part in hostilities at that point in time. Furthermore, as noted above, where there is doubt as to whether a person is a civilian or is taking a direct part in hostilities, the person is to be presumed as protected from direct attack.[95]

Moreover, all feasible precautions must be taken in determining whether a person is a civilian, and, if so, whether the person is taking a direct part in hostilities.[96] This obligation requires parties to the conflict to use all information that

[92] Decision of the German Federal Prosecutor of 20 June 2013 <https://www.generalbundesanwalt.de/docs/drohneneinsatz_vom_04oktober2010_mir_ali_pakistan.pdf> accessed 13 August 2019.

[93] See eg Watkin, 'Opportunity Lost' (n 83).

[94] Ibid.

[95] Art 50(1) of Additional Protocol I of 1977.

[96] ICRC, 'Interpretive Guidance' (n 83) 74.

is reasonably available in making the determination about whether a person is a lawful target. Where drones are used for targeting it could be argued that there is a greater degree of responsibility to take precautions than might otherwise be the case. This is because the technology and the way in which it is used in many cases make long-term surveillance possible. This means that more information is available about targets and more information can be made available than might otherwise be possible. Therefore, the assessment as to what information is reasonably available should take into account the relative ease with which information can be acquired.

It will not always be the case that evidence that a person is a member of an armed group or is directly participating in hostilities arises from information known about or which reveals the identity of the individual. In some cases, evidence about membership in an armed group or direct participation will arise from the characteristics associated with the individual or the activity that the individual is known to have performed or is performing. For example, where a non-state group has a particular uniform or insignia, evidence of membership may be derived from the wearing of that uniform or insignia. Strikes based on these 'signatures' or defining characteristics of an individual are not *per se* unlawful. What is crucial is whether the signatures or characteristics that are being used in making targeting decisions are the relevant characteristics as a matter of law.[97] The characteristics must be relevant to a determination that a person is a member of an armed group or that the person is taking a direct part in hostilities. The information must be such as to provide a high degree of confidence that the legal tests have been satisfied.

A determination that individuals are military-age males in an area of known terrorist activity does not provide a high degree of confidence that the individual is either a member of an armed group or that the person is taking a direct part in hostilities at that particular time. Indeed, mere presence in a given locality can never, in itself, amount to direct participation in hostilities. Some specific act would need to be engaged in for the person to be considered to be taking a part in hostilities. Furthermore, the fact that a person is armed, even in areas that are known to contain terrorists, is not sufficient to constitute evidence of loss of civilian status or direct participation in hostilities.[98] There are many parts of the world where it is lawful and/or common for individuals to carry personal arms. Carrying of such arms will not be sufficient to displace the presumption of civilian status. The public statements of states that they conduct threat assessments of individuals before targeting them in armed conflict should be welcomed

[97] Heller, 'One Hell of a Killing Machine' (n 11) 94ff distinguishing between 'legally adequate' and 'legally inadequate' signatures.

[98] See generally Heller, 'One Hell of a Killing Machine' (n 11); *Prosecutor v Simić* (Trial Chamber, Judgment) IT-95-9-T (17 Oct 2003) para 659.

and should be urged, as this helps to raise the floor of protection with respect to legitimate targets.[99] Of course, the situation must be correctly classified as an international or, as is more likely, a non-international armed conflict; if the requirements posed for an NIAC are not met, a loose threat assessment is not enough, and the more rigorous conditions of self-defence under IHRL would then exclusively regulate who can be targeted.

Finally, even in cases where lethal force is targeted at a member of an organized armed group or a civilian directly participating in hostilities, any such strike would need to comply with the principle of proportionality, the second cardinal principle of targeting in IHL. Drones come from the sky, but they leave the heavy footprint of war on the communities they target.[100] According to this principle, it is prohibited to carry out 'an attack which may be expected to cause incidental loss of civilian life, injury to civilians, damage to civilian objects, or a combination thereof, which would be excessive in relation to the concrete and direct military advantage anticipated'.[101] By implication, where the use of force is not excessive, such losses are regarded as incidental damage and are not prohibited provided the IHL rules have been respected.

The risk to civilians may be exacerbated where drone strikes are carried out far away from areas of actual combat operations, especially in densely populated areas, where unsuspecting civilians may suddenly find themselves in the line of fire. Avoiding harm to civilians requires taking all feasible precautions to prevent or minimize incidental loss of civilian lives and to gather information relating to possible civilian casualties and military advantages that might result from the proposed operation.[102]

C. The Possible Existence of an International Armed Conflict

As noted earlier, where there is an conflict between a state and a non-state group, it may qualify as a non-international armed conflict (should the conditions for an NIAC be met). Drone strikes may also take place in circumstances where there is no NIAC between the state and the non-state group, because the criteria for the existence of an NIAC are not met. However, the absence of a non-international armed conflict between the state and the non-state armed group does not necessarily mean that IHL will not apply to the use of force by a state. This is because the

[99] 'President Barack Obama's speech at National Defense University—full text' *The Guardian* (UK, 23 May 2013) <http://www.theguardian.com/world/2013/may/23/obama-drones-guantanamo-speech-text> accessed 13 August 2019.

[100] *Living Under Drones: Death, Injury, and Trauma to Civilians from US Drone Practices in Pakistan* (International Human Rights and Conflict Resolution Clinic, September 2012) <http://chrgj.org/wp-content/uploads/2012/10/Living-Under-Drones.pdf> accessed 13 August 2019.

[101] Art 51(5)(b) of Additional Protocol I of 1977.

[102] Art 57 of Additional Protocol I of 1977.

use of lethal force by a state directed at an armed group may still be governed by the law relating to international armed conflicts.

As noted earlier, international armed conflicts are limited to conflicts *between states*. When a state carries out drone strikes on the territory of another state, it will either do so with the consent of the territorial state or without that consent. Where the force is used with the consent of the territorial state, there can only be a non-international armed conflict between the state and the group against whom force is used (or indeed no armed conflict at all). However, where force is used without the consent of the territorial state, one of the present authors has argued elsewhere (as have others and the ICRC) that there would be an international armed conflict between the state using force and the state on whose territory force is used.[103] This would be an international armed conflict between the foreign state and the territorial state. This could be the case because the use of force by the intervening foreign state on the territory of the territorial state, without the consent of the latter, is a use of force *against* the territorial state. This, so the argument goes, is so even if the use of force is not directed against the governmental structures of the territorial state, or if the purpose of the use of force is not to coerce the territorial state in any particular way.

However, even on the view that there is an international armed conflict between the two states, such a conflict would exist in parallel with the non-international armed conflict between the state and the non-state armed group that is being targeted, if the criteria for an NIAC were met. The two conflicts would thus exist simultaneously. With regard to targeting of the members of the non-state group, it would be the criteria discussed earlier from the law of non-international armed conflict that would be determinative of the legality of the targeting of such members.[104] This is so because, as seen from the *Tadić* criteria already discussed,[105] the hostilities between the state and non-state group constitute the essence of a non-international armed conflict. Failure to apply the law of non-international armed conflict to targeting of members of the group would in effect be a failure to recognize the non-international armed conflict.

In cases where drone strikes occur outside the context of non-international armed conflicts and without the consent of the territorial state, on this view the individuals targeted would necessarily be classified as civilians, given that

[103] See eg Akande, 'Classification of Armed Conflicts' (n 59) 70–79 and *Commentary on the First Geneva Convention: Convention (I) for the Amelioration of the Condition of the Wounded and Sick in Armed Forces in the Field* (2nd edn ICRC Commentary to GC I, 2016), Commentary to art 2, paras 260–262.

[104] Arguably, matters regarding detention of persons taken from the territory of the non-consenting state or strikes that result in damage to objects or the natural environment would be governed by the law of international armed conflicts because, though those matters may be connected to the non-international armed conflict, the fact that they affect the territory of the state means they are also connected to the conflict between the two states.

[105] See *Tadić* (n 60) para 70.

they would not constitute combatants in the international armed conflict between the two states.[106] IHL prescribes that such persons would be protected from direct attack,[107] *unless and for such time as* they take a direct part in hostilities.[108] Drones strikes against them would, therefore, on this view only be lawful so long as they are directly participating in hostilities (on which, see earlier).

Finally, the fact that drone strikes would, according to this approach, take place in the context of an international armed conflict means that additional rules of international law to those discussed thus far would apply. For example, in addition to all the IHL obligations of the state using lethal force applying in such a situation, the applicable principles of international criminal law with respect to war crimes in an international armed conflict will also be relevant in determining individual responsibility for particular strikes. This conception of the relevant legal framework under IHL where drones are used abroad without the territorial state's consent thus has important implications both for substantive primary rules and for secondary rules on the responsibility of the actors involved.

D. Does IHL Require a Capture Rather Than Kill Approach?

Recent debates have raised the issue of whether IHL requires that a party to an armed conflict, under certain circumstances, considers the capture of an otherwise lawful target (ie a combatant, a member of an armed group with a CCF or a civilian directly participating in hostilities) rather than targeting with force. The ICRC has taken the view that it does, and in its Interpretive Guidance it states that 'it would defy basic notions of humanity to kill an adversary or to refrain from giving him or her an opportunity to surrender where there manifestly is no necessity for the use of lethal force'.[109]

The articulation of this principle has been controversial.[110] It has been criticized for its alleged misrepresentation of the current *lex lata*,[111] particularly on the basis that it suggests that the principle of military necessity sits above every rule of IHL

[106] Art 50(1) of Additional Protocol II of 1977 (effectively defining civilians negatively, as all persons who are not combatants).

[107] Art 51(2) of Additional Protocol I of 1977.

[108] Art 51(3) of Additional Protocol I of 1977. The Israeli Supreme Court has held that this constitutes a rule of customary international law and is therefore binding also on those States not party to API: *Public Committee Against Torture in Israel v Government of Israel*, Supreme Court of Israel, HCJ 769/02 (13 Dec 2006), para 30.

[109] ICRC, 'Interpretive Guidance' (n 83) 82.

[110] See Akande, 'Clearing the Fog of War?' (n 87) 191.

[111] See Michael Schmitt (2010) 'The Interpretive Guidance on the Notion of Direct Participation in Hostilities: A Critical Analysis' 1 Harvard National Security Journal 5, 39–43.

in a limiting manner, rather than simply as a consideration that has already been factored into the rules.[112] In other words, so the argument goes, states have already decided that it is necessary and proportionate to target combatants on the basis of their status, and in some cases, conduct alone.

It is too early to determine in which direction the controversy around this concept will be resolved. The impulse to move in the direction of the approach that in some cases capture rather than kill is required is likely to continue in the context of modern anti-terrorism measures where individuals or small groups may be isolated in territory far away from the conflict zone, which may even be controlled by the state party or its allies.[113] At least one state that uses drones has stated that, as a matter of policy, it will not use lethal force when it is feasible to capture a terror suspect.[114] At the same time it should be remembered that drones by their very nature will in most cases not allow capture.

E. Investigation and Accountability for Violations

The modern concept of human rights is based on the fundamental principle that those responsible for violations must be held to account. A failure to investigate and where applicable punish those responsible for violations of the right to life in itself is increasingly understood to constitute a violation of that right.[115] Legal, and indeed political, accountability are dependent on public access to the relevant information.[116] Only on the basis of such information can effective oversight and enforcement take place. The first step towards securing human rights in this context is transparency about the use of drones. A lack of appropriate transparency and accountability concerning the deployment of drones undermines the rule of law and may threaten international security.[117] Accountability for violations of IHRL

[112] Michael Schmitt (2010) 'Military Necessity and Humanity in International Humanitarian Law: Preserving the Delicate Balance' 50 Virginia Journal of International Law 795, 835.

[113] Ryan Goodman (2013) 'The Power to Kill or Capture Enemy Combatants' 24 European Journal of International Law 819.

[114] 'Fact Sheet: U.S. Policy Standards and Procedures for the Use of Force in Counterterrorism Operations Outside the United States and Areas of Active Hostilities' (White House, 23 May 2013) (hereafter White House, 'Use of Force in Counterterrorism Operations').

[115] *Kaya v Turkey* App No 22729/93 (ECtHR, 19 February 1998) paras 86–92; UNHRC 'General Comment No 31' (2004) CCPR/C/21/Rev.1/Add. 1326, para 15 (hereafter UNHRC 'General Comment No 31'); *McCann* and *others v United Kingdom* App No 18984/91 (ECtHR, 27 September 1995) para 169.

[116] See the OHCHR 'Principles on the Effective Prevention and Investigation of Extra-Legal, Arbitrary and Summary Executions (recommended by the UN Economic and Social Council resolution 1989/65, 24 May 1989)' para 16, and the companion UN Manual on the Effective Prevention and Investigation of Extra-Legal, Arbitrary and Summary Executions (sometimes referred to as the 'Minnesota Protocol').

[117] Melzer, *Targeted Killing* (n 11) 4.

(or IHL) 'is not a matter of choice or policy; it is a duty under domestic and international law'.[118]

The various components of transparency[119] require that the criteria for targeting and the authority which approves killings be known, and drone operations be brought within institutions which are able to disclose to the public the methods and findings of their intelligence, criteria used in selection of targets and precautions incorporated in such criteria. One of the criticisms levelled against the current drone programmes has been the absence of an official record regarding the persons killed. States must also give guarantees of non-repetition of unlawful drone strikes and realize the right of victims to reparations.

Drone victims, like any other human rights victims, and the society at large, have a right to access information related to allegations of human rights violations and their investigations.[120] Under IHRL, the UN Human Rights Committee has emphasized the need for transparency, highlighting victims' right to know the truth about the perpetrators, their accomplices, and the motives thereof.[121] Likewise, during an armed conflict, relatives of persons killed or missing have the right to know the fate of their relatives.[122]

A parallel obligation to investigate and where appropriate punish those responsible in respect of cases of alleged war crimes exists under IHL.[123] Whenever there are reasons to query whether violations of IHL may have occurred in armed conflict as a result of a drone strike, such as the incorrect designation of persons as targetable, or disproportionate civilian harm, full adherence to accountability demands at least a preliminary investigation.[124] Civilian casualties must be determined and should be disclosed.

118 United Nations, 'Report of the Secretary-General's Panel of Experts on Accountability in Sri Lanka' (12 April 2011).

119 See Philip Alston (2011) 'The CIA and Targeted Killings Beyond Borders' 2 Harvard National Security Journal 287.

120 See the *Case of Mapiripán Massacre v Colombia*, Inter-American Court of Human Rights Series C No 134 (15 September 2005) para 238.

121 UNHRC '9/11, Right to the Truth' A/HRC/9/L.12, preamble para 1; UNGA Res 61/177 (12 December 2007) art 24 (2); UNCHR Res 2005/66 (20 April 2005) E/CN.4/RES/2005/66.

122 Art 32 of Additional Protocol I of 1977; art 33 of Additional Protocol I of 1977; ICRC, 'Commentary to the Additional Protocols of 1977' (ICRC 1987) 350, para 1222; art 138 of the Fourth Geneva Convention of 1949.

123 See art 49 of the First Geneva Convention of 1949; art 50 of the Second Geneva Convention of 1949; art 129 of the Third Geneva Convention of 1949; art 146 of the Fourth Geneva Convention of 1949; art 85 of Additional Protocol of 1977; United Nations, Statute of International Criminal Tribunal for the former Yugoslavia, UN Doc S/RES/827 (1993) art 2; United Nations, Statute of the International Criminal Tribunal for Rwanda, UN Doc S/RES/955 (1994) art 4; 1998 Rome Statute of the International Criminal Court, 2187 UNTS 90, art 8(2)(a).

124 Second Turkel Commission Report, 'The Public Commission to Examine the Maritime Incident of 31 May 2010' 256.

V. International Human Rights Law

A. General Considerations

The final substantive area that must be considered in assessing the legality of the use of armed drones under international law is international human rights law (IHRL). It is under IHRL that the right to life is most clearly protected, as set out in the various international and regional human rights treaties,[125] and the rules of customary international law.[126] The right to life is sometimes described as the 'supreme right'.[127] Indeed, certain violations of the right to life are considered to be war crimes or crimes against humanity.[128] As discussed in the next subsection, IHRL applies not only in peacetime but also in armed conflict, both international and non-international. As such, the right to life under human rights law forms the default legal norm applicable to the protection of people affected by drone strikes.

As a general rule, international human rights law requires that any deprivation of life must be non-arbitrary.[129] The non-arbitrariness standard defining the scope of the right to life has generally been interpreted in human rights jurisprudence to require that intentional lethal force be used only as a last resort in order to *protect* life.[130] Thus, Principle 9 of the UN Basic Principles on the Use of Force and Firearms by Law Enforcement Officials provides that 'intentional lethal use of firearms may only be made when strictly unavoidable in order to protect life'. Indeed, Article 2 of the European Convention on Human Rights (ECHR) contains, rather than a general prohibition of arbitrary deprivation of life, an exhaustive list of grounds on which it is permissible to use lethal force.[131]

Under IHRL, any force must be necessary, that is, the least harmful means of achieving the particular legitimate purpose of protecting life. Whether that is the case is a factual assessment. Other avenues should be explored first and only when they are shown to be inadequate can there be resort to force.[132] Force must also be

[125] International Covenant on Civil and Political Rights (adopted 16 December 1966, entered into force 23 March 1976) 999 UNTS 171 (ICCPR) art 6(1); American Convention on Human Rights (adopted 22 November 1969, entered into force 18 July 1978) OAS Treaty Series No 36 (ACHR) art 4(1); art 4 of the African Charter on Human and Peoples' Rights (adopted 27 June 1981, entered into force 21 October 1986) CAB/LEG/67/3 rev 5, 21 ILM 58 (1982); art 5 of the Arab Charter on Human Rights (adopted 22 May 2004, entered into force 15 March 2008) 12 Intl Hum Rts Rep 893 (2005).

[126] UNHRC 'General Comment No 24 CCPR/C/21/Rev.1/Add.6, 10.

[127] UNHRC 'General Comment No 6: The Right to Life' (1982) HRI/GEN/1/Rev.9 (Vol I), para 1.

[128] See generally *Prosecutor v Mrkšić et al*, (2009) Appeals Judgment (IT-95-13/1-A).

[129] See references in n 125. Art 2 of the European Convention on Human Rights gives an exhaustive list of permissible grounds on which lethal force may be based.

[130] Cordula Droege (2008) 'Elective Affinities? Human Rights and Humanitarian Law' 90 International Review of the Red Cross 501, 525 (hereafter Droege, 'Elective Affinities?'); David Kretzmer (2005) 'Targeted Killing of Suspected Terrorists: Extra-Judicial Executions or Legitimate Means of Defence?' 16 Europan Journal of International Law 171, 179.

[131] Convention for the Protection of Human Rights and Fundamental Freedoms (entered into force 3 September 1953) 194 CETS (as amended) (ECHR) art 2(2).

[132] Art 3 of Code of Conduct for Law Enforcement Officials (General Assembly Resolution 34/169, annex, of 17 December 1979).

proportionate (ie the potential harm in using force does not outweigh the legitimate protective goal pursued). This entails making a value judgement. It is important to note that proportionality in this human rights law sense is a different test to the principle of proportionality in IHL (on which, see earlier). Moreover, *intentionally* lethal or potentially lethal force can only be used where strictly necessary to protect against an imminent threat to life: '[T]he police may shoot to kill only when it is clear that an individual is about to kill someone (making lethal force proportionate) and there is no other available means of detaining the suspect (making lethal force necessary)'.[133]

Proper precautions must also be taken to prevent, where possible, the resort to force. In *McCann and others v UK*, the European Court of Human Rights (ECtHR) held that the killing of members of the Provisional Irish Republican Army by state agents was a violation of their right to life as they could have been arrested on their arrival in Gibraltar, where the operation took place.[134]

Whether a particular drone strike satisfies these conditions must be examined on a case-by-case basis. It is important to emphasize, however, that, under these rules, alternatives to lethal force would need to be explored and shown to be inadequate for a drone strike to be lawful. In addition, it would need to be concluded that the use of lethal force is necessary on the basis that the person to be targeted constitutes an imminent threat to others.[135] It is here that conflation of different legal standards across different regimes often poses problems. It is important not to confuse this imminence requirement in IHRL with similar conditions under the *jus ad bellum*. As discussed earlier, according to the doctrine of anticipatory self-defence, a state can use force against another state where there is an imminent threat of armed attack emanating from the latter state. This, however, is a different legal threshold to the imminence requirement in IHRL. Whether a particular transnational drone strike is lawful would depend on demonstrating imminence in *both* of these senses in cases where the attacking state is claiming a right of anticipatory self-defence.[136]

133 UNHRC 'Report of the Special Rapporteur on Extrajudicial, Summary or Arbitrary Executions, Philip Alston' (2010) A/HRC/14/24, para 35.

134 *McCann* (n 115) paras 203–214; UNHRC, *Suárez de Guerrero v Colombia*, Merits (CCPR/C/15/D/45/1979) para 13.2.

135 See references to 'imminence' in the 2013 US Department of Justice White Paper (n 32) (although note the lack of clarity in the use of this requirement, discussed below); White House, 'Use of Force in Counterterrorism Operations' (n 114) 2 ('the United States will use lethal force only against a target that poses a continuing, imminent threat to U.S. persons'); see also the discussion of whether a US drone strike in Yemen fell foul of the arbitrary deprivation of life prohibition in IHRL, in Lubell, *Extraterritorial Use of Force* (n 52) 174–78.

136 The US White Paper on drones is an example where these categories of rules and the requirements under them are conflated, leading to an apparent misapplication of the imminence standard: see US Department of Justice White Paper (n 32); see a discussion of the 'imminence' requirement in the White Paper in Kevin Heller, 'The DOJ White Paper's Confused Approach Imminence (and Capture)' (Opinio Juris, 5 February 2013). The UK's more recent change of policy in targeting British citizens abroad using drones who are thought to be affiliated with ISIS also suggests some conflation in the government's invocation of self-defence: MacAskill, 'Drone Killing' (n 32).

B. Application of Human Rights in Armed Conflict

It is now well established that IHRL continues to apply in time of armed conflict, alongside IHL.[137] This has been confirmed in a number of decisions of the International Court of Justice (ICJ).[138] Indeed, the general applicability of human rights obligations in armed conflict is confirmed by the presence of provisions relating to derogations in certain human rights treaties. Those provisions permit state parties to derogate in time of war or public emergency from some of their human rights obligations arising under those treaties.[139] Such provisions confirm that, absent derogation, human rights obligations continue to apply in time of war or armed conflict. Thus, a state's conventional human rights obligations will only cease where that state validly suspends the rights in accordance with the treaty's derogation provisions. However, with the exception of the ECHR, the right to life is regarded as a non-derogable right under most major human rights treaties.

Where a particular drone strike falls within the context of an armed conflict, therefore, it will be governed by *both* IHL *and* IHRL. In certain cases, the right to life standard in IHRL might be interpreted in accordance with the relevant rules on the conduct of hostilities under IHL, explored above. Thus, the ICJ has stated that, while the right not arbitrarily to be deprived of one's life continues to apply in situations of armed conflict, what is an arbitrary deprivation of life under the ICCPR depends on the circumstances at hand and, in armed conflict, should be considered by reference to the IHL rules on the conduct of hostilities.[140] According to this view, where a state targets an individual in a drone strike that falls within an armed conflict, whether that state has violated its obligation not arbitrarily to deprive that individual of their life depends on whether the state has acted consistently with those IHL rules already discussed.

However, the ECHR, as noted, does not express the right to life by reference to *arbitrary* deprivation of life. Rather, it provides for a closed list of permissible bases for depriving a person of their life.[141] The extent to which one can read into this provision the IHL rules on the conduct of hostilities is, consequently, more limited than in the case of the arbitrariness standard found in the ICCPR and ACHR.[142] However, it is important to note that the ECtHR has interpreted te right not to be deprived of one's liberty under Article 5 of the European Convention by reference

[137] For an overview of the trend towards the consensus that IHRL continues to apply in situations of armed conflict, see Droege, 'Elective Affinities?' (n 130) 503–09.

[138] *Legality of the Threat or Use of Nuclear Weapons* (n 34) para 25; *Legal Consequences of the Construction of a Wall* (n 50) para 106; *DRC v Uganda* (n 31) para 216.

[139] See eg art 4 ICCPR; art 15 ECHR; art 27 ACHR.

[140] *Legality of the Threat or Use of Nuclear Weapons* (n 34) para 25.

[141] Art 2(2) ECHR.

[142] Marko Milanovic, *Extraterritorial Application of Human Rights Treaties, Law, Principles and Policy* (OUP 2011) 254ff (hereafter Milanovic, *Extraterritorial Application*).

to the IHL rules on detention in international armed conflicts.[143] This was done despite the fact that the relevant provision, like the provision on the right to life, is not expressed by reference to *arbitrary* deprivation, but rather a closed list of permissible bases for deprivation of liberty.[144] A similar interpretation of the right to life would allow the European Court to read the IHL rules on the conduct of hostilities into the right to life under the European Convention. In any case, Article 15(2) ECHR permits derogation from this provision 'in respect of deaths resulting from lawful acts of war'. This provision should, therefore, be used where states consider it necessary to resort to more permissive rules of IHL.

Where a drone strike is conducted outside the context of an international or non-international armed conflict, IHL will not apply; in such situations, there can be no claim that a state's human rights obligations must be interpreted in accordance with IHL. Instead, those obligations will apply according to their ordinary meaning as developed in human rights jurisprudence. That said, the arbitrariness standard remains context-specific and indeed has been applied in ways that are realistic to the context.[145] There are, however, limits to this. Importantly for our current enquiry, the view that mere past involvement in planning attacks is sufficient to render an individual targetable even where there is no evidence of a specific and immediate attack, distorts the requirements established in IHRL.[146]

This discussion relates to the potential responsibility of the state using the drone. But what about the state on whose territory it is used? It should be remembered, as noted at the outset of this article, that states cannot consent to the violation of their IHL or IHRL obligations. A state that consents to the activities of another state on its territory remains bound by its own human rights obligations, including the obligations not actively to violate the rights of those within its jurisdiction itself, and also to ensure respect for human rights within its jurisdiction and thus to prevent violations of the right to life, including by other states operating on its territory, to the extent that it is able to do so.[147]

C. Extraterritorial Application of the Right to Life

The fact that drones have been used with lethal effects by states against individuals *outside* their territory raises the additional question of whether states can be held accountable under those human rights treaties to which they are party, for their

[143] See *Hassan v United Kingdom* App No 29750/09 (Grand Chamber Judgment) (ECtHR, 16 September 2014).

[144] For a slightly critical reading of the judgment, see Lawrence Hill-Cawthorne, *Detention in Non-International Armed Conflict* (OUP 2016) 158–59.

[145] Melzer, *Targeted Killing* (n 11) 33.

[146] US Department of Justice White Paper (n 32).

[147] ILC, Articles on Responsibility of States for Wrongful Acts, (2001) UNYBILC vol II, Pt Two, art 23.

extraterritorial actions. Reference was made earlier to the status of the right to life, and the prohibition of the arbitrary deprivation thereof, as a norm of customary international law. In its customary form, at least the negative obligation not arbitrarily to deprive someone of their life appears not to be limited to application *within* a state's territory. Indeed, the Universal Declaration of Human Rights does not contain a limitation clause on its geographical application and simply states that '[e]veryone has the right to life'.[148]

In addition, in certain circumstances, states are bound by those human rights treaties to which they are a party even in relation to conduct they take outside their territory. The fact that human rights treaty obligations can apply in principle to the conduct of a state outside its territory has been confirmed, *inter alia*, by the ICJ,[149] the UN Human Rights Committee (UNHRC),[150] the Inter-American Commission on Human Rights,[151] and the ECtHR.[152] The applicability of such treaties is normally limited to those individuals within the 'jurisdiction' of a state party.[153] It is clear that all persons finding themselves within the territory of a state are presumed to be within its territorial jurisdiction.[154] Moreover, it is clear from the case law that, where a state is exercising effective control over a part of *another* state's territory, the former will be exercising 'jurisdiction' such that its obligations under those human rights treaties to which it is a party will apply.[155] Jurisdiction for the purposes of extraterritorial application of human rights treaties will additionally exist where, absent such territorial control, the state exercises, through its agents, 'authority or control' over the specific individual abroad.[156]

[148] Universal Declaration on Human Rights (adopted 10 December 1948 UNGA Res 217 A(III) (UDHR) art 3.

[149] *Legal Consequences of the Construction of a Wall* (n 50) para 109.

[150] UNHRC 'General Comment No 31' (n 115) para 10.

[151] *Coard and others v United States*, Inter-American Commission on Human Rights Case 10.951, Rep No.109/00 (29 September 1999) para 37.

[152] *Al-Skeini v United Kingdom* App No 55721/07 (Grand Chamber Judgment) (ECtHR, 7 July 2011) paras 106–186; *Loizidou v Turkey* (1997) 23 EHRR 513; *Ilascu v Moldoca and Russia* (2005) EHRR 46, para 392. *Al-Jedda v United Kingdom* App No 27021/08 (ECtHR, 7 July 2011); *Jaloud v Netherlands* App No 47708/08, (Grand Chamber Judgment) (ECtHR, 20 November 2014).

[153] In art 2(1) ICCPR, the obligation of states is further limited to 'all individuals within its territory'. However, since *Lopez Burgos v Uruguay*, Communication 52/1979, Views, 29 July 1981, the Human Rights Committee has held that State parties can also be held accountable for violations outside their territory. This is to be contrasted with the view of the United States and Israel, whereby those states reject the extraterritoriality of the ICCPR: HRC, 'Third Periodic Report: United States of America', CCPR/ C/ USA/ 3, 28 November 2005, 109–11; HRC, 'Second Periodic Report: Israel', CCPR/ C/ ISR/ 2001/ 2, 4 December 2001, [8]. Other states, such as the United Kingdom, disagree: HRC, 'Information Received from the United Kingdom of Great Britain and Northern Ireland on the Implementation of the Concluding Observations of the Human Rights Committee', CCPR/ C/ GBR/ CO/ 6/ Add.1, 3 November 2009, [24].

[154] This presumption may be rebutted, however, where the state is unable to exercise its authority over its territory.

[155] See eg UNHRC 'General Comment No 31' (n 115) para 10; *Loizidou v Turkey* (1995) Preliminary Objections, Series A No 310, paras 62–64. See the discussion in Melzer, *Targeted Killing* (n 11) 155–67.

[156] *Ocalan v Turkey* App No 46221/99 (ECtHR, 12 March 2003) para 93; *Issa and others v Turkey* App No 31821/96 (ECtHR, 16 November 2004) para 71.

One of the key difficulties posed by drones is that the attacking state can engage in targeted killing without exercising effective control over territory or without having the individual in custody, leading to questions over whether such persons fall within the 'jurisdiction' of the attacking state for the purposes of their human rights treaty obligations. There is limited case law on this matter. In the *Alejandre* case, the Inter-American Commission concluded that the shooting down of two private US-registered air planes by Cuban military aircraft in international airspace violated the right to life of the passengers.[157] At the same time, however, in *Bankovic*, the European Court held that persons killed during aerial bombings by NATO of a radio station in Serbia did not fall within the 'jurisdiction' of the participating states for the purposes of establishing whether they have violated the right to life.[158] The broad sweep of this decision has, however, increasingly been narrowed in subsequent cases of the Court,[159] and it is not clear that the position can be sustained. Indeed, the English High Court has held that 'whenever and wherever a state which is a contracting party to the [European] Convention [of Human Rights] purports to exercise legal authority or uses physical force, it must do so in a way that does not violate Convention rights'.[160]

It has been argued that the implication of this broader view of when an individual is within the jurisdiction of a state for the purposes of human rights treaties is that the deliberate killing of selected individuals through extraterritorial drone strikes is likely to bring the affected persons within the jurisdiction of the operating state.[161] Pursuing this line of reasoning, where a state targets individuals abroad with lethal force, one can argue that it intends to exercise ultimate control over the individuals concerned, resulting in those actions being governed by the state's human rights treaty law obligations.[162] Marko Milanovic is similarly of the view that the human rights treaty obligations of a state would apply to the deliberate killing of an individual through extraterritorial drone strikes.[163] However, Milanovic's reasoning is that the *negative* obligations owed by states under IHRL, for example, the obligation not arbitrarily to kill, should extend unbound by territorial constraints. This argument is based on the view that, in treaties that contain

[157] *Alejandre Jr and others v Republica de Cuba*, Inter-American Commission on Human Rights Case 11.589, Rep No 86/99 (29 September 1999) paras 23–25.

[158] *Bankovic and Others v Belgium* App No 52207/99 (Admissibility Decision, Grand Chamber) (ECtHR, 12 December 2001) para 82.

[159] *Al-Skeini* (n 152) paras 106–186.

[160] *Al-Saadoon and others v Secretary of State for Defence* [2015] EWHC 715 (Admin) para 106. This aspect of the decision was overturned in the Court of Appeal on the grounds that though it might follow from the *Al-Skeini* decision of the European Court of Human Rights, it is up to the European Court, and not domestic courts, to take the decisive step in spelling out this consequence from its decision. For comment on the High Court decision, see David Goddard (2015) 'Applying the European Convention on Human Rights to the Use of Physical Force: Al-Saadoon' 91 International Law Studies 402.

[161] See Melzer, *Targeted Killing* (n 11).

[162] See Droege, 'Elective Affinities?' (n 130); and Lubell, *Extraterritorial Use of Force* (n 52) 227–31.

[163] Milanovic, *Extraterritorial Application* (n 142) 209–21.

a jurisdiction clause, the negative obligation to *respect* rights is to be treated differently from the obligation to *ensure* those rights and that texts can and should be interpreted such that only the latter is confined to matters within the 'jurisdiction' of the state as that term has come to be interpreted. This appears to be a normatively desirable and principled basis for holding states to account in such situations, and it is in line with the position as set out earlier under customary international law. Importantly, to say that a state has human rights obligations with respect to conduct outside its territory does not, therefore, automatically mean that those obligations are the same as those that arise within its territory.[164] In principle, while control of territory means that a state has obligations not only to respect but also to ensure and to fulfil the human rights of those on the territory guaranteed by international law, the exercise of authority with respect to an individual by state agents in the absence of territorial control at a minimum triggers the state's obligation to respect the rights of those individuals.[165]

It has been held that human rights treaties 'cannot be interpreted so as to allow a State party to perpetrate violations of [the treaty] on the territory of another State, which it could not perpetrate on its own territory'.[166] The same must apply to the right to life under both custom and treaty law. In consequence, any positive action by a state, on its own territory or that of another state, should be carried out in compliance with its human rights obligations under both treaty and custom.

VI. Conclusion

The legal framework for maintaining international peace and the protection of the right to life is a coherent and well-established system, reflecting norms that have been developed over the centuries and have withstood the test of time. Even though drones are not illegal weapons, they can easily be abused. The central norms of international law need not and should not be abandoned to meet challenges posed by terrorism and 'new' forms of conflict. On the contrary, the fact that drones make targeted killing so much easier should serve as a prompt to ensure a diligent application of these standards, especially in view of the likely expansion in the number of states with access to this technology in the future. The use of drones by states to exercise what is essentially a global policing function to counter potential threats presents a danger to the protection of life, because the tools of domestic policing (such as capture) are not available, and the more permissive targeting framework of the law of armed conflict is often relied upon instead.

164 See the ECtHR in *Al-Skeini* (n 152) at para 137, holding (contrary to the *Bankovic* decision) that 'Convention rights can be "divided and tailored" on separating and tailoring obligations in extraterritorial contexts.'

165 Milanovic, *Extraterritorial Application* (n 142) 209–21.

166 *Issa* (n 156) para 71.

Though not inherently illegal weapons, drones do make the deployment of lethal force across borders much easier than before, and as such they pose significant risks to the protection of life. In this context the legal paradigm that is followed does make an important difference. If the assumption is that of a global non-international armed conflict, to which IHL applies as the dominant legal regime, then it becomes much easier to justify lethal force, than if one takes the default legal framework of IHRL as the governing regime. It was shown earlier that the notion of a global non-international armed conflict is controversial and in any event, the existence of any such conflict would have to be assessed against objective legal criteria rather than subjective self-interested claims. Moreover, even if IHL applies in a given situation, one should not be so quick to assume that IHL thereby modifies IHRL.[167] The question must be also be asked in each case where armed drones are proposed to be used whether it is wise to do so, in addition merely to being legal. Such an approach is the only way in which force remains the exception, thereby protecting the right to life in the long term.

There is an urgent need for the international community to gain greater consensus on the interpretation of the constraints that international law in all its manifestations places on the use of drones. This is important not only because of the implications for those who currently find themselves on the receiving end of drones, but in order to keep a viable and strong system of international security intact. A central component of such a security system is the rule of law. Drones should follow the law, rather than the other way around.

The following fundamental principles should, it is proposed, form the starting point of a search for greater consensus on the regulation of armed drones:

(i) The current international legal framework is adequate to govern drone strikes;
(ii) The right to life can only be adequately protected if all constraints on the use of lethal force abroad set out by international law are complied with individually and cumulatively, including the *jus ad bellum*, IHL (where applicable) and IHRL;
(iii) International norms on the use of lethal force must not be abandoned or modified to suit the current use of drones;
(iv) Any drone strike by a state outside of its own territory must comply with the *jus ad bellum*;
(v) Where a drone strike takes place within international or non-international armed conflict (a factual question governed by objective legal criteria), it is governed by both IHL and IHRL;

[167] Lawrence Hill-Cawthorne, 'Just Another Case of Treaty Interpretation? Reconciling Humanitarian Law and Human Rights Law in the ICJ' in Mads Andenas and Eirik Bjorge (eds), *A Farewell to Fragmentation: Reassertion and Convergence in International Law* (CUP 2015).

(vi) Outside the narrow confines of international or non-international armed conflict, any killing is governed solely by IHRL and must meet that body of law's requirements of strict necessity and proportionality as those terms have been developed in human rights jurisprudence;

(vii) There should be transparency surrounding all drone operations to enhance accountability.

These are merely a starting point, but the current authors would contend that the international community has a strong interest in ensuring that there is clearer agreement on the basis of our common security.

8
Application of the International Human Rights Law Framework in Cyber Space

*Helen McDermott**

I. Introduction

States are becoming increasingly dependent upon computer systems and networks to support vital services such as navigation, communications, defence systems, and the supply of electricity and water.[1] What flows from this is concurrent reliance of society, and the exercise of individual rights, on cyber infrastructure.[2] Cyber technology and the ability to rely upon it to support daily and long-term activities generate immense opportunities for economic activity and communications but at the same time, the increasing number of processes dependent on the interconnectedness of digital infrastructure has become a source of newly emerging threats for national, commercial, and private security. The novelty and unique character of cyber, in terms of the activities and geographical scope it encompasses, in turn presents challenges to the application and operationalization of the relevant international legal frameworks.

Digital technologies can advance human rights by creating a platform for expression and the exposure of human rights violations. Developments in this sphere, namely increased capacity of governments, businesses, and individuals to conduct surveillance, interception, and data collection, may also render certain rights vulnerable to interference.[3] In this context, privacy and freedom of expression are

* *The author writes in her personal capacity, the views expressed in this post are her own, and not those of the UK Foreign & Commonwealth Office, or any other Government Department.*

[1] It is estimated that in 2008, the number of devices connected to the Internet exceeded the number of people on earth. See Michael Ruhle, 'Preface', in Kasten Friis and Jens Ringsmose (eds), *Conflict in Cyber Space: Theoretical, Strategic and Legal Perspectives* (Routledge 2016) xi.

[2] 'Cybersecurity Strategy of the European Union: An Open, Safe and Secure Cyberspace', Joint Communication to the European Parliament, The Council, The European Economic and Social Committee and the Committee of the Region (Document 52013JC0001) 2013.

[3] Nick Hopkins, 'UK Gathering Secret Intelligence via Covert NSA Operation' *The Guardian* (7 June 2013) <https://www.theguardian.com/technology/2013/jun/07/uk-gathering-secret-intelligence-nsa-prism> accessed 14 August 2019; *Big Brother Watch and Others v the United Kingdom* (2014) ECHR 93; UNHRC 'Report of the Special Rapporteur on the Promotion and Protection of the Right to Freedom of Opinion and Expression' (22 May 2015) UN Doc. A/HRC/29/32 para 1.

Helen McDermott, *Application of the International Human Rights Law Framework in Cyber Space* In: Human Rights and 21st Century Challenges. Edited by: Dapo Akande, Jaakko Kuosmanen, Helen McDermott, and Dominic Roser, Published by Oxford University Press 2020. © Helen McDermott, 2020.
DOI: 10.1093/oso/9780198824770.003.0009

those most susceptible to infringement.[4] Accordingly, in describing the intersection between international human rights law (IHRL) and cyber operations, human rights advocates have focused the debate on this set of guarantees, and channelled efforts into increasing access to the Internet and pushing back against government interference in cyberspace.[5]

It is now well settled that IHRL can apply to cyber activities. However, uncertainty over its content and scope of application remains.[6] This chapter considers the application of the IHRL framework to extraterritorial cyber operations, and identifies certain characteristics of the cyber context that are likely to pose barriers to its operationalization. The issues that surface are not unique to this area in particular, the territorial scope of application of human rights law obligations,[7] the relationship between IHRL and the law of armed conflict,[8] and responsibility for conduct of non-state actors.[9] The chapter begins with a brief consideration of the tension between individual human rights and potential security threats posed by cyber operations. Section II provides a typology of cyber operations and identifies the primary rights affected. The discussion in section III offers a snapshot of the legal frameworks that regulate cyber operations before moving on to focus on the application of IHRL in section IV. The final section highlights two potential barriers to operationalizing human rights law in the cyber context, the extraterritorial scope of application of human rights obligations, and establishing responsibility for cyber conduct.

[4] UNHRC 'The Right to Privacy in the Digital Age, Report of the Office of the United Nations High Commissioner for Human Rights' (30 June 2014) A/HRC/27/37 (hereafter UNHRC, 'The Right to Privacy in the Digital Age'); See International Principles on the Application of Human Rights to Communications Surveillance (*Necessary & Proportionate*, May 2014), <https://en.necessaryandproportionate.org/text> accessed 14 August 2019 (thirteen principles drafted by civil society organizations that apply to both domestic and extraterritorial surveillance).

[5] According to US Presidential Policy Directive PPD/20, the term cyberspace refers to: The interdependent network of information technology infrastructures that includes the Internet, telecommunications networks, computers, information or communications systems, networks, and embedded processors and controllers.

[6] The White House, International Strategy for Cyberspace: Prosperity, Security and Openness in a Networked World (Washington 2011) 9 (hereafter The White House, 'International Strategy for Cyberspace').

[7] Marko Milanovic, *Extraterritorial Application of Human Rights Treaties: Law, Principles, and Policy* (OUP 2011) (hereafter Milanovic, *Extraterritorial Application of Human Rights Treaties*); Karen Da Costa, *The Extraterritorial Application of Selected Human Rights Treaties* (Martin Nijhoff Publishers 2012).

[8] Cordula Droege (2007) 'The Interplay between International Humanitarian Law and International Human Rights Law in Situations of Armed Conflict' 40 Israel Law Review 310; Marko Milanovic (2009) 'A Norm Conflict Perspective on the Relationship between International Humanitarian Law and Human Rights Law' 14 Journal of Conflict & Security Law 459; Jelena Pejic (2011) 'The European Court of Human Rights' Al-Jedda Judgment: The Oversight of International Humanitarian Law' 93 International Review of the Red Cross 883.

[9] Jean d'Aspremont, André Nolkaemper, Ilias Plakokefalos, and Cedric Ryngaert (2015) 'Sharing Responsibility Between Non-State Actors and States in International Law: Introduction' 62 Northern Ireland Law Review 49; Jan Hessbruegge (2005) 'Human Rights Violations Arising from Conduct of Non-State Actors' 11 Buffalo Human Rights Law Review 21; Daragh Murray, *Human Rights Obligations of Non-State Armed Groups* (Bloomsbury 2016); Andrew Clapham, *Human Rights Obligations of Non-State Actors* (OUP 2006).

II. Tension Between Rights and Security

In Chapter 6, Liora Lazarus sets out the relationship between rights and security:

> Security, a core rationale of the State, requires coercion and intervention from State actors for its realization. Human rights, on the other hand, are commonly associated with state limitation and, in particular, a structure in which to hold the State's coercive power to account.

The tension between the underlying objectives of human rights and security measures is very visible in the cyber context. Due to an increase in the use of hostile cyber activities and the level of harm that these can potentially cause, states have placed heightened attention on strengthening their defensive and offensive cyber capabilities.[10] Whether we are talking about hostile cyber activity or harmful conduct carried out in the real world, an appreciation of the operational environment and nature of threats and actors within it are important elements in ensuring defensive preparedness. The need for situational awareness lends a degree of justification for the introduction of security measures. Enhanced surveillance, data retention, and information sharing can facilitate the identification of the pattern and nature of cyber and real-time threats and, in turn, improve the public and private sectors' understanding of these threats. Although the motivation for employing such strategies may well be legitimate and their use highly effective in detecting, thwarting, and mitigating potentially harmful conduct, they can have a negative impact in other areas.

Human rights advocates tend to oppose proposals to expand governmental authority to conduct electronic surveillance and information sharing between governments and non-governmental entities.[11] This opposition, which is largely grounded in IHRL guarantees, is likewise justified. In 2015, the Council of Europe issued a report stating that based on the information disclosed by Edward Snowden, the former US Central Intelligence Agency (CIA) contractor who leaked details of extensive surveillance programmes, that these practices endanger fundamental

[10] In March 2016, the UK government announced plans to invest £1.9 billion over the next five years into 'protecting the UK from cyber-attack and developing our sovereign capabilities in cyberspace'; see Cabinet Office, The UK Cyber Security Strategy 2011–2016, Annual Report (April 2016); In February 2016, the United States announced its Cyber Security National Action Plan which provides for the investment of $19 billion into cyber security in 2017, a 35 per cent increase from 2016; see The White House, Fact Sheet: Cybersecurity National Action Plan (February 2016).

[11] For example, the UK Investigatory Powers Bill (also referred to as the Snooper's Charter) has been criticized for its overbroad and unchecked surveillance see Human Rights Watch, Written Evidence to the Joint Committee on the Draft Investigatory Powers Bill (January 2016); House of Lords House of Commons Joint Committee on Human Rights, 'Legislative Scrutiny: Investigatory Powers Bill: First Report of Session 2016–17'. A number of human rights organizations including Amnesty and Liberty launched campaigns to stop the Bill from becoming law.

human rights, including the rights to privacy, freedom of information and expression, the right to a fair trial, and freedom of religion.[12]

Therefore, a tension between rights and security exists; as stated in Fiona de Londras' Chapter 5 on sustainable security, 'a lack of security has negative implications for rights, and measures and actions taken ostensibly in pursuit of security can have negative impacts on rights'.[13] In the context of cyber, strong arguments can be made for enhancing surveillance and information sharing on the one hand, and limiting the authority of governments to employ practices that encroach upon the privacy of individuals on the other.[14]

III. Typology of Cyber Operations

One of the main complexities in determining the way in which cyber operations can affect individual rights stems from the breadth of activities that come under the 'cyber umbrella'.[15] The term encompasses conduct from malicious hacking and defacement of websites, to large-scale destruction of military and civilian infrastructures that rely upon cyber networks. It attaches to activities authored by different types of actors, both private and state entities, and to operations with varying degrees of consequences ranging from encroachment upon privacy and freedom of expression rights, to physical destruction and loss of life.

A. Restricting Online Content

A hostile cyber operation often takes the form of distributed denial of service (*hereinafter* DDoS) attacks.[16] These types of operations, which are becoming increasingly common, work by overloading websites or other online services with data traffic. A successful DDoS attack prevents legitimate Internet users from accessing websites and the information thereon for brief or prolonged intervals. Websites of

[12] Glenn Greenwald 'NSA Collecting Phone Records of Millions of Verizon Customers Daily' *Guardian* (6 June 2013) (hereafter Greenwald, 'NSA Collecting Phone Records')

[13] See Chapter 5, this book.

[14] Rolf Weber and Dominic Staiger, 'Privacy Versus Security: Identifying the Challenges in a Global Information Society' in Joanna Kulesza and Roy Balleste (eds), *Cybersecurity and Human Rights in the Age of Cyberveillance* (Rowman and Littlefield 2016) 63–84.

[15] Mathew Waxman (2011) 'Cyber-Attacks and the Use of Force: Back to the Future of Article 2(4)' 36 Yale Journal of International Law 421, 422; In 2014, the Swiss government funded a project to consolidate cyber security related definitions in the Global Cyber Definitions Database <http://cyberdefinitions.newamerica.org> accessed 25 April 2017; For definitions see also Presidential Policy Directive PPD-20 on US Cyber Operations Policy in the *Guardian* (7 June 2013) <www.theguardian.com/world/interactive/2013/jun/07/obama-cyber-directive-full-text> accessed 14 August 2019.

[16] Kim Zetter, 'Hacker Lexicon: What are DOS and DDOS Attacks?' *Wired* (1 January 2016) <http://www.wired.com/2016/01/hacker-lexicon-what-are-dos-and-ddos-attacks/> accessed 14 August 2019.

human rights organizations and independent media are frequently and increasingly becoming targets of DDoS attacks.[17]

International human rights law guarantees the right to hold and express opinions, and to seek, receive, and impart information.[18] These rights demand that there be as little interference by states as possible to freedom of expression and the flow of information. A DDoS attack that inhibits access to the Internet or the voicing of views, and is attributable to a state, may constitute an interference with the right to respect freedom of opinion and expression.

B. Electronic Surveillance

Surveillance involves the interception of digital communications and the collection of personal data. In 2013, Edward Snowden made public the existence and vast scope of electronic surveillance programmes run by the US National Security Agency and other government agencies, including the UK Government Communications Headquarters.[19] These revelations were met with intense public debate over the lawfulness and propriety of intelligence activities.[20]

The debate has come a long way since the initial revelations and it is now well settled that the practice of surveillance can trigger the right to privacy.[21] This applies to both domestic and foreign surveillance, with the latter subject to a determination that the obligations of the state conducting the surveillance apply extraterritorially.[22] The precise meaning and scope of the right to be free from arbitrary interference with one's privacy is unsettled, and a number of states deny that the associated obligations extend beyond their borders.

Human rights law requires that the integrity and confidentiality of communications be guaranteed: '[c]orrespondence should be delivered to the addressee

[17] Ethan Zuckerman, Hal Roberts, Ryan McGrady, Jillian York, and John Palfrey, 'Distributed Denial of Service Attacks Against Media and Human Rights Sites' (The Berkman Center for Internet & Society at Harvard University, December 2010).

[18] Universal Declaration of Human Rights (adopted 10 December 1948 UNGA Res 217 A (III) (UDHR) art 10; International Covenant on Civil and Political Rights (adopted 16 December 1966, entered into force 23 March 1976) 999 UNTS 171 (ICCPR) art 19; European Convention for the Protection of Human Rights and Fundamental Freedoms (European Convention on Human Rights, as amended) (ECHR) art 10; UNHRC 'Report of the Special Rapporteur on the Promotion and Protection of the Right to Freedom of Opinion and Expression, (16 May 2011) UN Doc. A/HRC/17/27.

[19] Greenwald, 'NSA Collecting Phone Records' (n 12).

[20] European Parliament Resolution on the US National Security Agency Surveillance Programme, Surveillance Bodies in Various Member States and their Impact on EU Citizens' Privacy (2013/2682(RSP)) 4 July 2013; Peter Margulies (2013–14), 'The NSA in Global Perspective: Surveillance, Human Rights, and International Counterterrorism' 82 Fordham Law Review 2137; Marko Milanovic (2015) 'Human Rights Treaties and Foreign Surveillance: Privacy in the Digital Age' 56 Harvard International Law Journal 81 (hereafter Milanovic, 'Human Rights Treaties and Foreign Surveillance').

[21] UNHRC, 'The Right to Privacy in the Digital Age' (n 4).

[22] Ibid, 11–12; see section IV on jurisdiction following.

without interception and without being opened or otherwise read'.[23] Therefore, if a state reads an email or listens in on a phone conversation, the right to privacy is triggered. As well as the content of communications, the collection and retention of metadata also constitutes a potential interference with the right to privacy, whether or not that content is consulted or used.[24] The European Court of Human Rights (ECtHR) has found that the mere existence of legislation which allows for covert monitoring of communications amounts to an interference with the right to privacy, irrespective of any measures actually taken against individuals.[25] In addition to the right to privacy, surveillance practices may also interfere with other rights, albeit indirectly. If an individual refrains from seeking or communicating sensitive health-related information based on the fear that his anonymity would be compromised, this could amount to an infringement of the right to health.[26]

C. Manipulation of Control Systems

To date, cyber operations have not been the cause of major humanitarian consequences. In saying that, cyber attacks against transportation systems, electricity networks, dams, and chemical or nuclear plants causing death and significant damage are technically possible. In testimony before US Congress in the late 1990s, then Deputy Defense Secretary, John Hamre, warned that the United States was facing the possibility of an 'electronic Pearl Harbor', adding that such an attack 'is not going to be against Navy ships sitting in a Navy shipyard; it is going to be against commercial infrastructure'. The threat posed to critical infrastructure by hostile cyber activity was again likened to 'Pearl Harbor' in 2010 by US Defense Secretary, Leon Panetta: '[Attackers] could derail passenger trains, or even more dangerous, derail passenger trains loaded with lethal chemicals. They could contaminate the water supply in major cities, or shut down the power grid across large parts of the country.'[27]

In 2015, a succession of technological outages temporarily grounded United Airlines flights, shut down the *Wall Street Journal* website, and halted trading on

[23] Ibid, 6. Official Records of the General Assembly, Forty-third Session, Supplement No. 40 (A/43/40), annex VI, para 8, as cited in Report of High Commissioner for Human Rights on the Right to Privacy in the Digital Age.

[24] UNHRC, 'The Right to Privacy in the Digital Age' (n 4) 19.

[25] *Szabo and Vissy v Hungary* App No 37138/14 (ECtHR, 12 January 2016). But see the earlier case of *Klass and Others v Germany* App No 5029/71 (ECtHR, 6 September 1978).

[26] Ibid, para 14. The right to health is included in the UDHR, supra note 17, Article 25 and ICCPR, supra note 17, Article 12.

[27] Elisabeth Bumiller and Thom Shanker, 'Panetta Warns of Dire Threat of Cyberattack on US' *New York Times* (11 October 2011) <http://www.nytimes.com/2012/10/12/world/panetta-warns-of-dire-threat-of-cyberattack.html> accessed 14 August 2019.

the New York Stock Exchange.[28] In March 2016, the US Department of Justice indicted a hacker based in Iran for gaining remote access to a computer controlling a dam in New York. [29] In December 2015, destructive malware is estimated to have knocked out more than thirty power stations across Ukraine for approximately six hours.[30] Policy-makers and cybersecurity experts predict that a cyber-attack on energy infrastructure could shut down water supplies, electricity, and gas, disrupt transportation and communication networks, and cripple financial institutions.[31] A report from the Congressional Research Service explains that modernization of the US electricity grid, while improving its efficiency, will increase its vulnerability to cyber attacks.[32] It is difficult to estimate the effect that a power outage might have on a major city but it is apparent that it could extend further than a temporary loss of production and transport delays.

It was the Stuxnet worm that first brought attention to the vulnerability of industrial control systems to remote manipulation and the potential for physical damage to facilities such as power plants, dams, and other critical infrastructure.[33] In that case, a worm inserted into the computer systems of a nuclear enrichment reactor facilitated the gaining of access to its internal network.[34] Through this access, the worm compromised the system's vulnerabilities, took control of the operating system, specifically affecting Iranian centrifuges.[35] The valves on these were manipulated so as to increase pressure, which in turn may have caused physical damage to the devices.[36] In 2015, a German report revealed that hackers had manipulated and disrupted control systems of a steel mill resulting in 'massive' damage due to an explosion at the site.[37] According to the report, the hackers may have

[28] Andrea Chang and Tracey Lien, 'Outages at NYSE, United Airlines, WSJ.com Expose Digital Vulnerabilities' *Los Angeles Times* (8 July 2015) <http://www.latimes.com/business/technology/la-fi-tn-technical-problems-united-nyse-20150708-story.html> accessed 14 August 2019.

[29] David Sanger, 'US Indicts 7 Iranians in Cyberattacks on Banks and a Dam' *New York Times* (24 March 2016) <https://www.nytimes.com/2016/03/25/world/middleeast/us-indicts-iranians-in-cyberattacks-on-banks-and-a-dam.html?_r=0> accessed 14 August 2019.

[30] Jordan Robertson and Michael Riley, 'How Hackers Took Down a Power Grid' *Bloomberg* (14 January 2016) <http://www.bloomberg.com/news/articles/2016-01-14/how-hackers-took-down-a-power-grid> accessed 14 August 2019.

[31] 'Cyber Attack on US Infrastructure' (*Council on Foreign Relations*) <http://www.cfr.org/global/global-conflict-tracker/p32137#!/?marker=2> accessed 14 August 2019.

[32] Richard J Campbell, 'Cybersecurity Issues for the Bulk Power System' (*Congressional Research Service*, 10 June 2015) <http://www.fas.org/sgp/crs/misc/R43989.pdf> accessed 14 August 2019.

[33] Jeremy Richmond (2012) 'Evolving Battlefields: Does Stuxnet Demonstrate a Need for Modifications to the Law of Armed Conflict?' 35(3) Fordham International Law Journal 841.

[34] The worm was reportedly inserted via a thumb drive, email, or a file share.

[35] Centrifuges are large cylindrical tubes that spin at supersonic speed to separate isotopes in uranium gas for use in nuclear power plants and weapons.

[36] It is not clear whether the Stuxnet worm did in fact cause damage of a physical nature. Iranian officials did not confirm any actual damage. See 'Stuxnet—Legal Considerations' (NATO Cooperative Cyber Defence Centre of Excellence, Cyber Defence Library) <https://ccdcoe.org/library/publications/stuxnet-legal-considerations/> 26 November 2019

[37] Robert Lee, Michael Assante, and Tim Conway, 'German Steel Mill Cyber Attack: ICS CP/PE Cyber-to-Physical or Process Effects Case Study Paper' (ICS Defense Use Case, 30 December 2014) <https://ics.sans.org/media/ICS-CPPE-case-Study-2-German-Steelworks_Facility.pdf> accessed 14 August 2019.

gained access through an email message containing malware or a downloaded file that enabled malware to install itself on a computer.

In both these cases, remote control of the infrastructure, and the resulting damage, was affected by way of the installation of malware onto the compromised system. Although these operations did not affect the rights of individuals, their destructive character indicates that such an outcome is possible. Manipulation of, or disruption to, the operation of critical infrastructure could interfere with the enjoyment of a number of rights; taking down a communications network might violate the right to freedom of expression; shutting off electrical supplies, manipulating navigation systems, or opening the flood gates of a dam, may result in loss of life; and interruption to infrastructures that support health services, water supplies, or sanitation systems, could potentially encroach upon the enjoyment of socio-economic rights.

IV. The International Legal Frameworks Applicable to State Conduct in Cyber Space

The emergence of any new form of technology calls for clarification of the legal frameworks regulating its use. This is as true in the context of cyber as it is in relation to drone technology.[38] Although the cyber field is relatively new and constantly developing, activities conducted by states within it do not exist in a legal vacuum. The UN Human Rights Council, the UN General Assembly, non-governmental organizations (NGOs), and states support the idea that cyber conduct is regulated by existing international law. The United States, for example, has asserted that 'development of norms for state conduct in cyberspace does not require a reinvention of customary international law, nor does it render existing international norms obsolete. Long-standing international norms guiding state behavior—in times of peace and conflict—also apply in cyberspace.'[39]

Cyber operations may implicate IHRL and to the extent that the conduct amounts to a use of force or is taken in the context of an armed conflict, *jus ad bellum* and IHL may also apply. These frameworks apply concurrently but are distinct bodies of law; the lawfulness of a cyber operation under the *jus ad bellum* will have no bearing on its legality under the applicable rules of IHL and IHRL. If a cyber operation is conducted in peacetime, the applicable rules of IHRL will govern the consequences. In a situation of armed conflict, whether of an international or non-international character, IHL and IHRL will apply concurrently.[40]

[38] See Christof Heyns *et al*, Chapter 7, this book.

[39] The White House, 'International Strategy for Cyberspace' (n 6) 9.

[40] On classification of conflict see Dapo Akande, 'Classification of Armed Conflicts: Relevant Legal Concepts' in Elizabeth Wilmshurst (ed), *International Law and the Classification of Conflicts* (OUP 2012) 72.

The nature and pattern of hostile cyber activities demonstrate the ability for the author to launch the operation from a state other than the one in which the consequences ultimately manifest. The weight of international jurisprudence and legal scholarship recognizes that states carry their human rights obligations with them where they exercise effective control over territory or an individual in their extraterritorial operations.[41] In situations of armed conflict, human rights law continues to apply alongside the laws of armed conflict subject to the application of the principle of *lex specialis*.[42] Parallel application of IHL and IHRL has been explicitly recognized by the ICJ,[43] scholars,[44] and is implied in the set-up of some human rights instruments. Some human rights treaties provide for derogations pursuant to which states can suspend certain human rights treaty obligations in situations of war or other public emergency.[45] Inherent in this system is an understanding that absent valid derogation, human rights obligations under the operative treaty continue. For a discussion on how the two frameworks interact in relation to the right to life, see Heyns, Akande, Hill-Cawthorne, and Chengeta, Chapter 7, this book.

While IHL will govern matters that it addresses, such as rules for targeting and for treatment and trial of detainees, it does not cover all matters related to armed conflict. For example, IHL presumes that persons will be detained in non-international armed conflict but in contrast with the rules regulating international armed conflict, it does not contain grounds and procedures for detention.[46] Accordingly, domestic law as informed by the state's human rights law obligations provides the relevant rules.[47] IHL may also be silent on other issues related to the armed conflict that are addressed by IHRL for example, surveillance, censorship, crimes against humanity, and genocide.[48] In the event that cyber activities are used in the commission of these crimes, human rights law may apply.

[41] *Legal Consequences of the Construction of a Wall* (Advisory Opinion) [2004] ICJ Rep 136, para 109 (hereafter *Legal Consequences of the Construction of a Wall*); UNHRC 'General Comment 31' (2004) CCPR/C/21/Rev.1/Add.13 para 10 (hereafter UNHRC, 'General Comment 31'); *Al-Skeini v United Kingdom* App No 55721/07 (Grand Chamber Judgment, 7 July 2011) paras 106–186; *Loizidou v Turkey* (1997) 23 EHRR 513; *Ilascu v Moldoca and Russia* (2005) EHRR 46, para 392. *Al-Jedda v United Kingdom* App No 27021/08 (ECtHR, 7 July 2011); *Jaloud v Netherlands* App No 47708/08 (Grand Chamber Judgment) (ECtHR, 20 November 2014).

[42] *Legality of the Threat or Use of Nuclear Weapons*, Advisory Opinion [1996] ICJ Rep 226, para 25; *Legal Consequences of the Construction of a Wall in the Occupied Territory*, ibid, para 106; *Armed Activities on the Territory of the Congo (DRC v Uganda)* [2005] ICJ Rep 116, para 216 (hereafter *DRC v Uganda*).

[43] *Legality of the Threat or Use of Nuclear Weapons* (n 42); *Legal Consequences of the Construction of a Wall* (n 41); *DRC v Uganda* (n 42).

[44] Cordula Droege (2008) 'Elective Affinities? Human Rights and Humanitarian Law' 90 (871) International Review of the Red Cross 501, 503–09; See references (n 8).

[45] See eg ICCPR art 4; ECHR art 15; ACHR art 27.

[46] For a thorough discussion on the topic of detention in non-international armed conflict see Lawrence Hill-Cawthorne, *Detention in Non International Armed Conflict* (OUP 2016).

[47] The ECtHR has been active in developing the law in this area. See *Hassan v UK* App No 29750/09 (ECtHR, 16 September 2014).

[48] Gabor Rona and Lauren Aarons (2016) 'State Responsibility to Respect, Protect and Fulfil Human Rights Obligations in Cyber' 8(3) Journal of National Security Law & Policy 32.

V. Challenges to Application of the International Human Rights Law Framework

The critical distinguishing characteristic of cyber space is that it has no physical borders. It exists almost everywhere, is accessible to anyone, and allows users to move across it with ease and varying degrees of anonymity. From the perspective of treaty law, it is difficult to contemplate the transposition of legal rules, the scope of which are traditionally understood in terms territorial demarcation, to a space where no system of geographical division exists. Cyber operations, whether it come in the form of surveillance, DDoS attack, or remote control of a critical infrastructure, can be initiated from a location far removed from where the effects of the operation ultimately manifest. As recent practice illustrates, hostile cyber operations are frequently of an extraterritorial nature.

Similar to lethal drones, one of the main difficulties in applying the IHRL framework extraterritorially to cyber operations is that the author can cause effects beyond its borders without exercising effective control over territory, or without having the affected individual in custody.[49] Cyber operations may even be achieved without the physical presence of the author on the territory upon which the consequences are ultimately felt. The unique characteristics of cyber operations raise a question as to whether those harmed fall within the 'jurisdiction' of the authoring state for the purposes of conferring human rights treaty obligations on that state. At the core of the issue is the concept of jurisdiction, what it means in the human rights law treaty regime and how, if at all, it translates to the cyber context.

A. Jurisdiction in Cyberspace

Article 1 of the European Convention on Human Rights (ECHR) states that the 'High Contracting Parties shall secure to everyone within their jurisdiction the rights and freedoms defined in Section I of this Convention'.[50] Article 2(1) of the International Covenant on Civil and Political Rights (ICCPR) provides that '[e]ach State Party to the present Covenant undertakes to respect and to ensure to all individuals within its territory and subject to its jurisdiction the rights recognized in the present Covenant'.[51] Unlike the ICCPR, the ECHR makes no mention of territory, nor does it explicitly distinguish between obligations to respect and to ensure human rights; the obligation to respect features in the title of Article 1, and the obligation to secure in the accompanying text. The application of IHRL treaties

[49] See Heyns *et al*, Chapter 7, this book.
[50] ECHR (n 18).
[51] ICCPR (n 18).

is ordinarily confined to individuals within the 'jurisdiction' of a state party.[52] All persons finding themselves within the territory of a state are presumed to be within its territorial jurisdiction.

It has been held that human rights treaties 'cannot be interpreted so as to allow a State party to perpetrate violations of [the treaty] on the territory of another State, which it could not perpetrate on its own territory'.[53] The ECtHR has produced the majority of jurisprudence on the issue of extraterritorial application of human rights law. The UN Human Rights Committee (HRC) has also contributed to the development of the area, albeit to a lesser degree. What emerges from the case law are two models whereby 'jurisdiction' can be established such that the state's obligations under the operative human rights treaty will apply; the spatial model and personal model. The spatial model grounds jurisdiction on the exercise of effective control over a part of another state's territory.[54] Absent such territorial control, the personal model dictates that jurisdiction will nevertheless exist in situations where the state exercises, through its agents, authority or control over the specific individual abroad.[55] Pursuant to both approaches, the concept of control is synonymous with jurisdiction. What distinguishes the models is how control is established.

B. Spatial and Personal Models of Control

The spatial model sees jurisdiction based on the exercise of effective control over areas. The ECtHR set out the model in *Loizidou*.[56] The HRC has also applied it.[57] In the *Namibia* Advisory Opinion, the ICJ stated that South Africa, which was at the time occupying Namibia was: '[a]ccountable for any violations ... of the rights of the people of Namibia ... Physical control of a territory, and not sovereignty or legitimacy of title, is the basis of State liability for acts affecting other States.'[58]

[52] Since *Lopez Burgos v Uruguay* Com 52/1979, Views, 29 July 1981, the Human Rights Committee has held that State parties can also be held accountable for human rights violations outside their territory.

[53] *Issa and others v Turkey* App No 31821/96 (ECtHR, 16 November 2004) para 71.

[54] See eg UNHRC, 'General Comment 31' (n 41) para 10; *Loizidou v Turkey* (1995) Series A Preliminary Objections, 310 paras 62–64. See the discussion in Milanovic (n 7). *Loizidou v Turkey* (n 40) para 62.

[55] *Öcalan v Turkey* App No 46221/99 (ECtHR, 12 March 2003) para 93; *Issa and others v Turkey* (n 53) para 71; UN Human Rights Comm, *Lopez v Uruguay*, Comm No R.12/52, paras 12.1–12.3, UN Doc Supp. No. 40 (A/36/40) at 176 (1981); UN Human Rights Comm, *Montero v Uruguay*, Comm No 106/1981, para 5, UN Doc. CCPR/C/OP/2.

[56] See n 54.

[57] Concluding Observations of the Human Rights Committee: Israel (18 August 1998) UN Doc. CCPR/C/79/Add.93, para 10.

[58] *Legal Consequences for States of the Continued Presence of South Africa in Namibia (South West Africa) Notwithstanding Security Council Resolution 276* (1970) (Advisory Opinion) [1971] ICJ Rep 16.

Although not a decision about human rights treaty law, it paved the way for the *Wall*[59] and *Congo v Uganda*[60] judgments in which the ICJ found that the ICCPR applied during occupation in these cases. The spatial approach is the least controversial of the models and the easiest to apply; human rights obligations towards another territory's inhabitants flow from the exercise of control over that territory by another state in a way that resembles its control over its own territory.

As just noted, the personal model dictates that jurisdiction will exist in situations where the state exercises, through its agents, authority or control over the specific individual abroad. As with the spatial model, the question as to what constitutes control over an individual, and whether that extends to non-physical control, requires consideration. If the personal model is limited by a requirement of physical custody, instantaneous acts such as an extraterritorial cyber operation, which interferes with an individual's privacy rights or results in loss of life would fall outside the state's jurisdiction.

Many ECtHR cases applying the personal model, including *Öcalan* and *Sanchez Ramirez*, have dealt with detention situations.[61] The model has also been applied in the absence of physical custody, as, for example, in *Pad*,[62] *Isaak*,[63] and *Solomou*.[64] In *Al-Skeini*, one applicant was killed by UK troops while in custody in a UK detention facility in Iraq, while the five other applicants were killed by British troops on patrol in Basra. The ECtHR's Grand Chamber found that all six were under the UK's jurisdiction pursuant to the personal model. At first blush this may seem like a broadening of the personal model, however the Court exercised a degree of restraint. Although the Grand Chamber found all of the applicants to be under the UK's jurisdiction conceived of in *personal* terms, it determined that this reasoning extended to situations where the state using force exercises some kind of 'public powers'. In this case public powers derived from the occupation of Iraq and relevant resolutions of the Security Council pursuant to which the United Kingdom 'assumed authority and responsibility for the maintenance of Security in South East Iraq'.[65] In other words, the power to kill must be coupled with public powers in order to constitute 'authority and control'; the power to kill in and of itself will not be enough to establish jurisdiction.

In 2015, the High Court of England and Wales gave *Al-Skeini* a broader interpretation.[66] In *Al-Saadoon*, it held that the ECHR applies to situations where

[59] See n 41.

[60] *DRC v Uganda* (n 42) 168.

[61] *Öcalan* (n 55); *Ramirez Sanchez v France* App No 59450/00 (ECtHR, 27 January 2005).

[62] *Mansur PAD and Others v Turkey* App No 60167/00 (ECtHR, 28 June 2007)—bombing an area from a helicopter.

[63] Beaten to death by a group of protesters at a protest; *Isaak v Turkey* App No 44587/98 (ECtHR, I November 1998).

[64] Shot and killed; *Solomou v Turkey* App No 36832/97 (ECtHR, 24 June 2008).

[65] *Al-Skeini* (n 41) para 149.

[66] *Al-Sadoon and Others v Secretary of State for Defence* [2015] EWHC 715 (Admin).

Iraqi civilians were shot during security operations carried out by British soldiers. In considering whether exercising the requisite control for the purposes of establishing jurisdiction under the Convention included shooting an individual, Leggatt J found:

> The essential principle that I derive is that whenever and wherever a state which is a contracting party to the Convention purports to exercise legal authority or uses physical force, it must do so in a way that does not violate Convention rights. That is still a far-reaching principle of jurisdiction ...
>
> When the lesser use of force involved in apprehending someone has been held to bring that person within the article 1 jurisdiction of a contracting state, it makes no sense to hold that the greater use of force involved in killing someone does not have that effect.[67]

Here, the High Court applied *Al Skeini* in a way that jurisdiction as authority and control over an individual exercised by a state agent encompasses the use of lethal force against that person. This approach would most likely extend extraterritorial obligations to lethal drones, and could potentially apply also to breaches of the Convention occurring as a consequence of cyber operations as physical control is not required.[68] In September 2016, the Court of Appeal of England and Wales disagreed with this aspect of the High Court's judgment finding that this was not the intention of the ECtHR in *Al-Skeini*, and that if the personal model were to incorporate uses of lethal force, it would be for the Strasbourg Court to interpret it accordingly.[69]

C. Applying the Models to Cyber Operations

Technological developments have largely rendered the exercise of physical control over a location or an individual unnecessary or less necessary and therefore, how traditional understandings of 'control' translate to operations conducted through cyberspace is a complex question to which only speculative answers can be offered. Most extraterritorial cyber operations will involve the author gaining 'virtual' control over certain functions of a computer, server, or other cyber-dependent machine. Therefore, existing case law, which has thus far involved only direct physical control over a location or person, is difficult to transpose to the cyber context, and

67 Ibid, para 106–107.

68 Marko Milanovic, 'English Court of Appeal Decides Al-Saadoon Case on the ECHR's Application Extraterritorially and in Armed Conflict' (EJIL: Talk!, 14 September 2016) <https://www.ejiltalk.org/english-court-of-appeal-decides-al-saadoon-case-on-the-echrs-application-extraterritorially-and-in-armed-conflict/> accessed 26 November 2019.

69 *Al-Saadoon & Ors v Secretary of State for Defence* [2016] EWCA Civ 811, paras 69–73.

may even preclude the extension of human rights law obligations to these activities when conducted extraterritorially.

In their current form, the spatial and personal models of extraterritorial jurisdiction do not accommodate extraterritorial cyber operations. A third model based on the distinction between the overarching positive obligation of states to secure or ensure human rights and the negative obligation of states to respect human rights, has been put forward by Marko Milanovic and is believed by a number of scholars to be the most satisfactory approach.[70] Pursuant to the third model, jurisdiction primarily means effective overall control over areas and where this is established, an overarching *positive* obligation to comply with human rights obligations. On the other hand, the *negative* obligation to respect human rights is territorially unlimited and not subject to any jurisdictional threshold. If this model were to be followed, a state's negative obligations not to interfere with rights would be triggered where its use of hostile cyber activities interfered with the rights of an individual wherever located.

Cases that have come before the ECtHR and HRC in this area have, to date, focused on situations involving the exercise of physical force by a state's security forces. Although the ECtHR and the HRC have yet to deal with the issue of extraterritorial application of human rights law to cyber operations, the UK specialized surveillance court, the Investigatory Powers Tribunal (*hereinafter* IPT), ruled in May 2016, that persons not present within the United Kingdom do not come within the jurisdiction of the United Kingdom for the purposes of Article 1 of the Convention.[71] Accordingly, an individual in France who is the target of a surveillance operation conducted by and from the United Kingdom, or a person in Ireland killed in an explosion at a nuclear power plant resulting from the remote control of its operation systems by a group operating in Russia, and whose conduct is attributable to that state, does not have an ECHR right to privacy vis-à-vis the United Kingdom, or right to life vis-à-vis Russia respectively.

The case law of the ECtHR supports the argument that human rights law applies where a state intercepts data on its own territory that belongs to an individual outside its territory. In *Liberty and Others v United Kingdom*, the ECtHR held that the United Kingdom violated the Convention right to privacy through legislation that afforded extensive powers to executive authorities to undertake extraterritorial surveillance.[72] The case related to communications between an NGO in Ireland and the United Kingdom that ran through a cable in the United Kingdom. The legislation allowed for the interception of emails originating from outside the United Kingdom in order to protect national security or economic interests. The fact that

[70] Milanovic, *Extraterritorial Application of Human Rights Treaties* (n 7) 209–21.

[71] *Human Rights Watch Inc and Ors v The Secretary of State for the Foreign & Commonwealth Office and Ors* [2016] UKIPTrib 15_165-CH.

[72] *Liberty and Others v the United Kingdom* App No 58243/00 (ECtHR, 2008) 1.

the claimant NGO was located in Ireland posed no barrier to the finding of an Article 8 violation of the ECHR. Therefore, contrary to the decision of the IPT, it is the location of the act causing the harm; that is, the interception that matters for the purposes of establishing jurisdiction.

Whether a state's control over a territory or a person through cyber means can also trigger the application of human rights law has yet to be clarified. However, the increase in cyber technologies may well see human rights law develop in a way that recognizes cyber operations, in addition to physical acts, as potential triggers for the extraterritorial application of IHRL. The HRC has suggested that extraterritorial surveillance does implicate the ICCPR[73] and the UN Office of the High Commissioner for Human Rights, has also asserted the opinion that human rights law would apply where a state exercises its power or effective control in relation to digital communications infrastructure wherever located, for example through direct tapping or interception of communication infrastructure located outside that state's territory.[74] The logic behind the extension of obligations to extraterritorial cyber operations is obvious, 'if virtual methods can in principle accomplish the exact same thing as physical ones, then there seems to be no valid reason to treat them differently and insist on some kind of direct corporeal intervention'.[75] If this approach is carried forward in the case law, it would not only extend states' obligations in the extraterritorial cyber arena but also in the context of lethal drones.

VI. State Responsibility for Cyber Operations

Cyber technologies and cyber space offer a relatively cheap, convenient, and effective means for both states and non-state actors to conduct hostile operations. It is therefore unsurprising that there are an increasing number of entities, both state and non-state, developing their cyber capabilities. These include the Syrian Electronic Army, the Iranian Cyber Army, CyberBerkut, and US Cyber Command. Because of the anonymity offered by cyber space, it will often be technically difficult to trace the author of a cyber operation, and even more challenging to rebut denials that hostile activities were directed or supported by a state.[76] As non-state actors do not have enforceable human rights obligations, redress for human rights

[73] UNHRC, *Concluding Observations on the Fourth Periodic Republic of the United States* (23 April 2014) UN Doc. CCPR/C/USA/CO/4 22.

[74] UNHRC, 'The Right to Privacy in the Digital Age' (n 4); UNHRC 'Report of the United Nations High Commissioner for Human Rights on the Protection of Human Rights and Fundamental Freedoms While Countering Terrorism' (22 January 2010) UN Doc. A/HRC/13/36.

[75] Milanovic, 'Human Rights Treaties and Foreign Surveillance' (n 20) 129.

[76] Peter Margulies (2013) 'Sovereignty and Cyber Attacks: Technology's Challenge to the Law of State Responsibility' 14 Melbourne Journal of International Law 496 (hereafter Marguiles, 'Sovereignty and Cyber Attacks'); Scott Shackelford and Richard Andres (2010–11) 'State Responsibility for Cyber Attacks: Competing Standards for a Growing Problem' 42 Georgia Journal of International Law 971 (hereafter Shackelford and Andres, 'State Responsibility for Cyber Attacks').

violations is dependent upon attributing the conduct to a state. Where the technical difficulties associated with tracing the author of the conduct and establishing a link between it and a state are overcome, the further hurdle lies in the satisfying the legal rules for attribution.

A. Distinguishing Attribution from Jurisdiction

Before turning to consider the substance of legal attribution and the complexities it attracts in the context of cyber, it is helpful to distinguish the concept from jurisdiction. The weight of the literature on extraterritoriality is in line with what was discussed earlier; extraterritorial jurisdiction is contingent upon the existence of effective control, and effective control is understood in terms of a nexus between the state on the one hand, and the territory or victims, on the other. Another interpretation holds that when a state causes a wrongful result, effective control has no other role in extraterritoriality than that of a criterion for attribution of the wrongful conduct.[77] The main difference here is that an attribution test is concerned with determining who should be held responsible rather than whether the ECHR is applicable abroad; where conduct is directly attributable, jurisdiction attaches. According to Tzevelekos, and contrary to the writings of scholars such as Milanovic: 'A State that is causing a breach of international law, including human rights, outside its territory is internationally responsible for that conduct, no matter whether it exercises effective control over that territory or not. Effective control should only come into play if the question of attribution arises.'[78]

This is an attractive position from a human rights standpoint as it presupposes that a state has human rights obligations when it conducts operations extraterritorially regardless of the level of control it has over the territory or the individual whose rights are affected. Having said that, this approach is not supported by the majority of the case law.

Whatever the role of effective control, it is apparent that the issue of attribution is central to each and every case because without it, there can be no state responsibility for the conduct and in turn, no redress. In most cases coming before human rights bodies, attribution is not explicitly dealt with. Instead, it is a preliminary inquiry that although important, does not require elaboration due to the obviousness of the answer. Take for example a situation where Irish state agents tap my phone

[77] Vassilis Tzevelekos (2015) 'Reconstructing the Effective Control Criterion in Extraterritorial Human Rights Breaches: Direct Attribution of Wrongfulness, Due Diligence, and Concurrent Responsibility' 36(1) Michigan Journal of International Law 129; Jane Rooney (2015) 'The Relationship between Jurisdiction and Attribution after *Jaloud v Netherlands*' 62(3) Netherlands International Law Review 407; Aurel Sari (2014) 'Untangling Extra-Territorial Jurisdiction From International Responsibility in *Jaloud v. Netherlands*: Old Problem, New Solutions? 53 Military Law of War Review 287, 318.

[78] Tzevelekos, ibid, at *fn* 63.

and listen in on my conversation while I am in the United Kingdom. I submit an application to the ECtHR alleging a violation of my right to privacy. Here, attribution is evident and the issue is dispensed with at the outset. The Court has determined, without need for discussion, that Ireland is responsible for the tapping and so the analysis begins with an inquiry as to whether the tapping of my phone constitutes an exercise of jurisdiction over me for the purposes of establishing whether Ireland had an obligation not to interfere with my privacy rights.

B. Attribution Test

Although the issue of attribution has in most cases been a preliminary consideration that is easily satisfied, the cyber context is likely to disrupt this pattern. The fact that non-state actors do not have human rights obligations could incentivize the use of proxy 'non-state' cyber entities; the link between it and the state masked by plausible deniability.[79] Responsibility for the 2007 cyber operations targeting Estonia was attributed to the Nashi youth activist group, but it has been speculated that Russia contributed to the efforts.[80] Operations targeting the US banking sector have been attributed primarily to the *Izz ad-Din al-Qassam* Cyber Fighters with the involvement of the Iranian government probable, but unconfirmed.[81] In 2013, China was accused of having supported a group of Chinese hackers in the carrying out of a series of cyber hacks on the *New York Times*.[82] These and other allegations of government-sponsored offensive activities in the cyber domain have been denied by China, and it was only in 2015 that it formally acknowledged the existence of specialized units for conducting cyber operations.[83] What these examples illustrate, is how difficult it can be to determine the author of a cyber operation and in turn, to allocate legal responsibility for any associated international law violations, including international human rights law.

In order to attribute conduct to a state for the purpose of establishing state responsibility, a connection must be established between the state and the unlawful conduct. Pursuant to the rules on state responsibility, conduct carried out by

[79] Michael Schmitt and Liis Vihul (2014) 'Proxy Wars in Cyber Space: The Evolving International Law of Attribution' 1(2) Fletcher Security Review 55.

[80] Declaration of the Minister of Foreign Affairs of the Republic of Estonia (1 May 2007) <https://valitsus.ee/en/news/declaration-minister-foreign-affairs-republic-estonia> accessed 14 August 2019.

[81] Nicole Perlroth and Quentin Hardy, 'Bank Hacking was the Work of Iranians, Officials Say' *New York Times* (8 January 2013) <http://www.nytimes.com/2013/01/09/technology/online-banking-attacks-were-work-of-iran-us-officials-say.html?_r=0> accessed 14 August 2019.

[82] Nicole Perlroth, 'Hackers in China Attacked The Times for Last 4 Months' *New York Times* (30 January 2013) <http://www.nytimes.com/2013/01/31/technology/chinese-hackers-infiltrate-new-york-times-computers.html> accessed 13 August 2019.

[83] Shane Harris, 'China Reveals its Cyberwar Secrets' *The Daily Beast* (18 March 2015) <http://www.thedailybeast.com/articles/2015/03/18/china-reveals-its-cyber-war-secrets.html> accessed 13 August 2019.

non-state actors will be considered an act of a state 'if the person or group of persons is in fact acting on the instructions of, or under the direction or control of that State in carrying out the conduct'.[84] There is ongoing debate over the standard to be used in determining the level of control required for attribution.[85] Some advocate for the *Nicaragua* 'effective control' test while others favour the less stringent 'overall control' formula.[86]

The *Nicaragua* effective control standard requires a finding that the state either directly influenced the commission of the act or enforced its perpetration. If *Nicaragua*'s formulation were to be applied to the relationship between a non-state actor engaged in harmful cyber activities and a potential state sponsor, it would mean that the latter could only be held responsible where effective control by the state could be proven beyond any doubt. This is a very high threshold and in the cyber context where technical difficulties will often mask the author(s) of conduct carried out within it, it is a burden of proof which may rarely be satisfied. The International Criminal Tribunal for the Former Yugoslavia (ICTY) introduced a lower standard in *Tadić*. It distinguished the case of individuals and unorganized groups where 'effective control' is the requisite standard from that of organized groups where 'overall control' is required. Overall control over a group can exist 'not only by equipping and financing the group, but also by coordinating or helping in the general planning of its military activity.' This test requires a showing that the state exerts general and direct influence over the group and its activities. Effective control on the other hand is established by control over the specific act.

In *Bosnian Genocide*, the ICJ dealt head on with the competing tests when it considered the question of whether the acts of genocide carried out at Srebrenica by Bosnian Serb armed forces must be attributed to the Federal Republic of Yugoslavia.[87] The Court applied the 'effective control' test set out in *Nicaragua* and reached a negative conclusion. Judge Antonio Cassese has criticized the ICJ's reasons for applying the effective control test and rendering the overall control test inapplicable in the circumstances.[88] In his article, Cassese notes that from a policy standpoint, the overall control test may prove helpful in legally appraising

[84] International Law Commission, Draft Articles on Responsibility of States for Internationally Wrongful Acts, November 2001, Supplement No 10 (A/56/10), chp.IV.E.1, art 8.

[85] Antonio Cassese (2007) 'The Nicaragua and Tadić Cases Revisited in Light of the ICJ Judgement on Genocide in Bosnia' 18(4) European Journal of International Law 649 (hereafter Cassese, 'The Nicaragua and Tadić Cases'); See Shackelford and Andres, 'State Responsibility for Cyber Attacks' (n 76) 971—the authors argue for a flexible test of attribution in the cyber context; Margulies argues for an even broader approach in the cyber context, one of 'virtual control' see Marguiles, 'Sovereignty and Cyber Attacks' (n 76) 496.

[86] The ICJ articulated the effective control standard for the first time in the *Nicaragua* Judgment. *Case Concerning Military and Paramilitary Activities in and Against Nicaragua* (Merits) [1986] ICJ Rep 14, paras 105–115; Tadić Case (Appeals) ICTY- 94-1-A (15 July 1999); see also Case Concerning the Application of the Convention on the Prevention and Punishment of the Crime of Genocide (Bosnia and Herzegovina v Serbia and Montenegro) [2007] ICJ Rep 43 paras 399–401.

[87] Ibid.

[88] Cassese, 'The Nicaragua and Tadić Cases' (n 85).

new trends in the use by states of armed groups or military units. Although he does not include non-state cyber operatives in this discussion, the points he makes nevertheless ring true to this context.[89] If the law of state responsibility is to apply to cyber activity and in turn facilitate accountability for human rights and other international law violations associated with them, an overall control standard should be adopted.[90]

The current structure of the law of state responsibility rests on the premise that the responsibility of a state attaches only to state or public acts. Considering the challenges faced when attempting to establish responsibility for cyber operations namely anonymity, plausible deniability, and technical complexities, along with the ever-advancing cyber capabilities of non-state actors, it is questionable whether existing understandings of state responsibility and attribution are adequate when applied to the cyber context. As it stands, international law presupposes that states are the dominant and most powerful entities in the international system however, the dynamics may be shifting in the cyber context. Cyber capabilities are relatively easy to acquire and therefore non-state actors can operate independent of states. Furthermore, the current models of attribution, which are grounded in notions of physicality, are not easily transposed to situations where anonymity abounds. As was contemplated in the section on extraterritorial application of human rights law obligations, it may well be the case that attribution standards adjust to accommodate the realities of the cyber context and the actors that operate within it.

VII. Conclusion

It is now well established that existing international law rules, including those coming within the international human rights law framework, apply to cyber operations. Recognizing this is, however, only one step in the direction of effective regulation of harmful cyber conduct. International law, which is based on traditional notions of physicality and state supremacy, does not easily transpose to cyber space, cyber operations, and the multiplicity of actors involved. Some of the barriers that arise are specific to cyber, while others are common to other areas. Long before the term cyber became commonplace, debates were underway about the scope of application of human rights law; does it apply to the conduct of a state beyond its borders? Does it apply in situations of armed conflict given the primacy of IHL in such situations? Does it apply to the conduct of non-state actors? These questions are likewise central to the cyber context and their reemergence here serves to highlight their persisting complexity and in turn, the need to further investigate these issues as they relate to all fields of international law.

89 Ibid.

90 See Shackelford and Andres, 'State Responsibility for Cyber Attacks' (n 76).

In relation to extraterritoriality, it is not always apparent where hostile cyber conduct originates; whether it is domestic or extraterritorial. In the case of the latter, current understandings of the effective control standard would seem to preclude cyber operations from ever triggering the human rights obligations of the responsible state. In order to accommodate cyber activities and properly regulate the harmful effect they can have on human rights, it is necessary to reconsider how jurisdiction is established.

The prevalence of non-state actors coupled with the practical difficulties in tracing the authors of cyber conduct poses an immense challenge to the current system of state responsibility. In order to ensure redress for violations associated with hostile cyber activities, reconsideration of the state-centric approach to international law is needed. Unlike conventional weaponry, destructive cyber technologies are just as accessible to non-state actors as they are to states. In addition to revisiting current tests of effective and overall control, the plausibility of conferring enforceable human rights law obligations on non-state actors requires serious consideration as the current landscape may breed proxy cyber armies with states operating behind a curtain of plausible deniability.

An ever-increasing amount of human activity, both public and private, rely upon cyber technologies. *Ergo*, the exercise of an ever-increasing number of human rights depend upon cyber technologies. This dependency raises an important and complex question: can international law effectively respond to advancements in technology so as to prevent and redress human rights violations in cyber space? This is a multifaceted question that requires unpacking a plethora of issues. It remains to be seen how each of the associated issues will be addressed and whether the responses themselves can avoid unwarranted interference with human rights.

III
POVERTY

9

State of Play and the Road Ahead

A World of Poverty and Human Rights

Margot E Salomon

I. Introduction

If Chapter 12 by Magdalena Sepúlveda Carmona and Kate Donald takes human rights as an essential component in advancing the Sustainable Development Goals (SDGs), Chapter 10 by Sandra Fredman reasons that a human rights approach to poverty needs to rethink its traditional assumptions if it is to transcend its limitations. Chapter 11 by Jaakko Kuosmanen explores the value of advancing human rights-based public budgeting through a deliberative process. In different ways, all three chapters in this part on poverty argue that, the in confronting poverty, human rights require a robust respect for democracy, equality, participation, and accountability. All three chapters seek to see human rights transform socio-economic deprivation and exclusion.

Varying degrees of human rights scrutiny condition the approaches that each of these chapters takes in assessing the fight against poverty. Sepúlveda Carmona and Donald offer examples as to what human rights norms require of the SDGs. Human rights, it is suggested, 'may assist in understanding and realizing the radical potential of the SDGs'. Kuosmanen outlines what human rights––in particular child rights––require of governments when it comes to deciding on public budgets. His proposals aim at closing the gap between human rights norms and the ambiguity of their guidance in concrete contexts. Fredman takes a step back to reflect on how traditional human rights theory and the interpretation of socio-economic rights by courts can work against poverty-reduction objectives. The role of law is also situated differently in each chapter––for Sepúlveda Carmona and Donald the mere reference to international human rights law in the SDG Declaration 'might be the lever to unleash the transformative potential of the 2030 Agenda' by linking the goals to legal standards. In Kuosmanen's chapter, the rights of the child provide a key starting point when it comes to the allocation of public funds, but the 'open-textured' nature of the legal obligations makes 'deliberative dialogue' around budgets vital if governments are serious about budgets that comply with human rights. For Fredman, the law is a weapon; its effectiveness in confronting poverty will depend on who is wielding it.

Margot E Salomon, *State of Play and the Road Ahead* In: Human Rights and 21st Century Challenges. Edited by: Dapo Akande, Jaakko Kuosmanen, Helen McDermott, and Dominic Roser, Published by Oxford University Press 2020.
DOI: 10.1093/oso/9780198824770.003.0010

The various efforts in these chapters to see human rights realized offer a basis for understanding the world human rights inhabit and thus what human rights can hope to achieve when it comes to confronting poverty. As the sociologist Anthony Woodiwiss explains, any rights regime may be seen as an 'index representing the disposition of power in the pertinent jurisdiction'.[1] This sociological reading of the law shows us not only who is protected and who is not but what is especially valued and what is not by the bodies responsible for 'constructing, approving and enforcing the regime'.[2] To read these three contributions on human rights and poverty with an eye to what they advocate and what they hope for is to shine a light on what impedes efforts to bring human rights to bear on poverty and material inequality. Tacitly or explicitly, all three chapters highlight several hard truths about human rights and the will of the powerful today, and through these insights a window on to what is valued. We undertake this exercise in disclosure by considering three key features that characterize the world today: a multilevel democratic deficit, a harmful commitment to growth, and a categorical absence of accountability for the state of poverty and inequality. This chapter reflects on each of these (interrelated) features in turn.[3]

II. Democratic Deficits

The deficit in democratic decision-making processes today manifests itself in many ways that bear on poverty. At the international level, it is no secret that the independence formally afforded states as sovereign equals under international law does not endow them with functional equality in the shaping of international rules and compliance mechanisms. Disparities, particularly in wealth, create power differentials between states that mock the idea of substantive sovereign equality, yet the 'fiction of equality' is preserved through international law's narrative of consent.[4]

1 Anthony Woodiwiss, *Human Rights* (Routledge 2005) XIII–XIV.

2 Ibid, XIV.

3 This brief introduction to the topic of poverty and human rights focuses largely, although not exclusively, on poverty in (so-called) developing countries . Given the role of influential developed countries (so-called) in shaping the global economy and shaping it to their benefit, the poverty in rich countries (here we can exclude, in part, the 'South in the North', such as Greece) can largely be understood as a result of their unwillingness to tackle it and not their inability. This invites a different investigation than the one that considers poverty in poor(er) countries. The SDG claim is that the 2030 Agenda is intended to apply to all countries but they reflect a half-hearted effort to think that through along with the familiar political compromises that get us nowhere. See eg para 41: 'We recognize that each country has primary responsibility for its own economic and social development' (read: if developing countries are poor it is their own fault). UNGA 'Transforming our World: The 2030 Agenda for Sustainable Development' (25 September 2015) A/Res/70/1 (hereafter UNGA 'Transforming our World').

4 Hilary Charlesworth and Christine Chinkin, *The Boundaries of International Law: A Feminist Analysis* (Manchester University Press 2000) 124; Thomas Pogge (2005) 'Recognized and Violated by International Law: The Human Rights of the Global Poor' 18 Leiden Journal of International Law 717, 732 ('Rational consent should not be mistaken for approval').

Perhaps as a consequence of international law's foundational commitment to the formal equality of states, the substantive inequality of states in the making of the international legal order is conveniently moved to the background.[5] Since the process of international law-making is a legitimizing one, ignoring the democratic deficit that comes from the failure to account for the substantive inequality among states in juridical fora has alleged 'anti-poverty' prescriptions and unjust rules cleansed through the sophistry of law.

SDG10 provides a cogent example of the function of sovereign inequality. SDG10 and its targets have as their declared aim to reduce inequality within and between countries. The inequality goal and targets in the SDGs are said to reflect the complementary and transformative structural counterpart to national duties and in particular to the basic needs approach that was criticized in the earlier Millennium Development Goals (MDGs) precisely for providing social safety nets as a response to the prevailing economic model that was and still is increasing inequalities.[6] But the 'transformative' nature of SDG10 is unconvincing because the SDGs endorse 'solutions' based on the status quo of international economic law prescriptions that--far from confronting poverty and inequality globally--have entrenched their violence for the benefit of rich countries and their transnational industries. While empirical findings challenge the suggestion that bilateral investment treaties have contributed even to the targeted objective of economic development in host states,[7] and there are grave concerns about a range of negative human rights and environmental impacts on host states and their people by the foreign investment legal regime,[8] SDG Target 10.b '[e]ncourages ... foreign direct investment to States where the need is greatest, in particular least developed countries' with the Goal on Global Partnerships for Sustainable Development committed to: '[a]dopt and implement investment promotion regimes for least developed countries'.[9] As for trade, the Global Partnerships in the SDGs restate the commitment of the international community to the liberalization of trade as currently practised

[5] Patrick Macklem (2015) 'Human Rights in International Law: Three Generations or One?' 3 London Review of International Law 61, 91. On the creation of misery by international law, John Linarelli, Margot E Salomon, and Mathucumaraswamy Sornarajah, *The Misery of International Law: Confrontations with Injustice in the Global Economy* (OUP 2018) (hereafter Linarelli *et al*, *The Misery of International Law*).

[6] Sakiko Fukuda-Parr, 'The 2030 Agenda and the SDGs—A Course Correction?' (Sheffield Political Economy Institute (SPERI) Blog, 30 September 2015) <http://speri.dept.shef.ac.uk/2015/09/30/the-2030-agenda-and-the-sdgs-a-course-correction/> (hereafter Fukado-Parr, 'The 2030 Agenda and the SDGs').

[7] Peter Muchlinski, 'Holistic Approaches to Development and International Investment Law: The role of International Investment Agreements' in Julio Faundez and Celine Tan (eds), *International Law, Economic Globalization and Development* (Edward Elgar 2010) 180–204, 186.

[8] On the perceived benefits flowing from FDI, Fiona Macmillan, 'The World Trade Organization and the Turbulent Legacy of International Economic Law-Making in the Long Twentieth Century' in Julio Faundez and Celine Tan (eds), *International Law, Economic Globalization and Development* (Edward Elgar 2010) 158–79, 170.

[9] UNGA 'Transforming our World' (n 3) SDG Target 17.5.

and thus to 'promote a universal, rules-based, open, non-discriminatory and equitable multilateral trading system under the World Trade Organization'.[10] But findings indicate that countries in the Global South that adopted trade liberalization, privatization, and fiscal discipline through the 1990s, even on the basis of the conventional marker of economic growth, had low growth rates both in absolute terms but also relative to other countries that did not follow such reforms or only partially, such as China.[11] More specifically, the regime of international trade is one defined by a lack of safeguards for domestic industry, labour,[12] and food security,[13] but still with plenty of backing for Northern industry at the expense of basic well-being in poorer countries, such as health.[14] Here we see another level of the democratic deficit at play: international economic law both regulates deep inside the state and is structured so as to be insulated from democratic processes.[15] Indeed, the basis of the legal regime of foreign investment is precisely to allow for

[10] SDG Target 17.10.

[11] See, among others, Henrietta L Moore (2015) 'Global Prosperity and Sustainable Development Goals' 27 Journal of International Development 801, 807–08. See also, Ha-Joon Chang, *Bad Samaritans: The Myth of Free Trade and the Secret History of Capitalism* (Bloomsbury Publishing 2008).

[12] Weak labour rights are the 'comparative advantage' of developing countries and tend to be defended by them in international fora. As Linarelli, Salomon, and Sornarajah explain: '[T]he rejection of labour standards in the WTO comes at the behest of developing countries who have ignored findings that compliance with international labour standards often accompanies improvements in productivity and economic performance ... International economic treaties in trade and investment combine in a way that providesmany benefits to capital but none to labour: capital is mobile and protected, but labour is immobile and unprotected.' Linarelli *et al*, *The Misery of International Law* (n 5) chapter 4, 110–44.

[13] Still no resolution was found at the latest WTO Ministerial Conference. WTO, *Public Stockholding for Food Security Purposes* (19 December 2015) WT/MIN(15)/44 <https://www.wto.org/english/thewto_e/minist_e/mc10_e/nairobipackage_e.pdf> accessed 14 August 2019. If the aim of international trade rules was to see the world well fed there would be a move to limit states' excessive reliance on international trade in the pursuit of food security and in increasing small-scale food production, particularly among women, and by pursuing economic policies that increase, rather than decrease, employment and livelihoods. See Timothy A Wise, 'Feeding the World: The Ultimate First World Conceit' (Triple Crisis, 2015) <http://triplecrisis.com/feeding-the-world-the-ultimate-first-world-conceit/> accessed 14 August 2019; Deborah James, 'Investing In Agriculture in Developing Countries: The World Says Yes, But the WTO Says No' (Alternet, 31 Mar 2015) <http://www.alternet.org/world/investing-agriculture-developing-countries-whole-world-says-yes-wto-says-no> accessed 14 August 2019; Olivier De Schutter, *The World Trade Organization and the Post-Global Food Crisis Agenda: Putting Food Security First in the International Trade System*, Briefing Note 04 (Nov 2011) <http://www.ohchr.org/Documents/Issues/Food/BN4_SRRTF_WTO_EN.pdf> accessed 14 August 2019.

[14] 23 January 2017 saw the entry into force of the first amendment to WTO rules since the organization was established back in 1995. The Protocol Amending the Agreement on Trade-Related Aspects of Intellectual Property Rights provides a legal pathway to ease access to affordable medicines in developing countries that mostly rely on imports for their medicinal needs. Unlike earlier efforts in the WTO to address this issue, the amendment gives legal certainty that generic versions of patent-protected medicines can be produced under compulsory licensing specifically for export to countries with limited or no pharmaceutical production capacity. It has taken over a decade for the amendment to enter into force after a huge and needless loss of life over years due to the unaffordability of, among others, patented anti-retroviral drugs under the WTO's Intellectual Property Agreement. The effect of the amendment remains an open question.

[15] Linarelli *et al*, *The Misery of International Law* (n 5).

challenging the outcomes of local democratic processes where they are seen to impact on the property rights of transnational corporations.[16]

While the inclusion of the stand-alone inequality goal in the SDGs is often considered to reflect 'a major paradigm shift',[17] what it gives with one hand it takes with the other. Ultimately, the SDGs endorse fully the current modus operandi of the democracy-subverting, rights-violating, inequality-generating transnational capitalist order. It is at one level surprising that the debate about the inclusion of SDG10 on addressing inequality was one of the most contentious political battles in the SDG negotiations.[18] The point is that when read together, the 2030 SDG Agenda does not support the poverty-reduction aspirations of developing countries and works against closing inequality gaps despite its claims to the opposite, and inequality and democracy are incommensurable.

As is well known, wealth concentration is incommensurable with democracy. A result of the extreme inequality today is the political costs of income concentration at the top whereby the rich get their preferences translated into government policy.[19] At the international level, the legal machinery has locked in many of the gains of wealthy and privileged states and their private actors. The assertion has been one of shared gain but the open secret is of course that the cost has been intolerably high to many. One of the grave consequences of this economic globalization under law is thus its triple democracy-subverting function: the impact that substantive sovereign inequality has on international law-making; the erosion of democratic control by national governments over economic and social policy, and; a move that has the autonomy of local communities to decide on their way of life pushed further and further away from the locus of influence.

III. Economic Growth

Wealth creation today makes the rich richer while dedication to profit generation through the expansion of (transnational) markets fails to take inclusive, fair, or sustainable growth into account. Conventional growth has sacrifices required to ensure it, the natural environmental being but one. That growth is not questioned as a foundational assumption of contemporary economics and global ordering renders

[16] See the insightful reflections by Margaret Somers in Conversation with Joshua Curtis, *Socially Embedding the Market and the Role of Law* (Series on Economics and Law in Conversation, Laboratory for Advanced Research on the Global Economy, Centre for the Study of Human Rights, *LSE,* March 2016) 12. <http://www.lse.ac.uk/humanRights/research/projects/theLab/Economics-and-Law-in-Conversation—Interview-with-Margaret-Somers-FINAL.pdf> accessed 14 August 2019.

[17] Sepúlveda Carmona and Donald, Chapter 12, this book.

[18] See Fukado-Parr, 'The 2030 Agenda and the SDGs' (n 6).

[19] This is a danger long recognized and captured in the famous remark by US Supreme Court Justice Louis Brandeis, 'We must make our choice. We may have democracy, or we may have wealth concentrated in the hands of a few, but we can't have both.' And see Robert Hunter Wade (2013) 'Capitalism and Democracy at Cross-Purposes' 28 (3) New Zealand Sociology 208.

it seemingly apolitical, beyond contestation and, as Bengi Akbulut and colleagues point out, largely 'insulated from any critical engagement with the myriad contradictory effects that economic growth necessarily entails'.[20] While it is now widely accepted that growth is not sufficient to alleviate poverty, the caution as to the role of growth in inevitably creating poverty is not heeded. The SDG global social protection floor initiative provides a cogent example.

A recent effort to secure human rights is through social protection floors, endorsed in the SDGs and by the United Nations Committee on Economic, Social and Cultural Rights. But while a social protection floor might confront the markers of poverty and inequality including lack of income,[21] at the same time it entrenches the capitalist growth economy that made possible the poverty and inequality in the first place. The problem is that the social protection floor and the socio-economic rights that are given effect through it serve to prevent or mitigate some suffering but not tochange the terms under which that suffering is made possible and reproduced. The transfer by the state of the profits of the capitalist growth economy to the subsistence economy legitimates the capitalist growth economy[22] and bolsters political support to the very policies that engender poverty and inequality. Fredman's insightful challenge to the 'background assumption' of human rights 'that freedom consists in the absence of state intervention' points up how freedom requires the state to play a role in the fulfillment of human well-being.[23] The warning here highlights how the economic status quo means social interventions risk working against their own objectives.[24]

It is also the case that the widespread turn to social protection does not challenge the commitment of international financial institutions (and of many

[20] Bengi Akbulut, Fikret Adaman, and Yahya M Madra (2015) 'The Decimation and Displacement of Development Economics' 46 (4) Development and Change 733, 734. See also, Sundhya Pahuja, *Decolonising International Law: Development, Economic Growth and the Politics of Universality* (CUP 2011). On wars and the decimation and reconstitution of value for capitalist use or disuse (bombs are commodities that get realized) in the developing world: 'The higher rate of value and resource dislocation resulting from the violence of war has been contravening the covenants of international law and the charter of the UN since 1945. In hierarchically articulated class structures, smelting together with finance and socially cutting across national boundaries, the consumption of humans and nature, often by brutal means, is necessarily but not exclusively a historical precursor to global economic growth. The Arabs and the Africans are not "wretched" (to use Fanon's expression) by historical coincidence. They are so as a result of all round and systemic imperialist assault... The key question is to investigate how wars through violent social order restructuring (inducing state collapse) decimate and reconstitute value for capitalist use or disuse in the developing world far beyond the salient wealth usurpation by which imperialism sets prices below value.' Ali Kadri, *Development Under Uncertainty in the Arab World* (SPEAK OUT! at The Laboratory for Advanced Research on the Global Economy, Centre for the Study of Human Rights, LSE, June 2016) 11 <http://www.lse.ac.uk/humanRights/research/projects/theLab/Kadri-Speak-Out-2-finalinsight.pdf> accessed 14 August 2019.

[21] *See* Sepúlveda Carmona and Donald, Chapter 12of this book, on what is required of social protection schemes in order to advance gender equality for example.

[22] Partha Chatterjee, 'Foreword' (2013) in Kalyan Sanyal (ed), *Rethinking Capitalist Development: Primitive Accumulation, Governmentality and Post-Colonial Capitalism* (Routledge India 2007) xii.

[23] Fredman, Chapter 10 of this book.

[24] Linarelli *et al*, *The Misery of International Law* (n 5) chapter 7, 226–70.

states) to liberalization and privatization––controversial prescriptions that continue unabated. Instead, supportof basic social services is reflective merely of an awareness that extremely poor people are unable to pay for those services at market-determined rates and as such cannot become customers.[25] In so far as social protection aims and succeeds in fulfilling human rights,[26] it leaves intact what Nancy Fraser refers to as the 'deep structures' allowing for the perpetual regeneration of the root causes of poverty and inequality and thus the need for 'surface reallocations time and again'.[27] Despite its claims, the SDG commitment to a social protection is, as Jayati Ghosh cogently captures, ameliorative of the conditions of those defined as poor, rather than transformative of the economies in which they live.[28]

IV. The Accountability Void

At the heart of the story of poverty is a conspicuous absence: accountability. There is an absence of accountability for the creation of poverty and inequality and for their perpetuation.[29] What might have become clear from this brief account is that the international legal regimes that regulate the global economy also regulate poverty and inequality. The promise of 'development' (still largely understood as a country's economic progress and industrialization) and the familiar trope of shared gains are the dual justifications under which international economic law operates and is central to the story that links poverty and human rights. While

[25] Arne Ruckert (2009) 'Towards an Inclusive-Neoliberal Regime of Development: From the Washington Consensus to the Post-Washington Consensus' 39 (1) Labour, Capital and Society 36, 42.

[26] In Brazil, it has reached more than a quarter of the population and 85 per cent of the poor. By 2014, 36 million Brazilians had been lifted out of poverty and Brazilians living in indigence had effectively been eradicated. As for inequality, the overall income gap was reduced by a third. Jonathan Tepperman (January/February 2016) 'Brazil's Anti-Poverty Breakthrough: The Surprising Success of Bolsa Família' Foreign Affairs 34, 41. But see Lena Lavinas: '[I]t is primarily rising labour earnings that have accounted for the decline in poverty in Brazil, as was the case elsewhere in Latin America. Brazil is also no exception to the wider continental tendency to concentrate social spending on cash transfers rather than expanding provision of decommodified services, such as public health, education, sanitation and other basic social goods... In short, in Brazil as elsewhere in Latin America, social infrastructure and access to state-provided, decommodified goods and services are growing at uneven tempos, exacerbating inequalities' Lena Lavinas (2013) '21st Century Welfare' 84 (5) New Left Review 32, 34.

[27] Nancy Fraser (1995) 'From Redistribution to Recognition: Dilemmas of Justice in a "Post-Socialist" Age' New Left Review 68, 85.

[28] Jayati Ghosh, 'From "Development" to "Poverty Alleviation": What Have We Lost?' (Frontline, 4 September 2015) <http://www.networkideas.org/news/aug2015/Development.pdf> accessed 14 August 2019.

[29] Poverty remains widespread. Claims of its global reduction rely on gains from India and particularly China, backdated to 1990, and an unrealistic international poverty line of $1.25 per day. See further, Jason Hickel (2016) 'The True Extent of Global Poverty and Hunger: Questioning the Good News Narrative of the Millennium Development Goals' 37 (5) Third World Quarterly 749. Inequality between states is widening rapidly while inequality has soared within nations with a surge of inequality in the West. In both the United States and China it is 'well-entrenched and self-reproducing'. Branko Milanovic, *Global Inequality: A New Approach for the Age of Globalization* (Belknap Press 2016).

it can be hoped that the international legal regime of human rights will bring to bear its demands on *national* efforts to reduce poverty--for example, substantive gender equality, participation, minimum socio-economic protections[30] --the emphasis on human rights realization through national efforts risks having structural causes downplayed and the causes of the problems localized and confused with effects.[31] At the same time, the economic regimes that sustain the systemic causes of poverty and inequality globally make wider change unlikely if not impossible.[32] Yet to critique development from a human rights perspective is to suggest that if human rights standards were brought to bear then development would be realized; this is an impossibility under current conditions that nonetheless implicate human rights in the never-ending drive for development.[33] The SDGs, like the MDGs that came before them, don't provide for a system of accountability when it comes to poverty-reduction,[34] this is hardly surprising. But the irony is that unless accountability for poverty and inequality were brought to bear on the international legal regimes of trade, investment, and finance[35]-- regimes that are anathema to addressing poverty and inequality and that are *endorsed through the SDG targets*--if accountability was included among the goals, it could serve to defend the mechanics of the economic order.

[30] See all three chapters for various considerations of what human rights require. For an interesting overview of empirical findings on the contribution of rights-based approaches see Malcolm Langford (2015) 'Rights, Development and Critical Modernity' 46 (4) Development and Change 777.

[31] Jason Beckett, 'Creating Poverty' in Anne Orford and Florian Hoffmann with M Clark (eds) *The Oxford Handbook of the Theory of International Law* (OUP 2016) 985, 1003 (hereafter Beckett 'Creating Poverty'); Susan Marks (2009) 'Human Rights and the Bottom Billion' 1 European Human Rights Law Review 37. Development at the United Nations has always exposed the perennial tension between South and North and the primacy each respectively gives to national versus international factors impeding development and poverty reduction. The language of the 1986 Declaration on the Right to Development offers a quintessential example of that tension. See Margot E Salomon, *Global Responsibility for Human Rights: World Poverty and the Development of International Law* (OUP 2007).

[32] See Margot E Salomon (2008) 'Poverty, Privilege and International Law: The Millennium Development Goals and the Guise of Humanitarianism' German Yearbook of International Law 39; Susan Marks, 'Exploitation as an International Legal Concept' in Susan Marks (ed), *International Law on the Left: Re-examining Marxist Legacies* (2008) 281, 281–307.

[33] '[T]he living standards currently enjoyed in the developed world are *subsidized by* the continuing exploitation of the developing world; there are not sufficient resources for everyone to enjoy our "developed" lifestyle.' Beckett 'Creating Poverty' (n 31) 1008. Emphasis in the original. On carbon emissions and poverty: '[R]egions that have seen extreme reductions in poverty, specifically East Asia and the Pacific and South Asia, have increased their carbon emissions by almost 200%. The only region that has decreased its carbon emissions over this time period [of the past 30 years], sub-Saharan Africa, has seen the number of people living in extreme poverty almost double.' Adam Goldstein, 'What is the Link between Carbon Emissions and Poverty' (World Economic Forum, 15 December 2015) <https://www.weforum.org/agenda/2015/12/what-is-the-link-between-carbon-emissions-and-poverty/> accessed 14 August 2019.

[34] As raised by Sepúlveda Carmona and Donald, Chapter 12, this book.

[35] On finance, see eg UNGA 'Transforming our World' (n 3) para 69. 'Maintaining sustainable debt is the responsibility of borrowing countries.' Cf Margot E Salomon (2015) 'Of Austerity, Human Rights and International Institutions' 21 (4) European Law Journal 521; Linarelli *et al*, *The Misery of International Law* (n 5) chapter 6, 175–225.

V. Conclusion

Let us return to the insight provide by Woodiwiss at the start of this chapter-- that we can hold up the law as a mirror through which to view the values of the powerful. What we see is that the schemes that claim to confront poverty and now material inequality (trade, investment, the SDGs, etc) offer, at best, an unconvincing route to their eradication. At worst, we are offered an audacious falsehood. On the reading of international law revealed by Woodiwiss, we are shown who is worthy of protection and who is not; it is not the poor and there is far too little human rights can do about that.

10

Poverty and Human Rights

A Peril and a Promise[1]

Sandra Fredman

> 'Human rights are not just about prisoners of conscience, they are also about prisoners of poverty.'
>
> Paul Hunt, previous Special Rapporteur for Health[2]

I. Introduction

Poverty has not traditionally been regarded as a human rights issue. While human rights are viewed as restraining the state from interfering in individual freedom, poverty has been characterized as due to individual misfortune, incompetence, or indolence and therefore the concern of charity, state welfare, or even disciplinary measures. The nineteenth-century Poor Laws in Britain offer a good example. They attributed unemployment and poverty to individual idleness,[3] placing responsibility squarely on the shoulders of the individual. However, there is growing recognition of a relationship between poverty and human rights. Clearly poverty affects the ability to exercise human rights, such as the right to a fair trial, the right to vote, freedom of speech, and freedom of assembly. At the same time, human rights violations can cause poverty. This is not only true of deprivations of the rights to food, education, health, or housing. Poverty can also be perpetuated when civil and political rights are not respected. As Amartya Sen has famously pointed out, it is when there is lack of full democratic accountability that famines occur.[4] Poverty has also been characterized as a human rights violation in itself. Thomas Pogge has argued

[1] Upendra Baxi, 'The Avatars of Indian Judicial Activism' in SK Verma and Kusum (eds), *Fifty Years of the Supreme Court of India: Its Grasp and Reach* (OUP 2000).

[2] Paul Hunt 'Statement to the Panel on Maternal Mortality and the Human Rights of Women' (2008) *UN Human Rights Council* 1 <http://repository.essex.ac.uk/9789/1/human-rights-council-statement-maternal-mortality-panel-june-2008.pdf> accessed 13 August 2019.

[3] Royal Commission Report in 1834, Sidney Webb and Beatrice Webb, *English Poor Law Policy* (Longmans 1910) 277 (hereafter 'Royal Commission Report in 1834').

[4] Amartya Sen, *Development as Freedom* (OUP 1999) 170–75 (hereafter Sen, *Development as Freedom*).

Sandra Fredman, *Poverty and Human Rights* In: Human Rights and 21st Century Challenges. Edited by: Dapo Akande, Jaakko Kuosmanen, Helen McDermott, and Dominic Roser, Published by Oxford University Press 2020.
DOI: 10.1093/oso/9780198824770.003.0011

that it is the current global order that perpetuates global poverty, which could be averted by feasible reforms. He argues further that our failure to make reforms implicates us in the violation of the rights of the poor.[5]

As the world continues to seek for answers to intractable problems of poverty in the twenty-first century, the central role of human rights is increasingly acknowledged. Thus, while the Millennium Development Goals agenda for addressing world poverty in the first fifteen years of the century made no mention of human rights, the new agenda signaled by the Sustainable Development Goals (SDGs) for 2030 is strongly grounded in human rights. The UN Office of the High Commissioner for Human Rights (OHCHR) regards the SDGs as marking a 'paradigm shift' towards a model of development which, echoing the Universal Declaration of Human Rights (UDHR), aims to secure 'freedom from fear and freedom from want' and puts the imperative of equality and non-discrimination at its core.[6] In a parallel trajectory, it has been recognized that development is not only about economic growth, but necessarily includes respect for human rights. Thus, the evolving right to development includes a central endorsement of the agency of each human being, and respect for human rights, equality, and non-discrimination.[7]

However, this relationship is not uncomplicated. Some human rights can favour the better off, either intrinsically or in the ways in which they operate and their relationship with social structures. The right to property is a paradigmatic example. As Sunstein argues, if homeless people lack a place to live, it is because the rules of property are enforced. Similarly, there is no law against eating in the abstract; it is the law which forbids a hungry person to eat any of the food which exists in the community.[8] Sen puts it even more strongly. People are hungry if they lack entitlements that enable them to eat; thus, 'the law stands between food availability and food entitlement. Starvation deaths can reflect legality with a vengeance'.[9] This is not only true of the right to property. The right to health has been shown to exacerbate inequalities in countries such as Brazil and Columbia.[10] In Quebec, a judicial determination of the right to health threatened to destabilize the public health system.[11] In India, claims of minority rights have blown a hole in provisions in the

[5] 'Global Justice' (*Stanford Encyclopedia of Philosophy*, 6 March 2015) para 2.4 <http://plato.stanford.edu/entries/justice-global/> 26 November 2019.

[6] OHCHR 'Transforming Our World: Human Rights in the 2030 Agenda for Sustainable Development' (2015) <http://www.ohchr.org/Documents/Issues/MDGs/Post2015/HRAndPost2015.pdf> accessed 13 August 2019.

[7] United Nations Secretary General (2013) 'The Emergence of the Right to Development' in OHCHR, Realizing the Right to Development: Essays in Commemoration of 25 Years of the UN Declaration on the Right to Development (United Nations) 8.

[8] Cass Sunstein, *The Second Bill of Rights* (Basic Books 2004) 23–24.

[9] Amartya Sen, *Inequality Reexamined* (OUP 1995) 165–66.

[10] Colleen Flood and Aeyal Gross (2014) 'Litigating the Right to Health: What Can We Learn from a Comparative Law and Health Care Systems Approach' 16 Health and Human Rights Journal 62 (hereafter Flood and Gross, 'Litigating the Right to Health').

[11] *Chaoulli v Quebec (Attorney General)* 2005 SCC 35 (hereafter *Chaoulli v Quebec*).

recently passed Right to Education Act, which required a set-aside of 25 per cent of places at independent schools for children of the most disadvantaged classes. Alternatively, long-term measures protecting human rights for future generations might be challenged as a breach of the human rights of current generations (see also Knox, Chapter 15, this book).[12] For example, greenhouse gas mitigation measures, put in place to prevent large-scale poverty in the future, might be challenged by those whose rights to housing are threatened by displacement due to renewable energy projects.

Are we then overloading the concept of human rights with too many expectations? This chapter argues that the limitations of a human rights approach to people in poverty can be attributed to a particular set of background assumptions, stemming from the notion that the primary aim of human rights should be to protect individual freedom against state intervention. Three basic premises underlie this assertion. The first is that freedom consists in absence of state intervention. Second, the individual is characterized as prior to society. Third, equality is regarded as consisting only in affording individuals the same treatment or formal equality before the law. The section II of the chapter explores the ways in which these background premises militate against a human rights approach which can include a poverty perspective. In the third section III, the chapter considers how these three basic premises might be reconfigured so that a human rights approach can genuinely address poverty. Drawing on Sen's capabilities approach, it is argued that instead of protecting individuals against state intervention, freedom should be understood as enabling individuals to live lives that they value. Second, individuals are essentially social beings and can only achieve their aims by collaboration in society. This means that social well-being is part of individual freedom, and that the value of solidarity should be regarded as complementing individual freedom. In this way, caring relationships are valued as well as autonomy advancing activities. Conversely, relationships of power and particularly imbalances of power need to be accounted for in human rights frameworks. Third, equality should be understood substantively, rather than formally. Substantive equality, as understood here, has four dimensions: the need to redress disadvantage, address stigma and stereotyping, facilitate participation, and to accommodate difference and bring about structural change.[13]

The chapter does not aim to present a fully fledged theory but instead seeks to begin to sketch a framework for evaluating and reshaping human rights in order to fulfil their promise for people living in poverty. Nor does the chapter present a comprehensive or systematic examination of comparable jurisdictions. Instead, it illustrates some of the challenges to a human rights approach to poverty by

[12] See Knox Chapter 15, this book.

[13] Sandra Fredman (2016) 'Substantive Equality Revisited' 14 International Journal of Constitutional Law 712.

examining a handful of cases from different jurisdictions where human rights litigation has had an adverse impact on people in poverty. While some of the reasons for these limitations might be specific to a particular jurisdiction, it is argued that these cases illustrate more generally the ways in which particular underlying assumptions about human rights operate.

II. The Peril

There are several interconnected and cumulative perils associated with a human rights approach to poverty. The first is the danger that human rights are only utilized to restrain state action, but poverty is regarded as a question of individual responsibility, or an aspect of the ordinary operation of the free market into which the state should not intrude. The second is the risk that human rights are treated as individualized entitlements, which trump utilitarian considerations and therefore should be protected against state intervention in the public interest. The third is the peril that human rights are used to protect formal rather than substantive equality, so that distributive consequences are ignored. These cumulative risks are aggravated in a system of judicially enforceable human rights, where the expense and complexity of legal claims might allow human rights to be captured by elites to entrench their position regardless of non-egalitarian implications for the poor. This part gives several major examples of human rights operating in this way. It is argued, however, that these problems are a result of a particular understanding of human rights, namely one based on the notion that human rights should create a space in which individuals can make choices free of state intervention. This in turn entails an understanding of human rights as individualistic, protecting negative freedom, and abstracted from the social context of power and inequality. If instead, an approach to human rights is adopted which incorporates the values of positive freedom, solidarity, and substantive equality, human rights can be appropriately fashioned to address poverty.

A. Rights as Restraint: Poverty as Individual Fault

Nineteenth-century notions of individual responsibility characterized poverty and destitution as the fault of the individual. This chimes with a 'negative' conception of freedom as absence of interference. In the famous words of Isaiah Berlin, the negative conception of freedom denotes that 'I am ... free to the degree to which no man or body of men interferes with my activity. Political liberty is simply the area within which a man can act unobstructed by others.'[14] Crucially, it is only interference by

[14] Isaiah Berlin, *Four Essays on Liberty* (OUP1969) 121.

others which impinges on liberty: 'Mere incapacity to attain a goal is not lack of political freedom.'[15] This means that I can be free even if I do not actually have the resources or opportunities to fulfil my choices, so long as no-one is deliberately interfering with me. Poverty is not viewed as lack of freedom unless it is caused by deliberate acts of others.

This approach has several consequences for human rights in general and for the relationship between human rights and poverty in particular. The understanding of political liberty as freedom from state interference maps directly onto a principle that the role of human rights is to protect individuals from state interference. Locke, for example, posited a set of 'natural rights' which ensured that individual liberty remained impervious to state power. It is as a fully formed person, clothed with 'natural rights', that the individual enters society, and it is only to secure those rights that political authority can use coercion. Such natural rights include the rights of individuals to life and liberty, to govern their own affairs, to dispose of their labour, and to possess property.[16] Rights are therefore essentially constraints on the state, functioning as limits on the extent to which state authority can be imposed.[17] At the same time, this view eschews state responsibility for creating the conditions in which individuals can exercise their rights. So long as poverty is regarded as due to individual laziness or ineptitude, it is not seen as a result of state interference in individual liberty, and therefore does not trigger human rights protection.

The result is not only that poverty is not viewed as a breach of human rights. It is also that the state can use punitive or disciplinary measures as a condition of welfare support without being regarded as intruding on individual freedom. A good example is the nineteenth-century Poor Law in Britain, which attributed unemployment and poverty to individual idleness.[18] State maintenance was punitive and disciplinarian, requiring destitute able-bodied persons to enter the workhouse and be put to work as a condition of relief.

By the end of the nineteenth century, unemployment came to be seen as a social and economic problem. This opened the way for the acceptance that the state should be under positive duties to contribute to individual welfare.[19] However, the resurgence of neo-liberalism has brought with it a renewed emphasis on liberty as absence of state intervention in a free market.[20] On this view, individuals should provide for themselves by pursuing their self-interest in the free market, and those who do not succeed are seen as a burden on those who do. Although there is now

[15] Ibid.

[16] John Locke, *Two Treatises of Government* (CUP 1963) 123.

[17] See further Sandra Fredman, *Human Rights Transformed: Positive Rights and Positive Duties* (OUP 2008) 16–17 (hereafter Fredman, *Human Rights Transformed*).

[18] 'Royal Commission Report in 1834' (n 3) 277.

[19] See further Fredman, *Human Rights Transformed* (n 17).

[20] See Friedrich Hayek, *The Constitution of Liberty* (Routledge and Kegan Paul 1960) (hereafter Hayek, *The Constitution of Liberty*).

a greater acknowledgement of the structural causes of poverty, there is still ready resort to the notion that poverty is the fault of the poor, and can be overcome with hard work and persistence. Conversely, welfare beneficiaries are portrayed as parasites and scroungers. Since poverty is not regarded as caused by the state, on this view, the state should only be responsible where the individual is disabled from working due to disability, illness, old age, or potentially natural disasters.

This has also resuscitated the view that it is not a breach of the human rights of those living in poverty to make welfare conditional on particular behaviours. Captured in the slogan 'no rights without responsibilities', we have seen the growing popularity of conditionality. Whether in the form of 'welfare-to-work' schemes or conditional cash transfers, such policies make the right to welfare dependent on fulfilling behavioural conditions such as looking for work, undergoing training, or taking children to health clinics or school. As one of its foremost proponents, Laurence Mead, puts it, the use of conditionality is 'an effort to return to the earlier view—to hold the dependent once again responsible for at least some behaviours, especially employment'.[21] Thus, instead of giving aid on the basis of 'impersonal economic criteria such as income', it was argued, it should be 'conditioned in some way on good behaviour'.[22]

This approach overstates the role of individual responsibility. As a start, it would be wrong to regard human rights as conditional on the exercise of personal responsibility and effort. There are also strong arguments against welfare to work from the value of substantive equality. Those who have enough means (through inheritance or otherwise) to live without undertaking paid work may share in the fruits of social cooperation without paying the same dues.[23]

Nevertheless, human rights-based challenges of such policies may not succeed so long as they continue to be based on a view that individuals should be expected to take responsibility for their own poverty. In both the United Kingdom and Canada, equality guarantees have been used to challenge welfare-to-work programmes which prescribe a lower welfare rate for claimants under a given age or make the full benefit conditional on participation in training or work programmes. In cases in both these jurisdictions, the court did not regard socio-economic disadvantage as itself infringing on an individual's dignity.[24] Thus in the Canadian case of *Gosselin v Quebec*,[25] the claimant challenged a scheme according to which welfare recipients under the age of thirty received only one-third of the welfare payable to older beneficiaries unless they participated in an education or work experience

[21] Lawrence Mead 'Summary of Welfare Reform' in Lawrence Mead and Chris Beem (eds), *Welfare Reform and Political Theory* (Russell Sage Foundation 2005) 13 (hereafter Mead *et al*, *Welfare Reform*).

[22] Ibid, 12.

[23] See e.g. Stuart White, 'Is Conditionality Illiberal' in Mead *et al*, *Welfare Reform* (n 21) 92.

[24] *Gosselin v Quebec* 2002 SCC 84 (Canadian Supreme Court); *R (on the application of Reynolds) v Secretary of State for Work and Pensions* [2005] UKHL 37.

[25] *Gosselin v Quebec* (n 24).

programme. The majority of the Court accepted the government's assertion that the most effective way to enable young people to join the workforce was to make increased benefits conditional on participation in such programmes. According to McLachlan J: 'This was not a denial of young people's dignity; it was an affirmation of their potential'.[26] Bastarache J, although he dissented on other grounds, took the view that the appellant's poverty 'was brought upon her by the vagaries of a weak economy, not by the legislature's decision not to accord her more financial assistance or to require her to participate in several programs in order for her to receive more assistance'.[27] The dissenting opinions, by contrast, cited evidence that there were not enough places available in the programmes to meet the needs of all welfare recipients under thirty. As L'Hureaux Dube put it, even if a claimant wished to participate in training programmes, there were intervals between courses, during which a claimant's social assistance benefit would have plunged. Any daily life choices would be made in the face of 'an imminent and severe threat of poverty'.[28]

A different manifestation of the background assumption that human rights should protect individual freedoms from state interference can be seen in cases which protect freedom of contract from state social policies, with detrimental effects for people living in poverty. In the well-known case of *Lochner v New York*,[29] the US Supreme Court struck down maximum working hours legislation on the basis that it:

> Necessarily interferes with the right of contract between the employer and employees, concerning the number of hours in which the latter may labour in the bakery of the employer. The general right to make a contract in relation to his business is part of the liberty of the individual protected by the Fourteenth Amendment of the Federal Constitution. Under that provision no State can deprive any person of life, liberty or property without due process of law. The right to purchase or to sell labour is part of the liberty protected by this amendment, unless there are circumstances which exclude the right.[30]

Importantly, the Court refused to countenance the possibility that the workers' freedom to contract was any more limited than that of the employers. 'There is no contention that bakers as a class are not equal in intelligence and capacity to men in other trades or manual occupations, or that they are not able to assert their rights and care for themselves without the protecting arm of the State, interfering with their independence of judgment and of action'.[31]

[26] Ibid, para 42.
[27] Ibid, para 217.
[28] Ibid, para 132.
[29] *Lochner v New York* 198 US 45, 25 S Ct 539.
[30] Ibid, 53.
[31] Ibid, 57.

The protection of individual freedom to contract has also been used to interfere with a universal right to healthcare. An example comes from the Supreme Court of Canada in the case of *Chaoulli*.[32] This case concerned the prohibition in Quebec on private medical insurance, a policy which had been adopted by the Quebec government to prevent doctors leaving the public system to practise private medicine, thus prejudicing the quality of public care. The court struck down the policy: by interfering with the individual's ability to enter into contracts to find healthcare, the state was violating the right to life and personal security. Lack of timely healthcare, where it could result in death, would engage the protection of the right to life in Section 7 of the Charter, which in turn included the freedom to use personal resources to find healthcare outside the state system. The result was that the right to health was closely tied to the availability of personal resources. The dissenting judgment put this well:

> In essence, the question is whether Quebeckers who are prepared to spend money to get access to health care that is, in practice, not accessible in the public sector because of waiting lists may be validly prevented from doing so by the state. But the liberty and security of Quebeckers who do not have the money to afford private health insurance, or who cannot qualify for it, or who are not employed by establishments that provide it, are not put at risk by the absence of 'upper tier' health care. It is Quebeckers who have the money to afford private medical insurance and can qualify for it who will be the beneficiaries of the appellants' constitutional challenge.[33]

B. Rights as Individual Entitlements: The Right to Healthcare

The second peril of a human rights approach to poverty is that human rights adjudication might focuses on the individual entitlements of the parties without accounting for wider public ramifications. A particularly troubling implication of such an individualized approach to human rights has been seen in relation to the constitutional right to health in Brazil and Colombia. The 'Brazilian model' as described by Ferraz consists of individualized claims demanding curative medical treatment (most often drugs) and an extremely high success rate for the litigant. As he describes it:

> in this interpretation, the right to health is an individual entitlement to the satisfaction of one's health needs with the most advanced treatment available, irrespective of costs ... the criterion for privileging litigants over the rest of the

[32] *Chaoulli v Quebec* (n 11).
[33] Ibid, 165.

> population is not based on any conception of need or justice but purely on their ability to access the judiciary, something that only a minority of citizens possess.[34]

Flood and Gross similarly situate the difficulty in the ways in which courts have individualized socio-economic rights, regarding them as immediate rights to a specific benefit.[35] Because of the myopia of courts, which are only able to see the two-way dispute before them, the complex distributive implications of this approach are not addressed, and particularly the consequences for equity in access to healthcare and medications.

The result has been that in these jurisdictions, the right to health has aggravated inequities in healthcare, and shifted attention away from the healthcare needs of people living in poverty. Thus in the Brazilian context, Ferraz has argued that 'the Brazilian experience should give us reason to be extremely cautious (if not sceptical) about the potential of the judiciary as a vehicle for social change in the health arena... [t]he courts might be worsening the country's already pronounced health inequities. I suggest that this is an almost inevitable corollary of the particular model of health litigation and adjudication in Brazil.'[36] Similarly Colombia has witnessed what Flood and Gross refer to as a 'tsunami' of litigation.[37] The experience in relation to rights to healthcare in Latin America leads Yamin to conclude that litigation on individual rights poses the greatest challenges to equity.[38] Spurred by low thresholds for standing, countries in this region have experienced high levels of litigation which exploit the system without transforming it. Indeed, Flood and Gross conclude from their study of sixteen countries that individual litigation can undermine the ability of governments to run fair and effective healthcare systems.[39]

C. Formal Equality

A third risk of a human rights approach in the context of poverty is that equality is interpreted as formal rather than substantive equality. Under this view, as long as individuals are equal before the law, it is irrelevant whether they have ability to exercise their rights. At its extreme neo-liberal end, liberty is formal and abstract: the extent to which a person can exercise real choice among a range of acceptable options is irrelevant. As Hayek put it: 'Liberty describes the absence of particular obstacles—coercion by other men ... it does not assure us of any

[34] Octavio Ferraz, (2009) 'The Right to Health in the Courts of Brazil: Worsening Health Inequities' 11 Health and Human Rights 33, 33 (hereafter Ferraz, 'Worsening Health Inequities').

[35] See Flood and Gross, 'Litigating the Right to Health' (n 10).

[36] Ferraz, 'Worsening Health Inequities' (n 34) 33.

[37] Flood and Gross, 'Litigating the Right to Health' (n 10) 68.

[38] Alicia Yamin (2014) 'Promoting Equity in Health: What Role for Courts' 16 Health and Human Rights 1.

[39] See Flood and Gross, 'Litigating the Right to Health' (n 10).

particular opportunities, but leaves it to us to decide what use we shall make of the circumstances in which we find ourselves.'[40] Even where there is widespread acknowledgement that the state can play a positive role in modern society, courts might take the view that distributive equality is a policy issue, outside of the purview of human rights. This can be seen in the approach of the US Supreme Court in *Rodriguez*, where the court held that policies which discriminate against poor people cannot attract heightened judicial scrutiny. Unlike racial classifications, which are suspect because they concern a 'discrete and insular minority',[41] poor people should not be regarded as discrete or insular.[42] Therefore a system which funded schools on the basis of local taxes, leading to under-resourced schools in poor areas, was not subject to the heightened scrutiny which would have been appropriate had the system provided inferior schools to African Americans.

Formal equality is also indifferent as to whether people are treated equally well or equally badly. It is therefore quite possible that the right to equality be fulfilled by 'levelling down', or removing benefits from the better off, rather than by levelling up. Rebell shows how in California, litigation requiring wealth-related disparities in educational expenditures to be minimized resulted in a 'dramatic levelling down of educational expenditures. Whereas California had ranked fifth in the nation per pupil spending in 1964–1965, by 1994–95 it had fallen to 42nd.'[43]

III. The Promise: Re-Envisaging Human Rights from a Poverty Perspective

For human rights to be able to address poverty, rather than cementing the *status quo*, it is therefore necessary to demonstrate that it is not inevitable that human rights are based on negative freedom, individualism, and formal equality. This part sketches out how such a system should look.

A. Positive Freedom and Positive Duties

As a start, from a human rights perspective, it is difficult to see why freedom should be seen only as an absence of deliberate state interference. If human rights are to be secured to all, it does not make sense to ignore other constraints on the ability of individuals to exercise their rights. Such constraints can arise as much from

[40] Hayek, The Constitution of Liberty (n 20) 19.

[41] *United States v Carolene Products Co* 304 US 144, 58 S Ct 788, footnote 4.

[42] *San Antonio Independent School District v Rodriguez* 411 US 959, 93 S Ct 1278.

[43] Michael Rebell, 'Ensuring Adequate Funding: The Role of Courts' in William Mathis and Tina Trujilo (eds), *Learning from the Federal Test-Based Reforms: Lessons for ESSA* (Information Age Publishing 2016) 4.

poverty, poor health, and lack of education as from tyranny and intolerance. This approach draws on the insights of modern theorists, in particular of Amartya Sen, who see freedom not as absence of coercion but as agency or the ability to exercise genuine choice and act on those choices. For Sen, freedom consists in being able to do and be what one has reason to value. As Sen argues: 'What people can achieve is influenced by economic opportunities, political liberties, social powers and the enabling conditions of good health, basic education, and the encouragement and cultivation of initiatives'.[44] Far from being irrelevant, the ability to achieve one's valued goals is essential to this conception of freedom. This necessitates the 'removal of major sources of un-freedom: poverty as well as tyranny, poor economic opportunities as well as systematic social deprivation, neglect of public facilities as well as intolerance or over-activity of repressive states'.[45] Similarly, Griffin stresses that human rights are grounded in the value attached to 'normative agency', or 'our autonomously choosing and freely pursuing our conception of a worthwhile life'.[46] Like Sen, he argues that '[t]he value [of normative agency] resides not simply in one's having the undeveloped, unused capacities for autonomy and liberty but also in exercising them—not just in being able to be autonomous but also in actually being so'.[47] Thus, in contrast to Berlin, poverty should be seen as the deprivation of basic capabilities and therefore a type of 'un-freedom'.[48]

This approach is strengthened by the recognition that the distinction between non-intervention and positive action is itself elusive. Poverty is always capable of being construed as an act of deliberate intervention by the state: it is the legal regime which creates property rights and protects them from theft and invasion. Bentham famously declared: 'Property is entirely the creature of law … [i]t is from the law alone that I can enclose a field and give myself to its cultivation … [b]efore the law, there was no property; take away the laws, all property ceases'.[49] To this Cohen adds the further insight, namely that lack of money is itself an act of deliberative intervention by the state. This is because the state has allocated a particular function to money, namely to give people the means to overcome interference with their liberty.[50] Thus, whether poverty is construed as deliberate state intervention, or as an obstacle to freedom which the state has the means to remove, it remains true to say that positive action is required from the state in order to ensure that an individual can exercise her human rights.

There are several ways in which reconfiguring the background assumption in this way can lead to judicial determinations which recognize violations of the

[44] Sen, Development as Freedom (n 4).

[45] Ibid, 3.

[46] James Griffin, *On Human Rights* (OUP 2009) 179 (hereafter Griffin, *On Human Rights*).

[47] Ibid, 183.

[48] Ibid, 90–91.

[49] Jeremy Bentham, *Principles of the Civil Code* (Simkin Marshall 1898) 1:307–08.

[50] Gerald Cohen, 'Freedom and Money' Lecture in Memory of Isaiah Berlin (1999) <http://www.howardism.org/appendix/Cohen.pdf> accessed 13 August 2019.

human rights of those in poverty. One way is to recognize that the right to property does not necessarily trump rights to housing or subsistence of people in poverty. Thus, the South African Constitutional Court and the European Court of Human Rights (ECtHR) have held that the right of property cannot be exercised to deprive people of a right to a home unless proper safeguards are in place.[51] Another manifestation is in the recognition of welfare rights as a species of property rights. Thus, the ECtHR has held that the statutory welfare rights fall within the ambit of the right to peaceful enjoyment of property in the European Convention on Human Rights (ECHR). Although a state need not provide social security benefits, if it does, it cannot do so in a discriminatory manner.[52]

This approach also raises the converse question of the extent to which human rights obligations bind non-state actors, particularly multinational companies and corporations. Human rights have traditionally been regarded as binding only the state, whereas some of the most serious violations of poor people's rights are committed by corporations. This too is embedded in a specific conception of freedom as non-interference with individual liberty, in this case, the liberty of corporations, or juristic persons. By contrast, a positive understanding of freedom as the ability to exercise one's human rights suggests that the correlative duty should fall on whoever is obstructing those rights, whether state or non-state, subject only to the human rights of the latter. Bilchitz argues that fundamental rights should be articulated from the perspective of the rights holder, which entails that it is incoherent to suggest that 'only states are bound not to violate human rights and all other entities may violate such rights at will'.[53]

There are two main ways in which human rights can be applied to corporations. The first is by recognizing that human rights require the state not just to refrain from violating human rights through its own actions but also to protect individuals from violations by third parties. The duty on the state is therefore threefold: to respect, protect, and fulfil human rights. The duty to protect can usually be discharged through legislation, for example, binding corporations to protect individual rights to fair conditions at work, minimum wages, environmental protection and other relevant requirements. A good example of the way in which this operates to protect the rights of people living in poverty is the case of *SERAC v Nigeria*,[54] which concerned a challenge before the African Commission

[51] *Occupiers of 51 Olivia Road v City of Johannesburg* Case CCT 24/07 [2008] ZACC 1 (South African Constitutional Court); *Connors v United Kingdom* App No 66746/01 (ECtHR, 27 May 2004); *Veloso Barreto v Portugal* App No 18072/91 (ECtHR, 29 June 1994).

[52] *Stec v United Kingdom* App No 65731/01 (ECtHR, 12 April 2006).

[53] David Bilchitz, 'The Necessity for a Business and Human Rights Treaty' (SSRN, 30 November 2014) 4 <https://papers.ssrn.com/sol3/papers.cfm?abstract_id=2562760> or <http://dx.doi.org/10.2139/ssrn.2562760> accessed 13 August 2019 (hereafter Bilchitz, 'The Necessity for a Business and Human Rights Treaty').

[54] Communication 155/96 *Social and Economic Rights Action Centre (SERAC) v Nigeria* (2001) AHRLR 60 (African Commission on Human and People's Rights).

on Human and People's Rights. The communication alleged that the government of Nigeria was responsible for failure to protect the Ogoni people from the environmental degradation and health problems resulting from the contamination of the environment caused by oil production by a consortium of oil companies. The oil companies had disposed of toxic waste into the environment and local waterways and caused numerous avoidable oil spills, thus poisoning much of the soil and water upon which Ogoni farming and fishing depended. The Commission reaffirmed that the duty on governments included the obligation to protect rights-holders against other agents by legislation and the provision of effective remedies.[55] However, as Bilchitz points out, the paradox of this finding is that while the state was liable, the responsible corporation was not held to account in any way.[56] In any event, many such corporations are powerful enough to find ways of avoiding state control.

The second approach is therefore to make businesses liable in their own right. At international level, this remains a contested issue, with the result that, thus far, only voluntary mechanisms have been agreed at UN level. The UN Guiding principles on Business and Human Rights, known as the Ruggie principles, reiterate the duty of the state to protect individuals against breach of rights by corporations; and the need for remedies to individuals whose rights have been violated but only a voluntary acceptance of corporate responsibility to respect human rights.[57] In 2014, the UN Human Rights Council established an intergovernmental working group with the mandate to elaborate an internationally legally binding instrument on Transnational Corporations and Other Business Enterprises with respect to human rights.[58] But this has not yet succeeded in producing a draft. In the meantime, some important dicta from regional human rights courts have been pointed to as paving the way for greater accountability of corporations. In the recent case of the *Kaliña and Lokono Peoples v Suriname*,[59] which concerned the adverse impacts on the human rights of indigenous peoples of corporate activity in Suriname, the Inter-American Court stated that both state and non-state actors can commit human rights violations. By using the term 'violation', rather than 'abuse', it arguably took an important step beyond the notion of voluntary assumption of responsibility

[55] Ibid, para 54.

[56] Bilchitz, 'The Necessity for a Business and Human Rights Treaty' (n 53) 7.

[57] UNHRC 'Report of the Special Representative of the Secretary-General on the issue of human rights and transnational corporations and other business enterprises, John Ruggie; Guiding Principles on Business and Human Rights: Implementing the United Nations "Protect, Respect and Remedy" Framework' (21 March 2011) A/HRC/17/31. See also <http://www.ohchr.org/documents/publications/GuidingprinciplesBusinesshr_en.pdf> accessed 13 August 2019.

[58] UNHRC 'Elaboration of an International Legally Binding Instrument on Transnational Corporations and other Business Enterprises with Respect to Human Rights' (25 June 2014) A/HRC/26/L.22/Rev.1.

[59] *Case of The Kaliña And Lokono Peoples v Suriname* (Merits, Reparations and Costs) Inter-American Court of Human Rights Series C No 12.639 (25 November 2015).

embedded in the Ruggie Principles.[60] However, since the Inter-American Court does not have jurisdiction to determine cases against non-state actors, these can only be suggestions.

B. From Individualism to Solidarity

Sen's normative framework places as its highest value the individual's capability to do or be what she has reason to value. However, this risks focusing too much attention on what individuals can achieve, giving the impression that the only function of human rights is to facilitate the ability of individuals to realize their own goals. It is important that this should not eclipse other human rights values, which are not based on choice but on interpersonal relationships and interdependence. Central among these is the value of caring, which comes, not as a matter of choice, but of responsibility. Human rights should not only value choices. They should also value relationships for themselves.[61] This is recognized more explicitly by Nussbaum, who includes in her definition of capabilities such values as affiliation and political participation.[62]

This suggests that a rights-based approach to poverty should also be shaped by the value of solidarity.[63] Critics of welfare rights argue that they impose a burden on productive members of society in order to benefit the unproductive. However, state responsibility for ensuring all reach a minimum capability threshold should be viewed as a contribution to the community as a whole,[64] not simply to particular individuals. Thus, Ritchie argued at the end of the nineteenth century that fundamental or natural rights were 'mutual claims which cannot be ignored without detriment to the well-being and in the last resort to the very being of a community'.[65] Even more forceful is the statement of Mokgoro J in the South African social security case of *Khosa*. As she stressed, 'sharing responsibility for the problems and consequences of poverty equally as a community represents the extent to which wealthier members of the community view the minimal well-being of the poor

[60] See Nicolás Carrillo-Santarelli, 'Part I: The intersection of Business and Human Rights at the Inter-American Court of Human Rights' (Oxford Human Rights Hub, 10 March 2016) <http://ohrh.law.ox.ac.uk/part-i-the-intersection-of-business-and-human-rights-at-the-inter-american-court-of-human-rights/> accessed 26 November 2019; Nicolás Carrillo-Santarelli, 'Part II: The Intersection of Business and Human Rights at the Inter-American Court of Human Rights' (Oxford Human Rights Hub, 11 March 2016) <http://ohrh.law.ox.ac.uk/part-ii-the-intersection-of-business-and-human-rights-at-the-inter-american-court-of-human-rights/> accessed26 November 2019.

[61] Fredman, *Human Rights Transformed* (n 17) 16–19; 25–30.

[62] Martha Nussbaum, *Women and Human Development* (CUP 2000) (hereafter Nussbaum, *Women and Human Development*).

[63] For a detailed defence of the value of solidarity see Fredman, *Human Rights Transformed* (n 17) 16–19.

[64] Michael Freeden, 'Rights, Needs and Community: The Emergence of British Welfare Thought' in Alan Ware and Robert Goodin (eds), *Needs and Welfare* (Sage 1990) 55.

[65] David Ritchie, *Natural Rights* (Allen & Unwin 1894) 87.

as connected with their personal well-being and the well-being of the community as a whole'.[66] From a legal perspective, incorporating these values into a rights-based approach is preferable to regarding solidarity as limiting rights. This is because limitations on rights are rightly construed strictly, placing the burden on the state, as the party claiming to limit the right, to show that the restriction is pursuing a legitimate aim, and is proportionate in the sense of being necessary to achieve this aim.

The move from pure individualism to a sense of community or solidarity can play a central role in counteracting the potential for human rights adjudication to favour elites at the expense of people living in poverty. Rather than a myopic focus on a bipolar dispute between the parties before it, this approach requires courts to recognize and account for the polycentric implications of decision-making. Yamin thus argues that the response to the inequitable results of health rights litigation in Colombia and Brazil should not be to remove the possibility of a justiciable right to health. Instead, she maintains that litigation should be structured in a way in which courts can consider the equity impacts of healthcare rights and create opportunities for public learning about health rights. Human rights litigation should include evidence of the broader impact of decisions in individual cases, an understanding of the complexity of the healthcare sector, and in particular, a reckoning with the asymmetries of power and information as between patients on the one hand and the insurance and pharmaceutical industry on the other. Courts should expect policy-makers to design healthcare plans to meet human rights-based criteria, not just for the litigants before them but for everyone affected. For example, the Colombian Court, after a period of intense individual litigation which threatened to skew the healthcare budget, issued a ruling in 2008, ordering the government to address the systemic factors behind the health litigation.[67] As part of this, the government was required to draw up a wider restructuring plan which included a participative process. The hope is that such an approach will achieve a greater balance between individual rights and the wider social interest.

The move from individualism to solidarity also suggests that justiciable human rights should be regarded as part of a wider civil society strategy to achieve the rights of people in poverty. A central example is the right to food litigation in India initiated by the People's Union of Civil Liberties in 2001. In this long-running case, the Indian Supreme Court has issued a series of innovative awards under its *interim mandamus* jurisdiction to direct the proper implementation of food distribution systems.[68] Possibly the most far-reaching is the scheme requiring a cooked midday meal at all public schools. A key dimension of the success of this case is

[66] *Khosa and Mahlaule v Minister for Social Development* 2004 (6) BCLR 569 (CC) para 74.

[67] Ruling T-760 of 2008.

[68] For a full discussion, see Sandra Fredman, *Discrimination Law* (2nd edn, OUP 2011) 130–33 (hereafter Fredman, *Discrimination Law*).

the recognition that a court-centred approach is not sufficient. Instead, the Court's continuing involvement is both a response to and a catalyst for a well-organized grass-roots activist campaign of fact-finding, compliance monitoring, and strategic litigations. These are supplemented by energetic Court appointed Commissioners. Initial resistance by state governments to court orders to provide midday meals in primary schools was met by a robust rejection by the Court of budgetary excuses. By the end of 2005, coverage of midday meals in state public schools was near complete, largely due to vigilance by civil society organizations and a responsive court. However, there remains much work to be done on the quality of such meals. On the instigation of the public interest litigants, the Court has issued further orders relating to quality of meals, infrastructure, and basic expenditure. According to the Right to Food Campaign, such orders have largely been implemented, although the quality of midday meals, content, variety, and health safeguards fall below national standards in some states.[69] This culminated in the Right to Food Act 2013.

C. Poverty and the Right to Equality: A Contested Terrain

It has been argued thus far that for human rights to be applicable to addressing poverty, three basic assumptions need to be refashioned: namely that freedom consists in the absence of state intervention, that the individual is separate from and prior to society, and that equality consists in formal equality before the law. The first two issues were dealt with in the previous two sections. This section considers the third issue, drawing on the move in recent years towards a more substantive conception of the right to equality. Since the right to equality is found in all major international human rights instruments, and is generally a centrepiece of domestic human rights instruments, the potential to interpret equality in a substantive way is of crucial importance to the applicability of human rights to addressing poverty. This in turn requires a deeper understanding of the relationship between poverty and the traditional constituency of equality rights, namely inequality on the grounds of race, gender, or other status. With the growing recognition of the concentration of poverty within status groups has come an increasing overlap between the areas of concerns of anti-poverty policy and equality law. Researchers and policy-makers continue to wrestle with the extent to which inequality should be part of the definition and measurement of poverty. Equally contested is the question of whether equality should be the desired outcome of anti-poverty measures, and if so, what this would entail. At the same time, deepening understandings of substantive equality have illuminated the continuities between 'status' inequalities

[69] See Midday Meals: A Primer (March 2014) <https://docs.google.com/viewer?a=v&pid=sites&srcid=ZGVmYXVsdGRvbWFpbnxoYXFyb3ppcm90aXxneDoxNDRmYmI2NWNjNWE0ODNj> accessed 13 August 2019.

(or inequalities on the grounds of race, gender, disability, etc) and poverty. Groups which suffer from discrimination on status grounds are disproportionately represented among people living in poverty. Conversely, people living in poverty experience many of the elements of discrimination experienced by status groups, including lack of recognition, social exclusion, and reduced political participation.

There are several aspects to this debate. The first concerns the conceptualization of poverty.[70] To what extent should poverty be defined in relative terms, focusing on inequalities between people, rather than in absolute terms, focusing on the ability to meet one's basic physical needs? This debate tends to focus on distributive inequalities, particularly income inequality. The second aspect brings inequalities of status into the frame, and examines the intersection between poverty on the one hand, and gender, race, disability, and age discrimination on the other. The aim of this section is to air these debates rather than resolve them. Since the conceptualization of poverty is closely related to the kind of policy prescriptions which might follow, it is important to ask how an equality perspective on poverty might enhance such policy responses.

1. Poverty and distributive inequality

The relationship between poverty and inequality is complex and contested.[71] In particular, there is an ongoing debate as to whether poverty should be defined in absolute or relative terms. A view of poverty as absolute focuses on basic needs or an existential minimum, such as the $1.25 a day standard used as the definition of extreme poverty in the SDGs, agreed in 2015.[72] On this view, poverty should be defined by the 'actual needs of the poor and not by reference to the expenditure of those who are not poor. A family is poor if it cannot afford to eat.'[73] However, it is immediately clear that it is impossible to keep inequality wholly outside the definition of poverty. In his path-breaking work, Townsend argued that a central mistake is to assume that 'physical efficiency of individuals can be divorced from their psychological well-being and the organization and structure of society'.[74] In particular, it is wrong to assume that there can be a be 'list of absolute necessities of life to maintain even physical efficiency or health which applies at any time and in any society, without reference to the structure, organization, physical environment and available resources of that society'.[75] Instead, he advocates a relative definition

[70] Ruth Lister, *Poverty* (Polity 2004) chapter 1 (hereafter Lister, *Poverty*).

[71] Ibid, chapter 1.

[72] See Sustainable Development Goals <https://sustainabledevelopment.un.org/?menu=1300> accessed 13 August 2019.

[73] Keith Joseph and Jonathan Sumption, *Equality* (John Murray 1979) 27; see also Lister, *Poverty* (n 70) 21.

[74] Peter Townsend (1962) 'The Meaning of Poverty' 13British Journal of Sociology 210, 218–19 (hereafter Townsend, 'The Meaning of Poverty').

[75] Ibid, 219.

of poverty, one which regards people as poverty stricken if 'their income, even if adequate for survival, falls markedly behind that of the community'.[76]

The relative definition of poverty has several advantages. Perhaps the most important is its ability to capture the ways in which social expectations can themselves structure poverty. Thus, as Sen shows, African Americans may well be many times richer in terms of incomes than poorer people in the rest of the world, even when taking account of price differences. However, they are decidedly poorer than American whites.[77] Even when one's income is high in terms of absolute standards, more income is needed to buy enough commodities to achieve the same social functioning:

> The need to take part in the life of a community may induce demands for modern equipment (televisions, videocassette recorders, automobiles and so on) in a country where such facilities are more or less universal (unlike what would be needed in less affluent countries), and this imposes a strain on a relatively poor person in a rich country even when that person is at a much higher level of income compared with people in less opulent countries.[78]

A relative approach to poverty also allows us to take account of important equality issues below the absolute threshold.[79] As Alcock shows, anti-poverty measures may appear successful because they increase the numbers of people above the poverty line. However, it is easier to move those just below the line to just above it than to achieve the same result with those well below the line.[80] It is therefore important to pay attention to the distribution of income among the poor themselves. This can be expressed in the form of an 'income gap', which measures the additional income that would be needed to bring all of the poor up to the level of the poverty line.[81] Similarly, inequalities above the minimum can be kept in focus on a relative approach. Recent research demonstrates that unequal societies have higher levels of social problems than more equal societies.[82] This affects not just the most deprived, but also the better off. Thus, an individual from the lowest-earning 20 per cent of society in a more equal society is more likely to live longer than her counterpart from a less equal society. By the same token, perhaps surprisingly, someone from the highest-earning 20 per cent in a more equal society has a longer life expectancy than an equivalently well-off person in a less equal society.[83] Similarly, more equal

[76] Ibid, 221 citing John Galbraith, *The Affluent Society* (Hamish Hamilton 1958) 252.
[77] Sen, Development as Freedom (n 4) 96.
[78] Ibid, 89.
[79] Mark Stein (2009) 'Nussbaum: A Utilitarian Critique' 50(2)(2) Boston College Law Review 489, 494–97, 508–09.
[80] Pete Alcock, *Understanding Poverty* (3rd edn, Palgrave Macmillan 2006) 85.
[81] Sen, Development as Freedom (n 4) 103.
[82] See Richard Wilkinson and Kate Pickett, The Spirit Level: Why More Equal Societies Almost Always Do Better (Penguin 2009) 15–24.
[83] Ibid, chapter 6.

societies tend to have lower infant mortality[84] and lower levels of crime[85] than more unequal societies, even where the latter have higher average rates of income.

This also suggests that income should not be the only measure of poverty. Even the earliest economists, such as Adam Smith, recognized that poverty entailed more than subsistence: lack of dignity can itself be an aspect of poverty. He therefore included in his notion of necessities, 'not only the commodities which are indispensably necessary for the support of life, but whatever the custom of the country renders it indecent for creditable people, even of the lowest order, to be without'.[86] For him, then, a linen shirt was indispensable. Townsend argues that inequitable distribution of housing, medical, educational, and other resources should also be taken into account.[87] This approach is now reflected in the European Commission's definition, adopted in 1984, which defines the poor as 'persons, families and groups of persons whose resources (material, cultural and social) are so limited as to exclude them from the minimum acceptable way of life in the Member State in which they live'.[88]

However, the relative definition of poverty is not without difficulty. Given that there will always be some sections of society that are badly off in relative terms, it would, on this approach, be impossible to eliminate poverty: a society might improve its general living standards without ever reducing the number of those in poverty. Sen therefore argues for an 'irreducible absolutist core in the idea of poverty'.[89] One particularly obvious element of the absolutist core is starvation and hunger: 'If there is starvation and hunger, then—no matter what the relative picture looks like—there clearly is poverty'.[90] Conversely, '[i]t would be absurd to call someone poor just because he had the means to buy only one Cadillac a day when others in that community could buy two of these cars each day. The absolute considerations cannot be inconsequential for conceptualizing poverty.'[91] It is through his capabilities theory that Sen achieves a synthesis between the absolute core and the relative characteristics of poverty. Deprivation of capabilities is absolute, whereas the resources needed to fulfil those capabilities are relative to the society. The same is true of the ability to participate in society, or the ability to be educated. Sen therefore sees poverty as 'the failure of basic capabilities to reach certain minimally acceptable levels'.[92] The relevant functionings range from 'such elementary physical ones as being well-nourished, being adequately clothed and sheltered,

84 Ibid, 82–83.

85 Ibid, chapters 10 and 11.

86 Adam Smith, An Inquiry into the Nature and Causes of the Wealth of the Nations (Bell 1892) Book V, ch 2, part I.

87 Townsend, 'The Meaning of Poverty' (n 74) 223–24.

88 Council of the European Communities 'Council Decision on Specific Community Action to Combat Poverty' (1984) 85/8/EEC, art 1(2).

89 Sen, Development as Freedom (n 4) 159.

90 Ibid.

91 Ibid.

92 Sen, Development as Freedom (n 4) 109.

avoiding preventable morbidity, [*et cetera*], to more complex social achievements such as taking part in the life of the community, being able to appear in public without shame, and so on'.[93] The specific form of these general functionings varies from society to society.

Drawing on these insights, Alkire and colleagues have developed a multidimensional measure of acute poverty, which focuses on three dimensions of poverty: education, health, and living standards. Each of these is broken down into indicators of deprivation. For example, a household is deprived in relation to education of no household member has completed 5 years of schooling or any school-aged child is not attending school up to class 8. The health indicators are child mortality and nutrition: a family is deprived if any child has died in the family and any adult or child is malnourished. The living standard indicators are electricity, improved sanitation, improved drinking water, flooring, cooking fuel, and assets ownership. A person is identified as poor if she is deprived of at least one-third of weighted indicators. Those deprived in 50 per cent or more of the dimensions are identified as in 'severe poverty'.[94]

2. Substantive equality and poverty: an analytic framework

The recognition that poverty is a multi-dimensional phenomenon has resonances in the rapidly developing theoretical and practical understanding of substantive equality. Poverty is not simply about insufficient income, although income is an important means to combat poverty. It is also about relative deprivation, absence of agency, stigma and exclusion. Putting the insights of the poverty analysis together with theories of substantive equality potentially yields a powerful analytic tool both to assess and to develop policy responses to poverty.

Substantive equality goes beyond formal equality in that it is not simply about equal treatment, or a comparison between two groups.[95] Some regard substantive equality as requiring a focus on equality of results; others stress equality of opportunity. In both cases, unequal treatment may be necessary to achieve the ultimate goal. However, both equality of results and equality of opportunity are vague and difficult to measure. A further potential 'substantive core' to the concept of equality is the concept of dignity. On this approach the ultimate aim of equality is to achieve equal dignity.[96] However, as the Canadian jurisprudence has shown, dignity on

[93] Ibid, 110.

[94] Sabina Alkire, Adriana Conconi, Gisela Obles, and Suman Seth, 'Multidimensional Poverty Index—Winter 2014/15: Brief Methodological Note and Results' (Oxford Poverty and Human Development Initiative, January 2015) <http://www.ophi.org.uk/wp-content/uploads/MPI-2015-Brief-Methodological-Note_1-5-15.pdf?0a8fd7> accessed 13 August 2019.

[95] For valuable analyses of substantive equality, see Catherine Albertyn (2007) 'Substantive Equality and Transformation in South Africa' 23 South African Journal on Human Rights 253; Christopher McCrudden, 'Equality and Non-Discrimination' in David Feldman (ed), *English Public Law* (2nd edn, OUP 2009); Gwen Brodsky and Shelagh Day (2002) 'Beyond the Social and Economic Rights Debate: Substantive Equality Speaks to Poverty' 14 Canadian Journal of Women and Law 185.

[96] *Law v Canada* [1999] 1 SCR 497 para 51.

its own may have the perverse effect of erecting barriers to claimants, who have to show not just that they have suffered disadvantage but that this reflects a breach of their dignity.[97] Drawing together these perspectives yields a multidimensional concept of substantive equality pursuing four overlapping aims.[98] First, it aims to break the cycle of disadvantage associated with status or out-groups. This reflects the redistributive dimension of equality. Second, it aims to promote respect for dignity and worth, thereby redressing stigma, stereotyping, humiliation, and violence because of membership of an identity group. This reflects a recognition dimension.[99] Third, substantive equality should facilitate full participation in society, both socially and politically. This is the participative dimension. Fourth, it should not exact conformity as a price of equality. Instead, it should accommodate difference and aim to achieve structural change. This captures the transformative dimension.

It can immediately be seen that this conception of equality is relevant to people in poverty in a number of important ways. The distributive dimension brings together status inequalities and poverty by recognizing that disadvantage is often disproportionately associated with status. The first aim of substantive equality is therefore to correct the cycle of disadvantage experienced because of status or other protected characteristic. However, focusing on disadvantage also carries with it some important challenges. The most important is to specify the nature of disadvantage. Disadvantage is most easily understood in the context of redistribution of resources and benefits, and therefore is of most relevance to poverty. However, as Iris Marion Young argues,[100] the distributive paradigm ignores social structures such as decision-making power, the division of labour and culture, or the symbolic meanings attached to people, actions, and things.[101] Thus disadvantage should encompass more than maldistribution of resources. It needs also to take on board the constraints which power structures impose on individuals because of their status. For example, women who are trapped in the private sphere will suffer disadvantage in this sense even if they live in affluent households.

Disadvantage can also be understood as a deprivation of genuine opportunities to pursue one's own valued choices. This again draws on the insights of Sen[102] and Nussbaum's[103] 'capabilities' theories, which stress the importance of considering the extent to which people are actually able to exercise their choices, rather than simply having the formal right to do so. It is not enough to treat everyone equally, since the same treatment of individuals with very different constraints can replicate

[97] See ibid; *Gosselin v Quebec* (n 24); *R v Kapp* 2008 SCC 41.
[98] Fredman, *Discrimination Law* (n 68) chapter 1.
[99] Nancy Fraser and Axel Honneth, *Redistribution or Recognition* (Verso 2003) 1.
[100] Iris Young, *Justice and the Politics of Difference* (Princeton University Press 1990) 16.
[101] Ibid, 16.
[102] Sen, Development as Freedom (n 4).
[103] Nussbaum, Women and Human Development (n 62).

disadvantage. Similarly, Griffin stresses that human rights are grounded in the value attached to 'normative agency', or 'our autonomously choosing and freely pursuing our conception of a worthwhile life'.[104] Like Sen, he argues that: '[t]he value [of normative agency] resides not simply in one's having the undeveloped, unused capacities for autonomy and liberty but also in exercising them—not just in being able to be autonomous but also in actually being so'.[105]

One of the aims of the redistributive dimension of equality therefore is to redress disadvantage by removing obstacles to genuine choice. At the same time, it needs to be recognized that choice itself can be problematic, since people often adapt their choices to their circumstances. For example, women might prefer part-time work even if it is insecure and low paid because it permits them to combine paid work and child-care. But this choice is made within a context in which women are assumed to be the primary child-carers. The fact that women make these choices should not imply that there is no further need for legal intervention. Substantive equality should also aim to remove the disadvantages attached to part-time work, and indeed to achieve more wide-ranging structural change, which includes an equitable division of child-caring obligations between mothers, fathers, and the broader community. Moreover, there are circumstances in which the concern is not solely to increase the range of feasible options but to address the disadvantage attached to the circumstances a person actually finds herself in. This is particularly true in the context of some kinds of disability; as well as of caring obligations.

Even in its most expansive sense, disadvantage does not cover all the wrongs associated with inequality. Stigma, stereotyping, humiliation, and violence on grounds of gender, race, disability, sexual orientation, or other status can be experienced regardless of relative disadvantage. Thus, the second main aim of substantive equality should be to promote respect for the equal dignity and worth of all. This is the dimension of equality which speaks to our basic humanity. Equality attaches to all individuals, not because of their merit, or their rationality, or their citizenship or membership of any particular group, but because of their humanity. Individuals should not be humiliated or degraded through racism, sexism, violence, or other status-based prejudice.

The particular value of the dignity or recognition dimension of equality is to highlight the fact that the stigma often associated with poverty is itself a harm which needs to be addressed. This was captured, as we have seen, in Adam Smith's recognition that a linen shirt might be a basic need because it signified the very minimum of respectability. Indeed, as we have seen, stigma can itself perpetuate poverty. Lister also points to the ways in which black people have been stereotyped and stigmatized through associating them with poverty and welfare dependency.[106]

[104] Griffin, *On Human Rights* (n 46) 179.

[105] Ibid, 183.

[106] Lister, *Poverty* (n 70) 64.

More generally, she argues, the ways in which the non-poor construct the poor as 'Other' can have a profound impact on how poverty is experienced.[107] The line between 'us' and 'them' is 'imbued with negative value judgements that construct "the poor" variously as a source of moral contamination, a threat, an "undeserving" economic burden, an object of pity or even as an exotic species'.[108] This also legitimates the privilege of the wealthy, defining and affirming their identity by diminishing others.

Locating dignity as one of several dimensions of equality also enables us to see that dignity is not a separate and additional element to socio-economic disadvantage in an equality claim. Socio-economic disadvantage is itself an assault on an individual's basic humanity. This was highlighted in the South African case of *Khosa v Minister of Social Development; Mahlaule v Minister of Social Development*,[109] which concerned a legislative measure which confined the right to child benefit and old-age pensions to South African citizens, to the exclusion of permanent residents. In striking down this measure as a breach of equality, Mokgoro J emphasized that the consequences of exclusion were not only socio-economic. In addition, the exclusion of permanent residents had a strong stigmatizing effect, creating the impression that they were inferior to citizens and less worthy of social assistance.[110]

The third dimension of substantive equality relates to participation. Given that past discrimination or other social mechanisms have blocked the avenues for political participation by particular minorities, equality laws are needed both to compensate for this absence of political voice and to open up the channels for greater participation in the future. Participation also refers to the importance of community in the life of individuals. Rather than the universal, abstract individual of formal equality, substantive equality recognizes that individuals are essentially social. To be fully human includes the ability to participate on equal terms in community and society more generally. Thus Young argues that the focus of theories of justice should be on structures which exclude people from participating in determining their actions.[111] Fraser puts particular emphasis on participation, regarding parity of participation as the normative core of her conception of justice, encompassing both redistribution and recognition without reducing either one to the other.[112] Collins, in searching for a justification for departure from the equal treatment principle, develops the concept of social inclusion as central to his notion of substantive equality.[113]

[107] Ibid, 100.

[108] Ibid, 101.

[109] *Khosa v Minister of Social Development; Mahlaule v Minister of Social Development* 2004 6 SA 505 (CC) 2004 6 SA 505 (CC).

[110] Ibid, para 77.

[111] Iris Young, *Justice and the Politics of Difference* (Princeton University Press 1990) 31–32.

[112] Nancy Fraser, 'Social Justice in the Age of Identity Politics' in Nancy Fraser and Axel Honneth (eds), *Redistribution or Recognition?* (Verso 2003) 36–77.

[113] Hugh Collins (2003) 'Discrimination, Equality and Social Inclusion' 66 Modern Law Review 16, 24.

Both the political and the social aspects of participation are similarly central to the characterization of poverty and therefore to the determination of appropriate policy. Indeed, the concept of social exclusion has to some extent eclipsed that of poverty in the European debate.[114] Social exclusion refers to those who are systematically excluded from participation in society, where participation refers to the capacity to purchase goods and services; participation in economically or socially valuable activities, political engagement, and social interaction.[115] The concept of social exclusion highlights the interaction between status and distributive equalities: it is closely correlated with living in a deprived area, suffering partnership breakdown, or being a member of an ethnic minority, the elderly, or disabled. It is particularly valuable in that its focus is on the relationship between the included and the excluded, and in particular on the role of the former in causing or perpetuating exclusion.[116]

The fourth dimension of equality, the transformative dimension, entails recognizing and accommodating difference. It also entails changing underlying structures, rather than expecting individuals to conform. This dimension of equality taps into a complex debate in relation to poverty: the relationship between agency and structure. The agency approach to poverty is based on the central assumption that, on the whole, people can be regarded as responsible for their own poverty. Only those who are genuinely incapacitated should be entitled to assistance from the state. This approach has directly influenced policy, from the punitive Poor Laws of nineteenth-century Britain to modern day welfare-to-work programmes in the United States and elsewhere. It puts people living in poverty in a double bind from which it is difficult to escape. Those who are regarded as capable of work are attributed more power and agency than they truly have. On the other hand, those who are regarded as incapacitated are deprived of all agency. In nineteenth-century Britain, this manifested as a distinction between the 'deserving' and the 'undeserving' poor. The undeserving poor were treated punitively, whereas the deserving poor were characterized as objects of charity rather than as individual agents. These epithets endure into modern-day debates.

At the other extreme, the structural approach recognizes that poverty is based on forces beyond the control of any one individual. However, there is a risk that such an approach leads to policy prescriptions which denude individuals of any agency. Instead, the object of policy should be to facilitate agency by removing some of the central constraints and obstacles. The transformative dimension thus frees individuals from constraints without expecting that they use their agency in predetermined ways.

[114] Lister, *Poverty* (n 70) 74.

[115] Tania Burchardt, Julian Le Grand, and David Piachaud, 'Degrees of Exclusion: Developing a Dynamic, Multidimensional Measure' in John Hills, Julian Le Grand, and David Piachaud (eds), *Understanding Social Exclusion* (OUP 2002) 30, 30–32.

[116] Lister, *Poverty* (n 70) 98.

IV. Conclusion

It has been argued here that a human rights approach to poverty needs to confront and reconfigure some of the basic premises behind traditional views of human rights. In particular, background assumptions of freedom as non-interference, individualism, and formal equality may in fact militate against effective engagement of human rights in addressing poverty. Instead, these background premises need to be reconfigured so that freedom requires the state to facilitate genuine fulfilment of individual capabilities; individuals are seen as achieving such fulfilment through their relationships with others in society; and equality is considered as substantive rather than formal. From these starting points, poverty can be seen to be a gross violation of human rights, requiring immediate and concerted action from state and non-state actors alike. The strong endorsement of human rights at the centre of the SDG agenda should require more than a rhetorical flourish. Most importantly, the goals articulated in the SDG agenda should be closely tied to legally binding human rights instruments which have been widely ratified by the vast majority of the world's nations. This means that, on the one hand, the goals become more than promises and policy aspiration, and are viewed as entitlements, empowering those in poverty to demand their fulfilment. On the other hand, the SDG content can be used to provide detailed content to binding human rights, which tend to be expressed in general terms. In particular, those rights which are subject to progressive realization should be pinned to the fifteen-year timetable of the SDGs, so that human rights instruments and the SDGs can work together to genuinely eliminate extreme poverty by 2030.

11
Uphill Battle
Deliberating Towards Human Rights-Compatible Public Budgets

Jaakko Kuosmanen

I. Introduction

Budgets and budgeting are generally thought to be an issue for political bargaining. However, the role of human rights, and particularly socio-economic rights, in relation to budgeting has become increasingly important. Human rights, especially where they give rise to positive duties on states, require appropriate budgets. This raises questions regarding the nature of the guiding framework that human rights set for budgets. Should human rights require a different kind of reasoning which stands apart from political or interest based bargaining, to legitimate the setting of budgets? This question is made more difficult because the obligations which arise from human rights are open-textured and at times contingent on the availability of budgets. Many socio-economic rights instruments specifically state that they are only realizable according to the availability of resources. Put differently, human rights do not set unambiguous quantified standards for public budgeting. Instead, they operate as general guiding principles that need to be interpreted in substantive terms. Therefore, in the context of budgeting human rights give rise to 'dialogues of contestation'. This chapter examines the role of deliberative approaches in addressing these difficult questions, and contrasts deliberative approaches 'with strategic' or 'interest-based' bargaining. Children's human rights will be used as a case example in the chapter. Section II of the chapter explores the open-textured nature of socio-economic human rights in the context of public budgeting. Section III makes a distinction between a 'strategic' and 'deliberative' approach to addressing dialogues of contestation, and examines one example of a 'strategic approach'. The focus will be on the implementation of the UK Child Poverty Act 2010. Section IV focuses on the general value of deliberation in the context of drafting 'human rights compatible public budgets', that is, budgets that adequately take into consideration the obligations set by human rights. It is argued that deliberation can have both intrinsic and instrumental value in the context of human rights budgeting. Section V considers some of the central challenges that remain for a deliberative approach to drafting human rights compatible budgets.

Jaakko Kuosmanen, *Uphill Battle* In: Human Rights and 21st Century Challenges. Edited by: Dapo Akande, Jaakko Kuosmanen, Helen McDermott, and Dominic Roser, Published by Oxford University Press 2020.
DOI: 10.1093/oso/9780198824770.003.0012

II. Budgets and Socio-Economic Human Rights: Emergence of Dialogues of Contestation

Public budgets enshrine in monetary terms particular domains of governance that are deemed by a government to be of importance. Due to resource scarcity, a public budget is always a statement on value priorities. In public budgeting, the pursuit of some ends receives more funds than the pursuit of other ends, and some ends are completely excluded from funding provisions. Human rights constitute ends that also compete for public resources. Ultimately, however, human rights should not be understood as constituting a mere 'policy option' that governments may or may not decide to keep on their strategic agenda. International human rights covenants and domestic constitutions and legislation set binding legal obligations to states that have ratified them, and these obligations also extend to budgeting.[1] Apart from setting legal procedural principles for public governance, socio-economic human rights also identify particular 'ends' or 'states of affairs' that have to be pursued through various governance measures, including budgetary measures. Put differently, bearers of socio-economic human rights have a claim that governments design and implement budgets that will contribute to the realization of certain ends in the future. These ends are linked to, among other things, health, education, housing, subsistence, work, and culture.

Consider the issue in the context of child poverty. In international human rights law, child poverty is tied centrally to two instruments, UN Convention on the Rights of the Child (CRC) and the International Covenant on Economic, Social and Cultural Rights (ICESCR). More specifically, Article 27 of CRC requires that 'States Parties recognize the right of every child to a standard of living adequate for the child's physical, mental, spiritual, moral and social development'. In turn, ICESCR enshrines the right to an adequate standard of living for everyone, including children (Article 11). The realization of Article 27 of CRC and Article 11 of ICESCR requires the design and implementation of particular policies in national contexts, which in turn require resources. The exact amount of resources that should be allocated from a particular budget to policy programmes targeting child poverty is context dependent. Article 4 of the CRC identifies a 'resource qualification', declaring that States Parties shall undertake all appropriate legislative, administrative, and other measures 'to the maximum extent of their available resources and, where needed, within the framework of international co-operation'. ICESCR obligations also include a resource qualification, requiring states to use their maximum available resources to pursue progressively (Article 2.1) the realization of the covenant rights.

[1] Some countries, such as South Africa and Colombia, have also constitutionalized socio-economic human rights, and rendered human rights obligations relating to them budgeting justiciable. See Malcolm Langford (ed), *Social Rights Jurisprudence* (CUP 2008).

At the national level, governments (here understood as consisting of the parliament and the executive) are responsible for the design and implementation of state budgets. This responsibility comes with an obligation to ensure that the process of drafting budgets and the implementation of budgets are compatible with human rights obligations. However, as human rights do not set clear quantified standards for budgeting (eg every budget, regardless of the economic climate, must allocate 2 per cent of GDP to children's healthcare), a government designing a budget needs to interpret what it means to put together a 'human rights compatible budget'. Particularly during the last two decades, plenty of invaluable work has been done by scholars, committees, and international organizations on the way socio-economic human rights will work in the context of economic and fiscal policy-making. This work effectively renders the relationship between human rights and public budgets more determinate for each particular context. The work was pioneered by International Human Rights Internship Program (IHRIP), which in 1999 released a paper titled 'A Rights-Based Approach towards Budget Analysis'. The conceptual framework for 'human rights budget work' has since been developed in various ways. Work has been done, for example, on the discharging of the various obligations enshrined in the ICESCR,[2] on the rights of women,[3] and on obligations relating to particular rights, such as the right to food.[4]

In the context of children's rights, UNICEF has produced a working paper that examines how rights have been implemented in different budgeting contexts, and what state resources should be utilized in efforts to realize rights enshrined in the CRC.[5] Further efforts to render human rights obligations more determinate in different budgeting contexts can be found in various treaty body commentaries. General Comments either focus on particular rights, on specific obligations, such as a on a minimum core or particular groups of right-bearers. The Committee on the Rights of the Child, for example, has drafted seventeen General Comments in total, focusing on, for example, general measures of implementation, the right of the child to the enjoyment of the highest attainable health, and the rights of children with disabilities. These specify, to a degree, the nature of obligations relating to children's socio-economic human rights, and therefore also provide guidance for national budgeting. The Committee also has prepared a draft General Comment

[2] See Rory O'Connell, Aoife Nolan, Colin Harvey, Mira Dutschke, and Eoin Rooney, *Applying an International Human Rights Framework to State Budget Allocations* (Routledge 2014) (hereafter, O'Connell *et al*, *Human Rights Framework*).

[3] See Diane Elson (2006) 'Budgeting for Women's Rights: Monitoring Government Budgets for Compliance with CEDAW' UNIFEM <http://www.internationalbudget.org/wp-content/uploads/Budgeting-for-Women's-Rights-Monitoring-Government-Budgets-for-Compliance-with-CEDAW.pdf> accessed 13 August 2019.

[4] FAO (2009) 'Budget Work to Advance the Right to Food: Many a Slip' <http://www.fao.org/3/a-i0717e.pdf> accessed 13 August 2019.

[5] Gore Radhika (2004) 'Influencing Budgets for Children's Rights' UNICEF Working Paper <https://www.unicef.org/policyanalysis/rights/files/Influencing_Budgets_for_Children_Rights.pdf> accessed 13 August 2019.

on public spending and the rights of the child, the aim of which is to specify in further detail what kind of guiding framework CRC sets for public budgeting in national contexts.

Although human rights are in constant state of evolution in terms of their content, ultimately this process of norm specification is yet to produce the kind of unambiguous and uncontroversial guidelines that would need to be applied in a particular budgeting context in some mechanical way. In the words of O'Connell and colleagues 'there is still some way to travel before sufficient consensus exists globally on definitional clarity'.[6] In fact, even if in the future there would be some kind of 'global consensus' on definitional clarity, this clarity may still leave space for interpretation and contestation. For the time being, at least, when interpreted in light of the law, all General Comments and supporting commentary, CRC and ICESCR do not set fully unambiguous spending requirements for child poverty-related policy programmes. Instead, they offer general guiding principles that require contextual interpretation and specification. The need for contextual interpretation provides a fertile ground for *dialogues of contestation* over the relationship between budgets and human rights. In general terms, contestation of budgetary decisions on human rights grounds may either focus on the budgeting process or on budgets. It may, for example, be questioned whether a budgeting process satisfies the human rights requirements of transparency and participation. Alternatively, it may be asked whether a budget adequately takes into account the substantive obligations that socio-economic human rights set (eg minimum core, progressive realization, non-discrimination).

In practice, dialogues of contestation occur in several different forums. Courts, for example, constitute one forum for dialogues of contestation. In many countries, such as Brazil,[7] South Africa,[8] and Colombia,[9] courts have been requested to consider whether a government has further resources available for the implementation of particular socio-economic rights.[10] Outside court rooms, dialogues of contestation occur, for example, in the context of the UN treaty framework. Country

[6] O'Connell *et al*, *Human Rights Framework* (n 2) 198.

[7] To date, the right to health in Brazil has garnered much attention and focus. See Octavio Luiz Motta Ferraz (2011) 'Harming the Poor Through Social Rights Litigation' 89 South Texas Law Review 1643, 1656–58.

[8] For further discussion of the South African context, see Nick Ferreira (2012) 'Feasibility Constraints and the South African Bill of Rights: Fulfilling the Constitution's Promise in Conditions of Scarce Resources' 129 South Africa Law Journal 274; See generally, Sandra Liebenberg, 'Adjudicating Social Rights Under a Transformative Constitution' in Malcolm Langford (ed), *Social Rights Jurisprudence* (CUP 2008).

[9] See Magdalena Sepúlveda, 'The Constitutional Court's Role in Addressing Social Injustice' in Malcolm Langford (ed), *Social Rights Jurisprudence* (CUP 2008) 144–62.

[10] For analysis on resource related human rights adjudication in the UK context, see eg Jeff King (2007) 'The Justiciability of Resource Allocation' 70 Modern Law Review 197. More generally on the link between rights and resources, see Stephen Holmen and Cass Sunstein, *The Cost of Rights—Why Liberty Depends on Taxes* (Norton 1999).

reviews by the Committee on the Rights of the Child serve as an example.[11] State parties to the CRC are required in accordance with Article 44 to submit an initial report on measures adopted which give effect to the enshrined rights, and then report on the progress every five years. Once a report has been received, the Committee identifies a list of issues/questions that forms the basis of dialogical review of state compliance. This list is developed on the basis of documents submitted by the government and information made available by other sources, eg other UN bodies and mechanisms, non-governmental organizations (NGOs), and national human rights institutions. On the basis of an interactive dialogue with State Party representatives, the Committee drafts and adopts recommendations in the form of Concluding Observations. Then the process moves to a follow-up procedure in which the implementation of the Committee's recommendations is monitored through reporting. Dialogues of contestation also take place in various public forums outside the UN Committees, including parliamentary assemblies, committees, specifically designed workshops, media outlets, and online. For example, the UN Special Rapporteur on Child Protection publishes reports for public discussion on various themes relating to children's human rights, including forced marriages, trafficking, and Internet safety. UN Special Rapporteurs also report on child protection developments in particular states, give policy recommendations, and invite public responses from the government.[12] Also, charities[13] and Ombudspersons/commissioners[14] publish reports and commentaries that contest governments' views on the compatibility between public budgets and rights enshrined in the international human rights covenants.

III. Addressing Dialogues of Contestation with a 'Strategic' Approach

So far it has been suggested that indeterminacy of socio-economic human rights provides a foundation for the emergence of dialogues of contestation in the context of drafting human rights compatible public budgets. Socio-economic human rights do not set unambiguous quantified standards for public budgeting. Instead,

[11] On the reporting process, see also UNICEF, 'Fact Sheet: The Committee on the Rights of the Child' <http://www.unicef.org/crc/files/Committee_fact_sheet.pdf> accessed 13 August 2019.

[12] For country reporting in the context of the United Kingdom, see Geoffrey Shannon (2011) 'Fifth Report of the Special Rapporteur on Child Protection: A Report Submitted to the Oireachtas' 104 <http://www.dcya.gov.ie/documents/publications/5RapporteurRepChildProtection.pdf> accessed 13 August 2019.

[13] See eg Child Poverty Action Group, 'Budget 2014: Child Poverty Action Group on the Impact on Families' (19 March 2014) <http://www.cpag.org.uk/content/budget-2014-child-poverty-action-group-impact-families> accessed 13 August 2019.

[14] See eg Office of the Children's Commissioner (2014) 'Child Right Impact Assessment of the 2013 Autumn Statement and 2014 Budget' <https://www.childrenscommissioner.gov.uk/publication/child-rights-impact-assessment/> 26 November 2019.

they operate as general guiding principles that need to be interpreted in substantive terms. In practice, dialogues of contestation can be addressed in various ways. To use Habermasian terminology, in a dialogue of contestation, the parties may be engaging in deliberative 'communicative action' the aim of which is to pursue mutual understanding between the parties through reasoned argumentation. Alternatively, dialogues of contestation may be addressed with interest-based 'strategic action'. Instead of a common understanding, the primary aim in these dialogues is the realization of each party's own goals. [15] The case of the UK Child Poverty Act 2010 provides an example of the latter.

The Child Poverty Act, which was adopted in 2010 as one of the outgoing Labour government's last statutes, set binding targets for future governments in relation to child poverty. A Bill was first introduced by the Labour government in 2008, and it arose from Prime Minister Tony Blair's 1999 commitment to end child poverty by 2020.[16] The Act's declared purpose was to 'define success in eradicating child poverty and create a framework to monitor progress at a national and local level'.[17] It placed a duty on the Secretary of the State to meet four specified child poverty targets by 2020: 'relative poverty',[18] 'combined low income and material deprivation',[19] 'absolute poverty',[20] and 'persistent poverty'.[21]

Scrutinizing the Bill in 2009, the Joint Committee on Human Rights emphasized that 'the statutory duty to meet these targets is absolute: it is not qualified by any reference to affordability or available resources. Nor is there any power to amend the targets.' In other words, the Act set the future governments an obligation to reach the enshrined targets by 2020, and there is no justification for diverting from the targets due to resource scarcity. The Act does not, however, set specific spending requirements for governments. In other words, the governments pursuing the realization of the targets enshrined in the Act may draft their budgets as they wish, as long as the targets are met by 2020. The Act, at its inception, was commendable from a human rights perspective, and it can effectively be understood as an attempt to render children's human rights more determinate through national legislative

[15] See Jürgen Habermas, *Toward a Rational Society* (Beacon 1970).

[16] Steven Kennedy, 'Child Poverty Act 2010: A Short Guide' (House of Commons Library, 4 July 2014) 3 <http://researchbriefings.parliament.uk/ResearchBriefing/Summary/SN05585#fullreport> accessed 13 August 2019.

[17] Explanatory Notes to the Child Poverty Act 2010, para 6 <http://www.legislation.gov.uk/ukpga/2010/9/notes/division/3> accessed 13 August 2019.

[18] Reduce the proportion of children who live in relative low-income families—that is, in families below 60 per cent of the median, before housing costs—to less than 10 per cent. Child Poverty Act 2010 s 1(3) paras 1–2 (hereafter CPA 2010).

[19] Reduce the proportion of children who live in material deprivation and have a low income—below 70 per cent of the median, before housing costs—to less than 5 per cent. CPA 2010 (n 18) s 1(4) paras 1–3.

[20] Reduce the proportion of children who live below an income threshold fixed in real terms to less than 5 per cent. CPA 2010 (n 18) s 1(5) paras 1–4.

[21] Reduce the proportion of children that experience long periods (at least three years) of relative poverty. CPA 2010 (n 18) s 1(6) paras 1–6.

measures. Although it doesn't set annual spending requirements, it enshrined binding human rights-based targets in national legislation, and provided a mechanism for the progressive realization of a child's right to an adequate standard of living in Article 27 CRC and Article 11 ICESCR.

The Act also set institutional mechanisms supporting the pursuit of the enshrined targets. It required the government to publish *ex ante* strategy on how the enshrined targets are to be met. The first child poverty strategy was published by the Coalition government in 2011[22] and a follow-up strategy was published in 2014.[23] In addition to obligations to draft plans of action, under the Act the government has an obligation to report *ex post* on the measures taken, and to 'describe the effect of all those measures on progress towards the targets'. The Act also set a requirement to establish the Social Mobility and Child Poverty Commission, which is an advisory non-departmental public body made up of ten commissioners and supported by a small secretariat. Furthermore, the Act established an obligation for the government to consult the Commission in order to ensure that the set strategy is an effective and credible plan for tackling child poverty. In turn, the Commission was mandated to publish an annual report setting out independent views on progress made in meeting the targets set in the Act.

As the UK government moved to implement the Act, it started to become increasingly clear that the set targets will not be met as envisioned in 2020. After the coalition government produced a draft version of its new Child Poverty Strategy 2014–2017, the Social Mobility and Child Poverty Commission was asked—in accordance with its statutory duty—to provide advice on the draft. In its response to the government, the Commission was critical. In other words, the Commission initiated a dialogue of contestation with the government. It criticized the government for a failure to draft a meaningful strategy of clear measures against which the government would consider it could be held to account during the implementation process by the Commission. The Commission stated that there was a 'credibility gap' at the heart of the government strategy, as it lacked a step-by-step plan to meet the set targets in 2020.[24] The Commission supported its argument with commissioned research. The research explored whether changes in parental employment

[22] HM Government, 'A New Approach to Child Poverty: Tackling the Causes of Disadvantage and Transforming Families' Lives' (Department for Work and Pensions, Department for Education, April 2011) <https://www.gov.uk/government/uploads/system/uploads/attachment_data/file/177031/CM-8061.pdf> accessed 13 August 2019.

[23] HM Government, 'Child Poverty Strategy 2014–2017' (Secretary of State for Work and Pensions, June 2014) <https://www.gov.uk/government/uploads/system/uploads/attachment_data/file/324103/Child_poverty_strategy.pdf> accessed 13 August 2019 (hereafter HM Government, 'Child Poverty Strategy').

[24] Social Mobility and Child Poverty Commission, 'Response to the Consultation on the Child Poverty Strategy 2014 to 2017' (Social Mobility and Child Poverty Commission, May 2014) para 54 <https://www.gov.uk/government/uploads/system/uploads/attachment_data/file/318062/2b_Poverty_Response_-_Final.pdf> accessed 13 August 2019 (hereafter Social Mobility and Child Poverty Commission, 'Response').

outcomes as planned by the government could enable the government to achieve the absolute and relative income targets set out in the Child Poverty Act 2010. The main finding of the research was that even with very optimistic assumptions (including no further welfare cuts in the next parliament), meeting the targets would require parental employment rates close to 100 per cent.[25] The Commission concluded that its research suggests that the targets will not be met unless the economy and labour market performs far better than the Office of Budget Responsibility anticipates over the next few years.[26]

The government responded to the initiated dialogue by publishing a consultation paper on the topic, declaring that 'there is a need for a revised set of child poverty measures which underlines its commitment to reducing child poverty but better reflects the evidence about its underlying causes and where action most needs to be targeted'.[27] The government then moved to propose a comprehensive reform of the targets, including abolishment of all income-related targets. In 2015 the government introduced a plan to adopt new targets focusing on 'the proportion of children living in workless household as well as long-term workless households', and on 'the educational attainment of all pupils and the most disadvantaged pupils at age 16'.[28] In January 2016 the House of Lords voted against the government's planned amendments to the Child Poverty Act, and in favour of an amendment that requires the government to publish annual figures on income-related child poverty.

Why is the approach adopted by the UK government an example of a strategic instead of a deliberative approach? The Commission initiated a dialogue of contestation over the budgetary measures needed to achieve the targets by 2020. It argued that the government had not made feasible budgetary plans to meet the targets. The government responded to the consultation not by redesigning its plan of action or by producing its own research with the aim of contesting the Commission's evidence but rather by strategically shifting the dialogue elsewhere. In other words, instead of engaging in a constructive dialogue with the Commission over the means of realizing the set targets, it strategically moved the discussion towards the nature of the ends. The government suggested that the enshrined targets are in fact problematic and proposed that these should be revised.[29] Admittedly,

[25] Ibid, para 56.

[26] Ibid, para 132.

[27] HM Government, 'Consultation on Setting the 2020 Persistent Child Poverty Target' (Secretary of State for Work and Pensions, June 2014) 5 <https://www.gov.uk/government/uploads/system/uploads/attachment_data/file/323974/Persistent_child_poverty_consultation_-_web_friendly_version.pdf> accessed 13 August 2019.

[28] HM Government, 'Government to Strengthen Child Poverty Measure' (Department for Work and Pensions, 1 July 2015) <https://www.gov.uk/government/news/government-to-strengthen-child-poverty-measure> accessed 12 August 2019.

[29] HM Government, 'Measuring Child Poverty: A Consultation on Better Measurements on Child Poverty' (Secretary of State for Work and Pensions, November 2012) <https://blogs.lse.ac.uk/politicsandpolicy/child-poverty-measures-why-academics-and-the-house-of-lords-challenge-the-government-proposals/> 26 November 2019 (hereafter HM Government, 'Measuring Child Poverty').

the government's argument that the targets enshrined in the Act should be subjected to revision is not fully without merits. It has been pointed out that legitimate questions can be asked about the design of some of the targets. Particularly the targets on relative poverty can be misleading in certain circumstances. In a recession, when average income falls poverty can also appear to be falling even if living standards have not improved for those at the bottom. Yet, although there would have been a case for a deliberative dialogue over the nature of the set targets, the government's approach was still essentially a strategic one. The government's proposal for new targets ignored expert advice in the process, which was almost unanimously against the move. During its consultation on child poverty measures the government received 257 responses. Of the 251 responses that could be accessed through a freedom of information request, only two recommended abandoning income-based measures.[30]

From a human rights perspective, there has also been a more fundamental failure in the dialogues of contestation in the implementation of the Child Poverty Act. The dialogues have essentially focused on budgetary measures sufficient and insufficient for realizing the set targets, and the nature of the targets. Yet, after the legislative scrutiny of the Joint Committee on Human Rights in 2009, the process of implementation has effectively been detached from *human rights*. For example, the government's consultation paper on redesigning the poverty targets does not discuss the proposal's compatibility with international human rights obligations at all.[31] The same applies to the government's Child Poverty Strategy 2014–2017.[32] It is important to note, however, that it is not only the government that has steered away from reflective consideration in relation to international human rights obligations. The Child Poverty Commission's consultation papers, in which the government's strategy for reaching the targets was considered, have also failed to offer an evaluation attentive to international human rights standards.[33]

IV. The Value of Deliberating Towards Human Rights Compatible Public Budgets

Ideally, dialogues of contestation about the relationship between human rights and public budgets would be addressed in a 'deliberative' instead of a 'strategic' manner, and this process reflect the content of general guiding principles in international

30 Kitty Stewart, 'Child Poverty Measures: Why Academics and the House of Lords have Challenged the Government Proposals' (London School of Economics and Political Science, 22 February 2016) <http://blogs.lse.ac.uk/politicsandpolicy/child-poverty-measures-why-academics-and-the-house-of-lords-challenge-the-government-proposals/>.

31 HM Government, 'Measuring Child Poverty' (n 29).

32 HM Government, 'Child Poverty Strategy' (n 23).

33 Social Mobility and Child Poverty Commission, 'Response' (n 24).

human rights law. But, in more general terms, what exactly is the value of a deliberative approach to the drafting of human rights-compatible public budgets? Deliberation is often suggested to have 'intrinsic' and 'instrumental' value. The same applies in the present context. The very act of deliberation—depending on how it is executed—is of importance from the perspective of the right-bearers. It can be understood to have a legitimizing function. Theorists defending the intrinsic value of deliberation often invoke 'publicity', 'mutual respect', 'right to participate', and a dialogue among 'free' and 'equal' citizens. In fact, according to some philosophers, justification constitutes the very heart of human rights. Rainer Forst, for example, argues that 'whenever human beings act, they are obliged to recognize every morally affected person as someone to whom they owe reasons justifying their actions'.[34] He also claims that a 'right to justification' forms the justificatory foundation for other human rights. In other words, on this philosophical approach the various more specific human rights can be normatively derived from the idea of a right to justification.[35] In sum, on the intrinsic approach, deliberation is not valuable only to the extent that it produces certain outcomes. Instead, it also has important value as process.

Apart from having a legitimizing function, there are various instrumental functions deliberation can potentially have. First, deliberation can potentially serve an important function in the promotion of public accountability.[36] In a non-ideal world, full compliance of duty-bearers cannot be accepted at face value. The requirement of a duty-bearer to demonstrate in a deliberative forum that human rights obligations have been discharged satisfactorily can simultaneously establish a mechanism for the scrutiny of compliance. For example, a requirement to produce plans of actions and *ex ante* assessments of the human rights compatibility of budgets and a requirement to have a deliberative public dialogue about their merits can remove a convenient excuse from a government antagonistic to human rights: 'we did not know that this would not be compatible with human rights obligations'. Second, deliberation can potentially serve a meaningful 'epistemic function' in efforts to render the relationship between human rights and public budgets more determinate in a particular context.[37] Deliberation can, for

[34] Rainer Forst, 'The Justification of Human Rights and the Basic Right to Justification' in Claudio Corradetti (ed), *Philosophical Dimensions of Human Rights* (Springer 2012) 81–106, 213.

[35] Ibid, 210.

[36] The idea of accountability denotes a relational term that involves at least two parties. In a relationship of accountability, one party is accountable to another party or parties. There are, of course, various different conceptions of the concept of accountability, including stronger and weaker. The various conceptions may be argued to include at least two invariable components: information and sanctions. In a relationship of accountability one party may under certain circumstances impose justifiable sanctions to the accountability holder. The form of sanctions can vary from public condemnation to coercive measures. See also Robert O' Keohane (2003) 'The Concept of Accountability in World Politics and the Use of Force' 24(4) Michigan Journal of International Law 1121.

[37] In the words of Amy Gutmann, 'to presume that we know what the right resolution is before we hear from others who will also be affected by our decisions is not only arrogant, but also unjustified in light of the complexity of the issues and interests' at stake. A refusal to subject priorities to deliberation

example, clarify the nature of rights and their correlative obligations in a particular context. As O'Connell and colleagues point out, much commentary 'in the public sphere continues to function with a degraded and impoverished version of human rights. There remains much basic misunderstanding of what the standards are. The result is that due regard is not paid to the nuanced nature of international human rights law.'[38] Misunderstandings of the content of rights can give rise to 'pseudo-conflicts', that is, clashes that turn out to be misconstrued for one reason or another.[39] Deliberation, which requires reasoned argumentation, can serve an instrumental function in identifying these conflicts. Deliberation can also clarify the actual circumstances of the right-bearers, their needs, and the more general policy environment for which public budgets are drafted. In light of new facts relating to a specific target or to the circumstances of implementation, particular policy measures deemed necessary by a government may turn out to be only one option among many. They may also turn out to be inappropriate, as the relationship between the means and ends may turn out to have been misconstrued.

V. From an Ideal Towards Reality: Four Challenges

It is important to emphasize that deliberation is not a magic wand that necessarily solves all contestation relating to human rights and budgets. Reasonable disagreement may be the final outcome of even a well-executed deliberative process. Therefore, at best, deliberation may provide an incomplete solution to the drafting of human rights-compatible public budgets. In addition, in practice the quality of deliberation can vary. In other words, it should not be understood as an 'either/or' issue.[40] Once we move away from ideal circumstances towards reality we can observe various challenges in the adoption of a deliberative approach to drafting human rights-compatible public budgets. In this final section, I will focus on four important challenges that can have a negative impact on the quality of dialogues of contestation. Even though the impact of these challenges varies from one policy context to another, in general terms each of these can be considered as an important twenty-first-century challenge that hinders the deliberative design of human rights compatible public budgets.

among those who are impacted effectively entails giving up 'the most defensible ground we could have for maintaining an uncompromising position: that we have fairly tested our views against those of others'. Amy Gutmann, *Why Deliberative Democracy?* (Princeton University Press 2004) 12.

---

[38] See O'Connell *et al*, *Human Rights Framework* (n 2) 198.

[39] See James Griffin, *On Human Rights* (OUP 2008) 58.

[40] Steenbergen *et al*, for example, have been developing a 'discourse quality index' for a quantitative measure of discourse in deliberation. See Marco Steenbergen, André Bächtiger, Markus Spörndli, and Jürg Steiner (2003) 'Measuring Political Deliberation: A Discourse Quality Index' 1 Comparative European Politics 21.

A. Transparency

Meaningful deliberation about human rights-compatible public budgets requires various different forms of transparency. One of the most important challenges that remain for human rights budget work is access to budget data. Those participating in a dialogue of contestation can have more as well as less relevant information available to them. This can have a qualitative impact on the nature of the dialogue. To put this in crude terms: 'how can you engage in meaningful deliberation if you don't know what you are talking about'? A government can, for example, be actively preventing the disclosure of data relevant to dialogues of contestation. A government can also fail (eg due to incompetence) to produce particular data in the first place, or the data can lack transparency because they are published in an aggregated form (eg there may be a failure to disaggregate the data at sub-sector level). In addition, there may be a failure to provide information on spending in relation to specific demographic groups. Fiscal data can also be produced methodologically in a way that lacks transparency, which in turn can complicate deliberation. A government may, for example, offer macroeconomic forecasts that it grounds in a specific forecasting methodology, but it can still fail to disclose this methodology and subject it to an independent public scrutiny.

Human rights set a normative foundation for transparency in policy-making, including public budgeting. The 'right to information', which sets general demands for *public* policy-making, appears in various places. During its first regular session in 1946 the UN General Assembly adopted Resolution 59(I), which states that '[f]reedom of information is a fundamental human right'. The right to information has thereafter been enshrined in various international and regional human rights covenants. The International Covenant on Civil and Political Rights (ICCPR) Article 19 recognizes the 'freedom to seek, receive, and impart information and ideas of all kinds'. A majority of the world's countries (168) have voluntarily ratified the ICCPR, and therefore are committed to the realization of the right to information. The European Covenant on Human Rights (ECHR) Article 10 states that everyone has the right 'to receive and impart information and ideas without interference by public authority and regardless of frontiers'. Article 13 of the American Convention on Human Rights (ACHR) enshrines the 'freedom to seek, receive, and impart information and ideas of all kinds' and Article 11 of the Charter of Fundamental Rights of the European Union (CFREU) recognizes the freedom 'to receive and impart information and ideas without interference by public authority and regardless of frontiers'. The Council of Europe (CoE) Convention on Access to Official Documents (CETS) No 205, which currently has fourteen signatories, recognizes in Article 2 that 'each Party shall guarantee the right of everyone, without discrimination on any ground, to have access, on request, to official documents held by public authorities'.

In the UN framework there have been some attempts to identify the kind of data that would be relevant for deliberation about budgets and human rights. The various treaty bodies have set their own guidelines for reporting, in addition to which the UN framework has Harmonized Reporting Guidelines for states.[41] In the context of children's human rights, the CRC identifies a general obligation to produce a review (Articles 44 and 45). The reporting guidelines by the Committee on the Rights of the Child give further specification on relevant budgetary information. According to the guidelines, 'States parties shall provide information on the amount and percentage of the national budget (at central and local levels) devoted annually to children, including, where appropriate, the percentage of external financing (through donors, international financial institutions and private banking) of the national budget, with respect to relevant programmes under each cluster'.[42] The guidelines also emphasize that 'where appropriate, States parties should provide information on poverty reduction strategies and programmes and other factors which impact or may impact the implementation of the Convention'. In addition to treaty specific guidelines, the Office of the High Commissioner for Human Rights has released a report on indicators, which provides guidance on the kind of budgetary data that are relevant from a human rights perspective.[43]

In practice, however, limitations in accessing data remain among the most important challenges for human rights budget work.[44] During the past two decades we have witnessed important developments in transparency relevant to human rights budget work, however much more work remains to be done. The disconnect between human rights and the work done on fiscal transparency by international organizations such as the International Monetary Fund (IMF) and the Organisation for Economic Co-operation and Development (OECD) provides a clear example of this. Even though these organizations have been systematically developing best practices guidelines for fiscal transparency for decades, this development work has been insulated from human rights work. The central fiscal transparency guidelines by IMF and OECD do not mention the phrase 'human rights'

[41] The general guidelines are somewhat vague and they do not set strong requirements for states to ensure that human rights related budgeting data will be publicly available. The guidelines for the 'Common Core Document' declare that states should report, '*where available*, budget allocations and budgetary trends, as percentages of national or regional budgets and gross domestic product (GDP) and disaggregated by sex and age for the implementation of the State's human rights obligations and the results of any relevant budget impact assessments' (emphasis added). UNHRI 'Compilation of Guidelines on the Form and Content of Reports to be Submitted by States Parties to the International Human Rights Treaties, Report of the Secretary General' HRI/GEN/2/Rev.6 (2009) 9.

[42] Ibid, 88.

[43] UNHRI 'Report on Indicators for Promoting and Monitoring the Implementation of Human Rights' HRI/MC/2008/3* (2008).

[44] As Ann Blyberg points out, 'in many countries researchers and communities face substantial difficulties in securing even basic budget information, and in most countries they can acquire only incomplete data'. Ann Blyberg, 'Government Budgets and Rights Implementation' in Jody Heymann and Adele Cassola (eds), *Making Equal Rights Real—Taking Effective Action to Overcome Global Challenges* (CUP 2012) Chapter 6, 209.

even once.[45] More methodical and cooperative development of guidelines for fiscal transparency on the basis of the content of various rights could potentially facilitate deliberative dialogues of contestation in national budgeting contexts. So far, however, this has been a missed opportunity from the perspective of human rights budget work.

B. Compliance

Deliberative forums can be designed in such ways that governments can shift from a deliberative approach to a strategic approach without meaningful sanction. For example, the UN human rights system lacks strong enforcement mechanisms, and states' compliance in review processes, which constitute forums for dialogues of contestation, varies. Currently, for example, only 16 per cent of States Parties submit their country report in the UN reporting framework on time. In fact, under the ICESCR, the ICCPR, and the Convention Against Torture, around 20 per cent of States Parties have never submitted an initial report.[46] Also, when reports are submitted their quality can vary. In the United Kingdom, for example, the Joint Committee on Human Rights has been critical of the reports the government has submitted to the UN Committee on the Rights of the Child. In its evaluative report, the Joint Committee has argued that the 2014 report submitted by the UK government 'is too abstract, its analysis too patchy, and there are some significant omissions from its content'.[47] The Joint Committee has also criticized the earlier consultation processes with non-governmental actors. It noted that the report 'fails to recognize those areas where there is still considerable disagreement outside government about whether its policy has indeed been compatible with the Convention, presenting a somewhat optimistic picture in places'.[48] Furthermore, the report does not 'represent the practical reality for many children, particularly the disadvantaged, in areas where policy may have been misjudged or good policies perhaps not properly implemented'.[49]

One possible avenue for further enquiries relating to compliance in deliberation is the scrutiny of judicial review as a deliberative process. The institutional set-up

[45] For more in-depth analysis on the issue, see Jaakko Kuosmanen (2016) 'Worlds Apart: Bridging the Gap Between Human Rights and Fiscal Transparency' 34 (1) Nordic Journal of Human Rights (2016).

[46] OHCHR Strengthening the United Nations Human Rights Treaty Body System, A Report by the UN High Commissioner for Human Rights (June 2012) 20–23 <http://www2.ohchr.org/english/bodies/HRTD/docs/HCReportTBStrengthening.pdf> accessed 13 August 2019.

[47] Joint Committee on Human Rights, 'The UK's Compliance with the UN Convention on the Rights of the Child' (Eighth Report of Session 2014–15, 18 March 2015) 53 <http://www.publications.parliament.uk/pa/jt201415/jtselect/jtrights/144/144.pdf> accessed 13 August 2019 (hereafter Joint Committee, 'UK's Compliance').

[48] Ibid.

[49] Ibid, 22.

for implementation in the context of the Child Poverty Act was essentially political, and there is no practical possibility for judicial review during the implementation process. In its review of the Bill, the Joint Committee on Human Rights suggested that the Act is effectively non-justiciable. It pointed out that a 'claimant would need to produce clear evidence that the targets will not be met by 2020, and this will be difficult to prove until quite close to 2020. The evidence capable of supporting such a claim is not likely to exist until the years immediately preceding 2020.'[50] Finally, it noted that in the United Kingdom, 'courts do not tend to interfere in matters of public spending when the Secretary of State has discretion as to how to allocate resources'.[51]

It can be asked whether the genuine possibility of judicial review could possibly have enhanced the dialogues of contestation relating to the Child Poverty Act. Some legal scholars see judicial scrutiny of human rights as potentially deliberative and democracy-enhancing. Sandra Fredman, for example, introduces a 'deliberative model' of decision-making for human rights, which comprises collaborative process involving the government and judiciary. She emphasizes that 'human rights should not be addressed on the basis of interest bargaining. If they were, those with superior numerical, political or financial power might always trump the rights of those without power.'[52] According to Fredman's deliberative model, 'when human rights are at issue, courts should augment democratic participation by steering decision-making away from interest bargaining towards value-oriented deliberation or indeed, by functioning as a forum for deliberation'.[53] According to this approach, courts can be understood as forums of public justification the aim of which is enhance the quality of dialogues between contesting parties. In practice, the quality of dialogues in judicial review of human rights has varied, and they effectively set along the lines of a continuum between 'strategic action and 'communicative action'.[54] Therefore, access to judicial review does not by itself guarantee that the dialogues of contestation relating to human rights and budgets are *in fact* done in a deliberative manner. Yet, at the very least it can be argued that judicial review holds the *potential* of improving the quality of the dialogues between a government and parties contesting budgetary decisions on human rights grounds. Courts can require decision-makers to lay out and substantiate their reasons for particular decisions and to produce evidence in support of their claims. This requirement can

[50] Joint Committee on Human Rights, 'Legislative Scrutiny: Child Poverty Bill' (HC Bill 155, 11 June 2009) 43 <http://www.publications.parliament.uk/pa/jt200809/jtselect/jtrights/183/18305.htm> accessed 13 August 2019.

[51] Ibid, 44.

[52] Sandra Fredman (2013) 'From Dialogue to Deliberation: Human Rights Adjudication and Prisoners' Rights to Vote' 2 Public Law 295 (hereafter Fredman, 'From Dialogue to Deliberation').

[53] Ibid, 295.

[54] In her inquiry on courts and deliberation, Fredman considers cases in South Africa, United Kingdom, and European Court of Human Rights, and discusses in detail successes and disappointments. See Fredman, 'From Dialogue to Deliberation' (n 51).

also potentially provide an institutionalized incentive for a government to conduct decision-making outside the courtroom in a (more) deliberative manner.[55]

C. Siloed Governance

The institutional set-up in which a government operates can be more or less conducive to a deliberative approach to drafting human rights compatible budgets. The design of plans of action—which constitute an important step in the drafting of human rights compatible budgets—serves as an example.[56] Plans of action concerning children's human rights are discussed in the 1993 Vienna Declaration and Programme of Action, adopted by the World Conference on Human Rights, which calls on states to integrate the Convention on the Rights of the Child into their national human rights action plans.[57] In addition, the outcome document of the UN General Assembly special session on children in 2002 commits states 'to develop or strengthen as a matter of urgency if possible by the end of 2003 national and, where appropriate, regional action plans with a set of specific time-bound and measurable goals and targets based on this plan of action'.[58] As well, the Committee on the Rights of the Child points out in General Comment No 5 that 'if Government as a whole and at all levels is to promote and respect the rights of the child, it needs to work on the basis of a unifying, comprehensive and rights-based national strategy, rooted in the Convention'.[59] Also, the Committee on Economic, Social and Cultural Rights discusses plans of action focusing on children's human rights in General Comment No 11 on Plans of Action for Primary Education (Article 14 of the Covenant).

Overall, however, the drafting of effective plans of action is not an uncomplicated process. The policy environment within which the drafting of plans of action takes place can be characterized with the concept of 'polycentricity'.[60] A non-polycentric issue may be characterized as an issue in which the link between a mean

[55] Ibid, 296.

[56] As well, review processes can serve an important deliberative function for plans of action. They not only provide information on progress, they also provide the governments an opportunity to reflect on the initial planning process, and to consider potential ways to enhance the subsequent processes for drafting plans of action. The Committee on the Rights of the Child has noted the complementary nature of plans of action and review. In General Comment No 5 the Committee states that it 'expects States parties to take account of the recommendations in its concluding observations on their periodic reports when developing and/or reviewing their national strategies'. UNCRC 'General Comment No 5 2003, General Measures of Implementation of the Convention on the Rights of the Child (arts 4, 42 and 44, para 6)' (27 November 2003) CRC/GC/2003/5, para 2.

[57] UNGA Vienna Declaration and Programme of Action (12 July 1993) A/CONF.157/23, para 47.

[58] UNGA A/RES/S-27/2, para 59.

[59] CRC/GC/2003/5, para 28.

[60] In the field of law, debates on polycentricity have been inspired by philosopher Michael Polanyi's work. See Michael Polanyi, *The Logic of Liberty: Reflections and Rejoinders* (Routledge and Kegan Paul 1951).

and an end is self-evident and the impact of the mean is limited only to the end. In turn, at least two components are among the broader set of necessary conditions for the occurrence of a polycentric issue or problem: *network* and *complexity*.[61] Consultation processes aiming towards plans of action can involve deliberation among various ministries, public officials, experts, and interest groups. If executed well, these processes can challenge the government to reflect on its capacities, the existing state of affairs, and the obstacles and opportunities in achieving set targets. Furthermore, they can feed into further deliberation about the design of budgets. The instrumental value of plans of action is emphasized by the UN Office of the High Commissioner for Human Rights, which notes that drafting them can contribute to 'better awareness and implementation of economic, social and cultural rights, leading to an improved quality of life, particularly for vulnerable groups'.[62]

Traditionally, however, governments have been structured in a way that department or ministries constitute 'silos' primarily responsible for certain policy areas. Furthermore, in practice, departments generally compete between each other of resources allocated by the Treasury. This can constitute a challenge not only for the delivery of policies aiming to address certain cross-cutting challenges but also an obstacle for deliberation. The UK's Public Administration Select Committee, for example, notes that one of the shortcomings in the drafting of governmental strategies has been the lack of integration. Drafting has been done department by department, and opportunities in linking strategies have been missed.[63] The same challenge has been recognized in the context of children's human rights. The Joint Committee on Human Rights has pointed out that 'some departments seem to believe that children's rights are only a matter for the Department for Education. More needs to be done across Government to spread knowledge and expertise and—more importantly—to impress upon ministers outside the Department for Education the central importance of children's rights for a just and healthy society'.[64] To sum up, deliberation towards human rights-compatible budgets requires cross-governmental effective communication and strategic planning. Furthermore, it requires the integration of human rights expertise in the deliberative processes. Within governments, human rights assessment of policies, including the drafting of budgets, can be sidelined to human rights committees that have a limited access to the budgeting process. This can constitute a substantial challenge to a deliberative approach.

[61] See also, Jaakko Kuosmanen (2016) 'Human Rights, Public Budgets, and Epistemic Challenges' 17(2) Human Rights Review 252.

[62] OHCHR 'Handbook on National Human Rights Plans of Action, (2002) Professional Training Series No. 10' (United Nations 29 August 2002) <http://www.ohchr.org/Documents/Publications/training10en.pdf> accessed 13 August 2019.

[63] House of Commons Public Administration Select Committee, Government Response to the Public Administration Select Committee's Second Report of Session 2006–2007 'Governing the Future' (Minister for the Cabinet Office and Social Exclusion, June 2007) 16.

[64] Joint Committee, 'UK's Compliance' (n 46) 47.

D. Participation

In addition to challenges relating to the institutional set-up of a government, there are also challenges relating to participation of those outside the government. Insulating deliberation within a government can lead to misinformed judgments about budgetary measures appropriate for pursuing a particular human rights end. Conversely, deliberative participation of right-bearers and/or their representatives can reduce epistemic uncertainties relating to the design of human rights-compatible budgets. Engagement with stakeholders can improve an understanding of the exact needs of the right-bearer and therefore provide crucial information for those preparing budgets. Participatory budgeting initiatives can be understood as attempts to promote a deliberative approach to budgeting. In principled terms, these initiatives have a supportive foundation in human rights. For example, the Committee on Economic, Social and Cultural Rights has emphasized that mechanisms of accountability should be 'accessible, transparent and effective', and that 'the international human rights normative framework includes the right of those affected by key decisions to participate in the relevant decision-making processes'.[65] In turn, the UN Human Rights Committee General Comment No 25 (on ICCPR Article 25, Participation in Public Affairs and the Right to Vote) emphasizes a state's obligation to allow citizens to 'take part in the conduct of public affairs by exerting influence through public debate and dialogue with their representatives or through their capacity to organize themselves'.[66]

Participatory budgeting initiatives have been adopted at the municipality level in various countries around the world to promote stakeholder participation, and they have been linked, among other things, to increased investments to sanitation, health services, and reduction in infant mortality.[67] However, participatory budgeting has not received unequivocal appraisal. In some contexts, there have been challenges in the promotion of participation, and in implementing the participatory processes in a cost-effective manner.[68] As well, although the number of participatory budgeting initiatives has been increasing—there are now between 1,500 and 2,500[69] cities and institutions implementing them in one form or another—it is still a fairly limited practice. In 2009 in most European countries, for

[65] UNCESCR 'Substantive Issues Arising in the Implementation of the International Covenant on Economic, Social and Cultural Rights: Poverty and the International Covenant on Economic, Social and Cultural Rights', Statement Adopted by the Committee on Economic Social and Cultural Rights (4 May 2001) E/C 12/2001/10, para 12.

[66] UNHRC 'General Comment No 25' (27 August 1996) CCPR/C/21/Rev.1/Add.7, para 8.

[67] Sónia Goncalves (2009) 'Power to the People: The Effects of Participatory Budgeting on Municipal Expenditures and Infant Mortality in Brazil' LSE Working Papers.

[68] Kai Masser, 'Participatory Budgeting as its Critics see it' (Buergerhaushalt, 30 April 2013) <http://www.buergerhaushalt.org/en/article/participatory-budgeting-its-critics-see-it> accessed 13 August 2019.

[69] Participatory Budgeting Project, 'PB Map and Process List' (2017) <https://www.participatorybudgeting.org/pb-map/> 26 November 2019.

example, only 1 to 2 per cent of the population lived in cities that used participatory budgeting.[70] This is a notable difference to Brazil, where it has been estimated that the same figure already in 2001–04 was around 22 per cent.[71]

An additional challenge that remains is the bridging of the gap between 'consultations' (in which opinions are merely heard) and between 'deliberation' (in which there is a genuine possibility of influencing government policies). Governments can organize formal consultative processes that effectively pay 'lip service' to deliberative processes, and following the consultations they can move towards policy design and implementation strictly on the basis of a pre-set agenda. For example, the consultations during the drafting of the UK government's report to the Committee on the Rights of the Child were criticized by the Joint Committee for lack of genuine engagement. In its evaluation of the reporting process the Joint Committee notes that the report produced by the UK government 'does not adequately reflect the 'grass roots' contact which the Government helpfully facilitated during the consultation'.[72]

VI. Conclusion

Ideally, parties disagreeing about what human rights require from public budgeting would have the necessary capacities and willingness to deliberate, they would have a well-functioning institutional set-up for deliberation, and they would have adequate epistemic clarity of the surrounding circumstances. They would set aside strategic concerns for the purposes of the dialogue, and engage in a reflective informed discussion aiming to render human rights more determinate in a particular budgeting context. Reality is, of course, always messier. Genuine deliberative dialogues can in practice be corrupted by interventions from powerful parties that aim to realize their strategic ends. In addition, as discussed in this chapter, there are further challenges for a deliberative approach to drafting of human rights compatible public budgets. It is important, however, to emphasize, that deliberation is not an 'either/or' issue. Dialogues of contestation can approximate more as well as less an ideal account of deliberation. Nor is the *status quo* a permanent state of affairs. Although socio-economic human rights are facing a challenging environment in the twenty-first century, there are still many avenues forward. Ultimately, human rights advocates can and should be pragmatists relating to the challenges for deliberation identified in this chapter, and push for incremental changes when and where possible.

[70] Yves Sintomer, Anja Röcke, and Carsten Herzberg, *Participatory Budgeting in Europe: Democracy and Public Governance* (Routledge 2013) 23.

[71] Adalmir Marquetti, 'The Characteristics of the Brazilian Cities with Participatory Budgeting' (Working Paper, 2005) 13 <http://cdn.fee.tche.br/jornadas/2/E12-01.pdf> accessed 13 August 2019.

[72] Joint Committee, 'UK's Compliance' (n 46) 67.

12

The Promise and Pitfalls of the Sustainable Development Goals*

Has the Time Come for a Rights-Based Approach to Poverty Reduction?

Magdalena Sepúlveda Carmona and Kate Donald

I. Introduction

The way that we think about poverty has changed hugely over the course of the late twentieth and early twenty-first century. Whereas before the archetypal image of poverty was of starving orphans in rural sub-Saharan Africa, now many people (especially in the development, social justice, and human rights fields) may think of a homeless person on the streets of bustling prosperous cities. Whereas before the charity and aid approach to tackling poverty predominated, now many more people are questioning the structural underpinnings of our economies and societies and the systemic injustices that may plague them. Today, in the public debate and public consciousness, poverty is not restricted solely to Africa or Asia, and poverty and inequality in countries such as the United States and austerity-hit Greece are widely acknowledged and discussed.

This considerable transformation is partly the result of success: the world has made great strides in reducing extreme poverty in the 'developing world' in the last few decades. Globally, the number of people living in extreme poverty declined by more than half from 1990 to 2015.[1] However alongside these laudable strides, certain failures have come more clearly into focus, not least the widening gap between the rich and the poor and the ever more intense concentration of wealth among a tiny number of elites.[2] Environmental degradation and the devastating current and future impacts of climate change are also coming further into focus and posing a profound challenge to an economic model which relies on continuous economic growth and expanding consumption.

* This chapter was originally submitted in February 2017. Only select references have been updated since then.

[1] United Nations, *The Millennium Development Goals Report 2015* (New York, 2015) (hereafter UN, *MDG Report 2015*).

[2] Oxfam, *An Economy for the 1%* (Oxfam 2017).

Magdalena Sepúlveda Carmona and Kate Donald, *The Promise and Pitfalls of the Sustainable Development Goals*
In: Human Rights and 21st Century Challenges. Edited by: Dapo Akande, Jaakko Kuosmanen, Helen McDermott, and Dominic Roser, Published by Oxford University Press 2020.
DOI: 10.1093/oso/9780198824770.003.0013

Meanwhile, the global demographics of poverty have shifted. Most of the world's (income) poor (those living below $1.90 dollar per day purchasing power parity (PPP)) now live in 'non-poor' countries, with middle-income countries now home to 73 per cent of the world's poor.[3] Extreme poverty in these countries is also very real—recent research shows that persons living below the international poverty line in middle-income countries have a similar standard of deprivation to those in the poorest countries.[4]

At the same time, austerity policies implemented in the aftermath of the 2007–08 financial crisis have driven up poverty rates (and related phenomena such as homelessness) in high-income countries.[5] The financial crisis and various political shifts have also impacted on aid flows. Intensified globalization has also in many cases shifted the locus of economic power (including from states to large transnational corporations), with profound and varied impacts on labour forces and wages worldwide.

Alongside other factors, the human rights approach has had some impact in changing norms and discourse around poverty, including by increasing recognition of the interrelationship of poverty with discrimination and entrenched inequalities (along lines of gender, class, race, migration status, religion, and others). However, in a world of widening economic disparity, in the aftermath of financial crisis, and with poverty increasingly recognized as manifesting in different pernicious forms, what next for the rights-based approach to poverty?

This chapter will discuss the question of how far we have come with regards to a rights-based approach to poverty through the lens of the Sustainable Development Goals (SDGs). The SDGs are likely to direct or at least frame poverty reduction and related development efforts until 2030. Moreover, in many senses the SDGs, their targets and the process of deciding and implementing them embody the peculiar

[3] World Bank, 'Middle Income Countries Overview' <http://www.worldbank.org/en/country/mic/overview> accessed 13 August 2019. The argument here is not to say that these people have moved from income poverty to secure lives. Most of them have joined what Guy Standing calls the 'Precariat' (Guy Standing, *The Precariat: The New Dangerous Class* (Bloomsbury Academic 2011)). The point we want to stress is about the change in the demographic of poverty. See Andy Sumner, 'The World's Two New Middles. Growth, Precarity, Structural Change, and the Limitations of the Special Case' (2016) WIDER Working Paper 2016/34 9 <https://www.wider.unu.edu/publication/world's-two-new-middles> accessed 13 August 2019.

[4] Chris Hoy and Andy Sumner (2016) 'Gasoline, Guns, and Giveaways: Is There New Capacity for Redistribution to End Three Quarters of Global Poverty?' Working Paper 433 Center for Global Development <https://www.cgdev.org/sites/default/files/gasoline-guns-and-giveaways-end-three-quarters-global-poverty-0.pdf> accessed 13 August 2019.

[5] Isabel Ortiz, Mathew Cummins, Jeronim Capaldo, and Kalaivani Karunanethy (2015) 'The Decade of Adjustment: A Review of Austerity Trends 2010–2020 in 187 Countries' 53 ESS Working Paper 35 (hereafter Oritz *et al*, 'The Decade of Adjustment') <http://www.socialprotection.org/gimi/gess/RessourcePDF.action?ressource.ressourceId=53192> accessed 13 August 2019; and Isabel Ortiz and Mathew Cummins (2019) 'Austerity: The New Normal. A Renewed Washington Consensus 2010-24' Initiative for Policy Dialogue, Working Paper <http://policydialogue.org/files/publications/papers/Austerity-the-New-Normal-Ortiz-Cummins-6-Oct-2019.pdf> accessed 15 October 2019. See also UNICEF Office of Research, *Children of the Recession: The Impact of the Economic Crisis on Child Well-Being in Rich Countries* (Innocenti Report Card 12, UNICEF Office of Research 2014).

mix of progress, challenges, and contradictions facing the field of poverty and human rights.

II. The SDGs—A Paradigm Shift?

On 1 January 2016, the world officially began the implementation of the 2030 Agenda for Sustainable Development after its adoption by 193 countries in September 2015.[6] With its 17 SDGs and 169 targets, the Agenda covers a comprehensive set of issues across the three dimensions of sustainable development: the economic, social, and environmental.

The 2030 Agenda is hugely ambitious: it seeks to 'end poverty and hunger, in all their forms and dimensions, and to ensure that all human beings can fulfil their potential in dignity and equality and in a healthy environment' (Preamble).

SDG1 aims to '[e]nd poverty in all its forms everywhere' by 2030. It has seven targets including: to 'eradicate extreme poverty for all people everywhere' (1.1); 'reduce at least by half the proportion of men, women and children of all ages living in poverty in all its dimensions according to national definitions' (1.2); and 'implement nationally appropriate social protection systems and measures for all, including floors; and by 2030 achieve substantial coverage of the poor and the vulnerable' (1.3). Target 1.4 includes one of the few explicit mentions of 'rights' in the goals and targets, aiming to 'ensure that all men and women, in particular the poor and vulnerable, have equal rights to economic resources' including land, property and inheritance. A brief analysis of some of these targets and their implications is made in the next section.

From a pragmatic point of view, while it is important to remain critical of the flaws of the SDGs, we argue that human rights advocates will achieve better results by working with it rather than ignoring it. Unfolding the potential of the SDGs might be a powerful vehicle for human rights realization and a feasible way to address the historic levels of inequality that are negatively impacting our societies.

Despite the progress made under the Millennium Development Goals (MDGs, 2000–15), the high levels of poverty and inequality today call into question the effectiveness and sustainability of several poverty reduction policies implemented in the past. Making further and better progress seems to require moving away from 'business as usual' by improving existing strategies and adopting new ones. Moreover, our increased knowledge of the devastating pace and impact of climate change requires an urgent turn away from models of poverty reduction which rely on continuous economic growth (with accompanying increases in consumption and carbon emissions) to lift large numbers of people out of extreme poverty.

[6] UNGA 'Transforming Our World: the 2030 Agenda for Sustainable Development' (21 October 2015) UN Doc A/RES/70/1 (hereafter UNGA, 'Transforming our World').

Instead, the daunting challenge is to find a way to tackle poverty while respecting planetary boundaries.[7]

The SDGs, which are self-proclaimed as 'transformative', prompt us to review all perspectives and approaches critically, including a human rights approach. In fact, the 2030 Agenda recognizes that a rights-based approach should underpin all poverty reduction efforts (2030 Agenda, paras 18–20).

However, despite the explicit anchoring of the new Agenda in human rights norms and principles in the Declaration, clear human rights language was resisted by some governments in the drafting of the goals and targets. This calls into question how far we have really come in bringing together the human rights and development agendas, and certainly how far-reaching the acceptance of the human rights-based approach to development has been even after several decades in place.

The exclusion of stronger human rights language undermines the international human rights framework adopted by the same states and contradicts the commitment they have made to a rights-based approach to development over decades, included in international instruments[8] as well as in national policy documents.[9]

Yet, even if the commitment to human rights in the SDGs is not as strong as one might wish, the references to human rights in the Declaration might be the lever to unleash the transformative potential of the 2030 Agenda, linking the SDGs with legally enforceable rights and internationally agreed standards. Such norms and standards limit the discretion of policy-makers in the design, implementation and evaluation of public policies. A human rights approach might be one of the essential elements needed to make comprehensive progress towards the goals, and can certainly provide alternatives to the approaches of the last decades.

III. A Human Rights-Based Approach to Unfold the Transformative Potential of the 2030 Agenda

This section examines how emerging contributions from a human rights perspective may assist in understanding and realizing the radical potential of the SDGs.

[7] Johan Rockstrom, Jeffrey D Sachs, Marcus Ohman, and Guido Schmidt-Traub (2013) 'Sustainable Development and Planetary Boundaries' Background Research Paper for the High Level Panel on the Post-2015 Development Agenda'.

[8] For example, in the Vienna Declaration and Programme of Action (1993); the Millennium Declaration (2000); 'The Human Rights Based Approach to Development Cooperation, Towards a Common Understanding Among UN Agencies' (2003) and 'In Larger Freedom: Towards Development, Security and Human Rights for all' (2005).

[9] See eg Republic of Ecuador, *Plan Nacional de Desarrollo 2017-2021. Toda una Vida* (SENPLADES 2017); Government of Namibia, *Vision 2030* (National Planning Commission 2004); Ministry of Foreign Affairs of Finland, *Human Rights Based Approach in Finland's Development Cooperation: Guidance Note 2015* (Ministry of Foreign Affairs 2015); and Ministry of Foreign Affairs of Norway, *Opportunities for All: Human Rights in Norway's Foreign Policy and Development Cooperation—Meld. St. 10 (2014–2015)* (Ministry of Foreign Affairs 2014).

There are of course many areas of the SDGs which would benefit from a human rights approach but we have chosen those we consider to imply the most significant step forward from the MDGs. Under each of them, a brief description is given of the dominant poverty reduction approaches that have been implemented over the last decades and then we examine how the SDGs might represent an improvement or a new approach—or where they might fall short. We then go on to describe what a human rights approach would imply in terms of strategy and policy, and where appropriate we analyse the likely obstacles to the flourishing of a rights based potential.

A. Anchoring the Concept of Universality

During the fifteen years of the MDGs Agenda (2000–15) there was a significant decline in global poverty. Yet, the results were very uneven. While in China and India there was a dramatic decrease in poverty, it remains stubbornly high in sub-Saharan African countries and South Asia.[10] Moreover, there are deep pockets of poverty within countries as well as an increase in poverty in developed countries, most notably in Europe, in recent years.[11]

The gains have also been uneven across population groups, with women and children disproportionately remaining stuck in poverty.[12] Even where progress has been made, gains remain fragile.

The 2030 Agenda recognized these significant shortfalls of the MDGs and committed 'to address their unfinished business'. To some extent, the SDGs were built on a different model of what development is and where it happens. They include several issues that human rights advocates have long recognized as intrinsic to equitable development but have been left out from the MDGs, such as inequality and discrimination, peace, violence against women, and good governance as well as the crucial environmental dimension.

A critical difference between the two agendas is the concept of universally. Unlike the MDGs which were largely focused on poor countries, all the SDGs are intended to apply to *all* countries. This provides a crucial recognition that no country in the world is sustainably developed; poverty and inequality and environmental degradation exist everywhere, and all countries must do their part both domestically and on the global stage. This concept of universality is also more in line with the international human rights framework and helps to correct the

[10] UN, *MDG Report* 2015 (n 1).

[11] International Labour Organization, *World Employment and Social Outlook 2016: Transforming Jobs to End Poverty* (ILO 2016) 10–11.

[12] UNICEF and the World Bank Group (2016) 'Ending Extreme Poverty: A Focus on Children' (UNICEF and the World Bank Group).

skewed power and accountability dynamics reinforced by the MDGs' focus on poor countries.

Target 1.2, which requires all countries to tackle multidimensional poverty with the national poverty line as a benchmark, is particularly important in the context of this universal approach, and in contrast to the MDGs' myopic focus on dollar-a-day extreme poverty in the developing world. In the SDGs, governments pledge to eliminate this extreme poverty (now measured as less than $1.90 a day) rather than just reduce it. Such 'zero targets', where states pledge to eradicate rather than just scale back grave injustices, occur at several points in 2030 Agenda (eg Target 5.1 to *end* discrimination against women and Target 5.2 to *eliminate* all forms of violence against women) and are certainly more in line with long-standing legal human rights obligations. Target 1.3 on social protection is also pertinent for all countries, given that austerity measures in many developed countries have resulted in cuts to social protection programs[13] and higher poverty levels.[14]

The fact that developed countries have committed to tackling poverty domestically as part of a global development agenda should be seen as an important opportunity to increase scrutiny of, and accountability for, poverty in these countries. In addition, developed countries also continue to have responsibilities regarding the ways in which their actions (and omissions) impact poverty levels in the developing world.[15]

While the MDGs included a goal on the Global Partnership for Development (MDG8), this was one of the most off-track and neglected MDGs.[16] Consequently, SDG17 seeks to 'revitalize the global partnership for sustainable development' with a more comprehensive approach that includes new elements that are important from a human rights perspective, including on policy space, policy coherence, macroeconomic stability, and civil society partnerships. Compliance with these targets should have strong implications for the actions of developed countries and their impacts overseas, requiring a robust political commitment from rich nations that was decidedly lacking under the MDGs.

The responsibilities of developed countries for the implementation of the 2030 Agenda overseas can be viewed in line with their extra-territorial human rights obligations and obligations regarding international assistance and cooperation. In particular, targets on policy coherence can be usefully interpreted through the obligation states have to refrain from any conduct that impairs the ability of another state to comply with its own human rights commitments, and to avoiding conduct that would foreseeably risk impairing the enjoyment of human rights by

[13] Oritz *et al*, 'The Decade of Adjustment' (n 5).
[14] Oritz *et al*, 'The Decade of Adjustment' (n 5) 35.
[15] For example, SDG targets 1.a, 4.c, 6.a, 7.a, 17.2.
[16] See eg United Nations, *The State of the Global Partnership for Development* (MDG Gap Task Force Report 2014).

persons beyond their borders.[17] Increasingly, human rights monitoring bodies are addressing the responsibility of states for extraterritorial impacts of tax abuses, as they may undermine the ability of another state to mobilize resources for the progressive realization of economic, social, and cultural rights and substantive equality.[18]

However, the political will around Goal 17 from rich nations remains very questionable, especially in light of the way many actors are emphasizing the role of 'partnerships' with the private sector for financing the agenda rather than 'the global partnership for development' between states.[19]

B. Giving Meaning to the Principle of 'Leave No-One Behind'

The 2030 Agenda centres on the pledge to 'leave no-one behind'. This promise was viewed as a paradigm shift as it commits to prioritize those who are most marginalized and disadvantaged rather than be satisfied with aggregate progress.[20] This was one of the major critiques of the MDGs,[21] where the indicators were consistently worse for disadvantaged groups in every region. However, the meaning of this new development mantra remains contested, with some actors seeming to interpret it as encapsulating only the need to reach the poorest people (in terms of income)—in essence recapitulating the MDGs' focus primarily on addressing extreme poverty.

To ensure that this commitment remains meaningful, it should be linked with the human rights obligations of equality and non-discrimination, and related human rights-based concepts such as substantive equality, horizontal inequalities, intersectional discrimination, and indirect discrimination.[22]

17 See ETO Consortium (2013) 'Maastricht Principles on Extraterritorial Obligations of States in the Area of Economic, Social and Cultural Rights' (FIAN International) principle 21.

18 UNHRC 'Report of the Special Rapporteur on Extreme Poverty and Human Rights, Magdalena Sepúlveda Carmona' (22 May 2014) UN Doc A/HRC/26/28. See also, CESCR, 'General Comment No. 24: on state obligations under the International Covenant on Economic, Social and Cultural Rights in the context of business activities' (2017) UN Doc E/C.12/GC/23, and Committee on the Elimination of All Forms of Discrimination Against Women, Concluding Observations on the Combined Fourth and Fifth Periodic Reports of Switzerland, UN Doc CEDAW/C/CHE/CO/4-5 (18 November 2016).

19 Aldo Caliari, 'Investing in the SDGs: Whose Business?' <https://business-humanrights.org/en/investing-in-the-sdgs-whose-business> accessed 13 August 2019.

20 'As we embark on this great collective journey, we pledge that no one will be left behind. Recognizing that the dignity of the human person is fundamental, we wish to see the Goals and targets met for all nations and peoples and for all segments of society. And we will endeavor to reach the furthest behind first.' UNGA, 'Transforming our World' (n 6).

21 For strong rights-based critiques of the MDGs, see Sakiko Fukuda-Parr and Alicia Yamin, *The MDGs, Capabilities and Human Rights: The Power of Numbers to Shape Agendas* (Routledge 2015). For a critique from a gender perspective, see Caroline Sweetman (ed), *Gender and the Millennium Development Goals* (Oxfam 2005).

22 See UN Chief Executives Board for Coordination, 'Equality and Non-Discrimination at the Heart of Sustainable Development: A Shared United Nations Framework for Action' (United Nations 2016) for a detailed explanation of how 'Leave No One Behind' could be operationalized through the lens of human rights standards.

1. Non-discrimination and substantive equality

The principle of 'leave no-one behind' can be given a more precise meaning by linking it with the human rights obligations of equality and non-discrimination. These principles have been included in many national legal systems (eg constitutions and anti-discriminatory laws) and international human rights instruments. Thus, these principles refer to an extensive array of legal obligations that states have voluntarily assumed through domestic, regional, and international human rights commitments. Their content has been further confirmed and developed by national courts and international tribunals.[23]

Looking at the principle of 'leave no-one behind' from a human rights perspective—in particular interpreting it through the specific understandings of non-discrimination and substantive equality that have been developed in human rights law and jurisprudence[24]—can help in a number of ways (see Chapter 20 in this book). For example, to reach *substantive* equality through the SDGs and beyond, we must examine the *outcomes* and not just the intentions of laws and policies,[25] 'ensuring that they do not maintain, but rather alleviate, the inherent disadvantage that particular groups experience'.[26] In addition, meeting SDG1 on poverty and SDG10 on inequality will certainly require the adoption of affirmative or positive actions to move towards equality in practice and eliminate conditions that cause or help to perpetuate discrimination.

At the same time, it will be critical to implement the commitment to leave no one behind in tandem with the universality principle that underpins human rights and the 2030 Agenda. This will require balancing prioritizing the situation of the worst-off with universal, inclusive policies. An approach which merely pinpoints those deemed the poorest in terms of income and seeks to address only one element of their deprivation is likely simply to repeat the results of the MDGs, and may also increase stigmatization and exclusion (see social protection section below).

From this perspective, 'leave no-one behind' requires much more than merely undertaking legal reforms (repealing or amending any discriminatory legislation),[27] improving data collection, and targeting poverty relief programs at

[23] See eg *Marckx v Belgium*, App no 6833/74, 13 June 1979; *Proposed Amendments to the Naturalization Provisions of the Constitution of Costa Rica*, Advisory Opinion OC-4/84, Inter-American Court of Human Rights (19 January 1984) para 57; *Government of the Republic of South Africa v Grootboom* 2001 (1) SA 46 (CC).

[24] See eg CESCR, 'General Comment No 16: The Equal Right of Men and Women to the Enjoyment of all Economic, Social and Cultural Rights (art 3 of the ICESCR)' (2005) UN Doc E/C.12/2005/4) (hereafter CESCR, 'General Comment No 16'); UN Committee for the Elimination of All Forms of Discrimination against Women 'General Comment No 25, on Article 4, paragraph 1, of the Convention on the Elimination of All Forms of Discrimination against Women, on Temporary Special Measures' (2004). See also Chapter 10 by Sandra Feldman, this book.

[25] As implicitly recognized in SDG target 10.3 which pledges to 'Ensure Equal Opportunity and Reduce Inequalities of Outcome'.

[26] CESCR, 'General Comment No 16' (n 24).

[27] See eg UNCHR 'The Limburg Principles on the Implementation of the International Covenant on Economic, Social and Cultural Rights' (1987) UN Doc E/CN.4/1987/17 para 37 and 'Maastricht Guidelines on Violations of Economic, Social and Cultural Rights' (1997) para 14 (b).

so-called vulnerable groups. It essentially requires looking at the political dimensions of exclusion and discrimination, seeking the transformation of the institutions and structures that inform and reproduce unequal power relations in the society along gender, race, ethnicity, class, disability, and other grounds.

2. Inclusivity through participation

Most importantly, the pledge to 'leave no-one behind' will be empty if it does not include a commitment to meaningful participation of the relevant communities in the design and implementation of policies and programs designed to affect them, and in monitoring progress. Too often, 'leave no-one behind' has seemed to be yet another top-down initiative and there has been very little recognition of the role the people in question might have to play.

Here, the human rights-based approach to participation can help to ensure that the most disadvantaged people are given a voice and meaningful influence.[28] Over the years, human rights monitoring bodies as well as several judgments of national and regional tribunals have further developed the content of the right to participation.[29] Moreover, human rights actors have a wealth of experience assessing and implementing participatory processes, for example, in budget formulation or service monitoring. These experiences could help to make participation in public policies operational and effective,[30] and might help to avoid the capture of governments by technocrats and to ensure poverty reduction policies reach the most vulnerable and disadvantaged.[31]

3. Addressing the complexities in conceptualizing and measuring poverty and inequality

In the effort to leave no-one behind, it will also be necessary to identify more accurately the most disadvantaged and excluded. To this end, careful efforts must

[28] The right to participation is enshrined in several human rights instruments, see eg the Universal Declaration of Human Rights (arts 21 and 27), the ICCPR (art 25), the ICESCR (arts 13.1 and 15.1), CEDAW (arts 7, 8, 13(c), and 14.2), CRC (arts 12 and 31), the Convention on the Rights of Persons with Disabilities (hereafter CRPD) (arts 3(c), 4.3, 9, 29, and 30).

[29] See eg UNHRC, 'Report of the Special Rapporteur on Extreme Poverty and Human Rights, Magdalena Sepúlveda Carmona' (2013) UN Doc A/HRC/23/36; UNHRC, 'Final Report of the Study on Indigenous Peoples and the Rights to Participate in Decision-Making: Report of the Expert Mechanism on the Rights of Indigenous Peoples' (2011); and UNHRC, 'CCPR General Comment 25: Article 25 (Participation in Public Affairs and the Right to Vote' (1996) UN Doc CCPR/C/21/Rev.1/Add.7 para 5. Judicial cases have focused particularly on participation regarding indigenous peoples. See eg ILO (2009) *Application of Convention No 169 by Domestic and International Courts in Latin America—a Casebook* (ILO).

[30] See eg ActionAid, 'People's Action in Practice: ActionAid's Human Rights Based Approach 2.0' (ActionAid 2012) and Lisa Veneklasen, Valerie Miller, Cindy Clarke, and Molly Reilly (2004) 'Rights-based Approaches and Beyond: Challenges of Linking Rights and Participation' IDS Working Paper No 235 5 <https://www.ids.ac.uk/files/Wp235.pdf> accessed 13 August 2019.

[31] For an SDG-specific initiative which sought to engage and seek the views of marginalized people, see the Participate 2015 initiative, in particular the 'Ground Level Panels' <http://participatesdgs.org/ground-level-panels/ > accessed 10 October 2019.

be made to collect better disaggregated data and capture their experiences.[32] The prohibited grounds of discrimination enshrined in international human rights law should help to guide identification of those groups which are most at risk of being left behind.

Furthermore, subjecting the measurements of poverty that have been used to critical examination can call into question the progress made in poverty reduction globally. The international poverty line included in the MDGs and SDG Target 1.1 (which defines the type of 'extreme' poverty to be eliminated) is a monetary measurement.[33] It does not consider the multiple dimensions of poverty that people experience (eg lack of access to good quality education and health services, clean water and sanitation facilities, or electricity).

In contrast, multidimensional approaches such as the Multidimensional Poverty Index (MPI)[34] and the Human Development Index (HDI)[35] take into account a number of different poverty dimensions and their links with social exclusion. As such, although they were not developed specifically as human rights monitoring tools, they are more in line with the normative framework of international human rights law, where basic needs such as access to food, shelter, drinking water and sanitation, education, and health are in fact legally binding human rights.[36]

Non-monetary measures of poverty are also more in line with the principle of equality and non-discrimination. By concentrating only on income and/or assets at the household level, monetary measures ignore intra-household power dynamics, including the distribution of resources within household. If complex intra-household dynamics are not taken into account, the specific needs and vulnerabilities experienced by some household members, such as children, women, older persons, and family members with disabilities are ignored and, as a result, public policies and interventions might not reach them.

Committing to implement the SDGs from a human rights perspective should be understood as a political commitment to reach consensus on a definition and a multidimensional measurement of poverty. However, despite the important inclusion of Target 1.2 in the SDGs which aims at reducing poverty 'in all its dimensions',

[32] UN Women, 'Turning promises into action: Gender equality in the 2030 Agenda for Sustainable Development' (UN Women 2018) <https://www.unwomen.org/-/media/headquarters/attachments/sections/library/publications/2018/sdg-report-gender-equality-in-the-2030-agenda-for-sustainable-development-2018-en.pdf?la=en&vs=4332> accessed 10 October 2019.

[33] The poverty line used by the World Bank was $1.25 purchasing power parity (PPP). Since October 2015, the updated international poverty line is $1.90 a day, using 2011 prices.

[34] Sabina Alkire and Maria Emma Santos (2010) 'Acute Multidimensional Poverty: A New Index for Developing Countries' OPHI Working Paper No 38 <https://www.ophi.org.uk/wp-content/uploads/ophi-wp38.pdf> accessed 13 August 2019.

[35] Sudhir Anand and Amartya Sen (1994) 'Human Development Index: Methodology and Measurement' Human Development Report Office Occasional Paper No 12 (UNDP).

[36] For example, the right to adequate housing is enshrined in UDHR art 25, ICESCR art 11, CEDAW art 14, CRC art 27, and CRPD art 28. The right to health is enshrined in UDHR art 25, ICESCR art 12, CRC art 24, CRPD art 25. The rights to water and sanitation are implicit components of the right to an adequate standard of living, ICESCR art 11.

the agreed global indicator for that target is '[p]roportion of population living below the national poverty line, by sex and age'. In most cases, national poverty lines are also purely monetary measurements; a multidimensional measure of poverty is not included among the agreed indicators. This is a major gap. A World Bank study has acknowledged that the MPI 'is one possible implementation' of Target 1.2 and that 'demand for harmonized multidimensional poverty assessment at the country and global levels is likely to rise'.[37] Of course, adoption of this indicator would be likely to make the poverty figures higher, but this would allow us to analyse and conceptualize the true scale and demographics of poverty far more accurately.

In line with the human rights obligations of equality and non-discrimination and progressive realization, the SDG indicators and their monitoring and review framework should also commit to monitoring the reduction of inequalities between social and economic groups regularly over time to ensure the gap is closing between the most disadvantaged groups and the rest of the population.[38]

C. Tackling Inequalities

Rising inequality is now widely accepted (including by the World Bank and International Monetary Fund (IMF)) as one of the defining challenges of our time.[39] Even as extreme poverty was being reduced in the MDG era, inequalities were persistent and even escalating; this has been one of the major critiques of the MDG project. For example, most countries which saw a decrease in under-five mortality (a target under MDG4) witnessed an *increase* in disparities in mortality rates between the richest and poorest.[40] Meanwhile, in advanced economies, the gap between the rich and the poor is at its highest level in decades.[41]

One of the major steps forward in the SDGs from a human rights perspective is the agenda's focus on inequalities, both through a cross-cutting commitment to prioritize equitable progress across the goals ('leave no-one behind', addressed earlier), and through a stand-alone goal (SDG10) on reducing inequalities within

[37] Marcio Cruz, James Foster, Bryce Quillin, and Philip Schellekens (2015) 'Ending Extreme Poverty and Sharing Prosperity: Progress and Policies' World Bank Group Policy Research Note (World Bank).

[38] See UNICEF-WHO Joint Monitoring Project on Equity and Non-Discrimination, 'JMP Working Group on Equity and Non-Discrimination Final Report' (UNICEF and WHO 2012) <http://www.wssinfo.org/fileadmin/user_upload/resources/JMP-END-WG-Final-Report-20120821.pdf> accessed 13 August 2019.

[39] See Era Dabla-Norris, Kalpana Kochhar, Nujin Suphaphiphat, Frantisek Ricka, and Evridiki Tsounta (2015) 'Causes and Consequences of Income Inequality: A Global Perspective' IMF Staff Discussion Note (IMF) (hereafter Dabla-Norris *et al*, 'Causes and Consequences of Income Inequality'); World Bank (2016) *Taking on Inequality: Poverty and Shared Prosperity 2016* (World Bank).

[40] UNICEF (2014) *The State of the World's Children 2015—Reimagining the Future: Innovation for Every Child* (UNICEF).

[41] Dabla-Norris *et al*, (2016) 'Causes and Consequences of Income Inequality' (n 39).

and between countries. There is also a separate goal (SDG5) on gender equality. Both goals have content which is closely related to human rights standards and priorities around equality and non-discrimination. The SDGs are intended to be an integrated agenda, and certainly both Goals 5 and 10 will be hugely important in maximizing progress under SDG1, as well as being inherently valuable goals in themselves.

1. Substantive gender equality

The 2030 Agenda is a significant improvement from the MDGs on issues of gender equality as it covers a more comprehensive set of issues. Moreover, 'gender equality and women's empowerment' is recognized as a 'crucial contribution to progress across all the goals and targets' (2030 Agenda, para 20) and is included as a cross-cutting theme and a stand-alone goal (SDG5). Meanwhile, the principle of 'leave no-one behind' has the potential to put the spotlight on women who experience multiple forms of discrimination and have been historically excluded.[42]

SDG5 builds on the gender goal in the MDGs but—thanks to the efforts of women's rights advocates—it is far more expansive and sensitive to women's rights and the major obstacles they face to equality and empowerment, including issues such as sexual and reproductive health and rights, unpaid care work, violence, and early marriage. Gender specific targets are also included in SDG11 and other goals. However, there are also several shortcomings in the 2030 Agenda's approach to gender equality. For example, several of the targets under Goal 5 (sexual and reproductive health and rights; unpaid care work, assets, and economic resources) are subject to qualifiers, in the form of references to national contexts and alignment with international policy outcomes.[43] In the negotiation process the efforts to introduce stronger language on the realization of women's and girl's rights in the title and content of the goal were resisted in favour of the more ambiguous concept of women's empowerment.

To ensure that the SDGs will be a vehicle for women's equal rights enjoyment, their implementation must be guided by the principle of substantive gender equality, drawn from human rights standards and in particular, the Convention on the Elimination of All Forms of Discrimination Against Women (CEDAW) (see Chapter 10, this book, for more on substantive equality). Women cannot lift themselves out of poverty if they are still subject to intense gender-related discrimination and lack of opportunities. Meanwhile, it is now widely accepted that gender inequality and discrimination are a significant drag on economic growth and

[42] Elisabeth Stuart and Jessica Woodroffe (2016) 'Leaving No-One Behind: Can the Sustainable Development Goals Succeed Where the Millennium Developed Goals Lacked?' 24(1) Gender & Development Journal 69–81.

[43] Shahra Razavi (2016) 'The 2030 Agenda: Challenges of Implementation to Attain Gender Equality and Women's Rights' 24(1) Gender & Development 25–41.

poverty reduction more broadly,[44] and therefore SDG1 and other SDGs will be out of reach without substantial progress on gender equality. The concept of substantive equality will be also an important lens to analyse whether efforts towards Goal 5 are sufficient and in line with women's human rights.

2. Reducing other forms of inequality

Goal 10 includes commitments to tackling various types of inequality, including targets on income inequality and social and political empowerment. It also explicitly acknowledges the need to tackle inequalities both of opportunity and outcome (much more in line with *substantive* equality), and to eliminate discriminatory laws, policies, and practices (Target 10.3). The inclusion of this stand-alone inequality goal in the SDGs is a major paradigm shift and unprecedented in previous global development agreements/frameworks.

Extreme income inequality slows poverty reduction,[45] and thus eradicating extreme poverty will be impossible without tackling economic inequality.[46] Indeed, if economic growth over the last thirty years had been more equally distributed, the world would already be on track to eliminate extreme poverty completely by 2030.[47]

An important part of SDG10 is tackling economic (income and wealth) inequality, which reinforces and overlaps with many other different types of inequality and produces many detrimental human rights effects.[48] Inequality is harmful to economic growth[49] and, moreover, high levels of inequality make it difficult to reduce poverty even when economies are growing.[50] To make progress on a human rights approach to poverty reduction under the rubric of the SDGs will

[44] Christian Gonzales, Sonali Jain-Chandra, Kalpana Kochhar, Monique Newiak, and Tlek Zeinullayev (2015) 'Catalyst for Change: Empowering Women and Tackling Income Inequality' IMF Staff Discussion Note (IMF).

[45] Martin Ravallion (1997) 'Can High-Inequality Developing Countries Escape Absolute Poverty?' 56(1) Economics Letters 51–7.

[46] See Christoph Lakner, Mario Negre, and Espen Beer Prydz (2014) 'Twinning the Goals: How Can Promoting Shared Prosperity Help to Reduce Global Poverty' World Bank Policy Research Working Paper 7106 <http://documents.worldbank.org/curated/en/2014/11/20377179/twinning-goals-can-promoting-shared-prosperity-help-reduce-global-poverty> accessed 13 August 2019. See also Peter Edward and Andy Sumner (2015) 'Philanthropy, Welfare Capitalism, or Radically Different Global Economic Model: What Would it Take to End Global Poverty within a Generation Based on Historical Growth Patterns?' Center for Global Development Working Paper 413 <http://www.cgdev.org/sites/default/files/Edward_Sumner_End_Global_Poverty_wp413.pdf> accessed 13 August 2019.

[47] Chris Hoy and Emma Samman (2015) 'What if Growth Had Been as Good for the Poor as Everyone Else?' (Overseas Development Institute) <http://www.odi.org/sites/odi.org.uk/files/odi-assets/publications-opinion-files/9655.pdf> accessed 13 August 2019.

[48] See eg United Nations Research Institute for Social Development (2010) *Combating Poverty and Inequality: Structural Change, Social Policy and Politics* (UNRISD) (hereafter UNRISD, *Combating Poverty*); UNHRC (2015) 'Report of the Special Rapporteur on Extreme Poverty and Human Rights, Philip Alston' UN Doc A/HRC/29/31 paras 11–13.

[49] Branko Milanovic (2011) 'More or Less' (Finance and Development) 48:3 <http://www.imf.org/external/pubs/ft/fandd/2011/09/Milanovic.htm> accessed 13 August 2019; IMF, Fiscal Policy and Income Inequality (2014).

[50] UNRISD, *Combating Poverty* (n 48).

require Goals 1 and 10 to be implemented in tandem, with a view to the synergies and interlinkages between them. As recent research has shown,[51] achieving SDG1 will simply not be possible without also determinedly tackling inequality, including economic inequality, and addressing the discrimination that people living in poverty face. Furthermore, if efforts under SDG10 focus only on boosting the incomes of the poorest rather than closing the gap between the rich and the poor through progressive measures, they will most likely fail. Ignoring the concentration of wealth at the top of the spectrum is short-sighted, not least because more progressive fiscal policies will be needed which collect more money from those who can most afford it in order to fund the policies and services that really work in addressing poverty and exclusion (see more detail in section on fiscal policies below).

Again, the human rights framework can help in providing a more holistic and far-reaching framework for identifying and tackling inequalities. As Fukuda Parr notes, '[h]uman rights norms and principles can help fill [the] ethical void in economics', providing 'an alternative framework for analysis of inequality, one that is based on the intrinsic value of equality as a social norm, and one that explores unjust institutions as the source of inequality'.[52] Drawing from human rights principles and practice should also help to improve the ways in which we measure poverty, inequality, and discrimination,[53] important given that many of the indicators currently proposed to underpin the SDG targets on inequality distort or depoliticize the policies and efforts necessary.[54]

D. Implementing Universal Social Protection Systems

Increasingly, there seems to be a clear understanding that to meet the SDGs, in particular 'ending poverty in all its forms everywhere' (SDG1), states must adopt social protection systems[55]. While the MDGs were silent about social protection,

[51] World Bank (2016) *Taking on Inequality: Poverty and Shared Prosperity 2016* (World Bank).

[52] Sakiko Fukuda-Parr, 'It's About Values: Human Rights Norms and Tolerance for Inequality' (OpenDemocracy, 22 December 2015) <https://www.opendemocracy.net/openglobalrights/sakiko-fukuda-parr/it-s-about-values-human-rights-norms-and-tolerance-for-inequalit> accessed 13 August 2019.

[53] CESR 'The Measure of Progress: How Human Rights Should Inform the Sustainable Development Goals Indicators' (Human Rights Policy Brief, October 2015) <http://www.cesr.org/measure-of-progress> accessed 13 August 2019.

[54] Kate Donald, 'SDG Targets Risk Missing the Mark on Inequality' (Center for Economic and Social Rights, 9 March 2016) <http://www.cesr.org/sdg-targets-risk-missing-mark-inequality> accessed 13 August 2019.

[55] ILO (2017), 'World Social Protection Report 2017–19. Universal social protection to achieve the Sustainable Development Goals' (ILO, 2017). (hereafter ILO, 'World Social Protection Report') <https://www.ilo.org/wcmsp5/groups/public/---dgreports/---dcomm/---publ/documents/publication/wcms_604882.pdf> accessed 10 October 2019.

the 2030 Agenda gives it unique prominence by including it in several targets (eg Targets 1.3, 3.8, 5.4, and 10.4).

Particularly relevant is Target 1.3, which requires states to achieve 'substantial coverage of the poor and the vulnerable' by social protection systems. This requires the implementation of social assistance measures, yet despite remarkable progress in the coverage of social assistance programs—now reaching more than 1.9 billion people[56]—many poor and vulnerable groups, which often include children, women, ethnic minorities, and persons with disabilities, remain uncovered, especially in lower-income countries.[57] The coverage gap is particularly acute in sub-Saharan Africa and South Asia, where most of the global poor live. In these regions, only one-tenth and one-fifth of the poorest 20 per cent have access to social safety nets, respectively.[58]

This means that the ways in which these programs have been implemented so far are actually excluding the majority of the poorest and most vulnerable. Reaching the poorest (as requested by the SDGs)[59] through social assistance programs requires new approaches or at least a considerable improvement in the way these programmes have been implemented.

A better understanding of the implications of human rights obligations for social protection[60] should assist in reaching the most excluded. A rights-based approach might assist not only in identifying the obstacles that prevent the most disadvantaged from accessing programs on an equal basis with the rest of the population, but also provide guidance on how to improve the design of the programs.[61]

From a human rights perspective, one particularly contentious policy measure is the Conditional Cash Transfers Program (CCT), and the excessive reliance on

[56] World Bank (2015) *The State of Social Safety Nets 2015* (World Bank Group) (hereafter World Bank, *Social Safety Nets*) <http://documents.worldbank.org/curated/en/415491467994645020/pdf/97882-PUB-REVISED-Box393232B-PUBLIC-DOCDATE-6-29-2015-DOI-10-1596978-1-4648-0543-1-EPI-1464805431.pdf> accessed 13 August 2019.

[57] World Bank (2012) 'Resilience, Equity and Opportunity: Social Protection and Labor Strategy 2012–2022' (World Bank) 32 <http://siteresources.worldbank.org/SOCIALPROTECTION/Resources/280558-1274453001167/7089867-1279223745454/7253917-1291314603217/SPL_Strategy_2012-22_FINAL.pdf> accessed 13 August 2019.

[58] World Bank, *Social Safety Nets* (n 56).

[59] See in particular Goal 1.3 and Indicator 1.3.1.

[60] The right to social security (social protection) is articulated in the UDHR arts 22 and 25; the ICESCR art 9; CERD art 11; CRC art 26; and the Convention for the Protection of Migrant Workers and their Families (CMW) art 27. It also appears in regional human rights instruments (eg Protocol of San Salvador, art 9; European Social Charter, art 12), and in several Conventions of the International Labour Organization (ILO), in particular Convention No 102 on Minimum Standards of Social Security. The CRPD art 28, explicitly refers to the right to social protection. For a human rights analysis of social protection, see CESCR 'General Comment No 19: The Right to Social Security' (2009) UN Doc E/C.12.GC/19 (hereafter CESCR 'General Comment No 19'); Magdalena Sepúlveda and Carly Nyst (2012) *The Human Rights Approach to Social Protection* (Ministry for Foreign Affairs of Finland) (hereafter Sepúlveda and Nyst, *Human Rights Approach to Social Protection*).

[61] Magdalena Sepúlveda, 'Ensuring inclusion and combatting discrimination in social protection programmes: The role of human rights standards' 70(4) International Social Security Review.

it as a social protection 'silver bullet'.[62] There are several aspects of the design and implementation of the CCTs which are in tension with a human rights approach, such as the imposition of conditionalities (also called co-responsibilities), the use of targeting methods, and the gender impacts.

For some authors, co-responsibilities in themselves infringe the principles of equality and non-discrimination as they entail behavioural control over the poorest segments of the population that is not imposed on other social and economic sectors that also benefit from public policies, such as high-income earners who enjoy tax credits.[63] In many countries, middle-class and high-income families are eligible for tax exemptions just because they have children. This tax credit which is, strictly speaking, a kind of transfer, comes with no conditions at all. In contrast, CCTs which are targeted at poor families with children, impose conditions and in some cases create stigma.[64]

Moreover, sometimes non-compliance with co-responsibilities can result in punitive sanctions (from suspension of benefits to exclusion from programs and services). Without appropriate mechanisms in place (eg the support of social workers) such punitive exclusion from the program might be discriminatory. For the most vulnerable families it is often more difficult to comply with conditionalities.[65]

The imposition of conditionalities often increases both community power imbalances and the opportunity for abuse of power by those involved in the monitoring of compliance with them (such as teachers, healthcare personnel, and program administrators). For example, requiring children to attend school and demanding minimum attendance or certain grades, gives teachers additional means to exert authority over students and parents, creating opportunities for abuse (eg if a teacher requests money or sexual favours in exchange for a certain grade or an

[62] The World Bank, for example, is a fervent promoter of CCTs as a major policy measure. See eg World Bank (2016) 'Poverty and Shared Prosperity 2016: Taking on Inequality' (World Bank Group) 140–45 (hereafter World Bank, 'Taking on Inequality') <https://openknowledge.worldbank.org/bitstream/handle/10986/25078/9781464809583.pdf> accessed 13 August 2019 This contrasts with the ILO, which systematically promotes universal social protection systems.

[63] Economic Commission for Latin America and the Caribbean (ECLAC) (2012) *Gender Equality Observatory of Latin America and the Caribbean: Annual Report 2012* (ECLAC) 59 (hereafter ECLAC, *Gender Equality Observatory 2012*).

[64] Simone Cecchini, Fernando Filgueira, Rodrigo Martinez, and Cecilia Rossel (eds) (2015) *Towards Universal Social Protection. Latin American Pathways and Policy Tools* (ECLAC) 101. It is worth noting that according to some researchers, there is no robust evidence about the value of conditions when compared with unconditional programs. See eg Stephen Kidd (2016) 'To Condition or Not to Condition: What is the Evidence?' *Pathways' Perspectives on Social Policy in International Development Issue No 20* (Development Pathways) <https://www.developmentpathways.co.uk/wp-content/uploads/2016/03/CCT-Evidence-PP20-1.pdf> accessed 10 October 2019.

[65] Stephen Kidd and Rebecca Calder (2011) 'Conditional Cash Transfer Programmes: Their Relevance for Nepal' (DFID) 12. <http://www.developmentpathways.co.uk/wp-content/uploads/2013/06/CCT-Nepal-2011-Final.pdf> accessed 10 October 2019. See also Stephen Kidd (2014) 'Social Exclusion and Access to Social Protection Schemes' (Australian Government, Department of Foreign Affairs and Trade) 24–25. <https://www.developmentpathways.co.uk/wp-content/uploads/2018/05/DFAT-Social-exclusion-and-access-to-social-protection-schemes-3.pdf> accessed 10 October 2019.

attendance certificate). Such situations can result in arbitrary exclusions of entire families from the program.

Despite the fact that many CCTs aim at enhancing the economic inclusion of women, when it comes to gender equality these programs have been strongly criticized on several grounds. First, due to their 'maternalistic' stance; it is considered that the focus on women is not based on recognition of their rights but rather as an instrument for benefiting their children.[66] Second, increasing unpaid care work: for example, a study shows that in Ecuador, poor women who were recipients of CCTs engaged in thirty-seven hours of unpaid care work per week, compared to thirty hours for women living in poverty who are not recipients of the program.[67] The additional demands on women's time created by these requirements has a discriminatory impact on women and on their enjoyment of several rights on an equal basis as men (eg right to education and health) and further deprives them of scarce leisure time.[68] Third, reaffirming socio-cultural norms that consider family caregiving to be women's sole or primary role, effectively relieving men of any responsibility for these tasks.[69] In this regard, CCTs are considered to do little to transform patriarchal power relations, attitudes, and stereotypes that cast the man as the family breadwinner, while the woman is left with responsibility for children's well-being and domestic chores.[70] Fourth, linked to the previous criticism, it is also considered that the conditionalities of CCTs hinder women's access to paid employment on an equal footing with men[71] and that they do nothing to reorganize gender roles in ways that would reduce or avoid tensions between paid and unpaid work, and in some cases they increase tensions in terms of equality of time use.[72]

Finally, another critical aspect of these programs is the use of targeting methods (mainly means tests and proxy means test mechanisms) as a way to reach specific income groups. While targeting mechanisms might be considered a way to give priority to the poorest, the problem is that there are few data on targeting outcomes and the existing evidence shows that many CCTs are not inclusive of the poorest sectors of society.[73]

66 ECLAC, *Gender Equality Observatory 2012* (n 63) 70–71.

67 Ibid, 62.

68 UNHRC 'Report of the Independent Expert on the Question of Human Rights and Extreme Poverty, Magdalena Sepúlveda Carmona' (2009) UN Doc A/HRC/11/9.

69 Simone Cecchini and Aldo Madariaga (2011) 'Conditional Cash Transfer Programmes: The Recent Experience in Latin America and the Caribbean' *Cuadernos de la CEPAL* No 95 (ECLAC).

70 ECLAC, *Gender Equality Observatory 2012* (n 63) 70–71.

71 Juliana Martínez Franzoni and Koen Voreend, 'Blacks, Whites or Greys? Conditional Transfers and Gender Equality in Latin America (2009)' Paper submitted for the RC19 Conference (Montreal, August 2009).

72 UN Women (2014) *Progress of the World's Women 2015–2016: Transforming Economies, Realizing Rights* (UN Women) 140–41.

73 See Stephen Kidd, Bjorn Gelders, and Diloá Bailey-Athias (2017), 'Exclusion by design: An assessment of the effectiveness of the proxy means test poverty targeting mechanism' ESS Working Paper No. 56 <https://www.social-protection.org/gimi/gess/RessourcePDF.action?ressource.ressourceId=54248> accessed 10 October 2019; and Stephen Kidd and Diloá Athias (2019), 'Hit and Miss. Church of Sweden and Development Pathways working paper' (hereafter Kidd and Athias, 'Hit

From a rights perspective, universal programs—those which provide benefits to all residents without conditions—are the best way to ensure that states meet their obligation to ensure that there is no discrimination in the selection of the beneficiaries.[74] These are the programs which truly 'leave no-one behind' and equalize upwards.[75]

When compared to targeted schemes, universal non-contributory programs have higher quality implementation, with fewer people living in poverty being excluded and with much more effective impacts on poverty and inequality reduction.[76] Universal programs also help avoid stigmatization and engender better social solidarity.[77]

In sum, a human rights approach to social protection which prioritizes universal, gender sensitive, and non-conditional social assistance measures is much more likely to ensure that all, in particular the most disadvantaged and vulnerable groups, are able to benefit. This is in fact, the objective behind the Social Protection Floors Initiative. Social Protection Floors (SPF) would play a major role in progress towards many of the SDGs, including the goals on poverty, gender equality, and reducing inequalities.

One critical problem here is that despite the formal appearance of collaboration between various players in the promotion of social protection, there are problems of coordination and significantly divergent agendas. Formally, the International Labour Organization (ILO) and the World Bank have declared that they 'share a vision of a world where anyone who needs social protection can access it at any time' and have jointly launched the Global Partnership for Universal Social Protection.[78] However, in practice, the social protection interventions of the World Bank continue to focus mainly on targeted CCTs, which are just one (limited) component of social protection systems,[79] often implemented without due consideration of

and Miss') <https://www.developmentpathways.co.uk/wp-content/uploads/2019/03/Hit-and-Miss-March13-1.pdf> accessed 10 October 2019.

[74] CESCR, 'General Comment No 19' (n 60) para 4.

[75] Sepúlveda and Nyst, *Human Rights Approach to Social Protection* (n 60).

[76] Kidd and Athias, 'Hit and Miss' (n 73).

[77] See eg UNICEF (2012) 'Integrated Social Protection Systems: Enhancing Equity for Children' (UNICEF), and Stephen Kidd and Emily Wylde (2011) 'Targeting the Poorest: An Assessment of the Proxy Means Test Methodology' (Australian Government, AusAid).

[78] Under this initiative, launched in September 2016, the World Bank and the ILO have formally committed to 'use their individual and collective resources and influence to support countries in their move towards providing universal coverage [of social protection]' in the next one to fifteen years.

[79] Universal social protection encompasses much more than social safety nets or cash transfers. It encompasses "a set of policies and programmes designed to reduce and prevent poverty and vulnerability throughout the life cycle. Social protection includes benefits for children and families, maternity, unemployment, employment injury, sickness, old age, disability, survivors, as well as health protection. Social protection systems address all these policy areas by a mix of contributory schemes (social insurance) and non-contributory tax-financed benefits, including social assistance". See ILO, 'World Social Protection Report' n 55 xxix and ILO and World Bank, 'A Shared Mission for Universal Social Protection: Concept note' (World Bank and ILO, n.d.) <http://www.ilo.org/wcmsp5/groups/public/---dgreports/---dcomm/documents/genericdocument/wcms_378996.pdf> accessed 13 August 2019.

the human rights framework leading to the problems described earlier. This is in contrast with the work of the ILO, which promotes universal access to social protection systems through a rights-based approach.[80] If the prevailing lack of coordination continues and major development partners do not fully embrace universal social protection, it is unlikely that the pledge to eliminate extreme poverty and leave no-one behind will be fulfilled.

E. Ensuring Fair and Progressive Domestic Resource Mobilization

In a major departure from the MDGs which focused on aid as the main source of financing for development, the SDGs—in particular SDG17 ('means of implementation') and the Addis Ababa Action on Financing for Development, also agreed in 2015—have put national fiscal policies ('domestic resource mobilization') at the centre of the development agenda.

Strengthening the revenue-raising capacity of governments is essential to ensure sustainability of poverty reduction measures. While international aid will continue to be critical for many countries and even essential for least developed countries, today domestic tax collection outweighs international aid including in low income countries.[81]

Human rights norms and standards can guide the adoption of more progressive and fair fiscal policies to ensure sufficient, equitable, and accountable financing for development. The adoption of these measures will also be critical to address inequality[82] in compliance with Target 10.4 which mentions the role of fiscal policies.[83] Particularly relevant is the principle of equality and non-discrimination, which may help to guide fiscal policies.[84] Respecting this principle in revenue collection requires setting up a progressive tax system with real redistributive capacity that preserves and progressively increases the income of poorer households. It also

[80] See eg ILO Recommendation R202: Recommendation Concerning National Floors of Social Protection (101st ILC session, 14 June 2012).

[81] Armando Barrientos (2015) 'Forget the Aid Obsession: Development Needs Redistribution Through Fiscal Policy' (Manchester Policy Blogs) <http://blog.policy.manchester.ac.uk/posts/2015/09/forget-the-aid-obsession-development-needs-redistribution-through-fiscal-policy/> accessed 13 August 2019.

[82] World Bank, 'Taking on Inequality' (n 62) 148–51.

[83] SDG10.4 calls to 'adopt policies, especially fiscal, wage and social protection policies, and progressively achieve greater equality'.

[84] See eg UNHRC 'Report of the Special Rapporteur on Extreme Poverty and Human Rights, Magdalena Sepúlveda Carmona' (2014) UN Doc A/HRC/26/28; International Bar Association Human Rights Institute Task Force on Illicit Financial Flows, Poverty and Human Rights, *Tax Abuses, Poverty and Human Rights* (IBAHRI 2013); Thomas Pogge and Krishen Mehta (eds), *Global Tax Fairness* (OUP 2016); and UNHRC 'Report of the Independent Expert on the Promotion of a Democratic and Equitable International Order, Alfred-Maurice de Zayas' (2016) UN Doc A/71/286 (hereafter UNHRC UN Doc A/71/286).

implies that affirmative action measures[85] should be adopted to assist the most disadvantaged individuals and groups that have suffered from historical or persistent discrimination. This would require, for example, the elimination of fuel subsidies which are proven largely to benefit richer groups in society[86] and the design of tax exemptions for the poorest. Increasing the tax base through progressive tax systems would enable states to invest in public goods such as education, legal aid, and health services that are critical for the enjoyment of human rights.

Unfortunately, there is a huge gap between these legal and political commitments and the fiscal policies currently implemented in most countries. In many countries, governments are imposing regressive tax policies, such as increasing value-added tax (VAT) and cutting corporate tax rates, with low revenue potential.[87] Moreover, there is widespread tax avoidance, both by wealthy individuals and by multinational companies. In addition, tax havens and secrecy jurisdictions —often presided over or facilitated by richer countries—continuously drain on national capital and government revenues. Thus, existing fiscal policies deprive developed and developing countries of critical resources to fight poverty, inequality, and ensure realization of human rights. Among the practices that deprives governments of much needed resources is the outdated and unfair international corporate tax system—which enables multinational companies to shift profits away from where they are generated to another country with lower or zero tax rates.[88] Some of these practices are also facilitating money laundering by criminal organizations.

The current international tax framework is certainly not fit for the development agenda of the twenty-first century. Among the central issues to change is to establish an appropriate institutional framework to bring more inclusive participation in global economic governance. While there has been some progress under the G20/OECD Base Erosion and Profit Shifting (BEPS) initiative, the process is not inclusive enough. Discussion related to international corporate tax reforms should move beyond a select number of countries to ensure global participation where developing countries can put forward their priorities with equal voting rights. A proposal has been made, for example, to upgrade the UN Committee of Experts on International Cooperation in Tax Matters to an intergovernmental Commission where all countries would have equal vote.[89] Such a measure would be more in line

[85] For a detailed explanation on how this principle applies to revenue collection see UNHRC A/HRC/26/28' (n 81) paras 12–17.

[86] Javier Arze del Granado, David Coady, and Robert Gillingham (2010) 'The Unequal Benefits of Fuel Subsidies: A Review of Evidence for Developing Countries' IMF Working Paper <https://www.imf.org/external/pubs/ft/wp/2010/wp10202.pdf> accessed 13 August 2019.

[87] Jose Antonio Alonso (2012) 'From Aid to Global Development Policy' DESA Working Paper No 121 <http://www.un.org/esa/desa/papers/2012/wp121_2012.pdf> accessed 13 August 2019.

[88] See eg Independent Commission for the Reform of International Corporate Taxation 'Declaration of the Independent Commission for the Reform of International Corporate Taxation' (hereafter ICRICT, 'Declaration') <https://www.icrict.com/icrict-documentsthe-declaration> accessed 10 October 2019.

[89] See eg ICRICT, 'Declaration' (n 88); UNHRC UN Doc A/71/286 (n 84).

with the fundamental human rights principle of participation[90] as well as with the commitments made in SDG16.8 ('broaden and strengthen the participation of developing countries in the institution of global governance').

While in recent years we have witnessed increased attention to fiscal policies from a human rights perspective, the engagement of human rights advocates on issues of taxation and economic activity is still limited, apart from some notable exceptions.[91] Applying human rights norms and standards to taxation policies requires an interdisciplinary approach. Human rights organizations and organizations that specialize in economic and fiscal policies such as tax justice organizations and trade unions, should strengthen their collaboration.

F. Protecting the Democratic Space

Under SDG16, states have committed to 'promote peaceful and inclusive societies for sustainable development, provide access to justice for all and build effective, accountable and inclusive institutions at all levels'. This goal is valuable in itself, but also essential to achieve other goals, including Goal 1 of ending poverty in all its forms. Goal 16 also represents a huge leap forward from the MDGs, which were silent on issues of governance or civil and political rights. The relevance of democratic freedoms and civil and political rights to development have long been documented,[92] and an approach which recognizes this is much more in line with the human rights framework which holds all rights to be interrelated and indivisible.[93]

While it does not use language that explicitly echoes civil and political rights standards, Goal 16 includes targets on effective, accountable, and transparent institutions (16.6), participatory decision-making (16.7), and promises to 'ensure public access to information and protect fundamental freedoms' (16.10). Yet, in spite of these persuasive commitments, today, in many countries the democratic space is shrinking[94] as a result of restrictions on freedom of expression (eg loose defamation laws, Internet censorship, impunity for killing of journalists); freedom of assembly (eg crackdown on activism and protests); restrictive controls over civil society organizations (eg making overseas funding illegal, excessive surveillance of their activities, and complex non-governmental organizations (NGOs)

[90] See n 29.

[91] Worth stressing is the work of the CESR, which is leading the debate on fiscal policies and human rights. For example, together with other organizations, including the Tax Justice Network, submitted a report to CEDAW Committee that was considered during the review of Switzerland at its 65th session in November 2015.

[92] Amartya Sen, *Development as Freedom* (OUP 1999).

[93] UNGA 'Vienna Declaration and Programme of Action' (12 July 1993) A/CONF.157/23.

[94] Civicus (2013) 'Global Trends on Civil Society Restrictions. Mounting Restrictions on Civil Society: The Gap between Rhetoric and Reality' (Civicus) <http://civicus.org/images/GlobalTrendson CivilSocietyRestrictons2013.pdf> accessed 13 August 2019.

registration procedures).[95] This reality poses a major challenge to the achievement of the SDGs. It is not possible to fight poverty and promote a progressive agenda comprehensively without a democratic civic space.[96]

If properly implemented, human rights norms and standards provide for freedom of expression, freedom of assembly, freedom of association, the right to seek, receive, and impart information, and the right to form and join trade unions and the right to strike, *inter alia*.[97]

At the individual level, these rights can empower people. At the collective level, these rights are critical preconditions for addressing the structural and institutional causes of poverty. For example, the protection of these rights would enable employers and workers' organizations to express their views and negotiate on more equal terms to achieve decent work conditions and minimum (or living) wage levels.

Overcoming poverty requires progressive measures such as minimum wages, increasing investment in public services, implementing progressive fiscal policies, and establishing or expanding social protection systems. Considering that those living in poverty —who stand to benefit most from such policies—are often not represented in political decision-making bodies, and governments may lack political will to enforce these measures, the support of middle classes is often essential. To ensure such support, the work of 'drivers of progressive change', such as women's organizations, representative and democratic trade unions, social movements, and independent media, are essential. Yet, the mere existence of these organizations depends on the respect of the rights and freedoms mentioned above. Thus, a critical challenge for reducing poverty in the twenty-first century is for human rights organizations and progressive organizations to act in solidarity to protect civic and democratic space worldwide.

G. Ensuring Better Monitoring and Accountability

The MDGs were chronically undermined by weak and asymmetrical accountability: a lack of clarity on who was responsible for what, a failure to create conditions in which 'beneficiaries' could meaningfully engage in shaping or challenging decisions, and inadequate, opaque systems to monitor and report on progress.[98]

[95] Civicus, 'Civic Space Initiative' <http://civicus.org/index.php/en/what-we-do-126/2014-04-25-03-26-23/cspi> accessed 13 August 2019.

[96] Andy Sumner (2011) 'Poverty in Middle Income Countries' Institute of Development Studies, The Resource Alliance and the Rockefeller Foundation <https://www.ids.ac.uk/files/dmfile/Bellagio_Sumner1.pdf> accessed 13 August 2019.

[97] See eg ICCPR arts 19, 21, and 22; CEDAW art 7(c); CRC art 15 and ICESCR art 9.

[98] See Philip Alston (2005) 'Ships Passing in the Night: The Current State of the Human Rights and Development Debate Seen Through the Lens of the Millennium Development Goals' 27(3) Human Rights Quarterly 755, 814–25; Kate Donald and Sally-Anne Way (2016) 'Accountability for the

Even the UN Secretary-General acknowledged that lack of accountability was one of the primary reasons for the MDGs' shortfalls.[99]

As a result, civil society and many other actors involved in the process to define the new agenda made it a priority to push for robust accountability for the SDGs[100]. However, in the final 2030 Agenda the content on monitoring and accountability is very weak, with only vague and voluntary commitments. This was a result of political resistance to accountability throughout the negotiations, with initial strong proposals being successively watered down in the face of resistance from many states.[101] Ultimately, the words 'monitoring' and 'accountability' were resisted in favour of the more anodyne phrase 'follow-up and review'. The final 2030 Agenda encourages Member States to 'conduct regular and inclusive reviews of progress at the national and sub-national levels, which are country-led and country-driven' (2030 Agenda, para 79), and proposes a number of principles for 'follow-up and review' processes, including that they will be 'people-centred, gender-sensitive, respect human rights' (para 74). However, the voluntary nature of reviews is stressed repeatedly, and only very tentative suggestions for review structures and processes at national, regional, and international levels are included. Among other weaknesses, the lack of recognition of the need for independent civil society monitoring, data collection, and reporting is striking, raising the risk of review mechanisms based entirely on government's official reports without any space for alternative views.[102]

At the international level, the High-level Political Forum on Sustainable Development (HLPF) was designated as the central platform for the follow-up and review of the SDGs.[103] The power of the HLPF to review and hold states accountable is weak and limited, especially given its reliance on voluntary self-reporting by states, and a meeting time of only eight days per year. At the 2016 HLPF (the first since the adoption of the SDGs), only a day-and-a-half was allocated to the national reviews, and the presentations by the twenty-two volunteer states seemed at times more focused on giving the most positive gloss than on really sharing implementation challenges and strategies[104]—not markedly different from the voluntary 'Annual Ministerial Reviews' of the MDG era.

Sustainable Development Goals: A Lost Opportunity?' 30(2) Ethics and International Affairs 201 (hereafter Donald and Way, 'Accountability for the Sustainable Development Goals').

[99] UNGA (2010) 'Keeping the Promise: A Forward-Looking Review to Promote an Agreed Action Agenda to Achieve the Millennium Development Goals by 2015' UN Doc A/64/665 para 116.

[100] See CESR and UNOHCHR (2013) 'Who Will be Accountable? Human Rights and the Post-2015 Development Agenda' (United Nations) (hereafter CESR and UNOHCHR 'Who Will be Accountable?') <http://www.ohchr.org/Documents/Publications/WhoWillBeAccountable.pdf> accessed 13 August 2019.

[101] See Donald and Way, 'Accountability for the Sustainable Development Goals' (n 98).

[102] Ibid.

[103] UNGA 67/290 (9 July 2013).

[104] CESR, 'Accountability Left Behind in SDG Follow-up and Review' <http://www.cesr.org/accountability-left-behind-sdg-follow-and-review> accessed 13 August 2019.

Without greater accountability for how poverty eradication/reduction policies are designed and implemented, and especially for their gaps and failures, poverty cannot be holistically tackled and measures are likely to be inappropriate or unsustainable. The lack of accountability for the SDGs at this stage may be the main factor that undermines their claim to be rights based, or their usefulness for human rights advocates.

However, as SDG implementation and monitoring evolves there will be opportunities to innovate new strategies for holding states and other actors accountable to their promises, building on existing human rights and social accountability tactics. The human rights normative framework—which has accountability as its cornerstone—may assist in providing new avenues for accountability of the SDGs, both in pursuing redress and corrective action in case of violations, but also in determining which aspects of implementation are working and what needed to be adjusted. Tactics and strategies used in the human rights field—such as the 'shadow reporting' to the UN treaty bodies—may also be usefully brought in to civil society monitoring of the SDGs.

The role of the existing human rights accountability system may also prove to be significant. Existing human rights mechanisms such as UN treaty bodies, the Universal Periodic Review (UPR) and Special procedures and, increasingly, regional bodies such as the European Commissioner for Human Rights and the European Committee for Social Rights are already monitoring compliance with obligations regarding economic, social, and cultural rights as well as civil and political rights. In many cases, the human rights cases that they examine and the recommendations they make have a large degree of overlap with the SDG commitments. Human rights mechanisms therefore have great potential for rigorously monitoring SDG progress—including on poverty and related human rights deprivations—through the lens of human rights obligations.

Engaging with human rights mechanisms could provide an alternative space for questioning some of the SDG data, methods, assumptions, and narratives, focusing on individuals and communities and drawing on civil society perspectives and expertise rather than relying solely on official statistics or 'big data'. Moreover, human rights standards can provide alternative (and in many cases more rigorous) benchmarks against which to judge progress.[105] This alternative space could prove particularly important for the inequality and 'leave no one behind' agendas. However, we can expect there will be political resistance to human rights mechanisms taking up this role.

Domestic human rights actors such as national human rights institutions may also be able to play a useful role in monitoring SDG progress through the lens of

[105] CESR (2016) 'From Disparity to Dignity: A Human Rights Agenda for Tackling Economic Inequality Through the Sustainable Development Goals' (CESR) <http://www.cesr.org/disparity-dignity-inequality-and-sdgs> accessed 13 August 2019.

human rights obligations, although many face constraints on their capacity, independence, and mandate.[106] Meanwhile, although the SDGs themselves are not legally binding, there are certainly legal avenues which could be brought to bear where their implementation (or lack thereof) creates or overlaps with a human rights violation.[107]

Given that the SDGs include a goal (16) on peace and governance, with targets on access to justice (16.3) and effective, accountable, and transparent institutions at all levels (16.6), it is somewhat of a contradiction that the SDGs themselves have little if any real accountability attached to them. However, at the domestic level advocates may be able to make use of Goal 16 to push for greater access to justice for people affected by development-related injustices, and to make the institutions responsible for implementing and monitoring the SDGs (from Ministries of Finance to National Statistical Offices) more transparent and accountable.

IV. Concluding Observations

There is no doubt that the ambitious and self-proclaimed transformative potential of the SDGs can be viewed with considerable scepticism. Similarly, the grand claims by international organizations,[108] financial institutions,[109] and philanthropic foundations[110] that (extreme) poverty can be eliminated by 2030 can be questioned. Such optimism seems not to match the entrenched challenges that the world faces today, such as unprecedented forced displacement and the increasing poverty in places affected by conflict and fragility,[111] climate change, and historically high levels of income and wealth inequality, among others.

[106] CESR and Danish Institute for Human Rights (2015) 'Realizing Rights Through the Sustainable Development Goals: The Role of National Human Rights Institutions' (CESR and DIHR) <https://www.humanrights.dk/files/media/dokumenter/udgivelser/research/nhri_briefingpaper_may2015.pdf> accessed 13 August 2019

[107] See CESR and UNOHCHR 'Who Will be Accountable?' (n 100) 39.

[108] The Secretary General of the United Nations has stated 'there is no question that we can deliver on our shared responsibility to put an end to poverty, leave no one behind and create a world of dignity for all'. UN, *MDG Report 2015* (n 1) 3.

[109] In 2013, the World Bank Group announced the goal of eradication of extreme poverty. More precisely, the goal is to bring the number of extremely poor people, defined as those living on less than 1.25 PPP-adjusted dollars a day, to less than 3 per cent of the world population by 2030.

[110] For example, Melinda and Bill Gates writing on the SDGs have noted: 'We are confident that [ending poverty in all its forms everywhere by 2030] is not only possible, but that we will see major breakthroughs along the way, which will provide unprecedented opportunities to people in poor countries. Indeed, we think their lives will improve faster in the next 15 years than at any other time in history—and that their lives will improve more than anyone else's.' See Bill Gates and Melinda Gates, 'Promises to Keep' (Project Syndicate, 20 January 2016) <https://www.project-syndicate.org/commentary/gates-foundation-2016-priorities-by-bill-gates-and-melinda-gates-2016-01> accessed 13 August 2019.

[111] As recorded in 2012, 39.9 per cent of population in fragile and conflicted-affected situations live below the international poverty line: World Bank <http://data.worldbank.org/topic/poverty> accessed 13 August 2019.

Moreover, as the result of a lengthy intergovernmental political process, the new development framework certainly includes worrying contradictions, compromises, and tensions. For example, despite its claim to be 'transformative' and inclusion of several goals and targets which would require major upheavals to the current economic model (eg a drastic shift to 'sustainable consumption and production'), SDG8 still expresses a vision of development dependent on economic growth.[112] In addition, it is yet not clear how implementation will unfold at the domestic level.[113]

Despite all these shortcomings, the adoption of the SDGs implied a significant departure from the MDGs. Not only was there an attempt to undertake a more participatory process in designing the goals and targets, including broad consultations,[114] but also there was a real effort to give attention to a broad range of urgent social, environmental, and economic challenges. The agenda has incorporated several elements, discussed in this chapter, that have the potential to change the course of development. Now, facing the challenge of meeting potentially transformative commitments such as the SDGs forces us to critically review all perspectives and approaches.

This chapter has examined how looking at some of the goals and targets from a human rights approach might assist in fulfilling their more ground-breaking aspects. Certainly, a rights approach does not provide answers to all the challenges the world confronts to overcoming poverty, but it does provide us with an opportunity to rethink some of the policy responses implemented so far.

The achievement of the SDGs will require unprecedented coordination among all different actors and stakeholders. Currently, the various players involved in the implementation of the SDGs seem to have divergent interests and agendas—as described earlier in the case of social protection. If this continues, the limited funds for implementation will be diffused and interventions fragmented. Human rights have the potential to provide a common language and framework for action.

While today most countries have ratified a range of relevant human rights treaties and many have formally adopted a rights-based approach to development, challenges remain in the application and enforcement of human rights norms and standards in development policies. Although some major actors have already expressed commitments to mainstreaming human rights in their work such as all UN agencies, funds, and programmes,[115] others—in particular international

[112] UNRISD (2016) *Policy Innovations for Transformative Change: Implementing the 2030 Agenda for Sustainable Development* (UNRISD).

[113] Moreover, considering that it is a very broad agenda, there could be selectivity and fragmentation in the implementation efforts at the domestic level, where the most challenging targets could be neglected for political or financial reasons.

[114] There were broad consultations globally, regionally, and by countries, that claim to have involved more than 1 million people across all countries and from all backgrounds. See United Nations Development Group (2013) *A Million Voices: The World We Want* (United Nations).

[115] See eg United Nations Development Group (2003) 'UN Statement of Common Understanding on Human Rights-Based Approaches to Development Cooperation and Programming' and the

financial institutions (IFIs)—have been actively reluctant to embrace human rights.[116] Undoubtedly, there are major gaps between the legal recognition of rights by governments and their compliance. The causes for this are broad and varied, ranging from limited policy space for national governments (eg due to constraints imposed by IFIs, trade deals, and the international tax system) to active resistance to a rights approach.

For us, the latter seems particularly relevant for the present analysis. Certainly, there are daunting political obstacles to the more widespread adoption of a rights approach in development. While many of those responsible for the design and implementation of the new agenda—from UN agencies to IFIs to national governments—pay rhetorical lip service to human rights, few if any seem actively poised to undertake the far-reaching rethinking of policies and economic models necessary. One manifestation of this tendency to fall back on the status quo is the considerable enthusiasm and attention given to partnerships with the private sector (in particular transnational corporations) for the implementation of the agenda[117]—far more than to partnerships with civil society. This poses several problems in terms of accountability and transparency, as well as giving huge power to actors who have an interest in maintaining the economic status quo rather than embracing 'transformation'.

Disciplinary dependency also seems to be a significant source of resistance to a human rights approach to development. Fully embracing a rights-based approach to poverty reduction requires policy-makers and researchers to overcome silos and embrace interdisciplinarity. There is a need to deepen the analysis of poverty and its causes, and to forge better collaboration between those working on human rights, social development, political science, and macro-economics.

As has been noted, compliance with the SDGs requires a 'change of mindset and some humility'.[118] Achieving the full realization of the SDGs does not only require major national and international efforts but also better collaboration among various disciplines. New policy interventions for poverty reduction require incorporating the work of a variety of specialists such as development practitioners, economists,

2013 'Rights Up Front' initiative, launched by UN Secretary-General Ban Ki-moon. An increasing number of UN agencies integrate human rights into their internal policies and actively advocate for human rights through their mandated work. For concrete examples on how this is done, see the UN Practitioners' Portal on Human Rights Based Approaches to Programming <http://hrbaportal.org/mainstreaming-hrba> accessed 13 August 2019.

[116] See eg UNHRC (2015) 'Report of the Special Rapporteur on Extreme Poverty and Human Rights, Philip Alston' UN Doc. A/70/274. In this report, the current Special Rapporteur concludes that the approach taken by the World Bank to human rights is 'incoherent, counterproductive and unsustainable'. He notes that 'the World Bank is a human rights-free zone'.

[117] Global Policy Watch (2016) 'United Nations and Business Community, Out-Sourcing or Crowding In?' (Global Policy Forum) <https://www.globalpolicywatch.org/wpcontent/uploads/2016/10/GPW13_2016_10_04.pdf> accessed 13 August 2019.

[118] Richard Jolly, 'Breaking the Cycle of Poverty' (UNA-UK, 1 March 2016) <https://www.sustainablegoals.org.uk/breaking-cycle-poverty/> accessed 10 October 2019.

human rights lawyers, tax specialists, political scientists, journalists, and sociologists. It is through a collaborative interdisciplinary approach that the complexities and scale of the challenges can be effectively addressed.

This interdisciplinary approach—expressly including human rights advocates—should be incorporated by all the actors that have a stake in implementing the 2030 Agenda. Thus, governments, UN system, international financial institutions, private sector and civil society organizations, should all be broadening their perspectives. Moreover, there is a need to break down intra-institutional silos and more rapidly incorporate the findings of emerging research into praxis and policy. For example, while the IMF's research branch is now steadily questioning the neoliberal model[119] (including trickle-down economics and austerity in response to financial crises), this has not translated into the IMF more broadly, critically reflecting on the conditions it imposes and the policies it demands when extending loans to countries.

Yet, as stressed in this chapter, overcoming this reluctance to meaningfully engage with the international human rights framework and its implications for development might be the key to unfolding the transformative potential of the SDGs. Certainly, we must be ready to admit that the dominant approaches to tackling poverty over the last several decades have had only limited success and in many cases have not been sustainable or comprehensive. Moreover, the manifestations of poverty continue to change and evolve, and due to environmental concerns and other considerations we can no longer rely on pure economic growth to lift people out of poverty. In order to meet the challenge of SDG1 and fully eradicate extreme poverty while also robustly tackling multidimensional poverty, we cannot expect the old models and policies to yield the results promised.

[119] Jonathan Ostry, Prakash Loungani, and Davide Furceri (2016) 'Neoliberalism: Oversold?' (International Monetary Fund) <http://www.imf.org/external/pubs/ft/fandd/2016/06/ostry.htm> accessed 13 August 2019.

IV

ENVIRONMENT

13

The State of Play and the Road Ahead

The Environment and Human Rights

Kerri Woods

Since they were established as a key part of the post-Second World War international order, human rights, as both an institutional framework and as an idea, have been adopted and adapted by those seeking to address the most pressing problems of their age. The framers of the Universal Declaration of Human Rights (1948) never dreamed of including environmental rights in the list of rights that are fundamental to a decent human life. However, by the early years of the twenty-first century, it had become clear that environmental problems generate profound human rights impacts and that a sustainable environment is essential to the enjoyment of all human rights.

Climate change has been widely regarded as the most pressing global environmental problem of the current age. If we are to address climate change adequately it seems inevitable that we must at least consider what insights might arise from doing so through the lens of human rights. Anthropogenic climate change is predicted to have severe impacts on human well-being. We expect to witness an increase in the frequency of severe weather events, a greater geographical spread of tropical diseases, increased risks of flooding, and the permanent loss of low-lying areas in some coastal areas, some Pacific Island States, and parts of Arctic regions. These impacts are all associated with climate change and will have clear implications for human rights to life, health, and subsistence.[1] Moreover, these human rights threats will be unevenly distributed, with women, children, the poor, and indigenous peoples recognized as being particularly vulnerable to the impacts of climate change.[2]

We should also note that while climate change is undoubtedly the most urgently discussed global environmental problem, it is not the only environmental issue that has a claim on those concerned with justice to future generations. For example, the alarming rate of biodiversity loss that we are witnessing at the beginning

[1] Simon Caney, 'Climate Change, Human Rights, and Moral Thresholds' in Stephen Humphreys (ed), *Human Rights and Climate Change* (CUP 2010) (hereafter Caney, 'Climate Change').

[2] UNHRC 'Report of the Independent Expert on the Issue of Human Rights Obligations Relating to the Enjoyment of a Safe, Clean, Healthy and Sustainable Environment' John H Knox (24 December 2012) A/HRC/22/43 (hereafter UNHRC, 'Human Rights Obligations').

Kerri Woods, *The State of Play and the Road Ahead* In: Human Rights and 21st Century Challenges. Edited by: Dapo Akande, Jaakko Kuosmanen, Helen McDermott, and Dominic Roser, Published by Oxford University Press 2020.
DOI: 10.1093/oso/9780198824770.003.0014

of the twenty-first century is a serious concern not only from our own point of view but perhaps even more so from the point of view of future generations.[3] However, it has received much less attention in both the scholarly literature on human rights and in international political debates. Yet, in so far as biodiversity performs important ecosystem services, it is fundamentally important to the maintenance of human rights. Indeed, we cannot enjoy any rights at all over the long term if our stocks of food, air, and water are not supported by sustainable and healthy ecosystem services.

Although Aldo Leopold's (1949) landmark work on environmental stewardship, *A Sand County Almanac*, was a contemporary of the Universal Declaration of Human Rights (1948), the close interconnection between human well-being and the sustainability of Earth's ecological systems was not widely understood at the point at which the International Bill of Rights was being drafted. Significantly, early articulations of environmental ethics tended not to draw upon the language of rights to make a claim for environmental protection. Indeed, the trend in environmental ethics was generally hostile towards, or at least suspicious of, institutions that have their roots in liberal ideology, as human rights undoubtedly do.[4] The reason for this is clear: the economic practices that have created systematic environmental degradation are themselves closely connected to the idea of rights, particularly property rights and national territorial rights, which posit a relation between the human and the non-human as one of ownership and legitimate exploitation. Environmental ethicists have sometimes been sceptical of the likelihood of being able to develop principles of sustainability that genuinely do justice to non-human nature and to future generations of humans whilst drawing on an ideological framework that is historically so steeped in attitudes that singularly failed to register the ecological dependence of humanity.[5]

On this view of the environment and human rights, the fact that biodiversity does not register immediately as a human rights concern might tell us something about human rights themselves. They are undeniably anthropocentric: they presuppose that the individual human is the relevant unit of moral concern. It is direct human interests and needs that are at the heart of human rights, as one would expect. The absence of explicit rights to environmental goods that are crucial for the support of human life amongst the pantheon of influential human rights treaties indicates that we have historically taken environmental goods for granted. We had not imagined that environmental problems might ever feature amongst the 'standard threats' to human dignity, from which human rights protect all humans.[6]

[3] Bradley Cardinale, Emmett Duffy, Andrew Gonzalez, David Hooper, Charles Perrings, *et al* (2012) 'Biodiversity Loss and Its Impact on Humanity' Nature 486, 56–67.

[4] Kerri Woods, *Human Rights* (Palgrave Macmillan 2014).

[5] John Barry, *Nature, Virtue, Progress* (Sage 1999).

[6] Henry Shue, *Basic Rights: Subsistence, Affluence and US Foreign Policy* (2nd edn, Princeton University Press 1990).

At the beginning of the twenty-first century, this is beginning to change. Human rights theory and practice are beginning to reflect the fact that humans are ecologically embedded beings. But even this emergent environmental sensitivity does not fully address the concern that in a human rights framework human interests will trump other concerns. That being the case, from an ecocentric point of view, the interests of non-human nature are likely to suffer to a greater or lesser degree.

Human rights theory and practice are of course connected, but they cannot be reduced to a single, coherent narrative. Human rights theory has been concerned at one level with the explanatory work of understanding the nature and function of human rights, and at another level with providing normative arguments in support of one or another vision of the scope and content of human rights and their associated duties. Human rights practice can be understood by examining the domestic laws and international treaties that constrain and place obligations on state governments and other relevant actors. But human rights practice is also in part to be found in the demands and processes of negotiation pursued by social movements, non-governmental organizations, and civil society actors. While human rights theorists have given greater attention to substantive environmental human rights, it is procedural environmental human rights that have often been most important for environmental activists, and which have arguably played the greater role in facilitating environmental protection.[7] Traditional civil and political rights, such as the rights to freedom of speech, rights against arbitrary arrest, rights to a fair trial, as well as rights to access information in relation to proposed development projects, have been crucial to the success of many environmental activists' campaigns.[8] In some contexts, in the face of authoritarian regimes pursuing environmentally damaging development policies, engaging in environmental activism presents a threat to the right to life. Of course, it may well be the case that the relative utility of procedural rights reflects not (or not only) the advanced state of such rights, but the relative failure of institutional actors to agree and enact substantive environmental human rights.

Indeed, having noted the practical value of procedural rights for environmental campaigners, we should also note that the symbolic importance of a new, distinct environmental human right or treaty is not lost on activists. As already noted, there is, as yet, no globally agreed declaration of, or treaty recognizing, distinctly environmental human rights. However, there are a number of laws and treaties at national, regional, and global levels that are relevant here, and we may well see international agreement in this area in the future. The constitutions of some 125 countries contain some reference to the environment, and 75 contain references

[7] Aaron Sachs (1995) 'Eco-Justice: Linking Human Rights and the Environment' (World Watch Paper 127); Ole Pedersen (2010) 'Climate Change and Human Rights: Amicable or Arrested Development?' 1(2) Journal of the Environment and Human Rights 236–51.

[8] Conor Gearty (2010) 'Do Human Rights Help or Hinder Environmental Protection?' 1(1) Journal of Human Rights and the Environment 7–22.

to a right to a safe, healthy, or clean environment.[9] Regional human rights bodies such as the Inter-American Commission on Human Rights, and global organizations such as the United Nations Environment Programme and the United Nations High Commissioner for Human Rights, have in recent years contributed significant work to emerging norms around environmental human rights. In the latter case, this is observable not least in the appointment of John Knox, first as an Independent Expert, and subsequently as a United Nations Human Rights Committee Special Rapporteur on the environment.

As Knox notes in his contribution to this volume, the recent Paris climate change conference was an intriguing focal point for the development of efforts to connect human rights and climate change formally in a binding international agreement. Indeed, Knox reads the Paris Agreement as a human rights treaty. The Paris talks gave rise to considerable debate amongst the state parties to the Agreement as to whether or not the obligations to which states would be committed could and should be framed in terms of human rights. Alongside this, transnational social movements and civil society actors vigorously lobbied state parties to include commitments to human rights in the final agreement.[10] Three networks of scholars, activists, and lawyers published texts of declarations of human rights and climate change to coincide with the Paris talks, undoubtedly moving forward efforts to realize substantive new environmental human right(s), and implicitly sidelining the extensionist approach (which sees environment rights extrapolated from existing rights). One of the declarations proposed explicitly sought to define environmental rights in ways that decentred the anthropocentrism hitherto inherent in human rights.[11] Although the Paris Agreement that emerged was not in any formal sense a human rights treaty, Knox nevertheless argues in Chapter 15 of this book that the Paris Agreement was deeply shaped by numerous developments in regional and international law in recent years that have built momentum towards much greater recognition of environmental human rights in global legal practice. As he has argued elsewhere, however, the status of rights of future generations remains less established.[12]

If we turn away from human rights practice and look at the fields of legal and political theory, since James Nickel's seminal essay (1993) on the right to a safe environment, we find that attention has focused on: (i) the justification of substantive environmental human rights as constitutional rights;[13] (ii) whether environmental

[9] Chris Jeffords and Joshua Gellers (2017) 'Constitutionalizing Environmental Rights: A Practical Guide' 9(1) Journal of Human Rights Practice 1.

[10] Kirsten Davies, Sam Adelman, Anna Grear, Catherine Lorns Magallanes, Tom Kearns, *et al* (2017) 'The Declaration on Human Rights and Climate Change: A New Legal Tool for Global Policy Change' 8(2) Journal of Human Rights and the Environment 217–53.

[11] Ibid.

[12] UNHRC, 'Human Rights Obligations' (n 2).

[13] James Nickel (1993) 'The Human Right to a Safe Environment: Philosophical Perspectives on its Scope and Justification' 18 Yale Journal of International Law 281–96; Tim Hayward, *Constitutional Environmental Rights* (OUP 2005); Richard Hiskes, *The Human Right to a Green Future* (CUP 2009).

human rights are best pursued by an extensionist approach, or by articulating a new, distinctly environmental right;[14] as well as on (iii) whether and how an intrinsically anthropocentric framework such as human rights can serve to realise environmental sustainability, given the role that anthropocentric ideologies are held to have played in perpetuating the ecological crisis we now face.[15]

However, the most striking feature of contemporary debates invoking intergenerational environmental human rights is that they are much less about rights than they are about duties. In this literature, the principal role of environmental rights is a justificatory one: environmental rights are used to underpin normative arguments concerning the duties of the current generation towards future ones. One reason this is intriguing is that it represents a distinct shift from previous work in environmental ethics that strived to radically reconceptualize both the content of ethics and the normative architecture employed to articulate it. While an earlier generation of green scholars was sceptical of liberal thought in general and rights in particular, a new generation of scholars has found in human rights a rich seam worth exploring. For example, Tim Hayward argues that, in the context of liberal democracies being the standard for legitimacy in international political practice, it is important to make the liberal case for taking full account of our environmental interests, and articulating this in the language of human rights given the normative weight associated with these rights.[16] As the urgency of climate change has intensified, the pro-liberal approach to environmental ethics has opened the door to an explicit focus on the interrelationship between human rights and climate change, which has in turn prompted sustained reflection on the question of whether and why future generations can be said to be bearers of rights.[17]

Dominic Roser's Chapter 14 in this book is an addition to the literature that uses the normative architecture of rights as a starting point for thinking through some of the complex issues that arise when we consider what we owe to future generations. Specifically, Roser looks at the relationship between rights and risks, and proposes a new way of evaluating risks, based on rights, which promises to clear much of the confusion in existing debates about the appropriate application of the precautionary principle to questions of what is owed to future generations. Roser's approach furthers the entrenchment of human rights (including rights held by

[14] Caney, 'Climate Change' (n 1); Kerri Woods, *Human Rights and Environmental Sustainability* (Edward Elgar 2010).

[15] Klaus Bosselmann, 'Human Rights and the Environment: Redefining Fundamental Principles?' in Brendan Gleeson and Nicholas Low (eds), *Governing for the Environment: Global Problems, Ethics and Democracy* (Palgrave Macmillan 2001) 118–34. Catherine Redgwell, 'Life, the Universe and Everything: A Critique of Anthropocentric Rights' in Alan Boyle and Michael Anderson (eds) *Human Rights Approaches to Environmental Protection* (Oxford Clarendon Press 1996) 71–88; Anna Grear (2011) 'The Vulnerable Living Order: Human Rights and the Environment in a Critical and Philosophical Perspective' 2(1) Journal of Human Rights and the Environment 23–44.

[16] Tim Hayward, *Constitutional Environmental Rights* (OUP 2005).

[17] Stephen Humphreys, *Human Rights and Climate Change* (CUP 2010).

future generations) as a key normative principle for tackling climate change in the twenty-first century.

Many would accept that status for human rights, but it does invite some questions about the scope of the community of rights-bearers that seems to be implied by the application of rights thinking to intergenerational issues. Richard Hiskes' distinct account of environmental human rights considers such rights to be properly group rights of future generations, not of all humans, but of the humans who will come to live under a given constitution––that is, future generations of Americans have rights against the current government of the United States but not against the government of China, and so on.[18] This is perhaps close to contemporary human rights legal practice, but it frames the rights of future humans as essentially parochial rights, which, of course, presents a challenge given the transboundary nature of environmental issues such as climate change. If human rights practice were to take full account of humans' status as ecologically embedded beings then we might expect the scope of the political community demarcated by membership of rights to stretch across time *and* space. The state-centrism of constitutional rights potentially limits the extent to which current generations have the power to protect future generations from environmental harms. Such rights, by definition, do not have global reach. Thus the rights thresholds for succeeding generations will be set not globally, but by each state, unless there is a global agreement (eg to limit greenhouse gas emissions to a given global level). Moreover, Jonas Brännmark agrees with Hiskes that future generations' environmental human rights are group rights, but he argues that the correlative duty-bearers today will in fact have much less influence than future generations' contemporaries will over the question of whether or not future people's environmental rights will be fulfilled.[19] While the total ecological inheritance of future generations will be determined by present actions, future decisions will make a significant difference to the socially produced distribution of benefits and burdens, and to inequalities, within future generations. Notwithstanding the profound impacts that current patterns of production and consumption have on the health and resilience of global ecosystems, socially created inequalities have considerable influence on the enjoyment of rights within the given ecological context. As noted earlier, it is expected that the impacts of climate change will fall disproportionately on many groups who are already vulnerable: women, children, and the poor among them. In so far as these vulnerabilities are significantly socially produced and maintained, Brännmark argues that it is future societies' distributive decisions that will have the biggest impact on whether or not members of future generations environment-related human rights will be secure.

[18] Richard Hiskes, *The Human Right to a Green Future* (CUP 2009).

[19] Jonas Brännmark (2016) 'Future Generations as Rights Holders' 19(6) Critical Review of International Social and Political Philosophy 680–98.

That conclusion invites reflection on a further set of issues that preoccupied environmental thinkers before the turn to liberalism: what does a green good life look like? The human rights approach would seem largely to leave these sorts of questions open––the freedoms protected in human rights offer the possibility of legitimately pursuing a diverse array of ways of life, supported by a diverse range of underlying values. In contrast, environmental ethicists have previously had much to say on the morality of sustainable ways of life, and of the core environmental values underpinning such ways of life.[20] Few serious commentators are prepared to condemn human rights these days; we take it for granted that such rights are a good thing and that all humans everywhere are entitled to these rights. But this privileged status for human rights sometimes leads us to overlook the fact that human rights do not represent the totality of ethics, nor does a human rights approach necessarily yield solutions where conflicts of rights emerge. For example, the human rights framework does not necessarily help us to resolve the conflicts which are increasingly apparent between current and future generations over rights to the use of resources, be those finite resources (such as fossil fuels) or renewables that can nevertheless be depleted through overuse (such as carbon sinks). We tend to think that human rights and environmental goals go together, but of course it matters a great deal how human rights like the right to development are pursued. Taking seriously the notion of environmental human rights seems to lead human rights advocates to a somewhat less open account of what a good life is, if we are committed to respecting the human rights of both current and future generations. Certainly, respecting the rights of future humans is not compatible with the continuation of currently dominant patterns of production and consumption. More troublingly, recent analysis shows that the Sustainable Development Goals are not in fact all mutually achievable for current and future generations if we continue on current trajectories of resource consumption.[21] In short, the stresses on global ecological systems are unsustainable. Along with the development of more substantive environmental human rights at the global level, this possible re-engagement with notions of a green good life through the prism of human rights is an intriguing area for future research. If nothing else, one might expect to find more critical reflection on the implications of the right to development, not just for developing countries but also in terms of the environmental obligations this may entail for developed countries.

One solution to conflicts around development, much favoured by somewhat misanthropic green scholars of the 1970s and 1980s focused on decreasing the numbers of human beings.[22] It seems intuitively obvious that if we cut the number

[20] Robin Attfield, *The Ethics of the Global Environment* (Edinburgh University Press 1999); John Barry, *Nature, Virtue, Progress* (Sage 1999) (hereafter Attfield, *Global Environment*).

[21] Viktoria Spaiser, Shyam Ranganathan, Ranjla Bali Swain, and David Sumpter (2016) 'The Sustainable Development Oxymoron: Quantifying and Modelling the Incompatibility of Sustainable Development Goals' International Journal of Sustainable Development and World Ecology 1–14.

[22] Attfield, *Global Environment* (n 20).

of people consuming environmental resources, then we will cut the volume of environmental resources being consumed, and pollution being produced. One might even make a case, based on the human rights of future generations, that current generations have a *duty* to limit their procreation. However, as Simon Caney demonstrates Chapter 16 of this book, there are grounds for rejecting this narrow reading of what rights entail, and there are, more importantly, good reasons not to isolate population as the salient variable in trying to manage levels of environmental pollution and degradation. Levels of technology and, crucially, the kind of lifestyle that current and future citizens consider acceptable and desirable, will have a massive impact on the realisation of environmental rights, both now and in the future. Surprisingly, then, Caney's argument prompts reflection on whether recognition of genuinely equal human rights to development, and equal rights to procreation, might direct us to return to the previously fashionable question of what kind of lifestyle is environmentally sustainable and therefore normatively justifiable.

It is evident, then, that the intersection of environmental issues and human rights presents both challenges and opportunities for understanding the rights of future generations. A common theme amongst the papers in this section is the presupposition that future generations are part of our community of rights-bearers, and, furthermore, that thinking through the implications of this status helps us better understand what intergenerational environmental justice demands of us and our governments, now. Understanding the environmental rights of future generations prompts us to confront difficult questions about what kinds of risks can be justified, what kinds of lifestyles can be pursued, and what kinds of political and legal obligations are required to deliver a just and sustainable future.

14

Don't Look Too Far

Rights as a Rationale for the Precautionary Principle

Dominic Roser

I. Introduction

Uncertainty matters. In the case of climate policy, which is the primary example for this chapter, any side in the current debate will typically defend its position at some point or other by reference to uncertainty.[1] In the latest Synthesis Report of the Intergovernmental Panel on Climate Change (IPCC), the first two pages are already devoted to the topic of uncertainty.[2] A rich and carefully crafted terminology is used to convey levels of confidence, degrees of agreement, and the extent of evidence regarding findings. Appreciating the extent of uncertainty makes all the difference for policy choice.

How precisely should uncertainty affect policy choice? This is the theme of precautionary principles. These principles capture the type and extent of cautiousness that seems appropriate in the face of uncertainty. Instinctively, we are averse to risk and endorse the idea of 'better safe than sorry'. If we could predict the future effects of current greenhouse gas emissions with certainty, there would still be much reason to reduce emissions—but add uncertainty and there is even more reason to do so. Precautionary principles come in many shapes and sizes and they are sometimes taken to be nothing more than a vague and general call for protection from environmental harm. But in so far as there is something distinctive about precautionary principles, their gist consists of expressing and specifying this intuition about a cautious response to uncertainty. Article 3 of the United Nations Framework Convention on Climate Change (UNFCCC) provides a prominent example of a precautionary principle: 'Where there are threats of serious or

[1] A terminological remark: Unless otherwise noted, I will use the expressions 'uncertainty' and 'risk' in a non-technical sense as catch-all terms for the opposite to certainty. They thus subsume more narrowly defined notions of risk, (Knightian) uncertainty, ignorance, ambiguity, etc. As far as risk is concerned, I will additionally use the term to denote (usually: bad) outcomes which do not happen with certainty.

[2] Rajendra Pachauri and Leo Meyer (eds), *Climate Change 2014: Synthesis Report. Contribution of Working Groups I, II and III to the Fifth Assessment Report of the Intergovernmental Panel on Climate Change* (IPCC 2014).

Dominic Roser, *Don't Look Too Far* In: Human Rights and 21st Century Challenges. Edited by: Dapo Akande, Jaakko Kuosmanen, Helen McDermott, and Dominic Roser, Published by Oxford University Press 2020.

DOI: 10.1093/oso/9780198824770.003.0015

irreversible damage, lack of full scientific certainty should not be used as a reason for postponing [precautionary] measures'.

Precautionary principles, however, are controversial. Their wording as well as the associated literature can be criticized as either demanding the obvious or else calling for the extreme, at least when taken literally.[3] The latter criticism about extremism can be interpreted not only to cover precautionary principles themselves but also the underlying intuition about cautiousness which they spell out. The worry is that the intuition does not track an important normative truth about the proper response to uncertainty but rather reflects an overly conservative, fear-driven, and irrational gut feeling. However, this chapter sets out to show that the 'cautiousness intuition' is basically sound by providing a rationale for it. Such a vindication not only counters the extremism charge but also provides the blueprint for a more carefully worded version of the precautionary principle.

If a precautionary principle is to be suitable for political practice it must fulfil two criteria (besides relying on a sound rationale). According to the first criterion, the recommendations derived from a precautionary principle must deviate from other prominent responses to uncertainty. If a precautionary principle does not call for more cautiousness than we would pursue anyway, there is no need for enshrining it in policy documents. Meeting this first criterion allows a precautionary principle to escape the charge of stating the obvious, that is, of being trivial, vacuous, or redundant. There are in particular two prominent approaches to uncertainty from which the precautionary principle must deviate.

- The Expectational Approach:The first approach from which a precautionary principle needs to deviate is the response to uncertain prospects that one would pursue if these uncertain prospects were evaluated the same as their expectation. In order to illustrate this approach by way of an oversimplified example, assume that there is uncertainty about the outcome of a climate policy: it might lead to a warming of either 1 °C or 3 °C, each with 50 per cent probability. The expected outcome of this policy—that is, multiplying each possible outcome by its probability and then adding up these products—is 2 °C. The expectational approach suggests evaluating the uncertain climate policy the same way that we would evaluate a climate policy that would lead to its expectation (ie 2 °C) with certainty. This is the basic version of the expectational approach. A more refined version of the expectational approach evaluates policies not in terms of their expected *outcome* but in terms of the expected *value of their outcomes*. For example: assume that value is measured in terms of welfare and that a 1 °C warming yields a welfare loss of 10 units, 2 °C warming yields a welfare loss of 20 units, and 3 °C warming yields (due to

[3] See Stephen Gardiner (2006) 'A Core Precautionary Principle' 14(1) Journal of Political Philosophy 33, 33–60.

having crossed a tipping point) a welfare loss of 100 units. In that case, the *expected* welfare loss of a warming of 1 °C or 3 °C (each with a 50 per cent probability) is more than the welfare loss associated with a certain warming of 2 °C. Thus, the uncertain policy would be evaluated less favourably than the certain policy.[4]

- The Tempting Approach:The second benchmark from which a non-trivial precautionary principle needs to deviate is the response to uncertainty that we are tempted to pursue given common human weaknesses and biases such as selfishness, myopia, or all kinds of probability-related irrationalities. The status quo manifested in current policies often reflects the tempting approach.

A second criterion for a politically useful precautionary principle is the suitability of its form (rather than its content). A precautionary principle must, for example, exhibit a certain simplicity, display neither too much nor too little flexibility in its wording, and achieve salience in the most important practical cases.

This chapter is primarily about a sound rationale for cautiousness and, to a minor extent, about the two criteria that a practically useful precautionary principle must fulfil. I claim that existing precautionary principles and the associated literature have provided questionable rationales for cautiousness (section II). The existing literature has looked too far for such rationales whereas a fairly straightforward rationale for cautiousness would have been in plain sight. This straightforward rationale is the asymmetry inherent in a rights-based morality. If increased uncertainty means that there is both an increased probability of implicating rights and an increased probability of providing benefits that go beyond the fulfilment of rights, then a rights-based approach will generally be averse to increased uncertainty. This is because rights implications and supererogatory benefits do not matter symmetrically as the former are not simply offset by the latter (section III). Section IV discusses the rights-based rationale in more detail and section V concludes.

II. Precautionary Principles and Their Problems

In this section, I provide examples of existing precautionary principles and the associated literature which have justifiably come under criticism. There is, metaphorically speaking, a treasure hunt going on for adequate rationales for the hard-to-grasp cautiousness intuition, but many have been misled onto non-promising tracks, thereby unearthing rationales which are *ad hoc*, incomplete, or far-fetched.

[4] Note that one could even define cautiousness such that it *means* evaluating uncertain prospects in comparison with their expectation less favourably than the expectational approach (in either its basic or refined version).

There is a shared structure in precautionary principles. They typically call for precaution if two types of triggering conditions are present: an effect condition and an epistemic condition.[5] The effect condition is about the type of negative effect (such as 'serious or irreversible damage') and the epistemic condition is about our epistemic situation with respect to this type of negative effect (such as 'lacking full scientific certainty') that should trigger a cautious response. I will first go through three examples of questionable instances of effect conditions and then mention a major questionable instance of the epistemic condition. I do not present a knock-down argument against any of these rationales for existing precautionary principles. The problems I highlight are meant to be examples and symptoms of the general difficulty of pinning down a sound rationale for cautiousness.

A. Serious Damage

Sometimes it is suggested that precautionary action be taken in case *serious* (or 'catastrophic') damage is possible.[6] However, it is unclear why cautiousness should be triggered by serious damage and not already by, say, 'significant' damage. Of course, serious damage and catastrophes are reason for concern. Any damage is reason for concern and in so far as serious damage amounts to extremely large damage, it is reason for extremely large concern. However, the extent of damage is a continuous quantity and—if the focus of the effect condition is put on damage—then there should thus be continuity in the strength of the response as well rather than a principled difference between the response to serious and non-serious damage. Why would a cautious response to uncertainty regarding small damages not be just as appropriate as a cautious response to uncertainty regarding serious damages? Treating serious or catastrophic damage in a fundamentally different way might lead us astray—to take just one example—in comparisons of policies of which one comes with a small probability of catastrophe but is most probably hugely beneficial and another policy has an even smaller probability of catastrophe but virtually certainly yields significant but not quite catastrophic damage. Some reason would have to be given why there should be a non-continuous treatment of damages as they get larger and larger and then cross the threshold to where they are 'catastrophic' or 'serious'. Otherwise, the suggested rationale is ad hoc.

It is of course conceivable that such a reason might come forth. The dimension in which damage is typically conceived of (say, degrees of warming or percentages of lost gross domestic product) might be associated with thresholds in the

[5] See Neil Manson (2002) 'Formulating the Precautionary Principle' 24(3) Environmental Ethics 263, 263–74.

[6] See eg Cass Sunstein (2007) 'The Catastrophic Harm Precautionary Principle' 6(3) Issues in Legal Scholarship 1539, or United Nations Framework Convention on Climate Change (opened for signature 9 May 1992, entered into force 21 March 1994) 1771 UNTS 107, art 3.

dimensions that really matter. For example, at a certain degree of warming, the extinction of humanity becomes a possibility, and losing all humans is morally fundamentally different from losing many or most humans. There would thus be reason for a non-continuous response to degrees of warming. There are also other thresholds. If one conceives of the extent of 'damage' simply as human lives lost, then important qualitative features are out of sight. For example, 'crimes against humanity'[7] are distinguished from equally great harm by some of their qualitative features and these features warrant a different response. However, if proponents of this type of precautionary principle have such thresholds in other dimensions than the dimension of mere damage in mind, then the wording of the principle ought to feature these thresholds rather than referring only to the general and vague notion of 'serious damage'.

B. Irreversible Damage

Irreversible damage is a *specific type* of damage and thus does not face the criticism of the last paragraph, or at least not necessarily so. Often, the intuitive basis for lamenting irreversible damage is that it is damage that lasts very long (to be precise: forever). And if that were all there is to irreversible damage—that it amounts to very large damage when added up—then there would be nothing specific about it: irreversible damage would just be another instance of serious damage.[8] But, if worked out carefully, there is something of additional moral relevance if a good has not only been lost but has been lost for good. Such irreversibility might well be a sound trigger for precautionary policies.

Still, irreversibility can at most be one minor reason among others for precautionary policymaking rather than its core triggering condition. First of all, many goods that are irreversibly lost have substitutes that serve the same purpose as the irretrievably lost good. This is not true for certain losses of cultural values, sacred spaces, or of biodiversity, but it is true of many goods that serve as resources to fulfil our material needs. These can in principle be substituted. Second, even in cases without substitutes, there are many straightforwardly justifiable reasons for irreversibly giving up goods. Irreversible loss is a common occurrence on which there is no absolute prohibition. Heritage conservation does not protect every building or valuable memory. Thus, cautiousness with respect to irreversibly lost values needs further argument. Third and importantly, cautiousness seems also warranted in case of risks in which the damage is in principle reversible.

All of this is not to deny that there are instances of irreversible damage which do constitute a specific class of damage to be prevented particularly urgently.

7 I thank Simon Caney for suggesting this.

8 Cass Sunstein (2010) 'Irreversibility' 9 Law Probability and Risk 227, 234–37.

However, the limitations show that this class of damage covers far too few cases to provide a comprehensive rationale for cautiousness.

C. Non-Linear Damage

Nicholas Stern claimed that the risk aversion implied by standard expected utility theory already involves a precautionary principle.[9] If Stern is right about this, then standard expected utility theory and thus also standard economics (both of which are examples of what the introduction labelled the 'refined expectational approach') can be interpreted to provide one way of spelling out the effect condition for a precautionary principle. To see how they do this, revisit the oversimplified example of the introduction where warming of 3 °C leads to *more than* three times as much welfare loss than warming of 1 °C. In other words: warming has a non-linear relationship to welfare loss. If we ultimately care about expected *welfare* loss rather than about expected *warming*, then an uncertain policy with an equal probability of 1 °C and or 3 °C warming should be evaluated as being worse than a policy that leads to 2 °C warming with certainty. The general logic is this: if there is damage in terms of an instrumental value (such as warming) which is non-linearly[10] related to damage in terms of an intrinsic value (such as welfare), then we should respond cautiously to uncertainty in terms of the instrumental value.

This simple effect condition—non-linear relationships between instrumental and intrinsic values—can explain significant parts of our cautiousness intuition. Many calls for cautiousness can be interpreted as tacitly presupposing this general logic and stressing just how non-linear the relationship between certain variables is (eg by highlighting tipping points) or just far the probability distribution regarding the size of damages extends into the territory where damages are highly non-linear (eg by highlighting fat tails). This general logic implies risk aversion in so many cases in which cautiousness is intuitively called for that economists are tempted to regard it as the only rationale for cautiousness that we need. However, there are two important reasons why this rationale is incomplete. First, it can only provide a rationale for cautiousness with respect to instrumental values.[11] It does not provide a reason for risk aversion with respect to intrinsic values (such as welfare or democracy—except in so far as they are also instrumentally valuable). However, intuitively, there also seem to be cases where we ought to be cautious with respect to intrinsic values. Second, this rationale for cautiousness makes no distinction

[9] Nicholas Stern, *The Economics of Climate Change: The Stern Review* (CUP 2007) 38.

[10] More precisely: concavely, i.e. in the standard case used in economics where wealth is the instrumental value and utility is the intrinsic value, we have diminishing (rather than increasing) marginal utility with rising wealth.

[11] Also, it justifies the opposite of cautiousness in case the instrumental value is related in a convex way to the intrinsic value.

between taking risks and imposing risks. However, there seem to be stronger grounds for cautiousness when the risks in question primarily affect others rather oneself.[12] Even apart from these two points, it is not clear that it justifies *enough* risk aversion, that is, enough to do justice to our cautiousness intuition.[13] Simply because it provides a good rationale for *much* risk aversion does not, of course, imply that it is a sufficient rationale for *all* instances of justified cautiousness.

D. Risk versus Uncertainty

It is sometimes claimed that there are two opposites to certainty: *risk* which allows for the ascription of probabilities and ('Knightian') *uncertainty* which does not allow for the ascription of probabilities.[14] Precautionary principles are then said to be principles for decision-making in the absence of probabilities, that is, for the context of uncertainty.

However, the distinction between risk and uncertainty is more problematic than it seems at first sight. If it is claimed that there are two kinds of decision contexts—one where probabilities are available and one where they are not—we first need to know what interpretation of probability is presupposed. Probability can mean very different things[15] but the relevant concept of probability for decision principles (such as the precautionary principle) is epistemic probability.[16] The somewhat misleading label 'epistemic probability' stands for the degree of evidential support that a hypothesis enjoys. Thus, the claim that there is a high probability of a certain glacier melting simply translates into the claim that the evidence strongly supports the hypothesis that the glacier will melt. The crucial point now is this: if we rely on a broad concept of evidence, then evidential support is almost always available. For any given hypothesis, there are almost always some propositions that we justifiably believe which speak for or against this hypothesis—even if these beliefs do not rely on well-tested models or scientific theories, extensive or precise data, or expert agreement. In other words, evidential support—that is, epistemic probabilities—exists in almost any conceivable circumstance. It is difficult

[12] See sections III and IV as well as Henry Shue, 'Deadly Delays, Saving Opportunities: Creating a More Dangerous World?' in Stephen Gardiner, Simon Caney, Dale Jamieson, and Henry Shue (eds), *Climate Ethics: Essential Readings* (OUP 2010) 147.

[13] In particular, it trivially does not provide more reason for cautiousness than the expectational approach.

[14] See eg Darrel Moellendorf, *The Moral Challenge of Dangerous Climate Change: Values, Poverty, and Policy* (CUP 2014) chapter 3.

[15] See eg David Mellor, *Probability: A Philosophical Introduction* (Routledge 2004).

[16] For an argument for this claim and qualifications regarding this claim, see Dominic Roser (2017), 'The Irrelevance of the Risk-Uncertainty Distinction' 23(5) Journal of Science and Engineering Ethics 1387–407 (hereafter Roser, *The Irrelevance of the Risk–Uncertainty Distinction*). The most relevant alternative interpretations are subjective probabilities (i.e. degrees of belief or credence) and objective probabilities (such as frequencies or propensities).

to imagine a decision situation in which we have strictly no evidence *at all*, not even casual observation or back-of-the-envelope calculations which yield vague, non-numerically expressed probabilities which are only marginally better than arbitrary probability ascriptions. Thus, since we almost always have probabilities, we are almost always in the context of risk. The distinction between risk and uncertainty seems irrelevant.

It could be objected that this characterizes the distinction between risk and uncertainty falsely. It could be said that the distinction is not really about whether probabilities are available *at all* but rather about whether *scientifically well-grounded, precise* probabilities are available or not.[17] It could be said that if there is only extremely scant or bad evidence, then this counts as a context of uncertainty rather than risk. In such a context, decisions should not be based on probabilities. Decisions should only be based on probabilities if these probabilities can be expressed numerically and if they arise from solid evidence (extensive data, well-tested models, scientific agreement, etc). However, if we were to draw the line between risk and uncertainty at this point—that is, depending on whether we have *scientifically well-grounded, precise* probabilities—then it would not be clear why the distinction between risk and uncertainty would be relevant. After all, if there is only scant and poor evidence, it is hard to see how we could make better decisions by disregarding this evidence than by making use of it (at least if we display epistemic humility in being aware of just how scant it is). After all, even scarce and shaky evidence is better than no evidence (a visually impaired driver would surely drive her car better by using whatever glimpse she gets than by closing her eyes on account of the impairment). But, according to the epistemic interpretation of probability, making use of evidence just *means* making use of probabilities. Deciding on the basis of bad probabilities is better than deciding without basis at all. This is particularly so since, as I argued elsewhere,[18] potential principles for deciding in the absence of probabilities—such as Maximin—come with grave problems.

Thus, the distinction between risk and uncertainty is irrelevant for either of two reasons. Either we distinguish risk and uncertainty according to whether probabilities are available at all. In that case, there do not (or hardly at all) seem to be any relevant cases of uncertainty (for the simple reason that at least *some* evidence pretty much always exists), or we distinguish risk and uncertainty according to whether well-grounded, precise probabilities are available. In that case,

[17] One might think that speaking of probabilities necessarily implies precision. But this is not so. In natural language, we often speak of probabilities in vague terms such as 'large' or 'sizeable' (and besides this, there is also philosophical and mathematical work on imprecise probabilities). Referring to *magnitudes* does not necessitate the use of *numbers*. And even if we do give precise numbers (such as a '50/50 chance' or a '33.3 per cent probability') this is often done for ease of exposition when vague expressions would be more adequate to convey orders of magnitude.

[18] Roser, *The Irrelevance of the Risk–Uncertainty Distinction* (n 16).

the distinction between risk and uncertainty is irrelevant because sound decision principles—including precautionary principles—should always make use of the best available probabilities, even if the best available probabilities have extremely weak grounds and are extremely vague. There should not be two different decision principles depending on whether the available evidence is gradually better or worse.

There are further problematic aspects of epistemic triggering conditions on which I will not expand here. For example, it is sometimes suggested that the allocation of the burden of proof is of crucial importance; that is, whether an activity that comes with uncertainty counts as 'innocent until proven guilty' or 'guilty until proven innocent'. However, if demonstrating guilt amounts to demonstrating that an activity's risks are intolerably large whereas demonstrating innocence amounts to demonstrating that its risks are not intolerably large then proving 'guilt' (danger) and 'innocence' (safety) are hardly two different tasks. Rather, they are, at least in principle, two sides of the same coin. Another instance of problematic aspects of epistemic conditions are duplicated references to uncertainty which some wordings in the literature display. Examples are expressions such as 'uncertain threats'[19] (a threat is just something bad happening with uncertainty), 'potentially dangerous'[20] (a danger is just something bad potentially happening), or 'doubts as to the safety'[21] (doubt refers to there being uncertainty, and safety refers to there being —sufficiently small—uncertainty).

Summing up, the examples suggest that many of the currently proposed triggering conditions for cautiousness run into problems. Both the effect conditions, such as catastrophes, irreversibility, or non-linear damage, as well as the epistemic conditions, such as the distinction between risk and uncertainty, often fail to contribute to a convincing and comprehensive rationale for cautiousness. The next section claims that a straightforward rationale for cautiousness with broad scope would have been right in front of our eyes the whole time. There would have been no need to dig for rationales in more obscure spots. Note, however, that the positive case in section III is independent of the negative case in this section. One can disagree on either the positive or the negative case without having to disagree on both.

[19] For example, Guidelines for Applying the Precautionary Principle to Biodiversity Conservation and Natural Resource Management, 67th Meeting of the IUCN Council (14-15 May 2007) <http://cmsdata.iucn.org/downloads/ln250507_ppguidelines.pdf> accessed 13 August 2019.

[20] For example, Commission, 'Communication from the Commission on the Precautionary Principle' Communication (COM) (2000) 0001 final.

[21] For example, Milieu Ltd, TMC Asser Institute, and PACE for DG Environment of the European Commission, 'Considerations on the Application of the Precautionary Principle in the Chemicals Sector' (August 2011) Annex I <http://ec.europa.eu/environment/chemicals/reach/pdf/publications/annex_cases.pdf> accessed 13 August 2019.

III. A Rights-Based Rationale for Cautiousness: The Basic Idea

High uncertainty means that the probability distribution over a policy's possible outcomes is spread out a lot rather than concentrated around the expected outcome.[22] High uncertainty thus implies both large 'downside risks' and large 'upside risks'. The reason why we should be averse to uncertainty is that, from a moral perspective, downside risks and upside risks do not necessarily cancel each other out. This is particularly so if the downside risks are risks to *rights*. Imposing risks to someone's rights is not simply justified by simultaneously providing this person with upside risks; that is, with a probability of benefits above and beyond the expected outcome. This is the basic rationale for cautiousness which I discuss in this and section IV. In order to make this basic idea more tangible, assume that the rights at stake in a policy decision are the rights of future people to be at least as well-off as people in the present. This assumption is purely for illustrative purposes.[23] Assume there is a choice between two policies. Policy A bequeaths the present welfare level to our descendants with certainty. Policy B comes with uncertainty: there is an equal probability of bequeathing a welfare level that is 50 per cent higher or lower than the present welfare level. Presented with such a choice, we should choose policy A. The reason is simply that policy A is certain not to implicate[24] rights whereas policy B has a 50 per cent probability of implicating rights. Imposing this 50 per cent probability on our descendants is not justified by simultaneously giving them, as policy B does, a 50 per cent probability of going beyond the call of duty and bequeathing a higher level of welfare to them than is owed. The reason is the same why it is not acceptable to pay back a £20 loan from a friend with a lottery ticket that pays £40 with a 50 per cent probability. Such a lottery ticket has a 50 per cent probability that the friend will end up ultimately not having his £20 paid back, and the countervailing probability of being paid back an extra £20

[22] 'Spread out a lot' must of course be fleshed out. Distinguishing between more or less spread out probability distributions could be done by reference to the standard deviation, the width of the range of possible outcomes around the central estimate, second-order stochastic dominance, or by visually assessing the graph of the probability distribution.

[23] See Caney, Chapter 16, this book). Personally, I am just as open to grant future people merely a right to be *sufficiently* well off. See Lukas Meyer and Dominic Roser, 'Enough for the Future' in Lukas Meyer, and Axel Gosseries (eds), *Theories of Intergenerational Justice* (OUP 2009) 219–48. The example in the text is highly simplified since, of course, future generations also have other rights besides the right to a certain level of welfare. The example is also simplified in the sense that whether a future individual enjoys its rights depends not only on what we do in the present but also on what its future contemporaries do. Johan Brännmark (2016) 'Future Generations as Rightholders' 9(6) Critical Review of International Social and Political Philosophy 680, 685.

[24] The terminology of implicating rights is used for the sake of precision in lieu of more common terms such as violating, infringing, or limiting rights. Douglas Husak gives the following definition: 'Actions "implicate" a right when they are contrary to that right. I intend this term to be neutral about whether those actions infringe or violate a right; that is, whether they are permissible or impermissible.' Douglas Husak (2011) 'Lifting the Cloak: Preventive Detention as Punishment' 48 San Diego Law Review 1173, 1190.

on top of the owed £20 does not make up for the risk of not being paid back at all. There is thus an asymmetry: Providing supererogatory benefits (or a probability thereof) does not make up for implicating rights (or a probability thereof), at least not in a straightforward way. This asymmetry speaks against policies that increase uncertainty in the sense of increasing the probability of both rights-implicating and supererogatory outcomes. Such downside and upside risks do not cancel each other out. I believe that it is the core rationale for cautiousness.

Moving on to a slightly less stylized example, assume that the choice is not between certainty and uncertainty but between *more* or *less* uncertainty. In the case of climate policy, we could, for example, imagine a mitigation and an adaptation policy which both have the same expected outcome in terms of future levels of welfare. The adaption policy, however, comes with more uncertainty. Its downside risks and upside risks are larger. The downside risk is runaway climate change for which our adaptation investments prove futile while its upside risk is manageable climate change for which adaptation investments prove to be the cheaper response than mitigation.

Referring to Figure 14.1, for example, in such a case even if the two policies have the same *expected* outcome (ie even if the bell curves have their centre at the same level of welfare), the mitigation policy is morally preferable. This is so because its potential to implicate rights (the black area) is smaller than the adaptation policy's potential to implicate rights (the grey area). Of course, the adaptation policy also exhibits a larger probability at the right-hand tail of the probability distribution; that is, a larger probability of very good outcomes. However, it is not justifiable to implicate someone's rights by simultaneously providing this agent with large supererogatory benefits, and this is also true in probabilistic terms: a certain probability of implicating rights cannot be justified by providing the agent in question with an equal probability of supererogatory benefits, at least not in straightforward ways.

In other words, the idea is simply that in a comparison of policies with the same expected outcome but different levels of uncertainty, the more uncertain policy

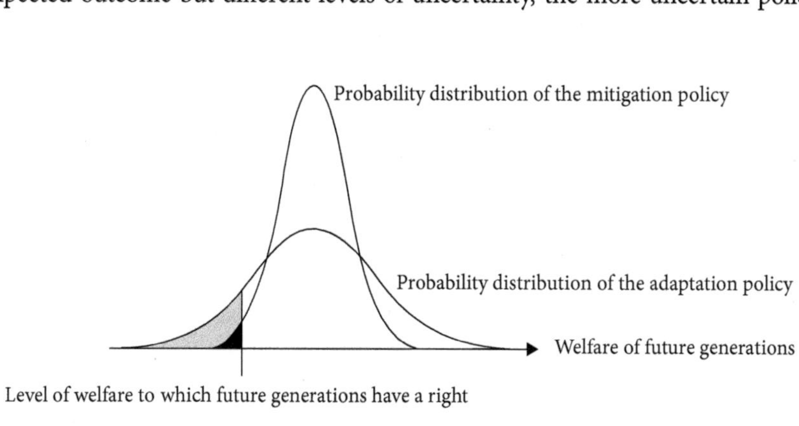

Figure 14.1 Comparing policies with different levels of uncertainty

will typically have a larger probability of implicating rights. It will also have a larger probability of very good outcomes, but since the two do not make up for each other, the more uncertain policy should be avoided. Note, however, that we can also make a stronger claim. Even if the mitigation policy had a *lower* expected outcome than the adaptation policy, it might still be morally preferable. This is so because—speaking in graphical terms—the black area can be smaller than the grey area *even if* the probability distribution of the mitigation policy were shifted to the left. A policy that is worse on expectation but has a lower probability of implicating rights can well be more choiceworthy than a policy with both a higher expected outcome and a higher probability of implicating rights.

In terms of the language of triggering conditions, my proposed effect condition thus amounts simply to *implicating rights*. My proposed epistemic condition amounts simply to a *probability* of doing so. It is important here to interpret probability in the sense of epistemic probability. According to this interpretation, the probability of a certain outcome corresponds to the degree of evidential support for the hypothesis that this outcome occurs. As argued in section III in the context of the discussion on risk and uncertainty, probabilities in this sense are pretty much always available. Of course, it is imperative to use the *best* available evidence for determining probabilities,[25] but if the best available evidence is very bad evidence, this does not undermine the fact that the degrees of support which this bad evidence gives for various hypotheses count as probabilities. The probabilities in question might stem from such shaky, scarce, and controversial evidence that they would never make it into peer-reviewed journals and that we would not feel comfortable expressing them by means of precise numbers. But as long as they represent the support given by the evidence, they are probabilities, and as long as they represent the best available evidence, they are the probabilities on which we ought to rely.

IV. A Rights-Based Rationale for Cautiousness: A Closer Look

Invoking rights might ring alarm bells about excessive cautiousness: should we avoid any policy that might, for all we know, implicate someone's rights even with the slightest probability and to the slightest extent? This would be a *reductio ad absurdum* of a rights-based approach to risk. A convincing precautionary principle will not require that the probability of implicating rights be kept to zero (which is impossible) or be minimized whatever the costs (which is implausible). The shape and extent of our cautiousness should make room for the idea that it is justifiable

[25] Of course, this must be fleshed out but for present purposes, 'best available' can be left as a placeholder into which various epistemologists can fill in their favourite theories.

to implicate rights with *some* probability to *some* extent in *some* circumstances. Fleshing out such a rights-based theory of risk imposition would go too far for this chapter. However, I will highlight certain constraints that such a theory must fulfil in order to actually call for cautiousness. I will focus in particular on the characteristics such a theory must exhibit in order to call for *more* cautiousness than the expectational approach and the tempting approach to uncertainty; for it to fulfil the introduction's first criterion for a politically useful precautionary principle mentioned.

An important ingredient of a rights-based theory of risk imposition is the claim that whether implicating someone's rights is permissible, depends, among other considerations,[26] on how large a good can be achieved by way of implicating the rights.[27] The benefits achieved by implicating someone's rights must be proportionate to the implication in order for the implication to be permissible. *Ceteris paribus*, more speaks for the permissibility of a specific rights implication if more benefits can thereby be achieved. This claim stands in tension with the intuition that rights are trumps or absolute. The general gist of this claim is reflected in such diverse principles as Judith Jarvis Thompson's 'tradeoff idea',[28] Shelly Kagan's 'sliding threshold',[29] the legal principle of proportionality, or the calculus of negligence in tort law. In order to make this idea more concrete, let us give labels to the considerations on the two sides of the scale of such a trade-off. On the downside, there is the Potential for Rights Implications (PRI) of a policy and, on the upside, there is the Potential for Supererogatory Benefits (PSB) of a policy. In terms of Figure 14.1, the PRI is the (grey or black) shaded area below the bell curve on the left-hand side and the PSB is the white area below the bell curve on the right-hand side. Depending on how a rights-based theory of risk imposition calculates the PRI and the PSB and depending on how it trades them off against each other, a rights-based theory calls for more or less cautiousness than the expectational approach. The expectational approach (in its refined form) simply multiplies the value of each possible outcome with its probability and adds them up. In order for a rights-based theory of risk imposition to call for more cautiousness than the expectational approach the rights-based theory must display (at least) one of the following two features.

First, a rights-based theory could—just like the expectational approach—calculate the PRI and the PSB each in expectational terms but then differ from the expectational approach by demanding that the latter must not merely outweigh the former in order for a policy to be justifiable but must *strongly* outweigh it.

[26] A particularly crucial further consideration which I bracket in this paper is necessity: Implicating someone's right is only justified by the benefits thereby achieved if the implication is necessary for achieving these benefits, i.e. if the benefits could not be achieved without implicating the right (or at least not without implicating it less).

[27] On tolerable levels of risk, see also de Londras, Chapter 5, this book, and Lazarus, Chapter 6, this book.

[28] Judith Thomson, *The Realm of Rights* (Harvard University Press 1990) 158.

[29] Kagan Shelly, *The Limits of Morality* (OUP 1989) 87–91.

Calculating the PRI of a policy in expectational terms just means that each possible rights-implicating outcome is evaluated by multiplying its disvalue with its probability and adding them up. Thus, if there is an equal probability of bequeathing a welfare level to our descendants that is 50 per cent lower than what we owe them or 50 per cent higher than what we owe them, the PRI and the PSB would count as equally large. However, the policy would not be justifiable because we would demand the PSB to be *much* larger than the PRI in order for the policy to be justifiable.

Second, a rights-based theory could claim that it is sufficient for the PSB to outweigh the PRI, rather than having to *strongly* outweigh it, but that either the PRI or the PSB or both should not be calculated in expectational terms. For example, one could posit a prioritarian theory for calculating the PRI but not for calculating the PSB. This would mean that large rights implications get disproportionately more weight than small rights implications. Bequeathing a welfare level 20 per cent below the owed level to our descendants counts as *more than twice* as problematic as bequeathing a welfare level 10 per cent below the owed level. One could also deny that any benefit should count for calculating the PSB. Rather, it could be said, only benefits for those whose rights are potentially implicated should count. In that case, too, a rights-based view would be more averse to uncertain policies than the expectational approach since the former takes only parts of the potential benefits of uncertain policies into account.

These are two ways for spelling out a rights-based theory such that it calls for more cautiousness than the expectational approach. However, one could in principle spell out a rights-based theory of risk impositions such that it does *not* (or not necessarily) call for more cautiousness than the expectational approach. One way of doing so would be to base the calculation of the PRI exclusively on the *probability* of implicating rights without taking note of how *gravely* the rights are implicated. Thus, a given probability of bequeathing an insufficient welfare level to our descendants would count as equally serious regardless of whether we bequeath them a little less or much less welfare than we owe them. If, at the same time, the PSB were still calculated in expectational terms (i.e. a probability of bequeathing large supererogatory benefits counts for more than the same probability of bequeathing small supererogatory benefits), we might well have a duty to choose more uncertain policies. Why is this so? According to the understanding proposed here, increasing uncertainty means that there is more probability at the tails of the distribution and less at the centre. This could mean that increasing uncertainty would leave the PRI unchanged in cases where we just shift probability from minor rights implications to major rights implications. In contrast, shifting probability from the centre to the tails would usually mean that the PSB is increased: there is an increased probability of large supererogatory benefits and a decreased probability of small supererogatory benefits. Thus, increasing uncertainty could increase the PSB but not the PRI according to this method of calculating the PRI and PSB. Of course, this method of calculating a policy's potential to implicate rights exclusively by the probability of implicating rights (and not at all by how serious the potential rights implications are) is not very plausible. However, it does reflect how we frequently speak in common parlance about uncertain rights implications. This might simply be due to the imprecision of everyday language. But it might also reflect a deeper feature of our intuitions about a rights-based morality: it is inimical to gradual thinking. For example, it could be claimed that the problem about violating a right is not primarily that something of value is thereby lost but rather that by violating a right, disrespect is shown. And disrespect, it might be said, does not (or hardly ever) depend(s) on how gravely a right is violated but rather on whether it is violated at all. The fact that disrespect only depends on *whether* a right is implicated could be said to translate in uncertain contexts into the idea that only the *probability* of a rights implication matters.[30] Note, also, that for most versions of a rights-based theory of risk imposition, there is another—and simpler—case in which it would not call for cautiousness, or at least not for more cautiousness than the expectational approach. This is the case if *none* of the possible outcomes of the policies under consideration implicate rights. The same holds if *all* the possible outcomes of the policies under consideration implicates rights, at least if the PRI is calculated in expectational rather than prioritarian terms.

Even if this section shows that plausible ways of spelling out a rights-based approach to risk impositions call for more cautiousness than the expectational approach, carrying out such a comparison comes with strong limitations. A first limitation is that the example I used was a specific *kind of right*: a right of future generations to a certain level of welfare. However, there are other and more complex kinds of rights: the right to life, the right to free speech, the right to receive a promised amount of money, the right not be discriminated against, the rights of animals, etc. These rights exhibit one or more of the following features. First, they are not necessarily rights to a certain *good* (such as welfare). Second, even if they are rights to goods, they are not necessarily rights to a certain level of a *single* good.[31] Third, they are not necessarily rights to *scalable* goods; that is, goods of which we can have gradually more or less. Fourth, they are not necessarily rights to goods that we value *intrinsically*. In these cases, it is much less straightforward to compare a rights-based view with the expectational approach and to claim that the former calls for more cautiousness than the latter. However, even in the case of

[30] There would be an even purer way of capturing the view that it primarily matters whether rights are implicated (rather than how much they are implicated): the PRI could be calculated simply as a *fixed* negative 'penalty' for any policy that comes with a *probability above some threshold* of implicating rights. This penalty must be weighed up against the PSB (calculated in expectational terms) which we can achieve by potentially implicating rights. If we evaluated policies according to this scheme, we might well end up welcoming an increase in uncertainty. This is so if the policy already incurred the negative penalty before the increase in uncertainty and thus increasing the probability of rights-implicating outcomes would not incur any further penalty.

[31] This raises problems along the lines described in Gregor Dorfleitner and Michael Krapp (2007) 'On Multiattributive Risk Aversion: Some Clarifying Results' 1(1) Review of Managerial Science 47, 47–63.

these more complex rights, the fundamental point about a rights-based cautiousness will often hold. *If* more uncertainty means that there is a larger downside risk in terms of implicating rights and *if* more uncertainty either does not mean that there is a larger upside risk in terms of supererogatory benefits or, if there is, that it is insufficient to outweigh the increased downside risk, *then* a rights-based approach will oppose increased uncertainty also for these more complex rights.[32]

In the introduction to this chapter, I mentioned that a precautionary principle should not only call for more cautiousness than the expectational approach but also for more cautiousness than the tempting approach; that is, for more cautiousness than we are tempted to display given our self-interest and cognitive biases. And indeed, a rights-based approach does seem to fulfil this criterion as well. For one, it puts the rights *of others* at the centre of attention. This speaks against self-interest which either overemphasizes the effects of a policy on *oneself* or, if it does take others into account, does not make a strong distinction between the different levels of cautiousness called for in *risk-taking* versus *risk-imposing*. In the case of risk-taking, we may permissibly display as little cautiousness as we like since there is no duty to respect our own rights (we can waive them) whereas rights must be respected in the case of risk impositions on others. Second, a rights-based approach can adequately explain why, in one standard case of relevance for the precautionary principle, we are typically prone to insufficient cautiousness: the case of imposing risks on future generations. The reason is this: our intuitions about justifiable risk impositions are formed in the context of risk impositions among contemporaries. But among contemporaries, the rights-based case for cautiousness is comparatively weaker than among non-contemporaries. This is due to three aspects of contemporaneity: *ceteris paribus*, more risk impositions are justifiable when the person on whom a risk is imposed *consents*, when risk impositions are *mutual*, and when *ex post* compensation is feasible (in case a potential rights implication materializes). None of this is possible in the case of future generations. Future generations cannot

[32] A second limitation of my comparison is that I relied on a quite specific interpretation of what it means for policies to exhibit more or less uncertainty: I equated 'more uncertainty' with a probability distribution that is more 'spread out'. It should be noted that most people would not disagree with me in the sense of proposing a different understanding of 'more uncertainty'. Most people simply do not make their understanding of the idea of more or less uncertainty precise. Still, alternative understandings are possible. Here is one contender: Assume that policy A and policy B come with the same probability distribution over possible outcomes but that there is less evidence to support this probability distribution in the case of policy A. (For example, in two tennis matches one could assess the probability of either player winning as 50 per cent, but in one case this could be based on extremely long track records of matches between the two players and in the other case this could be based on having seen a single match of each player many years ago; Cf Susan Hurley, *Natural Reasons: Personality and Polity* (OUP 1992). However, according to this understanding of 'more uncertainty' it would be difficult to provide an argument why choosing policy A would be worse than policy B. Note also that part of the intuition behind this proposal—i.e. that less evidence translates into more uncertainty—can be captured by my own proposal: often (but not always) scarce evidence means that the probability distribution is more spread out across various outcomes. When more evidence comes in, this allows for the probability distribution to narrow down to a smaller range of outcomes.

consent, they cannot *reciprocate* by imposing risks on us, and they cannot be *compensated* by us. Therefore we generally need to be more cautious about risk impositions on future generations than on contemporaries. Thus, a rights-based approach can explain how we are tempted to underestimate the required extent of cautiousness in a class of risk impositions that matters much for precautionary principles.[33]

V. Conclusion

If we are to face the big and novel risks of the twenty-first century, we must clean up our confused approach to uncertainty and find a plausible way to spell out and justify our cautiousness intuition. This chapter argued that this is possible without resorting to far-fetched rationales. The 'plain vanilla' building blocks of rights and probabilities are enough for devising a precautionary principle that is neither trivial nor extreme. Even though the last section showed that the case is not absolutely clear-cut, the proposed rights-based rationale for cautiousness plausibly supports more cautiousness than the expectational approach and the tempting approach.

If we want to devise an actual precautionary principle for political practice, the second criterion mentioned in the introduction must be given attention as well: the principle's form's suitability for political practice. For example, the principle must achieve salience in political debates about the most important cases for which it is relevant. This could be said to give a reason to limit its scope to, say, environment or health. While the general logic of rights-based cautiousness is relevant for a wide variety of uncertainties we face in private and public life, establishing the principle specifically for the domain of *environmental policy* gives it the attention it needs where it matters most. Also, it would give a precautionary principle much more bite if it did not refer to rights without specifying which rights are at stake. A restriction to *human rights* could be justified on pragmatic grounds since there is much less controversy on their content and stringency than there is regarding rights more generally.

[33] In this section, I focused on my proposed *effect* triggering condition (i.e. rights implications). Note, however, that my proposed *epistemic* triggering condition (i.e. epistemic probabilities, based on an ecumenical view of evidence) also supports more cautiousness than the 'tempting approach'. After all, there is a temptation to restrict the evidence on which we base our political decisions to *solid* evidence. This restriction makes us neglect many important risks. For example, scientists fear being accused of alarmism or of being proven wrong in retrospect if they publicly report on catastrophic risks for which the evidential basis is still fairly speculative Cf Kynyn Brysse, Naomi Oreskes, Jessica O'Reilly, and Michael Oppenheimer (2012) 'Climate Change Prediction: Erring on the Side of Least Drama?' 23(1) Global Environmental Change 327, 327–37. Against this temptation, I suggest always using the best available evidence and to use all of it, even when it is only minimally better than no evidence. Failing to embrace an ecumenical concept of evidence, and thus discounting the value of evidence that does not originate or is not processed within university walls, is one of the great enemies of cautious policy-making.

A resulting precautionary principle for environmental policy would put the effect condition of human rights implications at the centre, but could mention on a supplementary basis irreversible loss, non-linear damage, or any further plausible effect condition. In terms of the epistemic condition, it simply operates on the basis of probabilities, understood as degrees of support that the available evidence—in a broad understanding of evidence—provides. Extremely tentatively, a resulting principle could, for example, read: The probabilities of an environmental policy's outcomes should always be judged according to the best available evidence, regardless of the quality and extent of available evidence. Based on these probabilities, the potential of human rights implicating outcomes must be kept low and can only ever be justified as a necessary aspect of a policy that yields a much larger potential of important benefits.

15

The Paris Agreement as a Human Rights Treaty

John H Knox

I. Introduction

Climate change is one of the defining challenges of the twenty-first century. The Paris Agreement adopted in December 2015 is the most important effort yet undertaken to address that challenge. Together with the 1992 United Nations Framework Convention on Climate Change (UNFCCC),[1] the Paris Agreement establishes a legal framework that will shape climate actions at the national and international levels for decades to come. Remarkably, the Paris Agreement is also a human rights treaty. It states that '[p]arties should, when taking action to address climate change, respect, promote and consider their respective obligations on human rights,'[2] thereby making it the first global environmental agreement to recognize that human rights obligations are an integral element of the regime it establishes.

Of course, the Paris Agreement is not a human rights treaty in the usual sense. It does not define human rights obligations or create mechanisms to review and promote their compliance. Nevertheless, it makes an important contribution to the fulfilment of human rights. By clarifying that actions to address climate change should take human rights into account, the agreement helps to mainstream human rights norms into the ongoing implementation and evolution of the climate regime. In this respect, it sets a precedent for other international regimes as well. The effective protection of human rights requires more than strengthening the weak compliance mechanisms of the international human rights system. Even effective human rights tribunals will often be limited to responding to complaints of violations that have already occurred. An important complement to *post hoc* adjudication is building the capacity of international (and domestic) institutions

[1] United Nations Framework Convention on Climate Change (opened for signature 9 May 1992, entered into force 21 March 1994) 1771 UNTS 107 (hereafter 'UNFCCC').

[2] The Paris Agreement was adopted as a decision of the Conference of the Parties to the UNFCCC, and its text is included as an annex to that decision. UNFCCC (Conference of the Parties), 'Adoption of the Paris Agreement' (12 December 2015) UN Doc FCCC/CP/2015/L.9/Rev.1, 20 <https://unfccc.int/resource/docs/2015/cop21/eng/l09r01.pdf> accessed 13 August 2019 (hereafter 'Paris Agreement').

John Knox, *The Paris Agreement as a Human Rights Treaty* In: Human Rights and 21st Century Challenges. Edited by: Dapo Akande, Jaakko Kuosmanen, Helen McDermott, and Dominic Roser, Published by Oxford University Press 2020.
DOI: 10.1093/oso/9780198824770.003.0016

to comply *a priori*, by incorporating human rights protections into the institutions themselves. The Paris Agreement is a milestone along this path.

The first two sections of this chapter place the human rights language in the Paris Agreement in its historical and legal context: section II reviews the efforts over the previous decade to characterize climate change as a threat to human rights, and section III describes the evolution of human rights obligations relating to environmental harm in general and to climate change in particular. Section IV assesses the Paris Agreement in light of these norms. It concludes that the agreement is generally consistent with the human rights obligations relating to climate change, but that states must strengthen their commitments in order to fulfil those obligations completely. Section V examines how human rights law may further influence the climate regime, including through rights-based climate litigation, and through the adoption of social and environmental safeguards in international mechanisms to provide financial support to mitigation and adaptation measures.[3]

II. The History of Human Rights and Climate Change

The effort to apply human rights to climate change began a decade before the adoption of the Paris Agreement. In December 2005, members of the Inuit, an indigenous people in the Arctic, filed a petition with the Inter-American Commission on Human Rights alleging that the failure of the United States to restrict its greenhouse gas emissions violated its human rights obligations.[4] The submission described the effects of rising temperatures in the Arctic and explained that melting ice and permafrost were causing houses to collapse, making travel more dangerous, and harming the animals on which the Inuit depend for sustenance. The Inuit linked the rising temperatures to the failure by the United States to take effective steps to reduce its emissions, and argued that the failure violated their human rights, including their rights to life, health, and property. They asked the Commission to recommend that the United States '[a]dopt mandatory measures to limit its emissions of greenhouse gases and cooperate in efforts of the community of nations . . . to limit such emissions at the global level'.[5]

[3] For other recent analyses of the climate regime and human rights, see Lavanya Rajamani, 'Human Rights in the Climate Change Regime: From Rio to Paris and Beyond' and Sumudu Atapattu, 'The Right to a Healthy Environment and Climate Change: Mismatch or Harmony?' in John H. Knox and Ramin Pejan (eds), *The Human Right to a Healthy Environment* (CUP 2018).

[4] 'Petition to the Inter-American Commission on Human Rights Seeking Relief from Violations Resulting from Global Warming Caused by Acts and Omissions of the United States' (7 December 2005) <http://climatecasechart.com/non-us-case/petition-to-the-inter-american-commission-on-human-rights-seeking-relief-from-violations-resulting-from-global-warming-caused-by-acts-and-omissions-of-the-united-states/> accessed 25 November 2019.

[5] Ibid, 118.

The Inter-American Commission declined to accept the petition, stating only that 'the information provided does not enable us to determine whether the alleged facts would tend to characterize a violation of [protected human] rights'.[6] However, the petition raised awareness of the effects that climate change was already having on the Arctic, and of the possibility that those effects could be framed as a threat to human rights.[7]

The next step was taken by small island states in November 2007. Meeting in Malé, the capital of the Maldives, they adopted a Declaration on the Human Dimension of Global Climate Change. The Malé Declaration was the first intergovernmental statement that climate change has 'clear and immediate implications for the full enjoyment of human rights', including the rights to life, to an adequate standard of living, and to the highest attainable standard of health.[8] Rather than seek a quasi-judicial statement from a human rights tribunal, as the Inuit had, the small island states took the issue to the United Nations. The Declaration requested the UN Human Rights Council to convene a discussion on human rights and climate change, and the Office of the United Nations High Commissioner for Human Rights (OHCHR) to study the effects of climate change on the full enjoyment of human rights. The Declaration also asked the Conference of the Parties (COP) to the UNFCCC to seek the cooperation of the Council and of OHCHR in assessing the human rights implications of climate change.[9]

A few months later, the Human Rights Council responded by adopting its first resolution on climate change and human rights.[10] The Council expressed its concern that climate change poses an immediate and far-reaching threat to people and communities around the world and has implications for the full enjoyment of human rights, and it requested the OHCHR to conduct a detailed analytical study of the relationship, as the Malé Declaration had sought. Published early in 2009, the OHCHR report drew on the reports of the Intergovernmental Panel on Climate Change (IPCC) to describe how climate change threatens the enjoyment of a wide range of human rights, including the rights to life, health, food, water, adequate housing, and self-determination.[11] In response, the Human Rights Council

[6] Letter from Ariel Dulitzky, Assistant Executive Secretary, Inter-American Commission on Human Rights (IACHR) to Paul Crowley, Legal Representative of Sheila Watt-Cloutier *et al* (16 November 2006).

[7] Randall Abate (2007) 'Climate Change, the United States, and the Impacts of Arctic Melting: A Case Study in the Need for Enforceable International Environmental Human Rights' 43A Stanford Journal of International Law 3; Hari Osofsky (2007) 'The Inuit Petition as a Bridge? Beyond Dialectics of Climate Change and Indigenous Peoples' Rights' 31 American Indian Law Review 675.

[8] Malé Declaration on the Human Dimension of Global Climate Change (14 November 2007) <http://www.ciel.org/Publications/Male_Declaration_Nov07.pdf> accessed 13 August 2019.

[9] See John H. Knox (2009) 'Linking Human Rights and Climate Change at the United Nations' 33 Harvard Environmental Law Review 477.

[10] UNHRC Res 7/23 (28 March 2008) UN Doc A/HRC/RES/7/23.

[11] OHCHR 'Report of the Office of the United Nations High Commissioner for Human Rights on the Relationship Between Climate Change and Human Rights' (15 January 2009) UN Doc A/HRC/10/61 (hereafter 'OHCHR Report').

adopted another, more detailed resolution, in which it noted that the effects of climate change will be felt most acutely by those who are already in vulnerable situations, and affirmed that 'human rights obligations and commitments have the potential to inform and strengthen international and national policymaking in the area of climate change, promoting policy coherence, legitimacy and sustainable outcomes'.[12]

These themes were taken up by the special rapporteurs and independent experts mandated by the Human Rights Council to report on specific human rights issues. In December 2009, at the beginning of the fifteenth COP in Copenhagen, twenty United Nations human rights mandate holders issued a joint statement emphasizing that climate change poses serious threats to the full enjoyment of a broad range of human rights and urging that mitigation and adaptation measures should be developed in accordance with human rights norms, including with the participation of affected communities.[13] Although the outcome document of the Copenhagen COP did not refer to human rights, the next COP, which met in Cancun the following year, adopted a decision echoing the language of the 2009 Human Rights Council resolution. Specifically, the COP decision stated that the adverse effects of climate change have a range of implications for the effective enjoyment of human rights and that the effects will be felt most acutely by those segments of the population that are already vulnerable. Most important, the decision stated that, '[p]arties should, in all climate change related actions, fully respect human rights'.[14]

In subsequent years, the Human Rights Council has continued to adopt resolutions drawing attention to the effects of climate change on the enjoyment of human rights and encouraging its special rapporteurs and independent experts to consider the issue within their respective mandates.[15] The Council has also requested OHCHR to provide additional studies on the effect of climate change on the right to health and on children's health, and held panel discussions to focus attention on climate change.[16] In 2012, the Council created a new mandate on human rights and the environment, appointing the present author as the first independent expert. Over the next two years, he issued reports mapping statements by human rights bodies on the human obligations relating to the enjoyment of a safe, clean, healthy, and sustainable environment, and identifying good practices in the use of

[12] UNHRC Res 10/4 (25 March 2009) UN Doc A/HRC/RES/10/4.

[13] OHCHR 'Joint Statement of the Special Procedure Mandate Holders of the Human Rights Council on the UN Climate Change Conference' (Copenhagen, 7–18 December 2009) <https://www2.ohchr.org/english/bodies/chr/special/docs/Fifteenth_Issue_October-December2009.pdf> accessed 25 November 2019>.

[14] UNFCCC Dec 1/CP.16 (15 March 2011) UN Doc FCCC/CP/2010/7/Add.1 para 8.

[15] UN Doc A/HRC/RES/18/22 (30 September 2011); UN Doc A/HRC/RES/26/27 (27 June 2014); UN Doc A/HRC/RES/29/15 (2 July 2015); UN Doc A/HRC/RES/32/33 (18 July 2016); UN Doc A/HRC/RES/41/21 (23 July 2019).

[16] For example, in March 2015, it held a panel discussion that included participation by the President of Kiribati and the Prime Minister of Tuvalu.

such obligations.[17] In March 2015, the Council renewed the mandate for another three years and changed his title to special rapporteur.[18]

Over the same period, other mandate holders continued to publish reports describing the effect of climate change on particular human rights, including the right to food, the right to housing, the rights of internally displaced persons, and the rights of migrants.[19] In April 2015, at the request of the Climate Vulnerable Forum (a group of the states most vulnerable to climate change), several mandate holders published a joint report on the adverse effects that a 2 °C increase in average global temperature would have on the enjoyment of human rights.[20] Other international organizations, including the United Nations Environment Programme and the United Nations Children's Fund, also issued reports on the effects of climate change on human rights.[21]

In addition, the years before the adoption of the Paris Agreement saw a number of joint statements by mandate holders on human rights and climate change. In October 2014, twenty-seven mandate holders sent an open letter to the parties to the UNFCCC urging them to recognize the adverse effects of climate change on the enjoyment of human rights and to adopt urgent and ambitious mitigation and adaptation measures to prevent further harm. They proposed that the climate

[17] OHCHR 'Report of the Independent Expert on the Issue of Human Rights Obligations Relating to the Enjoyment of a Safe, Clean, Healthy and Sustainable Environment, John H Knox: Mapping Report' (30 December 2013) UN Doc A/HRC/25/53 (hereafter Knox, 'Mapping Report'); OHCHR 'Report of the Independent Expert on the Issue of Human Rights Obligations Relating to the Enjoyment of a Safe, Clean, Healthy and Sustainable Environment, John H. Knox: Compilation of Good Practices' (3 February 2015) UN Doc A/HRC/28/61.

[18] UN Doc A/HRC/RES/28/11 (26 March 2015). In 2018, the mandate was renewed for another three years. UN Doc A/HRC/RES/37/8 (22 March 2018). Professor David R. Boyd was appointed to the position in August 2018.

[19] OHCHR 'Report of the Special Rapporteur on Adequate Housing as a Component of the Right to an Adequate Standard of Living, and on the Right to Non-Discrimination in this Context' (6 August 2009) UN Doc A/64/255; OHCHR 'Protection of and Assistance to Internally Displaced Persons' (9 August 2011) UN Doc A/66/285; OHCHR 'Report of the Special Rapporteur on the Human Rights of Migrants' (13 August 2012) UN Doc A/67/299; OHCHR 'Interim Report of the Special Rapporteur on the Right to Food' (5 August 2015) UN Doc A/70/287. In June 2014, the then Independent Expert on Human Rights and the Environment summarized the statements made to that point by the mandate holders, the human rights treaty bodies, and others on climate change and human rights. OHCHR 'Mapping Human Rights Obligations Relating to the Enjoyment of a Safe, Clean, Healthy and Sustainable Environment: Focus Report on Human Rights and Climate Change (June 2014) <http://www.ohchr.org/EN/Issues/Environment/SREnvironment/Pages/ClimateChange.aspx> accessed 13 August 2019.

[20] OHCHR, 'The Effects of Climate Change on the Full Enjoyment of Human Rights' (30 April 2015) <http://www.ohchr.org/EN/Issues/Environment/SREnvironment/Pages/ClimateChange.aspx> accessed 13 August 2019 (hereafter OHCHR, 'The Effects of Climate Change'). The other authors of the report were Catalina Devandas Aguilar, the Special Rapporteur on the Rights of Persons with Disabilities; Philip Alston, the Special Rapporteur on Extreme Poverty and Human Rights; Virginia Dandan, the Independent Expert on Human Rights and International Solidarity; and Léo Heller, the Special Rapporteur on the Human Rights to Safe Drinking Water and Sanitation.

[21] UNICEF, 'Unless we act now: The impact of climate change on children' (November 2015) <http://www.unicef.org/publications/index_86337.html> accessed 13 August 2019; UNEP, 'Climate Change and Human Rights' (December 2015) <https://www.unenvironment.org/resources/report/climate-change-and-human-rights > accessed 25 November 2019(hereafter UNEP, 'Climate Change').

agreement then under negotiation include language stating that the parties 'shall, in all climate change related actions, respect, protect, promote, and fulfil human rights for all'.[22] On 10 December 2014, Human Rights Day, which fell during the twentieth COP, all seventy-three mandate holders issued a statement urging states to adopt the proposed language and underscoring that 'human rights must be pivotal in the ongoing negotiations and the new agreement must be firmly anchored in the human rights framework.'[23] On World Environment Day, 5 June 2015, twenty-seven mandate holders described the effects on human rights of even a 2 °C increase in temperature and again urged states to ensure that human rights are at the core of climate change governance.[24]

These resolutions, reports, and statements have clarified ways that climate change threatens the enjoyment of a vast range of human rights, including rights to life, health, food, water, and housing. The human rights perspective also emphasizes that climate change is inherently discriminatory: its effects will be felt disproportionately by those who are already among the poorest, the marginalized, and the least powerful, and who have done the least to contribute to the crisis.[25]

One possible result of these efforts, and of corresponding campaigns by indigenous peoples and civil society organizations (including the Center for International Environmental Law, Earthjustice, Human Rights Watch, the Interamerican Association for Environmental Defense, and the Mary Robinson Foundation for Climate Justice), has been to influence attitudes towards climate change among the public in general and decision-makers in particular. In this respect, the reports and statements in 2014 and 2015 sought to ensure that the comprehensive climate agreement to be adopted at the twenty-first COP, meeting in Paris in December 2015, would reflect and incorporate a human rights perspective. These efforts continued at the COP itself, where the then High Commissioner for Human Rights, Zeid Ra'ad Al Hussein, made a powerful statement that urgent,

[22] A New Climate Change Agreement Must Include Human Rights Protections for All: An Open Letter from Special Procedures Mandate-Holders of the Human Rights Council to the State Parties to the UN Framework Convention on Climate Change on the Occasion of the Meeting of the *Ad Hoc* Working Group on the Durban Platform for Enhanced Action in Bonn (20–25 October 2014) <http://www.ohchr.org/EN/Issues/Environment/SREnvironment/Pages/ClimateChange.aspx> accessed 13 August 2019.

[23] OHCHR 'Statement of the United Nations Special Procedures Mandate Holders on the Occasion of the Human Rights Day Geneva, Climate Change and Human Rights' (10 December 2014) <http://www.ohchr.org/EN/NewsEvents/Pages/DisplayNews.aspx?NewsID=15393&LangID=E> accessed 13 August 2019.

[24] OHCHR 'Joint Statement by UN Special Procedures on the Occasion of World Environment Day: Climate Change and Human Rights' (5 June 2015) <http://www.ohchr.org/EN/NewsEvents/Pages/DisplayNews.aspx?NewsID=16049&LangID=E> accessed 13 August 2019.

[25] For detailed descriptions of these effects see OHCHR, 'The Effects of Climate Change' (n 20); UNEP 'Climate Change' (n 21); OHCHR 'Report of the Special Rapporteur on Extreme Poverty and Human Rights' (25 June 2019) UN Doc A/HRC/41/39.

effective, and ambitious action to combat climate change was necessary to meet the obligations of states under human rights law.[26]

No-one should overestimate the effect that United Nations reports and resolutions can have on public attitudes or negotiating positions. Still, framing climate change in human rights terms may help to characterize its consequences as immediate rather than merely long term, to highlight local and regional impacts in particular, and to illustrate harmful effects on human health. These strategies, it has been suggested, increase the likelihood of effective communication with audiences that might otherwise dismiss climate change as a distant problem.[27] At the same time, it is likely that a human rights frame resonates best with audiences that are already predisposed to give weight to human rights claims.[28]

In this period, many governments also began to use human rights rhetoric in connection with climate change. For example, in February 2015, OHCHR and the Mary Robinson Foundation co-hosted a Climate Justice Dialogue in Geneva, which brought together delegates to the climate negotiations and the Human Rights Council. At the suggestion of Costa Rica, participants drafted the Geneva Pledge for Human Rights in Climate Action, a voluntary undertaking through which states promised to facilitate the sharing of knowledge and best practices between climate and human rights experts at the national level. By the time of the Paris conference, thirty countries had taken the pledge.

The efforts to bring human rights to bear on climate policy culminated in the Paris Agreement itself. The most obvious sign of their success was the inclusion of language on human rights in the text of the agreement. Until late in the negotiation, the reference was included in draft Article 2, but objections by some countries to including it in an 'operative' provision led to its being transferred to the preamble:

> Parties should, when taking action to address climate change, respect, promote and consider their respective obligations on human rights, the right to health,

[26] OHCHR, 'Burning Down the House' (3 December 2015) <http://www.ohchr.org/EN/NewsEvents/Pages/BurningDowntheHouse.aspx> accessed 13 August 2019; See also the Statement of the Special Rapporteur on Human Rights and the Environment, 'COP21: States' Human Rights Obligations Encompass Climate Change' (3 December 2015) <http://www.ohchr.org/EN/NewsEvents/Pages/DisplayNews.aspx?NewsID=16836&LangID=E> accessed 13 August 2019.

[27] Anthony Leiserowitz, 'Communicating the Risks of Global Warming: American Risk Perceptions, Affective Images, and Interpretive Communities' in Susanne Moser and Lisa Dilling (eds), *Creating a Climate for Change: Communicating Climate Change and Facilitating Social Change* (CUP 2007) 44. On the other hand, other research has indicated that, 'fear-inducing messages stressing the negative consequences of climate change failed to motivate individual engagement'. Seung Mo Jang (2013) 'Framing Responsibility in Climate Change Discourse: Ethnocentric Attribution Bias, Perceived Causes, and Policy Attitudes' 36 Journal of Environmental Psychology 27, 28.

[28] In terms of moral foundations theory, this would mean that a human rights framework would be more persuasive to those whose morality is grounded more on concepts of harm/care and fairness/justice than on loyalty, authority, purity, and patriotism. See Christopher Wolsko, Hector Ariceaga, and Jesse Seiden (2016) 'Red, White, and Blue Enough to be Green: Effects of Moral Framing on Climate Change Attitudes and Conservation Behaviors' 65 Journal of Experimental Social Psychology 7.

the rights of indigenous peoples, local communities, migrants, children, persons with disabilities and people in vulnerable situations and the right to development, as well as gender equality, empowerment of women and intergenerational equity.

As is not unusual in multilateral negotiations conducted under time pressure, the final language could have been more elegantly phrased. Nevertheless, the key points are clear: states have human rights obligations that are relevant to climate change; parties should respect, promote, and consider those obligations when taking actions to address it; the relevant rights include the right to health, the right to development, and gender equality, and also the rights of those who are most at risk from the effects of climate change; and additional considerations such as intergenerational equity are also relevant.

Lavanya Rajamani has pointed out that the drafters circumscribed this language in some respects, especially as compared to the more ambitious language proposed by human rights advocates.[29] For example, the phrase 'when taking action to address climate change' appears to have been intended to focus on the implementation of actions taken in response to climate change, rather than decisions as to the level of ambition and scope of states' mitigation and adaptation actions. Of course, the line between ambition and implementation is not always clear. More generally, every party to the UNFCCC belongs to at least one human rights treaty; as a result, all the parties already have human rights obligations that, where relevant, apply to all of their actions, including all of their climate change related actions, as the parties recognized in Cancun in 2010.

Rajamani notes the importance of the word 'respective' in the preambular paragraph, which she suggests means that no new human rights obligations are implied for states and that their existing obligations vary according to the human rights instruments that they have accepted. While it is certainly the case that, even without the use of the term 'respective,' a preambular paragraph in a climate agreement would not be the place to create *new* human rights obligations, the inclusion of the word does not preclude the application of *existing* human rights obligations to climate change. As this chapter has explained, states had generally accepted the idea that human rights are relevant to climate change even before Paris, and the language in the Paris Agreement will be taken—as Rajamani recognizes—as signalling increased openness within the climate regime to concerns and arguments based on human rights.

Indeed, such arguments were made by governments during the negotiation itself, when they used human rights rhetoric to argue for a tougher target for global average temperature. Speaking as the chair of the Climate Vulnerable Forum, the Philippines cited the report prepared by human rights mandate holders on a 2 °C

[29] See Rajamani, 'Human Rights in the Climate Change Regime' (n 3).

increase in temperature as an argument for adopting the lower target of 1.5 °C. In the event, then, the recognition of the devastating effects on human rights of even a 2 °C increase may have helped to convince the negotiators to adopt the stronger language in Article 2 that the Agreement 'aims to strengthen the global response to the threat of climate change ... including by holding the increase in the global average temperature to well below 2 °C above pre-industrial levels and to pursue efforts to limit the temperature increase to 1.5 °C above pre-industrial levels, recognizing that this would significantly reduce the risks and impacts of climate change'.

III. The Human Rights Obligations Relating to Climate Change

As the previous section explains, the 2010 decision of the COP at Cancun states that the parties to the UNFCCC should fully respect human rights in all climate change related actions, and the preamble to the 2015 Paris Agreement states that parties should respect their obligations on human rights when taking action to address climate change. But what are those obligations? What does human rights law have to say about climate change?

Since it is now almost universally acknowledged that climate change threatens the enjoyment of human rights, it may seem obvious that states should have duties to protect against that interference. However, it is less obvious exactly what those duties are, since no treaty, declaration, or other international instrument specifically describes them. It is therefore necessary to draw on the broader application of human rights norms to all types of environmental harm. Human rights bodies have created a detailed jurisprudence that clarifies the nature and scope of human rights obligations in the environmental context. While few of the relevant sources address climate change directly, the environmental human rights jurisprudence encompasses climate change as a particularly grave type of environmental harm. This section of the chapter describes first how human rights norms apply to environmental harm generally, then how the norms apply to climate change in particular.

A. Environmental Human Rights Law

Human rights law obligations have developed for the most part without reference to a human right to a healthy environment, which is not explicitly recognized in global human rights agreements.[30] Instead, human rights bodies have 'greened'

[30] The Convention on the Rights of the Child does refer to environmental pollution in the context of the right to health, requiring its parties to take appropriate measures, *inter alia*, to pursue implementation of the right to health through measures that include combating disease and malnutrition *inter alia* 'through the provision of adequate nutritious foods and clean drinking-water, taking into consideration

existing human rights, such as rights to life and health, by applying them to environmental issues. They have uniformly concluded that environmental degradation can interfere with the enjoyment of these and other rights, and they have reached remarkably congruent conclusions about the obligations of states to protect against such interference.[31] The obligations fall into three principal categories: procedural obligations; substantive obligations; and obligations relating to those who may be particularly vulnerable to environmental harm.

Procedural obligations include duties to assess the impacts of actions that may cause environmental harm interfering with the full enjoyment of human rights, to provide information relating to the environment, to facilitate full and informed public participation and protect the rights of freedom of expression and association in the context of environmental decision-making, and to provide access to effective remedies for states' failure to comply with these obligations. Human rights bodies have stated that implementation of these obligations is necessary to protect a wide variety of human rights, including rights to life and health, from environmental harm.[32]

These 'access rights' are also reflected in Principle 10 of the 1992 Rio Declaration, which states:

> Environmental issues are best handled with participation of all concerned citizens, at the relevant level. At the national level, each individual shall have appropriate access to information concerning the environment that is held by public authorities, including information on hazardous materials and activities in their communities, and the opportunity to participate in decision-making processes. States shall facilitate and encourage public awareness and participation by making information widely available. Effective access to judicial and administrative proceedings, including redress and remedy, shall be provided.[33]

the dangers and risks of environmental pollution'. Convention on the Rights of the Child (adopted 20 November 1989, entered into force 2 September 1990) 1577 UNTS 3 (CRC) art 24(2). The right is recognized in regional agreements, including the African Charter on Human and Peoples' Rights (adopted 27 June 1981, entered into force 21 October 1986) (1982) 21 ILM 58 (African Charter) art 24, and the Additional Protocol to the American Convention on Human Rights in the Area of Economic, Social and Cultural Rights (Protocol of San Salvador) (entered into force 16 November 1999) 28 ILM 161 art 11.

---

[31] See generally Knox, 'Mapping Report' (n 17); OHCHR 'Report of the Special Rapporteur on the issue of human rights obligations relating to the enjoyment of a safe, clean, healthy and sustainable environment (24 January 2018) UN Doc A/HRC/37/59 (setting out Framework Principles on Human Rights and the Environment that summarize the human rights obligations relating to the environment) (hereafter Knox, 'Framework Principles').

[32] Ibid, principles 5-10.

[33] UNCED Rio Declaration on Environment and Development (14 June 1992) UN Doc A/CONF.151/26/Rev.1 principle 10.

Many multilateral environmental agreements include provisions on one or more of these access rights.[34] The Aarhus Convention, which was adopted under the auspices of the United Nations Economic Commission for Europe, sets out particularly detailed requirements for information, participation, and remedy in the environmental context.[35] In addition, countries in Latin America and the Caribbean recently negotiated a new regional agreement on the implementation of Principle 10.[36]

With respect to substantive obligations, human rights bodies have been more deferential. Although they have made clear that states are expected to adopt and implement institutional safeguards against environmental harm to human rights, including such harm caused by private actors, human rights bodies have not tried to determine specific levels of emissions or concentrations of pollution that are allowed under human rights law. States have discretion to strike a balance between environmental protection and economic development. However, this discretion is not unlimited. States should avoid unreasonable, foreseeable infringements of human rights. Human rights bodies have identified factors that are relevant to determining whether the discretion has been exercised in a reasonable manner. For example, the decision should result from a process that satisfies the procedural obligations described above. Other relevant factors may include whether the end result accords with national and international environmental standards, and whether it is not retrogressive. Finally, states must implement and comply with the laws that they have adopted.[37]

A requirement that cuts across both procedural and substantive obligations is that states must not discriminate on prohibited grounds in their environmental law and policy.[38] In addition, states may have more specific obligations with respect to those particularly vulnerable to environmental harm, including women, children, and indigenous peoples. The obligations relating to indigenous peoples are especially well-developed. For example, the Inter-American Court of Human Rights has held that states must consult with an affected indigenous people regarding any proposed concessions or other activities that may affect their lands and

[34] See Rotterdam Convention on the Prior Informed Consent Procedure for Certain Hazardous Chemicals and Pesticides in International Trade (adopted 10 September 1998, entered into force 24 February 2004) 2244 UNTS 337 (Rotterdam Convention) art 15; Stockholm Convention on Persistent Organic Pollutants (adopted 22 May 2001, entered into force 17 May 2004) 2256 UNTS 119 (Stockholm Convention) art 10.

[35] Aarhus Convention on Access to Information, Public Participation in Decision-Making and Access to Justice in Environmental Matters (adopted 25 June 1998, entered into force 30 October 2001) 2161 UNTS 450.

[36] Escazú Regional Agreement on Access to Information, Public Participation and Justice in Environmental Matters in Latin America and the Caribbean (adopted 4 March 2018, not yet in force) https://www.cepal.org/en/escazuagreement.

[37] Knox, 'Framework Principles' (n 31) principles 10, 11.

[38] See *Mossville Environmental Action Now v United States*, Inter-American Commission on Human Rights No 43/10 (2010).

natural resources, ensure that no concession will be issued without a prior assessment of its environmental and social impacts, and guarantee that the community receives a 'reasonable benefit' from any such plan if approved. Moreover, the state must obtain the free, prior, and informed consent of the indigenous people with respect to 'large-scale development or investment projects that would have a major impact within [its] territory'.[39]

B. Applying the Environmental Human Rights Jurisprudence to Climate Change

In my previous work, I have set out a general framework for applying environmental human rights law to climate change.[40] In some respects, this application is quite straightforward. Every state has an obligation to protect against the adverse effects of climate change on human rights, just as it has an obligation to protect against the effects of other types of environmental harm.

However, it can be difficult to identify the causal chain between particular emissions of greenhouse gases and particular effects, and for this reason the Office of the High Commissioner, in its seminal 2009 report on human rights and climate change, cautioned that 'while climate change has obvious implications for the enjoyment of human rights, it is less obvious whether, and to what extent, such effects can be qualified as human rights violations in a strict legal sense.'[41] Ten years later, it has become clearer that tracing causation is more practicable than previously thought.[42] Moreover, as the OHCHR report acknowledged, the duty of a state to protect against the effects of climate change is not limited to those effects that it is particularly 'responsible' for causing. Even without a determination that a state has violated human rights law, 'human rights obligations provide important protection to the individuals whose rights are affected by climate change'.[43] Every state has an obligation to protect against the infringement of human rights by the effects of climate change, whether or not the state is directly responsible for the cause of the infringement.[44] This conclusion follows from the nature of their obligations to protect against environmental harm generally. Human rights bodies have made clear

[39] See *Saramaka People v Suriname*, Inter-American Court of Human Rights Series C No 172 (28 November 2007) paras 129, 134.

[40] See John H. Knox, 'Human Rights Principles and Climate Change' in Cinnamon Carlarne, Kevin Gray, and Richard Tarasofsky (eds), *Oxford Handbook of International Climate Change Law* (OUP 2016) 213; John H. Knox (2009) 'Climate Change and Human Rights Law' 50 Virginia Journal of International Law 163 (hereafter Knox, 'Climate Change').

[41] 'OHCHR Report' (n 11) para 70.

[42] See National Academies of Sciences, Engineering, and Medicine, Attribution of Extreme Weather Events in the Context of Climate Change (2016).

[43] 'OHCHR Report' (n 11) para 71.

[44] See John H. Knox (2009) 'Linking Human Rights and Climate Change at the United Nations' 33 Harvard Environmental Law Review 477.

that states should protect against foreseeable environmental impairment of human rights whether or not the states directly cause the harm.[45]

The more difficult obstacle to the application of environmental human rights principles to climate change is that those principles were largely developed in the context of environmental harm whose causes and effects are felt within a single country. As a global problem that requires a global response, climate change raises the question of the extraterritorial application of human rights norms, an issue on which governments and human rights authorities have not always agreed. The issue of extraterritoriality is common to other twenty-first-century challenges, including lethal drones and cyber operations, as discussed by authors elsewhere in this volume.[46] Although many human rights experts have concluded that states have extraterritorial obligations with respect to economic, social, and cultural rights, at least,[47] governments of developed countries have tended to disagree.[48]

Questions of extraterritoriality are not relevant to all aspects of the application of environmental human rights law to climate change. Even under a restrictive view of human rights obligations, in which states only have duties relating to those within their own territory or jurisdiction, states have clear obligations to take measures to help their own people adapt to the unavoidable (or simply unavoided) consequences of climate change.[49] This is the case even for states that contribute little or nothing to global levels of greenhouse gas emissions. These measures should meet the specific obligations set out above: they should make information available, provide for public participation and effective remedies, and adopt levels of protection that, *inter alia*, take into account the special situation of vulnerable people.

But this restrictive view is obviously inadequate with respect to the extraterritorial consequences of contributing to climate change. In particular, assessing states' obligations to mitigate their contributions to climate change only by reference to the effects of those contributions on those within their jurisdiction seems fundamentally unjust, since it ignores the substantial transboundary effects of such contributions by the major emitters. At the same time, no single emitter—even the largest—can prevent the effects of climate change on their own people merely by reducing their own emissions.

[45] See *Budayeva v Russia* App No 15339/00 (ECtHR, 29 September 2008).

[46] See Heyns, Akande, Hill-Cawthorne, and Chengeta, Chapter 7, this book, and McDermott, Chapter 8, this book.

[47] Knox, 'Mapping Report' (n 17) paras 62–68; Olivier de Schutter *et al* (2012) 'Commentary to the Maastricht Principles on Extraterritorial Obligations of States in the Area of Economic, Social and Cultural Rights' 34 Human Rights Quarterly 1084.

[48] Matthew Craven, 'The Violence of Dispossession: Extra-Territoriality and Economic, Social, and Cultural Rights' in Mashood Baderin and Robert McCorquodale (eds), *Economic, Social and Cultural Rights in Action* (OUP 2007) 71, 77. For a detailed analysis of the extraterritorial application of human rights law to climate change, see Knox 'Climate Change' (n 39) 40–52.

[49] Margaux Hall and David Weiss (2012) 'Avoiding Adaptation Apartheid: Climate Change Adaptation and Human Rights Law' 37 Yale Journal of International Law 309.

Therefore, in order for human rights to apply to mitigation, it seems necessary to treat climate change as a global problem. However, there are practical as well as legal objections to trying to address climate change merely through the extraterritorial extension of domestic obligations. Although climate change is in a sense a complex set of overlapping transboundary harms, it seems doubtful that the best way to address it would be for every state unilaterally to take into account its individual contribution to the effects of climate change in every other state in the world, in light of its human rights obligations. Nor has the international community attempted to address climate change in this way. Instead, states have treated climate change a global problem that requires joint action to solve.

This approach accords with, and can be seen as an application of, the duty of international cooperation.[50] The duty of international cooperation has support in the general practice of states and, more specifically, in the Charter of the United Nations. Article 55 of the Charter requires the United Nations to promote 'universal respect for, and observance of, human rights and fundamental freedoms for all', and in Article 56, 'all Members pledge themselves to take joint and separate action in co-operation with the Organization for the achievement of the purposes set forth in Article 55'. Similarly, Article 2(1) of the International Covenant on Economic, Social and Cultural Rights requires each of its parties to take steps not only individually, but also 'through international assistance and cooperation', towards the progressive realization of the rights recognized in the Covenant.

Although international cooperation is not the primary way that states address most human rights issues, states have repeatedly recognized that 'the global nature of climate change calls for the widest possible cooperation by all countries and their participation in an effective and appropriate international response'.[51] The duty of international cooperation provides a basis for applying the environmental human rights jurisprudence to the collective actions of states to address climate change. The obligation to protect against environmental interference with the enjoyment of human rights, including its subsidiary duties described in the previous section, can inform the content of the duty of international cooperation in addressing the threat to human rights posed by global climate change.[52] In other words, acting together, states should endeavour to meet the human rights obligations relating to environmental cooperation in relation to the specific challenge of climate change. They should, for example, ensure that their climate policy provides for access to information, public participation, and access to effective remedies; that it adopts standards that take into account international standards and are non-retrogressive;

[50] OHCHR 'Report of the Special Rapporteur on the Issue of Human Rights Obligations Relating to the Enjoyment of a Safe, Clean, Healthy and Sustainable Environment' (2016) UN Doc A/HRC/31/52 para 42 (hereafter Special Rapporteur, 'Climate Change Report').

[51] 'UNFCCC' (n 1) pmbl; UNHRC Res 26/27 (15 July 2014) UN Doc A/HRC/RES/26/27; UNHRC Res 29/15 (22 July 2015) UN Doc A/HRC/RES/29/15.

[52] Knox, 'Climate Change' (n 39) 52–58.

and that it safeguards the rights of the most vulnerable, in particular. Most important, they should do their best to avoid massive, foreseeable adverse effects on the enjoyment of human rights.

IV. Does the Paris Agreement Comply with Human Rights Law?

How well do the Paris Agreement and the climate regime of which it is an integral part comply with the human rights obligations relating to climate change?[53] The following first section examines how the climate regime supports the implementation of states' internal human rights obligations—that is, the obligations that each state owes to those within its own jurisdiction to help them adapt to the effects of climate change. The second section analyses whether and how the climate regime fulfils human rights obligations relating to the international cooperation necessary to take effective measures to mitigate climate change on a global scale. The sections argue that while the climate regime is generally consistent with the obligations of each state to protect against the effects of climate change within its own jurisdiction, it falls short of their collective obligation to cooperate to mitigate climate change. Most important, even if states fulfil their pledged commitments, they will not meet come close to meeting the 1.5 °C target set by the Paris Agreement.

A. Implementation of Internal Human Rights Obligations

The climate regime is generally consistent with and supportive of the obligation of each state to protect against the effects of climate change on the enjoyment of human rights within its own territory, but the regime falls short in some critical ways. The Paris Agreement builds on previous commitments in the UNFCCC concerning procedural obligations. With respect to the obligation to provide information, for example, Article 6(a) of the UNFCCC requires its parties to promote and facilitate educational and public awareness programmes, as well as public access to information. Article 12 of the Paris Agreement calls on its parties to cooperate in taking measures to enhance such measures. Many states are already taking significant steps to assess the impacts of climate change and to make this information publicly available.[54] Ideally, such assessments should include the transboundary effects of the activities. But even with respect to the effects of climate change that are felt within a state, assessments are an important method of clarifying impacts,

[53] This section draws on the analysis and language of my report to the Human Rights Council on climate change and human rights. See Special Rapporteur, 'Climate Change Report' (n 49).

[54] UNEP, 'Climate Change' (n 21) 34.

especially on vulnerable communities, and providing a basis for adaptation planning, as Article 7(9) of the Paris Agreement recognizes.

Article 6(a) of the UNFCCC also requires its parties to promote and facilitate public participation, and Article 12 of the Paris Agreement requires its parties to cooperate in taking appropriate measures to enhance public participation. Similarly, the UN General Assembly has recognized 'the need to engage a broad range of stakeholders at the global, regional, national and local levels, including national, subnational and local governments, private businesses and civil society, and including youth and persons with disabilities, and that gender equality and the effective participation of women and indigenous peoples are important for effective action on all aspects of climate change'.[55] Many governments have already provided for public participation in environmental decision-making, but they can often do more to solicit public input and ensure that it is taken into account.[56]

The requirements of information and participation apply not only to decisions about how much climate protection to pursue, but also to the measures through which the protection is achieved. Decisions on mitigation or adaptation projects must be made with the informed participation of the people who would be affected by the projects. Article 4(1)(f) of the UNFCCC encourages states to employ impact assessments of such measures, with a view to minimizing adverse effects on the economy, on public health and on the quality of the environment. However, the financial mechanisms the climate regime establishes to support mitigation and adaptation measures do not always protect human rights, including the rights of information and participation.

Ideally, every state should ensure that its legal system provides for effective remedies for all human rights violations, including those arising from climate-related actions. At the international level, states should work together to support the establishment and implementation of procedures to provide such remedies, including with respect to measures supported by international finance mechanisms. A report prepared by UNEP states that 'perhaps the largest procedural gap in this context is the lack of access to justice and remedies for climate-related harms.'[57] The climate regime currently does little to require states to provide effective remedies for climate-related violations of human rights.

As noted above, the substantive obligation of each state to protect those within its jurisdiction from the harmful effects of climate change is relatively straightforward with respect to the establishment and implementation of effective adaptation measures. States must adopt a legal and institutional framework that assists those within their jurisdiction to adapt to the unavoided effects of climate change. While states have some discretion as to which measures to adopt, taking into account

[55] UNGA Res 67/210 (12 March 2013) UN Doc A/RES/67/210 para 12.
[56] UNEP, 'Climate Change' (n 21) 34–35.
[57] Ibid, 35.

their economic situation and other national priorities, they should ensure that the measures: result from a process that provides for informed public participation; take into account national and international standards; and are neither retrogressive nor discriminatory. Finally, once the standards are adopted, states should ensure that they are implemented. Article 7 of the Paris Agreement calls on each party to engage in adaptation planning processes, including formulating and implementing national adaptation plans and building the resilience of socioeconomic and ecological systems. Like the UNFCCC, the Paris Agreement includes provisions designed to promote, in the words of Article 7, adaptation action that follows 'a country-driven, gender-responsive, participatory and fully transparent approach'.

With respect to obligations to those who are most vulnerable to the effects of climate change, states have procedural duties under human rights law to assess the effects of climate change, and of actions taken to mitigate and to adapt to it, on vulnerable communities. They should ensure that those who are in vulnerable situations and who are marginalized are fully informed of the effects of climate actions, that they are able to take part in decision-making processes, that their concerns are taken into account and that they have access to remedies for violations of their rights. Substantively, states should seek to protect the most vulnerable in developing and implementing all climate-related actions. Even if mitigation targets are met, vulnerable communities may still suffer harm as a result of climate change. Indeed, many are already experiencing adverse effects. The rights of the most vulnerable must be respected and protected in all actions, including actions taken to mitigate or adapt to climate change. Renewable energy projects and efforts to protect forests, while they may be highly desirable as methods of reducing or offsetting greenhouse gas emissions, are not exempt from human rights norms. When such projects are proposed for the territory of indigenous peoples, for example, the projects must accord with the obligations owed to those peoples, including, where applicable, the duties to facilitate their participation in the decision-making process and not to proceed without their free, prior and informed consent.

The Paris Agreement recognizes the importance of respecting the rights of the most vulnerable. Its preamble specifically refers to the rights of indigenous peoples, local communities, migrants, children, persons with disabilities, and people in vulnerable situations, as well as gender equality, in calling on the parties to respect, promote, and consider their respective obligations on human rights when taking action to address climate change. Article 7 of the Agreement emphasizes that, in addition to being country-driven, participatory and fully transparent, adaptation action should be gender-responsive and take into consideration vulnerable groups, communities and ecosystems.

B. Complying with the Duty of International Cooperation

Acting together, pursuant to the duty of international cooperation, have states collectively complied with their human rights obligations relating to climate change? Although the answer is yes in some respects, states are falling short of their most important obligation—to cooperate to reduce greenhouse gas emissions to levels that will avoid massive adverse effects on the full enjoyment of human rights.

Procedurally, states can point to some real successes. In particular, they have adopted an exemplary practice in the assessment and provision of information about climate change. Through the Intergovernmental Panel on Climate Change, states have provided for expert assessments of the scientific aspects of climate change, the vulnerability of socioeconomic and natural systems, and options for mitigation of and adaptation to climate change. By regularly publishing detailed reports summarizing the state of scientific and technical knowledge, the Panel has given governments and people around the world information about the effects of climate change and the consequences of various approaches to addressing it.

Substantively, the situation is more complicated. States agreed in the UNFCCC that their goal is to achieve 'stabilization of greenhouse gas concentrations in the atmosphere at a level that would prevent dangerous anthropogenic interference with the climate system'.[58] In the Paris Agreement, states went further, stating in Article 2(1) that they aim to hold the increase in temperature to well below 2 °C above pre-industrial levels and to pursue efforts to limit the temperature increase to 1.5 °C, 'recognizing that this would significantly reduce the risks and impacts of climate change.' This target is consistent with the obligations of states, acting together in accordance with the duty of international cooperation, to protect human rights from the dangerous effects of climate change.

Through the UNFCCC and the Paris Agreement, states have created a legal and institutional framework to try to reach this goal. As noted, human rights norms contemplate that states have some discretion to decide how best to balance their obligation to protect against environmental harm with their pursuit of other legitimate interests, but they should exercise that discretion reasonably in the light of all relevant factors, including those identified above. Applying those factors to the international climate regime indicates that states have struck a reasonable balance in many respects. They have conducted an international decision-making process based on detailed, publicly disseminated scientific assessments. The agreement that emerged from this process in 2015 takes into account international standards, including human rights standards, and is non-retrogressive. It also appears to be non-discriminatory, and it includes provisions designed to address the concerns of the most vulnerable countries and communities.

[58] 'UNFCCC' (n 1) art 2.

In the most critical respect, however, the Paris Agreement falls short. The Agreement addresses mitigation principally through requiring each party to prepare its own nationally determined contribution. The problem is not that the Agreement allows each state to decide for itself what contribution it commits to make; the problem is that the proposed contributions do not go far enough. Almost every state in the world has presented a nationally determined contribution, but even if fully implemented, they will not put the world on a path that avoids disastrous consequences for human rights. The UN Environmental Programme (UNEP) has determined that full implementation of the intended contributions would lead to emission levels in 2030 that will likely cause a global average temperature increase of well over 2 °C, and quite possibly over 3 °C.[59] Therefore, even if they meet their current commitments, states will not satisfy their human rights obligations.

From a human rights perspective, then, it is necessary not only to implement the current intended contributions, but also to strengthen those contributions to meet the target set out in Article 2 of the Paris Agreement. States are aware of the gap between their current commitments and their collective goal, and they agreed in Paris to review the adequacy of their commitments through stock-taking exercises every five years, beginning in 2018. However, it is already clear that states must move beyond their current commitments in order to close the gap between what is promised and what is necessary.

Other elements of the international climate regime are also integral to the implementation of the duty of international cooperation. To mention two of these elements in particular: (i) Article 7(7) of the Paris Agreement calls on the parties to strengthen their cooperation on enhancing action on adaptation, including with regard to sharing information, improving the effectiveness of adaptation actions and assisting developing countries; and (ii) developed countries reiterated in Paris their commitment to assist developing countries with respect to both mitigation and adaptation. The human rights norms relating to protection of the environment indicate that once states have adopted measures to protect human rights from environmental harm, they must implement those measures. The commitments made in relation to the Paris Agreement are elements of the collective decision of states on how to address climate change. All of them—the commitments for assistance as much as the commitments for mitigation and adaptation—should be implemented fully, as well as strengthened as necessary, to protect against the effects of climate change on human rights. Needless to say, backwards steps, such as the announcement by the Trump Administration that it will withdraw from the Paris Agreement in November 2020, are completely unjustifiable breaches of their human rights obligations in relation to climate change.

[59] UNEP, 'The Emissions Gap Report' (2016) xviii <http://web.unep.org/emissionsgap/> accessed 13 August 2019.

V. Human Rights in the Evolving Climate Regime

The Paris Agreement sets out a framework for further work that will take years to accomplish. This section focuses on two ways that human rights norms will continue to influence the evolution of the climate regime: in climate finance mechanisms, and in domestic litigation.

A. International Climate Finance

As noted above, human rights obligations apply not only to decisions about the level of protection from climate change but also to actions taken in response to climate change. States must take steps to ensure that mitigation and adaptation measures respect and protect the human rights of those who are most directly affected. Many of these measures will be facilitated by international climate finance mechanisms.[60] In Paris, the COP adopted a decision stating that developed countries intend to continue their existing collective mobilization goal, which is $100 billion per year as of 2020, and that, before 2025, the parties to the Paris Agreement will set a new goal from a floor of $100 billion, taking into account the needs and priorities of developing countries.[61] Whether these mechanisms have adequate environmental and social safeguards is therefore of critical importance to the protection of human rights.

Many climate finance mechanisms, including the Global Environment Facility (GEF) trust funds, the Adaptation Fund, the REDD+ program (operating through the Forest Carbon Partnership Facility and UN-REDD), and the Green Climate Fund, already have environmental and social safeguards in the form of criteria that proposed projects must satisfy in order to receive certification or approval. Although these safeguards should be strengthened, they do provide, when implemented, some significant protections for the human rights of those who may be affected by the projects.[62]

An exception is the Clean Development Mechanism (CDM), created under the auspices of the 1997 Kyoto Protocol as a way to encourage investment in renewable energy and other projects in developing countries that lead to emissions reductions. If certified by the CDM Board, a project can produce emissions credits that can be counted against the emissions reduction requirements

[60] On the relation of public finance and human rights more generally, see Kuosmanen, Chapter 11, this book.

[61] 'Paris Agreement' (n 2) para 54.

[62] UNEP, 'Climate Change' (n 21) 36–39. The REDD+ program, designed in principle to protect against deforestation and degradation of forests, has been a particular focus of concern about its effects on human rights of local communities. See David Takacs (2014) 'Environmental Democracy and Forest Carbon (REDD+)' 44 Environmental Law 71.

of a developed country. The CDM has facilitated funding for thousands of projects, but its certification process does not include safeguards to protect against violations of human rights. As a result, some of its projects have been implicated in grave human rights abuses, including the violent suppression of peaceful opposition to proposed projects, and the non-consensual displacement of indigenous and local communities to make way for dams and other projects.[63]

The Paris Agreement provides for the creation of a new mechanism, known as yet only as the mechanism established in Article 6, paragraph 4, which is expected to become the successor to the CDM. The December 2015 decision adopted by the Paris Conference recommends that 'the Conference of the Parties serving as the meeting of the Parties to the Paris Agreement adopt rules, modalities and procedures for the mechanism established by Article 6, paragraph 4, of the Agreement on the basis of [among other things] … (f) Experience gained with and lessons learned from existing mechanisms and approaches adopted under the Convention and its related legal instruments.'

To that end, the COP's Subsidiary Body for Scientific and Technological Advice (SBSTA) will make recommendations to the COP on the elements of the new mechanism. In his role as the Special Rapporteur on human rights and the environment, the present author urged the SBSTA to adopt social and environmental safeguards that reflect human rights obligations. Specifically, he recommended that it:

1. Include a requirement that every proposed project and programme produces an environmental and social assessment… at a minimum requiring: assessment of potential risks before approval, with management plans that identify the measures necessary to avoid, minimize, or mitigate the risks; monitoring of projects and programmes over time; and public disclosure of assessments and management plans….
2. Provide for effective public participation… The new mechanism should ensure that proposals identify interested stakeholders and involve them as early as possible in planning any project or programme for which support is sought, and that public consultations be timely, effective, inclusive, and held free of coercion and in an appropriate way for communities that are directly affected by the proposed project or programme….
3. Include effective remedial procedures… The Adaptation Fund, for example, requires implementing entities to identify grievance mechanisms that provide

[63] See Naomi Roht-Arriaza (2010) '"First, Do No Harm": Human Rights and Efforts to Combat Climate Change' 38 Georgia Journal of International and Comparative Law 593, 596–98; Carbon Market Watch, 'Human Rights in the CDM' < <http://archive.carbonmarketwatch.org/category/human-right-in-climate/human-rights/> accessed 25 November 2019.

people who are affected by projects or programmes with an 'accessible, transparent, fair and effective process for receiving and addressing their complaints about environmental or social harms caused by any such project/programme.' In addition, the new mechanism should establish its own grievance procedure, with the authority to review complaints that the mechanism failed to meet its own requirements. . . .

4. Require legal and institutional protections against environmental and social risks. The new mechanism should require that projects and programmes not only assess environmental and social risks, but also include effective measures to avoid, minimize, and mitigate those risks during implementation. The Adaptation Fund again provides a possible model. It provides that all projects and programmes supported by the Fund shall be designed and implemented to meet specific environmental and social principles, including: provision of fair and equitable access to benefits; avoidance of any disproportionate adverse impacts on marginalized and vulnerable groups; gender equity; protection of the rights of indigenous peoples; avoidance of involuntary resettlement; protection of natural habitats; conservation of biological diversity; avoidance of increase in drivers of climate change; pollution prevention; avoidance of impacts on public health; avoidance of harm to physical and cultural heritage; and conservation of lands and soil. . . .
5. Include requirements for the protection of the most vulnerable. The rights of the most vulnerable must be respected and protected in all climate-related actions, including actions taken to mitigate or adapt to climate change. The new mechanism should include a commitment that projects and programmes do not exacerbate existing inequities, particularly with respect to marginalized or vulnerable groups, and it should follow the lead of other mechanisms, including the Adaptation Fund, in ensuring that its projects and programmes avoid imposing any disproportionate adverse impacts on marginalized and vulnerable groups... The new mechanism should provide that it will not support projects and programmes that are inconsistent with the United Nations Declaration on the Rights of Indigenous Peoples and other applicable international instruments on the rights of indigenous peoples, and it should ensure that projects and programmes are designed and implemented in order to avoid the need for involuntary resettlement. . . .
6. Include a general commitment to respect all human rights. This paper focuses on human rights obligations that are particularly relevant to environmental protection, but other human rights, including labour rights, may also be relevant to social safeguards in climate mechanisms. Climate mechanisms should ensure that they comply with all relevant human rights norms. To that end, it is important to include a general provision, such as that in the Adaptation Fund Environmental and Social Policy, which states: Projects/programmes

> supported by the mechanism shall respect and where applicable promote international human rights.[64]

The author's letter to the Board pointed to existing models, particularly the safeguards of the Adaptation Fund. As noted earlier, however, work remains to be done to strengthen the protections of all of the climate mechanisms and to make them more uniform. For example, although most of the mechanisms provide for some type of procedure through which claims of violation can be filed, these procedures are generally either weak, or completely within the control of the implementing government, or both.

As of October 2019, the SBSTA has not yet recommended elements of the new financial mechanism to the COP, although it is expected to do so in the near future. The Green Climate Fund (GCF) adopted an overarching Environmental and Social Policy as well as an Indigenous Peoples Policy in 2018, but it is still using interim safeguard guidelines for the certification of projects, based on those of the International Finance Corporation. In July 2019, the GCF Board approved a plan to develop and adopt its own environmental and social safeguards by 2021. Since the Green Climate Fund is expected to be the principal means through which funding for mitigation and adaptation projects flows to developing countries, its safeguards will be of particular importance.

B. Domestic Climate Litigation

The international climate regime depends for its implementation on domestic climate law and policy. Two recent cases show how human rights claims in domestic courts can help to push governments towards more effective implementation of their international commitments.

The better-known is *Urgenda Foundation v Netherlands*, which has resulted in two decisions by Dutch courts that the Netherlands must ensure that Dutch emissions of greenhouse gases by the end of the year 2020 are at least 25 per cent lower than the level of emissions in 1990.[65] In the first decision, issued in June 2015, a district court grounded its analysis on the general duty of care under Dutch law. It stated that the scientific consensus was that to keep the average global increase in temperature below 2 °C, the maximum allowable without massive harm, developed countries must lower their emissions 25–40 per cent

[64] Letter from John H. Knox, United Nations Special Rapporteur on the Issue of Human Rights Obligations Relating to the Enjoyment of a Safe, Clean, Healthy and Sustainable Environment to Ambassador Carlos Fuller, Chair of the Subsidiary Body for Scientific and Technological Advice (SBSTA) (3 May 2016).

[65] *Urgenda Foundation v Netherlands* (2015), C/09/456689 / HA ZA 13-1396 <http://uitspraken.rechtspraak.nl/inziendocument?id=ECLI:NL:RBDHA:2015:7196> accessed 13 August 2019.

from 1990 levels. It noted that the government of the Netherlands itself had previously committed to that target, and it concluded that the government's subsequent decision to adopt weaker measures did not have sufficient justification to satisfy the duty of care.

Three years later, in October 2019, the Hague Court of Appeal affirmed the decision on the basis of articles 2 and 8 of the European Human Rights Convention, which protect the rights to life and to private and home life, respectively.[66] The appellate court stated that the state has a positive obligation to take precautionary measures to protect these rights from infringement by real and imminent threats, and that climate change poses a serious risk that the current generation of citizens will be confronted with loss of life and/or a disruption of family life.[67] It concluded that the Netherlands should reduce its greenhouse gas emissions by at least 25 percent by the end of 2020.[68] It seems very likely that *Urgenda* will be followed by similar suits in other countries, in which human rights arguments will again be employed to strengthen and supplement domestic legal claims.[69]

A decision from Pakistan illustrates another way that rights-based claims can support implementation of the international climate regime. In *Ashgar Leghari v Pakistan*, the Lahore High Court Green Bench considered a claim from a Pakistani citizen that the government's failure to implement its national policy on climate change violated his constitutional right to life, which has been interpreted by Pakistani courts to include the right to a healthy and clean environment. The high court agreed, and ordered specific government agencies to appoint focal persons on climate change and to prepare a list of adaption measures to be completed by the end of 2015. The court then established a Climate Change Commission, composed of the focal points, and maintained continuing jurisdiction to monitor its progress towards achieving the measures.[70]

VI. Conclusion

One of the great achievements of the twentieth century was the articulation of universal human rights and corresponding obligations on states to respect and protect them. For that achievement to bear fruit in the twenty-first

[66] *Netherlands v Urgenda Foundation* (2018), 200.178.245/01 <https://uitspraken.rechtspraak.nl/inziendocument?id=ECLI:NL:GHDHA:2018:2610>.

[67] Ibid, paras 43, 45.

[68] Ibid, para 76.

[69] See Tracy Bach (2016) 'Human Rights in a Climate Changed World: The Impact of COP21, Nationally Determined Contributions, and National Courts' 40 Vermont Law Review 561, 582–85.

[70] *Ashgar Leghari v Federation of Pakistan* (2015), WP No 25501/2015 <https://elaw.org/pk_Leghari> accessed 13 August 2019.

century, it will be necessary for human rights to be internalized within other international regimes. The Paris Agreement will be remembered not only as the first major climate agreement of the century, but also as the first international environmental agreement to recognize that human rights are part of the framework it creates.

16
Human Rights, Population, and Climate Change

Simon Caney

> Generally, it is to be foreseen that the population of a kingdom (especially if it be not mown down by wars) do not exceed the stock of the kingdom which should maintain them: neither is the population to be reckoned only by number; for a smaller number, that spend more and earn less, do wear out an estate sooner than a greater number that live lower and gather more; therefore the multiplying of nobility, and other degrees of quality, in an over proportion to the common people, doth speedily bring a state to necessity.
>
> Francis Bacon, 'Of Seditions and Troubles'.[1]

I. Introduction

A. The Challenge of Climate Change

Humanity faces several severe challenges in this century. Among these is climate change. In its Fifth Assessment Report, the Intergovernmental Panel on Climate Change (IPCC) records that:

> To limit the warming caused by anthropogenic CO_2 emissions alone to be *likely* less than 2°C relative to the period 1861–1880, total CO_2 emissions from all anthropogenic sources would need to be limited to a cumulative budget of about 1000 PgC since that period. About half [445 to 585 PgC] of this budget was already emitted by 2011.[2]

[1] This is from Francis Bacon 'Of Seditions and Troubles' in *The Essays, the Wisdom of the Ancients, & New Atlantis* (London: Cassell and Company, 1907 [1625]), 56.

[2] Matthew Collins and Reto Knutti, 'Long-term Climate Change: Projections, Commitments and Irreversibility' in Thomas Stocker, Dahe Qin, Gian-Kasper Plattner, Melinda Tignor, Simon Allen, *et al* (eds), *Climate Change 2013: The Physical Science Basis. Working Group I Contribution to the Fifth*

Simon Caney, *Human Rights, Population, and Climate Change* In: Human Rights and 21st Century Challenges. Edited by: Dapo Akande, Jaakko Kuosmanen, Helen McDermott, and Dominic Roser, Published 2020 by Oxford University Press.
DOI: 10.1093/oso/9780198824770.003.0017

At the time of writing, and assuming the current rate of emissions, humanity will exceed the trillion tonne budget by 2034.[3]

This is, in itself, a terrifying prospect. However, it understates the urgency of the problem for, as the authors of the above statement note, this appraisal omits a number of factors. First, this calculation ignores other greenhouse gases and only includes CO_2 forcing. Second, the analysis above is designed to limit the probability of dangerous climate change (defined as a more than 2 °C increase over pre-industrial times) to no more than 34 per cent––but that probability will strike many of us as too high a gamble.[4] Third, it excludes 'a possible release of GHGs from permafrost or methane hydrates'.[5] As the Fifth Assessment Report emphasizes, if we take these three further factors into account then humanity has 'a lower budget'.[6] The budget would be even smaller still if we take into account a fourth point, namely that the IPCC statement takes the appropriate target to be 2 °C, whereas many would also argue that this is too high. Indeed, Article 2.1(a) of the Paris Agreement (agreed at the 2015 climate negotiations) specifies the goal as '[h]olding the increase in the global average temperature to well below 2 °C above pre-industrial levels and to pursue efforts to limit the temperature increase to 1.5 °C above pre-industrial levels, recognizing that this would significantly reduce the risks and impacts of climate change'.[7] I say all of this to bring out the gravity of the situation facing humanity.

B. Human Rights and Climate Change

Many people have framed the ethical issues surrounding climate change in terms of human rights.[8] Human rights enter the picture in at least three ways. First, some have argued that we should judge climatic changes in terms of their impact on the enjoyment of human rights. On this view, climate change is unjust, in part, because it undermines human rights––such as human rights to food, water, health, and life, among others).[9] Second, some have argued that the policies employed to address

Assessment Report of the Intergovernmental Panel on Climate Change (CUP 2013) 1033 (hereafter Collins and Knutti, 'Long-term Climate Change').

[3] See <http://trillionthtonne.org/>.

[4] See Roser, Chapter 14, this book.

[5] Collins and Knutti, 'Long-term Climate Change' (n 2) 1033.

[6] Ibid.

[7] For the Paris Agreement, see UNFCCC (Conference of the Parties), 'Adoption of the Paris Agreement' (12 December 2015) UN Doc FCCC/CP/2015/L.9/Rev.1, 20 <https://unfccc.int/resource/docs/2015/cop21/eng/l09r01.pdf> accessed 13 August 2019 (hereafter 'Paris Agreement').

[8] See Knox (Chapter 15, this book).

[9] For my own view see Simon Caney, 'Climate Change, Human Rights and Moral Thresholds' in Stephen Humphreys (ed), *Human Rights and Climate Change* (CUP 2010) 69–90, (hereafter Caney, 'Climate Change, Human Rights and Moral Thresholds'). The 'in part' in the text is important. I do not claim that climate change matters *only* insofar as it harms human rights ('Climate Change, Human

climate change should be human rights-compliant[10]––a commitment that is reflected in the Preamble to the Paris Agreement.[11]

In this chapter, I propose to explore a third connection between human rights and climate change. This concerns the relationship between human rights, population size, and climate change. Why this focus? My answer is twofold.

The first point is that there is a causal link between population size and climate change. I will discuss the complex nature of the relationship in more detail shortly, but for the moment one salient point is simply that population size affects the volume of greenhouse gas emissions, and thus is one driver of climate change–, a point affirmed in the most recent IPCC report.[12] We can now introduce the second point: this is that some draw on the relationship between population and climate to make claims about people's human rights. They do so in two quite different ways.

First, some adopt what I shall term the *restrictivist approach*, where this holds that given the role that population size plays in contributing to dangerous climate change, we should question the assumption that people have a human right to unlimited procreation. This approach maintains that there are enforceable limits on people's rights to procreate.[13]

A second approach adopts what I shall term the *by-product approach*; this holds that we should realize human rights and, moreover, that realizing human rights (to reproductive choice, education, employment opportunities for women, and a decent standard of living) will, as a side effect, reduce population growth and thus contribute to combating dangerous climate change.[14]

Of the two, I think that the *by-product approach* is the more attractive. However, I shall argue that neither approach is satisfactory. I therefore outline and defend a third way of conceiving the relationship between human rights, population, and environmental sustainability. This builds on the *by-product approach* but goes beyond it.

Prior to introducing these approaches, it is salutary to begin with some figures about population change. Population increased dramatically over the twentieth century. In *A Concise History of World Population*, Massimo Livi-Bacci reports that world population has increased from 2 billion just after the First World War to 4

Rights and Moral Thresholds', 83). For example, I think that it also matters because, and to the extent that, it exacerbates global inequalities.

[10] Caney ibid, 89.

[11] See 'Paris Agreement' (n 7).

[12] Ottmar Edenhofer, Ramón Pichs-Madruga, Youba Sokona, Susanne Kadner, Jan Minx, *et al*, 'Technical Summary' in Ottoman Edenhofer, Ramón Pichs-Madruga, Youba Sokona, Jan Minx, Ellie Farahani, *et al* (eds), *Climate Change 2014: Mitigation of Climate Change. Working Group III Contribution to the Fifth Assessment Report of the Intergovernmental Panel on Climate Change* (CUP 2014) 47 (hereafter Edenhofer *et al*, *Climate Change 2014*).

[13] Sarah Conly, *One Child: Do We Have a Right to More?* (OUP 2016) (hereafter Conly, *One Child*).

[14] This view comes in different forms, and later I shall distinguish between a weaker and a stronger version.

billion in 1974, increasing to 5 billion by 1987, rising to 6 billion in 1998, and then 7 billion in 2012.[15] On current projections from the United Nations, it is expected to increase to 9.7 billion by the 2050s.[16] Given this, it is perhaps unsurprising that some have suggested that our focus should be on population size. This thought receives further support if we also bear in mind some of the claims made about the difference population reduction could make to combating climate change. For example, one recent paper reports that 'slowing population growth could provide 16–29 per cent of the emissions reductions suggested to be necessary by 2050 to avoid dangerous climate change'.[17]

II. The Restrictivist Approach

In light of the relationship between population size and climate change some have argued that individuals or couples are under a duty to limit the number of children that they have. For example, Christine Overall has argued that 'every individual adult has a moral responsibility to limit himself or herself to procreative replacement only'.[18] Overall is explicit that this duty is non-enforceable.

Some, however, have gone further and argued that government regulation to prevent population growth is justified. In her recent book, *One Child: Do We Have a Right to More?*, Sarah Conly argues that people do not have a right to unlimited procreation. Couples have a right to one child–, no more. Furthermore, 'there are restrictions that government can appropriately implement if voluntary efforts fall short'.[19] Conly's claim then is that the prospect of serious environmental catastrophe requires that we rethink our views on human rights to reproduce. In

[15] Massimo Livi-Bacci, *A Concise History of World Population* (6th edn, Wiley Blackwell 2017) 225.

[16] 'World Population Prospects' (*United Nations*, 2015) <https://esa.un.org/unpd/wpp/publications/files/key_findings_wpp_2015.pdf> accessed 13 August 2019.

[17] Brian O'Neill, Michael Dalton, Regina Fuchs, Leiwen Jiang, Shonali Pachauri, *et al* (2010) 'Global Demographic Trends and Future Carbon Emissions' 107 (41) Proceedings of the National Academy of Sciences 17521.

[18] Christine Overall, *Why Have Children? The Ethical Debate* (MIT Press 2012) 183–84.

[19] Conly, *One Child* (n 13) 3. Conly often makes statements such as 'we don't have a right to more than one biological child'. She then makes clear that what she means is that 'two people who procreate should limit themselves to one child between them' Conly, *One Child* (n 13) 2. I think that this focus on couples is problematic. What does it mean for individuals who do not wish to form a couple, or for the polyamorous? What if a woman has children with different men? Suppose that she has three children by three different men. Suppose that she wants to have a child with a fourth man (let us suppose that he has not fathered any children). May she have a child with this fourth man? On the one hand, she would then be the mother of four children. On the other hand, each man is father to a child each. What does her 'one child' approach entail here? These questions are of considerable practicable importance and we would need to have clear defensible answers to operationalize Conly's account, but I set them aside here. Conly's comment on what 'we' have a right to invites the further question as to who the 'we' includes. It is unclear whether it refers to Conly's contemporary American citizens, or the general audience for philosophy books, or everyone in the world. I come back to this second point later.

what follows, I argue that her argument, and that of restrictivists more generally, is deeply flawed. I present three concerns about her arguments.

A. Objection 1: Arbitrariness

The first problem is that her conclusion is arbitrary. To see this, we need to set out the normative framework that Conly would need to reach her conclusion. To derive a right (in this case a right to reproduce) and to establish what limits, if any, there are to it, we need to have an account that:

1. provides a plausible grounding of the right, and
2. explains the limits or parameters of the right.

This would give us an account of the *content* of any given right (what it is a right to—food, say, or health, or in this case, the right to reproduce) and the *extent* of the right (how much of the content a person has a right to—what level of health, or how many children a person may create). Using these terms, then, we can say that Conly's view is that a couple has a right to procreate (the content) but only up to one child (the extent).

Since her emphasis is on the effects that procreation has on the extent to which (current and) future people can enjoy the standard of living to which they are entitled her account of (2) above *must* include within it an account of our obligations to (current and) future generations.[20] Without this, her account is incomplete and her conclusions unfounded. This in turn requires two things:

(i) a normative account of (intra-generational and) inter-generational justice, which (a) specifies what principles of justice apply between contemporaries and future generations and which also (b) specifies the distribuendum of justice (happiness, material resources, human flourishing or something else); and,

(ii) an empirical account of the link between population and people's enjoyment of the standard of living to which they are entitled.

In short, we need to know what future generations are entitled to and what responsibilities that imposes on current generations. Furthermore, we need to know––empirically––what courses of action are required for current generations to fulfil

[20] In what follows I focus on intergenerational justice since climate change will greatly affect the level of the standard of living of enormous numbers of those who are alive in the future. Doing so suffices to bring out the problems in Conly's account. A comprehensive account would, of course, include both current and future generations.

this responsibility. Without this we simply cannot say how much current generations need to do for future generations.

Now the salient point here is that Conly does not supply a particular account of (i). She gives us no account of exactly what it is that we owe future generations, and thus the grounds of the constraints that she endorses. She thinks that we have a duty not to cause catastrophic climate change and her argument proceeds on this basis. However, this is insufficient. Some, for example, affirm more demanding accounts of what we owe future generations. If they are right, then, we owe future people more than Conly assumes. Compare three possible views.

Some hold that justice requires that everyone is above a decent minimum standard of living.[21] An important example of this kind of sufficientarian approach is the Brundtland Commission which holds that '[s]ustainable development is development that meets the needs of the present without compromising *the ability of future generations to meet their own needs*'.[22]

A second view holds that future generations should enjoy a standard of living that is at the same level or higher than that of current generations. Brian Barry, for example, writes that 'those alive at any time are custodians rather than owners of the planet, and ought to pass it on in at least no worse shape than they found it in'.[23]

A third view holds that we should maximize the total amount of well-being.

This list is, of course, not exhaustive. Nonetheless, if we reflect on just these three possibilities it is apparent that they will vary in the demands that they make on earlier generations. Consider, for example, the first view. How demanding this is will, of course, depend on how high or low the proposed minimum is. A threshold that simply calls for meeting people's physical needs for food, water, and shelter will make lesser demands than one that has higher ambitions. Furthermore, if we compare a sufficientarian approach focused on meeting the basic needs of future generations with the second and third views then it is very likely that it will require less onerous sacrifices than these others. Finally, if we compare the second and third view we can see that the third is very likely to require more sacrifice than

[21] See eg Lukas Meyer and Dominic Roser, 'Enough for the Future' in Axel Gosseries and Lukas Meyer (eds), *Intergenerational Justice* (OUP 2009) 219–48; Edward Page (2007) 'Justice Between Generations: Investigating a Sufficientarian Approach' 3(1) Journal of Global Ethics 3–20.

[22] World Commission on Environment and Development, *Our Common Future* (OUP 1987) 43.

[23] Brian Barry, 'Justice Between Generations' in Brian Barry (ed), *Liberty and Justice: Essays in Political Theory Volume 2* (Oxford Clarendon Press 1991) 258 (hereafter Barry, 'Justice Between Generations'). See also Brian Barry, 'Justice as Reciprocity' in Brian Barry (ed), *Liberty and Justice: Essays in Political Theory Volume 2* (Oxford Clarendon Press 1991) 240–41 (hereafter Barry, 'Justice as Reciprocity'). Similar views are expressed by James Woodward and Edith Brown Weiss. Woodward writes that 'each generation ought to leave for succeeding generations a total range of resources and opportunities which are at least equal to its own range of resources and opportunities' James Woodward (1986) 'The Non-Identity Problem' 96(4) Ethics 819 (hereafter Woodward, 'The Non-Identity Problem'); and Weiss that 'each generation is entitled to inherit a planet and cultural resource base at least as good as that of previous generations'. Edith Brown Weiss, *In Fairness to Future Generations: International Law, Common Patrimony, and Intergenerational Equity* (Transnational Publishers 1989) 25 (hereafter Weiss, *In Fairness to Future Generations*).

the second (and, of course, its demandingness is one reason that people give for rejecting utilitarianism). In short: different accounts of intergenerational justice—whether they are the modest or more ambitious kind of sufficientarianism, or whether they adopt the second or third view or some other view—diverge considerably in terms of the demands that they impose.

With this in mind, we can see that one cannot simply stipulate an upper limit on what current generations may do (in this case an upper limit on procreation) without having on hand principles of intergenerational justice which, when conjoined with the relevant empirical data, determine the precise level of the limit.

One cannot then merely assert that there is a limit of one child per couple. It might be, for example, that this is too low. Alternatively, it might be too high, and the choice to have children has to be even more severely rationed.[24] Suppose that our responsibilities to future generations require leaving future people at a level G, and suppose that it is simply not possible to honour this without limiting population to one child per six people, then Conly's proposal is too high. With no ethical guidance, it is simply impossible to say. We thus reach our first concern: the figure given by Conly is wholly arbitrary.

B. Objection 2: Its Monocausal Character

I turn now to a second problem. Someone might respond to the first objection that whilst this has force it does not fundamentally challenge the *restrictivist approach* for it shows only that an adequate *restrictivist approach* needs to make explicit its account of intergenerational justice, and then, on that basis, it can derive the upper limits on people's procreative liberty. This respondent thus says:

> It is true that *Restrictivists* need to add a specific account of intergenerational justice. They should supply such an account. Drawing on it, and using the empirical data about the determinants of the standard of living of future generations,

[24] Many treat the fact that people have an interest in being able to procreate as being sufficient to show that a couple has a right to at least one child. For example, Elizabeth Cripps, accepts that 'a genuine, secure opportunity to have and rear at least one child is necessary for a decent human life' (defending it on the basis that people have rights to 'some opportunity to develop and live by her conception of the good or plan of life, and that parenting is, for very many, integral to that', Elizabeth Cripps (2015) 'Climate Change, Population, and Justice: Hard Choices to Avoid Tragic Choices' 8(2) Global Justice: Theory Practice Rhetoric, 6 & 7. On this basis she treats 'the opportunity to parent' as a 'constraint' on any defensible demographic policy. 'Climate Change, Population, and Justice', 7. But we cannot make this kind of stipulation without knowing the social costs of this. The benefit to a would-be rights-holder, even if considerable, is insufficient to ground a right without examining its implications for potential duty-bearers. Suppose, for example, that ascribing a right for each couple to have a child would result in a situation where people did not have enough food to survive. Those interests are of a higher-order than an interest in procreation. Accordingly, in such a case people do *not* have a right to create one child. Second: it is also worth noting here that people can, of course, enjoy very many of the interests of bringing up children without bringing them into existence.

> they can work back to the responsibilities of current generation. However, this does not undermine the point that whatever the limits are they necessitate a limit on procreative autonomy. So, the figure might be 1 child per couple. Or it might be 2. Or it might be the case that for any 10 people, they can between them create 3 children and so the opportunity to procreate must, somehow, be rationed. Or it might be something else. But the point remains: there are limits on procreative choice.

I now want to show that matters are more complex than this response recognizes and are such that having an equal mandatory limit per person (or per couple, for that matter) is misconceived.

To do this I introduce a second objection: this is that the *restrictivist approaches* are objectionably monocausal. To see why we need to move from focusing on the normative principles examined earlier to the empirical question of what is needed to honour those normative principles. More specifically, we need to have an understanding of the empirical determinants of ecological sustainability. Now, analysts of environmental sustainability commonly use the so-called IPAT equation, where this states that Environmental Impact depends on the number of people (Population), their levels of consumption (Affluence) and the technology they employ (Technology).[25] This account has several important implications. I shall introduce the first here and return to the others in subsequent sections.

The first implication of the IPAT formula is that it shows that it is misconceived to move directly from normative commitments about what standard of living future generations are entitled to enjoy *directly* to any specific claim about how many children any person or persons should be entitled to have. As the IPAT formula makes clear, population is just *one* of the three crucial variables. One thus cannot make *any* inference *at all* about how many children persons are entitled to have without knowing the levels of consumption that people (including those to be born) would, or could enjoy (the A variable).[26] Similarly, one cannot reach any conclusion about how many children persons are entitled to have without knowing the levels of access to clean technology (the T variable) that people would, or could, enjoy.

To put the point another way: suppose that we accept that persons have responsibilities to future generations. Suppose we then think, on this basis, that:

[25] The IPAT equation was first formulated in debates in the early 1970s. See Barry Commoner, *The Closing Circle: Nature, Man, and Technology* (Alfred Knopf 1972) chapters 8 and 9 especially pp 175–77; Commoner 'Response' as part of 'A Bulletin Dialogue on "The Closing Circle"' 28(5) Bulletin of the Atomic Scientists, 17, 42–56; Paul Ehrlich and John Holdren (1971) 'Impact of Population Growth' 171(3977) Science 1212–17; Paul Ehrlich and John Holdren (1972) 'Critique: One Dimensional Ecology' as part of 'A Bulletin Dialogue on "The Closing Circle"' 28(5) Bulletin of the Atomic Scientists 16, 18–27. For a good overview of the debate see Marian Chertow (2000) 'The IPAT Equation and its Variants: Changing Views of Technology and Environmental Impact' 4(4) Journal of Industrial Ecology 13–29.

[26] See also Stephen Gardiner (2001) 'The Real Tragedy of the Commons' 30(4) Philosophy and Public Affairs 401.

> [1] Persons should limit their environmental impacts in order to fulfill their responsibilities to future generations (where the content of these responsibilities will depend on an as-yet-unspecified account of intergenerational justice).

If we think this then [1] should serve as our fundamental normative basis when seeking to derive specific and concrete practical implications about how persons should comply with their duties to future generations. For any practical prescription for people's conduct we would need to know whether it complies with [1] or not.

Now, given the IPAT formula, it follows that one cannot straightforwardly move from [1] to a specific conclusion, such as the following:

> [2] Couples may only have one child (Conly's conclusion); or persons may have only one child (Overall's conclusion).

One cannot because what the IPAT formula makes clear is that there are many different ways of honouring the requirements affirmed by [1]. And one cannot draw any conclusion about specific limits on procreative choice from the general claim affirmed by [1]. Before reaching any such conclusion we need to know what the current levels of consumption are and how much people use what kinds of technology. We would further want to know what the levels of consumption *could be* or *would be likely to be* (if strategies to limit environmentally harmful consumption were implemented) and what technology use *could be* and *would be likely to be* (if governments and other actors invested in clean technology and made it cheaper, if they fully utilized existing clean technology, and if they taxed non-clean energy more). Suppose, for example, that humanity can live within its environmental constraints by reducing aggregate consumption and/or by increased use of clean technology (and suppose, further, that these have no undesirable side effects).[27] In such circumstances, the ecological case for limiting population that is motivating Conly will fall away.

This gives us a further reason for thinking that Conly and Overall's figures are unwarranted since neither gives us a detailed empirical account of how their (different) proposed limits on procreation are both necessary to achieve their (underspecified) goal and sufficient to achieve it. Any specified limit on one variable (**P**) (combined with silence about the other two variables (**A**) and (**T**)) is arbitrary without this.

Now a *restrictivist* might make a number of responses to what I have said. For example, she might say:

27 Or suppose that there were some side effects but that they were small in comparison to the benefits brought about by clean technology (and small in comparison to laws that regulate people's reproductive choice).

Response 1: other methods for limiting environmental impact are ineffective and so limits on procreation are required.

This, however, is implausible, or, at the very least, unsubstantiated. It overlooks a number of important facts about consumption and technology. More specifically it ignores the role of:

1. *increased energy efficiency*. It is salutary to note that the most recent IPCC Assessment Report records that the environmental impact of the increase in world population between 2000 and 2010 was nearly outweighed by the increase in energy efficiency over the same period.[28]
2. *technology transfer*. We should also bear in mind that recent research concludes that the transfer of existing technology could reduce annual CO_2 emissions by greater than 10 gigatons—which is a quarter of humanity's annual CO_2 emissions.[29]
3. *expansion of renewables*. To this we should add that the greater deployment of renewables could considerably reduce humanity's greenhouse gas emissions. To give one example, recent studies of the United States reveal that it could achieve 80 per cent reductions in CO_2 emissions from electricity relative to 1990 levels by using wind and solar, and furthermore it could do so at no extra cost.[30]
4. *addressing deforestation*. A further factor is the reduction of deforestation. According to the IPCC, deforestation and other land use accounted for 12 per cent of annual greenhouse gas emissions between 2000 and 2009.[31] Eliminating this thus constitutes a further major step to a sustainable world.
5. *increasing electrification*. As well as the above, increasing electrification and the growth in the use of electrical vehicles will also greatly reduce greenhouse gas emissions.[32]
6. *consumption and infrastructure*. A further significant factor is the design of cities.

   To bring out the practical significance of the infrastructure, it is instructive to compare the per capita emissions of different cities. Compare, for example,

[28] Edenhofer *et al*, *Climate Change* 2014 (n 12) 48.

[29] 'More Efficient Technology can Reduce CO2 Emissions by up to One Quarter' (*Mercator Research Institute on Global Commons and Climate Change*, 29 May 2017) <https://www.mcc-berlin.net/en/media/press-information/press-release-detail/article/more-efficient-technology-can-reduce-co2-emissions-by-up-to-one-quarter.html> accessed 13 August 2019; Hauke Ward, Alexander Radebach, Ingmar Vierhaus, Armin Fügenschuh, *et al* (2017) 'Reducing Global CO_2 Emissions with the Technologies We Have' (2017) 49 Resource and Energy Economics 201–17.

[30] Alexander MacDonald, Christopher Clack, Anneliese Alexander, Adam Dunbar, James Wilczak, *et al* (2016) 'Future Cost-Competitive Electricity Systems and their Impact on US CO_2 Emissions' 6(5) Nature Climate Change 526–31.

[31] Pete Smith and Mercedes Bustamante, 'Agriculture, Forestry and Other Land Use (AFOLU)' in Edenhofer *et al*, *Climate Change 2014* (n 12) 825.

[32] James Wilson, Andrew DeBenedictis, Rebecca Ghanadan, Amber Mahone, Jack Moore, *et al* (2012) 'The Technology Path to Deep Greenhouse Gas Emissions Cuts by 2050: The Pivotal Role of Electricity' 335 (6064) Science 53–59.

Atlanta (characterized by a very low urban density) with the much more compact Barcelona. Whereas the average carbon emissions produced by public and private transport in Barcelona was 0.7 tonnes of $C0_2$ per person in 2004, the equivalent figure for Atlanta was a staggering 7.5 tonnes of CO_2 per person.[33] The same point is borne out by comparing cities within the United States. A Brookings Institution report found that Lexington's per capita transport and household emissions (which amount to 3.46 metric tons per person) were two-and-a-half times as much as Honolulu's (1.36), and Indianapolis's (3.36) were well over twice as much as those in Los Angeles, Long Beach, and Santa Ana (1.41).[34] What these empirical considerations demonstrate so forcefully is that focusing on the number of people can be misleading. If our concern is ecological sustainability, we must also focus on the infrastructure and built environment which shape and constrain how people go about their lives and define the parameters within which they have to operate.

One point worth stressing here is that changes to infrastructure and enhancements in energy efficiency at one point in time can affect the emissions of everyone affected for decades to come. For example, 'infrastructure and technology choices made by industrialized countries in the post-Second World War period, at low-energy prices, still have an effect on current worldwide GHG emissions'.[35]

This list is not exhaustive. In section IV, I will draw attention to other policies which focus on consumption–, such as abolishing fossil fuel subsidies and taxing the emissions of the wealthiest 1 billion people. When considered together these call into question Response 1.

A *restrictivist* might then argue that:

Response 2: Other methods for limiting environmental impact are politically infeasible.

If there are three policy instruments (tackling **A** or **T** or **P**) and if it is not politically feasible to tackle **A** or **T** then, it might be argued, we should focus our efforts on tackling **P**.

In reply: This does not follow for it might be the case that tackling **P** would be even more politically infeasible. This is surely likely to be the case. In many countries people have a very strong attachment to reproductive liberty, and it stretches

[33] The Global Commission on the Economy and Climate, *Better Growth, Better Climate: The New Climate Economy Report* (New Climate Economy World Resources Institute 2014) 61.

[34] Marilyn A. Brown, Frank Southworth, and Andrea Sarzynski (2008) *Shrinking the Carbon Footprint of Metropolitan America* (Washington DC: Brookings Institution Metropolitan Policy Program) 18–20.

[35] Gabriel Blanco, Reyer Gerlagh, and Sangwon Suh (2014) 'Drivers, Trends and Mitigation' in Edenhofer *et al*, *Climate Change 2014* (n 12) 355.

credulity to breaking point to imagine a party winning an election on a platform of coercively limiting reproductive choice. To put the point another way, suppose that we present people with the following two options:

Ecological liberalism: Persons should limit their environmental impacts in order to fulfil their responsibilities to future generations but can choose how to discharge this responsibility (selecting whether to do it through lowering consumption, enhanced use of clean technology, or limiting reproduction).

Restrictivism: Persons should limit their environmental impacts and to do so must accept limits on their reproductive choice.

Put like this: *ecological liberalism* is clearly more politically feasible than *restrictivism* since it gives people the choice as to how live within their ecological limits. Those who would rather limit their own reproduction can do so under *ecological liberalism*. Furthermore, in addition to this, they also have reason to prefer *ecological liberalism* because it respects their agency and grants them a choice in a way that *restrictivism* does not, and everyone else also has two reasons to prefer *ecological liberalism*. Those who would rather discharge their duties through limiting consumption and generating clean technology would prefer it because it accommodates their commitments. In addition, they too have reason to endorse it because it honours the value of liberty. Given this, a concern for political feasibility tells against the *restrictivist*.

If we turn now to consider the challenges facing contemporary political leaders—and crucially what they take to be central challenges, given the commitments of their citizens—we can see an additional reason why the feasibility argument is fatally flawed. For many, a central challenge of modern governance is how to cope with an increasingly ageing population. Most of Western Europe, Russia, Japan, and China are faced with the prospect of populations that are shrinking, and in which the proportion of the population which is over 65 years is dramatically increasing. In Europe, for example, '24 per cent of the population is already aged 60 years or over and that proportion is projected to reach 34 per cent in 2050 and 35 per cent in 2100'.[36] These demographic changes are putting immense pressure on the economy and the social security system, as a shrinking workforce is being required to pay for the health, social care, and pensions of increasing numbers of people who are retired. Given these pressures resulting from ageing societies, it is very unlikely that governments will be willing to enact policies which reduce the number of children being born, when doing so will exacerbate further already very difficult domestic problems. Now irrespective of whether this is justified or not, the relevant point here is that *restrictivism* lacks political feasibility. None of the

[36] UNDESAPD 'World Population Prospects: The 2015 Revision, Key Findings and Advance Tables' Working Paper No ESA/P/WP.241 (2015) 8.

governments facing the demographic challenges of ageing societies are likely to adopt a *restrictivist* approach.

C. Objection 3: An Unfair Egalitarianism

There is a further problem with *restrictivism*, namely that it is unfair. To see why, consider again the IPAT formula. Compare two societies. Suppose that one (A) uses technology which results in twice as much environmental impact per unit of consumption than the other society (B). Suppose further that A consumes twice as much as the other society. Per person then it has (other things being equal) four times as much of an environmental impact. Now if Society A and Society B have equal needs (and neither have ecologically less harmful options available to them) it would be unfair to impose identical population limits in this circumstance. Society B is generating much less environmental impact per person and so they can reasonably ask why they are required to make exactly the same population restrictions as Society A when Society B is causing so much more environmental impact per person.

This point applies at the global level: some countries have a much lower environmental impact per person than others. To get a sense of the enormous disparities it is instructive to compare different countries' per capita greenhouse emissions.[37] For example, if we turn to the data from US Department of Energy's Carbon Dioxide Information Analysis Center (CDIAC) we can see that in 2014 the United States was responsible for 16.5 metric tons of CO_2 per person. However, the relevant figure for Belgium was slightly over half of that (8.3 metric tons) and Italy was less than a third of that (5.3 metric tons). The United Kingdom was on 6.5 metric tons. Others are much lower: Brazil's figure is 2.6 metric tons. India's per capita emissions are a mere 1.7 metric tons (10 per cent of that of the average US citizen), and Pakistan is only 0.9 metric tons.[38] These are striking inequalities, and insisting on equal procreative limits given such disparities is both unwarranted from an ecological point of view and also *pro tanto* unfair.[39]

[37] In doing so a number of important caveats should be borne in mind. First, the data refer only to CO_2 emissions from fossil fuels and the manufacture of cement, and omits other greenhouse gases. Second, the data focus on whether the emissions are produced, not where they are consumed. Third, a fully comprehensive account of people's environmental impact would also, of course, not restrict itself to climate change but will include all environmental problems (such as ozone depletion, ocean acidification, biodiversity loss and so on). See Simon Caney, *On Cosmopolitanism: Equality, Ecology and Resistance* (OUP forthcoming) part II (hereafter Caney, *On Cosmopolitanism*).

[38] 'CO_2 emissions (metric tons per capita)' (*The World Bank*) <http://data.worldbank.org/indicator/EN.ATM.CO2E.PC?view=map> accessed 13 August 2019.

[39] Note: in the text I have assumed, for the sake of argument, that we should have an equal environmental impact. Someone might, however, query this. What is at stake is what is the fairest way of distributing the burdens of tackling climate change, and some might argue that a fair burden sharing scheme will impose greater burdens on some (those who have polluted the most and/or the wealthiest) than others (those who have polluted least and/or are the poorest). I completely agree: the view in the

Now if we accept this, then the next point to observe is that *exactly* the same reasoning would also apply *within* societies too since there are also major disparities in personal environmental impact within countries.

In both cases, the lion's share of the environmental impact comes from the wealthy.[40] Insisting on equal procreative limits here penalizes the poor for the lifestyles of the rich.

III. The By-Product Approach

Having criticized one account, I turn now to a second which I think is much more appealing, but which is nonetheless inadequate. This second account takes its cue from those like Amartya Sen who argue that realizing people's human rights (specifically the human rights of women) has the side effect of reducing population growth.

Sen's own discussion of this was not centred around climate change but on worries that overpopulation would lead to food insecurity. In a series of articles and books in the 1990s and early 2000s, Sen argued that securing human rights would result in lower population growth and that we thus need not adopt 'Malthusian' population policies. For example, he compared China and India and argued that literacy and educational opportunities bring down population size.[41] In addition to this, he argued that population size is greatly affected by 'the opportunity of women to earn an independent income, the property rights of women, and the general status and standing of women in the social culture'.[42] Sen thus emphasized the need to empower women, promoting their educational opportunities, their capacity to gain employment, and their social status in society.[43] Sen further argued that coercion not only limits freedom but it also leads to the ill-treatment of girls and their victimization. Furthermore, he argued, some of the positive results that some

text is a first approximation. However, if we accept this, it will not make it any easier to derive the conclusion that different societies should be subject to the same demographic constraints. If anything, it will make it much harder.

[40] As Dominic Roser pointed out to me, my argument here is structurally similar to an argument I made against the view that justice requires distributing rights to emit greenhouse gases equally (the equal per capita view). One of my challenges to the equal per capita view is that it is wrong to single out emissions for special treatment and apply an egalitarian principle to it considered in isolation. My challenge here is that it is wrong to single out one cause of environmental change for special treatment and apply an egalitarian principle to it considered in isolation. See Simon Caney (2012) 'Just Emissions' 40(4) Philosophy & Public Affairs 255–300 (hereafter Caney, 'Just Emissions').

[41] Amartya Sen (1997) 'Population Policy: Authoritarianism versus Cooperation' 10(1) *Journal of Population Economics* 3–22 (hereafter Sen, 'Population Policy').

[42] Ibid, 12.

[43] Amartya Sen (1996) 'Fertility and Coercion', University of Chicago Law Review 63(3) especially 1051–53.

might attribute to restrictive population policies may in fact result from other factors (eg literacy, jobs).[44]

Although Sen's focus was not on climate change, one could argue in a similar vein that it is important to secure human rights to reproductive choice, human rights to an adequate standard of living, human rights to education, and human rights to equal employment opportunities, and that furthermore, doing so will lead to reduced population growth in some countries. Philip Cafaro has argued along these lines. He argues for making birth control affordable or free, providing full information about reproductive choice, and for promoting access to reproductive choice more generally. He writes that 'policies which improve the lives of women have been shown to reduce fertility rates in many developing countries. These include guaranteeing girls the same educational opportunities as boys, promoting female literacy, and improving women's economic opportunities.'[45] Furthermore, he does so in the context of seeking to limit the demographic pressures on the climate system. Let us call this the *by-product approach*.

How persuasive is this kind of argument? If it can be successful in reducing population growth and thereby enable humanity to avoid dangerous climate change then this kind of response has a great deal of appeal. My starting point here is that we have very weighty reasons for promoting human rights and gender equality. This should be a fundamental objective of governments and other duty bearers (including citizens, non-governmental organizations (NGOs), international institutions, social movements, and corporations). So, irrespective of any benign side effects, justice requires these policies. It would thus be highly desirable if doing the right thing happened, as a by-product, to bring about ecological sustainability too. (Among other things, it would also give even more reason and motivation to promote human rights.)

To this we should add that there is a wealth of empirical evidence showing that meeting human rights to an adequate standard of living, women's rights to reproductive choice, to education, and to employment all result in reduced population.[46] For example, Abel and his colleagues report that ensuring Sustainable Development Goals results in 'population sizes between 8.2 and 8.7 billion in 2100'.[47]

[44] Sen, 'Population Policy' (n 41) 15–16. For further information see Sen *Development as Freedom* (New York: Anchor Books, 2000), chapter 9.

[45] Philip Cafaro (2012) 'Climate Ethics and Population Policy' 3(1) *Wiley Interdisciplinary Reviews, Climate Change* 47, footnote omitted.

[46] See generally, John Bongaarts (2016) 'Development: Slow Down Population Growth' 530 (7591) *Nature* 409–12; Massimo Livi-Bacci, *A Concise History of World Population* (6th edn, Wiley Blackwell 2017) chapter 5; Wolfgang Lutz, William Butz, and Samir KC (eds), *World Population and Human Capital in the Twenty-First Century* (OUP 2014).

[47] Guy Abel, Bilal Barakat, Samir KC, and Wolfgang Lutz (2016) 'Meeting the Sustainable Development Goals Leads to Lower World Population Growth' 113(50) Proceedings of the National Academy of Sciences 14294.

The problem, however, is that we lack sufficient reason to think it will be sufficient to tackle the climate crisis. It suffers from two problems that also afflicted the *restrictivist approach.*

The first is that before we endorse it we need to know what current generations owe to future generations. Without that it is simply not possible to know whether current generations are doing enough or not. We cannot know whether the affirmation of liberal rights is sufficient or not without a criterion by which to judge it.

Second, as I emphasized in the previous section, the extent to which humanity has environmental impacts depends not just on the number of people (including not just the numbers born but also their longevity) but also what kinds of technology are available to them and how much they engage in consumption. Given this, we cannot say whether any reduction in population growth will be sufficient until we know how much people will consume and what level of technology will be available.

Given these, we can have no assurance whether the liberal approach described above is sufficient or not. To put our faith in this alone is to gamble and keep our fingers crossed that it will work out all right.

Now a defender of the *by-product approach* might reply that these objections are not decisive. In response to my first objection, she might argue that this just shows that her account is incomplete and that it can be supplemented. She might also argue in response to the second objection that the liberal policies she advocates can also be combined with various policy instruments to reduce consumption (to the extent that it is necessary) and increase the generation and transfer of clean technology (again to the extent that it is necessary).

Both responses are, I think, plausible ones. However, note that they call for us to go beyond the *by-product approach*; they draw attention to the need for a more comprehensive approach that does not focus on population alone and includes consumption and technology within its remit too. If we accept (as I do) that we have good independent reason to endorse the rights of all to a decent standard of living and the rights of women to education, employment, and reproductive choice, then we should regard the liberal response described earlier as a necessary part of the appropriate response. But it cannot be a sufficient account. For that we have to go beyond it.

The point could be put another way. We can distinguish between *strong* and *weak* versions of the *by-product approach*, where the *strong* version holds that realizing the human rights (to a decent standard of living, education, and reproductive choice) is sufficient to bring about ecological sustainability, and the weak version holds merely that realizing these human rights helps contribute to bringing about ecological sustainability. Given what I have argued I believe that the strong version is implausible and the weak version is plausible but inadequate.

IV. Liberal Rights with a Sustainability Frontier

How then should we think about human rights, environmental sustainability, and demographic change?

A. The Proposal

My proposal builds on the criticisms made of the preceding views.[48] The idea is as follows.

1. Justice for current and future generations

First, we should identify what responsibilities people have to current generations and to those who will be born in the future. Elsewhere I have argued that current generations are required to act in such a way that future generations enjoy a standard of living that is no lower than the standard of living that they themselves seek to enjoy[49] and so, on my account this should be inserted here.[50]

2. The sustainability frontier

Second, we should draw on the empirical literature concerning the environmental impacts of human behaviour and the environmental preconditions of realizing justice, and then determine on this basis what are the ecological limits within which humanity must operate if it is to comply with the principles of justice identified in step (1). These ecological limits determine what we might call the 'sustainability frontier' where this demarcates the upper limit on the environmental impacts that people can impose on others (and it may call for revising (1) if (1) makes demands that violate the sustainability frontier).

Steps (1) and (2) establish the limits within which humanity must live. Our next two steps consider how we can do so, identifying *both* actions that we ought to perform for independent reasons but which also better enable us to live within the sustainability frontier and *also* actions which cause environmental impacts and thus may need to be regulated to ensure that we do not transgress the sustainability frontier.

[48] The view is set out in Caney, 'Just Emissions' 299 footnote 96; and Simon Caney, 'Tolstoy's Question' (2012) (unpublished Oxford Amnesty Lecture) (original title: 'Human Rights in a Finite World').

[49] Caney, *On Cosmopolitanism* (n 37).

[50] As noted earlier, versions of this view have been defended by Barry, 'Justice as Reciprocity' (n 23) 240–41; Barry, 'Justice Between Generations' (n 23) 258; Weiss, *In Fairness to Future Generations* (n 23) 25; Woodward, 'The Non-Identity Problem' (n 23) 819.

3. Realizing justice

Consider the first kind. When considering what we should do to ensure that we comply with the sustainability frontier, our starting point should be identifying and implementing policies which we have independent justice-based reasons to implement *and* which also happen to reduce environmental impacts. To give some examples, it would include the following four initiatives:

1. One has been discussed earlier, namely realizing rights to education, employment, and a decent standard of living, and women's rights to reproductive autonomy. Although doing so requires the use of energy and may thus involve greenhouse gas emissions, the expectation is that this can, and should, be done in such a way as to result in a net reduction of greenhouse gas emissions.
2. A second is tackling global inequalities and taxing the emissions of the most advantaged. From the point of view of egalitarian justice we have good reason to tax the most advantaged. In addition to this, however, Lucas Chancel and Thomas Piketty report that the top 10 per cent of the world are responsible for 45 per cent of global CO_2 emissions.[51] Taxing them (perhaps directly targeting their emissions-intensive lifestyles) can thus also promote the mitigation of climate change. As Chakravarty and his colleagues argue, one could make a major contribution to mitigating climate change ('reducing projected global emissions in 2030 by 13 $GtCO_2$') by sharing the emissions reductions among the top 1 billion emitters and this can be done without imposing costs on the world's poorest.[52]
3. A third policy is eliminating fossil fuel subsidies. These are unjust in a multitude of ways. They facilitate activities that inflict dangerous climatic change on others. They also use up enormous sums of money—in 2013 this amounted to $548 billion[53]—money that could be spent enabling the poor to meet their needs in a clean way. Furthermore, they cannot be justified on the grounds that they enable the poor to use energy since they are in fact regressive in their effects.[54]
4. A fourth kind of policy in this category is the regulation of transport and other emissions. Independent of their harmful effects on the climate system, such emissions result in poor air quality and thereby damage the health of those affected.[55]

[51] Lucas Chancel and Thomas Piketty, *Carbon and Inequality: from Kyoto to Paris* (Paris School of Economics 2015) 31.

[52] Shoibal Chakravarty, Ananth Chikkaturb, Heleen de Coninck, Stephen Pacala, Robert Socolow, *et al* (2009) 'Sharing Global CO_2 Emission Reductions among one Billion High Emitters' 106(29) Proceedings of the National Academy of Sciences 11884.

[53] International Energy Agency (2014) *World Energy Outlook 2014* (International Energy Agency) 314.

[54] Ibid, 317–18.

[55] Edenhofer *et al* 'Technical Summary' in Edenhofer *et al Climate Change 2014* (n 12) 61–63.

All these policies enable humanity to live within the *sustainability frontier*. We cannot, however, assume that these are sufficient to ensure that we do so. This takes us to the next step.

4. Freedom within the sustainability frontier

The next step holds that measures can be put in place to ensure that people pursue their conception of the good within the limits of the sustainability frontier but--and this is the key feature of the fourth step--they can choose (both at the individual level and at various societal levels) how they will live within these ecological limits. They can, that is, choose the extent to which they constrain their consumption and procreation and create and share clean technology.[56] This view corresponds to what I earlier termed *ecological liberalism*. It imposes limits on people's environmental impacts (and, as such, is ecological) but it permits agents to choose just how they comply with those limits (and, as such, is liberal). Some of these choices could be made at the individual level. For others, the relevant level might be at the level of the city or region or state.

5. Just burden sharing within the sustainability frontier

The account given so far is, however, incomplete. Suppose (i) that the net effects of people's consumption, procreation, and production of clean technology are such that current and future generations enjoy the kind of world to which they are entitled (in line with conditions (1), (2), and (3)); and suppose also (ii) that agents have choices about the mix of consumption, procreation, and technology (in line with condition (4)). A society could honour both (i) and (ii) and yet act unjustly. Why? The answer is that it could do so and yet distribute any sacrifices involved in realizing (i) unfairly among putative duty-bearers. We must, thus, add, that the sacrifices involved in ensuring that humans' ecological impacts do not exceed a fair level are distributed fairly.

What would this involve? On the egalitarian account of global distributive justice I affirm agents are entitled to equal opportunities to lead rich and fulfilling lives. Now, if and when agents have a genuine choice and they also enjoy a fair share of opportunities and resources, then such agents can be held accountable for their

[56] One question that might be raised is whether my proposal endorses the view that consumption and population are "morally equivalent" and, if so, whether that is a problem. See Thomas Young (2001) 'Overconsumption and Procreation: Are They Morally Equivalent?' 18(2) Journal of Applied Philosophy 183–92; Clare Heyward (2012) 'A Growing Problem? Dealing with Population Increases in Climate Justice' 19(4) Ethical Perspectives 703–32. Young, for example, holds that 'overconsumption and reproduction are (usually) morally equivalent: one should be opposed to both or in favour of both', Young 'Overconsumption and Procreation', 183–84. In reply: my claim is not that we should treat consumption, procreation (and technology) as morally equivalent *in all respects*. It is that they are morally equivalent in one specific sense--*namely that they are all determinants of environmental impacts*--and it is *only in that sense that* that they are treated as equivalent. So, one can--consistent with what I have said--treat them as morally disanalogous in other ways (such as their contribution to well-being or the extent to which their exercise leads to additional responsibilities).

choices, including reproductive choices.[57] On this view, then, those who wish to have children can do so, but they must pay for the privilege, and they must ensure that there is sufficient use of clean technology and reduction in consumption to ensure that humanity lives within the sustainability frontier.[58] By the same logic, others can choose to consume more, but they too must pay for the privilege and ensure that their population size and technology policy are such that they too live within the sustainability frontier.[59]

As I say, though, this reflects my own view on reproductive responsibilities. One could have a version of ecological liberalism that is identical to mine with the sole exception that it holds that the costs of reproduction should, as a matter of justice, be borne (in part or in total) by people other than the parents. What is crucial to ecological liberalism is that if people engage in reproduction, then the relevant duty-bearers must ensure that there is sufficient investment in (and transfer of) clean technology and/or reduction in consumption such that future generations inherit the world to which they are entitled and, furthermore, that any sacrifices incurred are borne equitably.

B. Three Virtues

This approach has three virtues. First, it sits better with the science than either the *restrictivist* or *by-product approaches* because it is predicated on the multicausal nature of the determinants of environmental change. Its thesis, that people are free to discharge their responsibilities in different ways, reflects the fact that environmental impacts are a function of three variables--population, consumption, and technology. As such, it is preferable to both the *restrictivist* and *by-product approaches* because both focus exclusively on one variable and ignore, or are silent about, the other two.

Second, my approach is attractive because it respects free choice. It imposes a duty on people (a duty demanded by intergenerational justice), but it gives people

[57] My views are indebted to the pioneering work of Eric Rakowski, *Equal Justice* (Oxford Clarendon Press 1991) 153–55, esp 153; Paula Casal and Andrew Williams (1995) 'Rights, Equality and Procreation' 17(1) Analyse und Kritik 93–116, esp 97–100, 108–14; Paula Casal and Andrew Williams, 'Equality of Resources and Procreative Justice' in Justine Burley (ed), *Dworkin and his Critics, with Replies by Dworkin* (Blackwell 2004) esp 152–54, 160–64; and Matthew Clayton, *Justice and Legitimacy in Upbringing* (OUP 2006) 69–70. The assumption is far from being uncontroversial. However, I cannot defend it here.

[58] It is important to emphasize that the responsibility principle applies when there is a fair share of opportunities and responsibilities. Where this does not apply then we should require those with more than their fair share to bear the burden (in proportion to the extent to which they have more than their fair share). On the egalitarian conception I endorse, it would be unfair to make disadvantaged parents—denied of their right to equality—pay for the full cost of their reproductive choices.

[59] My account is similar in spirit to that developed by Bruce Ackerman in *Social Justice in the Liberal State* and I am indebted to his discussion. For his illuminating analysis see Bruce Ackerman, *Social Justice in the Liberal State* (Yale University Press 1980) 112–13, 218–20.

leeway in how that they discharge that duty. It is not only possible for them to discharge it in different ways; it is also important to give people the choice to do so given the plurality of ways of realizing the duty. What reason could there be for some to prescribe to others how they should comply with their responsibility when, *ex hypothesi*, there are several different ways of discharging it?

This said, we do have special reason to put an emphasis on clean technology.[60] To see this consider the following. Given

1. that the impact of climate change is a function of Population (**P**), Affluence (**A**), and Technology (**T**);
   then, if
2. humanity is to continue into the future (so **P** will be, and should be, positive); and if,
3. people are to live the kinds of lives to which they are entitled (and thus **A** will be, and should be, positive);
   then, given
4. that humanity must reach a zero-carbon world;
   it follows that
5. humanity will have to develop technology (**T**) that is sufficient to support the kind of life to which people are entitled.

Ultimately, and soon, the budget of greenhouse gases that can be emitted will run out. Unless we think that humanity should cease to be (or, what is the same thing, consumption should be zero), that leaves us only technology to take us to zero emissions. The development and transfer of clean technology is thus of paramount significance. Even so, that leaves discretion on how high **P** or **A** can be.

This leads to a third virtue—one briefly mentioned above in section II—namely that my account enjoys much greater political feasibility than the *restrictivist* view. Precisely because it rejects the prescriptive approach endorsed by Conly, and because it grants a choice, it is much more likely to be adopted. By providing flexibility in how people discharge their responsibilities, it makes it much more likely than an approach which calls for everyone to engage in a specific course of action. It is true that it may impose greater constraints than the second approach considered, but recall the second approach is flawed because there is no assurance that it would yield environmental sustainability. As such, my ecological liberalism can claim to be the most politically feasible way of securing a just outcome.

Clearly much more needs to be said about this approach. My aim is to set out-- at the abstract level--how to think about population in the light of the threat to the climate system. A fuller, more comprehensive analysis, would need to specify the

[60] I am greatly indebted to Dominic Roser for pressing me on this, and for prompting the following line of reasoning (though he should not be held responsible for it).

principles of intergenerational justice and draw on the relevant empirics. It would also need to say more about exactly how we ensure that people live within the sustainability frontier and what measures should be adopted to ensure compliance. Thus, more detail needs to be supplied.[61]

V. Conclusion

However, what I hope to have done is to show how two common normative approaches to the environmental implications of population change—*restrictivist* and *by-product approaches*—are seriously flawed, and to have set out a third more systematic way of thinking about the challenges posed by climate change that overcomes the limitations of the previous two. It is animated by a respect for persons' human rights. It is designed both to protect people from being exposed to dangerous climate changes which compromise their human rights and also to find ways of preventing dangerous climate change that honour human rights and respect persons' agency and choice.

Acknowledgement

I am grateful to Dominic Roser for his extremely helpful comments.

[61] For a fuller development of the view see Caney, *On Cosmopolitanism* (n 37) Part II.

Index